Republics Ancient and Modern

Republics

Ancient and

Modern

VOLUME I

The Ancien Régime in Classical Greece

PAUL A. RAHE

The University of North Carolina Press

Chapel Hill and London

Republics Ancient and Modern was originally
published in hardcover in one volume by the
University of North Carolina Press in 1992. Both
the initial research and the publication of this
work were made possible in part through grants
from the Division of Research Programs of the
National Endowment for the Humanities, an
independent federal agency whose mission is to
award grants to support education, scholarship,
media programming, libraries, and museums in
order to bring the results of cultural activities to a
broad, general public.

Publication of this book was also aided by grants
from the Lynde and Harry Bradley Foundation,
the Earhart Foundation, and the John M. Olin
Foundation.

Library of Congress
Cataloging-in-Publication Data
Rahe, Paul Anthony.
Republics ancient and modern / by Paul A. Rahe.
p.   cm.
Includes bibliographical references and index.
Contents: v. 1. The Ancien régime in classical
Greece—v. 2. New modes and orders in Early
Modern political thought—v. 3. Inventions of
prudence: constituting the American regime.
1. United States—Politics and government—
1775–1783.   2. Political science—United States—
History—18th century.   3. Republicanism—
History.   4. Political science—Greece—History.
I. Title.
E210.R335   1994
321.8'6—dc20   94-5728
                                                                 CIP

ISBN 0-8078-4473-x (pbk. : alk. paper) (v. 1)
ISBN 0-8078-4474-8 (pbk. : alk. paper) (v. 2)
ISBN 0-8078-4475-6 (pbk. : alk. paper) (v. 3)

98   97   96   95   94
5   4   3   2   1

DONALD KAGAN

W. G. G. FORREST

Magistris Optimis

Contents

Preface

More than ten years ago, I set out to transform my dissertation into a publishable monograph. In the course of making the attempt, I paused in my work, unhappy with the conceptual framework into which I was trying to fit the pieces of the puzzle constituted by late fifth-century Sparta and Athens. I then thought that I would better be able to deal with those scattered fragments of information if I first clarified my own thinking about the character of ancient politics by composing a brief article comparing the constitution of ancient Lacedaemon with that of the modern United States. Had I had any notion at the time of the enormity of the task that I was then taking on, I would no doubt have jettisoned the project right then and there.

When I began that essay in comparative politics, I presumed that I knew virtually all that I needed to know about modern republicanism. I had been born in such a republic. I had grown up there, and I had spent three glorious years in Great Britain, studying ancient history and observing the politics of that remarkable polity at close hand. But, as I pursued my new project, I lost my way—or, rather, discovered that I had never had a very good grasp of where I was—and gradually I came to find strange and mysterious that which had always seemed familiar and obvious. The more I learned about the foundations of modern politics, the less I found that I could depend upon that which I had been taught and had always been inclined to take for granted. And so what began as an attempt to elucidate the character of ancient politics became as much, if not more, a study of modernity.

So, let the reader be warned. This three-volume work is not a summary of the received wisdom concerning the republics of ancient Greece, the political speculation of early modern Europe, and the character of the American founding. Moreover, it is unlikely that the arbiters of intellectual fashion will ever find my thinking congenial. In the three spheres discussed, I have not only broken with the orthodoxy currently reigning in the academy; I have also eschewed the latest trends; and I suspect that many, both in and outside our universities, will find what I have to say unsettling. Thus, for example, where present-minded ancient historians are inclined to place emphasis on the institutions or to stress the sociology of the ancient Greek city and to treat Athens as an exemplar, I present the world of the *pólis* in the light cast by the regime-analysis of Thucydides, Plato, Aristotle, and the like, and I try to show that the ancient tendency to prefer Sparta to Athens made considerable sense. Similarly, where students of early modern political thought now stress the continuity between the ancients and the moderns, I contend that there was a decisive break, disguised somewhat by the need of the latter to circumvent censorship and to make the new thinking more persuasive by presenting it in a fashion designed to soothe rather than shock, and I argue, therefore, that Machiavelli, Harrington, the radical Whigs, and Lord Boling-broke were as much opposed to classical republicanism as Hobbes, Locke, Hume, and Montesquieu. And finally, where American historians debate whether the regime produced by the American Revolution was republican or liberal, ancient or modern, or simply confused, I argue that it was a deliber-ately contrived mixed regime of sorts—liberal and modern, first of all, but in its insistence that to vindicate human dignity one must demonstrate man's capacity for self-government, republican and classical as well. In short, it is my contention that we cannot understand our own situation without think-ing a great deal about the politics of antiquity and the speculation of early modern times. Moreover, if I am correct, the modern social science that cus-tomarily guides our reflections with regard to this question is itself the chief obstacle to our understanding that which we most need to know. To put it bluntly, these volumes are intended solely for those willing to pause and rethink.

Because I address in these pages questions of permanent public interest, I have tried to make my argument and the evidence on which it is based as accessible as possible to the general reader. To that end, I have cited, where available, English translations of the secondary works which I have found useful, and I have in every case provided translations of the pertinent pri-mary source material. Moreover, where the inclusion of a critical word or phrase in the original language may alert readers familiar with that language to my particular interpretation of the passage or to something going on in the text cited that I have been unable to capture fully in translation, I have provided such information as well. All of the translations, unless otherwise indicated, are my own. In quoting works published in English, I have nearly always retained the original spelling, punctuation, and emphasis. Exceptions are specified in the notes or marked by brackets in the text. In the last note to the introduction to each volume, I have listed books and articles, pertinent to the themes of that volume, which have appeared or come to my attention since the original edition went to press.

Washington, D.C.
18 December 1993

Acknowledgments

En route to publishing these three volumes, I have accumulated a great many debts. Some are exclusively professional. As anyone who peruses my notes will discover, I have read widely in the secondary literature of the three fields covered in this work, and I have learned a great deal from those who have preceded me—not least, let me add, from those whose opinions I challenge here. As will be evident, I owe much to the late M. I. Finley and Louis Gernet, to G. E. M. de Ste. Croix, Jean-Pierre Vernant, Pierre Vidal-Naquet, Marcel Détienne, and to their many students and associates; to John Dunn, Quentin Skinner, J. G. A. Pocock, and those who have succumbed to their influence; to the late Leo Strauss and his many, intrepid admirers; and to the late Hannah Arendt, to Bernard Bailyn, Gordon S. Wood, Joyce Appleby, Lance Banning, and to those who have further elaborated their various arguments.

Many of my debts are personal as well. Donald Kagan first introduced me to ancient history when I was a freshman at Cornell University, and a decade later he directed my dissertation at Yale University. Though rightly inclined to think that I should turn my thesis into a book before embarking on a project as ambitious as this one, he was always generous in his support and encouraging. At one time or another, he read every word printed below. From the outset, he has been my model of what a scholar should be. Allan Bloom first introduced me to the study of political theory and, while tolerating a sophomore's stubborn resistance to his arguments, he taught me how to read. At Oxford's Wadham College, I profited from the tuition of W. G. G. Forrest and I. M. Crombie, and I learned a great deal as well the term I was shipped out to Oswyn Murray of Balliol. Not the least of my Oxford acquisitions was my friendship with Peter Simpson, once my tutorial partner in philosophy, then a boon companion, and a generous reader of everything that I have written since, always ready to make a suggestion, to supply a reference, and to dig up an article. I was always fortunate in my colleagues while a student: Jonathan Erichsen, Julius Grey, and Gibson Kamau Kuria have all been a great help. In graduate school at Yale, I learned at least as much from my colleagues Barry Strauss, Brook Manville, Peter Krentz, Michael Cadden, Williamson Murray, and Stephen Holmes as I learned in class; and in one fashion or another, they have all been helpful since. To Douglas and Roseline Crowley, I owe more than I can say.

I began this work while a fellow at the Center for Hellenic Studies in Washington, D.C. I owe much to Bernard Knox, who was the first to suspect that the story now told here might be well worth telling, and I gained greatly from exchanges with Nicholas Richardson, Peter Burian, Maria Dzielska, Richard Kraut, Jan Bremmer, and Tessa Rajak. That year saw the beginning of the many pleasant conversations that I have had with my former student William Connell on this subject. He has been very generous with his time, reading drafts of various chapters and sending me articles and references that he has come across.

While teaching at Franklin and Marshall College, I encountered Joel Farber, who never denied me his time and advice, and met James W. Muller, who has gone over every word I have written since, sharing with me his deep knowledge of political theory, correcting me when I am wrong, pointing out errors in spelling and grammar, and encouraging me to get on with the task and finish my work. To no contemporary do I owe a greater debt; from no friend have I learned more. In some ways, this is his work as much as it is mine.

I learned something as well from a National Endowment for the Humanities Summer Seminar on slavery which I took with Orlando Patterson at Harvard University before trekking out West to the University of Tulsa. My colleagues at that institution have always been free with their time and advice and tolerant of my frequent absences. I am particularly indebted to Lawrence Cress, Robert Rutland, David Epstein, Marvin Lomax, Thomas Buckley, Patrick Blessing, Joseph C. Bradley, Mary Lee Townsend, Thomas Horne, Michael Mosher, Eldon Eisenach, and Jacob Howland, and I have mercilessly exploited the generous leave policy pioneered by Thomas Staley and reaffirmed by Susan Parr.

While a fellow at the National Humanities Center, I profited from conversations with Charles Blitzer, J. H. Hexter, Timothy Breen, John Shelton Reed, Donald Horowitz, Marc Plattner, Michael Alexander, Josiah Ober, and Shaul Bakhash, who read and commented on divers chapters. Thanks to Charles Blitzer and Kent Mullikin, I was later able to return to the center for three summers running to test my ideas in a national institute for high school teachers on ancient and modern republicanism taught with Christine Heyrman and Peter Riesenberg, who saved me from many a blunder.

While pondering the questions addressed here, I spent two years in Istanbul as a fellow of the Institute of Current World Affairs, thinking and writing about contemporary politics in Greece, Turkey, and Cyprus, and often wondering whether the hypotheses advanced in this work accurately describe contemporary republics in the eastern Mediterranean. While abroad, I drew on the wisdom of Peter Bird Martin, Dennison Rusinow, Nicholas

Rauh, Charles and Marie Henriette Gates, Joan and Patrick Leigh Fermor, and Antony Greenwood.

I finished the initial draft of this work while a fellow of the John M. Olin Foundation, and I revised much of the manuscript while a fellow at Washington University's Center for the History of Freedom. There I was saved from errors by criticism and suggestions advanced by Richard Davis, David Wootton, Blair Worden, Maurice Goldsmith, and Herbert Rowen. Along the way, I became acquainted with Hiram Caton and Lance Banning, who looked over the entire manuscript and gave me detailed and helpful advice, and with Alvin H. Bernstein, Carnes Lord, William and Susan Kristol, Eugene D. Genovese, Elizabeth Fox-Genovese, Bertram Wyatt Brown, Harvey C. Mansfield, Jr., Mark Golden, Kurt Raaflaub, and Father Ernest Fortin—who read and commented on particular chapters.

In writing this volume, I have drawn freely on the following, previously published work: "The Primacy of Politics in Classical Greece," *The American Historical Review* 89 (1984): 265–93.

My research and the writing of these volumes were aided greatly by generous support from the Center for Hellenic Studies, Franklin and Marshall College, the National Endowment for the Humanities, the National Humanities Center, the University of Tulsa, the Oklahoma Foundation for the Humanities, the John M. Olin Foundation, and Washington University's Center for the History of Freedom. Publication was made possible by subventions from the John M. Olin Foundation, the Earhart Foundation, the Lynde and Harry Bradley Foundation, and the National Endowment for the Humanities. The introductions to the three volumes were written while I was a fellow of the National Endowment for the Humanities and of the Woodrow Wilson International Center for Scholars. To these institutions and their officers, I owe a great debt.

It is with pleasure that I thank Lewis Bateman, of the University of North Carolina Press, and my three readers for suggestions and encouragement, as well as Alice Kauble, Gail Newman, and David Pettyjohn, all students at the University of Tulsa, who helped me check the notes.

Suppose that we were to define what it means to be a people (populus) *not in the usual way, but in a different fashion—such as the following: a people is a multitudinous assemblage of rational beings united by concord regarding loved things held in common. Then, if we wished to discern the character of any given people, we would have to investigate what it loves. And no matter what an entity loves, if it is a multitudinous assemblage not of cattle but of rational creatures and if these are united by concord regarding loved things held in common, then it is not absurd to call it a people; and, surely, it is a better or worse people as it is united in loving things that are better or worse. By this definition, the Roman people is a people, and its estate* (res) *is without doubt a commonwealth* (res publica). *What this people loved in early times and what it loved in the ages that followed, the practices by which it passed into bloody sedition and then into social and civil wars, tearing apart and destroying that concord which is, in a certain manner, the health and welfare* (salus) *of a people—to this history bears witness. . . . And what I have said concerning this people and concerning its commonwealth, this also I should be understood to have said and thought concerning the Athenians, the rest of the Greeks, . . . and the other nations as well.*

AUGUSTINE

Introduction

No man can be a Polititian, except he be first an Historian or a Traveller; for except he can see what Must be, or what May be, he is no Polititian: Now, if he have no knowledge in story, he cannot tell what hath been; and if he hath not been a Traveller, he cannot tell what is: but he that neither knoweth what hath been, nor what is; can never tell what must be, or what may be.
—James Harrington

On the fifth of October 1938, Winston Churchill rose to address the House of Commons. It was not, in his estimation, an auspicious occasion. Four days before, Neville Chamberlain had returned from the Munich Conference to announce to nearly everyone's applause and relief that he had brought "peace in our time." To the consternation and annoyance of many within his own party and many without, Churchill insisted on throwing cold water on the prime minister's claim. He started off in an almost apologetic tone. "If I do not begin this afternoon," he said, "by paying the usual, and indeed almost invariable tributes to the prime minister for his handling of this crisis, it is certainly not from any lack of personal regard. We have always, over a great many years, had very pleasant relations, and I have deeply understood from personal experiences of my own in a similar crisis the stress and strain he has had to bear." Churchill then drew attention to the candor of others, and having fortified himself from their example, he came to the point: "I will, therefore, begin by saying the most unpopular and most unwelcome thing. I will begin by saying what everybody would like to ignore or forget but which must nevertheless be stated, namely, that we have sustained a total and unmitigated defeat, and that France has suffered even more than we have." Initially, he claimed, "One pound was demanded at the pistol's point. When it was given, £2 were demanded at the pistol's point. Finally, the dictator consented to take £1 17s. 6d. and the rest in promises of good will for the future." As for Czechoslovakia, "All is over. Silent, mournful, abandoned, broken, [she] recedes into the darkness."

More important from Churchill's perspective was his own country's descent in the brief span of time that had passed since Adolf Hitler had come to power. Czechoslovakia's disappearance was merely, he insisted,

the most grievous consequence of what we have done and of what we have left undone in the last five years—five years of futile good intentions, five years of eager search for the line of least resistance, five years of uninterrupted retreat of British power, five years of neglect of our air defenses. Those are the features which I stand here to expose and which marked an improvident stewardship for which Great Britain and France have dearly to pay. We have been reduced in those five years from a position of security so overwhelming and so unchallengeable that we never cared to think about it. We have been reduced from a position where the very word "war" was considered one which could be used only by persons qualifying for a lunatic asylum. We have been reduced from a position of safety and power—power to do good, power to be generous to a beaten foe, power to make terms with Germany, power to give her proper redress for her grievances, power to stop her arming if we chose, power to take any step in strength or mercy or justice which we thought right—reduced in five years from a position safe and unchallenged to where we stand now.

He could not believe "that a parallel exists in the whole course of history" for such a squandering and neglect of combinations and resources. By allowing the remilitarization of the Rhineland, by standing idly by while Austria was seized, by giving away Czechoslovakia, by opening the way for a Nazi domination of Eastern Europe, "we shall find that we have deeply compromised, and perhaps fatally endangered, the safety and even the independence of Great Britain and France." He feared that his own country would fall "into the power, into the orbit and influence of Nazi Germany" and that its "existence" would become "dependent upon their good will or pleasure." He predicted that there would be additional demands. He foretold that a "policy of submission" would "carry with it restrictions upon the freedom of speech and debate in Parliament, on public platforms, and discussions in the Press, for it will be said—indeed, I hear it said sometimes now—that we cannot allow the Nazi system of dictatorship to be criticized by ordinary, common English politicians. Then, with a Press under control, in part direct but more potently indirect, with every organ of public opinion doped and chloroformed into acquiescence, we shall be conducted along further stages of our journey."

He concluded his oration by saying that he did not grudge "our loyal, brave people . . . the natural spontaneous outburst of joy and relief when they learned that the hard ordeal would no longer be required of them at the moment." But he added that "they should know the truth." Above all else, they should know "that there has been gross neglect and deficiency in our defenses; they should know that we have sustained a defeat without a war, the consequences of which will travel far with us along our road; they should know that we have passed an awful milestone in our history, when the whole equilibrium of Europe has been deranged, and that the terrible words have for the time being been pronounced against the Western democracies: 'Thou art weighed in the balance and found wanting.' "[1]

Churchill's greatest speech makes strange reading today. Fifty years before he delivered it, liberal democracy appeared to be the wave of the future, its victory inevitable, its triumph almost at hand. In the first half-century that passed after the Munich crisis, the western democracies were time and again weighed in the balance; and though they were not ultimately found wanting, they were generally on the defensive. Indeed, for a long time, it seemed by no means certain that the future would be theirs. Then, suddenly, in the wake of Mikhail Gorbachev's rise to power in the Soviet Union, events took a new turn in that country and in Poland, in Hungary and Czechoslovakia, in East Germany and Bulgaria, in Romania, Yugoslavia, and ultimately even in Albania. The totalitarian regimes in Europe collapsed; the long, twilight struggle dubbed the Cold War came to an end; and it became evident that the patient postwar American policy of containment had actually worked. There were even grounds for the hope that communism would someday soon be regarded as a stage on the way to liberal democracy—not just in Europe, but in Asia and in the Caribbean as well.[2]

At a moment so fraught with hope for the future, it may seem untimely to resurrect past failures and to remind readers that the welcome events which have transpired need not have taken place. But I would submit that a certain sobriety is in order on our part and that it is not entirely fortuitous that the West has greeted the transformation of the East with a comparative lack of euphoria. It is essential to remember that it is in large part an accident that at the end of the Second World War liberal democracy was not in effect restricted to the continent of North America. Churchill's fears for his country no doubt seemed overly dramatic when he expressed them; they may seem so as well today. But this was not the case during the Battle of Britain, for, in truth, he was right in every particular. As a consequence of what Churchill called "an improvident stewardship," Western Europe fell to Nazi aggression and Britain was left all but defenseless. If Hitler had staked everything on an invasion of the British Isles, or if he had simply been content to consolidate his hold on Western and Central Europe, build submarines, and await his opportunity, there can be little doubt that he would eventually have prevailed, and Churchill's worst suppositions would have been translated into fact. One can, of course, imagine Hitler succumbing to Stalin. But a Soviet domination of the continent would hardly have improved Britain's prospects for survival as an independent, liberal democracy. It took direct

American intervention in the war to change the fundamental situation, and that intervention was entirely due to the Japanese attack on Pearl Harbor and the German declaration of war. Had the Japanese high command chosen to avoid a confrontation with the United States, the war would have had a different outcome—and not just in the Pacific. Indeed, if Hitler had held back from declaring war on the United States, there would have been no obvious occasion for an American military intervention in Europe, and one may wonder whether the United States would ever have involved itself directly in the conflict raging on that continent. The grave blunders of democracy's enemies obscure the fact that the world's first and most firmly settled liberal democracy was also then weighed in the balance and found very much wanting.[3]

The events of the 1930s and the 1940s proved to be a sobering experience for many of those who lived through them, and that costly education served them well when the time came for forging the postwar world. But that generation has now all but passed from the scene, and it is not difficult to imagine that liberal democracy in Europe, in North America, and elsewhere might once again suffer from "an improvident stewardship"—especially if faced with a challenge as unexpected, as formidable, and as terrifying as the one mounted some fifty years ago. This may seem unlikely in the wake of communism's collapse, but it is by no means impossible: modern military technology is dynamic; and where inattention, complacency, and wishful thinking are the rule, unforeseen developments can quickly and decisively alter the balance of power. In the 1930s, five years made all the difference. Nothing prevents such an eventuality in our own time. Indeed, as Saddam Hussein's abortive lunge for power should serve to remind us, the proliferation of nuclear, biological, and chemical weapons may well render the coming decades much more unstable than those in the recent past. There is every reason to suspect that, in one fashion or another, we will continue to be weighed in the balance.

But even if my misgivings prove unjustified, even if now, for the first time in more than half a century, we have nothing to fear from the appeasement of evil, there is little to justify self-satisfaction on our part, for there are clouds of another sort forming on our horizon. As Alexis de Tocqueville warned us long ago, the prosperity engendered by the modern republic and its remarkable success do not in any way preclude a fall: if the "decent materialism," which he found regnant in America, was unlikely to corrupt those exposed to it, it could nonetheless "soften the soul and without noise unbend its springs of action," and it could thereby prepare the way for a species of tyranny all the more horrifying because welcome and unremarked.[4] Something of the sort may be in wait for us, for over the last few decades a noiseless revolution has been under way; and as countless commentators on both left and right have repeatedly pointed out, domestic developments in all of the modern republics have been disheartening in one critical regard. There is a drift toward a species of soft, administrative despotism evident nearly everywhere—not least in the United States, the oldest, the least centralized, and most democratic republic in the world.

This point needs particular emphasis, for one can hardly think a liberal democracy in good health that acknowledges no limits to the expansion of public "entitlements," government services, and controls; that eats up an ever increasing proportion of the national income; that effectively relegates all severely contentious political decisions to a court of men and women appointed to office for life; and that leaves much of public policy to be determined by a dialogue between tenured bureaucrats and judges who never have to justify to the voters or even to one another in a public forum the decisions they have made. Nor can one be heartened to discover that those elected to the polity's most popular branch have so effectively entrenched themselves in office that death and retirement account for virtually all changes in personnel. These are straws in the wind. Like the gradual disappearance of the state and local autonomy that Thomas Jefferson and Alexis de Tocqueville thought so important for the maintenance of political freedom, they are indicative of a decline in democratic vigor, and this is a phenomenon which should give us pause.

There is, then, reason to ask what has gone wrong, what accounts for the modern republic's long period of vulnerability in the international sphere, and what explains the malaise now besetting it at home, for one must wonder whether modern republicanism suffers somehow from a debilitating, genetic disorder. These are, however, questions that it is far easier to pose than to answer, for the very character of modern republicanism is cast into the shadows by its brilliant, initial success when pitted against the old order. The men who made the American Revolution were arguably the most self-conscious legislators in human history. They claimed that they were initiating "a new order of the ages," and subsequent events in France and throughout the world suggest that they knew whereof they spoke. One consequence of their remarkable accomplishment is that the ancien régime is no longer with us, and that makes it extremely hard for us to adequately understand the political options that were open to them and the reasoned choices that they made. In past ages, one could gain perspective on one's own regime and come to discern its peculiarities by traveling, as Herodotus, Machiavelli, and James Harrington did, and thereby one could attain an awareness of the very considerable range of human possibilities. But when we travel today, we encounter polities by and large constructed in our own image and peoples uncannily eager to imitate our ways. Those polities which are not like ours are with the rarest of exceptions decidedly, if to our way of thinking, strangely, modern; and they are, in nearly every instance, tyrannies. For the comparative study of republicanism, historical inquiry is our only recourse. In no other way can we liberate ourselves from the tyranny of the familiar. In no other way can we come to see our own world with the discerning eye of a visitor from abroad.[5]

Here, however, we encounter another difficulty. The way that human beings tend to read the past is for the most part decisively shaped by the regime in which they live. In our case, this penchant is strengthened and fortified by a phenomenon peculiar to the modern age. The republicanism and the tyranny familiar to us are unique in human history in that they are explicitly grounded on a species of political science; and, as I will try to show in the chapters of this three-volume work, that political science is, despite its pretensions, quite partial to those very regimes. Like all peoples, then, we warm to what is familiar and we instinctively tend to prefer that which is our own. What distinguishes us is the partisan character of our political science, which serves chiefly to reinforce our prejudice in our own favor and which cannot, therefore, emancipate us from our natural sense of our own superiority. In sum, our status as children of the Enlightenment provides us with an elaborate and highly plausible rationalization of our own way of life—which tends to prevent us from seeing the polities of the past as their citizens saw them, and which in turn virtually rules out our seeing ourselves and our own regime as they would have seen us. Above all else, we lack a sense of our own peculiarity, and the most obvious sign of this fact is that the species of servitude which we think of as the peculiar institution our more distant ancestors considered a perfectly normal state of affairs.

The extended essay that stretches through this and the two successive volumes is not intended as a thoroughgoing diagnosis of the strengths and weaknesses of modern republicanism. Its goals are more modest and per-haps more easily achieved. It is designed to make the present discontents more comprehensible by making visible their roots. It is aimed at preparing the way for the requisite diagnosis by bringing the ancient Greek republic back on stage, by doing justice to the legitimate appeal and moral purchase of the way of life which it fostered, and by setting the modern republic along-side it so that the elements of continuity and discontinuity in the history of republicanism can become visible. In this regard, this three-volume work is an essay in comparative politics. But it is something else as well: for in the process of trying to lay bare the fundamental principles of self-government in antiquity and today, it seeks to clarify and weigh the reasoning that led the Founders of the first and paradigmatic modern republic to deliberately turn their backs on the ancient model and to reject, or at least transform, classical politics; and it aims, therefore, at casting new light on the peculiar foundations on which they purposed to construct modern political life. In this regard, it is an attempt to study the influence of one epoch on another, and it is an appreciative exa.nination of the thinking of a remarkable group of men.

To achieve these ends, I might have sought a premodern exemplar for self-government elsewhere, in ancient Rome or in medieval and Renaissance Europe. A case can no doubt be made for according priority to each. I would not want to suggest that one can make full sense of the history of the struggle for self-government in early modern Europe without referring to the influence of Roman institutions and law or that one can do so without considering the medieval heritage of corporate liberty. Nor would I argue that little or nothing can be learned from an extended comparison between modern republicanism and these earlier forms of self-government.[6] I would merely contend that classical Greece has a special claim on our attention. It was in Hellas that the first republics known to the West appeared and flourished. There is reason to suppose that it was their example that inspired the subsequent appearance of republicanism in ancient Italy; and Roman institutions provided, in turn, the impetus for medieval corporatism and, thereby, for the development of representative assemblies and for the emergence of the medieval commune in the Latin West. In Greece, one encounters premodern republicanism in its pristine and purest form. Moreover, there survives from ancient Hellas a sophisticated body of theoretical writing concerning politics that knows no equal in any subsequent time and place. To the extent that modern political reflection draws on and responds to the political thought of the ancient Greeks, Hellas must be accorded primacy.

The great oracle of those Americans who labored long and hard in the late eighteenth century to establish just and workable political constitutions was the French philosophe the baron de Montesquieu. "To comprehend modern times well," he warned his readers, "it is necessary to comprehend ancient times well; it is necessary to follow each law in the spirit of all the ages."[7] That piece of advice they took to heart, and so, I would suggest, must anyone who really desires to understand their remarkable achievement. If at least some of the readers of these three volumes emerge from pondering my long and labyrinthine argument with a new sense of detachment from their own world and with an inkling of what it is that makes modern republicanism so wondrous, so vulnerable, and so very strange, I will have achieved my goal. Wonder is, as Plato suggests, a very philosophical passion[8]—and until we are in its grip, we cannot even begin to understand. In the words of the greatest of the American poets,

> We shall not cease from exploration
> And the end of all our exploring
> Will be to arrive where we started
> And know the place for the first time.[9]

Before entering on the first and most difficult stage of our voyage of self-discovery, our examination of classical republicanism in ancient Greece, we will have to pause briefly to provide ourselves with the requisite intellectual equipment and to acquire the services of a guide intimately familiar with the most important of ancient Hellas's political landmarks. To see clearly what it is that distinguishes the republics of antiquity from those of modern times, one must first make one's escape from the intellectual prison constituted by modern social science and then come to grips with what Aristotle had in mind when he insisted on interpreting the character of a given community in light of what he called its political regime (*politeía*).[10]

VOLUME I

The Ancien Régime in Classical Greece

We are no longer able to enjoy the liberty of the ancients, which consisted in an active and constant participation in the collective power. Our liberty, for us, consists in the peaceful enjoyment of private independence. The share which, in antiquity, each had in the national sovereignty was not, as with us, an abstract supposition. The will of each had real influence: the exercise of that will was a pleasure intense and often repeated. In consequence, the ancients were disposed to make many sacrifices for the preservation of their political rights and their share in the administration of the state. Each, sensing with pride all that his suffrage was worth, found in this consciousness of his own personal importance an ample recompense. This compensation no longer exists today for us. Lost in the multitude, the individual hardly ever perceives the influence he exercises. Never does his will leave any impression on the whole; nothing establishes in his own eyes his cooperation. The exercise of political rights, then, offers us no more than a part of the enjoyment which the ancients found there; and, at the same time, the progress of civilization, the commercial tendency of the epoch, and the communication of the various peoples among themselves have multiplied and have given an infinite variety to the means of personal happiness. It follows that we ought to be more attached than the ancients to our individual independence. For the ancients, when they sacrificed that independence for political rights, sacrificed less to obtain more—while we, in making the same sacrifice, would give more to obtain less. The purpose of the ancients was the sharing of the social power among all the citizens of the same fatherland. It is this to which they gave the name liberty. The purpose of the moderns is security in private enjoyment; and they give the name liberty to the guarantees accorded by the institutions to that enjoyment.

BENJAMIN CONSTANT

———

They were free states; they were small ones; and the age being martial, all their neighbors were continually in arms. Freedom naturally begets public spirit, especially in small states; and this public spirit, this amor patriæ, must encrease when the public is almost in continual alarm, and men are obliged, every moment to expose themselves to the greatest dangers for its defence. A continual succession of wars makes every citizen a soldier: He takes the field in his turn: And during his service he is chiefly maintained by himself. This service is indeed equivalent to a heavy tax; yet it is less felt by a people addicted to arms, who fight for honour and revenge more than pay, and are unacquainted with gain and industry as well as pleasure.—David Hume

There is an elevation natural to man, by which he would be thought, in his rudest state, however urged by necessity, to rise above the consideration of mere subsistence, and the regards of interest: He would appear to act only from the heart, in its engagements of friendship, or opposition; he would shew himself only upon occasions of danger or difficulty, and leave ordinary cares to the weak or the servile. The same apprehensions, in every situation, regulate his notions of meanness or of dignity. In that of polished society, his desire to avoid the character of sordid, makes him conceal his regard for what relates merely to his preservation or his livelihood. In his estimation, the beggar, who depends upon charity; the labourer, who toils that he may eat; the mechanic, whose art requires no exertion of genius, are degraded by the object they pursue, and by the means they employ to obtain it. . . . Women, or slaves, in the earliest ages, had been set apart for the purposes of domestic care, or bodily labour; and in the progress of lucrative arts, the latter were bred to mechanical professions, and were even intrusted with merchandise for the benefit of their masters. Freemen would be understood to have no object besides those of politics and war. In this manner, the honours of one half of the species were sacrificed to those of the other; as stones from the same quarry are buried in the foundation, to sustain the blocks which happen to be hewn for the superior parts of the pile. In the midst of our encomiums bestowed on the Greeks and the Romans, we are, by this circumstance, made to remember, that no human institution is perfect.—Adam Ferguson

In the Greek cities, where one did not live under that religion which establishes that, among men also, purity is a part of virtue; in the Greek cities, where a blind vice reigned in a manner unbridled, where love took a form which one dare not mention, while in marriage only friendship could be found: there, the virtue, the simplicity, the chastity of the women was such that one has hardly ever seen a people that was, in this regard, better policed.—Montesquieu

An Ancient Science of Politics

*The Greek political writers (politiques), who lived under popular government, acknowledged
no other force able to sustain them except that of virtue. Those of our own day speak of nothing
else but of manufactures, of commerce, of finance, of wealth, and of luxury itself.—Montesquieu*

In her novel *The Nice and the Good*, Iris Murdoch introduces her readers to
a wealthy, remarkably fastidious, forty-three-year-old bachelor civil servant
named John Ducane. In the course of delineating his character, she makes a
series of observations regarding the man's favorite pastime that might serve
also as an appropriate introduction to any inquiry addressed to classical antiquity:

> The immense literature about Roman law has been produced by excogi-
> tation from a relatively small amount of evidence, of which a substantial
> part is suspect because of interpolations. Ducane had often wondered
> whether his passion for the subject were not a kind of perversion. There
> are certain areas of scholarship, early Greek history is one and Roman
> law is another, where the scantiness of evidence sets a special challenge
> to the disciplined mind. It is a game with very few pieces, where the
> skill of the player lies in complicating the rules. The isolated and unelo-
> quent fact must be exhibited within a tissue of hypothesis subtle enough
> to make it speak, and it was the weaving of this tissue which fascinated
> Ducane.[1]

What Iris Murdoch says, in passing, about Roman law and early Greek history could be applied to ancient history simply. The evidence for life in ancient Greece and Rome is not just scanty. Not seldom, it reflects a bias; and,
more often than not, the modern researcher is ill placed to discern the nature
of that bias and to fathom its depths. In effect, scholars find themselves in
the position of children eager to reconstruct a vast jigsaw puzzle—who are
aware that the great majority of the pieces are missing and that many of those
which have survived are broken, and who then discover, to their great dis-
may, that their situation is complicated by yet another, perhaps even graver
deficiency: for they have not the vaguest notion of what the puzzle would
look like if they actually managed to piece it together.

In short, the ancient Greek *pólis* poses an almost insuperable obstacle to
the modern understanding. To begin with, as one acute observer pointed out
not so many years ago,

We must imagine houses without drains, beds without sheets or springs, rooms as cold, or as hot, as the open air, only draughtier, meals that began and ended with pudding, and cities that could boast neither gentry nor millionaires. We must learn to tell the time without watches, to cross rivers without bridges, and seas without a compass, to fasten our clothes (or rather our two pieces of cloth) with two pins instead of rows of buttons, to wear our shoes or sandals without stockings, to warm ourselves over a pot of ashes, to judge open-air plays or lawsuits on a cold winter's morning, to study poetry without books, geography without maps, and politics without newspapers.[2]

But we must do much more as well, for the difficulty posed by the ancient Greek *pólis* is, in no small measure, conceptual. Few of the terms coined to describe the political experience of the West in the last two hundred years can properly be used to make sense of the regimes of classical antiquity. The scientific revolution and the technological upheaval that grew out of it, the Enlightenment's popularization of philosophy and the concomitant emergence of ideology, the foundation of representative democracy and the development of the capitalist economy—these events, which decisively shaped the republics of modern times, have altered the range of political options so radically that we find much in the world of antiquity almost unrecognizable.

This profound transformation has not escaped the notice of the ablest of the modern political analysts. For example, in 1816, Thomas Jefferson commented on the problem:

So different was the style of society then, and with those people, from what it is now and with us, that I think little edification can be obtained from their writings on the subject of government. They had just ideas of the value of personal liberty, but none at all of the structure of government best calculated to preserve it. . . . The introduction of this new principle of representative democracy has rendered useless almost everything written before on the structure of government; and, in a great measure, relieves our regret, if the political writings of Aristotle, or of any other ancient, have been lost, or are unfaithfully rendered or explained to us.[3]

About twenty years later, when Alexis de Tocqueville had completed his tour of the United States, he advanced an even more general claim: "When I compare the republics of Greece and of Rome with those in America; . . . when I call to mind all the attempts that are made to judge the latter with the aid of the former, and to foresee what will happen in our day by considering what took place two thousand years ago, I am tempted to burn my books in order to apply none but novel ideas to so novel a condition of society."[4] What Jefferson and Tocqueville say regarding the application of ancient political thought to the modern situation can far more aptly be said about the application of modern paradigms to ancient circumstances. Thus, for example, it makes little sense to ask whether the Lacedaemonian regime was totalitarian or liberal. It was, properly speaking, neither. In its heyday, Sparta was never subject to a tyrant—least of all to a tyrant in command of a party animated by a revolutionary ideology, intent on using propaganda to impose a particular worldview on the populace, and willing to employ terror to snuff out every hint of political and cultural dissent. Nor was classical Lacedaemon an open society where the citizen was able to live his life for the most part as he pleased, free from external restraint insofar as his behavior was consonant with the maintenance of public order. Like the regime described in Jean Jacques Rousseau's *The Social Contract*, the Spartan polity was at the same time a closed society and a participatory democracy.[5]

It is a measure of the depths of the chasm that separates the republics of Greek antiquity from those of recent modernity that we find it difficult to understand how a polity could deny its citizens any rights against the community and concurrently foster their participation in its governance. In contrast to their heirs, the founders of the first great liberal democratic republic were acutely aware of this possibility. They were witnesses to the decay of a world in certain, decisive respects closely akin to that of the ancients; they were self-conscious proponents of an alternative to classical republicanism; and they were ideally situated to profit from the institutional political science established by Thomas Hobbes on a foundation laid by Niccolò Machiavelli and then further developed in various ways by James Harrington, Henry Neville, John Locke, John Trenchard, Bernard Mandeville, the baron de Montesquieu, Viscount Bolingbroke, David Hume, William Blackstone, Adam Smith, Jean Louis de Lolme, and the like. Perhaps as a consequence, the men who launched the American Revolution and founded America's various governments were able to draw the distinction between the ancient and the modern regimes with a modicum of precision. With their help, one would think that it would be possible to achieve that critical distance from current affairs prerequisite for initiating an attempt to understand antiquity in its own terms.

Even here, however, a word of caution is in order, for it is doubtful whether the institutional political science of early modern Europe and revolutionary America can, in fact, provide "a tissue of hypothesis subtle enough" to elicit fully intelligible speech from "the isolated and uneloquent" facts available

to the student of antiquity. In stressing the formative influence of political
institutions, that political science is less narrow than the modern social science devised by figures such as Karl Marx and Max Weber and developed by
their various disciples, and it is no doubt superior to it. Certainly, no one can
accuse John Adams, Thomas Jefferson, James Madison, Alexander Hamilton, and their colleagues of underestimating the degree to which political
architecture shapes civil society and the classes and social groupings within
it. But like the social science of quite recent times, the institutional political
science of early modernity is reductionist at heart.[6] Both are predicated on
a questionable assumption: that what Machiavelli once called "the effectual
truth of the matter (*la verità effettuale della cosa*)" is not a half-truth but the
truth, the whole truth, and nothing but the truth.[7] Both presuppose that
the Florentine's distinguished English disciple the Marquis of Halifax said
all that really needs saying on the subject when he began by observing that
"men's resolutions are generally formed, by their appetite or their interest"
and then added that "reason is afterwards called in for Company, but it hath
no Vote."[8] As a consequence, institutional political science shares with contemporary social science a predilection for dismissing opinion as a matter
of secondary concern and for treating what Augustine called "concord regarding loved things held in common" largely as a reflection of social and
political arrangements rather than as the element constituting civil society
and underpinning its many institutions.[9]

I do not mean to suggest that classical historians have little to learn from
comparative ethnography and political science. In fact, given the poverty of
the evidence available to them, they desperately require such instruction.
But from the homogenized products of contemporary social science, they
are quite unlikely to be able to derive what they need most. Indeed, to the
extent that they succumb to the reductionist project that animates the various social science disciplines, their history will be little more than a pack
of tricks played on the dead. The *method* systematically applied by all but a
few modern students of these subjects deconstructs and reduces the phenomena in a fashion that disarms the past and obscures its true character.
These disciplines, which pretend to be impartial, are in their very impartiality profoundly partisan. Behind their studied neutrality lies an arrogance
unchecked because unremarked. For what poses as a rejection of all ethnocentricity is, in fact, an ethnocentricity fully victorious: the one thing that
contemporary researchers are taught to take for granted and never to question is that the men and women whom they study were wrong, and deeply
wrong, above all else because these individuals were unaware of their own
ethnocentricity—unaware, that is, that the beliefs for which they claimed to

live and for which they were sometimes willing to die were arbitrary and nonsensical, if not self-serving. Almost never are well-trained modern researchers open to the possibility that the moral and political visions guiding the communities they study are, in fact, superior to those which inspire their own research. Almost never are they willing to apply to their own disciplines, to the presuppositions of those disciplines, and to the aspirations of social scientists like themselves the reductionist method to which they subject the opinions of those on whom they do their research. To do so would be to unmask the prejudices and the ambitions which inspire the project in which they are engaged. To do so would be to debunk the priestcraft of our modern clerks.[10]

It matters little whether the modern social scientist takes as a mentor Marx, Freud, Weber, Durkheim, or some figure less well known. His task is, typically, to "explain" the words and deeds of those whom he studies by tracing those words and deeds to crude passions and material interests familiar to one and all. As a consequence, much of what passes as scholarship in our time is an attempt—more or less unconscious, and almost always devoid of self-critical awareness—to debunk the past and to legitimate the trends of the last two hundred years.[11] In the process of domesticating the past and rendering what was once thought noble and sublime familiar and banal, this scholarship deprives that past of anything but antiquarian interest. If, for example, "the fundamental vectors of Athenian society" were simply "the needs for food, shelter, security, and conflict resolution," as one distinguished classical scholar has recently argued,[12] classical Athens would be a proper subject for idle and self-congratulatory curiosity alone, for not much more than the accident of circumstance would distinguish the ancient Greek citizen from the modern bourgeois, and the latter could justifiably take considerable pleasure and pride in contemplating the remarkable advances that have been made in the course of the intervening centuries in meeting those fundamental needs.

In recent years, to their credit, a number of Marxist historians—ordinarily restricted to a narrow and unenlightening species of class analysis—have betrayed an awareness of some of the weaknesses inherent in their approach.[13] Many speak of "false consciousness" and unwittingly confess that a class lacking class consciousness is for all practical purposes no class at all. Some resort to Marx's distinction between "a class-in-itself" and "a class-for-itself" in trying to make sense of the absence of open class warfare within a given political community and in effect concede that the concept of class is of little use in the analysis of that particular polity.[14] But only a very few take the final and fatal step, join with Antonio Gramsci in emphasizing the "hegemony" of the ruling class, and acknowledge that "once an ideology arises it alters profoundly the material reality and in fact becomes a partially autonomous feature of that reality." In practice, the ablest and most resolute of these historians tacitly abandon anything recognizable as a "theory of class determinism"; and then, largely unawares, they approach a purportedly outmoded and virtually forgotten, pre-Machiavellian species of political analysis that recognizes the partisan character of all class rule but insists, above all else, on giving opinion its due.[15]

Well over a century ago, John Stuart Mill touched on what deserves to be considered the critical feature of all political life. One of the conditions of "permanent political society," he observed, "has been found to be, the existence, in some form or other, of the feeling of allegiance, or loyalty." The English philosopher was aware that "this feeling may vary in its objects." He knew that it "is not confined to any particular form of government." But he insisted that, "whether in a democracy or in a monarchy, its essence is always the same; viz. that there be in the constitution of the State *something* which is settled, something permanent, and not to be called in question; something which, by general agreement, has a right to be where it is, and to be secure against disturbance, whatever else may change." Mill thought the "necessity" self-evident that there be "some fixed point: something which men agreed in holding sacred; which, wherever freedom of discussion was a recognised principle, it was of course lawful to contest in theory, but which no one could either fear or hope to see shaken in practice; which, in short (except perhaps during some temporary crisis), was in the common estimation placed beyond discussion." To be sure, he explained, no community was or could be "exempt from internal dissension." It is, in fact, inevitable that there be "collisions . . . between the immediate interests and passions of powerful sections of the people." But if nations and peoples have generally been able "to weather these storms, and pass through turbulent times," it is precisely because, "however important the interests about which men fell out, the conflict did not affect the fundamental principles of the system of social union which happened to exist; nor threaten large portions of the community with the subversion of that on which they had built their calculations, and with which their hopes and aims had become identified."[16] Fortunately for the student of self-government in the ancient Mediterranean world, Mill's insight was the fundamental premise of premodern political science, which had its origins in classical antiquity and came to fruition while trying to make sense of the ancient Greek *pólis*.

The emergence of this first political science can easily be traced. In the fifth century B.C., Herodotus traveled about the eastern Mediterranean and the Black Sea, investigated the *nómoi*—the customs, habits, and laws—of the Hellenes and the barbarians, and attempted to make sense of the *nómoi* of each nation with an eye to the political regime (*politeía*) within which those customs, habits, and laws found their place.[17] At the end of that century, Thucydides depicted the great war between the Athenians and the Spartans as an epic contest between two different republican regimes and used his history to analyze the strengths and weaknesses of each.[18] In the decades that followed, Xenophon employed the same approach in interpreting the Persian monarchy; Plato pioneered the study of political psychology with regard to the rise and the decay of the different regimes; and then Aristotle brought regime analysis to full maturity, applied it to an assortment of the polities in existence in his time, and left it as a legacy to Theophrastus, Polybius, Diodorus Siculus, Dionysius of Halicarnassus, Cicero, Sallust, Livy, Tacitus, Dio Cassius, Plutarch, Ammianus Marcellinus, and the other great writers responsible for recording so much of the little that we know concerning the ancient world and for making sense of the changes that took place.[19] It is to the picture that these authors draw that the modern scholar must turn if he is to piece together the jigsaw puzzle of ancient history from the very few pieces of evidence that have survived, and it is the conceptual framework provided by ancient political science that he must employ as a tool if he is to weave "a tissue of hypothesis subtle enough" to entice fully intelligible speech from "the isolated and uneloquent" facts now available. Only with regard to the sphere of religion, where their partisanship for nonpartisanship occasioned a deliberate and misleading silence on the part of some of the ancient philosophers, must he remain on his guard.[20]

Except, on occasion, in that one sphere, it was not the practice of the ancient political scientists to ignore public opinion or to explain it away—dismissing it as false consciousness, treating it as mere ideology, or interpreting it simply as a product of the historical process.[21] Instead, typically, they gave the views of ordinary men a respectful hearing and attempted to make sense of them by showing that, when considered as a systematic whole, they point beyond themselves to something both nobler and more intelligible. In fact, doing justice to popular opinion was one of the principal goals of ancient political science. Thus, where the modern political science of Thomas Hobbes and his successors, like the modern physical science of Descartes and his admirers, aims at the achievement of an absolute, quasi-mathematical certainty and begins with the categorical rejection of "those opinions which are already vulgarly received,"[22] Aristotle customarily started off with a careful consideration of what he called *éndoxa* or "reputable opinions."[23] The task of political science as he understood it was identical with that of science in general as understood by Plato and his followers: both aimed at making sense of the ordinary man's perceptions; both sought, in this way, "to save *tà phainómena*."[24] As a consequence, Aristotle and his disciples managed— religion aside—to record, examine, and analyze the deepest convictions of their contemporaries and to give them as full and as coherent an expression as those convictions could sustain.

Because they treated the opinions of ordinary men with such respect, the ancient students of political affairs understood well what Marx, Weber, and modern social scientists in general have managed to forget: that the articulation of humanity into nations and political communities is of greater fundamental importance and deserves more careful study than its articulation into economic and social classes.[25] And they recognized that to make this assertion is to give primacy to the political regime and to deny the tyranny of circumstance. They were sensitive to the severe limits imposed on human freedom by the need to eke out a livelihood, to be sure; and they paid careful attention to the formative influence of political institutions. But they accorded these elements secondary standing. Though much may separate Plato from Aristotle, on this fundamental point they were agreed: to understand the ancient Greek *pólis*, one must be willing to entertain two propositions—that the political regime (*politeía*), rather than economic or environmental conditions, is the chief determinant of what one acute, ancient observer called "the one way of life of a whole *pólis*" and another dubbed "the city's soul,"[26] and that education in the broadest and most comprehensive sense (*paideía*) is more important than anything else in deciding the character of the regime.[27]

In one passage of *The Politics*, Aristotle suggests that it is the provision of a common education (*paideía*)—and nothing else—that turns a multitude (*plêthos*) into a unit and constitutes it as a *pólis*; in another, he indicates that it is the regime (*politeía*) which defines the *pólis* as such. Though apparently in contradiction, the two statements are in fact equivalent.[28] It is not fortuitous that Polybius's celebrated discussion of the Roman *politeía* is, in fact, a discussion of the *paideía* accorded the ruling element (*políteuma*) at Rome. Precisely the same observation can be made regarding Xenophon's account of the Persian *politeía*.[29] As both Polybius and Xenophon recognized, if certain opinions reign within a given community, it is simply because their advocates have consolidated dominion there and, in the process, have managed to persuade themselves and their subjects of their right to rule by an appeal to their own preeminence in honoring these same opinions in speech and in deed.[30]

The ancients were by no means naive. In fact, if anything, they were harder headed than the putative realists of our own day. Though they insisted on the primacy of *paideía*, they recognized that there is a strong case to be made for institutional balances and checks;[31] and though they made a point of judging human affairs from the perspective of the best regime, they conceded that, in politics, one must nearly always settle for the lesser evil. Concerning the manner in which human beings can normally be expected to behave, the classical writers harbored no illusions: they knew that ordinary, uninstructed human desire tends to be insatiable, and they acknowledged that most of those who enter the political arena do so for the sake of money and material advantage.[32] Consequently, they took it for granted that the justification advanced by the *políteuma* within any actually existing *políteía* would, at least in some measure, be partisan, partial, and self-serving.[33] But a sober appreciation of human weakness was merely their starting point, for they understood as well that, for the purposes of regime analysis, the partisan character of the *políteía* is of secondary importance.

This needs emphasis. La Rochefoucauld may have been the first to remark that "hypocrisy is an homage that vice renders virtue."[34] But he was hardly the first to recognize the fact.[35] And in any case, as that great disciple of Machiavelli would have been perfectly ready to concede, vanity normally dictates that opinions at first hypocritically embraced should come to be cherished sincerely as well.[36] The marquis of Halifax was, then, surely right to assert that, while a "Good man, for his own sake, will not bee guilty of hipocrisy, . . . for the sake of the world, hee will not discourage it in others." Hypocrisy really is "a Paradox; It is rayled at, and deserveth it; yet doth more good to Mankind, than the best of the vertues they commend."[37] For Otto Hintze hit the nail on the head when he observed that "man does not live by bread alone; he wants to have a good conscience when he pursues his vital interests; and in pursuing them he develops his powers fully only if he is conscious of simultaneously serving purposes higher than purely egotistical ones."[38] Odd though it may seem, the fact that hypocrisy and self-delusion are needed to mask the partisan character of the political order is a sign of man's innate generosity and of his capacity for impartiality, for they are the dark shadows cast by the tension within human nature between the desire for private advantage and a genuine public-spiritedness.

This argument can be restated in different terms. In pondering the character of a given political community, one must always keep in mind the fact that Plato's Thrasymachus was at least partially correct in thinking that, within every regime, political justice embodies "the advantage of the stronger." But one must still give primacy to the insight inherent in Polemarchus's conviction that justice is inseparable from the sort of friendship that is grounded in a common, cooperative pursuit of the noble and the good: for even if the political community is really just a gang of thieves or a band of pirates, if it is unsustained by some such vision of the whole, it will quickly fall apart.[39] When Sir Lewis Namier dismissed opinion, remarking that, in politics, "what matters most is the underlying emotions, the music, to which ideas are a mere libretto, often of very inferior quality," he missed the point.[40] If an opera is to be effective, the music and the words must sound the same theme, and the same can be said for emotions and ideas in the political realm.

In the end, then, the modern distinction between materialism and idealism makes little practical, political sense—for what really matters most with regard to political understanding is this: to decide who is to rule or what sorts of human beings are to share in rule and function as a community's *políteuma* is to determine which of the various and competing titles to rule is to be authoritative; in turn, this is to decide what qualities are to be admired and honored in the city, what is to be considered advantageous and just, and how happiness (*eudaimonía*) is to be pursued; and this decision—more than any other—determines the *paideía* which constitutes "the one way of life of a whole *pólis*."[41] This decision may be a matter of chance, to be sure. Nations and peoples tend to stumble on what Edmund Burke called "establishments" and John Stuart Mill termed that "*something*" in their constitution "which is settled, something permanent, and not to be called in question." As even Alexander Hamilton was forced to concede, few, if any, "societies of men" have ever established "good government from reflection and choice"; most, if not all, have been "destined to depend, for their political constitutions, on accident and force."[42] But where circumstance predominates—as, the ancients fully recognized, is usually the case—it is either because the citizens have been overwhelmed by the sheer momentum of events or because they have managed affairs quite ineptly and have allowed things to drift so that fortune comes to function as a lawgiver (*nomothétēs*) in arranging that distribution and disposition of the polity's offices and honors (*táxis tôn archôn*) which, more than anything else, determines the *paideía* that makes them a political community. What counts most from the vantage point assumed by Plato, Aristotle, and their successors is the fact that circumstance need not be absolutely predominant. Thus, if ancient political science stresses the limits of human mastery, it nonetheless presupposes the possibility of statesmanship.[43]

Of necessity, the chapters that follow draw on the great body of recent classical scholarship. Much of the best of this scholarship has been to one degree or another influenced by the political science of the early moderns or by the social science of more recent times. Where profit can be gained from institutional and sociological studies designed to reveal "the effectual truth of the matter" and that alone, I have not been hesitant to do so.[44] But I have been careful throughout to stress what such studies *methodically* ignore. Thus, as one would expect from what has been already said, I take a substantially, if not entirely, unfamiliar approach and exhibit the surviving evidence within a schema largely borrowed from the ancient analysts of political change. In the sense in which Iris Murdoch uses the terms, these chapters constitute an attempt to "complicate" and even alter the rules of the scholarly "game." To meet what is just in the penetrating criticism leveled at social history by scholars of distinction often otherwise opposed,[45] I have incorporated much of what passes today as social history within political history understood in a much more comprehensive fashion than is now the norm. This I have done by once again making the political regime as such, the ruling element within that regime, and the "loved things held in common" that animate both the central object of historical research.[46] Thus, what follows could perhaps best be described as an attempt to recapture the spirit of life in the first republics known to man by means of an historical essay in the recovery and application of Aristotelian political science. I begin by considering what it was that the citizens of an ancient Greek *pólis* embraced when they treated political liberty as "*something* . . . settled, . . . permanent, and not to be called in question" and made it central to the "concord regarding loved things held in common" which transformed them from "a multitudinous assemblage of rational beings" into what Augustine described as "a people" possessed of "a commonwealth."[47]

CHAPTER 1

The Primacy of Politics in Classical Greece

To act in the view of his fellow-creatures, to produce his mind in public, to give it all the exercise of sentiment and thought, which pertain to man as a member of society, as a friend, or an enemy, seems to be the principal calling and occupation of his nature. . . .

Animals less honored than we, have sagacity enough to procure their food, and to find the means of their solitary pleasures; but it is reserved for man to consult, to persuade, to oppose, to kindle in the society of his fellow-creatures, and to lose the sense of his personal interest or safety, in the ardour of his friendships and his oppositions. —Adam Ferguson

I.i.1

At the turn of the century, the Irish-American journalist Finley Peter Dunne wrote a column of political and social satire for a Chicago newspaper. On one occasion, he touched on the ancient world, attributing the following observation to his character the sage of Halsted Street Mr. Dooley:

> I know histhry isn't thrue, Hinnissy, because it ain't like what I see ivry day in Halsted Sthreet. If any wan comes along with a histhry iv Greece or Rome that'll show me th' people fightin', gettin' dhrunk, makin' love, gettin' marrid, owin' th' grocery man an' bein' without hard-coal, I'll believe they was a Greece or Rome, but not befure. Historyans is like doctors. They are always lookin' f'r symptoms. Thos iv them that writes about their own times examines th' tongue an' feels th' pulse 'an makes a wrong dygnosis. Th' other kind iv histhry is a postmortem examination. It tells ye what a counthry died iv. But I'd like to know what it lived iv.[1]

Mr. Dooley's complaint deserves quotation because it reflects with great precision the dilemma faced by modern historians of antiquity and by their readers as well. Like Mr. Dooley, we are eager to know more about ancient domestic life—and not only about family quarrels, drinking bouts, love, marriage, and the never-ending struggle to make ends meet. But on these and related matters, we have very little reliable information: for the things which Mr. Dooley could see every day on Halsted Street in Chicago are the very things which the ancients took great care to hide from each other—and ultimately from us.[2]

The dearth of evidence regarding the private sphere does nothing to assuage our curiosity, but it may, in itself, be revealing. We may not be able to say what the Greek cities died of, but the relative silence of our infor-

mants regarding domestic affairs suggests that the citizens of the *pólis* lived
for something which Mr. Dooley and the residents of Halsted Street would
have had a great deal of trouble comprehending. Benjamin Constant hinted
at the source of our difficulty when he pointed out that modern circumstances deny us many of the pleasures associated with participation in public
affairs while, at the same time, multiplying and invigorating those derived
from attentiveness to matters lying outside the political realm.[3] As the economy has expanded, shattering the relationship between *oikonomía* and the
simple management of a household and its attached estate, so the polity has
contracted: in a representative democracy situated on an extended territory,
politics is but seldom the focus of popular concern; on the ordinary day,
family matters and money-making engage the passions of the ordinary citizen. If we sometimes find ourselves sharing Mr. Dooley's incomprehension
and disbelief, it is because of the world that we have lost and because of all
that we have gained. To recover that world and to revive some sense of the
spirit that animated it requires a forgetfulness of contemporary concerns and
an imaginative effort at repossession that may, at times, tax our intellectual
and even our moral resources. Prudence dictates that we begin by pondering the eclipse in ancient Greece of that private sphere which Mr. Dooley
considered the chief locus of human endeavor. If Xenophon is to be trusted,
it was the peculiar character of the distinction which the Greeks drew between public and private and the relative weight they gave to each of the two
spheres that set them apart from the barbarians.[4] That understanding and
that evaluation separate them from us in much the same way.

I.i.2

In recent years, it has become commonplace for scholars to allude to the
Greek quest for political solidarity (*homónoia*) and to the attendant hostility
to commerce by saying that the ancient economy was embedded in society.[5]
This formulation has the great virtue that it draws attention to the Greek practice of rigidly subordinating those concerns generated by the market to the
larger needs of the community. But although this phrasing is enlightening to
a degree, it masks the true character of the *pólis*. At least in classical Greece,
the concerns that were primary were not social; they were political. The economy was not embedded in society; the economy and the society were both
embedded in the polity.[6] The love of money was not subordinated to the
desire for social status; they were alike secondary to the quest for office, for
power, and for glory.[7] It was only in postclassical Greece that war ceased to
be the chief concern of the citizen and something akin to social competition

replaced political rivalry.[8] When the Macedonians and their Roman successors destroyed the full independence of the political community, ultimately
reducing the *pólis* to little more than a unit of local administration, politics
lost much of its dignity.

There is another, perhaps more telling way to make this point. Those who
speak of the economy being embedded in society take for granted the distinction between government or state and society; and this distinction, prepared
if not explicitly introduced by John Locke, belongs to the world of the modern
republic and is inapplicable to the ancient city.[9] There was no Greek state.[10]
The ancient Hellenic republic was, as James Madison noted, "a pure democracy, . . . a society consisting of a small number of citizens, who assemble
and administer the government in person."[11] The *pólis* was, as the Greeks
often remarked, the men.[12] In one poem, Alcaeus of Mytilene contended that
"warlike men are a city's tower of defense." In another, which survives only
as paraphrased by later authors, he played variations on the same theme:

> Neither stone blocks (*líthoi*)
> Nor ships' timbers (*xúla*)
> Nor even the carpenter's art (*téchnē tektónōn*)
> Can make a *pólis*.
> But where there are men (*ándres*)
> Who know how to preserve themselves
> There one finds walls and a city as well.[13]

Because they shared the poet's conviction, the Hellenes never spoke in an abstract way of the deeds of Athens, Corinth, and Megara. These were places,
not polities. As the public inscriptions assert, the real actors were the Athenians, the Corinthians, and the Megarians.[14] The people wielded the power,
and they constituted both state and society wrapped up in one. With only
trivial exceptions, the Greek cities had no bureaucracies, no magistrates
blessed with long tenure, no professional armies. It was futile to try to distinguish the governors from the governed; the *pólis* itself depended on the
identity of soldier and civilian;[15] and the farmer had the right to own land
solely by virtue of his status as a citizen.[16] The differentiation of roles which
the distinction between state and society presupposes simply did not exist.
In principle and to a substantial degree in practice, the citizen body was
homogeneous.[17]

Just as there was no Greek state, so there was no civil society. The city was,
as Aristotle argued, a political community (*koinōnía*):[18] it was a *Gemeinschaft*,
not a *Gesellschaft*.[19] The *pólis* was not a conspiracy of self-seeking individuals
joined for mutual profit and protection in a temporary legal partnership that

would be dissolved when it ceased to suit their interests; it was a moral community of men permanently united as a people by a common way of life. As a human being, the Greek possessed no rights against the commonwealth; as a citizen, he might demand and be granted certain privileges—but these would be more than outweighed by his duties to the community at large. Here, as is often the case, language is the shadow of political reality: it is by no means fortuitous that the English word *idiot* is derivative from the Greek term employed to designate those who preferred private pleasure to public endeavor. Because they were shirkers who took what the city had to offer and gave little or nothing in return, men of this stripe incurred scorn and ill will. In short, the peculiar division between a narrow public and a broad private realm characteristic of bourgeois regimes was utterly alien to the Greek experience. The civic community's claim was, in principle, total: only the household (*oîkos*) proved capable of resisting absorption, and this was solely because the city depended on the preservation of this one refuge of privacy for the procreation, rearing, and nourishment of its future citizens.[20]

This design left little room for women. Throughout antiquity, the female members of the human race shared the fate of the *oîkos*: physically, they were not up to the rigors of hoplite warfare, and the biological function they performed in reproduction relegated them of necessity to the realm of procreation and childrearing (though it need not have confined them there forever). Prior to the emergence of the *pólis* and after its decline, when the household was strong and the political community relatively weak, custom and law accorded women a certain modicum of personal freedom and independence. But in the classical period, when the *pólis* was in full vigor, they occupied what we must regard as an unenviable status.[21] Women were everywhere denied political rights, and in some cities, they could on their own neither bring suit in the courts nor legally dispose of the property that was in effect theirs.[22] In at least one such community, it was considered bad form for a male citizen to mention a woman by name in court, on the stage, or in any setting where men from outside the family were present unless, of course, she held civic office as a priestess.[23] And while the men of the town spent their leisure hours loitering about grand public spaces within sight of marble or stone buildings possessed of a magnificence still striking today, their wives and daughters were virtual prisoners, segregated within the world of women, kept in seclusion to the degree that the family could afford it, and then locked within the squalid, dark, and damp confines of relatively primitive mud-brick houses.[24] Though free by law, as Montesquieu reminds us, Greek women were held captive by custom.[25]

In a community that denied full dignity to private affairs, women had a semblance of public existence through the role they played in the city's religious rites, but they otherwise secured honor and recognition almost solely through the accomplishments of their male offspring. A young girl of fourteen who suddenly found herself wed and thrust into the arms of a seasoned warrior more than twice her own age might find the experience disconcerting and even traumatic,[26] but she dared not complain.[27] In all likelihood, this was her one opportunity to achieve that for which, she was repeatedly told, she had been born. If a woman married, became pregnant, survived the ordeal, and bore her husband a son, she would assure for herself by the risk of her life a position of respect within the family and the community at large; but by the same token, if she failed, whatever the reason, the life that remained hers would be hardly worth living. The ancient medical writers inform us that women denied marriage or unable to conceive were unusually susceptible to "the sacred disease." For this malady, when contracted under these circumstances, there was only one cure: marriage, pregnancy, and the birth of a child. This is precisely what we would expect. Psychosomatic illness is by no means a modern discovery: even in antiquity, it was known that the fear of dishonor could generate hysteria and, through it, epilepsy and other disorders.[28] For the wholehearted commitment to public life which the laws and customs of the city sought to elicit from their husbands, brothers, and fathers, the women of Greece paid what must inevitably seem to us a very high price.[29]

As the first book of Aristotle's *Politics* makes clear, they were not alone.[30] The primacy accorded political life presupposed more than one hierarchy. The *oîkos* served an essential productive as well as a procreative function. Just as the city needed women for the replenishment of its steadily dwindling stock of citizens, so also it required laborers to provide for their nourishment. The visible *pólis* constituted by the citizen-men rested on an invisible and politically inarticulate body of slaves condemned to labor in private so that their masters might be free to devote their time and efforts to speech and action in public.[31] "As free men," Euripides observes, "we live off slaves."[32]

Nearly a century after Euripides' death, the comic poet Menander composed a variation on the same theme. To support his contention that "farming is work fit for a slave," he argued that it is not through labor, but "in matters pertaining to war that a real man (*anér*) must outdo his rivals (*huperéchein*)."[33] Though brutal in tone, the verses of the Cretan poet Hybrias echoed the aspirations of the citizens active in every Greek *pólis*:

> In my great spear and my sword lies my wealth,
> And in my fine shield, a screen for the body.

With these, I plow; with these, I reap; and
With these, I trample out sweet wine from the vine;
For it is with these that I am called the master of churls (*mnoía*)
And those who dare not bear the spear and the sword
And the fine shield, a screen for the body,
All fall down, grasping my knee and
Calling me master and Great King.[34]

In antiquity, virtually all of those within the political class belonged to what Tocqueville so aptly calls "the aristocracy of masters."[35] These men could do without slaves, Aristotle remarked, but only if they possessed automatons like the statue of Daedalus or the tripods of Homer's Hephaestus—each able to perform its particular function when ordered and even to anticipate the need.[36] The desire to be at leisure for political action explains why a world requiring no labor at all was one of the abiding fantasies of the Greek imagination.[37]

Menander's quip and Hybrias's poem are important for more than one reason, for they capture not only the situation but the Greek outlook as well. Heraclitus touched on the central issue: to support his claim that "war is the father of all and king over all," he noted that it was combat that "made some men slaves and some men free."[38] Of those condemned to labor for others, the houseborn (*oikogeneîs*) and the foundlings were but a small minority.[39] Throughout Hellas, the ordinary slave was a barbarian taken in war, kidnapped by pirates, or sold by his kin;[40] and even where some form of dependent labor other than chattel slavery prevailed, the servile class was held down by force. As a result, its members—by displaying cowardice in accepting their fate—became objects of scorn. "The race of slaves is ignoble (*kakón*)," one Euripidean character argues. "They observe everything from the perspective of the stomach (*gastér*)."[41]

This claim was not peculiar to the last of the great tragedians. In the *Plutus*, Aristophanes sketches the gulf separating the outlook of the master from that of his slave in strikingly similar terms. While still under the delusion that wealth is the only good thing of which no human being has ever secured a sufficiency, Chremylus provides by way of reinforcing his point a list of desirables that a man can only too easily possess in excess. One can have a surfeit of sex, poetry, and honor, of courage, ambition, and even of high office as general, he remarks; and his slave adds in responsion that one can have enough and more than enough of bread, sweet meats, placenta, dried figs, barley cakes, and even lentil soup. The juxtaposition—underlined by the antiphonal form which the poet adopts—was intended to elicit a laughter bred of prior contempt: for, in keeping with the dictates of convention, the citizen intent on mentioning the good things in life can think only of eros, poetry, and politics, while the slave in precisely the same situation ponders nothing but subsistence and the pleasures of filling his belly. The root of servility was taken to be an obsessive and degrading love of mere life.[42]

Thus, when Plato's Socrates suggested that men educated for freedom must be accustomed to fearing slavery more than death, he was not saying anything out of the ordinary: he was merely echoing the most profound convictions of a martial and slave-owning people.[43] More than a century before, on the eve of the battle of Plataea, the Hellenes united against Persia had purportedly taken an oath "not to hold life dearer than liberty (*eleuthería*)."[44] The document recording the oath may well be a forgery,[45] but this matters very little. The point is that the oath's authenticity seemed plausible to the Greeks. Throughout Hellas, men who preferred servitude to the sacrifice of life were regarded as little better than the beasts of the field. The Euripidean character who asked whether "it was not better not to live at all than to live ignobly (*kakôs*)" spoke for his fellow nationals.[46] For the Greeks, courage was more than merely a prerequisite for citizenship; like freedom, it was virtually a precondition for the possession of humanity itself.[47]

I.i.3

The presence of the women and the slaves was a permanent reminder to the citizens that privacy is privative and that a life centered on domestic concerns—on Mr. Dooley's family quarrels and his drinking bouts, on love, marriage, and the never-ending struggle to make ends meet—is a life of deprivation.[48] No one would query Xenophon's claim that the citizens served each other as bodyguards against their own slaves,[49] and no one would deny that the emergence of republican institutions during the archaic period was in large part occasioned by the desire of the peasantry for equal protection under the law.[50] Indeed, more than a century and a half after the close of that age, a comic poet could still speak of "freedom of speech (*parrhēsía*)" as "the shield of poverty" and suggest that "anyone who loses this freedom has thrown away the shield of life."[51] But to suppose, as many scholars do, that political liberty was for the ordinary citizen of the Greek *pólis* merely or even primarily instrumental would be to surrender to the very incredulity that so blinded Mr. Dooley.[52]

Here, as in nearly all things, Aristotle is a more dependable guide than Karl Marx or even Max Weber. The peripatetic philosopher was perfectly prepared to acknowledge that the political community owed its existence to private concerns—to the need for common defense against attack and to the desire for economic cooperation. But he was too respectful of the convictions of ordinary men to be willing to suppose that such an account of the origins of the city would explain its true nature.[53] If the desire for mere life brought the *pólis* into being, he observed, it is the desire to live nobly and well that sustains it. Thus, when Aristotle describes man as being, by nature, a political animal, he is not simply asserting that human beings are gregarious. Such a claim would fail to distinguish mankind from the ants and the bees. He is contending, instead, that it is only in the *pólis* that gregarious beings of this sort "have a share in the good life."

To understand what Aristotle means by the good life, we must take careful note of those faculties which distinguish man from the beasts. In Aristotle's view, human beings are set apart from the other animals not by their capacity for self-expression, but rather by their capacity for rational speech (*lógos*). Man possesses more than mere voice (*phōnē*); he can do more than just intimate that he feels pleasure or pain. Thus, his humanity is in no way constituted by his ability to speak out, to get a load off his chest, to give vent to his spleen. He could just as well accomplish a purge of emotion by the inarticulate utterance of the beast. For Aristotle, *lógos* is something more refined than the capacity to make private feelings public: it enables the human being to perform as no other animal can; it makes it possible for him to perceive and make clear to others through reasoned discourse the difference between what is advantageous and what is harmful, between what is just and what is unjust, and between what is good and what is evil. It is the sharing of these things, Aristotle insists, which constitutes the household and the *pólis* each as a community (*koinōnía*).

This analysis of human nature explains why Aristotle singles out as mankind's greatest benefactor the human being who first organized the *pólis*, and it accounts as well for his assertion that someone who, by nature, belongs outside the political community must be either a god—or a hunted animal (*thēríon*) alone and at war with the world. It matters little whether the individual lives in solitude, in slavery, as a metic, or under the rule of a tyrant or king. Human beings, other than philosophers, are rendered servile and virtually subhuman by the circumstances or fully conscious choices that deny them participation in the political life. They are rendered servile and virtually subhuman because they are prevented from developing fully those faculties of rational argument (*lógos*) and cooperative action (*práxis*) which men possess and the other nonpolitical animals lack altogether. We exclude slaves from the political community, Aristotle explains, because some men are by nature lacking in the capacity for prudential deliberation (*tò bouleutikón*) regarding the advantageous, the just, and the good; we exclude women, though they possess this capacity, because it is without authority (*ákuros*) over them; and we exclude children because they possess it in incomplete form. For all but the handful of men capable of that quasi-divine existence devoted to *theōría*, the fully human life is a life of *práxis* conducted in accord with the dictates of *lógos*.[54]

Aristotle was by no means the only Greek writer to suppose that man is fully human only when engrossed in public deliberation. Among Aristotle's contemporaries, Isocrates advanced similar claims.[55] And a quarter of a millennium prior to the appearance of *The Politics*, Alcaeus had betrayed much the same outlook. In his song of exile, this poet mourns the loss of his native Mytilene, but he does not dwell on the pleasures of the hearth and the comforts of domestic life. He intones, instead, a dirge with a political theme. "What a wretch I am," he writes,

> Condemned by fate to live the life of a country boor.
> I yearn, Agesilaidas, to hear the herald summon the assembly
> And the council. These things which my father and my father's father
> Grew old possessing among the citizens (who do each other harm)—
> From these I am cast out: an exile on the frontiers. Like Onomacles,
> I have made my home in solitude here, and I [plot] war as one
> In whose veins flows the blood of the wolf (*lukaimíais*).

There was evidently nothing novel in Aristotle's conviction that men destined by nature to live outside the *pólis* were, like Homer's Cyclops, little better than beasts of prey. Alcaeus even suggests that fortune can act in nature's place and make a hunted animal of a man.[56]

The Mytilenian poet was not alone in his understanding of exile. Euripides touches on the same issue in *The Phoenician Women* and deals with it in a strikingly similar way. When Jocasta asks her banished son Polyneices whether "being deprived of one's fatherland is really a great evil," the young man responds that it is "the greatest of evils—worse when experienced than when depicted in speech." When urged to explain in detail what he means, Polyneices does not at first mention that physical insecurity which was in antiquity and is so often today the constant companion of a man without a country. He notes, instead, that "the most annoying aspect" of his plight is that the exile lacks "freedom of speech (*parrhēsía*)." Of course, when pressed by his mother, Polyneices does allude to the hardships he faced in the days immediately following his departure from Thebes. Like Aristotle, he is more than willing to grant the desire for survival its due. But even when confronted with maternal concern, he makes only passing reference to what

James Madison would later call "the great principle of self-preservation." Death by violence is not, for men of Polyneices' mettle, the summum malum that it would be for Thomas Hobbes and for the liberal tradition in political thought that he inspired: this Theban exile nowhere treats citizenship and the political rights that go with it in the fashion of Locke, the radical Whigs, and the American Founding Fathers—as simply, or even chiefly, an instrument for the protection of man's inalienable right to life, liberty, and property. He treats political freedom, instead, as an end in itself.

As the son-in-law of Argos's king, Polyneices is in secure possession of life and the means to sustain it in comfort: what he lacks is that "freedom of speech" which belongs solely to men of independent means participant in politics. Thus, when Jocasta compares the exile's fate to that "of a slave unable to say what he thinks," her son signals his assent by remarking that a man without a country "must bear with the brute ignorance of those who wield power." This is "a painful thing," Jocasta responds, "—to share in the folly (*sunasopheîn*) of fools." In such circumstances, Polyneices sadly acknowledges, "one must be servile for the sake of advantage (*kérdos*)—and this contrary to nature (*parà phúsin*)." Even when freed from material want, the exile is really no better off than the merchant, artisan, or slave. All three lack the dignity of public existence; and even under the best of circumstances, all three remain trapped within the narrow world of the household: for they are forced by human necessity—by the fear of violence and death, or by the love of money and the sense of security it brings—to pursue *kérdos* at the expense of all honor.[57]

The value which Alcaeus, Polyneices, and men like them accorded freedom of speech and the weight they gave to political participation help explain why the Greeks harbored such contempt for the barbarians. Even before the appearance of the Mede, when Hellas was but a scattering of obscure settlements hidden in the shadow of distant Assyria, Phocylides could write:

> A small *pólis* on a headland
> Is superior to senseless Nineveh
> If its affairs are conducted
> In an orderly manner.[58]

After the Greeks had exhibited their prowess against the conquerors of all Asia, there was no stopping them. Aeschylus was not the first to suggest that men who submitted to the rule of a king were slaves,[59] and he was by no means the last. Herodotus picked up the refrain—and in Aristotle's day, the great minds of the age were disputing whether the subjects of the Great King were obsequious by nature, by education, or because of the climate.[60]

This mentality was remarkably resilient. For a considerable period after Macedon's rise to predominance, men of talent and ability who abandoned the cities of Hellas to seek fortune and fame in the service of Alexander the Great and his successors could count on incurring the contempt of their one-time compatriots and on being dismissed as flatterers, parasites, and slaves. This posed a dilemma for cities deeply indebted to such men; and it is striking that, in the early years of the Hellenistic period, communities intent on displaying their gratitude tended, in the decrees they passed, to allude only in the vaguest of terms to their benefactors' association with the monarch they served—while politely avoiding all mention of their rank or status at court. It was only late in the Hellenistic period that serving a king became sufficiently respectable to be mentioned in the civic decrees.[61] If the spirit of republican liberty only slowly gave way, it was presumably because, over the course of centuries, it had laid down deep roots. In the classical period, the attitude evidenced by Aeschylus, Herodotus, Aristotle, and the like actually surfaced at the court of the Great King. Persia's monarch governed his vast empire as a household; for this reason, where the king spoke of *manā badaka* ("my subject or vassal"), his Greek scribe—lacking a vocabulary for feudal relations—employed the term *doûlos*. The great magnates of the royal house were not women; they were not children; and so they could only be slaves.[62]

Much the same outlook colored the Greek view of poverty. What the Greeks feared most from penury was not the discomfort, but the indignity; not the lack of security, but the loss of independence. When Plato equated "being poor" with "lacking power over oneself" and when Demosthenes wrote that "destitution (*penía*) compels free men to do many things that are slavish and base," they were restating a theme announced by Theognis centuries before. "To die, my dear Cyrnus," he wrote, "is better for a poor man than to live worn out by an indigence hard to bear."

> Poverty does more to bring a brave (*agathós*) man under the yoke
> Than anything else—more, Cyrnus, than grizzled age and the ague.
> To flee poverty, such a man must hurl himself from the high rocks
> Into the vastness of the sea. For poverty will subdue any man,
> And he will be unable to say or do anything of note:
> For his tongue will be tied.[63]

It is easy to see why Alcaeus described *penía* as the sister of helplessness (*amachanía*).[64] Destitution was, for the poor man, what exile had been for the Mytilenian poet and for Polyneices: because these rendered a man subservient to the wealthy and the powerful, they robbed him of his capacity for great deeds and political speech. Cicero—in paraphrasing a treatise by the Greek philosopher Panaetius of Rhodes—summed up the situation brilliantly when he wrote that "the workman's wage is itself the pledge of his servitude."[65] In Greece, a proud man facing old age in straitened circumstances might choose day labor over begging; but for the sake of his freedom, he was expected to sacrifice every prospect of receiving support when weak and no longer fit for work and to prefer the instability of the labor exchange to the dependency bred of prolonged employment in the service of another.[66] To be brief: the ancient hierarchy is the reverse of the modern. The Greeks did not value political freedom for the sake of life, liberty, and property. If they valued the last three, it was for the sake of the first.

This, more than anything else, explains Mr. Dooley's confusion: for the opposition of priorities is the root cause of many of the differences which distinguish the world of Halsted Street from that of ancient times. As we shall explore in detail, the founders of the liberal tradition explicitly rejected Aristotle's conviction that the human being is a political animal. They took their bearings not from man's capacity for public deliberation and cooperative action, but rather from his fear of death and aversion to pain. As a consequence, they considered the Greeks' set of preferences to be a travesty of common sense. No one stated this more clearly than Montesquieu. The Hellenes were guilty, he contends, of having "confounded the power of the people with the liberty of the people." They established republics which were "not in their nature free states." Had they understood political freedom in light of its true purpose, they would have recognized that it is not first and foremost a sharing in power, but that it "consists in security, or at least in the opinion that one has of one's security." In Montesquieu's view, the Greeks placed far too much emphasis on public-spiritedness and rendered the citizens of their polities insecure by subjecting them to the purview of their fellows. "Virtue itself has a need for limits," he argues. True "political liberty is to be found only in moderate governments"—and even then, only in those of a commercial character which leave the citizens by and large to themselves. Not Sparta, Athens, and Rome, but Great Britain and, ultimately, the United States of America: these were to be the models for the constitution of liberty in modern times.[67]

Although neither Mr. Dooley nor many of the other residents of Halsted Street would have had much use for a theory so abstract, they would certainly have been in agreement with the spirit of Montesquieu's observations. The citizens of liberal republics are left pretty much to their own devices, and they live in commercial and technological societies that multiply the possibilities of private enjoyment; they possess freedom of speech, but the very size of the polities in which they reside generally robs that speech of all consequence. As a result, the citizens develop a taste for domesticity: they are quick to resent any invasion of the broad realm of privacy which the regime guarantees them, and they often express the fear, even on the slightest of pretexts, that there will be a wholesale abrogation of their rights as individuals. As long as there are free elections, this fear may lack substance—but, as both Montesquieu and Tocqueville note, it is the impatience and anxiety of the citizens which promotes the vigilance that obviates the danger.[68] Even in time of war, the liberal democracies have shown remarkable respect for the privacy of the ordinary citizen. No ancient community would ever have considered sparing the principled opponents of war the burden of serving in the ranks. But in the course of the American Revolution, conscientious objection was established as a constitutional right in Pennsylvania, Delaware, Vermont, New Hampshire, and, in the case of Quakers, New York;[69] and the First Federal Congress came quite close to including such a provision in the Bill of Rights.[70]

The founders of the liberal tradition foresaw trouble, but not from an excess of political spirit. They worried, instead, that the citizenry would eventually lose all semblance of public vigilance.[71] Adam Ferguson sounded the warning on the eve of the American Revolution. Perhaps because he was a Gaelic-speaker reared in close proximity to the clans in the wild highlands of eighteenth-century Scotland, and perhaps because he had passed nearly a decade in service as chaplain to the Black Watch, Ferguson was more acutely aware than even his friends and colleagues David Hume and Adam Smith that the emergence of commercial society would inevitably be accompanied by a decline in that martial fervor which was the ultimate guarantor of political freedom.[72] Ferguson feared "that remissness of spirit, that weakness of soul, that state of national debility, which is likely to end in political slavery." "Every successive art, by which the individual is taught to improve on his fortune, is, in reality," he observed, "an addition to his private engagements, and a new avocation of his mind from the public." Thus, "if to any people it be the avowed object of policy, in all its internal refinements, to secure the person and property of the subject, without any regard to his political character, the constitution indeed may be free, but its members may likewise become unworthy of the freedom they possess, and unfit to preserve it." Indeed, "if the pretensions to equal justice and freedom should terminate in rendering every class equally servile and mercenary, we make a nation of helots, and have no free citizens."[73] Benjamin Constant made the same point: "The danger is that we will be so absorbed in the enjoyment of our private independence and in the pursuit of our particular interests that we will renounce too easily our right of participation in political power."[74] In modern times, the household and the skein of economic and social relations to which it gives support threaten to eclipse the polity altogether.

This danger existed also for the Greeks, but it was not nearly as great. Throughout the classical period, they were in accord with the judgment rendered two millennia later by Giambattista Vico. After reading and rereading the powerful opening paragraphs of Tacitus's *Histories* and *Annals*, this great Neapolitan philosopher and student of rhetoric paused to consider the polities of his own day and observed that when "the majority of the citizens no longer concern themselves with the public welfare, . . . the citizens have become aliens in their own nations."[75] For those who observe everything from the perspective of the stomach, for human beings interested chiefly in what Thomas Hobbes once called "commodious living," the establishment of great states on extended territories and the other circumstances that inhibit day-by-day participation in political affairs on the highest levels are matters of little concern.[76] But for men like Alcaeus, Polyneices, and Theognis, to live under such conditions would have been the most bitter of fates. For them, the fatherland was more than a place of repose; for them, it was an all-encompassing and all-absorbing way of life.

I.i.4

How this could be the case remains difficult to see. In a nation that concedes primacy to the concerns generated by the marketplace, in a polity whose citizens are dedicated to the quest for "over-all security," politics becomes "a field of work for punier heads." Nietzsche made this observation, and we tend to agree.[77] In liberal democracies, politicians—particularly on the local level—inspire little respect. There is something dreary and even sordid about much of the business done by the government. The awarding of contracts and the apportionment of jobs, the leasing of public lands and the purchase of equipment, the raising of taxes and the distribution of subsidies: these and similar mundane matters are the stuff and substance of modern-day political life.[78] Their predominance reflects the degree to which administration has supplanted deliberation as the chief function of public officials. It should not be surprising that human beings reared in such an environment have some trouble understanding the extraordinary appeal exercised in antiquity by political life.

In *The Suppliants*, Euripides gives us an inkling of what it was that aroused the Greeks' ardor. There, he stages a debate over the relative merits of democracy and tyranny between Theseus, the leader of the "free city" of Athens, and the herald dispatched by Creon, the monarch of Thebes. In attacking one-man rule, Theseus sounds all the familiar themes: the citizens' need for equal protection under the law, the absence of safeguards in a monarchy, and the penchant of tyrants for the murder of the able and hot-blooded young, for the pillaging of those with property, and for the abduction and rape of young virgins. The tone of his discourse verges on the melodramatic, but there is nothing here that the judicious Montesquieu would not have endorsed. However, when Theseus comes to speak of political freedom itself (*tò eleútheron*), he gives it a definition that goes well beyond simply guaranteeing the safety and well-being of the citizens. "Being free is this," he argues: "Whoever wishes to bring useful advice before the public (*es méson*) may do so. In this way, whoever longs for eminence can shine (*lamprós estì*)—while the man lacking this desire remains silent. What could be more equitable in a city than this?"[79]

The metaphor Euripides employs to depict the public sphere deserves attention: for, if the body is the ground of privacy, intelligible speech (*lógos*) is the middle ground (*tò méson*) of publicity.[80] This is why *tò méson* comes to be identified with the political community itself,[81] and it accounts for the fact that the middle ground was thought to be the proper sphere in which to weigh and determine what is measured, fitting, timely, needful, and the like.[82] It also helps explain much that would otherwise be puzzling about ancient life—why, for example, rightful authority was thought to emanate from *tò méson*,[83] why the middle position was deemed the seat of honor,[84] why a Greek proverb associated occupation of the middle or common ground with the assumption of risk and a rolling of the dice,[85] why departure from the middle ground (*ek mésou*) was synonymous with withdrawal from the contest for rule, and why neutrals who distanced themselves from the debate taking place in the common council were described as sitting or standing *ek mésou*.[86] If the Greek *pólis* of the archaic and classical periods was peculiar, it was because it offered its citizens more than mere protection. It provided them, in addition, with middle ground in which to display those qualities which distinguished them from animals. "Learn the political art well," Democritus of Abdera advises his fellow Hellenes, "for it is the greatest of the arts; and pursue its toils—from which human beings secure greatness and brilliance (*tà lamprá*)."[87]

To be great and to be brilliant, to shine, to be *lamprós*:[88] this was the desire that animated the Greek *pólis*. Long before Euripides and Democritus voiced the sentiments of their contemporaries, and even longer before Aristotle fully articulated the meaning of citizenship, Homer depicted a luminous world in which men shared in the nature of the gods and sought to shed all mortality through action on the public stage. Again and again, in his two great epics, the circle of warriors gathers on the middle ground (*es méson*) to deal with questions of concern to one and all.[89] There, in public assembly, Homer's heroes deliberate in common.[90] There, in full view of all, they parcel out the booty gained in war and make public reparation for injustice done.[91] And there, in all solemnity, they set out the rich prizes which will be claimed by those victorious in the funeral games put on to honor their dead.[92] It is not fortuitous that *agōn*—the Homeric word for "public assembly" and "assembly place"—meant "contest" as well. To occupy the middle ground was to enter an agonizing struggle for preeminence and renown.[93]

With all of this in mind, Plato called Homer "the education (*paídeusis*) of Hellas,"[94] and so he was—for the spirit that he propagated later gave content to a political freedom he might himself have been unable to imagine.[95] For the development of this understanding of freedom, the Greek conception of the divine opened up the way. It was here that the greatest of the epic poets and his disciples made the decisive contribution: in one passage, Herodotus tells us that Homer and Hesiod were the poets responsible for giving the Greek gods their titles, their honors, their functions, and even their looks (*eídea*); in another, he hints that the paramount difference between the religion of the Greeks and that of their barbarian opponents the Persians was the fundamentally human character (*anthropophuéas*) assigned Hellas's divinities.[96] When the Greeks bowed down, they bowed down before something to which they themselves could aspire.[97] Dionysus and Heracles, though born of mortal women, had both crossed the boundary separating men from the gods.

Thus, the poet Pindar spoke for his compatriots when he restated Homer's great theme:

> There is one race of men, and one race of gods
> Yet from a single mother, we both draw our breath.
> A division of all power keeps them asunder.
> The one is nothing—while, for the other,
> Brazen heaven remains forever a safe seat.
> We bear, this notwithstanding, a certain resemblance
> To the immortals (*athanátois*) either in our nature
> Or in greatness of mind.
> Yet we do not know
> To what goal

Fate has written that we,
By day and by night,
Must run our great race.[98]

They, too, believed that a species of immortality lay within man's reach, even if it was almost always beyond human grasp. And for that reason, they adopted the Heracles of Hesiod's *Theogony* and the Achilles of Homer's *Iliad*, even over the wily Odysseus, as the models for Greek manhood.

Resplendent in victory (*kallínikos*) and renowned for defending both men and the gods against evils (*alexíkakos*), Heracles was famous for his exploits and his labors. By freeing Prometheus from his bonds and by slaying dread monsters like Geryon, the Lernaean Hydra, the Nemean Lion, and the Gigantes, "the strong son of beautiful-ankled Alcmene" transcended the merely human, achieved apotheosis, and came to "live among the immortals as a being blessed (*ólbios*): freed for all time from pain and from age." Because of these accomplishments, Heracles exercised an unparalleled sway over the Greek imagination. At least in the archaic period, he was more often celebrated in Greek poetry and art than any other figure; throughout antiquity, he was honored as a patron and chosen as a model not just by athletes, but as well by those whom the Greeks termed the ephebes: these were young men undergoing military training and a ritual initiation into the body of full citizens.[99]

Homer's hero played no less important a role in the citizen's education. Taught from youth to be "a speaker of words and a doer of deeds," Achilles tried "always to be the best (*aristeúein*) and to be superior to others." [100] He neither sought nor achieved godhead. But he was willing to embrace an untimely death in exchange for the promise of undying glory, and those who came after would regard this defiance of necessity as the distinguishing feature of those who deserved to be free. "The best men," Heraclitus would write, "choose one thing above all others—everlasting fame among mortals." "The many," he continued, "are easily satisfied—like cattle." [101]

Heraclitus's metaphor abides.[102] But the contempt which the sixth-century Ephesian aristocrat had showered on the many, the fifth-century Athenian democrat was to reserve for the barbarians. In *The Persians*, Aeschylus's chorus compares the Great King Xerxes with a herdsman and his army with "a divine flock driven over the entire earth—both by foot and on the sea." When Xerxes' mother Atossa asks who is the "shepherd" of the Greeks and who "serves as master (*epidespózei*) over their army," the chorus replies that the Hellenes "are said to be the slaves and subjects of no man." The coming of democracy has evidently opened up to the many the very quest for ever-

lasting glory which Heraclitus had made the preserve of the few. Thus, when
Aeschylus speaks of what has been won with the defeat of the Mede, he
mentions not only freedom from the demeaning necessity to pay tribute to a
master and to bow down to a man as if to a god; he adds the political dimension as well. "No longer will the tongues of mortals be held under guard,"
he writes, "for the commoners (*lâos*) are released and left free (*eleúthera*) to
make speech." Political liberty was nothing more and nothing less than the
opportunity to do or say something of note.[103]

Xenophon grasped this. In his dialogue *The Hiero*, he ascribes to the poet
Simonides the opinion that "man (*anér*) is distinguished from the other animals by his desire for honor." To establish the truth of this claim, the poet
notes that "all creatures seem in a similar fashion to take pleasure in food,
drink, sleep, and sex. But the love of honor (*philotimía*) does not grow up
(*emphúetai*) in animals lacking speech (*alógois zóois*). Nor, for that matter, can
it be found in all human beings (*hápasin anthrópois*). The lust (*éros*) for honor
and praise grows up only in those who are most fully distinguished from
the beasts of the fields (*boskémata*): which is to say that it grows up only in
those judged to be real men (*ándres*) and no longer mere human beings."[104]
Plato echoed this understanding of *philotimía*. He too believed that it was the
yearning for renown that distinguished man from the animals. "The human
race," he writes, "possesses by nature a certain share in immortality, and the
desire for this belongs naturally to all—for the desire to become famous and
not to lie nameless after death is the desire for just such a thing."[105] In *The
Symposium*, Plato suggests that this longing can be satisfied in a variety of
ways. Those who most resemble animals, he hints, will live solely through
their offspring, but ambitious women and men like Alcestis, Achilles, and
Codrus "are ready to run every risk, to spend their substance, to undergo
every sort of labor, and even to die for the sake of achieving a deathless fame
for all time." Among the ambitious, Plato includes the men of intelligence
(*phrónēsis*) like the poets and those responsible for discoveries in the mechanical arts, but he reserves his most emphatic praise for the practitioners of
the political art. As he puts it, "By far the greatest and the most noble form of
phrónēsis is that which deals with the ordering of cities and of households."[106]

To comprehend fully what Plato had in mind, one must recognize that the
pólis was itself a memorial to those who had shaped it. If the classical political philosophers were in accord with their forefathers and contemporaries in
supposing that politics is a pursuit endowed with great dignity, it is because
they shared the popular belief that the conscious, purposive political action
of the lawgiver (*nomothétēs*) can give form to a people.[107] Thus, when Plato
comes to give examples of the supreme practitioners of the political art, he

mentions most prominently not the lawgivers Solon and Lycurgus, but the epic poets Homer and Hesiod.[108] The latter were the education of Hellas. They contributed more than anyone else to the ordering of its cities and house-holds. By providing the Greeks with a common pantheon and with a shared understanding of what constitutes the good life, Homer and Hesiod formed the scattered communities of Greece into a single nation and defined the horizon within which the ancient legislators were to go about the business of imposing order on the various *póleis* and their constituent parts. In the quest for the immortal, the ordinary lawgiver falls short of the epic poet—and as an educator, the epic poet is destined to fall short of the philosopher alone.[109]

The ordinary citizen of the *pólis* might well have queried the claim which Plato and Aristotle made on behalf of the philosopher, but the rest he took for granted. Throughout Hellas, there was general accord: an existence eked out on the periphery of things, outside the middle ground of the political arena, was a subhuman life and hardly worth living. As Aristotle put it, the city existed "for the sake of noble action"; its dignity as a moral community derived from the fact that it made possible for men "the sharing of words and of deeds."[110] Only a handful of Greeks could seek to rival Homer and Solon, and no one supposed that every man could become an Achilles; but as a warrior band in republican form, the *pólis* offered the ordinary citizen a participation in greatness inconceivable under a monarchy, in a commercial society, or in a polity the size of a nation (*éthnos*). The existence of middle ground multiplied the opportunities to display eloquence in council and courage in battle; because the city constituted an audience with the prospect of permanence, it provided the citizen with the hope of achieving through his contributions to its welfare at least a shadow of the eternal fame which Hesiod gave Heracles and Homer, Achilles.[111] "We should not follow those who exhort us, being human, to think human thoughts and, being mortal, to think mortal thoughts," writes Aristotle, "but, as far as is possible, we should make ourselves immortal (*athanatízein*) and do everything in life in accord with the most powerful thing in us."[112] It was this straining after im-mortality that distinguished a human life (*bíos*), constituted by *práxis* and possibly worth recounting, from mere animal existence (*zōḗ*),[113] and it was the *pólis* which made the maintenance of this distinction intelligible.

The fact that the political community was itself the repository of memory served to distinguish freedom of speech (*lógos*) from mere freedom of expres-sion (*phōnḗ*). The citizen aimed at glory, not at notoriety; he wanted to be famous forever and not merely to be a celebrity. When Pindar remarked that the "excuse given" by a particular individual "for sidestepping established contests (*titheménōn agṓnōn próphasis*) has hurled his reputation for manly virtue (*aretá*) into utter darkness," he assumed without argument that the battle for renown was actually a struggle for excellence. Theognis could even claim that

> Reputation is a great evil for human beings; trial (*peîra*) is the best!
> For many who are untested nonetheless possess a reputation as good
>   men.
> But when brought against the touchstone and rubbed on the black lead,
> Gold that has been refined and is pure reveals its nobility to all.

Among the Hellenes, as Aristotle emphasized, honor was esteemed not for its own sake but as "virtue's prize."[114] This conviction underlay the Greeks' willingness to face and, sometimes, even welcome war. If the gods "gave up the bodies" of their offspring "to the necessities of nature," Isocrates observed, then, by way of compensation, "they made immortal the memory of their *aretê*." In similar fashion, he was prepared to suggest, "one of the gods" had brought on the Persian Wars "out of admiration for the *aretê* of those involved—lest those by nature so blessed escape notice and end life deprived of renown (*akleôs*)." In this way, his countrymen had had the opportunity to "be deemed worthy of the same honors as those born of gods and dubbed demigods."[115]

In practice, of course, it was the *pólis*, not the gods, that put the words and deeds of the citizen to the test; long after his death, it remembered all that he had accomplished for good or for ill. By demonstrating this mnemonic capacity, the community redirected that *philotimía* which grows up naturally in men endowed with *lógos*, and it caused this powerful yearning to point beyond mere transient opinion to lasting glory—and, thereby, toward the just, the noble, the good, and virtue entire.[116] For this reason, the citizen's speech and deeds were tempered and directed by a prudent concern with the common good. On the eve of Salamis, when Aristeides crossed over from Aegina to warn the Greeks that Xerxes' navy had them surrounded, he is said to have defended his fierce rivalry with Themistocles on just these terms. "At other times and especially now," he reportedly told his ancient enemy, "it is right (*chreón*) for us to stand opposed (*stasiázein*) as to which of us will do the city more good"—and Themistocles concurred.[117] Not surprisingly, then, when Euripides' Theseus comes to define *tò eleútheron*, he links the quest for eminence with the provision of useful advice (*tà chrēstá*). And, in similar circumstances, Sophocles does the same. "Where one is not allowed freely (*eleuthérōs*) to give voice to *tà chrēstá*," the great tragedian observes, "worse advice (*tà cheírona*) will triumph in the city and the men will trip up its safety with their blunders."[118] Prudence is as much the standard for political speech as it is for political deeds. The *pólis* of Phocylides' poem is "superior to senseless Nineveh" precisely because the opportunity for public deliberation allows its affairs to be conducted "in an orderly manner (*kosmíōs*)."

The subordination of the quest for immortality to the needs of the political community is perhaps most strikingly evident in the one field of endeavor which modern thought links most closely with an untrammeled freedom of expression.[119] Euripides may have been at odds with Aeschylus over a good many things—but if Aristophanes is to be trusted, the two would have been in agreement on the standard by which poetry should be judged. In *The Frogs*, when Aeschylus asks why the poet deserves to be an object of wonder, Euripides makes no mention of aesthetic imperatives. Instead, he suggests that the poets should be admired "for cleverness and for advice— and because we make the human beings in the cities better."[120] From Aristophanes' Aeschylus, this reply elicits no objection—and rightly so. For there is no greater indication of the primacy accorded politics and war by the city's provision of middle ground than the example set by the poet himself: on the epitaph he wrote for his monument, Aeschylus made no mention of his tragedies. These were, he elsewhere claimed, mere "slices from the banquet of Homer." When the time of reckoning came, this great tragedian simply recorded that he had been among those who had fought on Athens's behalf with the Mede in the battle on Marathon's plain.[121]

I . i . 5

Despite the general accord that reigned throughout all of Greece, there were men who rejected the primacy of politics and war. Euripides' Theseus hints at their presence in Athens when he remarks that, in a free city, a man lacking the desire for eminence can choose to remain silent.[122] Lycophron appears to have been such a man, and Aristippus another. If Aristotle and Xenophon can be trusted, neither had much use for the middle ground provided by the public arena. Yet, to the best of our knowledge, no Greek thinker, not even these, ever elaborated a *public-spirited political* philosophy grounded in liberal principles. Lycophron did treat the *pólis* as little more than "a military alliance (*summachía*)," and he reportedly argued that the law was merely "a covenant . . . a pledge to respect each other's rightful claims" and not an instrument "able to make the citizens good and just."[123] This denial that the *pólis* is a moral community certainly foreshadows the social-contract theories developed by Thomas Hobbes and his successors. But there is something missing: Lycophron's account is wholly descriptive and never prescriptive.

In the seventeenth and eighteenth centuries, those who embraced the notion of the social contract did so in order to advocate what the designers of the Great Seal of the United States called "a new order of the ages." Among these was Britain's Thomas Pownall, once the royal governor of Massachusetts Bay Colony. In 1783, Pownall chose to indicate his support for the American Revolution in a fashion that underlined the radical character of the Founding Fathers' break with the past. He did so by attacking what he termed "the grand *Desideratum* of all the ancient Legislators and Institutors of Republics." As he put it, the great statesmen of ancient times

saw the necessity that there was of an exact conformity between the Constitution of the State and the *Species of Individuals*, the *form of the community* and [the] *nature of the basis* on which such [a] State must be founded. No such Basis was there in Nature; they therefore tried a thousand different projects to form such in Art. They forced Nature. Not finding the natural situation of men to be what it was necessary to the System of their Polity it should be, they endeavoured to make it what it never could be, but under force and violence done to nature. They destroyed or perverted all Personal Liberty, in order to force into establishment Political Freedom. While Men were taught by Pride, and by a prospect of Domination over others, to call the State Free, they found themselves cut off from, and from the use of, many of the essential inalienable rights of the Individual which form his happiness as well as freedom.[124]

Pownall's critique of the ancient city deserves notice because there is nothing comparable to be found in Lycophron or in any other ancient writer. In antiquity, no one ever asserted "the inalienable rights of the Individual." No one ever claimed that the attempt to establish a moral community on the political plane leads to the destruction or perversion of "all Personal Liberty." The ethical perspective adopted by admirers of the American experiment and advocated by liberal political theory in general is absent from Lycophron's argument altogether.[125]

Nor can such an outlook be found in Aristippus. There is, in fact, no indication that he was interested in political problems at all. Yet he was a devotee of personal liberty. He reportedly argued that, lying between the alternatives of slavery and rule, there was a middle path of freedom (*eleuthería*)—of freedom from the agony of servitude and from the burdens of political participation as well. "Not for a moment do I place myself in the ranks of those wishing to rule," Aristippus remarks.

For, in light of the great effort required to provide for oneself, it seems to me to be the height of folly not to be satisfied with this, but to take on as well the additional burden of making provision for the needs of the other citizens. How would it not be great folly for a man to give up many of the things that he wants and to incur, as head (*prostátēs*) of the city, the danger of trial if he fails to accomplish all that the city wishes? The cities think it proper to make use of their rulers just as I make use of my household slaves. For I think it proper for my servants to equip me in abundance with those things I need, but not themselves to lay hands on anything; and the cities think it necessary for their rulers to provide them with as many good things as possible and to abstain themselves from their enjoyment. Should there be those wishing to make trouble for themselves and for others, I would educate them and class them with those fitted to rule. But I would rank myself with those wishing to live as easily and as pleasantly as possible.

Socrates found this argument unsatisfactory. It would be fine, he retorts, if one encountered no human beings on the path intermediate between slavery and rule. The strong, he warns, have a way of enslaving those who abstain from political life. For Aristippus, however, the danger of enslavement was not a serious problem: "To avoid it," he explains, "I do not lock myself up in my own city, but am a stranger (*xénos*) everywhere." When Socrates responds that the *xénos* is, in all cities, an easy mark with little chance of defending himself, Aristippus shifts his ground, tacitly acknowledging that the middle path of personal liberty is an illusion. He is apparently unaware that the polity itself can be refashioned to provide for the needs of those "wishing to live as easily and as pleasantly as possible." Many centuries would pass before the invention of "a new science of politics" aimed solely at the protection of life, liberty, and the pursuit of happiness.

The subsequent exchange between Socrates and Aristippus is even more revealing than the first. Defeated on his own ground, Aristippus attacks Socrates on his. Having been forced to concede that the path of personal freedom eventually merges with that of slavery, he argues that the distinction traditionally drawn between the path of slavery and that of rule cannot intelligibly be maintained. Here again, the standard he adopts is that of pleasure—or, rather, of the avoidance of pain. When Socrates has gone through all the evils associated with being a slave, Aristippus responds, "But Socrates! What about those educated in that royal art which you seem to equate with human flourishing (*eudaimonía*)? If they are to go hungry, to be thirsty, to endure cold, to pass sleepless nights, and voluntarily to undergo every other hardship, how does their condition differ in reality from that of men whose sufferings are forced on them? I cannot understand what difference it makes whether the victim is willing or unwilling if the same back gets flogged and the same body is besieged by all these torments—except, of course, that folly is attributable to anyone who freely chooses to endure pain." To answer this charge, Socrates must establish that the life devoted to politics offers greater satisfaction than that devoted to pleasure. He begins by noting two advantages which the man who toils voluntarily has over the slave: such a man can choose when and under what circumstances to cease, and like the hunter in search of game, he works with pleasure in anticipation of reward. The slaughter of game may not be worth the effort, but other prizes are: "Consider those who labor in order that they might possess good friends, master their enemies, or gain the physical and spiritual capacity to manage their own households well, to help their friends, and to become benefactors of the fatherland. How would they not take pleasure in toil for all this— and live lives full of joy, looking on themselves with admiration and being praised and envied by others!" The man who avoids participation in public life and sidesteps the burdens of politics and war has no opportunity to exercise the faculties which give him dignity and a sense of his own worth. As a consequence, even the mundane pleasures of life lose their attraction.

Socrates illustrates this last point by retelling the parable in which the sophist Prodicus had staged a debate between Virtue (*Aretē*) and Vice (*Kakía*). When Heracles was a young man still on the verge of beginning his labors and had not yet become a god, Virtue and Vice presented the model for ephebes with a choice. *Kakía* offered him "a short and easy road to happiness (*eudaimonía*)." To her blandishments, *Aretē* responded,

Wretch! What do you possess that is any good? What can you know of real pleasure—when you have no wish to do any work for pleasure's sake? You do not even wait for the desire for pleasant things to come on; you fill yourself full of everything before you even feel the need. Before feeling hunger, you eat; before feeling thirst, you drink. In order that you may take pleasure in dining, you contrive the presence of chefs; in order that you may take pleasure in drinking, you equip yourself with expensive wines and rush about in search of snow in summer; and in order that you may take pleasure in falling asleep, you provide yourself not only with soft bedding, but with a frame for your couch as well. You desire sleep—not because you have labored, but because you have nothing to do; and you force sex before it is needed, contriving everything and using men in place of women. So, you train up your friends, behaving arrogantly at night and sleeping through the most useful hours of the day. . . . You never hear praise, the most pleasant of all things to hear; and you never see the most pleasant of all things to see: for nothing is more pleasant to see than one's own noble work.

Socrates' point is much the same as before, but he manages here to draw attention to the emptiness and the self-contradictory nature of a life devoted to material comfort and pleasure. The short and easy road to *eudaimonía* does not lead there at all: it leads, instead, to an existence fraught with boredom and marked by an almost desperate search for diversion.[126]

In pondering the emerging bourgeois regime of eighteenth-century Britain, Montesquieu noticed a similar phenomenon. In England, he observed, "all the passions are left free." There, "each individual, always independent, follows his caprices and his fantasies." The majority care little, if at all, what anyone else thinks; for that reason, they tend to "abandon themselves to their own humours." But this freedom, though it is as complete as anyone could ask, brings them little satisfaction. In bourgeois society, the people have a "restless spirit"; the men try to lose themselves in debauchery; and "the majority of those blessed with wit and intelligence (*esprit*) are tormented by that very *esprit*: in the disdain and disgust they feel for all things, they are unhappy in the midst of so many occasions for felicity," and they demonstrate a marked propensity for committing suicide.[127] This observation is striking and strange, and it would be easy to dismiss it as yet another French discovery of *la maladie anglaise*—were it not for the remarks made some years later by a student of commercial society no less acute.

Nearly a hundred years after the publication of Montesquieu's *The Spirit of the Laws*, Tocqueville paid a visit to a new nation even more thoroughly bourgeois than eighteenth-century Great Britain. On this occasion, he took note of "that peculiar melancholy which the inhabitants of democratic countries often exhibit in the bosom of abundance, and the disgust with life which sometimes seizes them in the midst of an easy and tranquil existence." In America, he wrote, "I saw the freest and most enlightened men placed in the happiest condition that there is in the world; it seemed to me as if a kind of cloud habitually covered every visage, and I thought them grave and almost sad, even in their pleasures." Tocqueville did not find the Americans prone to debauchery; indeed, he feared "much less for democratic societies from the audacity than from the mediocrity of desires." Equality tended to foster in the United States "a kind of decent materialism" aimed at wealth and comfort, but not at magnificence. The danger was not that this would corrupt, but that it would "soften the soul and without noise unbend its springs of action."

Montesquieu left it ambiguous whether the peculiar unhappiness which afflicted English men of *esprit* was caused by England's climate or by the mores and manners inspired by her laws. With regard to the Americans, Tocqueville took the latter course. Upon reflection, he attributed their "secret disquietude" and the danger they ran of becoming dispirited to the same two causes: to "their taste for material enjoyments" and to the "universal competition" which democratic society opens up. The first sends democratic man on a bootless chase in "the single-minded pursuit of the goods of this world," and the fact that "he has but a limited time at his disposal to find, to lay hold of, and to enjoy them . . . fills him with care, with fears and regrets, and maintains his soul in a kind of ceaseless trepidation." The second of the two causes only aggravates his frustration:

> When all the prerogatives of birth and of fortune are eliminated, when the professions are open to all, and a man may reach by his own efforts the summit of each, an easy and unbounded career seems to open itself up to the ambition of men, and they readily suppose that they are called to destinies grand. But this is an erroneous view which experience corrects all the days of their lives. The very equality that permits every citizen to conceive vast hopes renders all the citizens, as individuals, weak; it circumscribes their powers on every side at the same time that it permits their desires to increase. . . . When men are almost alike and all follow the same route, it is quite difficult for any one from among them to walk swiftly and cut through the undifferentiated mob (*la foule uniforme*) that surrounds and presses in on him. The constant opposition between the inclinations to which equality gives birth and the means which it furnishes for their satisfaction torments and wearies the soul.[128]

For this problem, Tocqueville suggests no completely satisfactory solution. He was acutely aware that, for all but a handful of men, the very size of the extended republics of modern times rules out the provision of middle ground adequate as a space accessible for the display of the human capacity for rational deliberation and cooperative action, and he knew as well that the commercial orientation of these regimes inevitably deprived that handful of politically active men of the public attention they craved. In pondering ways to prevent the soul's enervation under these conditions, Tocqueville drew attention to the few opportunities that remained for the ordinary citizen to participate in the political process. In the United States, he discovered, local government was vigorous and the citizens were free to form public associations for almost any purpose. As a consequence, where local government impinged on the interests of individuals, they were willing and able to band together to resist encroachments and to force reform. By the expedient of self-interest rightly understood, ordinary men were drawn out of their shells and into a public arena still existent, though diminished in dignity. Their concern with their own long-term interests might even infect them with a passion for public affairs less robust than the longing for glory which had animated the Greeks, but invigorating nonetheless.[129]

These observations of Montesquieu and Tocqueville deserve heed largely because they accord so well with the remarks of Xenophon's Socrates. Ordinary human beings, born into fully bourgeois societies, may not be prone to the vanity and to the taste for magnificence which hurl those of aristocratic temper into ever-greater refinements of pleasure; but, particularly when blessed with affluence, they tend to wander aimlessly, lacking all purpose and afflicted with a weariness of the world. Where men are "accustomed to consider personal fortune as the sole object of care," Adam Ferguson observes, "they, who, in the vulgar phrase, have not their fortunes to make, are supposed to be at a loss for occupation, and betake themselves to solitary pastimes, or cultivate what they are pleased to call a taste for gardening, building, drawing, or music. With this aid, they endeavour to fill up the blanks of a listless life, and avoid the necessity of curing their languors by any positive service to their country, or to mankind." The way of life advocated by Xenophon's Socrates is by no means above reproach—particularly in a world made safe for the likes of Aristippus. But for all save the women, the slaves, the metics, and the very poor, the Greek *pólis* did have one great advantage: it may not have eased the provision for mere life and for "animal enjoyment," but it did give men of *esprit* something to live for by opening up a middle ground on which they could develop and display their capacities for courage, for wisdom, and for eloquence. "Happiness," Adam Ferguson argues, "is not that state of repose, or that imaginary freedom from care, which at a distance is so frequent an object of desire, but with its approach brings a tedium, or a languor, more unsupportable than pain itself. . . . It arises more from the pursuit, than the attainment of any end whatever; and in every new situation to which we arrive, even in the course of a prosperous life, it depends more on the degree to which our minds are properly employed, than it does on the circumstances in which we are destined to act, on the materials which are placed in our hands, or the tools with which we are furnished." If, in echoing Aristotle, Ferguson is right, his remarks go a long way toward explaining the strangest omission from the ancient Greek language: the lack of a specific term for what Finley Peter Dunne's Mr. Dooley would have called boredom.[130]

CHAPTER 2

Opinions, Passions, and Interests

Men are so far from valuing society on account of its mere external conveniencies, that they are commonly most attached where those conveniencies are least frequent; and are there most faithful, where the tribute of their allegiance is paid in blood. . . . Hence the sanguine affection which every Greek bore to his country, and hence the devoted patriotism of an early Roman. Let those examples be compared with the spirit which reigns in a commercial state, where men may be supposed to have experienced, in its full extent, the interest which individuals have in the preservation of their country. It is here indeed, if ever, that man is sometimes found a solitary being: he has found an object which sets him in competition with his fellow creatures, and he deals with them as he does with his cattle and his soil, for the sake of the profits they bring. The mighty engine which we suppose to have formed society, only tends to set its members at variance or to continue their intercourse after the bands of affection are broken.—Adam Ferguson

I.ii.1

For the excitement of political life, the Greeks paid a very high price. Honor, fame, and glory are, by their very nature, the rarest and the most fragile of all the goods accessible to man. To distribute them in equal measure to all is to annihilate them altogether; indeed, to make any concession to the claims of equality in this regard is to debase the coinage of distinction. Unavoidably, then, the quest for immortality and the longing to be the best and to be superior to all others set political communities and the individuals within them at each other's throats.[1]

Moreover, *lógos* is, as its range of meanings implies, a double-edged sword: the faculty which brings men together also drives them apart; a creature capable of speech and reason will be inclined to argument and disputation as well. Plato observes that human beings infrequently get into serious squabbles regarding matters of number, size, or weight; he remarks that they can generally reach accord with respect to what they mean when they speak of stone, wood, iron, or silver; and he rightly emphasizes over and over again that they are rarely able to agree with one another concerning "the just and the unjust" and the other "things in which we are apt to go astray." Because their arguments regarding what is just and unjust, what is admirable (*kalón*) and shameful, and what is good and evil inevitably give rise to the question as to who is competent and therefore entitled to decide; because these arguments just as inevitably turn on the competing claims to rule, the distribution of offices, and the touchy subject of honor, glory, and fame; and because human beings are least inclined to be objective, fair-minded, and impartial where their own worth, opinions, and interests are at stake, such disputes can rarely, if ever, be simply or even largely academic. Indeed, contentions of this kind are, the Greek philosopher warns us, the chief sources of the anger and hostility which men feel toward one another, and they are, therefore, the principal roots of war and of civil strife as well. "The tongue of man is," as Thomas Hobbes would later justly remark, "a trumpet of warre, and sedition."[2]

In antiquity, there was little, apart from the fear of total defeat, to prevent communities endowed with a prickly sensitivity to questions of civic honor and devoted to different and opposed notions of justice and human excellence from coming to blows. In contrast, the citizens of a particular *pólis* could hope that the common understanding of justice and virtue that set their city at odds with its neighbors would work to obviate conflict within. Even then, however, the two-dimensional nature of the ancient political community would inevitably spawn disappointment, distrust, and recrimination. As Aristotle took care to emphasize in his *History of Animals*, man "plays a double game (*epamphoterízei*)." He is political and nonpolitical at the same time. Like the bees, the ants, and the other political animals that lack the critical faculty of speech, men share a common purpose, function, or task (*érgon*); but, unlike the dumb animals, they also pursue private interests that set them at odds. It is, in fact, the two-faced nature of man that gives rise to the double-edged faculty of speech. According to the peripatetic philosopher, *lógos* serves initially to clarify the advantageous and the harmful; only thereafter and "as a consequence (*hóste*)" of this essentially private concern is the faculty of rational speech applied to the just and the unjust as well. The *pólis* may survive because men wish to live nobly and well, but it comes into being in the first place out of necessity and for reasons of material interest. Once the community has been established, the two impulses continue to exist side by side and in considerable tension with one another, and they contribute in roughly equal measure to shaping the relations that join the community's members. As a result, fellow citizens come to look upon one another as friends and almost as members of a single family (*phíloi*); quite naturally, they expect far more of one another than they do of the foreigners they meet; and yet, all too often, they pretend to be pursuing the common good and even persuade themselves that they are doing so—when they are, in fact, looking out solely for their own interests and for those of their family or clan. In these situations, the more tightly knit the community and the stronger the sense of moral obligation uniting it, the greater the conviction of betrayal and the attendant bitterness will in due course become. In one passage, Aristotle tells us that the type of friendship (*philía*) linking fellow citizens is mixed; it is a legal or contractual relationship designed to provide for the private interests of the parties involved, and it is a moral or ethical relationship aimed at the pursuit of excellence. Elsewhere, he intimates that this mixture is extremely unstable and that civic friendship is therefore so fragile that one might describe it as contrary to nature.[3]

For the Hellenes, the consequences of all this were grievous and lasting: where a community gives primacy to politics and devotes itself not just to the attainment of security and well-being, but also to the achievement of immortal fame, to the noble conduct of life, and to the exercise of *lógos* in prudential deliberation (*tò bouleutikón*) regarding the advantageous, the good, and the just, that community incurs the clear and present danger of *stásis* and it insures the eternal prevalence of war. It is by no means fortuitous that the earliest surviving theoretical critique of republican government lays great stress on the grave danger posed by the prevalence of faction. The ancient democracies really were apt to fall prey to the conspiracies of evil men; and in oligarchies, it was all too common for "powerful private hatreds to develop between the many men practicing virtue in pursuit of the common good," for each public-spirited man had entered the political arena "wishing to take the lead and seize victory by speaking his mind (*boulómenos koruphaîos eînai gnômēsí te nikân*)."[4] As a consequence of the never-ending contest for superiority, it was purportedly much more difficult for fellow citizens to remain friends than for men drawn from different communities.[5] In a sense, the history of Hellenic civilization is simply a recapitulation of Homer's *Iliad*.

As a result, Greek policy was, in practice, chiefly concerned with the preparation for armed conflict, with the actual conduct of war, and with the prevention of civil strife. This focus served only to heighten still further the political spirit of the ancient Greek *pólis*. Politics and war were mutually supportive: for, while politics bred conflict, the never-ending fear that the city would be defeated in battle and destroyed and that its citizens would be enslaved or dispersed powerfully reinforced the primacy accorded public affairs and gave particular impetus to the tendency to subordinate the concerns of the individual and his household to those of the city as a whole. This bias was, as we shall see, especially evident in what we would be inclined to call the economic sphere.

I.ii.2

Modern liberal democracy and the ancient Greek *pólis* stand, in their fundamental principles, radically opposed. The ancient city was a republic of virtue—first by its very nature, and then also because it had to be one in order to survive. Its cohesion was not and could not be a mere function of incessant negotiation and calculated compromise; it was and had to be bound together by a profound sense of moral purpose and common struggle. Alexander Hamilton captured the difference between the two regimes succinctly when he wrote, "The industrious habits of the people of the present day, absorbed in the pursuits of gain, and devoted to the improvements of agriculture and commerce are incompatible with the condition of a nation of soldiers, which was the true condition of the people of those [ancient Greek] republics."[6] The point is a simple one: the modern citizen is a bourgeois; his ancient counterpart was a warrior.[7] Commerce defines the terms on which life is lived in the liberal polity founded by George Washington, John Adams, Thomas Jefferson, James Madison, Alexander Hamilton, and their associates: the ordinary American may not be a merchant himself, but the concerns of trade and industry regulate his labor with respect to time and govern the relations that unite him with his compatriots.[8] In contrast, commerce was peripheral to the ancient economy: the ordinary Greek was a more or less self-sufficient peasant proprietor,[9] and he needed his fellow citizens as unpaid bodyguards against the city's slaves[10] and for the defense of his family and land against foreigners far more than for any exchange of goods and services.[11] Many communities took steps to exclude those engaged in trade and industry from participation in politics;[12] even where the marketplace was allowed to intrude upon political life, the merchant and craftsman were generally objects of contempt, ridiculed on the stage, if not banished from respectable society.[13]

Under these circumstances, the spirit of commerce could not perform the historical task, set for it by Samuel Ricard, Montesquieu, William Robertson, and the marquis de Condorcet, of softening men's manners and rendering them anxious, peaceable, and bland.[14] Nor could trade serve the purpose, assigned it by François Veron de Forbonnais, Joseph Priestley, Thomas Paine, and Benjamin Constant, of making war unthinkable by rendering potential enemies economically interdependent.[15] In antiquity, armed struggle was a mode of acquisition far more respectable and often more profitable than trade.[16] At the beginning of a later and more enlightened age, Thomas Sprat might suggest that "*Trafic,* and *Commerce* have given mankind a higher degree than any title of *Nobility,* even that of *Civilty,* and *Humanity* itself."[17] Thereafter, Bernard Mandeville might link the propagation of "good Manners or Politeness" with vanity and the growth of "Luxury,"[18] and David Hume might argue that the "vulgar arts . . . of commerce and manufactures" foster an atmosphere conducive to "mildness and moderation";[19] Adam

Smith might write of the producer and trader in movables as being "properly a citizen of the world and . . . not attached to any particular country,"[20] and Montesquieu might conceive of eighteenth-century England as a country in which such mild-mannered cosmopolitans were predominant. This matters not a whit. No ancient thinker could have written of any Greek city what Montesquieu said of England—that it was a nation devoted to a "commerce of economy," that it sought "gain, not conquest," and that it was so "pacific from principle" that it would sacrifice "its political interests to the interests of its commerce."[21] The Enlightenment vision of the benign effects of trade— so central to the understanding of political economy which guided America's revolutionary generation—would have seemed absurd to the ancients.[22] The Greeks were not a nation of shopkeepers.[23] Their cities were brotherhoods of peasant warriors, not associations of merchants, and one community's freedom was understood to entail another's subjection.[24] As a consequence, Hellas rarely knew peace—and when she did, it was generally a peace purchased at the price of freedom. Greek history was a struggle for mastery: turmoil was the norm, and tranquillity the exception.

The citizens of a tiny, warrior community in such a world needed a unity that an extended, bourgeois republic endowed with a dynamic economy and located on a vast and nearly empty continent could afford to dispense with.[25] Pythagoras is said to have compared faction (*stásis*) in the city with disease in the body, ignorance in the soul, division within the household, and a lack of proportion (*ametría*) in general. "One must avoid these things," he reportedly observed, "with every means at one's disposal, and one must root them out with fire and sword and with every sort of contrivance."[26] The philosopher from Samos was not at all peculiar in holding this opinion. The testimony of Herodotus on the matter is, if anything, more forceful. The historian from Halicarnassus not only wrote that "civil strife within the tribe (*stásis émphulos*) is a greater evil (*kákion*) than war waged by men thinking as one (*polémou homophronéontos*)"; he added that this was true "to the very degree that war itself is less desirable (*kákion*) than peace."[27] For the cities of Hellas, the presence of the enemy without required the suppression of dissidence within.

For this reason, James Madison's well-known antidote for faction could never have been applied within the Greek *pólis*. No one in antiquity would have countenanced economic differentiation and the multiplication of religious sects. If the commonwealth was to survive, it was vital for the citizens "to act in unison with each other." As a consequence, the ancient republic sought to solve the problem of *stásis* not "by controlling its effects," but rather "by removing its causes." As Madison himself had occasion to observe, the Greeks attempted this not by granting free rein to opinion and by encouraging a proliferation of special interests, but rather "by giving to every citizen the same opinions, the same passions, and the same interests."[28] *Homónoia*—unanimity, solidarity, or like-mindedness regarding the advantageous, the just, and the good: this was the goal;[29] and the market economy, though tolerated as a necessity, was perceived as a threat. Where the Greeks distinguished the free from the commercial *agorá*,[30] where they excluded the merchant and the craftsman from political life, and where they simply held the tradesman in disdain, the cause was not some bizarre and irrational prejudice against men of business. Instinctively, the Greeks recognized that the differentiation of interests inevitably fostered by trade and industry was a danger to the hard-won solidarity that enabled them to survive.

Among the theorists, this recognition was more than merely instinctive: looking back on the experience of the Greeks as well as the Romans, Cicero observed that "it is easiest for there to be concord in that republic in which the same thing profits (*conducat*) everyone; from a diversity of interests (*ex utilitate varietatibus*), when one thing is of advantage to some and another to others, discord is born."[31] Cicero was by no means the first man to reach this conclusion. Centuries before, Xenophon, Plato, and Aristotle had directly addressed the corrupting influence of the marketplace,[32] and the last two members of this threesome had even discussed the geographical issue that would later so plague the proponents of the American Constitution. Alexander Hamilton and James Madison would have understood perfectly well why Plato and Aristotle proposed assigning to every citizen two plots of land—one on the periphery of the civic territory, the other near its center.[33] The circumstances that give rise to the clash of interests were as fully apprehended in antiquity as they were to be in 1787.[34] Some Greek cities even excluded those owning land on the border from participating in deliberations regarding war against their immediate neighbors.[35]

I.ii.3

To combat the natural propensity of human beings for forming factions, the communities of Hellas sought, by a variety of expedients, to prevent a serious differentiation of interests. The Greeks perceived that merchants and craftsmen would be less willing to defend the civic territory than farmers,[36] and they were acutely aware of the difference between what we still instinctively call real estate and what they termed invisible wealth (*aphanès ousía*).[37] The latter distinction is particularly instructive, for it is the predominance of invisible wealth which sets the modern apart from the ancient political economy.

In the eighteenth century, Montesquieu and his disciples treated the invention of the bill of exchange as a turning point in world history. "By this means," Montesquieu argued, "commerce was able to elude violence and to maintain itself everywhere—since the richest merchant had no possessions other than invisible goods which could be conveyed anywhere and left not a trace." As a consequence, the princes came to fear that "great and arbitrary actions (*les grands coups d'autorité*)" on their part might drive out the men who conducted the trade on which they depended for revenues. This, in turn, made it necessary for the sovereigns of Europe "to govern themselves with greater wisdom than they themselves could have imagined." By making it possible for a man to conceal his substance, the techniques of modern banking were a bulwark against arbitrary rule.[38]

What the proponents of modern republicanism saw as a virtue their ancient counterparts viewed as a vice. The Greeks knew nothing of the bill of exchange, and their system of accounting was primitive in the extreme.[39] But they did recognize that riches easily hidden and spirited abroad are not subject to political control, and for that very reason they regarded invisible wealth with considerable distrust.[40] Adam Smith touched on the central issue, for he not only contended that merchants and their like were cosmopolitans unattached to any particular community; he added as well that "the proprietor of land is necessarily a citizen of the particular country in which his estate lies."[41] If the ancient farmer was a figure far more respectable than the potter, the huckster, and the money changer, it was not just because he was free from a degrading dependence on customers.[42] Above all else, he was a man securely tied to the territory of the community.

If war brought defeat in battle, the ancient Greek farmer might save his life by flight but in the process lose whatever slaves, domestic animals, and stored crops he had been unable to gather up and drive or cart off to the hill country or to a fortified place of refuge. If the enemy eventually withdrew (as was the general practice), this same man might well return home to find his house leveled; his barn demolished; his fields of grain harvested, torched, or flattened; his vines trampled or cut; and his olive and fig trees burned, chopped down, or entirely uprooted.[43] Such were the fortunes of war—but only for those who tilled the soil. Except if the urban center or the port was in danger of falling, those who made their living from trade and industry had comparatively little at risk; even in the rare instance where an enemy victorious in battle attempted a siege, had the resources to sustain it, and ultimately captured the town, those among the surviving artisans who escaped captivity and enslavement could seek refuge and continue to pursue their professions abroad. Much the same could be said for those merchants able to smuggle out whatever they possessed of silver and gold, but not for the citizens who cultivated the soil. In recognition of all this, some Greek *póleis* denied political rights to the landless[44]—and even where this practice was contrary to established tradition, the prolonged experience of war might occasion advocacy of its adoption.[45] The poet Menander summed up the Greek outlook when he wrote that "for all human beings the cultivated field (*agrós*) is a teacher of virtue—and of the life devoted to freedom (*bìos eleútheros*)."[46]

The distinction between professions which anchor a man to the soil and those that do not was of fundamental psychological importance to the *pólis*. Among other things, this goes a long ways toward explaining why it was shameful to tan leather and not so to lease mines.[47] But the inevitable tension between those who could abandon the city without losing their livelihood and those who could not was hardly the root of the Greeks' most serious and abiding fears. The assembly of a relatively commercial and radically democratic community might well encompass bronzesmiths, shipwrights, and wheelwrights; fullers, tailors, and cobblers; builders, brickmakers, and merchant-travelers. It might even include those who peddled their wares in the public market, forever pondering what to buy cheap and sell dear.[48] But—despite the bewildering variety of professions represented—the citizens who actually practiced a trade or made their living from commerce were remarkably few,[49] and the likelihood that these men would, in fact, betray the city or lead it far astray was really quite small.

For the Greeks, the principal danger lay elsewhere. The comic poet Amphis identified the realm. "For human beings (*anthrópois*)," he wrote, "the father of life is the cultivated field (*agrós*); it alone knows how to conceal utterly the neediness (*penía*) of man."[50] But, unfortunately, though the vast majority of the citizens within every Greek community drew their sustenance from the soil, good farmland was no more abundant in the mountainous peninsulas and islands of the Mediterranean world in ancient times than it is today. In *The Federalist*, James Madison was essentially correct: in the cities of Hellas, there was always a serious threat that an unbridgeable gap would open up within the agricultural sphere between "those who hold and those who are without property" at all.[51]

Within each Greek community, Plato tells us, there were at least "two cities at war with each other—the *pólis* of the poor and that of the rich."[52] His depiction is exaggerated for dramatic effect, but not excessively so. In a speech designed to appeal to popular sentiment, Lysias praises *homónoia* as "the greatest good for the city" and describes *stásis* as "the cause of all evils." When he describes the principal sources of civil strife, the orator makes no mention of the distrust incurred by artisans and merchants. *Stásis* is most likely to plague a city, he contends, "if some desire what is not their own while others are deprived of their possessions."[53] The historical record bears Lysias out. The cancellation of debts and the redistribution of land was already a revolutionary slogan in the archaic period.[54] From the middle of the fourth century on, the chant was raised with renewed fervor;[55] and in the rare city where such agitation was absent, those with land might still be at odds over matters of foreign policy with those who had none.[56] From enemy raiders, some had much and others relatively little to fear.

I . i i . 4

To head off the onset of *stásis*, many communities took steps to obviate the concentration of wealth by preventing land from becoming a commodity.[57] Oftentimes, the founders of independent colonies (*apoikíai*) or of dependent settlements abroad (*klērouchíai*) would specify that the original allotments of farmland be inalienable from the outset.[58] Some newly established communities limited the size of holdings conveniently situated in the immediate vicinity of the assembly place, markets, and fortifications of the town; these same communities sometimes set aside land on the periphery of the civic territory for latecomers and for further acquisition. Other *póleis* simply restricted the acreage that any given individual might own.[59] One lawgiver went further: to inhibit the growth of that inequality which naturally arises over the course of generations from the division of estates, he sought to regulate procreation.[60]

Even where measures of this sort were never enacted, the city took precautions to prevent the wealthy from using their influence to dispossess the smallholder and his heirs. There was little chance that a peasant would willingly court disgrace and choose to imperil his own livelihood by selling or giving away the family farm.[61] But it made good sense to restrict the size of the dowry he might bestow and to deny him the testamentary freedom to disinherit or make unequal division of his property among his legitimate sons.[62] One city imposed a fine and, for repeated infractions, a loss of citizenship rights on anyone who squandered his inheritance.[63] Another limited the proportion of a man's estate that he could encumber as security for loans,[64] while a third barred his sons from selling or mortgaging their patrimony in anticipation of receipt.[65]

The laws designed to safeguard the smallholder from expropriation had as their principal aim not the protection of the individual citizen's rights but the welfare of the city as a whole. Thus, when the Sicilian Greek writer Diodorus outlined the rationale for measures prohibiting loans with the person as security, he made no mention of the suffering of citizens sold abroad, held in prison, or subjected to debt bondage at home. His point was that, while ordinary possessions might belong to those who had worked for them or had accepted them as gifts from their original owners, "the bodies [of the citizens] should rightfully belong to the *póleis* so that the cities can exact the services (*leitourgíai*) that are properly theirs in war and in peace." It would be "absurd (*átopon*)," he went on, "if a man should happen to be seized for a debt by his creditor just as he was marching into danger on the fatherland's behalf." It would be "absurd to risk the safety common to all for the sake of the greed of private individuals (*pleonexía tôn idiotôn*)." Thus, the Athenian lawgiver Solon deserved praise for his famous "lifting of burdens (*seisáchtheia*)," and "the majority of Greek lawgivers were not unreasonably blamed for prohibiting the seizure as security for loans of weapons, plows, and other indispensable items while allowing those who employed these objects to be treated as moveables subject to seizure or sale (*agôgimoi*)." [66]

The testimony of Diodorus is a salutary reminder of the chaotic character of much of Greek legislation. The law codes adopted by the individual Greek cities were various and confused. Each was adapted (however ineptly) to the particular circumstances of the community for which it was designed, and each was shaped (often decisively) by the peculiar history and traditions of that community. Moreover, each made a great many concessions to the private interests of those within the city's *políteuma*. But this is all beside the point, for the consideration to be grasped is that these codes derived what little coherence they possessed from the very concerns which Diodorus outlined. It is that common understanding which allows him to distinguish what is absurd and utterly "out of place (*átopon*)" from that which is not. [67]

Guided by this understanding, a number of communities placed orphans, heiresses, and—in at least one case—pregnant widows under the protection of the eponymous archon or of special magistrates appointed to see to their welfare. [68] In each case, guardians were to be selected, and great care was taken to prevent them from enriching themselves at the expense of those entrusted to their charge. [69] One city carried this principle an additional step: where a man's children had inherited property from some other source, he too was subject to legal controls. He could manage their inheritance, but he was barred from selling or mortgaging the estate. [70] As a brotherhood of warriors, the *pólis* had a stake in maintaining the number of viable citizen households; and if liberty was to be preserved, it was essential to facilitate the establishment of that modicum of economic equality prerequisite for the growth of fraternal affection within the community.

This seems to have been what Philolaus of Corinth and Solon of Athens intended when they set down legislation concerning inheritance and adoption. Aristotle does not describe in detail the law code instituted by the former at Thebes, but he does specify that the regulations dealing with adoption were aimed chiefly at preserving the number of households already existing in the community.[71] Concerning the legislation of Solon, we are somewhat better informed. Prior to the adoption of the changes that he recommended, the property of a childless Athenian automatically reverted to his *génos*. Lest this practice contribute to a decline in the number of independent households and to excessive concentrations of wealth, Solon granted those without legitimate sons the right to pass on their property through testamentary adoption. If a son was adopted, he had to give up his right to share in his natural father's estate and could recover that right only if he left behind a legitimate son of his own to succeed his adoptive father.[72] As the celebrated Athenian legislator knew, a man of even ordinary piety, who contemplated the prospect of death through disease, old age, or war in the absence of a legitimate son, had a powerful motive for including such a provision in his will, for otherwise there was no guarantee that there would be anyone to tend his grave and maintain the family cults.[73]

The Solonian regulations regarding *epíklēroi* had precisely the same function, for the sons of a woman left without brothers at the time of her father's death were destined to be their maternal grandfather's heirs. As the legal term *epíklēros* suggests, the fatherless girl or woman was less an heiress than a vehicle for the transfer of her father's allotment of land (*klêros*). She was literally "on the allotment": it went with her, and she went with it. Even where a man's natural or adopted daughter was his sole survivor, she did not secure the right to dispose of the property that she could be said to have inherited; and though her husband might manage the estate while her sons were still quite young, he had to hand over the appropriate part of the *klêros* as soon as each boy came of age and took up his responsibilities as his maternal grandfather's successor.[74] In these matters, the *génos* still possessed certain rights: the closest living male blood relative of the deceased could claim the man's daughter as his wife even if she was already married but had not yet borne a son. In such a situation, the woman and the community were not entirely without protection, for the law did seek to prevent the man from claiming her merely in order to secure control of the estate: if he was to retain the *epíklēros*, he had to risk fathering her son by having intercourse with his wife at least three times a month.[75]

The need for safeguards was particularly evident to the Greeks where the disablement or death of a citizen in battle threatened the well-being of his family, for such an event called into question whether the interests of the household and those of the community were one and the same. At least one city addressed this problem by granting a modest pension to invalids possessing little in the way of property.[76] There and elsewhere, it was the custom to make provision for the kin of those killed in the city's wars. If Diogenes Laertius is to be believed, the lawgiver Solon may have been the originator of the latter scheme. He reportedly stipulated that Athens assume the financial burden of rearing those left fatherless in this way.[77] The town planner Hippodamus of Miletus later incorporated the Athenian practice into the design of his ideal constitution, and many, if not all, of the Greek *póleis* eventually adopted the measure.[78]

Though, in other respects, the cities were quite various, their policies were, on one point, remarkably uniform. In every case where detailed evidence survives, the community provided more than just a daily allowance. When the daughter of a war hero reached majority, the city supplied her with a dowry; when the son of such a man attained manhood, the *pólis* not only conferred on him the greaves, breastplate, dagger, helmet, shield, and spear that made up the hoplite panoply: to bring home to him and to his fellow citizens the debt owed his father and the honor due those who had made the ultimate sacrifice for the community, the magistrates paraded the young man, dressed in full armor, before the populace at a public festival and then sent him off to his ancestral hearth to take up his inheritance and his responsibilities as a citizen and soldier.[79] The ultimate purpose of the regulations regarding those left fatherless by war was hidden from no one. As the comic poet Cratinus took occasion to remark, the *pólis* "educated and nourished them through adolescence at public expense—in order that they would ward off the city's ruin in turn."[80]

In special circumstances, the privilege of support might be extended to a wider circle. When faced with a crisis, the Rhodians chose to guarantee sustenance not only to the children of the man killed in battle, but to his parents as well.[81] In one instance, the Athenians went even further. In the months immediately following their loss of the Peloponnesian War, Athens had suffered terrible civil strife. In the process, more than fifteen hundred Athenians had been murdered or otherwise killed.[82] To promote *homónoia* among the ultimate victors, the survivors voted to confer on the children of those citizens who had given their lives fighting in defense of the ancestral democratic constitution the maintenance fee customarily reserved for the disabled and for those orphaned by war. The sum—an obol a day—was by no means trivial: at the end of the fifth century, an unskilled laborer could expect to earn three times and a skilled craftsman only four times as much.[83] The measures of this sort adopted in such situations no doubt differed a great deal from community to community, but their purpose was always and everywhere the same.

I.ii.5

Hippodamus may have been the first, but he was not the only theorist to address such concerns. The problem of gross inequality and its relation to civic defense engaged the attention of a good many others as well. Some paid special notice to the role which individual benefactors might play in the promotion of civic solidarity.[84] In the fifth century, Democritus of Abdera was one among these. He contended that jealousy (*phthónos*) was "the origin (*archē̌*) of *stásis*." But "whenever the powerful take heart and advance money to those without property, assisting and gratifying them," he argued, "at such a time there will be fellow-feeling (*tò oiktírein*), a sense of companionship, and an end to isolation. Then, the citizens will protect each other (*amúnein allḗloisin*) and be of like mind (*homonóous*)—and they will gain other goods more than anyone could list."[85]

In the fourth century, Archytas of Tarentum pondered the same problem and made much the same claim. "Upon discovery," he wrote, "right reason (*logismós*) brings an end to civil strife (*stásis*) and promotes solidarity (*homónoia*)—for where *logismós* comes into play there is equity (*isótas*) and no grasping at excess (*pleonexía*). Through calculation (*logismós*), we come to terms over contracts; and because of it, the poor (*pénētes*) receive from the powerful while the rich give to those in need—with both parties trusting that because of right reason they will be treated in an equitable fashion."[86] It would be easy to dismiss Archytas's praise of *logismós* as mere posturing, but there seems to have been more to it than that. In *The Politics*, Aristotle advances three propositions: that property should be privately held, that no citizen should have to do without sustenance, and that the citizens should— in the manner of friends (*philikȭs*)—share in common the use of what they possess. "Where the notables (*gnȭrimoi*) are gracious and possessed of good sense (*noûs*)," he remarks, "they divide up those at a loss for livelihood (*apórous*) and provide them with the resources needed so that they can work." In this context, he singles out Archytas's Tarentines as an example for emulation. The leading citizens of that philosopher's *pólis* "secured the goodwill of the multitude by treating their private possessions as public property available for the use of those without means (*koinà poioûntes tà ktḗmata toîs apórois epì tḕn chrȇsin*)."[87]

The comportment of the more prosperous Tarentines was by no means an isolated example. Isocrates claims that the sharing of wealth by the rich with the poor was commonplace in archaic Athens. His testimony on the matter may seem exaggerated, but it should not be too quickly dismissed. Even in Isocrates' own time, a citizen of some substance who assisted one or two of the men from his village in securing the equipment necessary for war could do so on the assumption that his example would be followed.[88] In earlier periods, it appears to have been taken for granted that the local gentry would aid fellow demesmen in need. It is only when great magnates like Peisistratus in the sixth century and Cimon in the fifth exhibited a spectacular hospitality within their home district and extended their largesse to those from other localities that their generosity was thought to warrant particular attention; and though these two men were evidently the most liberal of patrons, they were by no means alone: it is striking that an Athenian aristocrat on trial for his life just after the close of the fifth century did not hesitate to appeal to the fact that generosity of this sort was a family tradition.[89]

The same pattern is evident elsewhere as well. Aelian records the benefactions of particular Corinthians and Mytilenians, and there is epigraphical and literary evidence for such contributions on the part of the rich in Hellenistic Olbia, Erythrae, Priene, Samos, and Rhodes.[90] In *The Characters*, Theophrastus depicts the braggart as a recognizable social type—the sort of man who would not only boast that he had donated over five talents to support those citizens in need when food fell short, but go on to remark that "he simply cannot say no."[91] One late fifth-century writer summed up the situation in brief compass: where the *pólis* was in good order (*eunomía*), the first result was the generation of an atmosphere of trust (*pístis*). "From this," he remarked, "comes the holding of wealth in common—and even where it amounts to very little, it suffices because it circulates about—while without such trust, not even great wealth is enough." Where "men hoard money and do not hold it in common," it is a sign of "distrust (*apistía*) and of a general breakdown in social relations (*ameixía*)."[92]

There is, unfortunately, no way to assess with any certainty just how widespread a phenomenon local patronage actually was. The evidence does suggest that the estates of wealthy landowners were widely dispersed, and one can make an educated guess. In doing so, one must keep in mind not just the need to maintain public morale in time of war, but also what was entailed by the absence of police. Plato's Socrates understood the consequences perfectly: to impress upon his interlocutors the disadvantages of tyranny, he compared the situation of the tyrant with that of a wealthy slaveholder deprived of the protection which neighbors afford or fated to live among men violently hostile to the very notion of one man's claiming to be the master of another.[93] In antiquity, an individual threatened with violence or theft was expected to see to his own protection: he had no one to turn to other than his fellow citizens, and in an emergency, he would naturally look first to his nearest neighbors and then only later to more distant kin. Needless to say, the *pólis* took an interest in the local enforcement of law and in the maintenance of public order. To accustom "the citizens to feel and suffer with one another like the parts of a single body," Solon is said to have included a provision in his law code empowering any citizen to file charges on behalf of any compatriot who had suffered an injustice.[94] This practice may have been peculiarly Athenian, but we do hear of communities passing decrees penalizing citizens who fail to come to the aid of political exiles and of other foreigners singled out as guests deserving public hospitality, and these decrees appear to have been modeled on statutes making assistance to resident aliens under attack a legally enforceable duty.[95] It is not likely that citizens were less well protected. At least one *pólis* enacted legislation imposing collective responsibility in cases of theft: that city exacted contributions from a man's neighbors to cover the cost of replacing property stolen from his home or estate.[96] But though laws of this sort were probably not uncommon and undoubtedly of importance, so was goodwill. The rich man was an obvious object for attack and could not easily survive the hostility or even the indifference of those dwelling nearby. If he raised a hue and cry (*boế*) in the night, he expected his neighbors to run to his aid (*boế-theîn*), and the most simple application of Archytas's *logismós* will have taught him that he had an interest in earning their loyalty, friendship, and trust. Above all else, it was imperative that he persuade them to defend his life and his property as if these were somehow also their own. In these circumstances, it is not likely that the local gentry neglected to cultivate those living within easy reach.[97]

In pondering the overall political efficacy of private patronage, we should never forget the small size of the ordinary *pólis* and the close, personal relations that characterized life within its bounds. Plato makes a point of cautioning the public-spirited that they should avoid the civil strife associated with the redistribution of wealth and the canceling of debts—for once the process has begun, it cannot be stopped, and the bitterness to which it gives rise might imperil defense. As he puts it, "It is neither possible for a city forced to revise its laws to leave ancient practices intact nor to alter them in any way—and one is left, so to speak, only with prayer and small changes cautiously undertaken over a long period of time." In a great and turbulent nation established on an extended territory, the abandonment of traditional practices might not be an invitation to anarchy; but by the same token, the actions of individuals would have little or no impact on the whole. Within the tiny communities of Greece, Plato argues, incremental change might accomplish much "if there existed over a long period of time a body of reformers within the class of those possessing an abundance of land and having many in their debt. Out of a sense of fairness, these reformers would have to be willing to share their wealth in some fashion with those lacking means—perhaps by remitting debts and making distributions—and to hold on in some way or other to moderation (*metriótēs*), regarding as poverty (*penía*) not the diminution of a man's substance but rather the addition to his greed." In Plato's view, the comportment of such reformers "becomes the greatest source of security for a city (*sōtērías archè megístē*)," and he adds that "on this solid a foundation it becomes possible for someone later to construct a political order (*kósmon politikón*) befitting such a state of affairs." [98]

The ancient students of political science might place great emphasis on the voluntary, public-spirited action of individual citizens—particularly where a regime was already well established. But they did not do so to the absolute exclusion of all recourse to law and public policy. Aristotle is a case in point. With aristocratic largesse and the example of the tyrant Peisistratus in mind, he argued that democracies should employ public revenues to purchase land for the poor or to help them set up shop. [99] Phaleas of Chalcedon is another. Intent on promoting a gradual redistribution of concentrated wealth, he urged that dowries be given only by the rich and be received only by the poor. [100] Gorgias, Lysias, and Isocrates were no less practical than Aristotle and Phaleas, but they thought such expedients grossly insufficient. These three renowned orators considered the situation in fourth-century Greece so desperate that it demanded concerted action on the part of the various cities. Gorgias first sounded the theme in 392; Lysias took it up shortly thereafter; and, again and again, over a period of more than forty years, Isocrates returned to the same point: calling for a cooperative Panhellenic effort to conquer the Persian empire, appropriate its great wealth, and populate its vast reaches with colonies of Greek poor. [101] Well before Alexander the Great did just that, Plato urged Dionysius II of Syracuse to repopulate the cities of Hellenic Sicily in much the same fashion; in due course, Timoleon of Corinth managed the feat. [102]

The Greeks were characteristically more radical when given the chance to devise institutions for an entirely new foundation. In the immediate aftermath of the Persian Wars, apparently under the guidance of Hippodamus of Miletus, the Hellenic cities took up a novel species of town planning, adapting the orthogonal grid, already employed in many of the Greek colonies, for the purpose of giving architectural form to the new democratic principle of political equality (*isonomía*). To this end, they constructed new towns

out of a series of city blocks rectangular in form, built to the fixed propor-
tions of Pythagorean number theory, and containing a predetermined number of dwellings equal in size and similar in plan. The egalitarian logic of this
development Plato carried to its conclusion. In constructing his imaginary
Cretan city, he proposed a comprehensive body of legislation aimed at sta-
bilizing the division of wealth. To foster concord, he made the original allotments of farmland roughly equal in product and decreed them inalienable;
to maintain harmony, he outlawed dowries and restricted the acquisition of
movable wealth; and to prevent inequality, he specified that a man's public
allotment pass intact to his favorite son and encouraged childless couples to
adopt an heir from among the male children of their more prolific compatriots. Finally—with Aristotle's endorsement—he sought to sustain the fragile balance between population and the means of production by encouraging
family planning.[103] As the two philosophers recognized, the half-measures
taken by most Greek cities were woefully inadequate.

Yet, even where the distribution of property was left almost entirely to
chance, the Greeks took steps to curb class resentment. In antiquity, grain
was the chief source of nutrition,[104] and communities suffering from a shortage or afflicted by overpopulation sometimes sought to prevent profiteering
by prohibiting its export.[105] In some *póleis*, an egalitarian regimen was enforced, and men were expected to take the main meal of the day together in
one or another public mess and to contribute from their estates to its support.[106] Virtually all of the cities enacted sumptuary laws to stop the wealthy
from making offensive display of their opulence,[107] and many required or
pressed the prosperous to devote part of their substance to public works
adorning the *pólis* or filling its needs.[108] In at least one such community, a citizen saddled with heavier responsibilities than he thought just had recourse
to the law; if he could demonstrate in court that another citizen who had
shirked the performance of liturgies actually possessed greater wealth, he
could force the individual to take up the burden or submit to an exchange of
estates (*antídosis*).[109] Here, an important principle was at stake: in antiquity,
no one supposed that a man had a natural or god-given right to the fruits of
his own labor; if a given individual possessed property, he held it in privilege
and as a public trust.[110] A particularly acute observer summed up the situation at the time by saying that public policy had two guiding principles: that
"the laws turn the multitude away from plotting against those possessing
property, and that they engender in the wealthy a love of honor (*philotimía*)
sufficient to cause these men to spend their riches in liturgies serving the
public (*koinaì leitourgíai*)."[111]

The *pólis* was not always and everywhere dependent on the generosity of

the rich. On occasion, the city itself had the means for the promotion of a
salutary equality: where a community could afford it, there might be public
pay for the performance of jury duty or for attendance at the assembly [112] and
public provision for wrestling grounds, changing rooms, and gymnasia. [113]
Quite often, at festivals, rich and poor alike would feast on meat at public
expense; [114] and where the city's income from mines or from foreign largesse
exceeded the demands made on the public treasury, the surplus was customarily distributed equally to all. [115] In the extreme case, a maritime city,
governing a large empire and drawing tribute from a host of subject allies,
could grant the needy land in settlements abroad [116] and provide a small
army of men with public employment as rowers in its fleet or as petty officials charged with overseeing minor matters at home or the affairs of subject
communities abroad. [117]

These were the measures taken under ordinary circumstances. In moments of great danger, more might be done. At the beginning of the sixth
century, a group of political refugees from Cnidus and Rhodes settled on
Lipari in the Aeolic isles just off the coast of Sicily. At first, they appear to
have divided the land on the island among themselves in the customary fashion. But when they came under persistent Etruscan assault, these colonists
abolished private property, took their meals in common, and split the citizen
body into two groups—one of which cultivated the soil while the other fitted
out a fleet to ward off the foe. When in due course the danger receded, they
divided the land on Lipari into individual allotments but continued to farm
the outlying islands as property common to all. Not until somewhat later did
they subdivide the remaining territory, and even then they chose to redis-
tribute the wealth again at the end of every twenty-year cycle by casting lots
for estates. [118]

The case of Lipari is extreme, but the principle was supported elsewhere.
In a crisis, the affluent were expected to place their property at the disposal
of the *pólis*; [119] and to guarantee *homónoia* during a siege, Aeneas Tacticus suggests a cancellation of debts and special provision from the wealth of the rich
for feeding the poor. [120] At all times, but particularly then, it was vital that the
citizens all consider their interests the same.

I. ii. 6

The threat posed to communal solidarity by the market economy had more
than one aspect. The ancients feared commerce not simply because it encouraged economic specialization and contributed to a differentiation of interests.

They worried also that trade would erode the fragile moral consensus of the community by exposing its citizens to a flood of foreigners and to the alien notions these travelers brought with them. Cicero argued that maritime cities risked not only seaborne assault, but also "a corruption and degeneration of morals." In such polities, he remarked, "there is a mingling of strange tongues and practices; and with foreign merchandise, they import foreign ways—so that nothing in their ancestral institutions remains intact. Those who reside now in these cities do not cling to their dwelling places, but are always being seized and carried off by winged hope and flying thought— and even when they remain bodily at home, they wander in an exile of the mind." In Cicero's opinion, this spiritual deracination was a danger not only for trading centers like Corinth, but for the rest of Greece as well: "Even the Peloponnesus itself—almost in its entirety—lies next to the sea," he wrote. The Hellenes had dispatched colonies to a great many places—"to Asia, to Thrace, to Italy, to Sicily, and even to Africa"—but the Roman orator could think of only one such settlement that "the waves do not wash." As for "the Greek islands," he noted, "girdled as they are by the flood, they seem almost to swim—and the institutions and the mores of their cities swim with them." It was difficult for the citizens of such communities in flux to hold to the same opinions. Patriotism thrives on isolation, and trade imperils like-mindedness.[121]

Cicero's claim may at first appear strange, but it should not upon reflection seem all that uncanny. It is not fortuitous that the modern English word *speculation* has two different meanings. The commerce in goods inevitably gives rise to a commerce in ideas,[122] and subsequent history justified as prescient the stress which Edmund Burke laid on the critical role played by speculators of both kinds in overturning the ancien régime in France.[123] Nor is it an accident that, just a few decades after coinage became commonplace in Greece, Heraclitus should expound his physics by means of a mercantile metaphor, depicting "an exchange (*antamoibé*) of all things for fire and fire for all things like the exchange of goods (*chrémata*) for gold and gold for goods."[124] If Aristotle is to be trusted, the first philosopher may well have been the first man to have conceived of the market as an abstraction. When reproached for his poverty, Thales is said to have resolved to demonstrate once and for all that philosophy is by no means utterly helpless (*anōpheloús*) in the world of practical affairs. So, for a time, he abandoned his cosmological speculations in order to pursue speculation in a somewhat more vulgar and familiar vein. Having determined in winter that the following year would bring a bumper crop in olives, Thales managed to lease for a pittance all the olive presses in

Miletus and on Chios. When a rich harvest came in just as he had predicted, his patience was rewarded, for he employed his corner on the olive-press market to establish a monopoly and to make himself a very rich man.[125]

Greek linguistic practice provides additional evidence for the connection which Aristotle's anecdote suggests. A century and a half after Thales, the poet Aristophanes would depict the philosopher Socrates as a man suspended in a basket, his head in the clouds, his feet far from the ground. This absentminded figure was said to be devoting his time to the investigation of "the things aloft (*tà metéōra*)."[126] It is revealing that the same term recurs in a third-century Ephesian inscription recording a law in which a deceased man's intangible assets—the money he has deposited in a bank, a credit unsecured by a mortgage—are referred to as *metéōron*: "something aloft."[127]

The point may seem farfetched, but it should not be dismissed out of hand. As Aristotle points out, it can hardly be an accident that the Greek word for coinage (*nomísmata*) is derived from the Greek term for that which exists solely by convention (*nómos*), solely in thought (*nomízein*). In 1689, John Locke would draw attention to the fact that "Fancy or Agreement" far "more than real Use, and the necessary Support of Life" assigns value to "Gold, Silver, and Diamonds,"[128] and the shrewdest students of economic affairs in the generation following the Glorious Revolution would make much of the dependence of credit and the stock market on the human imagination. Though a defender of the Junto Whigs and their financial revolution, the novelist Daniel Defoe would write:

> Trade is a Mystery, which will never be compleatly discover'd or understood; it has its Critical Junctures and Seasons, when acted by no visible Causes, it suffers Convulsion Fitts, hysterical Disorders, and most unaccountable Emotions—Sometimes it is acted by the evil Spirit of general Vogue, and like a meer Possession 'tis hurry'd out of all manner of common Measures; today it obeys the Course of things, and submits to Causes and Consequences; to morrow it suffers Violence from the Storms and Vapours of Human Fancy, operated by exotick Projects, and then all runs counter, the Motions are excentrick, unnatural and unaccountable—A Sort of Lunacy in Trade attends all its Circumstances, and no Man can give a rational Account of it.[129]

An institution as unstable as commerce could not provide a proper foundation for a martial republic. The suspicion which the Greeks reserved for the philosopher and that which they directed at the merchant have the same root.

I . ii . 7

A differentiation of interests and opinions was not the only danger recognized to be attendant on trade. Commerce posed a similar threat to public-spiritedness. By accustoming its practitioners to dickering and haggling, it engendered a mean-spirited and selfish individualism inconsistent with the wholehearted commitment to the common good which the *pólis*, as a brotherhood of warriors, demanded. Though easily overlooked, this last point is important: because they habitually calculate how best to profit from those with whom they deal, human beings "absorbed in the pursuits of gain and devoted to the improvements of agriculture and commerce" find it remarkably difficult "to act in unison with each other." For this reason, Plato argued that a well-governed city should be situated some distance from the harbors of the coast. He acknowledged that "proximity to the sea" had material advantages, but he added that, because it "fills a place with buying and selling (*emporía*) and with the money-making that goes with retail trade, such proximity breeds in men's souls unstable and undependable dispositions and makes a city distrustful and unfriendly towards itself." [130] This same attitude manifests itself in an anecdote related by Herodotus. When the Spartans warned him not to trouble the Ionians, the Persian king Cyrus reportedly replied that he had no fear of the Greeks. He could not take seriously the threats of "the sort of men who set aside a place in the center of their city, where they swear oaths and cheat each other." Men of this sort would be useless in war. [131]

To appreciate fully the import of the observations made by Plato and Herodotus, we must take heed of the manner in which different regimes shape the dispositions of those subject to them. Commercial societies, despite the veneer of bourgeois propriety which they display, are predicated on an emancipation of greed. Over time, they tend to substitute contractual relations—what Thomas Carlyle called "the cash nexus"—for every other human tie. [132] Of course, acquisitiveness does generate a utilitarian morality all its own. The bourgeois virtues are not a fraud perpetrated on an ignorant public; they have a certain content. In Hamilton's liberal polity, the merchant will be assiduous; the husbandman, laborious; the mechanic, active; and the manufacturer, industrious. Montesquieu's "democracy founded on commerce" will foster "frugality, economy, moderation, labor, prudence, tranquillity, order, and regularity." Its citizens will exhibit a "politeness of morals" and "a certain sentiment of exact justice." [133] The habit of honesty, and the expectation that it will be reciprocated, link the merchant with his suppliers and with his customers: he assumes that they will abide by their contracts and pay their bills, but he does so only because it is in their interest to sustain their own credit and because he can ultimately depend on their dread of punishment as a guarantee. He does not look for generosity from his fellows, and in the course of hammering out deals, he rarely encounters it. Except (if he is fortunate) within the bosom of his immediate family, his is a life governed by self-interest, by caution, and by distrust. The businessman's anxious hunger for money and his sense of propriety mask a more fundamental and less respectable passion—the love of mere life. As one Greek writer of the late fifth century had occasion to note, most men hold possessions and money dear (*philochrēmatoúsin*) because of the things that cast them into fright: things like disease, old age, and the losses caused by fire; things like the deaths of animals and of members of the household—as well as other misfortunes.[134] If the tradesman craves lucre and supports law and order, it is only because he senses that both are a hedge against death. As Madison acknowledged, the foundation of liberal theory and practice is "the great principle of self-preservation."[135]

Warrior communities embody an entirely different morality. They tend to emphasize friendship and honor even in the realm of commodity exchange. This propensity helps explain the remarkable character of the discussion which Aristotle devotes to the function of coinage in the *Nicomachean Ethics*. The Stagirite was perfectly aware that the introduction of money eased considerably the task of the profiteer, but—when assessing the import of coinage—he chose to underline, instead, the role that it played as an instrument of reciprocity within the political community: standing in place of need (*chreía*) and enabling each citizen to share with his fellows through something like an exchange of gifts (*metádosis*) his own contribution to the common weal. "This is why," Aristotle explains, "we establish a temple for the Graces (*Chárites*) where the citizens will stumble across it—in order that there might be reciprocal giving (*antapódosis*). Exchanges of this sort are a peculiar characteristic of graciousness (*cháris*), for it is required of a man who has received a boon that he serve in turn—and again subsequently repay the debt by taking the initiative in conferring a favor himself." Aristotle's discussion of coined money may seem strange to us, but his understanding of the place reserved within the community for what we might mistake for commerce would not have been thought odd in ancient times.[136] To grasp Aristotle's point, we must keep in mind that it is camaraderie which links the citizen-soldier with his fellows. When he is in danger, he expects them to risk their lives to come to his aid, and he knows that the greatest obstacle to their support is that very fear of violent death which sustains the minimal decency at home in the autonomous marketplace of the liberal polity. If a soldier is not joined to his compatriots by bonds of warmth and trust on the day before battle, he may not be able to depend on them in his hour of need.

The contrast between these two regimes and the radically different ways of life that they foster can be put simply: the passions nurtured by commerce are at odds with those required by a warrior band. As Montesquieu put it, the "sentiment of exact justice" is opposed not only to "brigandage," but also to "those moral virtues" which make men "able to neglect their own interests for those of others." The spirit of commerce causes men "to forget the laws of friendship and those of hate"; it renders them "confederates rather than fellow citizens." [137] Herodotus made this point with a parable: in the aftermath of the Persian conquest of Asia Minor and the subsequent Lydian revolt, when Cyrus the Great pondered the means for preventing future rebellion, he was purportedly advised to ban the possession of arms at Sardis and to require luxurious dress, musical training, and the profession of retail trade. "If you do this," he was told, "the Lydians will quickly become women instead of men, and there will no longer be any danger that they will revolt." [138]

Similar reasoning caused men in the late eighteenth century such as Adam Ferguson and, less emphatically, Adam Smith to worry that the emerging capitalist order would be accompanied by a decay in national spirit fatal to the long-term prospects of political liberty. [139] As they recognized, liberal democracies are forever in danger of degenerating into what Aristotle called "an association for residence on a common site existing for the sake of exchange and for the prevention of mutual injustice." In such a polity, Aristotle had warned, "the law" is "unable to make the citizens good and just" because it is nothing more than "a covenant . . . a pledge to respect each other's rightful claims." [140]

The recognition that the unleashing of the commercial instinct would undermine the moral foundations of classical republicanism by destroying every vestige of martial spirit did not provoke consternation in all circles. Bernard Mandeville was a Dutchman: he had come to maturity among "a people" once proudly described by their countryman Hugo Grotius as "unsurpassed in their greed for honourable gain," and he was, in consequence, intimately familiar with the most fully commercial regime known to mankind prior to the transformation of England in the eighteenth century. [141] As early as 1705, he reported with glee that the "publick benefits" derivative from trade had their source in "private vices." His celebrated satire *The Fable of the Bees* was a direct assault on the inherited moral code that stood as an obstacle to the full emancipation of the lust for profit. His purpose was "to shew the Impossibility of enjoying all the most elegant Comforts of Life that are to be met with in an industrious, wealthy, and powerful Nation, and at the same time be bless'd with all the Virtue and Innocence that can be wish'd for in a Golden Age." Though a proponent of the new economic order, he did not hesitate to echo the charges lodged against trade by Cicero, Plato, and Herodotus. He cared little whether the citizens harbored the same opinions and passions; he cared even less that they be "good and just"—as long as they were rich:

> The Root of Evil, Avarice
> That damn'd ill natur'd baneful Vice
> Was Slave to Prodigality,
> That noble Sin; whilst Luxury
> Employ'd a Million of the Poor
> And odious Pride a Million more:
> Envy it self, and Vanity
> Were Ministers of Industry;
> Their darling Folly, Fickleness
> In Diet, Furniture and Dress
> That strange ridi'lous Vice, was made
> The very Wheel that turn'd the Trade
> Their Laws and Clothes were equally
> Objects of Mutability;
> For, what was well done for a time,
> In half a Year became a Crime;
> Yet while they alter'd thus their Laws,
> Still finding and correcting Flaws,
> They mended by Inconstancy
> Faults, which no Prudence could foresee.
> Thus Vice nurs'd Ingenuity,
> Which join'd with Time and Industry,
> Had carry'd Life's Conveniencies,
> It's real Pleasures, Comforts, Ease,
> To such a Height, the very Poor
> Liv'd better than the Rich before,
> And nothing could be added more.

If Mandeville viewed the emergence of commercial society with pleasure, it was at least partly because he was confident that such a society, though divided against itself, would be successful in war. Despite the fact that he lived well after Francis Bacon, he was, with John Locke, among the first to appreciate fully the military advantages attendant on the possession of a dynamic economy.[142]

The debate begun in Mandeville's time continues in our own. It remains an open question whether his confidence was fully justified. In the early nineteenth century, Tocqueville expressed fear that a liberal democracy could not "brave for long the great storms that mark the political life of peoples." "This relative weakness of democratic republics in times of crisis is perhaps the greatest obstacle to the foundation of such a republic in Europe," he contended. "In order that the democratic republic should subsist without difficulty for one European people, it would be necessary that it be simultaneously introduced among all the others." [143] A hundred years later, George Orwell brooded over the same phenomenon. "Right at the end of August 1939," he wrote, "the British dealers were tumbling over one another in their eagerness to sell Germany tin, rubber, copper, and shellack—and this in the clear, certain knowledge that war was going to break out in a week or two." [144] Neither man was a reactionary, hearkening back to a preliberal golden age; both welcomed recent modernity's democratic tide. But they echoed the fears of Adam Ferguson and Adam Smith nonetheless.

CHAPTER 3

The Political Economy of Hellas

Within aristocracies, it is not precisely labor (travail) that one despises; it is labor with a view to profit. Labor is glorious when it is undertaken for the sake of ambition or virtue alone. Under an aristocracy, it happens again and again that he who labors for honor is not insensible to the greed for gain. But the two desires meet only in the depths of his soul. He takes great care to conceal from all eyes the place where they unite. He voluntarily hides it even from himself.
—*Alexis de Tocqueville*

Among the ancients, we never come upon an investigation as to which form of landed property . . . is the most productive [and] creates the greatest wealth, do we? Wealth does not appear as the aim of production—though Cato may well investigate which mode of cultivating the fields is the most profitable, and Brutus may even lend his money at the most favorable rates of interest. The question is always which kind of property creates the best citizens. Wealth appears as an end in itself only among the handful of commercial peoples—monopolists of the carrying trade—who live in the pores of the ancient world, like the Jews in medieval society.—*Karl Marx*

I . iii . 1

The Greeks could not contemplate trade with the equanimity of a Mandeville or even with the muted misgivings of a Tocqueville or an Orwell. For the citizens of the *pólis*, the tension between commerce and war posed an insuperable difficulty. They had no reason to suppose that a grant of autonomy to the marketplace would indirectly generate progress in military technology, and they could not survive without trade. This last point is vital: poverty has, in all ages, been the scourge of Hellas.[1] The citizens of the *pólis* were not great magnates able to incorporate within their households all the skills and resources needed to sustain well-being. From year to year, most of them eked out a bare living from a rocky and infertile soil.[2] Like peasants in other times and places, they may have dreamed of complete self-sufficiency, but few, if any, actually possessed it.[3] In good years, most could no doubt get by—if not solely on the produce they grew for themselves on the scattered plots they farmed, then on the meager return they received for seasonal labor performed on the estates of their wealthier neighbors. But some years were lean years: when there was excessive rainfall or a drought, or when invaders ravaged the land, the harvest could easily fall short, and the stocks carefully stored away as a hedge against disaster would quickly dwindle.[4] Furthermore, many of the poorer farmers depended for their livelihood on marginal land best suited to the production of items such as olive oil, which could be exchanged for the grain exported in great abundance by the Greek colonies situated in the colder climes along the Black Sea where the olive will not grow.[5] Moreover, all of the citizens needed finished goods—pottery, armor, metal tools—which they could not easily make for themselves, and often they had to import from abroad the materials from which these were fashioned.[6]

The degree to which the Hellenes were dependent on maritime trade is suggested by the peculiar geographical configuration of the Greek diaspora of classical times. Plato's Socrates touches on the central point when he remarks that "we dwell in a small part of the world between the Pillars of Heracles and Phasis, living about the sea like ants or frogs around a pond."[7] It was, Cicero observed, "as if a Greek seacoast had been stitched on as a border about the lands of the barbarians."[8] In antiquity, overland trade in most staples was prohibitively expensive: if the edict issued by Diocletian in 301 A.D. is a dependable guide, the price of wheat transported in bulk by road doubled every three to four hundred miles; and to carry grain by wagon, donkey, or camel a mere seventy-five miles cost as much as to ship it from Syria clear across the Mediterranean and through the straits of Gibraltar to Portugal.[9] Put simply: except in time of emergency, the rivers, oceans, and seas were the only plausible highways for commerce over any substantial distance in most items; and that is why, throughout antiquity, the Greeks clung so tenaciously to the shore. Late in the fifth century B.C., one Athenian observed, "Those powerful on land suffer terribly when maladies sent by Zeus strike the crops, but those powerful on the sea cope well—for not all of the earth is ill at any given time, and so food from a flourishing place reaches those ruling the sea."[10] In the three-quarters of a millennium that passed thereafter, the situation altered not a whit: when a famine struck the Cappadocian city Caesarea in the mid-fourth century A.D., Gregory of Nazianzus was led to remark, "Coastal cities bear up under shortages of this kind without great difficulty—simply by giving what they produce at home in exchange for what they can import by sea (*didoûsai tà par' eautôn, kaì tà parà tês thalássēs dechómenai*). To those of us on the mainland in the interior, producing a surplus is senseless (*tò peritteûon anóēton*) and securing what we need is out of the question (*tò endéon anepinóēton*) since we do not have the means to dispose of what we possess and to bring in what we lack."[11] Thus, while the quest for *homónoia* may have dictated the abandonment of overseas commerce, no Hellenic city was ever able to eliminate the marketplace altogether.

The Greeks attempted only what was possible: to insulate the political community from the influence of the market by suppressing or restricting the passion for profit and by deliberately putting psychological distance between citizens and traders—as well as other outsiders. To achieve this, a community might ban gold and silver coinage[12] or simply regulate the market;[13] it might prohibit the citizens from becoming artisans and merchants[14] or merely deny full political rights to those who soiled their hands in endeavor so sordid.[15] At least one city forbade travel abroad; two restricted all visits by foreigners,[16] while a third went even further: fearful lest fraternization with the Illyrians undermine the city's ethos and spark a revolution, Epidamnus appointed an official, called "the seller," to administer all trade with its barbarian neighbors.[17] Aristotle even urged that all commerce with the outside world be filtered through a port of trade some distance from the urban center so that the magistrates could oversee all contact between citizens and aliens.[18]

Many communities were hospitable to immigrant craftsmen and merchants, but they all appear to have denied their metics the right to own land. Most evidently subjected these resident aliens to the stigma of a special tax, and at least one confined them to a ghetto within the town.[19] In the most cosmopolitan of cities, the individual metic—one distinguished by wealth, by education, or by nobility of birth—might find a welcome among citizens similarly blessed. But, even in such a community, he and his fellow immigrants were the object of a measure of popular disdain. In the public imagination, they were so closely associated with trade that the lexicographer Hesychius later thought it adequate to gloss *merchant-traveler* (*empórios*) simply with *metic*.[20] Though perhaps novel, Plato's suggestion that a time limit be placed on the immigrant's sojourn was entirely in keeping with the spirit of Greek practice.[21]

I.iii.2

The establishment of institutions conforming to that same spirit goes some distance toward explaining the extraordinary stagnation of technique that characterized the two great civilizations of classical antiquity.[22] Though the ancients were perfectly cognizant that progress in the arts (*téchnai*) was possible and had in the past been beneficial, no city is known to have done much of anything to encourage the spirit of invention and enterprise within its own population. This neglect reflects an indifference to and even a suspicion of further progress in the arts, not gross ignorance regarding the potential effectiveness of this sort of political intervention. The admiration which Sir Francis Bacon reserved for the pre-Socratics may have been exaggerated, but it was not entirely misplaced. There was, in fact, one ancient writer who did call for public encouragement of the inventor. In his plan for an ideal constitution, the town planner Hippodamus of Miletus included legislation conferring an honorarium (*timê*) on any citizen who made a discovery of benefit to the community at large. But while Hippodamus's other scheme (the provision of public maintenance for children left fatherless by war) seems to have given rise to emulation, this particular recommendation inspired little or no enthusiasm—and Aristotle makes it clear why.

In this discussion, the Stagirite takes for granted a premise, underlying Greek practice, that he makes explicit elsewhere. Politics is, as he puts it, the architectonic art: because the *pólis* is the association most efficacious in promoting "the human good," political science has the right and duty to determine "which sciences and disciplines (*epistêmai*) are needed in the cities, which are to be learned by which sorts of persons, and up to what point." It is with the responsibility of the political scientist in mind that he ponders the suggestion put forward by his Milesian predecessor.

Aristotle readily acknowledges that Hippodamus's proposal will seem attractive at first hearing. But he argues vigorously against its adoption and does so on the grounds that such a law can all too easily promote turmoil, malicious prosecution (*sukophantías*), and even revolution (*kinêseis politeías*). The Stagirite's discussion is extremely compressed. He does not spell out his argument in every detail. But his point seems clear nonetheless: in his view, the spirit of innovation engendered by the practice of conferring public honors on the inventor cannot be restricted to the arts alone; in due course, it will inevitably impinge on the political realm. In particular, this practice, by fostering a taste for novelty, must ultimately undermine that irrational attachment to custom and that blind reverence for inherited institutions which secure for the laws popular obedience and provide them with their only real and lasting support. Thus, like Bernard Mandeville, Aristotle seems to have been persuaded that the "Fickleness / In Diet, Furniture and Dress" occasioned by a process of constant technical innovation is inconsistent with the maintenance of traditional institutions. But, unlike the Dutchman, the Greek philosopher was by no means sanguine that, when "Laws and Clothes" are "equally / Objects of Mutability," men will in fact be better off. He conceded that new discoveries might in rare circumstances justify legal or even constitutional reform. But, in general, he urged caution, contending that lawlessness and disorder might well be the consequence of change. The solidarity of the warrior community had to be protected no matter what it cost.[23]

In less rational form, this distrust of innovation was remarkably widespread. The city of Cnidus was situated on a peninsula stretching into the

Mediterranean from Asia Minor. In the middle of the sixth century, the citizens sought to head off a Persian attack by cutting a canal through the neck of the peninsula to make of their homeland an island. When a good many of the men engaged in the digging were wounded by splinters of stone, the authorities decided to consult the Delphic oracle, and according to Herodotus, Apollo then forbade the project. "If Zeus had wanted to make an island of Cnidus," the Pythia chanted, "he would have done so himself." In antiquity, men were more likely to try to propitiate a river than to change its course. They lived within a universe rendered sacred by the simple fact that it was literally full of gods. Within the pious, warlike, and tradition-bound republics of ancient times, virtually any attempt to tamper with the existing order of things might be judged tantamount to impiety.[24]

In defending Socrates against just such a charge, Xenophon depicts him as a figure who had studied geometry and astronomy in depth and then concluded that "a man rightly educated" would pursue such disciplines only to the extent that they might prove useful for surveying land or computing its yield, for planning a journey, for setting the city watch, for judging what should be done in a given season, or for some such purpose. After attending lectures on these subjects, the Athenian philosopher had "turned away from becoming a deep thinker about the heavens and the manner in which the deity contrives each part, for he thought that these things were not to be known by human beings, and he considered displeasing to the gods a man who seeks to learn what they did not want to reveal." Anyone who "thought earnestly about these things" would "risk becoming deranged" in the manner of the mad Anaxagoras who had so "prided himself on his interpretation of the contrivances of the gods."[25]

The same respect for what is given and the same suspicion of change presupposed by Herodotus's tale and by Xenophon's defense of Socrates is found again in a story told by Plutarch. In the fourth century, the Spartan king Archidamus was among the first of those residing in the Peloponnesus to witness the newfangled catapult launch a projectile. Though impressed by the event, he did not welcome what it portended. Archidamus's only reaction was to swear by his putative ancestor Heracles that "manly virtue (*andròs aretá*) has perished from the earth." As the Macedonian conquest of Hellas would soon reveal, progress in the art of war could only too easily signal the obsolescence of the hoplite militia—and, with it, the demise of the *pólis* and the entire Greek way of life.[26]

Archidamus was no doubt extreme, but he was hardly peculiar in his dread of change. By Greek standards, late fifth-century Athens was, in fact, a far stranger place than the king's own homeland Lacedaemon. Radically democratic, relatively commercial, and dependent for her very survival on the import of foodstuffs from far distant shores, this community looked in matters of defense less to the time-tested phalanx of her farmers than to the technical innovations and tactical flexibility of a fleet of ships rowed by landless natives and by hirelings from abroad.[27] It should not be surprising that the Athenians had a reputation throughout Hellas for taking pleasure in all that was new.[28] That much stands to reason. What is strange is that, at Athens, an engineer (*mēchanopoiós*) known to have contributed through his ingenuity as much to the city's safety as a general would nonetheless be so much held in contempt that a well-born citizen would deem it unthinkable that he should marry his daughter to the man or marry the man's daughter himself.[29] Moreover, it is odd and more than a bit disconcerting to find one of Athens's leaders presenting to her assembly much of what would later reappear as Aristotle's argument against innovation—and this not from a country boor, but from a man of the town, not from a member of the landed gentry, but from a demagogue by trade a tanner, a man thoroughly familiar with at least one of the industrial arts. Even at Athens, public opinion tended to identify ignorance (*amathía*) with moderation (*sōphrosúnē*) and cleverness (*dexiótēs*) with a lack of restraint (*akolasía*). Even there, a man could appeal to popular prejudice by arguing that "a *pólis* employing inferior laws that remain unchanged is stronger and better off (*kreísson*) than a city governed by fine laws lacking authority and force (*nómois . . . akúrois*)."[30]

This argument was made in the early years of the Peloponnesian War. The fourth century brought change but not in this particular regard. In the 350s, the great Demosthenes could still seek the favor of an Athenian jury by appealing to the same attachment to and trust in ancestral custom and long-established laws. In a forensic oration written for an associate, he heaped praise on a Locrian statute which purportedly specified that anyone who proposed a change in the law had to present his arguments while encumbered with a halter around his neck. "If the law seemed noble and useful," Demosthenes went on, "the proposer was allowed to live and to depart; if not, he was hanged by the neck until dead."[31] Novelty remained suspect in the most innovative and open-minded of the ancient martial republics.

This does not mean that technology is a uniquely modern phenomenon. But to the extent that there was in antiquity a deliberate and systematic application of scientific reasoning (*lógos*) to the development of the mechanical and industrial arts (*téchnai*), it took place under the patronage of tyrants and kings, not republics—and even then the promotion of applied science by men like Dionysius of Syracuse and the Ptolemies in Egypt was an extraordinary phenomenon virtually restricted to the stratagems of war.[32] The ancient monarchs had no stake whatsoever in maintaining the fragile military infrastructure that had made republicanism viable, and the most ambitious among them were fully prepared, even eager, to take advantage of every new weapon that their technicians and engineers could devise.

To other forms of technical innovation, even the ancient princes were notoriously resistant. On one occasion, when the emperor Vespasian was in the process of reconstructing the Capitolium, an engineer (*mechanicus*) approached him with a plan (*commentum*) for reducing considerably the costs of moving great marble columns to the building site. Vespasian gave the man a reward but did nothing to implement the plan. He reportedly explained that he wished only to "be allowed to feed the mob (*plebicula*)." The engineer's *commentum* was apparently some sort of labor-saving device, and the emperor rejected it because he had no desire to reduce the number of workmen which the project required.[33] Vespasian's response to the engineer's suggestion was by no means peculiar. The emperor Tiberius is said to have been even more resistant to innovation. When an artisan (*faber*) seeking a reward presented him with a goblet made of some flexible and unbreakable glass-like substance, Tiberius at first stood aghast and then purportedly inquired whether there was anyone else familiar with the process for producing the marvel. Upon learning that the craftsman had kept the formula a secret, the emperor had the man beheaded without further ado. "If this were to become common knowledge," he reportedly remarked, "we would treat gold as dirt (*lutum*)."[34]

Needless to say, the anecdote concerning Tiberius is of doubtful authenticity. Though frequently repeated, it was thought suspect even in antiquity. In truth, however, it matters little whether the event actually happened or not, for the fact that the story was told and retold over and over again throws a great deal of light on the outlook dictating the public policy actually followed. That much is confirmed by the tack taken in the treatise *De rebus bellicis* addressed to the emperors in late Roman times. The author, a vigorous and ingenious proponent of technological reform, took care to preface his remarks with the denial that he sought praise or reward. "It would be more than sufficient," he explained, "if I were to avoid stirring up your indignation at my presumption." It can hardly be fortuitous that the tract's author remains nameless: as his preface suggests, military inventions could themselves be judged controversial—even where monarchy had long prevailed.[35]

There was, of course, one republic that might be cited as an exception to the ancient rule: a city that occupied a particularly favorable location in a region of southern Italy so Hellenic in character that the Romans called it Magna Graecia. In the archaic period, this community was extraordinarily prosperous, and it became sufficiently famous for luxury that the name Sybaris has been a byword for decadence in every age since. There, Aristotle tells us, the wealthy trained their horses to dance at their banquets to a particular air; and if the story be credited, the Pythagorean leaders of Croton, the city's nearest neighbor and her deadly enemy, learned the tune from a renegade flutist and had it played to distract the Sybarite cavalry in the midst of what proved to be a decisive battle sealing the community's fate. There, too, if we are to believe Phylarchus, the world's first patent law was devised, for the chef who concocted a new and previously untasted culinary marvel was not just the recipient of great honors; he was granted a temporary monopoly lasting a full year. This privilege was extended, we are told, "to encourage others to be devoted to toil (*philoponoûntas*) and to make them vie with each other in contriving such things." The moral is too obvious; the various tales, even if there is some truth in them, can hardly be free from embellishment. But this is essentially irrelevant, for these anecdotes reveal in a remarkable way the degree to which the ancients linked technical innovation with self-indulgence, frivolity, and the decay of the martial virtues necessary for the city's survival.[36]

The stories concerning Sybaris may seem bizarre, but the outlook which they evidence was by no means uncommon. In the waning years of the second century A.D., Pertinax, a senator of republican temper, succeeded as emperor at Rome upon the assassination of Commodus, the degenerate son and heir of Marcus Aurelius, a sybarite by inclination if not by birth. According to report, the new emperor found among his predecessor's prized possessions a carriage equipped with a primitive odometer. Shortly thereafter, he had this particular vehicle of Commodus destroyed, treating the instrument for recording the distance traversed just like "the other means for gratifying the vices of the man." Pertinax apparently paid no attention to the manner in which the odometer might benefit those who built, maintained, or simply traveled on the public roads. For him, as for all but a handful of the ancients, inventions were suspect as novelties and playthings; they were nothing more.[37]

The reaction of Pertinax should give us pause. More than six centuries prior to that emperor's brief reign, Herodotus had concluded *The Histories* with a paragraph striking an oddly similar note. The transition to that paragraph is abrupt and jarring. Herodotus ends his narrative of the Persian Wars with a description of the fate meted out to the Persian governor Artayctes—whom the Athenians had nailed to a plank as punishment for pillaging the tomb of the hero Protesilaus. Then, suddenly and without warning, the father of history transports us two generations back in time to the court of

Cyrus the Great. There, he tells us, an ancestor of this same Artayctes had once approached the Great King with the suggestion that the Persians should take advantage of their newly won empire by migrating from their homeland, confined and harsh as it was, to a territory more favorable to human habitation. "It befits men who are rulers to do this sort of thing," the man purportedly argued. "What finer time could there be—for we now rule over many men and all Asia?" Herodotus's Cyrus was not much impressed. The Persians might take up this suggestion, he remarked, but only if they wished to rule no longer and to be ruled by others. "From soft countries," he explained, "come soft men: it does not happen that the same soil produces an admirable harvest and men good in war." If the ancient republics and the monarchies that lived on as their relics viewed technological progress with a jaundiced eye, it was because the ancients sensed that a science pledged "to come to the relief of man's estate" was a science that promised to make of all countries "soft countries" and that thereby threatened to make of all men "soft men." It can hardly be fortuitous that the last word of Herodotus's great work is the infinitive *douleúein*—"to be enslaved." [38]

I . iii . 3

The legal constraints imposed on the marketplace and on those who frequented it, on the one hand, and the absence in the ancient republics of any official encouragement of technical progress, on the other—these were, in truth, merely the tip of the iceberg. Far more important was the public sentiment which they both reflected and shaped.[39] Here, as in so many other matters, Aristotle is the best guide. A metic himself, this peripatetic philosopher was acutely aware of the tensions generated by the warrior community's lack of economic autarky, and he managed to articulate what others only felt.

In *The Politics*, Aristotle distinguishes the art of household management (*oikonomía*) from the art of money-making (*chrēmatistikē*). The former aims at self-sufficiency. Because it responds to concrete human needs, it is in accord with the dictates of nature. What its practitioner cannot use to help his family or to serve the city he does not covet. In the village, he will barter what he has in abundance for those things which he needs for survival, for comfort, and for the performance of his duties as the head of a household and as a citizen. In the city's *agorá*, he may find it convenient to exchange produce for currency and to employ that medium, as needed, to secure what he lacks. He does not by any means despise riches, but he fears disgrace; and for him, wealth is a means, not an end in itself. If secured in sufficient amount, it will leave him relatively free from household responsibilities and enable him to devote his time to the only pursuits endowed with real dignity—war, politics, and the life of the mind.

In contrast, the art of money-making aims at securing riches without limit. In the village, where barter prevails, this art cannot be practiced; but in the city *agorá* or in international commerce, where a man can amass coinage or store up precious metals and stones, the art of money-making often appears in conjunction with retail trade. The practitioner of this art cares little for an object's use; he is concerned almost solely with its value in exchange—and because he treats wealth as an end in itself and not as a means, his behavior is unnatural; it smacks of dishonor; it arouses contempt.[40]

Few Greeks could have delineated the matter in as a clear a fashion as Aristotle, but this moral understanding governed their conduct nonetheless. Though Epicurus was not at all inclined to speak in praise of political ambition and the pursuit of lasting fame, even he was prepared to acknowledge that "the life of freedom (*eleútheros bíos*) is incompatible with the acquisition (*ou dúnatai ktésasthai*) of great wealth." For, like his more politically oriented compatriots, he was persuaded that riches cannot be gathered "without servile behavior (*thēteía*) towards dynasts (*dúnastai*) or mobs."[41] As Homer's testimony shows, the measured distaste which human beings still harbor, in the most commercial of societies, for the executioner and the undertaker, for the purveyor of pornography and the prostitute, and for the professional gambler and the reader of palms was at the outset extended in Greece to all those who were driven by avarice and greed.[42]

As a result, the marketplace served rarely, if ever, as a mechanism for price formation.[43] This is why there was so little speculation in land—or, for that matter, in anything else. The natives with the necessary resources generally lacked entrepreneurial spirit,[44] and the metics and other noncitizens were barred from the ownership of houses and farms and could not even lend money with real property as security.[45] This prohibition effectively drove a wedge between the world of visible and that of invisible wealth, for it severely restricted the sources of credit for the poorer citizens who lacked movable property to put up as security.[46] Of course, as a consequence of the existence of real estate owned by the community, by orphaned children, and by wealthy men who preferred to devote their time to public affairs, there was within the Greek city a considerable market in farms and houses for lease.[47] But there was no comparable market for the sale of real estate, and there were no real estate brokers. For only rarely could a man expect to be presented with the opportunity to buy a neighbor's estate. The ordinary peasant or gentleman farmer would certainly save what he could, and if given the chance, he might well purchase an additional parcel of land. But he did not have it in mind to resell it later at a profit. He might plant fig trees, olive trees, or vines, but not because the introduction of new crops would improve the market value of his estate.[48] By the same token, when he bought additional slaves, he did so because he needed them to work the land, to serve as artisans, or to dig for silver or gold—and not because he hoped to breed them or expected the price to increase. For the most part, he valued his property for use and for barter or for the rents which accrued—and not for the profits it would bring in exchange.

The subordination of economic concerns to the larger needs of the community is particularly evident where lending was involved. In a city utterly dependent on trade, some citizens might join with the metics and with the other foreigners as merchant venturers, risking their capital in bottomry loans contracted for the duration of a voyage on precise terms at very high interest. But these were the exception. Only the wealthy had money to spare;[49] and according to Xenophon, men with an overabundance of silver would ordinarily bury the surplus in the earth. Neither he nor anyone else suggests that they were apt to invest it in enterprises likely to add to their wealth. Indeed, long after war had ceased to be a function of the ancient Greek *pólis*, the younger Pliny reported to Trajan that the notables of Nicomedia in Asia Minor preferred to leave their money idle when there was no opportunity to add to their holdings in land.[50]

Those few, brave souls who did venture their capital in maritime loans could justify their incursions into the market on the grounds of public need. The one city where we have substantial evidence for bottomry loans was a community that subsisted to an extraordinary extent on imported grain. As one citizen had occasion to point out, the greater part of "the resources" that made provisioning the city possible came not from the merchants who actually conducted the trade, "but rather from the lenders—and if the share provided by the lenders was taken away neither ship nor captain (*naúklēros*) nor passenger (*epibátēs*) would be able to set sail."[51]

The bottomry loan was not just an instrument for securing credit; it was also a species of maritime insurance designed to spread the risk of the voyage. If the ship was lost at sea or if the cargo was seized by pirates or jettisoned in a storm, the obligation binding the merchant to the man whose capital he employed was extinguished, and each lost his share.[52] The degree to which this institution reflected the needs of the community at large is evident from the laws governing the practice, for no resident of the city, whether citizen or metic, was allowed to participate in a venture transporting grain to any other place, and all of the grain brought to the port was intended for local consumption.[53] Those who risked their substance to bring grain to the city no doubt hoped to make a profit, but they sought gain in the particular fashion they chose perhaps chiefly because, in the process, they could demonstrate their loyalty and dedication to the community as a whole. Citizens thus engaged were certainly not hesitant to present themselves to the public as benefactors of the city.[54] The typical braggart, as depicted in Theophrastus's *Characters*, boasts not only of the liturgies he has performed for the *pólis*, but also of the profits he has gained *and the losses he has incurred* in the making of maritime loans.[55]

Apart from the exception just canvassed, usury was generally regarded with distaste. "Where there is a debt, there is no friend," one contemporary observer remarked, "for if a man is a friend, he does not lend; he gives."[56] Thus, generally, when a citizen advanced money to a compatriot, he did so out of public-spiritedness, for reasons of friendship, and from a desire to make an impressive display of generosity. Ordinarily, he accomplished this in conjunction with a group of his fellow citizens by making a contribution to a sum collected equally from all. Normally, the contributors charged little or no interest; generally, the borrower paid back the sum in regular installments; and only rarely would there be a contract recording the loan and stipulating the terms. Friendly loans of this sort were so common that they bore a special name (*éranoi*) linking them with the aristocratic tradition of reciprocal gift-giving, with the potluck suppers of humbler folk, and with the religious corporations of later times.[57] Though the institution could be employed to provide for the emancipation of slaves, it was essentially political in character. That much is evident from the metaphor to which it gave rise: at the end of the first year of the Peloponnesian War, when Pericles delivered his famous funeral oration, he reportedly spoke of those who had died that year in Athens's defense as "having advanced the most noble of *éranoi*." Here, too, the ethos of reciprocity was predominant: Athens's citizens had given their lives; everlasting fame would be theirs in return.[58]

The spirit of the *éranos* dictated not just the comportment of the contributors (*eranistaí*), but that of the borrower as well. Ordinarily, when a citizen sought the help of *eranistaí*, it was because he was temporarily in difficult financial straits for political reasons: in need of money to ransom himself or a relative captured by pirates or in war, obligated to pay for public works, or simply eager to make a noteworthy contribution to the common weal. Whatever the source of his problems, he was always intent on spending the sum in a way that would safeguard or improve his standing and that of his household in the community at large. For the city concerned, the evidence is far too limited to be conclusive. But it is suggestive nonetheless. Citizens seem rarely to have borrowed money for the purchase or improvement of real estate, and this occasioned the absence of an institution well known in polities where property of this sort is an object of speculative investment: though loans might be secured by land, the land thereby encumbered served as a substitute, not as collateral, for the sum borrowed.[59]

Of course, a good many of the artisans and retail merchants working in the commercial *agorá* found it necessary from time to time to borrow money to cover the ordinary expenses of conducting business,[60] and there were others (though apparently few in number) who deemed it expedient to do so in order to set up shop.[61] Here, too, political concerns circumscribed behavior. A number of Greek cities may have prohibited the sale of citizen debtors abroad and their subjection to bondage at home, but we know only of one— and there are excellent grounds for supposing that Athens was the exception, not the rule.[62] Long and bitter experience had made the Hellenes acutely aware that a man unable to pay what he owed was liable to become his creditor's dependent.[63] "For a human being born to freedom," so goes the Roman proverb, "indebtedness (*aes alienum*) is a bitter servitude." The Greeks saw the matter in precisely the same light. It can hardly be an accident that where we first learn of land put up as security for a loan, the debtor bears the epithet *stigmatías*, indicating that his debts are a stigma like the tattoo on the forehead of a criminal or a captured runaway slave. By the same token, land unencumbered is called *ástikton chōríon*—land untattooed.[64]

To avoid the stigma of servitude, even an Athenian would endeavor to collect an *éranos* from a group of his compatriots rather than from an individual; and for the same reason, men in need of business loans tended to sidestep their fellow citizens altogether and turned more often than not to the freedmen working as money changers and small-scale bankers in the commercial *agorá*. No one feared becoming the bondsman of a metic: in case of default, the latter could seize neither the debtor's person nor the real estate that gave him the independent standing to perform his duties as a citizen and soldier.[65] Similar concerns account for the willingness of a man who has lost his patrimony to accept from foreigners gifts and favors that he would not take from his fellow citizens at home. "To accept a favor (*beneficium*) is to sell one's freedom": though a maxim culled for schoolboys from the mimes of a Syrian freedman writing in Latin at Rome, the line could just as easily be Greek.[66]

Those who incurred debts for business purposes appear generally to have employed the sum borrowed to maintain or (in a few instances) to organize an enterprise; they seem rarely, if ever, to have used it for the extension or intensification of production. This simple fact was part of a much larger picture: like the Greeks' complete ignorance of amortization and depreciation, and like their failure to devise negotiable instruments and their employment of primitive accounting methods designed chiefly to ease the detection of negligence and fraud, the virtual absence of borrowing for productive purposes speaks volumes about the secondary role played by economic concerns and about the consequent lack of an emphasis on entrepreneurship.[67]

It would be tempting to attribute the absence of so many of the economic practices familiar to the citizen of the modern republic to the inelasticity of demand within the ancient polity.[68] The two phenomena are no doubt related, but it would be a mistake to treat either as if it were independent of the martial community's moral economy. If Aristophanes can be trusted, an ordinary peasant driven from his village and forced for a time to reside in the town could be expected to loathe urban life and to yearn for his country deme precisely because the latter

> Never cried out "Buy Coal!"
> Nor "Buy Vinegar! Buy Oil!"
> It had no notion of buying at all,
> But produced everything itself—
> And so the Buyer was not
> To be found in that place.[69]

Much the same outlook seems to have been prevalent throughout the ancient world. Columella—a Roman writer of the first century A.D.—takes note of a tendency widespread among the landowners of his own age to "run away from annually recurring charges and to count the complete avoidance of expenditure (*impendere nihil*) as the first and most certain source of income (*reditum*)."[70] Pliny's testimony indicates that this had been conscious Roman practice from at least the time of Cato the Elder.[71] The ancients kept in mind what human beings reared in an economically prosperous and technologically dynamic republic often tend to forget: that a man can reduce his neediness (*penía*) by simply restricting his needs.[72] Throughout much, if not all, of antiquity, the dictates of the reigning ethos were as simple as simple can be: the primary goal was not to maximize production, but to minimize consumption. As a consequence, the ancient householder was far more likely to fall prey to the vice of avarice than to be driven by a lust for acquisition. To the degree that circumstances allowed, the ordinary citizen aimed at self-sufficiency (*autárkeia*)—and ultimately at freedom from the need to work at all.

This aversion to toil deserves particular attention, for it points to the principle determining the citizen's priorities. The artisan might take a certain pride in the quality of the object he produced through his skill;[73] but—however much men might admire his workmanship—few envied him his lot, and no one attributed any particular dignity to his labor or to that of anyone else. "Oftentimes," Plutarch remarks, "we take pleasure in the work, but despise the workman (*dēmiourgós*)—as in the case of perfumes and dies. For we enjoy these things, but regard dyers and perfumers as unfree men (*aneleuthérous*) and as rude mechanicals (*banaúsous*). . . . No young man of good natural disposition, contemplating the statue of Zeus at Olympia, would desire to be Pheidias; nor would he want to be Polycleitus after seeing the figure of Hera at Argos; nor would he wish to be Anacreon, Philetas, or Archilochus because he took pleasure in their poems." It is not fortuitous that Greek vases tended to depict artisans—even free potters and the vase painters themselves—in the unflattering poses normally associated with slaves. Where the modern factory produces goods for exchange in distant and largely abstract markets, the ancient workshop generally did so for the immediate use of patrons whom its owner knew only too well, and that fact caused his compatriots to assimilate his efforts, as well as those of his employees, to the labor of men condemned to serve the needs of others. In addition, as Demosthenes had emphasized centuries before Plutarch took up the theme, the only life considered worthy of esteem was the life of virtuous action in the public realm. That is why the great biographer could add Anacreon, Philetas, and Archilochus to the list of *dēmiourgoí* that a young gentleman would not wish to join. Unlike the bards who had fashioned the epics, tragedies, and comedies that form so important a part of our legacy from Greece, these three lyric poets had devoted their attention chiefly to the subject of love and to other private and inconsequential affairs.[74]

In keeping with this outlook, the distinction between rich and poor, as we understand the terms, simply did not exist. The relevant distinctions were, in fact, political in character. The hard-working *pénēs* had a considerably higher status than the idle beggar (*ptōchós*) chiefly because, as a smallholder, he was freed from an abject dependence on the kindness of others, equipped with the substance required for the purchase of the heavy infantryman's hoplite panoply, and able to devote at least some of his time to the performance of his responsibilities as a citizen and soldier. By the same token, it was leisure, settled independence, and the opportunity to take a more active part in the affairs of the community—rather than the simple possession of wealth—that distinguished the *ploúsios* from those lacking the necessary means.[75] It was because the men of property provided leadership on the battlefield and in public council that they were customarily called "the best (*hoi béltistoi*)," "the useful (*hoi chrēstoí*)," "the gracious (*hoi charíentes*)," or simply "the noble and good (*hoi kaloì kagathoí*)." The notables (*gnōrimoi*) of the city might not live up to their responsibilities; as the Greeks were perfectly aware, excessive wealth could easily breed arrogance and pride or even engender softness and cowardice. But the *kaloì kagathoí* had at least one distinctive advantage. Unlike "the base, cowardly men (*hoi ponēroí*)" who were driven by poverty to endless toil (*pónos*), to shameful behavior, and perhaps even to treason, those endowed with large estates possessed all the equipment prerequisite for the practice of civic virtue.[76] Aristotle had these men in mind when he made a point of remarking that, although the management of slaves might be a science, it was not as a pursuit particularly grand (*semnós*) or worthy of respect. That is why, he explained, "those who have the resources to avoid suffering this annoyance confer the honor (*timḗ*) of this office on a steward (*epítropos*) and devote themselves to politics and to the life of the mind (*philosophoûsin*)."[77]

Aristotle describes one way in which the well-to-do freed themselves from the burden of household responsibilities. There were others as well. It was not at all uncommon for a man of considerable means to purchase slaves, lease them out to craftsmen or those working the mines, and live off the proceeds.[78] For one locality, there is epigraphical evidence suggesting the presence in rural areas of a substantial body of metic farmers (*geōrgoí*)—probably freedmen—working as tenants on fields owned by landlords presumably absent in the town.[79] In that same community and apparently elsewhere as well, citizens appear to have been much less eager than foreigners to oversee the work of the slave artisans they owned. A good many preferred, instead, to have these skilled laborers live and work on their own; and to encourage diligence on the part of those "dwelling apart (*chorís oikoûntes*)," the citizen masters allowed their slaves to set aside a portion of their earnings toward the eventual purchase of their own manumission.[80] When the Greeks dreamed of a world without the need for servile labor, what they longed for was less the emancipation of the slave from servitude than the liberation of his master from care.[81]

I. iii. 4

The prevalence in antiquity of so marked a distaste for all aspects of *oikonomía* had profound practical implications—for, like the cities in which they lived, few if any of the private individuals blessed with the necessary resources to act on their own displayed any inclination to devote their wealth and attention to fostering progress in the arts. Theophrastus does mention one entrepreneur—an Athenian named Callias—who devised a way to extract cinnabar from a particular kind of sand, but the man must have been a very rare bird.[82] In general, the well-to-do neglected even to adopt the few really significant advances in technique that were actually made. We know, for example, that the water mill was devised and employed for the grinding of grain sometime before the end of the first century B.C.; and in the Greek anthology, there is a poem from the period celebrating its virtues as a labor-saving device:

> Stay, servant girls, the hand that turns the mill.
> Sleep on—even if the cock's crow foretells the dawn.
> For Demeter has imposed the work of your hands
> On the river nymphs—who leap on the topmost wheel
> And turn the axle with its revolving spokes,
> Moving the heavy concave form
> Of the Nisyrian millstones round.
> Once more, we taste the life of olden days
> If, aloof from toil,
> We learn to feast on Demeter's works.

But despite the poet's clear and certain grasp of the water mill's import, the great landowners who might have profited most from its introduction generally ignored the contrivance. In a treatise dedicated to the emperor Augustus, the architect Vitruvius did make brief mention of the invention, but it was evidently not yet actually in use in Caligula's Rome. In fact, we have very little evidence for the employment of water mills before the third century A.D., and they became widespread only when classical civilization was virtually at an end.[83]

Those who actually practiced the mechanical and industrial arts seem to have been no more likely to pay careful attention to productivity and economy of effort than men of great property. When craftsmen took occasion to celebrate their skills, they always emphasized the quality, never the quantity, of what they produced. Vitruvius's treatise on architecture conforms to this pattern. Only once (and then only in passing) does the author recommend a particular design because it is sparing of labor and resources. Near the end of his lengthy tome, he proudly describes a host of machines—some of which enabled the engineers and architects of his own age to achieve what had never been possible before. Yet, never in the course of this particular discussion does Vitruvius bother to draw attention to the labor-saving features of a single device (the water mill included).[84] His silence and that of the craftsmen in general should not be all that surprising. On the few occasions when more reflective men took note of the arts, they were reticent in exactly the same way. Xenophon managed to discuss the division of labor solely in terms of its contribution to the improvement of quality; and though Plato did mention that specialization makes production "easier (*hrâon*)" and results in things being "more plentiful (*pleíō*)," he did so only as an afterthought.[85] In antiquity, to the extent that technical advances were made at all, necessity— military necessity above all else—does really seem to have been the mother of invention.[86] Certainly, no one ever paid much attention to dreaming up more efficient ways to accomplish everyday tasks. Otherwise, it would be impossible to explain why neither the farmers who employed the lever and the wheel nor the engineers who understood the mechanical principles underlying their use ever managed to join the two together and fashion a machine as simple and as useful as the wheelbarrow.

Men began paying greater attention to mundane matters of this sort only later—and not, as admirers of Max Weber may be wont to suppose, with the birth of Protestantism, but centuries before, in the so-called Dark Ages, when the spread of Christianity desacralized the universe and the advent of monasticism introduced a new ethic of toil. As was only natural, the warrior aristocracy of that epoch shared the contempt for work so evident in the martial republics of earlier times. But the monks were steeped in a biblical tradition that represented man as being formed in the image and likeness of a divine artificer who had labored for six days to create the heavens, the earth, and everything on it. Within this tradition, God's only begotten son appears as a lowly carpenter and his disciples as ordinary workmen. The monks were accordingly taught to regard labor as a form of prayer, and they were quick to adopt and perhaps, on occasion, even to devise contrivances that would enable them to increase their productivity. Furthermore, they did so not out of necessity in response to an evident shortage of hands, but simply by choice. Because work was demanded of men by God as penance for sin, it deserved a certain attention and had a dignity and importance all its own. As a consequence of this profound alteration in outlook, the arts were anything but stagnant—at least by the standards of classical times.[87]

Of course, those standards were extremely low. Neither the Dark Ages in particular nor the medieval period as a whole can bear comparison with the epoch of the scientific and industrial revolutions to which Sir Francis Bacon's great project eventually gave rise, and it is easy to see why. The Bible taught that men and women were made in the image and likeness of a divine creator who commanded them to increase, multiply, replenish, and subdue the earth. It taught that God had imposed on His sinful and disobedient creatures the curse: "In the sweat of thy face shalt thou eat bread." But it did little to glorify labor as such and nothing to recommend and sanction man's acquisitive instincts and productive impulse. In fact, Christ suggested that it would be easier to slip a camel through the eye of a needle than to smuggle a rich man into heaven. "What is a man profited," he asked, "if he gain the whole world, and lose his own soul?" He blessed not the inventors, but the poor in spirit, the meek, the peacemakers, and those persecuted for righteousness, and he promised them a reward in heaven. He warned his followers against "covetousness," and he denounced as "a fool" the rich man, eager to increase his holdings, who pulls down his barns to build greater and allows his soul to take its "ease, eat, drink *and* be merry." "Take no thought for your life, what ye shall eat; neither for the body, what ye shall put on," he said. Though the ravens "neither sow nor reap," they are fed. The lilies "toil not, they spin not; and yet I say unto you, that Solomon in all his glory was not arrayed like one of these." In the judgment of God's son, it made more sense for men to "sell" what they had, to "give alms," and lay up for themselves "a treasure in the heavens that faileth not, where no thief approacheth, neither moth corrupteth." In this spirit, St. Paul denounced "the love of money" as "the root of all evil." The wealthy he urged neither to be "highminded" nor to "trust in uncertain riches." They were to "flee these things: and follow after righteousness, godliness, faith, love, patience, meekeness."[88]

More than anyone else, the monks took the Christian message to heart. They were therefore concerned first and foremost with achieving salvation in the next world, not progress and material prosperity in this one. For their part, the great men of property were no more anxious to foster the development of the arts than their predecessors in Greece and in Rome, and the craftsmen in the towns were concerned with regulating markets and were deeply hostile to innovations aimed at promoting productivity. Most important of all, neither in antiquity nor in the Middle Ages did the learned seek "to come to the relief of man's estate." The contempt for *chrēmatistikē*, the distaste for *oikonomía*, and the resulting disinterest in the practical utility of scientific knowledge were by no means restricted to those deeply engaged in war and political affairs. In antiquity, the critical tenets were part of the city's ethos. In the Christian epoch, they were preached from the pulpit. And throughout both ages, they were accepted by all or nearly all.[89] As Bacon himself emphasized again and again in his spirited attacks on Plato, Aristotle, and their subsequent disciples, it was of the greatest significance for explaining the failure of the ancients and their immediate successors to make a systematic application of *lógos* to the *téchnai* that the same contempt, the same distaste, and the same disinterest were especially evident among those who devoted their time to the life of the mind.[90]

In *Democracy in America*, Tocqueville provides an explanation for this phenomenon which should for the moment suffice. There, he observes that "the majority of the human beings" who live in the modern democratic republics "dream solely of the means for altering their fortunes and making them grow. For minds thus predisposed, every new method which shortens the road to wealth, every machine which cuts down on labor, every instrument which reduces the cost of production, and every discovery which eases and adds to life's pleasures seems the most magnificent effort of the human intelligence." Those resident in the martial republics of antiquity—regimes rendered aristocratic by the ownership of slaves—looked on the sciences in an entirely different way. They turned to such studies, seeking only "gratification for the mind (*l'esprit*)." Within societies of this sort, "the class which directs opinion and manages public affairs" finds itself placed permanently by birth in a status well "above the mob." This class is prey to lofty notions, and its members "display a certain proud disdain for the little pleasures at the very moment when they surrender to them." This set of prejudices, as Tocqueville is at pains to explain, "raises all to a very high level. In aristocratic times, men generally entertain grand ideas of the dignity, power, and greatness of man. These opinions influence those who cultivate the sciences as they do others. They ease the natural impulse of the mind to the higher regions of thought and naturally dispose it to conceive a sublime and almost divine love of the truth." That ardor ultimately becomes an obstacle to progress in the arts; for "the savants of such an age are drawn towards theory, and it often happens that they conceive an unreflective (*inconsideré*) contempt for the practical (*la pratique*)." [91]

So it was within the ancient city. The philosophers of antiquity would certainly have disputed Tocqueville's contention that this contempt was unreflective, but no one among them would have challenged its existence or denied its kinship with aristocratic hauteur. If anything, they may have exaggerated its import. Aristotle claims that Thales cornered the olive-press market solely to demonstrate two related propositions: first, "that it would be very easy for philosophers to enrich themselves if they so wished"; and second, "that money-making is not an activity which men of this kind think worthy of serious concern." Though the skeptic might be tempted to question Aristotle's imputation of motive, he would certainly agree that this was the attitude of the Stagirite himself—and Aristotle was not peculiar in holding this view. [92]

Under the influence of Plato, Archimedes carried the same outlook to extremes. This man was, by all accounts, the greatest mathematician of ancient times; and during the Second Punic War, when his native Syracuse came under Roman siege, he performed wonders, designing machines that frustrated the enemy's every attack. Despite all of this, his accomplishments as an engineer evidently gave Archimedes very little satisfaction. Plutarch reports that he even refused to compose a treatise on the subject. "Archimedes regarded pursuits of a mechanical character and every *téchnē* intimately bound up with human need (*chreía*) as ignoble and vulgar," the biographer explains. "His love of honor (*philotimía*) was focused solely on those studies endowed with a nobility (*tò kalón*) and magnificence (*perittón*) to which the demands of necessity had made no contribution." For this reason, the Syracusan dedicated his writings to pure mathematics alone: "Here, the subject rivals the proof—the former displays grandeur and nobility (*tò kállos*); and the latter, a precision and power exceeding nature itself."

Archimedes' death was, so Livy reveals, in accord with his belief. On the day that Syracuse fell to the Romans, the great mathematician was so "intent on some geometrical forms that he had scratched out in the dust" that he was oblivious that the city was being put to the sack. As a consequence, he did nothing to protect himself, and a Roman soldier caught him unawares. One version of the story stipulated that the soldier tried to arrest Archimedes and conduct him to his commander, but the great mathematician was so wrapped up in the geometrical problem at hand that he refused to budge until he had finished his proof; in anger, the soldier drew his sword and killed him on the spot. On Archimedes' instructions, his friends and relations placed a distinctive monument over his grave. On the top, there was a sphere enclosed by a cylinder. Below it was inscribed a formula specifying by how much the volume of the solid exceeded that of the sphere it contained. Archimedes was not a self-effacing man; but despite all the marvelous feats he had managed in that remarkable struggle with Rome, this scientist and mathematician did nothing to insure that he be remembered for his wondrous machines.[93]

There were others, of course, who had little sympathy for Plato's crusade to keep mathematics pure. But though Ctesibius, Hero, and the other scientists associated with the Museum at Alexandria were far less contemptuous than Archimedes regarding the status of the science of mechanics, they never applied their expertise to any practical matter other than war. They did devise primitive engines worked by steam, and they used these to open doors and to awe the multitude with magical effects; but neither they nor anyone else ever did anything to apply these discoveries to easing the burdens imposed on their fellow men by the need for endless toil. At the end of antiquity, when the author of the *De rebus bellicis* paused to reflect on the stagnation of technique that characterized the age, he found it easy to pinpoint the cause. "It is agreed by all," he observed, "that neither noble birth nor abundant wealth and neither power founded on high office nor eloquence acquired by the study of letters has aimed at and achieved (*consecuta est*) anything of use in the mechanical and industrial arts (*utilitates artium*). . . . For, though the barbarian nations neither excel in eloquence nor gain glory from rank, they are by no means strangers to mechanical invention when nature comes to their aid."[94] As Sir Francis Bacon and his disciples (Benjamin Franklin, John Adams, Thomas Jefferson, Alexander Hamilton, and James Madison among them) were to recognize, to change the situation identified by this anonymous observer would require a profound revolution in human affairs. Until that happened, progress in the arts would be haphazard at best.

I.iii.5

In antiquity, those with the ability and resources to contribute to a project like that sketched out by Bacon tended to regard *oikonomía* as annoyance and the *téchnai* with disdain. Aristotle was essentially correct: those able to do so preferred to devote their time to politics and the life of the mind. But there were, needless to say, a good many exceptions to the rule. The Athenian Callias can hardly have been an isolated case. What was true for Tocqueville's aristocrats seems to have been true for the Romans, and it was no doubt true for the Greeks as well:[95] even those who labored solely for honor cannot have been entirely insensible to the longing for gain, and there were shameless men who took less care to conceal their regard for what related merely to preservation, to comfort, and well-being. Greed and vulgarity find a home in every community; and where the standards demand great restraint, not a few will fall short. In surveying the world in which he lived, Xenophon's Socrates claims to have noticed that "many private individuals (*idiôtai*) who possess a great deal of money nonetheless consider themselves so poor that they subject themselves to every sort of toil (*pónos*) and risk (*kíndunos*) in the expectation of getting more," and no doubt he did encounter such men among the metics, the foreign traders, and even the citizens of the town.[96] The last-mentioned may have shied away from the less respectable professions; but where there were productive mines, there was certainly no shortage of citizens eager to bid for the leases.[97]

Xenophon's Socrates was by no means alone in drawing attention to the acquisitive instincts of those about him. The protagonist of Aristophanes' *Plutus* makes much the same claim and puts it in particularly bald terms. In trying to persuade the proverbially blind Ploutos—the god Wealth—that he is a divinity "much more powerful than Zeus," Chremylus argues that the love of lucre is, in fact, the true motive for all human activity. One can have an excess of virtually all the noble and good things in life, he observes, but one can never have a surfeit of wealth. "Of you," Chremylus tells Ploutos,

> No one ever has enough.
> For if a man possesses thirteen talents,
> He desires to have sixteen all the more.
> And once he has that,
> He'll want forty
> And say that for him
> Life is not worth living
> Without such a sum.

One might be tempted to accuse Aristotle of gross exaggeration were it not for a later scene in the same play.

At the central moment in Aristophanes' drama, Penía—the goddess Poverty—appears to Chremylus and confronts him with a statement and a series of rhetorical questions that leave him dumbfounded. "If sight were restored to Wealth," she contends,

> And he were to distribute himself equally among all,
> No human being would ever practice a trade (*téchnē*)
> Or make use of a skill (*sophía*);
> And once *téchnē* and *sophía* had disappeared
> From among you,
> Who would wish
> To be a bronzesmith, a shipwright, or wheelwright;
> To stitch clothing, fashion shoes, or make bricks;
> To run a laundry or engage in the tanning of leather?
> Who would want
>   "Breaking up the earth with his plough
>   To harvest Demeter's fruit"
> If it were possible for you
> To live without effort
> And pay no care to all these pursuits?

Though comic poetry tends to represent men and women as being less noble than they in fact are, Aristophanes leaves little doubt that at heart even those whom he terms "lovers of toil (*erastaì toû poneîn*)" were household-managers—and not money-makers.[98]

As citizens, the humble folk that tilled the soil treasured what little independence they had; and like almost everyone fated to live in an age that judged each by his contribution to the community in politics and war, these men longed for the education and—above all else—the leisurely life of the *kaloì kaguthoí*. If Aristophanes' peasants yearned for wealth, it was not in an infinite amount and for its own sake. Men of this sort would have had little trouble understanding the distinction which Rousseau had in mind when he first wrote that "money which one possesses is the instrument of liberty" and then carefully qualified his statement by adding that "money which one pursues is the source of servitude."[99]

Karl Marx was evidently on the right track when he drew attention to the absence in antiquity of any theoretical "investigation as to which form of landed property . . . is the most productive [and] creates the most wealth." Of course, Cato did consider "which mode of cultivating the fields is the most profitable"; Brutus did "lend his money at the most favorable rates of interest";[100] and these Romans had their counterparts in Greece.[101] Very few among the Hellenes had the means necessary to live as rentiers,[102] and no man of affairs—eager to provide himself, his children, and his children's children with the equipment necessary for survival and for the performance of their civic responsibilities—could afford to ignore altogether the condition of his estate. With an eye to this fact, a contemporary admirer of the one Greek *pólis* able from public resources to support all of its citizens at leisure might express disdain for those living elsewhere. Such a man might charge that "in the other cities all men are money-makers (*chrēmatízontai*) and make as much as they can." Though exaggerated, the claim would no doubt have seemed plausible to many at the time, for such an observer would have been correct in contending that, in the ordinary *pólis*, "one man farms, another captains ships, and a third travels as a merchant—while some even subsist from the crafts." For all but those blessed with an overabundance of rich land and a numerous population of dependent laborers to work it, household management was a necessary art. This is important; it should not be neglected, but here it is beside the point: for the key to understanding the ancient political economy is not the heavy burden of necessity, but the simple fact that money-making was so rarely in itself the paramount concern.[103]

"The mighty advantages of property and fortune, when stript of the recommendations they derive from vanity, or the more serious regards to independence and power, only mean a provision that is made for animal enjoyment." Though composed by Adam Ferguson more than two thousand years after the decline of the *pólis*, the words could easily have been written by a Greek.[104] The Hellenes had little use for all the advantages we associate with life in bourgeois society, and they would have been appalled at the sacrifices we have made for mere "animal enjoyment." If they acknowledged "the mighty advantages of property and fortune," it was almost entirely for the sake of "independence and power." This fact can hardly have been lost on the most brilliant and courageous of the staff officers to serve under George Washington in the Revolutionary War. Alexander Hamilton had tasted glory at the battle of Yorktown, and he understood only too well the call of ambition. Though he helped establish a commercial (in preference to a martial) regime, the overall point can be made in terms with which he was perfectly familiar. The Greeks were devoted to the quest for honor, not "to the improvements of agriculture and commerce." They were absorbed in public affairs, not "in the pursuits of gain." They were, after all, "a nation of soldiers." [105]

CHAPTER 4

Paideía—The Preparation for Battle

In simple or barbarous ages, when nations are weak, and beset with enemies, the love of a coun-
try, of a party, or a faction are the same. The public is a knot of friends, and its enemies are the
rest of mankind. Death, or slavery, are the ordinary evils which they are concerned to ward off;
victory and dominion, the objects to which they aspire. Under the sense of what they may suffer
from foreign invasions, it is one object, in every prosperous society, to increase its force and to
extend its limits. In proportion as this object is gained, security increases. They who possess
the interior districts, remote from the frontier, are unused to alarms from abroad. They who are
placed on the extremities, remote from the seats of government, are unused to hear of political
interests; and the public becomes an object perhaps too extensive, for the conceptions of either.
They enjoy the protection of its laws, or of its armies; and they boast of its splendor, and its
power; but the glowing sentiments of public affection, which, in small states, mingle with the
tenderness of the parent and the lover, of the friend and the companion, merely by having their
object enlarged, lose great part of their force.—Adam Ferguson

I.iv.1

Within the ranks of the students of antiquity, Friedrich Nietzsche holds a special place. In his brief career, he exhibited a grasp of the nature of Hellenic civilization that has only rarely been rivaled in the years that have passed since his untimely death. On one occasion, the German philosopher spoke of the ancient Greek *pólis* as "an aristocratic commonwealth" and suggested that it be considered "an arrangement . . . for the purpose of *breeding (Züchtung)."* In such a community, he wrote,

> one finds—joined together and left to their own devices—men who want their race (*Art*) to prevail, generally because they *must* prevail or run a fearful risk of being rooted out altogether. . . . The race holds itself, as a race, indispensable; it considers itself as something that can actually prevail and make itself lasting by dint of its hardness, its uniformity, its simplicity of form, in constant struggle with its neighbors or with the oppressed who rebel or threaten rebellion. Its many-sided experience teaches the race to which qualities it is especially indebted for the fact that—in spite of all the gods and men—it is still there and has always won out: these qualities it calls "the virtues," and these virtues alone it cultivates on a large scale. It does this with hardness, indeed it wants hardness: every aristocratic morality is intolerant in the education

of the youth, in its disposition of the women, in the marriage customs, in the relations of old and young, in the penal laws (which consider deviants only)—under the name "justice," it reckons among the virtues intolerance itself.[1]

One may query Nietzsche's use of biological metaphor, and one should point out that his treatment of classical virtue as an instrument forged solely to provide for the community's survival is one-sided, incomplete, and therefore ultimately inadequate; but one need not doubt that virtue was essential for the preservation of the *pólis*, and one must acknowledge that it was universally esteemed by the citizens and cultivated as such. The fostering of *homónoia* required much more than the mere containment and channeling of what Adam Smith termed "the propensity to truck, barter, and exchange one thing for another."[2] Indeed, when James Madison considered the forces which the ancients thought capable of giving to men the same opinions, the same passions, and the same interests, he made almost no allusion to such a containment and channeling at all. Instead, he emphasized what he chose, in one passage, to call "moral" and "religious motives" and what he elsewhere dubbed "the superstition of the times" and identified as "one of the principal engines by which government was then maintained."[3] Here, in a feature of ancient Greek life studiously ignored by contemporary admirers of participatory politics,[4] lies the key to identifying the means by which the ancients sought to limit and direct the commercial instincts which Smith so emphasized; and it is to this subject that we must now turn.

I.iv.2

In antiquity, the model for political relations was not the contract; it was kinship. The ancient city was, like the household, a ritual community of human beings sharing in the flesh of animals sacrificed, then cooked at a common hearth.[5] The citizens were bound together by the myth of common ancestry and linked by a veneration for the gods and the heroes of the land.[6] The *pólis* was not and could not be the household writ large; but, as Plato makes clear in *The Republic*, this is what it tried to be.[7] The city was not a circle of friends; but, as both Plato and Aristotle imply, this is what it strove to become.[8] The citizens were tied to each other not by a web of compromise; they were, as Augustine puts it, "united by concord regarding loved things held in common."[9] Theirs was a permanent, moral bond: they were brought into association (*sociatus*), as Cicero remarks, not only by a community of interest (*utilitatis communione*), but also by fundamental agreement regarding the character of justice (*iuris consensu*).[10]

This fundamental like-mindedness was itself sustained by that steadfast adherence to tradition (*mos maiorum*) and that pious veneration for the ancestral (*là pátria*) which the common civic rituals and legends were intended to foster.[11] "The *pólis* teaches the man." So wrote Simonides, the well-traveled poet from Iulis on Ceos. And when the Cyclops of Euripides' satyr play wants to know the identity of Odysseus and his companions, he asks whence they have sailed, where they were born, and what *pólis* was responsible for their *paideía*.[12] As long as the citizens were relatively isolated from outside influence, it mattered little, if at all, that the religious beliefs and rites of a particular city were irrational and incoherent: what mattered most was that the beliefs and rites peculiar to that city inspired in the citizens the unshakable conviction that they belonged to each other.[13] And where it was difficult, if not impossible, to engender so profound a sense of fellow-feeling, as in colonies which drew their citizens from more than one metropolis, *stásis* was all too often the consequence.[14] Put simply: in antiquity, the political community was animated by a passion for the particular. The patriotism which gave it life was not a patriotism of universal principles like those enshrined in the Declaration of Independence; it was a religion of blood and of soil. If the commonwealth was to flourish, the citizens had to sense in their dealings with each other that they were engaged in a common endeavor peculiar to their community, sanctioned by time, and somehow of greater dignity than they were. Plato's Protagoras alluded to this with a parable: though fearful of attack and skilled in the mechanical arts, men were in the earliest times constitutionally incapable of living peacefully in towns. "Zeus, fearing that our race would be destroyed altogether," the sophist explained, "sent Hermes to human beings with reverence (*aidôs*) and with justice (*díkē*) in order that these might be regulators (*kósmoi*) of cities and bonds uniting in friendship."[15] There was more to communal solidarity than the need for military cooperation and the desire for those advantages derivative from the division of labor.

Of course, the *pólis* no doubt came into being in the first place because of the need for common defense. The word itself appears to be derived from an Indo-European term employed to designate the high place or citadel to which the residents of a district ordinarily retreated when subject to attack.[16] But that high place was more than just a refuge; even in the narrow, pristine sense of the word, the *pólis* was also an enclosure sacred to the gods who lived within the city's walls.[17] Thus, when a city pondered the establishment of a colony, it was customary for the founder (*oikistês*) to consult the oracle of Apollo at Delphi regarding the site.[18] The failure to seek or a decision to ignore the advice of the god was thought likely to be fatal to the entire enterprise.[19] In fact, the act of establishing a new community was itself an elaborate religious rite specified in detail by the laws;[20] and in keeping with the divine origin and character of the new *pólis*, the citizen designated as *oikistês* could expect to be buried with all solemnity in the *agorá*, to be worshipped as a demigod and divine protector of the *pólis* from the moment of his decease, and to be honored thereafter in an annual festival complete with public sacrifices and athletic games.[21]

The political community's sense of common endeavor was grounded in its particular *pátrioi nómoi*—its ancestral customs, rites, and laws. These practices and institutions marked one city off from other, similar communities and defined it even more effectively than the boundaries of the civic territory (*chóra*) itself. Though forced to abandon its *chóra*, a *pólis* could nonetheless retain its identity.[22] Heraclitus took this for granted when he wrote that "the people must fight for the *nómos* as if for the walls of the *pólis*."[23] When a Greek city went to war, the citizens battled not just to expand their dominion and to protect their wives, their children, and land; they fought also to defend their *pátrioi nómoi* and the entire way of life which these embodied. To Bias of Priene, one of the Seven Sages of Greece, Plutarch attributes the conviction that "popular government (*dēmokratía*) is strongest where all fear the *nómos* as a tyrant."[24] The anecdote is no doubt apocryphal: Bias was in his prime in the mid-sixth century at the time of Persia's conquest of Lydia, while the term *dēmokratía* seems to have been coined not much earlier than the 460s, if that.[25] But the fact that the story seemed plausible to Plutarch and well worth retelling is itself revealing. Within the confines of ancient Hellas, Pindar's oft-quoted dictum undoubtedly applied: *nómos* was always and everywhere "King of all."[26]

This spirit carried over as well into the conduct of foreign affairs.[27] Even where military cooperation was the only end sought, the Greeks tended to invest with moral and even religious foundations any confederacy they joined. This is why cities that formed such a connection often adopted each other's gods, founded a common festival, or sent delegations to take a share in each other's principal rites.[28] In 428, when the Mytilenians were intent on securing aid from Sparta and her Peloponnesian allies, they couched their request in terms which, they knew, would find favor. "We recognize," they remarked, "that no friendship between private individuals will ever be firm and no community (*koinōnía*) among cities will ever come to anything unless the parties involved are persuaded of each other's virtue and are otherwise similar in their ways (*homoiótropoi*): for disparate deeds arise from discrepancies in judgment."[29]

Fifty years before, in a time of like trouble, their Athenian opponents resorted to similar rhetoric. On the eve of the battle of Plataea, the Spartans expressed fear that the citizens of Athens would come to terms with the Persians. The Athenians, in response, mentioned two reasons why they could not conceive of abandoning the struggle against the Mede. First, they explained, it is our duty to avenge the burning of our temples and the destruction of the images of our gods. "Then," they added, "there is that which makes us Hellenes (*tò Hellēnikón*)—the blood and the tongue that we share, the shrines of the gods and the sacrifices we hold in common, and the likeness in manners and in ways (*ētheá te homótropa*). It would not be proper for the Athenians to be traitors to these."[30] In neither case was the presence of a shared enemy deemed adequate. Though separated by half a century, the two speeches were in accord: the only secure foundation for alliance was a common way of life.

The conviction so firmly stated by the Mytilenians and the Athenians contributed in a variety of ways to the actual making of policy. Cities with a common origin and extremely similar *nómoi* rarely went to war.[31] The ordinary Greek colony, for example, generally had customs, rites, and laws closely akin to those of the mother city.[32] Even where the two were fully autonomous, they usually maintained close ties, and the colony was expected to defer in most matters to the metropolis and to send a delegation with gifts of symbolic import to join in celebrating the principal festival of that community.[33] The failure of a colony to perform what were seen as its moral obligations was deemed shocking in the extreme, and it could give rise to a bitterness that might easily overshadow the cold calculation of interests. As Thucydides makes abundantly clear, one cannot make sense of the origins of the Peloponnesian War without paying close attention to the deep-seated anger that shaped the Corinthians' policy toward their renegade colonists the Corcyraeans.[34]

The forceful response which the Spartan expression of distrust elicited from the Athenians in 479 B.C. deserves a second glance. The great struggle against Persia did in fact bring home to the Hellenes all that they held in common—the blood and the tongue that they shared, the shrines of the gods and the public sacrifices, and their similarity in manners and ways. It was natural in the aftermath of that war, particularly when the Great King of Persia started once again to meddle in Hellenic affairs, for some Greeks to begin to argue that wars within Hellas were not properly wars at all, but examples of *stásis* and, as such, reprehensible. But though such arguments were made, they had remarkably little effect.[35]

If the Greeks were nonetheless inclined to make war on each other, it was at least in part because the disparate communities were never sufficiently similar in manners and in morals. What brought the citizens of a particular *pólis* together set them apart from others; what united them as a people set them in opposition to outsiders. They held their land at the expense of slaves and foreigners, and they pursued the way of life peculiar to them in defiance of notions elsewhere accepted.[36] When, in Plato's *Republic*, Polemarchus ("war-leader") defines justice as "doing good to friends and harm to enemies," he is merely reasserting on the personal level the grim civic ethic suggested by his name.[37] In ancient Greece, patriotism went hand in hand with xenophobia. If "civil war (*stásis*) is not to thunder in the city," Aeschylus's divine chorus warns the Athenians, the citizens "must return joy for joy in a spirit of common love—and they must hate with a single heart."[38]

The implications of all of this were not lost on the American Founding Fathers. Perhaps because of his own experience as a soldier, Alexander Hamilton recognized the warlike demeanor of the ancient agricultural republics more clearly than many who have come after, and this recognition played no small role in determining his adherence to Madison's bold project. When confronted by the arguments of those who believed that no viable republic could be constructed on an extended territory, he replied that the American states were themselves already too large. Those who took such arguments seriously would have to choose between embracing monarchy and dividing the states "into an infinity of little, jealous, clashing, tumultuous commonwealths, the wretched nurseries of unceasing discord, and the miserable objects of universal pity or contempt."[39]

On more than one occasion, the Greeks were forced to choose between the alternatives posed by Hamilton; and in all but the most difficult of circumstances, most, if not all, preferred the jealousy, the tumult, the unceasing discord, and the excitement of life in the fully autonomous *pólis* to the relative tranquillity promised in exchange for their absorption into a great empire. In considering the character of the *pólis*, we must never lose sight of the permanence of conflict that afflicted Greek life. The ordinary Hellene would have nodded his approval of the opinion attributed by Plato to the lawgiver of Crete: "What most men call peace, he held to be only a name; in truth, for everyone, there exists by nature at all times an undeclared war among all the cities."[40] Such was the human condition in Greece, where political freedom took precedence over commodious living.

James Madison was certainly right when he observed that the ancient republics attempted through moral and religious motives to expunge the human propensity to form factions. These communities had no choice: one might be able to promote domestic tranquillity and secure obedience to the law by balancing interests and negotiating trade-offs, but one cannot easily persuade men to risk their lives for each other by a naked appeal to economic interest. Madison may even have been correct when he argued that these same moral and religious motives are inadequate as a control. Plato, for one, believed that the institutions of the various *póleis* had failed in this particular regard.[41] If true, this is important—but it cannot be decisive. In the final analysis, it matters little whether morality and religion are sufficient to move men or not: these are the only means available when life and death hang in the balance. For profit, men may kill. It is for love and glory that they will sometimes die.[42]

I.iv.3

In advising would-be orators on the manner in which they should argue for the adoption of particular pieces of legislation, Anaximenes of Lampsacus once noted that "it behooves one to show that the law is equitable, that it accords with the other laws, and that it is particularly beneficial to the city with regard to *homónoia*." Where it is not possible to make a plausible case based on this last point, Anaximenes went on, one should argue that the law benefits the *pólis* in other ways. It might, for example, promote the excellence (*kalokagathían*) of the citizens or increase the public revenues. It might foster the city's good repute as a self-governing community or augment its actual political power. It must, in any case, be supposed to do something of the sort.[43]

As one would expect, Greek lawmaking aimed at achieving a variety of goals. But among these one purpose was preeminent: when a *pólis* pondered the shaping of its institutions, the solidarity of the community generally took precedence over all other concerns. The prospect of war dictated this hierarchy of priorities. If the city was to survive, the citizens would have to be taught to think as one. Xenophon described the situation elegantly by posing a rhetorical question. "How could human beings be more easily defeated in battle," he wrote, "than when each begins to take counsel in private concerning his own safety?"[44] This was the type of deliberation which the *pólis* had to attempt to suppress.

Because the ancient city was a brotherhood of warriors and not an association of merchants, the principal task of legislation was the promotion of public-spiritedness and not the regulation of competing interests. It is revealing that, in Plato's *Republic*, a discussion of the best regime rapidly turns into a dialogue on character formation.[45] "It is necessary," Aristotle took occasion to remark, "that the *pólis*, which is multitudinous (*plêthos*), be made through education (*paideía*) communal (*koinê*) and one."[46] Unfortunately, even under the best of circumstances, the nurturing of civic virtue was a difficult under-taking—one that called for the deliberate shaping of the citizen's passions and opinions. Even when everything needed to insure that the citizens have the same interests has been done, there remains a tension between private inclination and public duty, between individual self-interest and the common good that it is impossible fully to resolve. Death and pain are the greatest obstacles: they bring a man back upon himself, reminding him all too power-fully that, when he suffers, he suffers alone. As a consequence, the quality which Plato and Aristotle called civic or political courage is rare: it is not by natural instinct that a man is willing to lay down his life for his fellow citizens. He must be made to forget the ineradicable loneliness of death. The fostering of courage, self-sacrifice, and devotion to the common good requires artifice, and this is why Plato's discussion of character formation rapidly turns into a dialogue on poetry and its chief subject: man's relations with the gods.[47]

James Madison was little interested in such artifice. He could take pleasure in "the multiplicity of sects" constituting the American republic precisely be-cause he was far more concerned with increasing the number of factions than with establishing *homónoia* and promoting civil courage. His ancient counter-part could not afford to be so latitudinarian. It is true that ancient polytheism lacked the priestly establishment, the proselytizing fervor, and the passion for doctrinal purity that have, at various times, characterized monotheism (particularly in its Christian form); and for this reason, Hellas was relatively receptive to foreign cults and generally free from the waves of persecution, the sectarian strife, and the religious wars that so disrupted early modern Europe and that still disturb India, Sri Lanka, northern Ireland, Cyprus, and much of the Middle East. Religion was not the political obstacle for the an-cient lawgiver that it would be for his modern successor, but this does not mean that the study of Greek religion is of trivial importance for understand-ing Greek politics: even the most skeptical of the Greeks acknowledged the religious roots of that "reverence (*aidōs*) and justice (*díkē*)" which served as the "regulators (*kósmoi*) of cities" and the "bonds uniting" the citizens "in friendship."

The Athenian Critias is a case in point. He was a student of Socrates, an essayist, and a playwright of note—all this long before he achieved infamy as a member of the oligarchy called The Thirty. In Critias's satyr play *The Sisy-phus*, the protagonist has occasion to discuss the origins of that cooperative capacity which makes political life possible. "There was a time," he notes, "when the life of human beings was without order (*átaktos*) and like that of a hunted animal (*thēriōdēs*): the servant of force. At that time, there was neither prize for the noble nor punishment for the wicked. And then human beings, so it seems to me, established laws in order that justice (*díkē*) might be a tyrant (*túrannos*) and hold arrogance (*húbris*) as a slave, exacting punishment if anyone stepped out of line." This stratagem worked well in most regards, but it was of limited effectiveness in one decisive respect—for "though the laws prevented human beings from committing acts of violence in the full light of day, men did so in secret."

It required "a real man (*anḗr*), sharp and clever in judgment," to overcome this deficiency; and when he finally appeared, he "invented for mortals (*thnētoí*) dread (*déos*) of the gods, so that there would be something to terrify (*ti deîma*) the wicked even when they acted, spoke, or thought entirely in secret." To this end, the man

> brought in the divine (*theîon*), saying that there is a divinity (*daímōn*) thriving with immortal life, hearing and seeing all with its mind, thinking and reflecting much on these things, and possessing the nature of a god—who hears all that is said among mortals and is able to see all that is done. Even if you plot evil in silence, this will not escape the gods— for much intelligence is in them. In speaking these words, the man introduced the most pleasant of teachings, concealing the truth with false argument. And he claimed that the gods dwelt there where, by suggesting the place, he could most strike panic into human beings. Whence, he knew, there would be terrors (*phóbous*) for mortals and compensation for the hard life: all this from the heavens, where he knew there was lightning, the dread crashing of thunder, and the starry frame of heaven (the beautiful embroidery of the clever workman Time) whence comes forth the shining (*lamprós*), starry hot mass and the damp thunderstorm to the earth. Round about human beings, he placed terrors of this sort. By these, nobly and with speech, he established the divinity in a fitting place, and quenched lawlessness (*anomía*). . . . And in this fashion, so I think, someone persuaded mortals to believe in the race of divinities.[48]

Critias's Sisyphus was by no means alone in making this assertion. In *The Metaphysics*, Aristotle sketched out a similar analysis, suggesting that human beings had invented gods "human in form (*anthrōpoeidḗs*)" in order that these deities might be "a means for persuading the multitude and a support for the laws and the public advantage (*tò sumphéron*)."[49] In one fashion or another, Isocrates, Polybius, Diodorus, Strabo, Quintus Mucius Scaevola, Marcus Terentius Varro, and Marcus Tullius Cicero all echo his claim.[50]

The skepticism voiced by Critias's Sisyphus, Aristotle, and Isocrates; by Polybius, Diodorus and Strabo; and by Scaevola, Varro, and Cicero was foreign to the ordinary Greek, but the political importance which these men ascribed to religion was not. Well before Critias was even born, Theognis had stressed the dependence of lawful order on piety.[51] When asked what would please the gods, the Delphic oracle reportedly replied, "[Obedience] to the city's law"; and Plato claimed that "enslavement to the laws" was "really enslavement to the gods."[52] Demosthenes agreed. When he found himself called upon to explain the chief reasons why "it is proper that all obey the law," he not only told his fellow citizens that they should do so "because every law is a discovery and gift of the gods"; he mentioned that consideration before any other. Demosthenes did go on to stipulate that the law reflects "the settled opinion (*dógma*) of prudent men"; he did specify that the law is "a corrective for transgressions both voluntary and involuntary"; and he did emphasize that the law is "a covenant shared in common by the city."[53] These concerns were important, even vital. But in Demosthenes' estimation the gods always came first.[54]

In establishing this hierarchy, the great Athenian orator was in no way peculiar; he was, in fact, merely following the dictates of convention.[55] The ancient city was not constituted by a "multiplicity of sects"; it was itself akin to a sect. The *pólis* had a civil religion, and that religion was one of the chief sources of its unity and morale. The tepid religiosity so favored by Thomas Jefferson and James Madison would have been a positive danger to the Greeks; as a warrior community, the *pólis* had no room for the lukewarm. The ancient city demanded from its citizens a devotion wholehearted.

For the Greeks, the gods were a constant presence. The Olympians might be thought to stand above the fray, but the gods and heroes of the land were taken to be the city's protectors, sharing in its glory and suffering its reverses.[56] In Greece as well as in Rome, it was commonly believed that no town could be captured prior to the departure of its patron deities.[57] For this reason, some cities chained their gods down,[58] and it was an event of profound political importance when a citizen managed to discover abroad and remove to a final resting place within the territory of his own *pólis* the bones of a hero.[59] Securing and maintaining divine favor was vital.[60] As a consequence, propitiation of the gods could never be simply a private matter; piety was a public duty. In an ode celebrating the election of a Tenedian to the city's council, Pindar invokes Hestia, the goddess of the public hearth. "In honoring you, by propitiating the first of the goddesses with many libations and again often with the savor of burnt offering," he writes, the new councillor and his companions "guard Tenedos and hold her upright."[61]

Just as the piety of the citizens was thought to protect the city, so also their misdeeds could threaten her survival. Indeed, the whole community might be made to suffer for the sins of a single man.[62] "Oftentimes," Hesiod writes,

It has happened that an entire city
Shares in the fate of a bad man who commits transgressions
And contrives reckless and presumptuous deeds.
On the citizens of this man's *pólis*,
The son of Kronos inflicts from heaven
A great calamity—famine together with plague.
The commoners (*laoí*) waste away, suffer, and die.
The women bear no children.
The number of households dwindles—
All because of the shrewdness of Olympian Zeus.
Elsewhere, the son of Kronos
Exacts the penalty by destroying
The wide army of a people,
Their walls,
Or their ships floating at sea.[63]

In a similar context, Pindar compares divine vengeance to "a fire on a mountainside: though begotten of a single seed, it removes a great forest entirely from sight."[64] As a consequence, men were unwilling to take ship with an individual deemed guilty of offending the gods,[65] and cities found it necessary to expel or even execute the impious and those who had incurred pollution by murder, manslaughter, or some other infraction.[66]

It is correct, but not sufficient, to observe that in antiquity patriotism required piety, for the converse was likewise true. Treason was more than a political act—at least as politics is narrowly defined in modern times. The man who turned coat or simply abandoned his city in time of crisis betrayed not just his fellow citizens; he betrayed the gods as well. This explains why one peripatetic writer chose to list "offences against the fatherland" under the category of "impiety."[67] It also explains why the law of Athens equated treason with the robbing of temples. The Athenians dealt with the two crimes in a single statute that called not just for the guilty party's execution but also for the confiscation of his property and a denial to him of burial in his native soil.[68] As one Athenian orator put it, traitors "commit acts of impiety in depriving the gods of the ancestral cults stipulated by custom and law." The citizen who brings to trial a man who has abandoned the city in its time of need can therefore justly tell his fellow citizens that he is prosecuting "a man who has betrayed the temples of the gods, their shrines and precincts, the honors ordained by the laws, and the sacrifices handed down from your forefathers."[69] There was nothing novel in his contention. As the battle of Salamis began, Aeschylus tells us, a great shout could be heard from the Greek ranks:

"Go on, sons of Hellas! Liberate the fatherland! Liberate your children and wives! Liberate the seats of your ancestral gods and the tombs of your forefathers! For the contest at hand is over these things."[70] In classical Greece, patriotism and piety overlapped a great deal, and their near-identity had consequences that go far toward explaining the roots of public-spiritedness among the Hellenes.[71]

To reinforce the conviction that the gods required of the citizens a total devotion to the common good, the ancient cities resorted to the administering of oaths. Fortunately for us, an Athenian orator took the trouble to explain in detail the logic of this practice to the members of a jury. "The oath is the force holding the democracy together," he observed. "Our regime is composed of three elements: the magistrate, the juryman, and the private individual. Each of these is required to give his pledge, and quite rightly so. For many have deceived human beings and escaped notice, not only by eluding immediate dangers but also by remaining unpunished for their crimes through the rest of the time allotted to them. But no oath-breaker escapes divine notice; no man of this sort can avoid the vengeance that the gods exact. Even if a perjurer manages to escape retribution himself, his children and his entire family will fall upon great misfortunes."[72] This religious understanding guided civic policy throughout all of Hellas. To support his claim that "*homónoia* is considered by the cities to be the greatest good," Xenophon pointed to the fact that "everywhere in Greece there is a law requiring the citizens to swear that they will maintain *homónoia*—and in every place they take such an oath."[73]

Only a handful of the civic oaths mentioned by Xenophon actually survive. Typical in most respects is the pledge inscribed on stone by the magistrates of the city of Itanos on the island of Crete. During the Hellenistic period, when most of the Greek communities fell under the sway of Alexander the Great's various successors and lost something of their martial character, the *póleis* of Crete generally retained their freedom and continued to squabble among themselves. In what seems to have been a time of crisis, the authorities at Itanos imposed a loyalty oath and made it a prerequisite for the retention of citizenship.[74] Some elements of the pledge were no doubt traditional: for example, the men of the town had to swear by the city's gods never to betray the community, its territory, its islands, its ships, its citizens, or their property; and they had to promise that they would give first consideration to the public interest, that they would observe the laws then in force and those that would be promulgated in the future, and that, to the best of their abilities, they would never desert the *pólis* whether in peace or in war. Other elements hint at the possibility of trouble: the citizens were also required to swear that they would not propose any redistribution of land or cancellation of debts, that they would never themselves engage in conspiracy, and that they would report to the authorities the activities of all those who did. To add to the oath's force, the magistrates appended a solemn curse. Those tempted to break faith had to ponder the prospect of being denied the fruits of the earth, the enjoyment of children, and the growth of their flocks; they had to consider whether to risk being destroyed altogether along with their offspring. Taken as a whole, the inscription from Itanos reflects something of the difficulties faced by a tiny community in an age fraught with war.[75]

Except during an emergency, it was probably not the norm for a community to exact from all of its citizens at once a pledge of their loyalty. It was common within the Greek cities to make public provision for the military training of the young.[76] Ordinarily, it seems to have been deemed sufficient that these youths be called upon to swear once and for all at the time of their formal initiation into manhood that they would stake their lives to protect the community, their fellow citizens, and the institutions which they held in common. In Hellenistic Crete, this practice was apparently universal: inscriptions alluding to the ritual survive for Cnossus, Dreros, Hierapytna, Lato, Olous, Lyttos, Malla, and probably Axos as well.[77] The only oath extant is that which was administered at Dreros. Each year, those among the young men of the town who had reached the age of eighteen seem to have undergone an ordeal and then doffed the garments of childhood. Thereafter, they gathered at a specified place to participate in a rite of passage marking their attainment of manhood. These neophytes first took as witnesses not just the deities familiar from Homer, but also the heroes and heroines of the land, the springs and rivers, and all the gods and goddesses. Then, they called down a curse on themselves if they failed in any way to defend the city, its territory, and its allies with all their might, or if they neglected to do all possible harm to its enemies, to oppose *stásis*, and to warn the magistrates of any conspiracies that might become known.[78]

Of all the civic oaths, that from Athens is the best-attested example. From time immemorial, the ephebes of that *pólis* gathered for their induction as citizens in the sanctuary of Aglaurus, daughter of Cecrops, the city's legendary founder and king. In that sacred place, each young initiate was first fitted out with a shield and spear, and then he solemnly swore,

I will not disgrace these sacred arms. Nor will I desert the man posted at my side—no matter where in the battle line I shall be placed. I will ward off harm from the holy and sacred things, and I will pass the fatherland on [to those who come after] not diminished, but greater and better, in-

sofar as I together with all the other citizens am able. I will obey those at
any given time exercising rule as long as they remain within the bounds
of reason (*émphronos*). I will obey the laws—both those established now
and those within the bounds of reason that shall be established here-
after. If anyone shall act to destroy these, I will not permit it, insofar
as I together with all the other citizens am able. And I shall honor the
holy places handed down by our ancestors. For my oath, I take as witnesses the gods Aglaurus, Hestia, Enyo, Enyalius, Ares and Athena
Areia, Zeus, Thallo, Auxo, Hegemone, Heracles, the boundary stones of
the fatherland, the wheat, the barley, the vines, the olive trees, and the
fig trees.[79]

These oaths deserve to be treated with the greatest seriousness. When a truly
god-fearing hoplite lined up with his fellows in his city's phalanx, he had
things to worry about that were far more terrifying than the spears bran-
dished by those in the enemy line. The virtue which the ancient city fostered
was not a rational courage founded on the recognition that some lives are
too degrading to be worth living; it was a political courage rooted in religious
awe and sustained by civic orthodoxy.

Plato expounds the nature of this virtue with a clarity unparalleled elsewhere. In concluding his discussion of religion in *The Republic*, he calls civil
courage a "preservation through everything, of the correct and lawful opinion (*dóxēs orthês te kaì nomímou*) concerning what is to be dreaded (*deinôn
te péri*) and what is not"; in the *Phaedo*, he draws attention to the irrational
and artificial foundation of this courage, arguing that "all brave men, except
the philosophers, are brave by virtue of dread (*déos*) and cowardice (*deilía*)."
"The brave," he suggests, "endure death only because they fear evils greater
than death." Plato makes the meaning of these enigmatic statements clear in
The Laws where he distinguishes two opposed sorts of fear—the natural fear
of ordinary evils like death, and that salutary, but artificially induced fear
of public opinion called shame (*aischúnē*). The first he considers the root of
cowardice; the second, of courage—and the latter can be extremely effective
where reverence (*aidôs*) informs it.[80]

In his subsequent discussion of the remarkable display of civil courage
made by the Athenians at Salamis, Plataea, and Mycale, Plato illustrates the
power of a shame reinforced by reverence:

At that time, when the Persians made their attack on the Greeks, . . .
we had reverence (*aidôs*) as a despotic mistress; and because of this, we
were willing to live as slaves to the laws then in existence. In addition,
the magnitude of the expedition, both by land and by sea, inspired in

us a sense of helplessness and fear; and this made us to an even greater degree slaves to the magistrates and the laws. Because of all this, a sense of our friendship (*philía*) fell upon us with great force. . . . If dread (*déos*) had not then seized hold of the Athenians, they would never have come together to defend themselves, nor would they have defended the temples, the tombs, the fatherland, and their kin as well as their friends, coming to their aid as they then did—but each of us would have been scattered at that time and little by little dispersed here and there.[81]

The touchstone of this civic virtue was not the truth known to the philosophers concerning man's place in the natural scheme of things, but the laws and conventions of the particular community to which the citizen belonged. The brave man was moved not by reason, but by an inculcated fear of the city's gods and by shame. It was not dishonorable and vicious behavior itself that he regarded as terrible; it was divine wrath and ill repute.[82] In his lyric nome *The Persians*, the fifth-century, Milesian poet Timotheus rightly identified *aidós* as a "coworker of spear-battling virtue (*sunergòn aretâs dorimáchou*)." To exhibit the courage required of free men, to remain steadfast in the presence of danger, to face the enemy down, and to establish his right to rule thereby, the ancient citizen-soldier had to stifle all self-doubt; and to do so effectively, he had to remain unaware of his own ignorance and impervious to wonder, the passion animating the truly rational man.[83]

I.iv.4

To the layman, this analysis of the nature of courage may seem strange. Though commonplace in antiquity,[84] the notion that reverence and shame cause bravery in combat is as foreign to the experience of civilians reared and educated in Madison's bourgeois republic as combat itself. This would not have been the case with veterans of Oliver Cromwell's New Model Army, and it is not entirely the case with the warriors of our own day. Reverence has less of a place in the ruminations of the latter than it would have had in those of the former, but that is only because ideology, with its claim to full rationality, has supplanted revelation as the foundation of legitimacy. Even in our own age, armies at war devote considerable time and effort to the indoctrination of troops, and liberal democracies, though uncomfortable with such propaganda, find it difficult to sustain foreign wars not treated as crusades. Except with regard to religion, contemporary military theory endorses the outlook of the Greeks.

The French infantry officer Ardant du Picq advanced in the late nineteenth century what was then a revolutionary hypothesis: the notion that men in the heat of battle are moved to fight not by love of country or by principles held dear as much as by the relations that bind them to each other. Persuaded that the battlefield was a place of terror for all, he argued that the true foundation of the soldier's courage was his friendship with his comrades—that "mutual acquaintanceship of long standing between all elements" which engenders moral cohesion and company spirit. As Picq put it, "We animate with passion, a violent desire for independence, religious fanaticism, national pride, a love of glory, a madness for possession." But these motives are somehow in themselves insufficient. For most men, military discipline and martial fervor depend "on surveillance: the mutual supervision" natural and inevitable within small "groups of men who know each other well." In the end, "the science of making men fight with their maximum energy" can be mastered only by those who know how to give the soldiers "an organization with which to fight fear."[85]

The twentieth century provided ample opportunity to test the thesis of Picq, and American studies, conducted by a team of historians during the Second World War, confirmed his suggestion. As S. L. A. Marshall put it in his classic work *Men against Fire*, "Men who have been in battle know from first-hand experience that when the chips are down, a man fights to help the man next [to] him, just as a company fights to keep pace with its flanks. Things have to be that simple. An ideal does not become tangible at the moment of firing a volley or charging a hill. When the hard and momentary choice is life or death, the words once heard at an orientation lecture are clean forgot, but the presence of a well-loved comrade is unforgettable." This devotion to others stems from friendship, but its power is quite deeply rooted in shame: in the American army, camaraderie was effective precisely because it gave rise to a strong sense of honor. "Wherever one surveys the forces of the battlefield," Marshall remarks, "it is to see that fear is general among men, but to observe further that men are commonly loath that their fear will be expressed in specific acts which their comrades will recognize as cowardice. The majority are unwilling to take extraordinary risks and do not aspire to a hero's role, but they are equally unwilling that they should be considered the least worthy among those present. . . . When a soldier is . . . known to the men who are around him, he . . . has reason to fear losing the one thing he is likely to value more highly than life—his reputation as a man among men." In the end, the role played by self-respect and by a man's personal sense of honor is always decisive.[86]

The claims of Picq and of Marshall should not be taken to mean that armies can do without indoctrination altogether. It is not enough that the military promote mutual acquaintanceship. Familiars can be at odds, and an army divided against itself is worse than useless. If acquaintances are to become well-loved comrades, their friendship must be grounded in something deeper and more stable than the pleasure men ordinarily take in the company of men. If they are to risk their lives for each other in combat, they must be convinced that the struggle is just and the prize worth the fight. Though his emphasis lies elsewhere, even Marshall acknowledges that "belief in a cause is the foundation of the aggressive will in battle." If a nation "is to endure the test of centuries," he adds, "men must feel themselves a part of something greater than themselves."[87] Victory in war depends on those who are born leaders: if the soldiers are to conquer, these men—exceptional for their natural boldness in battle—must be willing and eager to press on their fellows. Indoctrination can never substitute for intimacy, but patriotism and belief in the cause can provide a foundation for friendship and give effective content to shame. The attention which officers pay to morale is not wasted: it can determine whether the men accept with enthusiasm the missions assigned them or sullenly resist direction from above.

The modern infantryman, sent to do battle by a modern bourgeois republic, has far less reason to fight than his ancient counterpart.[88] Reared and educated in a commercial society with little sympathy for the soldier's calling, able to live the better part of his life in peace and in comfort, and sheltered throughout from the presence of death, the former is in no way inured to the loss of life and to the shedding of blood.[89] Typically, he is a private man, with opinions and interests, if not passions, that bring him into conflict with his comrades; normally, he is a conscript, ripped untimely from civilian life; and, more often than not, he is called on to fight not at home on his native soil in defense of his family and land, but abroad in a country far away of which he and his fellows know little or nothing. The modern foot soldier is the citizen of a large state: during a particular campaign, he may be posted with a small group of his familiars; but when that campaign is done, he can retreat to anonymity in a world wholly ignorant of his comportment in combat. On the battlefield, the modern infantryman is almost alone. When confronting the enemy, he finds himself isolated: within shouting distance, but often out of sight of his comrades, crawling on his belly from one place of cover to another, and never quite sure when he will himself come under fire. It should not be surprising that many, when caught in such circumstances, betray a marked reluctance to fight, but the discovery of the American investigators is shocking nonetheless. In the battles of the Second World War, a good many of the GI's confronting the enemy never even managed to fire their guns at all.[90] Some would not fight under any circumstances; others, only when goaded. For the rest, the support of their fellows seems to have been decisive. As Marshall observes,

> The thing which enables an infantry soldier to keep going with his weapons is the near presence or the presumed presence of a comrade. The warmth which derives from human companionship is as essential to his employment of the arms with which he fights as is the finger with which he pulls a trigger or the eye with which he aligns his sights. The other man may be almost beyond hailing or seeing distance, but he must be there somewhere within a man's consciousness or the onset of de-moralization is almost immediate and very quickly the mind begins to despair or turns to thoughts of escape. In this condition he is no longer a fighting individual, and though he holds to his weapon, it is little better than a club.

Friendship and shame: although modern conditions undermine their great strength, these remain in our age, as much as ever, the sources of courage in combat.[91]

The demands placed on the ordinary Greek hoplite and the moral support afforded him in his moment of trial went far beyond anything imagined by the normal soldier today. As Aristotle emphasizes, mutual acquaintance-ship was one of the features that distinguished the Greek *pólis* from a nation (*éthnos*). If the *pólis* was to function properly, he suggests, it had to be "easily surveyed" so that the citizens might know each other's characters.[92] Most of the cities were small towns, and in only a few did the citizen body exceed a few thousand.[93] There was little, if any, privacy, and the citizen's entire exis-tence was bound up with his participation in the religious and political affairs of the community. The Greek soldier was well known to the men around him. He had spent the better part of his leisure time in their company: when not in the fields, he would leave the household to his wife and loiter about the blacksmith's shop, the palaestra, the gymnasium, or the *agorá*, discuss-ing politics and personalities, testing his strength and his wit against the qualities of his contemporaries, and watching the boys as they grew up.[94] He lived for those hours when, freed from the necessity of labor, he could exercise the faculties—both moral and intellectual—that distinguished him from a beast of burden and defined him as a man.[95] When deprived of repu-tation, he was deprived of nearly everything that really mattered. In classical Greece, the absence of a distinction between state and society was as much a practical as a theoretical matter: it meant that the citizen lived most of his life in the public eye, subject to the scrutiny of his compatriots and dependent on their regard. To be identified as a draft evader, accused of breaking ranks, or branded a coward and, in consequence, to be shunned or deprived of one's political rights could easily be a fate worse than death.[96]

In time of war, the Greek citizen could not escape combat: no allowance was made for conscientious objection, there were no desk jobs, and slaves and metics performed whatever support functions the hoplite could not perform for himself.[97] More often than not, he was fighting near his home in defense of his children and his land; and even when he was posted abroad, he was acutely aware that the city's safety and his family's welfare depended on the outcome of the struggle.[98] On the field of battle, this foot soldier would be posted alongside his fellow citizens as they advanced, shoulder to shoulder, marching in step—in some communities, to the tune of a flute. The phalanx was generally eight men deep, and it extended as far as the numbers and the terrain permitted. There was no place to hide: ancient battles took place on open terrain, and this infantryman's behavior under stress would be visible to many, if not to all. The phalanx might be subject to attack by the primitive artillery then available; if he disrupted the formation, desperate to avoid the javelins and arrows, everyone would know. The phalanx might be threatened by a cavalry charge on the flank where he was stationed; if he turned to run for the cover of rough ground, his fellows would see it. Eventually, the phalanx would meet the enemy's spears; if he gave way and, running for life, threw away his shield, his cowardice would be noted. Whether he stood his ground and did his part was not a matter of indifference to his comrades; it was a matter of life and death. For success, the modern army depends on the courage of the minority of men who actually fire their guns; the Greek phalanx depended on the effort of every man. The strength of this chain of men was no greater than that of its weakest link, for it took a breach at only one point for the formation to collapse. As a result, the behavior of a single hoplite could sometimes spell the difference between victory and rout. The man who betrayed his fellows, leaving them to die by breaking ranks and opening the way for the foe, would not soon be forgiven and could never be forgotten. In a sense, he had spent his entire life preparing for this one moment of truth.[99]

I.iv.5

The process of preparation for that moment of truth required a great deal of time and effort. Toil (*pónos*) undertaken for the sake of profit might be regarded as shameful, but *pónos* undertaken for the sake of good order (*táxis*) and victory in battle was not only honorable; its avoidance was a source of unending shame. This fact explains the centrality of athletics in ancient Greek life. If the wealthy young men of the town spent their idle hours at the palaestra and the gymnasium, it was not simply or even chiefly because they were driven by narcissism. Indeed, their primary concerns were public, not private. In a tyranny, such as the one established by Aristodemus at Cumae on the northern marches of Italy's Magna Graecia, there was to be no middle ground, and it might therefore seem prudent and even appropriate for the despot to do what he could to suppress the noble and manly disposition of the young by closing the gymnasiums and banning the practice of arms, by draping the young boys of the town in finery and keeping them out of the hot sun, and finally by sending them off, their long hair curled, adorned with flowers, and doused with perfume, to study with the dance masters and the players of flutes.[100] But where the middle ground survived, this would never do: for republics needed real men, and citizens with the leisure in which to ready themselves for the ordeal of battle were quite rightly expected to do so. "It is necessary," as Montesquieu observes, "to look on the Greeks as a society of athletes and warriors."[101]

Herodotus hammers away on the need for *pónos* with particular vehemence. The manner in which he turns his description of the battle of Lade into a parable is a case in point. In 499, the Greeks who inhabited the coastal communities of Asia Minor and the islands of the eastern Aegean had joined together in rebellion against their royal master the Great King of Persia. A few years later, they sent naval contingents to the island of Lade, which lay off Miletus, the largest and most prosperous of the coastal towns. There, the rebels intended to make a concerted effort to prevent the Phoenician fleet of the Mede from regaining control of the sea and putting an end to their revolt. Upon the arrival of the various contingents, Dionysius of Phocaea reportedly addressed them in the following fashion: "Men of Ionia, our affairs— whether we are to be free men or slaves (and fugitive slaves at that)—stand balanced on a razor's edge. If, for the time being, you are willing to subject yourselves to hard work, you will have to submit to toil (*pónos*) on the spot, but you shall be able to overcome those opposed to you and so go free. If, however, you prefer softness (*malakía*) and disorder (*ataxía*), I have no hope that you can avoid paying to the King the penalty for your revolt."[102]

The Ionians initially took Dionysius's advice. According to Herodotus, they toiled for seven days from dawn to dusk, rowing their ships and practicing maneuvers under the Phocaean's direction. But because the men of the islands and coast were soft and unaccustomed to *pónos*, many among them soon became ill; and in due course, the rowers wearied of hardship and rebelled. Then, they labored no more but instead erected tents on the island

and took shelter there from the harsh rays of the sun. The Ionians paid dearly for their weakness. The Persians generals had promised to pardon any among the rebels who turned coat; and as a consequence of the rowers' indolence and insubordination, the Samian generals became persuaded that the cause was hopeless and elected to accept the king's offer. Thus, just as the battle began, the contingent from Samos—followed quickly by the triremes from Lesbos—sailed off, leaving the remaining Ionians to certain defeat. Herodotus might have added that these men got precisely what they deserved, but he had no need to spell out his point.[103]

Needless to say, toil, endurance, and good order were no less necessary for those destined to engage in combat on land. When Xenophon singles out farming as a profession likely to prepare men for war, he has more in mind than the fact that those who cultivate the soil have an interest in its defense. "The earth," his Socrates remarks, "supplies good things in abundance, but she does not allow them to be taken by the soft (*metà malakías*) but accustoms men to endure (*kartereîn*) the wintry cold and summer's heat. In exercising (*gumnázousa*) those who work with their own hands, she adds to their strength, and she makes men (*andrízei*) of those who, in farming, take pains, getting them up early and forcing them to march about with great vigor (*sphodrôs*). For in the country as in the town, the tasks most fitting to the time must be done in season." Xenophon's Ischomachus even asserts that agriculture teaches generalship, noting that victory generally depends less on cleverness than on the thoroughness, diligence, and care exhibited by the sort of men who have learned from long experience the necessity of taking precautions.[104]

Courage, strength, endurance, and diligence were vital, but they were not the only virtues demanded of the citizen-warrior in classical times. In fact, in certain crucial respects, the hoplite was quite unlike the heroes of *The Iliad*. He and his opponents fought not on their own, but in formation; and, therefore, he could not afford to be a berserker, driven by rage (*lússa*) to run amok among the enemy host, for he could not break ranks to charge the enemy line without doing himself and his own side great harm. To achieve victory, the hoplite and his comrades had to display what the Greeks called *sōphrosúnē*—the moderation and the self-restraint expected of a man required to cooperate with others in both peace and war.[105] Consequently, in considering the *paideía* to which young Greeks were customarily subjected, one would err in dwelling on athletic contests and military maneuvers to the exclusion of all else, for Greek boys were expected to toil at music as well. In fact, to judge by the remarks made by the greatest of the ancient philosophers, the study of music played a vital role in giving a young man the psychological preparation he needed for the assumption of his duties as a citizen and soldier.[106] In Plato's *Republic*, the interlocutors of Socrates take it for granted that education consists of gymnastic exercise and musical training. Initially, Socrates treats exercise at the gymnasium as a hardening of the body. But as the argument unfolds, he introduces another, more important consideration—the effect of that hardening on the soul, and the danger that Guardians subjected to gymnastic training alone will be savage toward one another and toward their fellow citizens as well. Poetry set to music he presents as an instrument capable of moderating and harmonizing—in short, of civilizing—the all-important quality of spiritedness.[107] In *The Laws*, Plato's Athenian Stranger takes a similar tack, arguing at length and with considerable psychological insight that participation in choral singing and dancing can habituate the young and the not so young to take pleasure in that which is good and to feel loathing and disgust when presented with that which is not.[108] Even Aristotle thought such pursuits an antidote to the savagery bred of the ancient city's constant and obsessive preoccupation with war. In fact, like his mentor, he was persuaded that a *pólis* devoted to music and the arts would be a far healthier and saner polity than a community dedicated to conquest and imperial rule and consequently riven by political ambition and strife.[109]

Plato and Aristotle were neither the first nor the last to think of music and poetry in so political a fashion. The testimony of Aristoxenus, Theophrastus, Chamaileon, Claudius Ptolemy, Varro, Cicero, Strabo, Quintilian, Plutarch, and Aristides Quintilianus suggests that the founders of the Academy and Lyceum were merely elaborating variations on what was in Hellas the common sense of the matter.[110] To the bard blessed by Apollo with the kithara and with the Muse, Pindar attributed a capacity to "infuse into [the citizens'] hearts and minds that good order and lawfulness which frees men from war (*apólemon agagòn es prapídas eunomían*)."[111] Aristophanes was no less persuaded of the formative capacity of song; and in his poems, Socrates is said to have remarked that "those who honor the gods most nobly in choruses are the best in war."[112] Moreover, if the words that Plato puts into the mouth of the sophist Protagoras can be trusted at all, ordinary Greeks sent their sons to study music in the hope that they would thereby imbibe *sōphrosúnē* and become not only more gentle (*hēmeróteroi*) but also, through rhythm and harmony, effective and useful in speech and in deed (*chrḗsimoi . . . eis tò légein te kaì práttein*).[113] Damon of Athens, who was a member of Pericles' kitchen cabinet, carried this analysis considerably further. He observed that singing and the dance arise, of necessity, when the soul is moved, and he concluded that singing and dancing of a liberal and noble sort (*hai mèn eleuthérioi kaì kalaí*) engenders souls of a similar character, while singing and dancing of an illiberal and ignoble sort has a parallel effect. He was even prepared to suggest that, wherever a change in musical modes (*trópoi*) is introduced, a revolution in the city's most important customs and laws (*nómoi*) will follow.[114]

To us, the claims initially advanced on music's behalf by Pindar, Damon, Protagoras, Aristophanes, Socrates, Plato, and Aristotle and later taken up by Aristoxenus, Theophrastus, Chamaileon, Claudius Ptolemy, Varro, Cicero, Strabo, Quintilian, Plutarch, and Aristides Quintilianus may well seem bizarre. Even in ancient times, some deemed them preposterous.[115] And yet, when one pauses to think about the question, it is not difficult to see how a young man nurtured exclusively on Bach would be likely to develop tastes, habits, and a general disposition distinguishing him from a counterpart similarly reared on John Philip Sousa. Nor, to take an even more striking example, is it hard to see how the former and the latter would differ from a comparable young man subjected to a steady diet of rock and roll. A detached observer would, in fact, be hard put to deny that the ethos fostered by rock and roll music had a great deal to do with the sea change in middle-class mores which legitimized sexual promiscuity among young Americans and led to the widespread use of hallucinogenic drugs and other illegal intoxicants.[116] It is, in any case, noteworthy that the ancient poets, philosophers, and music theorists were not peculiar in their estimation of music's power.

The historian whom Montesquieu calls "the judicious Polybius" was a hardheaded man, perfectly familiar with the trials and tribulations of political life and utterly intolerant of arrant nonsense. So daunting a figure can hardly be accused of simplemindedness. Yet when he finds himself called upon to explain the prevalence of civil strife within Cynaetha, a *pólis* set in the mountains of Arcadia, Polybius attributes to the city's neglect of music and to nothing else the massacres and banishments, the seizures of goods and redistributions of land, and the general savagery, cruelty, and lawlessness which had come to characterize the life of that particular community. As he puts it, one must study the music of the Arcadians if one wishes to account for their general reputation for virtue and for piety in particular, and one must do the same if one is to understand the humanity and hospitality which the inhabitants of Arcadia generally evidence in their characters and lives. From the very beginning, he tells us, those resident within that cold and rugged mountainous region had incorporated music into every aspect of public life (*eis tền holền politeían*); in particular, they had required boys and even young men up to the age of thirty to learn, first, the ancestral hymns and the paians honoring the gods and heroes of the land and, then, the measures of Philoxenus and Timotheus. Every year, in the theater, they held contests at public expense in choral singing and in the dance. They also learned to march to the sound of the flute. By these means, they softened the harsh, austere national character to which the rugged nature of their land and climate would otherwise have given rise. By these means, they tried and in large measure succeeded in avoiding *stásis*.[117]

The avoidance of civil strife and the preparation for war—these were the goals of ancient Greek education. Democritus summed up the civic outlook elegantly when he remarked, "Children left free from the requirement of toil will learn neither their letters, nor music, nor gymnastic struggle (*agōníē*), nor that which more than anything else encompasses virtue: the practice of reverence (*tò aideîsthai*). For it is especially from these pursuits that reverence (*aidṓs*) is inclined to be born."[118] As we shall soon see, the need for a *paideía* capable of instilling *aidṓs* and of reinforcing civil courage shaped sexual practices as well.

I.iv.6

One of the most telling indications of the degree to which the warrior ethos permeated every aspect of Greek life is the prevalence of pederasty through-out Hellas. No ancient author gives us a full and detailed report of the conventions that guided Greek behavior in the various cities, and the surviving plays, courtroom harangues, philosophical dialogues, and vase representations that throw light on the elaborate code of homosexual courtship pertain chiefly to Athens.[119] But though the evidence is fragmentary, the general pattern is clear: the Greeks seem normally to have practiced pederasty as a rite of passage marking a boy's transition to manhood and his initiation into the band of citizen-soldiers; and even in those communities where wooing adolescent boys was the fashion only among men of leisure, pederasty was conceived of by its many proponents as a reinforcement of those ties of mutual acquaintanceship which were universally recognized to be the foundation of civil courage.[120]

The Greeks were unusual, but not unique, in this practice. Remarkably similar folkways have appeared under somewhat similar circumstances in several places, particularly among the aborigines of Australia and the various tribal peoples of Melanesia. Within the various martial communities, the customs vary a good bit, but the elements and their import are very much the same. The sexual relationship is always temporary, and it always marks the transition to manhood; typically, it involves young, unmarried men and boys; and although either sodomy or fellatio may be the norm, the man always plays an active and the boy a passive role in the sexual act.[121] In all these respects, the Keraki tribesmen of Papua New Guinea are typical. At the age of thirteen, Keraki boys would be taken from their villages into the forest to be subjected to a series of trials and to rituals of submission including whipping and sodomy. The last of these rites was thought vital: like the tribesmen elsewhere, the Keraki considered insemination a prerequisite for the communication of manliness and strength from one generation to the next. For the boys, the period of withdrawal lasted one year. Thereafter, when they had undergone the Bull-roarer's ceremony, they would return to their homes—no longer members of the world of women and children, but initiates into that of the men. Only then would they receive the belt of manhood and the arrows that would set them apart within the tribe as hunters and warriors from that moment on.[122]

Precisely the same pattern is evident in Ephorus's extraordinary description of prevailing practice in the region of Greece where the *pólis* as a religious and military community governed by constitutional forms (*politeía*) seems first to have emerged.[123] In Crete, the younger boys attended the men's mess with their fathers; and under the direction of the *paidonómos* associated with that mess, those slightly older learned their letters, memorized the songs prescribed by the laws, and tested their strength against each other and against those associated with other messes. When the boys had turned seventeen,[124] the most distinguished among them gathered their less wellborn contemporaries into herds (*agélai*), each collecting as large a personal following as possible. Fed at public expense and subject to their recruiter's father, they practiced hunting, they participated in foot races, and—at appointed times— they joined in battle against rival *agélai*, marching in formation to the cadence of the flute and the lyre.[125] This period of apprenticeship in hunting and war reached completion when a man of distinguished family took as his beloved the boy who had gathered the herd in the first place. "In matters of *érōs*," Ephorus informs us,

> their custom is peculiar—for they secure their loved ones (*erṓmenoi*) not by persuasion, but by abduction (*harpagḗ*). Three or four days before the event, the lover (*erastḗs*) informs the friends of the boy that he intends an abduction. For them to hide the boy or not to allow him to journey by the appointed path is deemed shameful in the extreme, for it is a confession that the boy is unworthy of the *erastḗs*. When they meet, if the abductor is the boy's equal or superior in honor and in other respects, the boy's friends pursue him and take hold of him in a gentle manner, thus satisfying the demands of custom; and, then, they happily turn him over to the abductor to lead away—but if the abductor is unworthy, they take the boy away from him. The pursuit ends only when the boy

arrives at the men's house (*andreîon*) of the abductor. The Cretans regard as worthy of love not the boy who excels in physical beauty, but rather the one distinguished by courage or manliness (*andreía*) and by orderly behavior.

This ritual abduction marked the first stage in the process by which an aristocratic boy and his followers were prepared for initiation into manhood. Together, they were forcibly withdrawn from the community of ephebes; for a transitional period, they slipped off to the wilds; and when they came back, they immediately married and joined the community of men.

> When the abductor has given the boy gifts, he leads him into the countryside wherever he wishes; those present at the abduction follow them; and after feasting and hunting for two months (for the abductor is not allowed to hold onto the boy for a longer period), they make their return to the city. The boy is, then, released and receives as gifts the equipment needed for war (*stolèn polemikèn*), an ox, and a drinking cup (for these are the gifts required by law [*katà nómon*]) as well as other presents so many in number and so expensive that his friends chip in because of the greatness of the cost. The boy sacrifices the ox to Zeus and prepares a feast for those who have returned with him; then, he makes known the facts regarding his intimacy with the *erastếs*, indicating whether it pleased him or not (the law allows this so that, if force was applied at the time of the abduction, he can now take his revenge and rid himself of the *erastếs*).[126]

The gifts evidently symbolized the boy's coming of age.[127] The cup signified his recruitment into the *andreîon* of his abductor—where, for the rest of his life, he would take his meals and drink his wine. The military outfit indicated his acceptance into the army where he would be numbered among the *parastathéntes*—"those posted alongside" their lovers in combat. And the ox enabled him to conduct the final initiatory rite of celebration honoring the beardless Zeus of Crete—patron of ephebes, protector of the *andreîon*, and abductor of Ganymede.[128] It was thought to be a sign of bad character if a handsome and well-bred boy lacked admirers; and while still young men, those who had completed the entire ritual process were singled out to hold prominent positions in the choruses and at the footraces and were allowed to wear the uniform that distinguished them as *parastathéntes*. Even when they were much older, they would still wear special garments reserved for those dubbed "the famous (*kleinoí*)."[129] It should be no surprise that, when the Cretans arranged their hoplites in the phalanx for battle, they called on the most handsome of their soldiers to make sacrifice to Eros.[130] Pederasty was evidently one of the central institutions of the martial communities of Crete, and it was probably from this island that the custom spread to the remainder of Greece.[131]

Concerning the other Hellenic cities, we are less well informed, but all that we do know suggests that pederasty elsewhere served precisely the same function.[132] Hunting, which was everywhere considered a form of training for war, and homosexual courtship appear to have been as closely connected at Athens as they were on Crete.[133] On Thera, sodomy seems to have been linked with rituals honoring Apollo Delphinios and marking the boy's transition to manhood.[134] At Thebes, when the *erōmenos* was enrolled as a man, his *erastēs* conferred on him the hoplite panoply;[135] and in fourth-century Elis, as well as in Thebes, the couple would fight as a pair in the ranks.[136] "It is the part of a prudent general," Onasander would later remark, to encourage his heavy infantrymen to take risks on behalf of those alongside them in the battle line by stationing "brothers next to brothers, friends next to friends, and *erastaí* next to their *paidiká*."[137] In this spirit, the Greeks of the Thracian outposts would sing,

> Ye lads allotted grace and noble birth!
> Do not begrudge to brave men (*agathoísin*)
> Intimacy (*homilían*) with the charms of your youth!
> For Eros, the looser of limbs, thrives
> Alongside courage (*andreía*) in the cities
> Of the Chalcidians.[138]

Érōs and *andreía* were everywhere linked:[139] Aeschylus and Sophocles even devoted tragedies to the theme, with the former reinterpreting the story of Achilles and Patroclus in this vein.[140]

Throughout Greece, pederasty seems to have been a part of the gentleman's *paideía* as a citizen.[141] The friendship was, as Aristotle acknowledges, both unequal and unstable: at least initially, the *erastēs* entered the relationship in search of pleasure, and his *erōmenos* was concerned with the educational benefit he might receive.[142] When the latter became bearded, the friendship would inevitably change character, and the former might move on to another youth, while his *erōmenos*, come to manhood, began his own pursuit of the young.[143] There was a season to their dalliance, and propriety dictated the rule which Pindar set to verse: that a man "love and yield to love in due course" and never "pursue the matter beyond measure."[144] For a boy come of age to remain an *erōmenos* was a disgrace, and for a man to continue his courtship of adolescents when he had passed his twenties seemed silly. As Timon the satirist quipped, "There is a time for *érōs*, a time for marriage, and a time for stopping entirely."[145] If two men remained devoted to each other after the hour of their passion had passed, so much the better for the *pólis*.

Pederasty may have been, in origin, an aristocratic practice; but by the fifth century, it had been tamed and subordinated to the cities' interest in the promotion of friendship. As a consequence, we are told, Eros was enshrined in the public gymnasium along with Hermes the god of eloquence and Heracles the patron of physical strength.[146] Within the *pólis*, the gymnasium served as the training ground for war.[147] That is why the cities of Crete barred slaves from exercise there just as they barred them from the bearing of arms.[148] Thus, it is symptomatic of pederasty's civic function that Athens prohibited slaves from taking on *erōmenoi*—just as she prohibited them from working out in the public gymnasium. The two prohibitions were evidently part of the same statute,[149] and draft evaders, cowards, and traitors seem to have been included as well.[150] This was only fitting. Pederasty and the gymnasium lay, as institutions, in the public and political realm: like the hunt, both served to prepare the citizens for service in war; and the two were connected, for it was in the gymnasium ("the place of nakedness") that a comely young man would exhibit his charms to older admirers.[151] Because he had no discernible stake in the city's defense, the slave had no place in the public arena; because they had failed in their civic duty, draft evaders, cowards, and traitors were banned from this arena as well.

Pederasty was not the only instrument suitable for reinforcing the sense of shame which was at the root of civil courage. There were other, equally effective ways to do this. It is characteristic that Roman legend conceived of the household as the bulwark of liberty: to avenge the rape of Lucretia, Brutus led her father and husband in ousting the Tarquins and then founded the republic; to preserve Virginia's virtue, Verginius took his daughter's life and then employed this public act to stir up the plebeian secession that toppled the decemvirs and restored political freedom to Rome.[152] Such a sequence of events would hardly have been conceivable in Greece: the matrons and virgins of Hellas were not easily accessible. Except at festival time and on other solemn occasions, the women of respectable households were kept in seclusion. At the evening gatherings which they were allowed to attend, they would encounter only close relatives, and under most circumstances, they were confined to the women's quarters and excluded even from the public rooms of their own homes.[153]

The role allotted Lucretia and Virginia at Rome was assigned to *erōmenoi* in

Greece. In verses that would be sung at symposia for generations, the poets of Hellas celebrated the feats of *erastaí* who fought to protect their favorites from tyrannical lust and were subjected to torture or killed in the end. Antileon was remembered in South Italy; in Agrigentum, Melannipus and his *erómenos* Chariton were honored for their plot against Phalaris and for their steadfast refusal, when caught, to divulge their fellow conspirators' names.[154] The case of the Gephyraioi is well known: despite the best efforts of Herodotus, Thucydides, and Aristotle to persuade the Athenians that Cleisthenes and the Spartans were responsible for expelling the Peisistratid tyrants,[155] the man in the street persisted in attributing the foundation of Athenian liberty to the tyrannicide lovers Harmodius and Aristogeiton. The Athenians set up statues of these men in the *agorá*. To the eldest descendants of the pair, the citizens granted the privilege of dining at the city's expense in the public prytaneum—an honor otherwise restricted to Olympic victors, the priests of Demeter and Kore, foreign dignitaries, returning ambassadors, and the like. The Athenians even stipulated by law that the polemarch, that "archon of war," make sacrifices to the Gephyraioi at regular intervals.[156] If the Roman republic was represented in its founding myth as a coalition of families, Athens was, by the same token, a men's club.[157]

Strange though it may seem, the Greeks regarded the homoerotic passion linking a man with a boy as the cornerstone of political liberty. That is why the Samians, in dedicating a gymnasium to Eros, decided to establish a festival entitled the *Eleuthería*.[158] The Stoic philosopher Zeno of Citium is said to have described Eros as "the god who made provision for friendship (*philía*) and concord (*homónoia*)—and for political freedom (*eleuthería*) besides." Hence, he added, "the god Eros is a coworker (*sunergón*) devoted to the preservation (*sōtēría*) of the *pólis*."[159] There is every reason to suppose that Zeno got it right. Prior to the emergence of the *pólis* as a self-governing community of citizen-soldiers, pederasty had not been a public institution;[160] and after the decline of the ancient Greek republics as fully independent entities organized for war, homosexual relations between men and boys gradually lost the support of the laws, and the rules of decorum underwent a noiseless revolution.[161] Throughout much of the archaic period and the entire classical age, pederasty was one of the means by which martial communities of ancient Hellas sought "to remove the causes of faction" and to promote civil courage "by giving to every citizen the same opinions, the same passions, and the same interests."

I . i v . 7

Plato's testimony regarding the Greek diaspora deserves repetition: "We dwell in a small part of the world between the Pillars of Heracles and Phasis, living about the sea like ants or frogs around a pond."[162] Classical Hellas encompassed an array of independent communities stretching from the east coast of the Black Sea to the far reaches of the western Mediterranean. Language, literature, religion, culture, republican institutions, proximity to the sea, and diminutive size—these common characteristics made the ancient *póleis* much alike and very different at the same time. The last on this list of characteristics may well be the most important. Smallness in size gives rise to familiarity, and familiarity breeds contempt in more than one way: for the defense of familiarity requires xenophobia, since all outside contact is a threat to the integrity of the community.

The *pólis* was akin to a party of zealots. The tendency to smother internal conflict, the intensity of the relations binding citizen to citizen, and the almost familial quality of the polity itself—these gave to what James Madison called "the most frivolous and fanciful distinctions" a powerful impulse able to inflame the disparate *póleis* "with mutual animosity" and to render them, like factions grounded in passionately held opinion, "much more disposed to vex and oppress each other than to cooperate for their common good."[163] Alexander Hamilton was right: Hellas was "an infinity of little, jealous, clashing, tumultuous commonwealths." There was variety enough in the local circumstances and traditions of these apparently similar communities to set them incessantly at odds; and strange to tell, the unity of the Greek world owed much to this very variety and to the conflicts which it engendered. Radical particularity makes for a certain uniformity. Athenaeus rightly made no distinction between *póleis* when he wrote that "the men of olden times thought courage the greatest of the political virtues," and what he had to say was as true for Rome as it was for the republics of Greece.[164] Even where the institutions of the various cities were structurally different, the constant threat of war made them functionally similar. As a type of community, the *pólis* rested on its citizen militia and fell only when that militia was overwhelmed.

If we are to grasp with any degree of certainty the unity underlying all the diversity within Hellas and to see with any degree of clarity the fashion in which the disparate institutions of the *pólis* meshed and formed a whole, it will be necessary for us to examine in detail a single example. Unfortunately, the options are severely restricted. Of many *póleis*, we know little but the name. Most of the others now possess only a shadowy existence: we do recognize their names, and we can locate them on a map; we may even be able to relate an anecdote or two, cite a snatch of poetry, peruse a fragmentary inscription, and perhaps point to a scattering of physical remains. But rarely can we reconstruct much of anything of the life of the town or even of its political constitution. Athens is, of course, an exception to this rule, and so is Sparta. But neither was typical, and we must choose.

Most scholars would select Athens: we know much more about this community than about any other, and she is far more congenial to our tastes. But, unfortunately, in matters ancient our tastes are the least reliable of guides. In fact, it is Sparta which deserves our attention. In many respects, the men of Lacedaemon were no doubt very peculiar, but only because they had systematically sought and perhaps even in large measure achieved that for which their fellow Greeks so hungered. This much can be inferred from Josephus's report that "all hymn the praises of Sparta."[165] About no other Hellenic city could an ancient writer legitimately have advanced a similar claim.

CHAPTER 5

The Spartan Regimen

Patriotism is conducive to good morals, and good morals contribute to patriotism. The less we are able to satisfy our private passions, the more we abandon ourselves to those of a more general nature. Why are monks so fond of their order? Precisely because of those things which make it insupportable. Their rule deprives them of all the things on which the ordinary passions rest: there remains, then, only that passion for the rule which torments them. The more austere the rule, that is, the more it curbs their inclinations, the more force it gives to the one inclination which it leaves them.—Montesquieu

What gives rise to human misery is the contradiction found between our condition (état) and our desires, between our duties and our inclinations (penchans), between nature and social institutions, between man and citizen; render a man one and you shall render him as happy as he is able to be. Give him entirely over to the state or leave him entirely to himself—but if you divide his heart, you shall tear it asunder (déchirez).—Jean-Jacques Rousseau

I. v. 1

In the eighteenth century, Jean-Jacques Rousseau made a brief stab at writing a history of Sparta. It would not be, he concluded, an easy task.

> The greatest inconvenience associated with my endeavor is that here one sees men who resemble us almost in nothing, who seem to us to be outside of nature—perhaps as much because we are in that state ourselves as because they are in fact there. Their crimes inspire in us horror. Sometimes their virtues themselves make us shiver (*frémir*). Because we are weak and pusillanimous in good times and in bad, everything that bears a certain character of force and vigor seems to us impossible. The incredulity that we parade is the work of our cowardice rather than that of our reason.[1]

Rousseau's indictment does not make pleasant reading today, but it should be kept in mind nonetheless. For Sparta presents us with an almost insuperable obstacle to analysis, and the humble citizen of Geneva may have understood her better than anyone since.

Lacedaemon troubled even the ancients. In antiquity, some thought her a democracy; others, an oligarchy.[2] In one passage of Plato's *Laws*, the Athenian stranger describes her constitution as a mixture of monarchy and democracy; a few pages later, the Spartan Megillus admits that even he is at a loss for a name to give the polity: when considering the ephorate, he is tempted to call it a tyranny; when looking at the regime as a whole, he is led to think Sparta the most democratic of all the cities; and it would be altogether strange to deny that she is an aristocracy. But there is a kingship in the place, for her *basileîs* rule for life, and theirs is the oldest of kingships.[3] Aristotle suffered a fate similar to that of Plato's Megillus. When reflecting on the strife between rich and poor that wracked most Greek cities, he could describe the Lacedaemonian regime as a mixture of democracy and oligarchy; when thinking of the Spartan way of life, he found it necessary to term the city an aristocracy somehow both democratic and oriented toward the pursuit of virtue.[4]

The confusion persists. In the age stretching from Machiavelli to Rousseau, Sparta was often considered a model for the constitution of liberty.[5] In the aftermath of the French Revolution, with the advent of liberal democracy, this view seemed discredited; and since the 1930s, scholars have tended to see in Sparta a forerunner of the modern totalitarian state.[6] This recent trend has not entirely stifled debate. But the range of respectable opinion remains narrow and is perhaps best illustrated by remarks made in the mid-1960s by the Wykeham Professor of Ancient History at Oxford and by his counterpart at Cambridge. The former introduced a study of Spartan government with the observation that "Sparta had in some ways a more open constitution than most oligarchies." The latter asked himself whether the Spartans, when assembled for debate on a public policy, were likely to be able to drop the habit of unquestioning obedience instilled in them by their military training. He concluded with the guess that "the Spartan assembly was much closer to the Homeric than to the Athenian in function and psychology."[7] It would not be hyperbole to appropriate for Sparta Winston Churchill's famous description of Russia: Lacedaemon was in antiquity and remains today a riddle wrapped in a mystery inside an enigma.

The quandary in which we find ourselves is partly a function of the Spartan secretiveness that so frustrated Thucydides.[8] Even in antiquity, it was difficult to obtain precise information. In consequence, as one scholar recently put it, "many of the problems, and not only those of the remote archaic period, are in a sense insoluble: that is, the evidence is limited and often enigmatic, the range of possible solutions is wide, and there is no criterion but general plausibility to help one judge between them."[9]

Our difficulties are also partly a consequence of the idealization of Sparta already evident in the writers of the fifth century B.C. In recent times, scholars have done a great deal of work in attempting to separate out what is trustworthy in the ancient sources from that which is a product of the Spartan mirage.[10] But even this yeoman service has not sufficed to remove the obstacles entirely. Indeed, the skepticism so evident in the modern literature on the subject may even have compounded our difficulties. David Hume identified the source of the problem when he remarked, "Ancient policy was violent, and contrary to the more natural and usual course of things. It is well known with what peculiar laws SPARTA was governed, and what a prodigy that republic is justly esteemed by every one, who has considered human nature as it has displayed itself in other nations, and other ages. Were the testimony of history less positive and circumstantial, such a government would appear a mere philosophical whim or fiction, and impossible ever to be reduced to practice."[11] There is so much in Spartan life that is repugnant to the tastes fostered by the modern regime of liberal democracy that it is, in truth, far harder for us to achieve clarity on this subject than it was for the ancients themselves.

In any case, the establishment of a Spartan empire at the end of the fifth century made it impossible effectively to maintain the regimen of secrecy, and the fourth-century writers Plato and Aristotle were extremely critical of Sparta and can hardly be accused of having been taken in by the Spartan legend.[12] If they too had trouble accurately describing the Lacedaemonian polity, it is probably because the mystery is not itself a mirage.

In the end, the only proper conclusion to reach is that advanced more than two centuries ago by a man who grew up among the Gaelic-speaking Highlanders of Scotland—a people not much less warlike than the ancient Spartans had been. "After all," Adam Ferguson observed, "we are, perhaps, not sufficiently instructed in the nature of the Spartan laws and institutions, to understand in what manner all the ends of this singular state were obtained; but the admiration paid to its people, and the constant reference of contemporary historians to their avowed superiority will not allow us to question the facts."[13] It would, then, be presumptuous to assume without extensive discussion that we can somehow improve upon the efforts of Plato and Aristotle, but it should be possible to come closer to understanding their Delphic remarks by attending first to the Spartan way of life and then by carefully sifting what we know and what we can surmise regarding the day-to-day government of classical Sparta. The latter task has been made easier by the appearance in recent years of a number of specialized studies elucidating the working of particular institutions and the importance of particular practices.[14] If it is not within our power to dispel entirely the mystery of the Spartan regime, it still may be possible to shed some light on the subject.

I . v . 2

If the more commercial Greek cities stood at one end of the ancient spectrum, Sparta stood at the other. Of all the Hellenic communities, she came the closest to giving absolute primacy to the common good. She did this by turning the city into a camp, the *pólis* into an army, and the citizen into a soldier.[15] She did it by taking the institutions and practices embryonic in every *pólis* and developing them to an extreme only imagined elsewhere. Except with the express permission of the magistrates, her citizens were prohibited from traveling abroad and foreigners were forbidden to visit Lacedaemon.[16] As a consequence, she was able to exert an almost absolute control over the circumstances which shaped her citizens' lives. Everything that she did in this virtually self-contained world was aimed at a single end: nurturing what Macaulay referred to as "that intense patriotism which is peculiar to members of societies congregated in a narrow space."[17] This radical fidelity to the principles particular to the *pólis* explains why a city so rarely imitated was so universally admired.[18]

To prevent the emergence of factions, Sparta took great care to insulate the polity from the influence of the marketplace. Fearful that competition for wealth would set the citizens at odds, she coined no money and outlawed the possession of silver and gold.[19] Eager to prevent a differentiation of interests, she barred her citizens from engaging in commerce and prohibited their practice of the mechanical arts.[20] She even banned visits to the commercial *agorá* by men under the age of thirty.[21] The Spartans were, as Plutarch remarks, "the servants of Ares," not Mammon. They were "the craftsmen of war," not the makers of pots.[22] They had but one purpose in life: to gain a reputation for valor.[23] From childhood on, they trained to secure victory in battle by land.[24]

To eliminate those unfit for this endeavor, the city practiced infanticide, subjecting the newborn to a careful scrutiny and exposing those who were deformed or otherwise lacking in vigor.[25] To enable those who survived this initial test to pursue the chief goal set by the regime, the city granted to every citizen an equal allotment of public land and servants called helots to work it.[26] The rent determined by the *pólis* and paid in kind by these dependent peasants was sufficient to support a small household,[27] and the labor of this depressed class made it possible for the Spartans to devote their time and efforts to mastering the martial arts and to gaining that confidence which fortifies civil courage.[28] When asked why they placed their fields in the hands of the helots and did not cultivate the soil themselves, one Spartan is said to have replied that "it was not by caring for the fields but by caring for ourselves that we came to possess those fields."[29] Centuries after the city's decline, Josephus would look back and remark that "these men neither tilled the soil nor toiled at the crafts—but freed from labor and sleek with the palaestra's oil, they exercised their bodies for beauty's sake and passed their time in the *pólis*. To take care of all the needs of life, they employed other men as servants and drew ready nourishment from these. And they were ready to do all and suffer all for this one accomplishment—noble and dear to human kind—that they might prevail over all against whom they marched."[30] While the ordinary Greek city was a community of peasants, Lacedaemon was a legion of men-at-arms.

She was also an aristocracy of masters, a city of seigneurs, a commonwealth of leisured gentlemen.[31] The Spartans called themselves *hoi hómoioi*: "the equals, the similars, the peers."[32] In a sense, they were equal. By means of the land grants, the *pólis* abolished the distinction between "those who hold and those who are without property" at all and thereby eliminated "the most common and durable source of factions."[33] Some of the soil did stay in private hands;[34] but although there remained a "various and unequal distribution of property," the gap between rich and poor was not great. As men of property, the Spartans had essentially the same interests.

To remove any lingering doubts, the city exercised close control over the education of children and the daily comportment of the citizens.[35] The rich and the poor grew up together, subject to the same regimen,[36] and they took their meals together in the common mess (*sussitía*) thereafter, partaking of the simple fare.[37] The giving of dowries was strictly forbidden,[38] but women were able to inherit private property;[39] so, the magistrates were empowered to fine those who paid more attention to opulence than to virtue in matters of love and marriage.[40] To the same end, there were severe sumptuary laws to deny the great families the public display and use of their riches.[41] An exception was made for the breeding and racing of horses,[42] but this served a military function; and the ordinary citizen was allowed the free use of the slaves, horses, and hounds of his wealthier fellows-in-arms.[43] As Thucydides, Xenophon, and Aristotle all emphasize, the Spartans shared a common way of life.[44]

Those with scanty resources apart from the civic allotment may still have felt envy—but if so, it was a jealousy dampened by fear. The helots who tilled the soil were a permanent threat to the city's survival.[45] The "old helots" descended from the ancient Achaean stock resided near their masters within Laconia and gave every appearance of being docile. In time of need, some from among them were even freed and recruited as hoplites into the army of Lacedaemon.[46] Those seized when the Thebans invaded Laconia in 370/

369 B.C. were so thoroughly broken in spirit that, when their captors asked them to sing the verses of Terpander, Alcman, and Spendon the Laconian, they resolutely refused to do what their Spartiate masters did not allow.[47] And yet—when the opportunity presented itself—many of these Laconian helots nonetheless proved to be fully capable of rebellion.[48] Aristotle rightly speaks of them as a hostile force "continuously lying in wait for misfortune" to strike.[49] And in this regard they were by no means alone: throughout much of the archaic and nearly all of the classical period, the Spartans controlled not just Laconia, but the neighboring province of Messenia as well. The latter region was fertile and well watered but extremely difficult of access, shut off as it was from Laconia's Eurotas valley by the rugged peaks of Mt. Taygetus. There, where the Spartans themselves were few, the helots were numerous, conscious of their identity as a separate people, bitterly hostile to their masters, and prone to revolt.[50] The danger posed by the helots of Laconia and perhaps even that posed by those in Messenia might have been managed with relative ease had Lacedaemon lacked foes abroad, but unfortunately for her that was not the situation: on Sparta's northeastern border, the ancient enemy Argos, a large and powerful city, stood poised, watching and waiting to take advantage of any disaster that might strike.[51] Even in the best of times, the helots of the two regions outnumbered their masters by a margin of seven-to-one or more;[52] and in an emergency, the Spartans could never be fully confident that their allies would rally to their cause. The "dwellers-about (*períoikoi*)," the class of non-Spartiate Lacedaemonians who resided in the subject villages of Laconia and Messenia and retained in privilege a measure of local autonomy, may generally have been loyal—but only out of fear.[53] And the city's allies elsewhere within the Peloponnesus were often disaffected and sometimes in open revolt.[54]

One Corinthian leader summed up Sparta's strategic position elegantly by comparing her to a stream. "At their sources," he noted, "rivers are not great and they are easily forded, but the farther on they go, the greater they get—for other rivers empty into them and make the current stronger." So it is with the Spartans, he continued. "There, in the place where they emerge, they are alone; but as they continue and gather cities under their control, they become more numerous and harder to fight." The prudent general, he concluded, will seek battle with the Spartans in or near Lacedaemon where they are few in number and relatively weak.[55] The structure of Sparta's defenses was fragile in the extreme, and the Lacedaemonians understood from the beginning what history was eventually to reveal: that it took but a single major defeat in warfare on land to endanger the city's very survival.[56]

As a consequence of the community's strategic situation, fear was the fundamental Spartan passion.[57] It was fear that explained why Lacedaemon was notoriously slow to go to war,[58] and it was fear that accounted for the remarkable caution that she so conspicuously displayed on the field of battle.[59] This omnipresent fear lay behind her flagrant inability in matters of state to distinguish the dictates of interest from the biddings of honor,[60] and it was fear that made the distrust and the deceit that governed her relations with other communities so pronounced and so glaring.[61] Fear, the great equalizer, rendered the Spartan regime conservative, stable, and—despite the survival of a wealthy, landed aristocracy—socially harmonious. The Spartans were well aware of this fact: as Plutarch remarks, they established a temple to *Phóbos*— not to ward off panic in battle, but because they recognized that fear held the polity together.[62] The Spartans had to be friends: as members of a garrison community, they desperately needed each other.

That awareness of need the Spartans magnified by sentiment. Because piety was understood to be the foundation of patriotism, Spartans were from an early age imbued with a fear of the gods so powerful that it distinguished them from their fellow Greeks.[63] Plato had a better understanding of this than anyone since. With the promotion of civic virtue in mind, he wrote, "One of the finest of [Sparta's] laws is the law that does not allow any of the young to inquire which of the laws are finely made and which are not, but that commands all to say in harmony, with one voice from one mouth, that all the [city's] laws are finely made by gods."[64] Sophocles' Menelaus speaks for Sparta when he asserts,

> Not in a city would the laws ever succeed unless dread (*déos*) was there established; nor would an army ever show restraint and be ruled (*sóphronos árchoit' éti*) unless it had a protective screen of fear and of awe (*aidoûs*). And even if a man develops great strength, he should be of the view that he can be felled by an evil quite small. For, where there is dread together with shame (*aischúnē*), know that you have safety. But where it is permitted to be arrogant (*hubrízein*) and to do whatever one wishes, be aware that such a city will run before favorable winds and finally into the deep. For me let there be a seasonable dread.[65]

Reverence and dread came easily to a people living in fear. More effectively than any other Greek city, Sparta used superstition to reinforce that total obedience to the law which constituted civic virtue.[66]

Superstition was by no means the only force employed. The Spartans gave to the citizens the same opinions and fostered in them the same passions by means of the *agōgē*, their much-celebrated educational system.[67] When a male child reached the age of seven, he was taken from his mother, classified as a *paîs*, and added to a herd of boys his age.[68] When he returned home thereafter, he returned as a visitor: his true home was to be the community of his contemporaries. In this new home, he would learn to think of himself not as an individual, nor as a member of a particular household, but as a part of the community. Apart from that community, he was nothing.[69]

In the herd, the boys were subjected to a regimen of exercise interspersed with sessions dedicated to learning the communal dances, the poetry, and the songs of Sparta.[70] Because endurance and craft were necessary for success when on campaign, they were inured to pain, hardship, and short rations; for additional sustenance, they were forced to steal, and those who were caught were severely punished.[71] Because physical stamina and the ability to march to the music of the flute were required for victory in hoplite warfare, they were encouraged to compete in athletics, in mock battles, in dancing, and in musical contests.[72] Music was, in fact, central to Spartan life.[73] That much is clear from Pindar's brief celebration of Lacedaemon: for the Theban poet praises Sparta not only for the prudence of her leaders and the achievements of her warriors, but also for her prowess in the arts.

> There the Counsels of the Elders
> And the Spears of the Young Men are the Best
> And the Choirs and the Muse and the Splendor.[74]

Pindar was not peculiar in linking these notions. By his day, this depiction of Sparta had come to have a familiar ring. Two centuries earlier, when the Karneia was purportedly first held, Terpander of Lesbos had written of Lacedaemon that "there the spears of young men blossom, and music with a clear tone, and justice in the broad streets—ally of noble deeds."[75] Later in the seventh century, Alcman had sounded much the same theme, describing Sparta as a place where "playing the cithara well rivals the wielding of iron swords."[76] By the end of the archaic period, the Lacedaemonian zest for music had become proverbial. "The cicada," wrote Pratinus of Phlius, "is a Laconian: ever ready for a chorus."[77]

This phenomenon deserves respectful attention, for it would be a mistake to underestimate the integrating force of the choral performances, the dancing, and the other public rituals that marked the Karneia, the Gymnopaidiai, and the other great festivals of Sparta.[78] Terpander is himself credited with having brought an end to civil strife in the city, and Plutarch suggests that music in general played a vital role in the prevention of *stásis*.[79] Moreover, when Pindar attributed to the poet indebted to Apollo and inspired by the Muse an ability to "infuse into [the citizens'] hearts and minds that good order and lawfulness which frees men from war (*apólemon agagṑn es prapí-*

das eunomían)," Sparta was the city that he had foremost in mind.[80] Though the Lacedaemonians neglected the technical study of this art, Aristotle tells us, they claimed an expertise in distinguishing songs that were serviceable from those that were not.[81] The standard depiction of the Spartan way of life as grim and forbidding no doubt has a great deal of merit, but such a depiction can scarcely do full justice to the place of honor which the Lacedaemonians accorded sports, music, and the dance. As virtually all who have been comrades-in-arms can easily testify, the army camp does have its own peculiar charms.[82]

To grasp the true nature of Spartan life, one must ponder the connection of music with war. The poetry which the Lacedaemonians taught their young was vital for the overall process of indoctrination through which they sought to achieve that total subordination of the individual to the community which the law commanded.[83]

I . v . 3

It is not easy for the citizens of modern, liberal republics to imagine, much less assess, the influence which poetry exercised over the Lacedaemonians. For the most part, modern political life is prosaic, and our literature reflects little but private concerns. At best, it exists—or at least is generally thought to exist—on the margins of the larger public world. As a result, we tend to forget that there was a time when this was not the case at all. Without Dante, there would arguably never have been an Italian people. Luther's translation of the Bible shaped not only the German language but the generations of men and women who were to speak it. Much the same could be said of the impact of the King James Bible and Shakespeare on English and the English-speaking peoples. To begin to grasp the importance which poetry had at Sparta, we must remember that it was once considered the supreme form of rhetoric—a form with more immediate power and far greater longevity than ordinary writing and speech.

Though utterly foreign to us, this understanding of the dignity of poetry was still very much alive when Goethe remarked to his companion Eckermann that

> if a great dramatic poet is at the same time productive and occupied by
> a powerful, noble way of thinking, which runs through all his works,
> he may achieve the result that the soul of his plays becomes the soul of
> the people. I should think that this would be something well worth the
> trouble. From Corneille proceeded an influence capable of forming the
> souls of heroes. This was a matter of no small consequence for Napoleon,

who had need of a heroic people; for this reason, he said of Corneille that, if he were still alive, he would make him a prince. A dramatic poet who knows his intended purpose should therefore work without ceasing at its higher development in order that his influence on the people may be beneficial and noble.[84]

As the example set by Dante, Luther, and those who composed the King James Bible suggests, Goethe's claim can be applied not just to drama but to poetry in general—and similarly to a prose so elevated in tone that it transcends the form. The Greeks shared Goethe's conviction. That is why they habitually employed the same word—*idiótēs*—to point out both the private individual and the writer of ordinary prose. In their world, political life was anything but prosaic, and for them, poetry was the public speech par excellence. As the Greeks recognized, the propagation of the works of a particular poet had public consequences of untold importance.[85] The soul of Spartan verse was to become the soul of the Spartan people.

Of the examples of Spartan poetry surviving in his own time, Plutarch remarked, "They were for the most part eulogies of those who had died on Sparta's behalf, celebrating their happiness; censure of those who had fled in battle, depicting their painful and unfortunate lives; and professions and boasts of virtue of a sort proper for the different age-groups."[86] Although the Spartans were quite familiar with *The Iliad* of Homer and *The Odyssey*, they are said to have regarded these works as depicting the Ionian, not the Laconian way of life.[87] There is, in fact, no indication that the young Spartan followed the normal Greek practice of memorizing extended passages selected from Homer; he seems, instead, to have concentrated on the verses of Tyrtaeus.[88] When on campaign, the Spartans would chant this poet's songs as they marched.[89] In the evening after dinner, they would first raise the paean, and then each, in turn, would sing something by Tyrtaeus—with the polemarch acting as judge and awarding extra meat to the victor.[90]

The poetry of Tyrtaeus did much to reinforce the exaggerated piety that was the foundation of Spartan morale. In one of his poems, the bard praised Lacedaemon as a law-abiding community, well-ordered, possessing what the Greeks called *eunomía*. In a passage replete with allusions to oracles, to prophecy, and to men dear to the gods, he justified the Spartans' control over their vast domain by an appeal to divine right, singing,

> The son of Kronos, husband to splendidly crowned Hera,
> Zeus himself gave this city to the sons of Heracles,
> The men with whom we made our journey, when we left
> Windy Erineus for the broad isle of Pelops.[91]

For the Heraclid kings and their Dorian followers, the Eurotas valley was precisely what Israel had been for Moses and the Jews of the exodus. Laconia was a fertile and well-watered territory ripe for the taking. Like Canaan, it was "a good land, a land of brooks of water, of fountains and depths that spring out of valleys and hills; a land of wheat, and barley, and vines, and fig trees, and pomegranates; a land of oil, olive, and honey."[92] The Eurotas valley was all this and more. For a people reared on Tyrtaeus, Laconia was nothing less than the promised land.

In another passage, almost certainly drawn from the same work, Tyrtaeus attributed Sparta's political order not to human action, but to the intervention of the gods, tracing its origins to advice sought from the oracle of Apollo. Of a trip undertaken to Delphi by Sparta's two kings, the poet wrote,

> Having listened to Phoebus, they carried home from Pytho
> Oracles of the god and words certain of fulfillment:
> "To rule in council is reserved for the god-honored kings,
> To whom the lovely city of Sparta is entrusted as a care.
> It is reserved also for the *gérontas*, men elder in birth.
> Then the commoners, making reply with straightforward decrees,
> Shall speak and accomplish all that is noble and just,
> Not giving to the city a counsel that is crooked.
> So shall victory and power attend the multitude of the *dêmos*.
> For thus has Phoebus spoken of these things to the *pólis*."[93]

By trusting in the authority of Tyrtaeus, the Spartans could rest assured that they had the same divine sanction for the organization of their community that they possessed for their acquisition of the southeastern Peloponnesus.

Tyrtaeus's poetry was evidently wide ranging. In one of the small handful of surviving fragments, he celebrated Sparta's original conquest of Messenia; in two others, he alluded to the fate suffered by her helots. The members of this servile class were not simply men "distressed with great burdens like asses, carrying to their masters under painful necessity half of all the fruit that the fields bear." They suffered insult in addition to injury, for they were forced "themselves (and their bedfellows likewise) to mourn for their masters" when one such encountered "the sad fate of death."[94] The poet presumably had more to say on the subject. He may even have gone on to describe the manner in which the Spartans ritually reinforced the boundary between master and servant by deliberately humiliating the helots—making them appear in public in a costume suggesting their kinship with animals, whipping them at regular intervals for no apparent reason, getting them disgustingly drunk, and even requiring that they sing degrading songs. The presence of a servile class, the derisive treatment to which its members were forced to submit, and the manner in which they actually comported them- selves—these contributed much to the education of the Spartan young. As Tyrtaeus seems to have recognized at the start, the helots were a permanent reminder to the Spartans of their own exalted status and a warning of the fate that might be theirs if they failed to justify their claim to superiority and dominion by victory on the field of battle.[95]

Young Spartans could hardly fail to appreciate the point. While undergoing the *agōgḗ*, they occupied a liminal status intermediate between that of the helots and that of the *hómoioi*, and they sampled both worlds. Much was done to remind them of the distance separating them from the Spartiates and to suggest at least the possibility of their kinship with those already set perma- nently apart as their fathers' inferiors. The hair of these young Spartans was short-cropped, not long. They slept under the stars rather than in the men's house or with the women at home. Like country bumpkins, they were filthy and rarely bathed, and they wore no tunic (*chitōn*), just a cloak (*himátion*), which was replaced but once a year. Like calves and colts, by which names they were known, they were gathered in herds (*agélai*) under the direction of herdsmen (*Bouagoí*). But like foxes and wolves living on the margins of a village or town, they stole food from the men's mess. If these boys learned the martial dances for which Lacedaemon was famous, that was apparently not all: for, adorned with masks, they are thought to have performed a great variety of less dignified dances—some terrifying, some comic, some obscene, some violent. And if we can trust the scattered testimonia and the evidence provided by the surviving ex-voto terracotta masks, they mimed not just men but animals, satyrs, and grotesque members of the female sex. These Spartan youths were sometimes armed, but only with weapons of the sort issued to helots on campaign: for the hoplite panoply was reserved for citizen-men. Like the helots of Tyrtaeus, these neophytes were distressed with toil (*pónos*); and like that subject race, they had ample experience of the whip. They suffered flagellation if judged soft or fat. They were flogged if caught stealing food. In one famous ritual, which was solemnly reenacted as an ordeal each year, two groups of boys waged battle about the shrine of Artemis Orthia: one intent on running off with the cheeses piled high on the altar, the other wielding whips in defense of the agricultural products prepared for the virgin goddess. If these young Spartans repeatedly endured injuries and insults like those to which the helots were subjected, it was to establish—by the fact that they were utterly unfazed—their worthiness to pass on from the threshold and join the ranks of free men.[96]

The bulk of Tyrtaeus's poetry dealt neither with just conquest nor with the proper form for organizing rule nor even with the suffering inflicted on the helots. He composed his verse in the middle of the seventh century— much of it during the Second Messenian War, when the Spartans fought dog- gedly to recover the rich province they had acquired on the western side of Mt. Taygetus some two generations before. Tyrtaeus's principal subject was not peace, but war. In one of his hortatory elegies, he drew the attention of his compatriots to the manner in which their well-being depended on the fate of the city itself.

> It is a noble thing for a brave man to die,
> Falling in the front ranks, doing battle for the fatherland.
> But for a man to forsake his city and his rich fields
> And to go begging is of all things the most grievous
> As he wanders with his dear mother and his aged father,
> With his small children and his lawful, wedded wife.
> For he is hated by those among whom he goes as a suppliant
> Yielding to need and loathsome penury;
> He disgraces his lineage; he refutes his splendid appearance,
> And every dishonor and evil follows in his train.
> Now if no heed is paid to a wandering man
> And neither reverence nor regard nor pity is his,
> Let us then fight with spirit for our land and children
> And let us die, not sparing our lives.

In the young men posted in the phalanx's front ranks, the poet sought to in- still what he called "a spiritedness great and firm." He encouraged them not to hold life dear as they did battle with the foe; he exhorted them to stand closely bunched; and he warned them never "to make a start of fear and shameful flight." There is something splendid, he argued, about the death in battle of a young man, blessed with the bloom of youth, admired by his fellows and beloved of women. But there is no sight quite as disgraceful and none as horrid as that of a greybeard fallen in the front ranks, "sprawled on the earth before the young men, breathing out his life in the dust, and clasp- ing his hands to a bloodied groin." The Spartan king Leonidas reportedly spoke of Tyrtaeus as "a good poet for stirring up the young (*néoi*)." It is not difficult to see why.[97]

In a similar poem, Tyrtaeus reminded his compatriots of their descent from "Heracles the unconquered." There, he urged them to treat "life as some- thing hateful" and to hold "the black ruin of death as dear as the beams of the sun."

Of those who dare to stand by one another and to march
Into the van where the fighting is hand to hand,
Rather few die, and they protect the host behind.
But for the men who are tremblers all virtue is lost.
No one can describe singly in words nor count the evils
That come to a man once he has suffered disgrace.
For in dread war it is alluring to pierce from behind
The back of a man in headlong flight,
And disgraceful is the corpse laid out in the dust,
Thrust through from behind by the point of a spear.

After issuing this admonition, the poet urged each of the hoplites to close with, wound, and take out his foe. "Placing foot against foot, shield against shield, crest against crest, helm against helm, and chest against chest, let him struggle with the man, grasping the handle of his sword or the long spear." [98]

Tyrtaeus's debt to Homer was enormous. That much is obvious from his diction alone. But despite all that he owed his great predecessor, the Spartan poet rejected the Homeric precedent and radically altered the heroic ethic. Tyrtaeus did not glorify that Achilles who had valued his own honor above the interest of the Achaean host; nor did he celebrate the exploits of Odysseus "the man of many ways" who wandered through "the cities of many men and learned their minds." He heaped praise not on the great individual who sought "to be the best and to excel all others," but on the citizen who never traveled abroad except on campaign and who fought gamely alongside his companions in the city's hoplite phalanx. [99]

To make his point in the boldest possible fashion, Tyrtaeus turned to the mythological tradition. To bring home to his listeners the inadequacy of the traditional understanding of human excellence, he provided them with a list of legendary individuals who exhibited qualities and faculties universally admired but who nonetheless performed in a fashion that called into question the esteem conventionally conferred on those very qualities and faculties. As the poet indicated in the priamel of his most famous work, there was only one trait truly worthy of celebration:

I would not call to mind a man nor relate a tale of him
Not for the speed of his feet nor for his wrestling skill
Not if he possessed the stature and force of a Cyclops
And could outpace Boreas, the North Wind of Thrace
Not if he were more graceful in form than Tithonos
And exceeded Midas and Cinyras in wealth

Not if he were more fully a king than Tantalid Pelops
And possessed the soft-voiced tongue of Adrastus
Not if he had reputation for all but prowess in battle.[100]

Quickness, agility, brute strength, physical beauty, the golden touch, regal
bearing, and even the eloquence evidenced by the poet himself—though
men longed for these, they were of little import when distinguished from
and compared with capacity in war.

To support this revolutionary notion, Tyrtaeus introduced a new, fully
political standard for measuring the merit of men. No longer would the Spartans assess a man's status by anything other than his contribution to the
welfare of the *pólis* as a whole. After dismissing those qualities which were
so widely thought to be virtues, the poet went on to explain,

For no one ever becomes a man good in war
Unless he has endured the sight of the blood and slaughter,
Stood near, and lunged for the foe.
This is virtue, the finest prize achieved among human kind,
The fairest reward that a young man can carry off.
This is a common good, shared by the entire city and people,
When a man stands his ground, remains in the front ranks
Relentlessly, altogether forgetful of disgraceful flight,
Nurturing a steadfast, patient spirit and soul,
And heartening with words the man posted alongside.
This is a man become good in war:
With a sudden attack, he turns the rugged phalanx
Of the enemy host, sustaining with zeal the wave of assault.[101]

Tyrtaeus was the supreme poet of civil courage. The virtue he admired with
so passionate an intensity is the particular excellence of the man who sub-
ordinates not just his own mundane concerns but even his ambition and his
yearning for immortal fame to the larger and enduring needs of the community at large. It would be tempting to conclude that Tyrtaeus simply preferred
Hector to Achilles and Odysseus. But it is virtually certain that the Spartan
poet would have faulted the Trojan champion for the foolish pride evident
in his rejection of Priam's appeal to prudence and in his decision to meet
Achilles alone in single combat apart from the forces of Troy.[102]

To reinforce his celebration of bravery in the city's cause, Tyrtaeus added
encouragement and an admonition—for, in the end, justice was to be done:
the brave would be rewarded, and the coward punished. Even death would
lose its sting. What made this achievement possible was not the activity of the

poet in calling to mind the feats of the heroes. Here, too, Tyrtaeus broke with Homer. If death was to rule no more, it was because of the public memory guaranteed by the continued existence of the *pólis* itself. While ordinary Spartans were buried in a manner both simple and frugal,[103] the city's champions were treated like those honored in its hero cults:[104]

> And he who falls in the front ranks and gives up his spirit
> So bringing glory to the town, the host, and his father
> With many a wound in his chest where the spear from in front
> Has been thrust through the bossy shield and breastplate:
> This man they will lament with a grievous sense of loss
> The young and the old and the city entire.
> His tomb and his children will be noted among human kind
> And the children of his children and his lineage after them.
> Never will his shining glory perish, and never his name,
> For he will be an immortal though under the earth, the man
> Who excels all others in standing his ground in the fight
> For his children and land, he whom the raging Wargod destroys.[105]

Tyrtaeus then devoted the final ten lines of this remarkable poem to recounting the honors that were customarily showered on those brave men fortunate enough to survive.[106] By the end, it has become evident that courage in battle confers on a man all of the advantages normally attributed to the qualities and faculties conventionally admired.

> But if he eludes the doom of death, which lays bodies out,
> And, conquering, seizes by spearpoint the shining object of prayer
> All will honor him, the young together with the old,
> And he will enter Hades after enjoying many delights
> Having grown old in distinction among the men of the town.
> Nor will any wish him harm, denying him reverence or right.
> And all—the young, those his own age, and those
> Older than he—will yield him place on the seats.
> This virtue a man should attempt with whole heart to attain,
> Straining for the heights and never ceasing from war.[107]

This was a communal poetry fit for the education of citizen-soldiers who would be expected to spend their lives at home in Laconia and to risk them abroad on the city's behalf. The Spartans committed these and similar verses to memory and recited them about the campfire and while on the march for the same reason that they prepared for combat in ritual fashion by combing out their long hair and donning cloaks of royal purple.[108] Like the wine which the Lacedaemonians customarily imbibed before battle, like the strains of the flute which accompanied their steady march into combat, and like the paean which they chanted as they closely approached the enemy phalanx, the songs of Tyrtaeus were an intoxicant intended to reduce tension, dull pain, and make men—at least momentarily—forget the specter of death.[109] With the city's poets in mind, Plutarch suggests, the Spartan king would sacrifice to the Muses at the onset of battle. His purpose was to remind Lacedaemon's warriors to accomplish feats worthy to be remembered by the city in song.[110]

I. v. 4

The young men who survived the *agōgē* and became Spartans were a highly select group.[111] On their journey to manhood, they had been subjected to a formal magisterial scrutiny (*dokımasía*) at regular intervals: initially, at birth; then, probably, as boys (*hoı paîdes*) at seven and twelve; again, as youths (*hoı paıdískoı*) at eighteen; and finally, at twenty, when they joined the young warriors variously called *hoı hēbôntes* and *hoı néoı*.[112] As a *paîs* approached adolescence and, then, the threshold of manhood, his physical training became more and more rigorous and the tests of his strength and courage more and more severe.[113] The final test, the period of concealment (*krupteía*), appears to have taken place when he was a *paıdískos* approaching his twentieth birthday. For a full year, the young man withdrew from the community and was thrown back entirely on his own resources. Armed with a dagger, he hid in the wilds during the day, only to emerge at night to secure provisions by theft and to kill any helots found roaming about after curfew. The *krupteía* helped head off servile rebellion, and it functioned as a rite of passage marking the boy's initiation into manhood.[114] His performance in this ordeal might determine his fate: he could become a citizen only if he submitted to the Spartan regimen, successfully completed the *agōgē*, and was accepted into a *sussıtía*.[115]

Composed of about fifteen men of all ages,[116] the *sussıtía* was an elite men's club, a cult organization, and, at the same time, the basic unit in the Spartan army.[117] If a single member found a candidate objectionable and blackballed him, the young man would be denied entrance.[118] If admitted, he would dine for the rest of his life in what one ancient writer called "a small polity (*políteuma*) of sorts," [119] eating what his companions ate and drinking only a moderate portion of wine, discreetly discussing public affairs and more private concerns, gently teasing his comrades, and otherwise comporting himself always in the dignified, respectful fashion which the old demand of the young and the young nearly always expect from the old.[120] Until he was forty-five, except when he was on active service abroad or doing garrison duty elsewhere in Laconia or Messenia,[121] he would spend his nights in the men's house of his *sussitía* or camped under the stars "with the other young men (*metà tôn állōn néōn*)."[122]

The rationale behind these arrangements was perfectly evident to the shrewdest of the ancient observers. "In time of peace," Dionysius of Halicarnassus remarked, the *sussitía* "greatly aided the city by leading men towards frugality and moderation (*sōphrosúnē*) in their daily lives." That advantage he thought important, but not decisive. The Spartan institution accomplished something of at least equal, if not greater importance. "In time of war," Dionysius explained, "it instilled in every man a sense of reverential shame (*aidôs*) and a prudential concern (*pronoía*) that he not desert the man posted beside him in the city's battle line (*parastátēs*)—for this man was a comrade with whom he had made libations, conducted sacrifices, and shared in common rites."[123] At Lacedaemon, the pressure to perform never let up.

In fact, acceptance into a *sussitía* marked not the end of competition, but its intensification. From among the *hēbôntes* who had reached the height of their powers (*ek tôn akmazóntōn*)—Spartiates who had survived the *krupteía*, joined a men's mess, and distinguished themselves in service to the city in peace and war—every year the magistrates chose as *hippagrétai* the three whom they judged the ablest. Each of the three then had the privilege of electing from among their fellow *hēbôntes* a battalion of precisely one hundred men. In every case, he had to specify why a particular individual was chosen and another excluded. The three hundred select men were called the *hippeîs*, and it was their duty and privilege to accompany the king into battle and to fight by his side. After the initial choice was made, each of those within this royal bodyguard had to defend—sometimes by force—not just the exalted status of his elite unit, but also his own particular right to membership in it. There was, in short, an unending competition with all among the *hēbôntes* who had been denied the honor of admission.[124]

A further rivalry existed within the ranks of the royal bodyguard itself. When a man reached the age of forty-five, he graduated from the class of *néoi* and was therefore no longer eligible to serve among the *hippeîs*. The five members of the graduating class who had most distinguished themselves during their years of service as *hippeîs* were then singled out, given the honorific title "doers of good (*agathoergoí*)," and made available to the *pólis* and the magistrates for a full year as special agents prepared to take on any mission that might be deemed appropriate.[125] Thereafter, they would permanently rejoin the *sussitía* to which they had been elected so many years before. Only at this stage in life, when a Spartan had joined the ranks of the older men (*hoi presbúteroi*), did he become eligible to serve as *paidonómos* and to hold what Xenophon called "the greatest offices (*hai mégistai archaî*)" of the city.[126]

In general, when a boy became a man, his *sussitía* supplanted the herd as his true home. His ties to his parents, his wife, and his children were intended to be weak: he had left his mother's care and had been removed from his father's authority when he was seven; and although he was expected to take a spouse well before he reached the age of forty-five and was subjected to civic disabilities and to rituals of harassment and humiliation if he failed to do so, he would not as a husband then live with his wife. During the initial period of their marriage, shame and dread governed the comportment of the couple. The *néos* visited his bride's bedroom in secret at night, and all their relations were conducted under the cover of darkness.[127] The Spartan might beget a child. But at least until he had himself joined the *presbúteroi*, he would not live within his own household; and even then, his sons would depart from that household at a tender age. As Plutarch remarked, the institution of marriage existed at Sparta solely for the procreation of children.[128]

The tendency evident in these arrangements was exacerbated by the Spartan practice of pederasty.[129] In Lacedaemon, the *erómenoi* were neither shy nor coy: when a boy reached the age of twelve, he aggressively sought out and eagerly took an older lover (*erastês*) who would be his patron, his protector, his friend.[130] This was not just a practice sanctioned by custom; as among the tribesmen of Australia and Melanesia, it was a political institution. It was not only the case that a boy lacking lovers was an object of disdain: a young man of distinguished background could, in fact, be severely punished by the magistrates for refusing to select a *paidiká* or for preferring a wealthy boy to one of virtuous character; and as a surrogate father, the *erastês* would be held personally responsible for the behavior of the boy that he chose.[131] The Spartans dubbed the *erastês* an *eispnélas* or "breather-in," apparently because they believed that, by his example and probably by insemination, the *eispnélas* could breathe manliness and courage into his charge.[132] It was his task to prepare the boy for his duties as a citizen and soldier, and he was probably expected to ease his *paidiká*'s admission into a *sussitía*. When this was accomplished, the younger of the two would in turn become an *eispnélas* himself and take on a surrogate son, abandoning the passive for the active homosexual role as the entire process repeated itself in accord with the elaborate rituals and rules of decorum that governed its course. Finally, when the time came for marriage, the young man carried off his bride in a ritual abduction, then left briefly to dine with his mess, and returned to find her waiting in the dark, dressed in the cloak of a man, her hair cut short in the style of a boy.[133] For some, this transvestism no doubt eased what must have been an awkward transition to heterosexuality.[134]

The institution of pederasty did not preclude affection between husband and wife,[135] but it seems to have been designed to ensure that the emotional ties to the homosexual be stronger than those to the subsequent heterosexual partner. The ultimate purpose was that a young man's loyalty be fixed neither on the parents he had left, nor on the wife and son he so rarely saw, but rather on his *erastés* and *paidiká*: in normal circumstances, both were apparently members of his *sussitía*;[136] and as a consequence, the two would usually be stationed in his immediate vicinity, if not on either side of him in the battle formation.[137] It is not fortuitous that the Spartans customarily sacrificed to Eros before drawing up their phalanx. They apparently thought that victory and their safety would depend on the love that united the men about to be posted.[138]

The attempt to loosen familial ties was part of a larger scheme. The household was the chief obstacle to the city's complete psychological absorption of the individual. For the ordinary Greek, the *oîkos* represented a focus of loyalty independent of the community in arms; it provided him with an identity separate from his citizenship; and it consoled him, as his death approached, with the prospect of living on through his offspring. Essential though it may have been for the production and early rearing of children, this rival stood in the way of the city's giving "to every citizen the same opinions, the same passions, and the same interests." As long as men felt the desire to increase their property and to pass it on to their progeny, they would be at odds.

The social and economic arrangements at Sparta seem to have been aimed at suppressing the private element in human life, at making the Spartan an almost entirely public being by eliminating to the greatest degree possible the last refuge of privacy—the family. Thomas Jefferson came close to the truth when he borrowed Montesquieu's metaphor and called Spartan government "the rule of military monks."[139] Like a monastery, the city itself attempted to fill most of the functions elsewhere conceded to the household: it granted the citizen landed property and servants; it secured for him both surrogate father and surrogate son; and it provided him with bed, board, and lover, integrating him into the larger community by means of an all-male social unit of a size perfect for engaging and keeping his loyalties.[140] He spent his entire life in the public eye, being judged and praised or blamed by his fellows. For this reason, it is true to say that Sparta exercised greater control over her citizens than any regime that has existed anywhere else at any time. It exercised this control not through terror, but rather through the power of public opinion in a tiny, close-knit community that never included more than ten thousand male adults: a *pólis* in which everyone knew virtually everything that there was to know about everyone else.[141] The force of public opinion—powerful as it is in any small town—was magnified at Sparta by a set of institutional arrangements designed to make it fully dominant. The Spartans outlawed gold and silver coinage and encouraged homosexuality for the same reason. The *agōgē* and all that followed it were aimed at forming the completely public-spirited man—the man who would return from every battle with his shield or on it.[142]

No one understood this better than Herodotus. In *The Histories*, he represents the exiled Spartan king Demaratus as having been in attendance at a review of Xerxes' troops on the eve of the battle of Thermopylae. When Xerxes asks whether the Greeks would dare to resist Persia, Demaratus replies that the Spartans would fight to the end. He concludes by saying: "As for the Spartans, fighting each alone, they are as good as any, but fighting as a unit, they are the best of all men. They are free, but not completely free—for the law is placed over them as a master, and they fear that law far more than your subjects fear you. And they do whatever it orders—and it orders the same thing always: never to flee in battle, however many the enemy may be, but to remain in the ranks and to conquer or die."[143] The Spartan was to be brave and steadfast even in the face of certain death. That was the goal which the institutions of the Lacedaemonians attempted to achieve.

I . v . 5

There was, of course, a gap between ideal and performance. It is striking just how many Spartan anecdotes presuppose close ties between mother and son,[144] and it is very revealing that the Spartans were notorious for corruption when abroad and for being open to bribery when freed from the purview of their fellows.[145] This gap should not come as a surprise; it is what we would normally expect. Spartan institutions ran against the grain; as even Rousseau was forced to acknowledge, the attempt to suppress altogether the private element in human life required doing violence to human nature.[146] This is why the poet Simonides gave Lacedaemon the epithet "man-subduing (*damasímbroton*)."[147] It is impossible entirely to expunge the normal preference for one's own flesh and blood and to eliminate the universal desire of human beings to amass wealth as a hedge against hardship and as a legacy for their offspring.

To these propensities, the Spartans were themselves forced to give a grudging recognition. In describing the shortcomings of the Spartan regimen, Dionysius of Halicarnassus acknowledges that "the Lacedaemonians allowed those who were the oldest to strike with their canes citizens who were behaving in a disorderly fashion in any public place." But then he immediately adds that, in one critical respect, they were much more like the Athenians than the Romans: "They made no provision for and took no precaution against what might take place in the home; instead, they regarded the door to each man's house as a boundary stone marking out the sphere where he could conduct his life freely and as he wished."[148] The contradiction between desire and duty, between unaccommodated human nature and the needs of the *pólis*, and between a man's character as an individual and his status as a citizen—ultimately, the contradiction cannot be resolved. Try as one may, it remains as impossible to give a man entirely over to the community as it is to leave him entirely to himself.

The chief effect of the attempt at a suppression of the private element in human life was to make the pursuit of wealth dishonorable. But what the Spartans disdained in public they longed for when alone. Unlike the heavenly city of Plato's *Republic*, the Spartan regime did not eliminate private property and the family altogether. The Spartiate could distinguish between the children and the estate which belonged to him and the children and the estate which did not. He had a stake in protecting those children and in increasing that estate which brought him into conflict with his peers. This was the very conflict which the abolition of coinage, the encouragement of pederasty, the *agōgé*, and the *sussitía* were designed to expunge. The Lacedaemonian legislator sought to form a man who loved toil, victory, and honor—toil for the common cause, victory in the struggles of his people, and the honor which only his city and fellow citizens could confer on him.[149] The lawgiver sought to redirect, transform, and harness the spirit of competition to serve the city; he tried to replace as much as possible the love of one's own property and progeny and the hatred of those outside the family implicit in that attachment with the love of one's own city and citizens and the hatred of foreigners implicit in that commitment.

Plato rightly regarded this project as a partial failure. It produced men torn between their public duties and the private wants engendered by the remnants of the distinction between mine and thine. "Such men," he observed, "will long for money just as those in oligarchies do; and under the cover of darkness, like savages, they will pay honor to silver and gold."[150] The consequence was a Spartan disobedience of the law against the possession of gold and silver so widespread that there was "not in all of Hellas as much gold and silver as is held privately in Lacedaemon; through many generations, it has been entering that place from every part of Greece and often from the barbarians as well, but to no other place does it ever depart. As in the fable of Aesop, what the fox said to the lion is true: the tracks left by the money going into Lacedaemon are clear, but nowhere can one any see traces of it going back out."[151] To this result, the custom of treating a man's home as a realm truly private made a profound contribution. The Athenian philosopher speaks of the "magazines for storage and domestic treasuries" of the Spartiates, and he mentions the "walls surrounding their houses" which are "exactly like private nests where they can make great expenditures on women and on whomever else they might wish."[152]

Aristotle shared Plato's judgment of what the latter termed the timocratic regime. He took note of the sumptuary laws limiting the expense and specifying the character of funerals, and he was aware of the regulations governing the comportment of the women and denying them the right to let their hair grow long, to wear jewelry in public, and to otherwise adorn themselves.[153] But he thought these and the other similar *nómoi* grossly inadequate, and he contended that the Spartan legislator had, in fact, mixed "the love of honor" with "the love of money" and had thereby formed "private individuals covetous of wealth." Like Dionysius, the peripatetic philosopher attributed this, in part, to the absence of laws regulating the household. In particular, like Plato, he faulted Spartan institutions for their failure to bring under control "the women, who live intemperately in every kind of licence and luxury," observing that "the necessary consequence is that riches are held in honor, especially when the citizens fall under the rule of their women, as tends to happen among peoples devoted to soldiering and war. . . . The arrangements regarding the women not only introduce an air of unseemliness into the regime; they tend to foster avarice as well."[154] The Spartans may have been grudging when it came to making concessions to the private needs of mankind, but the concessions which they were forced to make nonetheless had an extraordinarily important effect. In fostering public-spiritedness, the Lacedaemonians went further than any other community before or since, but they inevitably fell far short of that at which they aimed. It is not at all surprising that Sparta eventually succumbed. Nor is there anything odd in the fact that she lost her hold on Messenia just over a generation after the ephor Epitadeus had persuaded his compatriots that it was perfectly proper for a citizen to be able to give or bequeath his public allotment of land to whomever he pleased.[155] From the outset, the Spartan *politeía* was fragile in the extreme, and the oracle which is said to have warned that "the love of money (*philochrēmatía*) and nothing else will destroy Lacedaemon" was right on the mark.[156]

I. v. 6

What is truly surprising, then, is not Sparta's ultimate failure but, rather, her long years of success. What was extraordinary was her capacity to produce public-spirited men. When Isocrates wrote that the Spartans "think nothing as capable of inspiring terror (*deinón*) as the prospect of being reproached (*tò kakôs akoúein*) by their fellow citizens," he was not just mouthing a cliche.[157] In 480, when Lacedaemon consulted the Delphic oracle on the eve of Persia's advance, she was told that a king must die if the city was to be saved. The Spartans did not shirk what was demanded, but dispatched Leonidas soon thereafter with the customary royal bodyguard of three hundred, taking care only to preserve the number of citizen households by enrolling as *hippeîs* to accompany the king none but mature men with surviving sons.[158] In sacrificing their lives for the city, Leonidas and his companions did no more than their compatriots expected.

According to the fourth-century Athenian orator Lycurgus, there was a law at Sparta "expressly stipulating that all those unwilling to risk their lives for the fatherland be put to death." The rationale behind the statute was straightforward. "The fear of one's fellow citizens is strong," Lycurgus explained. "It will force men to undertake risks when confronted with the city's enemies. For who, seeing that the traitor is punished with death, would desert the fatherland in its time of peril? And who, knowing that this would be the punishment awaiting him, would value his life contrary to the city's advantage?"[159]

One may justly wonder whether such a law existed or was even required. Xenophon makes it clear that in Lacedaemon cowards were formally expelled from the ranks of the *hómoioi*, then generally shunned;[160] and Plutarch tells us that they were subject to assault from passersby and that, as a sign of their degraded status, they were required to wear cloaks with colored patches and to go about unbathed with one cheek shaven and the other not.[161] Something of the sort was apparently the fate of the two members of the three hundred who missed dying at Thermopylae. One had been sent to Thessaly as a messenger: on returning to Sparta, he found himself in such disgrace that he hanged himself. The other had a similar excuse, suffered similar reproach, and was expelled from his *sussitía* and deprived of his political rights. No Spartan would give him a brand to kindle his fire; no one would speak to him; and echoing Tyrtaeus's description of those who sacrificed all virtue by wavering in battle, the Lacedaemonians called him "the trembler." In due course, he too chose to commit suicide. Within the field of vision of the entire army at Plataea, this man thrust himself forward alone in front of the Spartan line against the spears of the oncoming Persians.[162]

The battle of Thermopylae was the most dramatic, but not the first such occasion. Well over a half-century before Leonidas's last stand, the Spartans had sent out on a special mission another three hundred picked men (perhaps the *hippeîs* this time as well). Their task was to defend the Lacedaemonian claim to the borderland Cynuria against Argos by defeating a like number of Argive champions. At the end of the battle, there was but one Spartan alive; and though his survival was the ground for Sparta's continuing claim to the disputed province, that very survival had rendered him suspect of cowardice. The man apparently found insupportable the prospect of living his life in disgrace, and he ultimately chose death instead.[163] At Lacedaemon, a life without honor in the eyes of one's fellow citizens was a life not worth living.

This ethic was still very much alive early in the fourth century when a regiment (*móra*) of Spartans suffered ambush in the Corinthiad near Lechaeum. That much is made strikingly clear by a passing remark in Xenophon's report. Early in the skirmish, a number of Spartans were wounded by javelins hurled by enemy peltasts; the polemarch immediately ordered that these men be carried to safety by the helots who ordinarily bore their shields. The remaining members of the *móra* were less fortunate: roughly two hundred and fifty hoplites lost their lives in the encounter, while only a handful managed to flee, some by plunging into the sea and others by seeking refuge with the cavalry. To the latter, Xenophon gives remarkably short shrift. In speaking of those who had been wounded and then borne to Lechaeum, he observes, "In truth, these were the only members of the *móra* who were saved." It mattered not a whit that the battle had already been lost when the other survivors took to heel. Any Spartan who managed to preserve his life by taking refuge in flight was classed as a trembler. As such, he might as well have been dead.[164]

The enviable reputation that they had earned greatly aided the Spartans in the conduct of war. By the same token, when these men failed to live up to that reputation, the event could have a devastating impact on the morale of the city and of its allies as well. In 425, when the Lacedaemonian contingent on the island of Sphacteria surrendered to the Athenians, a shudder ran through Greece. According to Thucydides, "The Hellenes supposed that the Lacedaemonians would never surrender their arms in response to starvation or to any other form of compulsion, but that they would instead hold fast to their weapons, fight to the best of their abilities, and so give up their lives. The Greeks simply could not believe that those who had surrendered were *hómoioi* like those who had died." To bring home to the prisoners the enormity of what they had done, one citizen of a community allied with Athens is said to have posed to one of the men captured on the island a simple question—whether "those of the Lacedaemonians who had died were not the *kaloì kagathoí*." The arrow, he was told in reply, that could pick out the brave men would be worth a great deal.[165]

The presence of tremblers in substantial numbers could pose a serious political problem for the Spartans. The men captured on Sphacteria returned home just a few years later after the Peace of Nicias had been ratified. Though the *pólis* suffered from an increasingly severe shortage of manpower, those taken prisoner in 425 were for a time deprived of their citizen rights. Some of the captives had come from families of particular prominence, and the citizens reportedly feared that out of bitterness at suffering disgrace these men would be eager to start a revolution. In due course, the Spartans reversed their decision, but a certain sense of awkwardness must have remained.[166]

The same problem presented itself again after the battle of Leuctra but this time in a fashion far more severe. For the Spartan army itself had on this occasion suffered a decisive defeat, and a very large proportion of the surviving adult male citizen population had been guilty of flight. To inflict on so many men the disabilities required by the law would be to risk revolution at a time when the city itself might be in danger of being destroyed. The king Agesilaus provided the solution, proposing simply that the laws be allowed to sleep for a day but that they be enforced thereafter with the same rigor as in the past.[167] Even then, the survivors could expect to be held in disgrace.

Xenophon tells us that the news of the disaster at Leuctra reached Lacedaemon on the last day of the festival of the Gymnopaidiai. Upon being informed, the ephors chose not to suspend the choral performance of the men which was then under way, but they did in due course report to the various families the names of those who had lost their lives. The women were instructed at this time to make no lament and to bear the calamity in silence. Xenophon's description of what followed reads like an eyewitness report. "On the next day," the Athenian observes, "it was possible to see those whose relatives were among the deceased walking about in the full light of day, their faces bright and beaming. But one saw few of those who had been told that their kin had survived, and these few were making their way with countenances sullen and dejected."[168] After a defeat in battle, the Spartans were more likely to mourn the living than the dead.

The ancients wondered at this spectacle, and so should we. The first and most important step that anyone can take in attempting to understand the structure of Spartan politics is the recognition that, of all the Greek cities,

Sparta went the furthest in promoting civil courage. By giving "to every citizen the same opinions, the same passions, and the same interests," her social and economic institutions were intended to foster that *homónoia* which Rousseau called the General Will.[169] Her political constitution served precisely the same function.

CHAPTER 6

The Structure of Politics in Classical Sparta

Nothing is better suited for the maintenance of mores than an extreme subordination of the young to the old. They are both restrained—the former by the respect they have for the old; and the latter by the respect they have for themselves.—Montesquieu

I.vi.1

Over a half-century ago, Lewis Namier prefaced his now-classic study *The Structure of Politics at the Accession of George III* with a brief discussion of the reasons why he had at least temporarily abandoned an attempt to write a narrative history of British public life in the age of the American Revolution. "Too much in eighteenth-century politics requires explaining," he explained.

> Between them and the politics of the present day there is more resemblance in outer forms and denominations than in underlying realities; so that misconception is very easy. There were no proper party organizations about 1760, though party names and cant were current; the names and the cant have since supplied the materials for an imaginary superstructure. A system of non-Euclidean geometry can be built up by taking a curve for basis instead of the straight line, but it is not easy for our minds to think consistently in unwonted terms; Parliamentary politics not based on parties are to us a non-Euclidean system, and similarly require a fundamental readjustment of ideas and, what is more, of mental habits. A general explanation registering the outstanding differences may be understood but cannot be properly assimilated; one has to steep oneself in the political life of a period before one can safely speak, or be sure of understanding its language.[1]

With the advantage of hindsight, one may reasonably question whether Namier actually managed in the end to sort out the politics of late eighteenth-century England. His failure no doubt owes much to the contempt he exhibited for what he calls "party names and cant" and to his resulting neglect of the central importance always occupied by opinion in political life. Even if one were seriously to entertain the absurd supposition that public figures rarely mean what they say and say what they mean, it is surely the case that their rhetoric is designed to secure the support of their listeners, and the need to retain that support inevitably places limits on the speakers' subsequent freedom of action.[2]

This objection should be noted and assimilated, then safely put aside, for much of what Namier had to say nonetheless remains apt, and his strictures against anachronistic reconstructions apply not just to public affairs in the Augustan age, but—with even greater force—to politics within the ancient cities of the Hellenes. To be sure, it would hardly be proper to speak of classical Greek politics as a non-Euclidean system; in fact, there may well be something to the view that the "new science of politics," pioneered by Hobbes, Harrington, and Locke and further developed by Montesquieu, Hume, and the American Founding Fathers, is a creation which bears a striking resemblance to a system of geometry "built up by taking a curve for basis instead of the straight line." As we shall see, the framers of the American Constitution certainly broke in their fundamental conception with premodern precedent.[3] But, though true, this begs the point to be made here—for, revolutionary though it once was, their application of this "new science of politics" has decisively shaped subsequent history and thereby our own expectations, and that fact may be the greatest obstacle to our comprehension of earlier times. It really is difficult for our minds to think in unwonted terms, and the attempt to understand the character of ancient political life does, in fact, require of us a fundamental readjustment of ideas and of mental habits as well. One might even say that one has to steep oneself in the political language of a period before one can safely describe or be sure of understanding its political structure.[4]

Adam Ferguson followed the correct procedure when he took the ancients at their word and prefaced his observations regarding the Spartan constitution with the remark that "we may easily account for the censures bestowed on the government of Sparta, by those who considered it merely on the side of its forms. It was not calculated to prevent the practice of crimes, by balancing against each other the selfish and partial dispositions of men; but to inspire the virtues of the soul, to procure innocence by the absence of criminal inclinations, and to derive its internal peace from the indifference of its members to the ordinary motives of strife and disorder."[5] Rousseau did the same when he drew attention to the absence of "partial societies" in ancient Sparta.[6]

There were, in fact, no organized political parties in any of the republics of archaic and classical Greece; there was no formed opposition. Indeed, prior to the appearance of Edmund Burke's *Thoughts on the Present Discontents*, which was published in the very period which elicited Namier's interest, partisanship and party government were all but universally held in bad odor. Of course, before that time, when emergencies had presented themselves, would-be statesmen had openly banded together in associations at least putatively aimed at preserving or restoring the traditional rights of the citizens and the ancestral constitution. But these alliances never acknowledged partisan purpose; they always claimed to speak for the whole and to be strictly defensive in character. In principle, they were intended to be temporary, for they were explicitly directed at eliminating the need for party divisions altogether. They would otherwise have had to present themselves as conspiracies—which was a characterization that they reserved for those against whom they had mounted their assault. Prior to 1770, no respectable figure had ever even dared to argue that party government, formed opposition, and a lasting division of the community into political parties could ever be condoned, much less merit esteem.[7]

In this respect, the Greeks were typical. The Greek language actually lacks a word to designate such a formed and lasting opposition.[8] In the *póleis* of ancient Hellas, men sometimes attached themselves to a recognized leader able to benefit them or committed to the cause they espoused; they did not join permanent associations, and—even when embroiled in conspiracy—they never publicly admitted to partisan design. The ancient authors acknowledge the political importance of the divisions defined by wealth and birth when they refer to "the many" and "the few," to "the commoners" and "the notables," to "the mob" and "the gentlemen."[9] But when they wish to identify the politically active groupings, these writers speak of "those about Thucydides," they mention "the friends of Pericles," and they offer remarks in a similar vein.[10]

Within this world, Lacedaemon formed something of an exception, and she did so in precisely the fashion which Adam Ferguson and Rousseau indicated. On the whole, the Spartans of the sixth and fifth centuries really do seem to have been indifferent to the *ordinary* motives of strife and disorder: the politically disruptive social divisions within the citizenry, which so afflicted the other Greek cities, were apparently unknown in Lacedaemon. In any case, we hear little of them. Their absence, however, did nothing to preclude the give and take of political struggle and the fleeting formation of factions around prominent figures.[11] There is no dearth of evidence for political disputation at Sparta.[12] The measures taken "to give to every citizen the same opinions, the same passions, and the same interests" might reduce the bitterness of controversy, but they could not eliminate it altogether. Despite the fundamental consensus regarding ends, the Spartans could always dispute over means; and although the regime sought to channel ambition (*philotimía*), it did nothing to stifle that breeder of quarrels.[13] Indeed, as Aristotle points out, it made the citizens "greedy for honor (*philótimoi*),"[14] and Plutarch is surely right when he contends that this was deliberate. "The Spartan legislator," he observes, "seems to have introduced the spirit of ambition (*to philótimon*) and the fondness for strife into the regime as a fuel for virtue, supposing that there should always be a certain disagreement and contest for superiority among good men and believing that it was not right to call like-mindedness (*homónoia*) that lazy complaisance which yields without debate and contention." [15]

At least while the Atlantic and Pacific oceans sufficed to isolate and protect it, the liberal republic established by James Madison, Alexander Hamilton, and their colleagues could almost do without men of warlike demeanor; but to defend the city, Sparta needed spirited men—and to maintain solidarity within the ranks, she had to keep their rivalry firmly under control. Among the Greek writers, there was no one who praised the competitive spirit with greater vigor than Pindar. But he, too, could preach moderation, chanting, "The men in the *póleis* who court *philotimía* to an excess—they stir up a visible and palpable grief." [16] Their own warlike character posed a problem for the Spartans, and they dealt with that problem through their *politeía*, encouraging ambition and at the same time subordinating the pursuit of honor to the needs of the *pólis*.[17] The Lacedaemonian constitution was designed—above all else—to reinforce the fundamental consensus and to regulate the struggle for office, for power, and for glory.

Sparta was neither a monarchy nor a democracy. We hear little of court intrigue and even less of demagoguery. The most subtle of the ancient authors described it as a mixed regime. According to Aristotle, the two kings (*basileîs*) represented the monarchical element; the *gerousía*, the oligarchic element; and the ephorate, the democratic element.[18] In order to secure the consent of the governed, Sparta ensured the participation of every element of the citizen population in the administration of the city; in order to prevent the emergence of an overmighty subject, she employed an elaborate system of checks and balances to restrain her magistrates from excess. These safeguards were essential. In general, ancient policy was violent—and nowhere more so than at Lacedaemon. The fostering of citizen virtue and the enforcement of the Spartan regimen necessitated the establishment and maintenance of a vigorous inquisitorial tribunal. This could not be accomplished without the concentration of extraordinary power in the hands of Sparta's officials.

I . v i . 2

The most dangerous element within the Spartan regime was the kingship. Even a cursory glance at the privileges and prerogatives associated with that office is adequate to demonstrate the truth of this proposition.[19] Two Spartiates were not among "the equals." Two held office for life;[20] two escaped the *agōgē*;[21] two took their meals outside the barracks.[22] Other Spartiates served in the *gerousía*, but only a king or his regent could serve in that venerable body before his sixtieth year.[23] Other Spartiates sacrificed to the gods, but only a king or regent could do so year after year on the city's behalf.[24] Other Spartiates commanded troops, but only a king or his regent could normally lead out the Spartan army and the forces of the Peloponnesian League.[25] Prior to the last few years of the sixth century, the two *basileîs* ordinarily shared the command; and when acting in concert, they could reportedly wage war against any territory they wished. It was apparently a sacrilege for a Spartiate to resist their authority to do so.[26] As hereditary generals and priests with life tenure, the Agiad and Eurypontid kings stood out from the ranks.[27]

In the strict sense, the two kings were not Spartiates at all. Envoys sent on missions abroad could claim to represent two entities at the same time: "the Lacedaemonians and the Heraclids from Sparta."[28] Tradition taught that the Spartiates were Lacedaemonians precisely because they were adherents of men who traced their ancestry back to Heracles, the son of Zeus. The Athenians and the Arcadians might think of themselves as autochthonous: "always possessed of the same land," and even "born from the earth."[29] But the Spartans were acutely aware that they were interlopers in the Peloponnesus, that they had invaded and seized Laconia by force, and that their servants—the "old helots" of the province—were descended from the original Achaean stock. As Dorians, the Spartans had no legitimate place in what was, in fact, an alien land. The righteousness of their cause and its continued success were founded on the quasi-feudal relationship binding the citizens to their two kings: for the first Dorians to call themselves Spartans had purportedly been among the followers of the sons of Heracles, and the latter had inherited from their illustrious father and had passed on to their descendants the right to rule the Peloponnesus. As long as their *basileîs* were Heraclids, the Spartans of later times could rest confident in the legitimacy of their tenure in Laconia and in the support of the gods. But if they expelled their charismatic kings or countenanced an illegitimate succession, they could expect to suffer the fate which the gods had reserved for their Dorian neighbors in Messenia. The Spartans justified their conquest of that province and their reduction of its inhabitants to a servile condition on the grounds that the Dorians of Messenia had extinguished their own claim to the land when they drove out their Heraclid king. The Spartan conquerors had merely reasserted Heraclid control.[30]

At the start of each generation, the conquest community experienced a rebirth. While a *basileús* lived, he was sacrosanct.[31] And when he died, there were elaborate burial rites—"more majestic," Xenophon tells us, "than properly accords with the human condition."[32] The market was closed; assembly meetings and elections were temporarily suspended; and the entire community—the Spartans, the *períoikoi*, and even the helots—went into mourning for a period of ten days.[33] "In this fashion," Xenophon observes, "the laws of Lycurgus wish to show that they give the kings of the Lacedaemonians preference in honor not as human beings, but as demigods."[34] The renaissance came with the choice of a new *basileús*—normally the eldest surviving son of the deceased.[35] When this man assumed the royal office, there was a cancellation of all debts owed his predecessor or the public treasury, and the citizens purportedly celebrated the man's accession with the same choral dances and sacrifices which they had employed in instituting their founders (*archagétai*) as kings of Lacedaemon at the time of the original conquest.[36] At Lacedaemon, history was an eternal return of the same. The king's death brought one cycle to an end; ritual alone could guarantee its repetition. It is not fortuitous that the Spartans sometimes referred to their current kings as *archagétai*:[37] the Heraclid *basileîs* of each new generation refounded the *pólis* by renewing its claim to the land. If the magistrates exhibited an almost obsessive concern to insure a legitimate succession, they had good reason.[38] The same concerns dictated the law barring the Heraclids from having children by any woman from abroad.[39]

In a community in which military concerns predominate and in which there is a popular element in the constitution, generals—even hereditary generals—are men of great power and influence.[40] A soldier's opportunity to distinguish himself on the field of battle and to gain the admiration and support of his comrades depends more often than not on the goodwill of his commander. This was particularly true among the Lacedaemonians. When on campaign, a Spartan king or regent conducted the sacrifices[41] and exercised an almost absolute sway: he had the power to appoint his own officers, to issue orders to all and sundry, to send troops wherever he wished, to raise fresh forces, to execute cowards, and even to levy money.[42] No matter what happened, until the army returned home, his word was law.[43] One need only reflect on the political consequences of replacing the consulship at Rome with a dyarchy to start to grasp the importance that the Spartan kings must have had. And after that beginning, one must ponder the same issue anew: for in Rome a man was arguably first a citizen and then a soldier, while in Sparta the priorities were without a doubt reversed.

The two kings possessed other politically important prerogatives as well. One of these privileges was symptomatic of royal preeminence in the making of foreign policy.[44] In antiquity, it was not the practice for a city to maintain resident ambassadors in the polities with which its citizens had frequent dealings. Instead, the Greeks adapted the traditional aristocratic institution of guest-friendship (*xenía*) to serve the needs of the political community as a whole:[45] ordinarily, the citizens of one community selected from among the citizens of another one or more vice-consuls called *próxenoi* to provide hospitality when they dispatched embassies and, in general, to look after their interests in that particular locality.[46] Here, in typical fashion, Lacedaemonian practice diverged from the norm. For the Spartans insisted on regulating and controlling all intercourse with outsiders, and they were therefore unwilling to allow foreigners to choose their own representatives from among the citizens of Lacedaemon.[47] We may suspect, but we cannot be certain that the two kings selected those who served as Sparta's *próxenoi* abroad.[48] What we do know is that they appointed vice-consuls at Sparta for the various cities that had relations with her.[49] Thereby, they not only conferred honor on the men selected for the posts; they also secured for themselves, even in time of peace, a formal role in the conduct of foreign affairs.

In similar fashion, the *basileîs* appointed the four officials known as the *Púthioi*—each naming two to keep the records of the oracles for him and to share his mess. When the city itself wished an oracle from Delphi concerning a given matter, it chose its messenger from among these four men.[50] This practice assured royal predominance in religious matters and made the manipulation of religion for political purposes almost the sole prerogative of the two dyarchs.[51] In a community as traditional and as pious as ancient Lacedaemon, this could have extraordinary consequences. A wily man like Cleomenes could use religion to control the city.[52]

The kings were also responsible for maintaining the public roads, for legalizing the adoption of children, and for securing husbands for heiresses left unbetrothed by their fathers.[53] The last two functions were of untold importance: because the Spartiates were barred from commerce and the possession of coinage, the only legal way open to them for the amassing of a fortune was to inherit privately owned land or to marry its owner. The rights of the kings in matters of adoption and with regard to heiresses provided them with substantial patronage. To grasp fully the political leverage which this gave the two *basileîs*, one need only reflect once again on the contradictory nature of the man produced by the Lycurgan regime.

On one occasion, the historian Macaulay paused to consider the licentiousness that prevailed in the arts in England in the wake of the restoration of Charles II. "In justice to the writers of whom we have spoken thus severely," he remarked, it must be acknowledged

> that they were, to a great extent, the creatures of their age. And if it be asked why that age encouraged immorality which no other age would have tolerated, we have no hesitation in answering that this great depravation of the national taste was the effect of the prevalence of Puritanism under the Commonwealth. To punish public outrages on morals and religion is unquestionably within the competence of rulers. But when a government, not content with requiring decency, requires sanctity, it oversteps the bounds which mark its proper functions. And it may be laid down as a universal rule that a government which attempts more than it ought will perform less. . . . And so a government which, not content with repressing scandalous excesses, demands from its subjects fervent and austere piety, will soon discover that, while attempting to render an impossible service to the cause of virtue, it has in truth only promoted vice.[54]

Something of the sort could be said of ancient Sparta. But there the dividing line between excessive discipline and reactive license was marked out in space and not in time. One Athenian wag summed up the situation nicely: in public, he observed, the Lacedaemonians were clearly the better men; in private, however, the Athenians surpassed them.[55]

The Spartans resembled their houses. They were austere without, but not so within.[56] These were men torn between their public responsibilities and their private inclinations. They openly pursued honor and fame. But, in secret, they coveted wealth. Plato's description merits repetition: under the cover of darkness, like savages, the Spartans paid honor to silver and gold. It should not be surprising that these men were susceptible to bribes, and bribes were precisely what the two kings were in a position to bestow. Through their exercise of oversight with regard to adoptions and through their tutelage over unbetrothed heiresses, Sparta's dyarchs were able in the most important of ways to help their friends and deny their enemies aid.

The royal power to shower with property those who were cooperative and to punish those who were not was undoubtedly of great import in the archaic period and in the fifth century. Thereafter, it may even have increased—at least for a time. In the late fourth century, when Aristotle published *The Politics*, the two kings had apparently been deprived of the right to dispose of unbetrothed heiresses.[57] Precisely when the girl's father was given the right to appoint a tutor to handle this task remains unclear. But it is reasonable to suspect that this reform followed in the wake of the general liberalization of property law at Sparta that took place shortly after the Peloponnesian War. It was at this time, we are told, that Epitadeus—who was apparently unfriendly to his own son—managed to secure the passage of legislation granting the holder of a *klêros* the right to leave his estate to whomever he pleased or even give it away.[58] The consequences were startling: no Spartan who failed to make the required contribution to his *sussitía* could retain his rights as a citizen;[59] and as time passed, property came to be concentrated in the hands of the few—many of them women. To explain this development, Aristotle alluded to the greed of the Spartan notables, to the size of the dowries that came to be given under the new dispensation, and to the great "multitude of heiresses," observing that, in his own time, "nearly two-fifths of the entire country" was "owned by women."[60]

Corruption evidently contributed much to the concentration of property, but the wars of the fourth century were presumably important as well. The measure carried by Epitadeus, in effect, legalized the giving of dowries, and it also made possible a disguised sale of the civic allotment. This enabled citizens too foolish to foresee the consequences or too eager for private enjoyment of the pleasures that money can buy to trade the patrimony of their sons for the means of their own delight.[61] At the same time, the disasters which struck Sparta in the wars of the period eliminated a good many men and left the land in the hands of their wives, sisters, and daughters. These women, inured to "every kind of licence and luxury," were hardly likely to be eager to confer their estates on the impoverished sons of the prolific. They were no doubt much sought after by the surviving Spartiates, both the landless men intent on securing the property needed if they were to make the required contributions to a *sussitía* and those possessed of an estate but caught in the grips of an unquenchable thirst for additional wealth. Prosperous Spartiates with only daughters for heirs would naturally try to find the best possible match, and money no doubt tended to marry money. But if a girl's father died before she was betrothed, her fate may still for a time have become the responsibility of the two kings. We do not know whether Sparta's dyarchs disposed also of widows, but—while it lasted—the power to oversee adoptions and to marry off unbetrothed heiresses was power enough.

These two functions contributed greatly to the influence which the two kings exercised over the allocation of property, but they by no means exhausted that influence. The two *basileîs* had other resources from which to benefit their political allies. Of all the Spartans, the wealthiest were the two kings. They owned choice land in many of the perioecic towns.[62] In addition, they received anywhere from one-tenth to one-third of the booty captured in battle; they claimed the hides and chines of whatever animals were sacrificed; and they took a piglet from every litter raised in Lacedaemon.[63] At the same time, they benefited from a special tax levied on the citizens and the *períoikoi*; and of course, because of the power they exercised in the conduct of foreign affairs, they gained more from the gold and silver that flowed into Sparta from abroad than any other citizens.[64] No one was in a better position to bestow gifts.

From the coincidence of what the Spartiates desired and what the kings could provide, it would be easy to suppose, but wrong to conclude, that the two *basileîs* were virtual tyrants within Lacedaemon. To be sure, the dyarchs were capable of working great harm. Aristotle stresses this fact himself.[65] But caution is required regarding this matter, for things would have been much worse had there not been two circumstances working to prevent tyranny—the power of the ephors and the rivalry between the two kings.

I . v i . 3

The Spartan ephors were magistrates of no mean importance. On two different occasions, Cicero compared them with the tribunes of the Roman plebs, suggesting that they were a check on the kings in much the same sense that the tribunes were a check on the consuls at Rome.[66] Rousseau fleshed out the Roman's description when he denied that the ephorate existed solely to protect the sovereign people against the government and went on to suggest that, while the office was a regulator of and restraint on (*modérateur*) the executive power, it served also to safeguard the laws and "to maintain the equilibrium" between the government and the populace.[67] The tribunes represented the plebs only; the ephors were chosen from the political community as a whole.

No one could be ephor more than once,[68] and the board of five held office for only a year[69]—but during that year, they exercised by majority vote arbitrary, almost unchecked power.[70] It was only at the end of their period in office that the ephors were called to account for their deeds and subjected by their successors to a formal, judicial examination (*eúthuna*) of the sort employed in other Greek cities to guarantee that magistrates remained responsible to the political community.[71] In the period before that day of reckoning, the ephors played a predominant role in the making and implementing of public policy. They were empowered to summon the probouleutic *gerousía*[72] and the Spartan assembly;[73] they could introduce laws, decrees, and declarations of war and peace to the assembly through the *gerousía*;[74] and when the assembly met—whether on an extraordinary occasion or at the regular monthly time[75]—they decided who would present a particular proposal.[76] One of their number then presided, put the question, and determined whether those shouting for the measure outnumbered those shouting against.[77] It is an indication of their central importance that Xenophon—the ancient writer most intimately familiar with Spartan practice and parlance—thrice ascribes important decisions to "the ephors and assembly."[78] It would not be an exaggeration to say that the ephors governed Sparta with the advice and consent of the *gerousía* and assembly. Aristotle rightly observes that a magistracy empowered to convene a city's assembly, set its agenda, and preside over it is virtually "sovereign (*kúrios*) within the regime."[79]

The ephors were particularly influential in the sphere of foreign relations. It was within their prerogative to determine when and for how long a foreigner might visit Sparta and a Spartan might go abroad.[80] They ordinarily received embassies, conducted negotiations with foreign powers, and decided when to place matters before the *gerousía* and assembly.[81] They had influence, if not control, over the appointment of the harmosts who administered communities under Sparta's dominion, and they were competent to issue these officials directives.[82] In time of war or civic emergency, the ephors called up the army,[83] and they determined which age groups were to march.[84] In foreign affairs, there were few functions that these magistrates did not perform—other than serve as Sparta's commanders in the field.

At home, the ephors' chief task—as their name suggests—was oversight. They enforced the sumptuary laws and determined which pieces of music and poetry would be tolerated within the community.[85] They kept tabs on the *agōgē*, checking each day to see that the youth observed the regulations regarding clothing and bedding and subjecting them every tenth day to a physical examination.[86] Ultimately, they appointed three outstanding young men who had reached their prime to select from among their fellow *néoi* and command the three hundred *hippeîs* that formed the royal bodyguard.[87] Likewise, the ephors controlled the treasury, disbursing necessary funds, overseeing the collection of taxes,[88] and receiving the proceeds from the sale of prisoners and other booty captured in war.[89] They also manipulated the calendar, intercalating months when this was deemed necessary.[90] At Sparta, the ephors controlled virtually every aspect of daily life.

Each year, when they took office, the ephors declared war on the helots, employing the young men of the *krupteía* to eliminate the obstreperous and those menacingly robust.[91] At the same time, Aristotle tells us, they reissued the famous decree calling on each Spartiate to obey the law, to comply with the customs of the land, and to observe the ancient practice of shaving his upper lip.[92] According to Plutarch, this last injunction was intended as a reminder to the young men that they were to obey the city even in the most trivial of matters.[93]

In overseeing the many aspects of Spartan life and public policy for which they were responsible, the ephors exercised broad judicial powers. At the time they took office, they apparently subjected all of the retiring magistrates to the *eúthuna*.[94] Thereafter, they had the authority to suspend their fellow officials at any time.[95] Individually, the ephors judged civil suits;[96] as a board, they functioned as moral censors and criminal justices empowered to impose fines on malefactors[97] and, in capital cases, to hold preliminary, fact-finding hearings before joining the thirty members of the *gerousía* to form a jury competent to banish or execute the accused.[98]

The importance of the ephors is perhaps most obvious from their relationship with the two kings. Here, they had clearly defined prerogatives designed to make manifest and to enforce the sovereignty of the political community as a whole. They alone remained seated in the presence of a king;[99] they alone had the power to summon the kings and even to fine them for misconduct;[100] and when one of the kings led out the army, two of their number accompanied him to observe his every action and to give advice when asked.[101]

One Eurypontid king is said to have remarked that "the magistrate rules truly and rightly only when he is ruled by the laws and ephors."[102] His coupling of the rule of law with the rule of the ephors is not an accident. At the time of his institution, the Spartan *basileús* swore to maintain the *nómoi* of the *pólis*.[103] Each month thereafter, the ephors exchanged oaths with the kings, the latter swearing to reign in accord with "the established laws of the city," the former pledging to "keep the kingship unshaken" as long as the latter abided by their "oath to the city."[104] There was a threat implicit in the ephors' part of the bargain, and they had the power to make good on it. Every ninth year, the five chose a clear and moonless night and remained awake to watch the sky. If they saw a shooting star, they judged that one or both kings had acted against the law and suspended the man or men from office. Only the intervention of Delphi or Olympia could effect a restoration.[105]

Similarly, if the ephors judged that a king or regent had acted against the interests of the city, they could arrest him and bring him to trial on a capital charge just like any other Spartan citizen.[106] In the course of the turbulent fifth century, they were to exercise this prerogative time and time again: Cleomenes and his colleague Leotychides, Pausanias the regent and his royal son Pleistoanax, Agis and his younger contemporary Pausanias the king—all of these were brought to trial (some repeatedly) and all but Agis were eventually convicted and banished or executed.[107] Of the fifth century kings, only three—Leonidas, his son Pleistarchus, and Archidamus—are not known to have been tried for capital crimes, and even this statistic may be misleading. Leonidas and Pleistarchus bore the full weight of royal responsibility for periods so brief that their escape could not be deemed significant.[108] And neither of their reigns nor that of Archidamus is sufficiently well attested to justify our being certain from the silence of the sources that none of them was ever in danger.[109] The only reasonably safe conclusion is that none of them was ever convicted of a capital crime.

The fact that Sparta's kings were so often tried and so often convicted should not be taken as evidence of congenital criminality. Sometimes, of course, there was wrongdoing, but even here the motive for prosecution was more often than not political. Theophrastus stresses that even at Sparta "the lust for victory (*philonikía*)" played a substantial role in trials, and this is precisely what we would expect when the kings were involved.[110] There is no evidence that the Spartans distinguished between the judicial and the political functions of their magistrates, and the removal of a king was a matter of enormous political consequence.

It is a measure of the ephors' importance that the kings had to court them.[111] It would no doubt be an exaggeration to say that the Spartan kings lived in terror of the ephors, but they cannot have been unaware of their vulnerability.[112] Polybius claims that the kings obeyed the ephors as children their parents.[113] This may be hyperbole—but Xenophon, Plato, and Aristotle are surely not far from the truth when they compare the powers of the ephors to those of tyrants.[114]

It might seem that the kings were virtual prisoners of the ephors. Two sets of circumstances precluded this. In the first place, the kings were kings for life, while the ephors held office but for a year and apparently could never again serve. And, equally important, the kingships were hereditary, while the ephorate seems to have been filled by lot from an extremely large elected pool.[115] Thus, as board after board of ephors served, then retired, and as the *gérontes* slowly died off, a strong king endured, exercised his prerogatives, and worked the political and social system to benefit his friends and to impose a burden of gratitude on those judged to be politically prominent.[116] Quite often, Aristotle tells us, the ephors were poor men and were easily bribed.[117] In a given year, a particular king might find himself in difficulties and might deem it prudent to remain quiet, but he knew that the annual game of chance by which the ephors were chosen always offered the hope for a board more favorable to his cause or more easily corrupted.[118] The institution of the ephorate would not alone have staved off tyranny. The fact that the kingship was dual was essential for accomplishing that feat.[119]

In his account of the foundation of the Roman republic, Dionysius of Halicarnassus depicts the great Brutus as a somewhat scholarly advocate of dividing the royal office between two consuls. The Lacedaemonians have done so
"for many generations," he explains.

> And because of this arrangement of their constitution (*políteuma*), they
> have maintained the best order (*eunomeîsthai*) and they have been the
> most successful (*eudaimoneîn*) of all the Hellenes. If the power is divided
> in two and each has the same strength, those who hold sway will be less
> arrogant (*hubristaî*) and less oppressive. From this equal sharing of honor
> and lordship (*isotímou dunasteías*), the most likely result would be that
> each will feel a sense of reverence and shame (*aidôs*) before the other,
> that each will be able to prevent the other from conducting his life in
> accord with the dictates of pleasure, and that each will compete with the
> other in seeking a reputation for virtue.

Centuries after the decline of Lacedaemon, this was the historian's analysis
of the kingship at Sparta.[120]

It was almost inevitable that there be rivalry between the two *basileîs*. As
Dionysius's testimony suggests, the aristocratic ethos virtually dictated the
conflict between the two houses which came to be the norm.[121] It is symptomatic of the situation that, in the fourth century, each Spartan house appears
to have had clients of differing political persuasion in each of the cities of the
Peloponnesus.[122] If the leading men in those cities looked to the two kings
for aid and comfort in their struggles against each other, the same is likely
to have been true for the Spartiates. The two thrones were natural foci of
power and influence. The character of the political and social organization of
Lacedaemon strongly encouraged the political class to group itself into two
factions around the two thrones.[123]

A division along these lines did not always come to pass: Theopompus and
Polydorus were allies, not rivals, in the early seventh century and succeeded
in carrying out a thorough reform against bitter aristocratic opposition.[124]
Cleomenes' success in eliminating the hostile occupant of the rival throne
and in replacing him with a dependent of his own did not end all opposition to his schemes in the late sixth and early fifth centuries.[125] Sthenelaidas
the ephor pushed Sparta into war in 432 despite the firm opposition of the
Eurypontid monarch Archidamus and almost certainly without the support
of the rival house.[126] Sparta's *basileîs* were important, not all-important. In
general, they were at the center of conflict—and where the two kings are not
known to have been friends and allies or proponents of the same policy, it is
reasonable to suspect that they were at odds.

I. vi. 4

The *gerousía* was the least-dangerous branch of the Spartan government, but not the least important. In fact, Plutarch came very close to the mark when he described the Spartan regime as a mixture "of democracy and kingship, with an aristocracy to preside over it and adjudicate in the greatest affairs (*tền epistatoûsan kaì brabeúousan tà mégista*)." [127] In normal circumstances, when the ephors were nonentities and the two kings were rivals of no particular talent, the *gérontes* were in a position to exercise great influence, though not to initiate policy. One measure of their authority is the fact that Demosthenes speaks of this body of men as "the master (*despótēs*) of the many." [128] Dionysius of Halicarnassus advances a similar claim, contending that, while Sparta retained her independence, "the kings of the Lacedaemonians were not autocrats able to do whatever they wished, for the *gerousía* possessed full power (*krátos*) over public affairs (*tà koiná*)." [129] Even if we were to discount these assertions and to suppose them hyperbolic, as we probably should, we would still have to acknowledge that the *gerousía* was a formidable instrument of government. Even if it had been effectively divorced from the exercise of power, the prestige of its members would have been sufficient to guarantee that its recommendations were generally honored. Demosthenes and Aristotle both speak of election to membership in the *gerousía* as "the prize (*âthlon*) allotted to virtue," and Plutarch makes it clear that being selected was the highest honor which could be conferred by the *pólis* on a citizen.[130] Elsewhere, by means of an anecdote, he makes manifest the political import of being in this fashion esteemed. On one occasion, when a certain Demosthenes, a Lacedaemonian notorious for his lack of self-discipline, brought a sensible measure before the Spartan people, they voted its defeat. Fearful lest the opportunity pass, the ephors acted quickly, selecting by lot one of the *gérontes* to present the proposal once again. "So great," the biographer concludes, "is the influence that can be attributed in a republican regime (*politeía*) to confidence in a man's character and to its opposite." [131]

As the Spartan name suggests, the *gerousía* was a council of the aged. Twenty-eight of its thirty members—all but the two kings—were always men of experience and proven worth over the age of sixty. Drawn exclusively from the priestly caste that seems to have constituted the city's ancient aristocracy, directly elected by popular acclamation, and guaranteed the office for life,[132] the *gérontes* performed three functions: the first, probouleutic; the second, judicial; and the third, sacerdotal. With the ephors presiding, the "old men" met to set the agenda for the assembly, and thereafter they could annul any action on its part that exceeded the authority which they thereby conferred.[133] In capital cases, the *gerontes* joined the ephors in form-ing a jury,[134] and in circumstances left unclear, they apparently functioned as augurs.[135] No legislation could be enacted and no war declared without their permission, and it was prudent for magistrates to consult the *gérontes* on all matters of administration entrusted to their care.

The kings and the ephors had particularly strong reasons for heeding the advice of these old men. Whether a king or former official was eventually indicted for malfeasance of office, because left to a board of ephors annu-ally and more or less arbitrarily chosen, was largely a matter of chance. But whether the defendant would then be convicted, because entrusted to a tri-bunal dominated by *gérontes* elected for life, was a subject for calculation.[136] It is no wonder that aging Spartan nobles canvassed for the office.[137] There were limits to what they could accomplish: except perhaps in a period of gen-eral disarray, the "old men" could not have pushed legislation through the assembly releasing their fellow aristocrats from the egalitarian restrictions that so limited their wealth and its use. But, much of the time, albeit within clear confines, the *gerousía* was in a position to be the arbiter of events. If great seriousness was attached to the selection of the *gérontes*, Isocrates tells us, it was because this handful of elderly men "presided over the disposition of all public affairs."[138]

Like the Nocturnal Council of Plato's *Laws*, the *gerousía* was the guardian of the constitution.[139] It served a function comparable to that which Alexan-der Hamilton would later attribute to England's House of Lords. The *gérontes* had a greater stake in stability than any other group at Sparta. As wealthy aristocrats, they had no pressing need to tamper with the system of land allotments; as recipients of the city's highest honor, they should generally have been satisfied with existing political arrangements; and as old men on the threshold of death, they had little to hope for from revolution or reform. In short, they had "nothing to hope for by a change, and a sufficient inter-est by means of their property, in being faithful to the National interest." In consequence, they formed "a permanent barrier agst. every pernicious inno-vation" and endowed the government with "a permanent will." Their very "duration" in office was "the earnest of wisdom and stability." Though the turnover must sometimes have been rapid as death took its toll, the funda-mental character and bias of the *gerousía* must have been always the same.[140] So, at least, one would judge after reading *The Rhetoric* of Aristotle.

In that great, but neglected work, the peripatetic makes much of the fact that an orator, called upon to address a particular group and eager to achieve a particular end, must pay careful attention to the character of his listeners and couch his rhetoric in a fashion that will move them in the way he intends.

There are many differences which distinguish types of men—even within a particular political regime—and the statesman must pay attention to them all. Among these differences, Aristotle singles out age. His awareness of its importance causes the philosopher to dedicate an extended digression to a discussion of the qualities which separate young men in the cities of Greece from those, like the *gérontes* of Sparta, who have lived for a long time, observed many events, learned much from experience, and then finally entered their twilight years. The result is a psychological portrait of considerable subtlety which may throw a great deal of light on the nature of the Spartan regime.

"In character," Aristotle observes, "the young are guided by desire and prepared to act in accord with its dictates." They are particularly vulnerable to sexual license because they lack full self-control. At the same time, "they are quick to change and fickle in their desires"; and because "their impulses are keen but not grand," they tend to oscillate between violent passion and sudden disinterest. In addition, "young men are spirited, sharp-tempered, and apt to give way to anger." They are unable entirely to restrain the spirited part of their souls; and "owing to *philotimía*, they cannot endure being slighted and become indignant when they suppose that they have been wronged." But although the young love honor, "they love victory even more" because they desire the "superiority" which only victory can bring. Accordingly, they attach little value to money "because they have never experienced the trials arising from want." This dearth of unpleasant experience has other consequences as well. In particular, the young are good-natured, quick to trust, and full of hope. In addition, "they are hot-blooded—like men drunk on wine." They have themselves had little opportunity to blunder, and because the future before them seems open, they are guided by hope. "In the first days of one's life," Aristotle observes, "one has nothing to remember and everything to look forward to."

Both because the young are hot-blooded and because they so easily give way to hope, they tend to be courageous. "An angry man is not likely to know fear," Aristotle explains, "and hope is good for generating confidence." This courage is balanced by a certain vulnerability to shame, a certain natural bashfulness; and since the young "have been educated in accord with convention and have not yet conceived of other things as honorable," they can easily be kept under control. Furthermore, because they have "not been laid low by life and are as yet untried by harsh necessity," young men tend to be high-minded and magnanimous—to be what the Greeks called "men of great soul (*megalópsuchoi*)"—and to think themselves "worthy of great things." As a consequence, the young choose "to perform deeds of nobility rather than works of advantage and to govern their conduct in accord with the dictates of good character rather than in accord with those of calculation." This distinction is important because "calculation aims at the advantageous while virtue seeks the noble." Furthermore, men are more likely when young to "hold friends and companions dear." In their early years, "they take delight in living together and do not yet judge anything with an eye to advantage (not even their friends)."

The blunders characteristic of young men are linked with vehemence and excess. "They do everything in excess," the peripatetic observes. "They love too much, and they hate too much, and they do all things in a similar fashion." This quality he attributes to the passionate attachment which the young exhibit for their own opinions. They think they know everything. Accordingly, when young men "treat others unjustly, they do so out of arrogance (*húbris*), not wickedness." In similar fashion, the young like to laugh, and they are particularly fond of jesting, which Aristotle calls "the arrogance of the educated man." This arrogance would be intolerable were it not balanced by pity. According to Aristotle, the young measure those about them by their own lack of malice, and they quite naturally assume that men unjustly suffer all that they have to endure.[141]

Aristotle structures his description of elderly Greek men in much the same fashion, juxtaposing their tendencies with those of the young. "Because the old have lived through many years," he observes, "they have often been deceived and have made many more blunders than the young." Most matters involving mankind turn out badly, so that their experience of the world causes the aged to be hesitant.

> They "suppose" only; nothing do they "know." And being of two minds, they always add a "possibly" or a "perhaps." They speak of everything in this fashion and say nothing without reservations. The old are, in addition, ill-disposed—for this trait is grounded in the assumption that all things tend to get worse. They are suspicious because of mistrust and mistrustful because of experience. And because of these things, they neither love nor hate with any vehemence, but . . . they are always loving in the expectation of hating and hating in the expectation of someday loving again. They are, in fact, pusillanimous (*mikrópsuchoi*). Life has laid them low, and they desire nothing great or out of the ordinary but, rather, only those things which support staying alive. As a consequence, the old are anything but liberal with their substance (*aneleútheroi*): property is a necessity and experience has taught them that wealth is difficult to get and easy to lose. They are also cowardly and foresee danger from

everything—for they are in temperament opposed to the young. Where the latter are hot-blooded, the former are cold-blooded—so that old age has paved the way for their becoming cowards (cowardice being a certain coldness of blood).

This cowardice has deep roots. Sensing that they are near death, "old men hold life dear," and they tend also "to be fonder of themselves than is proper." Because they are selfish in this fashion, "the old live for advantage and not for the noble," and they prefer what is good for themselves to what is good in and of itself. They are not bashful like the young, but shameless; and "in concerning themselves less with the noble than with the useful, they exhibit a contempt for reputation."

Aristotle contends that their position in life affects even the time orientation of the elderly. Where the young thrive on hope, the old look to memory; where the young live in the future, the old live in the past. They tell stories because "they love to remember." Aristotle emphasizes also that, while old men "are sharp in temper, they are weak in their anger." In fact, their desires are in general weak, and their "actions owe less to passion than to profit." For this reason, the philosopher can remark that "such men only seem to be moderate (*sōphronikoî*)—for their desires have waned and they are enslaved to gain." Accordingly, the old are strikingly different from the young.

> They live more by calculation than in accord with the dictates of moral character—for calculation aims at the advantageous and character aims at virtue. And they treat others unjustly out of wickedness, not out of arrogance (*húbris*). The old may be prone to pity but not for the same reasons as the young. The latter feel pity out of a sense of fellow-feeling (*philanthrōpía*); the former out of weakness—for the old think that they, too, may suffer everything and this inspires pity—whence they are disposed to complain and are neither jesters nor lovers of laughter. For querulousness is the opposite of the love of laughter.[142]

As should be evident, the young and the old are opposed in virtually every respect—and the young are not only far better suited to war because of their physical strength; they are better suited to such pursuits by temperament as well.

But the very qualities which make it proper that young men serve in the front lines in time of battle render them unfit for rule, particularly in a regime like that of Lacedaemon. Fighting and the actual conduct of war may favor the passionate and the bold, but diplomacy and statecraft generally require caution and precise calculation. The qualities which render old men less generous and more selfish than the young render them also shrewder, less trustful of foreigners, and far less apt to embark on grand but foolish ventures. In foreign affairs, where interest presides, pusillanimity is certainly not a virtue, but then neither is the excessive high-mindedness of the young. Statesmen should not be bashful. They must, in fact, be prepared to be shameless on occasion. In particular, they must be ready to sacrifice the noble for the sake of advantage, for they must care more for the city's survival than for its reputation. Furthermore, in making peace and in preparing for war, the rulers of a community must neither love nor hate with any real vehemence. Instead, they must cherish the city's friends and allies in the full expectation that someday enmity will be required, and they must be hostile to her foes in the full knowledge that these may well become friends and allies at some point in the not too far distant future.

Similarly, the young are hardly fit for rule in any regime aimed at fostering *homónoia* and at achieving stability. Young men are in all places an unsettling element. Even where reared in accord with the spirit of the laws and encouraged to deem honorable precisely what convention prescribes, they rarely display that reverence for the past and that veneration for tradition which is the foundation of communal solidarity. In contrast, because the old are backward-looking and enslaved to memory, they tend naturally to assume that precedent should govern in all cases and that what has been done from time immemorial has an authority and a sanction almost religious in character.

It is not fortuitous that the Spartans rarely conferred political responsibilities on anyone young.[143] Within any community, Aristotle observes, there are two functions—the martial and the deliberative—and both justice and good sense dictate that they be distributed to the young and to the old respectively: for the young are generally strong, and the old are often prudent.[144] Nor is it an accident that the Spartans were famous throughout ancient times for the exaggerated respect which they paid to age.[145] Where they received such attention, the old were in a position to do great service. Because they were at leisure, they could act as censors willing to oversee not just public affairs, but private matters as well. Plutarch emphasizes that the old men of Sparta kept watch over the young, attending their workouts in the gymnasium and their games and taking note of their general comportment throughout the day. Simply by their presence, they inspired fear in those likely to transgress and reinforced the shame and the yearning for excellence which guide those inclined to be virtuous. In these circumstances, he notes, "the young tend to cultivate and follow the lead of the old, and the latter, in turn, manage to strengthen and encourage the innate orderliness and nobility of their disciples without incurring envy thereby." [146] The Spartans were fully aware of the character and import of this relationship: an older man who witnessed wrongdoing on the part of a young man and failed to administer the proper reproof was subject to punishment himself.[147]

The depiction in Aristotle's *Rhetoric* of the differences between the young Greeks and the old is perhaps overdrawn; it may introduce more clarity into the matter than actually exists. But his discussion is, nonetheless, strikingly reminiscent of the one description we have of a member of the *gerousía* addressing the Spartan assembly. In that account, the Heraclid Hetoimaridas is represented as having gone to great lengths in attempting to persuade his compatriots and, in particular, the bold and impetuous young that it is imprudent for a land power like Sparta to go to war against a maritime power like Athens for the hegemony of the sea.[148] In truth, most of the time, the *gérontes* must have been a force for that caution for which Sparta was so notorious. Most of the time, the *gerousía* must have been a bastion of tradition. Precisely because the *gérontes* were not in a position to initiate positive action, they could exercise extraordinary influence and even power without becoming themselves a threat to the regime; and in the end, their oversight was the best guarantee against any disruption of that set of social and economic arrangements that fostered Spartan *homónoia*.[149]

I.vi.5

There is little purpose in disputing whether the Spartan regime was aristocratic or egalitarian and whether its constitution was democratic, monarchical, or oligarchic. As Plato, Aristotle, and the other ancient writers understood, the truth was more complex. In the "well-mixed" regime, the peripatetic tells us, "each of the extremes is revealed in the mean." [150] For those within the Lacedaemonian citizen body, the social and economic arrangements were far more egalitarian than any known elsewhere in Greece.[151] But that citizen body was itself recruited by a weeding-out process in which prowess and courage, cunning and hardiness, and physical beauty and charm all played a great part. As a *pólis* that placed greater emphasis on civic virtue than any other community in Hellas, Sparta was—even by Greek standards—extremely aristocratic. At the same time, however, Lacedaemon was a republic. Ultimately, it referred all fundamental decisions to a popular assembly, and it selected its most powerful magistrates from the entire citizen body by a procedure akin to the lot.[152] In this respect, it was—by those same Greek standards—extraordinarily democratic. Nonetheless, the presence of hereditary *basileîs* claiming descent from Zeus points to divine-right kingship, and that of a small, elective council drawn from a narrowly defined pool and endowed with broad probouleutic and judicial powers suggests oligarchy. It is no wonder that the ancient writers were perplexed and found it necessary to jettison the familiar terminology. To speak of Sparta as a kingdom, an aristocracy, an oligarchy, or even a democracy would be to take the part for the whole.

Lacedaemon was, in fact, all and none of the above. It was, as the ancient writers ultimately concluded, a mixed regime—an uneasy compromise between competing principles that managed to prevent or at least retard the emergence of partial societies by somehow admitting and somehow denying the claims of all. As a mixed regime, the polity attempted (with considerable success for an extended period) to protect each element within the community against the others and to secure loyalty and devotion from all. The prerogatives conferred on the *basileús* and the influence that went with those prerogatives bolstered kingship and satisfied in some measure the ancient Heraclid claim to rule; the sharing of those prerogatives and that influence between two rival houses and the subjection of both kings to the oversight of the ephors prevented one-man domination. By its very existence, the *gerousía* guaranteed that noble birth would be honored, and the responsibilities reserved for that council prevented not just the wholesale redistribution of the land inherited by the traditional aristocracy but the public discussion of any such measure as well. At the same time, the ephorate and assembly safeguarded the property, the political rights, and the other privileges of the common people. While it all lasted, each element had its rights and dignity reinforced, and that fact goes a long way toward explaining the stability of the constitution and its capacity safely to concentrate in the hands of the magistrates the extraordinary power that was required for the enforcement of the Spartan regimen.

Eventually, of course, that regimen—and, with it, the Spartan constitution—collapsed. Tacitus came reasonably close to the truth when he claimed that "all nations and cities are ruled either by the people, or by the leading men, or by individuals; the form of commonwealth that is selected and composed from these types, it is easier to praise than to achieve, and, if achieved, it will hardly last for long." But, here again, Lacedaemon's real failure is less striking than her remarkable success, and Rome's greatest historian admitted as much when he conferred on Sparta a distinction he resolutely denied the Roman republic: inclusion among what he termed "well-constituted civic communities (*civitates*)." [153]

One would be hard put to charge John Stuart Mill with being a partisan of Sparta. Lacedaemon was, in his view, "memorable for the peculiar pettiness of its political conduct." Furthermore, Mill gave great emphasis to the fact that, when temporarily liberated from supervision by his fellow citizens, a Spartan "was not only the most domineering and arrogant, but in spite of, or rather by a natural reaction from his ascetic training, the most rapacious and corrupt of all Greeks." And yet, despite the distaste that he consistently displayed, the great nineteenth-century liberal could not help being moved by "the steadiness of the Spartan polity, and the constancy of Spartan maxims." He was even prepared to acknowledge that the "habitual abnegation of ordinary personal interests, and merging of self with an idea"—so evident at Lacedaemon—"were not compatible with pettiness of mind. Most of the anecdotes and recorded sayings of individual Lacedaemonians breathe a certain magnanimity of spirit." To these concessions, Mill ultimately added another of equal or even greater importance: "There is indeed no such instance of the wonderful pliability, and amenability to artificial discipline, of the human mind, as is afforded by the complete success of the Lacedaemonian legislator, for many generations, in making the whole body of Spartan citizens *at Sparta* exactly what he had intended to make them." [154] In making this admission, John Stuart Mill joined distinguished company. The accomplishments of the legendary Lycurgus were indelibly impressed on the minds of the men who initiated the American Revolution and subsequently wrestled with the difficulties involved in the establishment of republican government in the New World. When Francis Scott Key wrote *The Star-Spangled Banner* and described America as "the land of the free and the home of the brave," he was adopting a phrase which his countrymen had hitherto reserved for ancient Lacedaemon. [155]

CHAPTER 7

Athens's Illiberal Democracy

The Athenians pretended to the first invention of agriculture and of laws: and always valued themselves extremely on the benefit thereby procured to the whole race of mankind. They also boasted, and with reason, of their warlike enterprises; particularly against those innumerable fleets and armies of Persians, which invaded Greece during the reigns of Darius and Xerxes. But though there be no comparison in point of utility, between these peaceful and military honours; yet we find, that the orators, who have writ such elaborate panegyrics on that famous city, have chiefly triumphed in displaying the warlike achievements. Lysias, Thucydides, Plato, and Isocrates discover, all of them, the same partiality; which, though condemned by calm reason and reflection, appears so natural in the mind of man.—David Hume

I.vii.1

It may seem strange that the American Founding Fathers should single out Lacedaemon for admiration, for there were other ancient communities that future generations would think better suited to liberal democratic taste. Within the framework of the *pólis*, there was ample room for deviation. Just as no liberal democracy ever accorded complete autonomy to the economy, so no Greek *pólis* ever fully worked out in practice what was implicit in the absolute primacy accorded the transcendent common good. The very existence of the commercial *agorá* ruled out the complete subordination of economic to political concerns; and where local circumstances made a particular city a mercantile center, there was no way to preserve completely the integrity of the political community. It was one thing for the peasant occasionally to visit the *agorá* to exchange grain, olive oil, or wine for metal, pots, clothing, or other finished goods; it was something altogether different for the craftsman and the merchant to depend on the market for their entire livelihood. Where these last two groups were relatively numerous, as in Corinth, they might achieve something approaching respectability;[1] and where they were influential, as in Chios, they might occasionally even determine policy.[2]

Despite these aberrations, the fundamentals of civic life remained everywhere the same. For subsistence, the Corinthians were probably more dependent on commerce and the provision of services than any other Greek community. They possessed a fertile territory, but it was quite limited in extent; and because Corinth was located on a narrow neck of land separating the Saronic from the Corinthian gulf, she possessed two separate harbors. The character of the terrain prevented the Corinthians from linking the two harbors by a canal, but they were able to carry goods overland and even to convey triremes and small merchantmen from one gulf to the other by means of a dragway some five miles long. As a consequence of her location, Corinth was from very early times the chief port of transit between the Black Sea and the Aegean on the one hand and the western Mediterranean on the other. There simply cannot ever have been very many Corinthian peasants, and a sizable minority of the citizens must from early times have depended for livelihood on the city's position as an *empórion*.[3] Cicero compares this *pólis* with Carthage, suggesting that the ultimate downfall of both cities was due to "the wandering and dispersion of the citizens." This phenomenon was, in turn, rooted in the "lust for trade and navigation" which had led the Corinthians and Carthaginians to abandon not just "the cultivation of the fields" but that of "arms" as well. There is good reason, then, to think of Corinth as a bourgeois polity like Montesquieu's England: dedicated to a "commerce of economy," inclined to seek "gain, not conquest," and so "pacific from principle" that it would sacrifice "its political interests to the interests of its commerce."[4] But one may nonetheless doubt whether there is reason enough: twice in the fifth century the Corinthians displayed a prickly sense of honor and allowed relatively trivial border or jurisdictional disputes with minor powers to catapult them into war with the one city in Greece capable of blockading their eastern and western ports.[5]

The Chian story is less dramatic, but similar. From the archaic period on, Chios seems to have been a major center of the lucrative slave trade.[6] As a consequence, she was rich and notably cautious.[7] Yet no Ionian community proved more fiercely resistant to Persian domination;[8] and in the course of the fifth century, the Chians always fielded a large navy and never succumbed to the almost irresistible temptation to substitute a monetary contribution for the ships they had agreed to supply to the Delian League.[9] Indeed, on the eve of the century's last decade, when it seemed that they had a serious chance to free themselves from Athens's hegemony, the Chians leapt at the opportunity and readily sacrificed their prosperity and the relative independence they had retained for so many years in exchange for the futile hope that they could somehow be totally free.[10]

Though deeply implicated in trade, the Corinthians and the Chians showed no lack of martial spirit. When put to the test, they consistently preferred honor, freedom, and the pursuit of dominion to the pusillanimous retention of the wealth they already possessed or could hope to earn by the available commercial and industrial means. Despite the changes worked by the marketplace, no classical Greek city ever seems fully to have given way to the dictates of the commercial way of life. Throughout the classical period, the *pólis* remained a republic of virtue, obsessed with politics and caught up in incessant war; in that regard, there was no reason why the American Founding Fathers should have preferred any other ancient Greek republic to the most stable of them all: Lacedaemon.

I . v i i . 2

It would be tempting for us to suppose that there was an exception to the general rule. In the archaic period, Athens had been a relatively traditional backwater; but by the late fifth century, she was the preeminent trading center in Hellas and the capital of a great empire.[11] Even in the immediate aftermath of the Peloponnesian War, when the plague, her great losses in battle, and the famine that gripped her during the Spartan siege had wreaked demographic havoc, Athens was still the most populous city in all of Hellas.[12] She remained by modern standards a diminutive and even tiny community, and it makes no sense to think of her as a mass society, for the Athenian *dêmos* could not be termed passive, weighty, difficult to move, and practically inert.[13] And yet, in truth, the territory of Athens was too large, her citizen population too numerous, and her streets too full of foreigners for the city to function properly as an integral, face-to-face community.[14] In addition, she was a democracy: as such, she accorded full political rights to her citizens simply by dint of their status as free men of Athenian descent, paying relatively little heed to whether they possessed the equipment and virtues requisite for performance of their civic duties;[15] and in filling magistracies in which no particular talents or technical skills were required, she joined the other democracies in employing the lot.[16] Apart from military officials, who could be reelected again and again, and the members of the probouleutic council, who could serve twice in the course of their lives, the city prohibited a man from occupying any given office for more than one term.[17] Moreover, to insure that everyone could participate fully and to encourage them to do so, she provided pay for public office, for service on a jury, and ultimately even for attendance at the assembly.[18] As a consequence of all this, Athens became the least illiberal of the ancient republics.[19] Neither her circumstances nor the *paideía* implicit in her comparatively cavalier disposition of political offices and honors (*táxis tôn archôn*) gave strong support to the ethos of deference, reverence, and shame that she had inherited from earlier times.[20]

  In the mid-fifth century, before Athens's transformation had reached completion, Aeschylus could still, without any sign of awkwardness or embarrassment, appeal to the religious foundations of civic solidarity, writing,

> Neither anarchy nor the rule of a single master
> Do I counsel my townsmen, upholding, to reverence (*sébein*).
> Nor do I urge that they cast all dread (*tò deinón*) from the city.
> For who among mortals, dreading (*dédoikos*) nothing, is just?
> Should you be thus justly fear-stricken,
> You shall have for the land's bulwark and the city's salvation
> A reverential awe (*sébas*) such as no one possesses
> Among the Scythians or in Pelops's domains.[21]

But by the time of the Peloponnesian War, the tide of skepticism had so undermined belief in some quarters that Sophocles, Euripides, and Aristophanes all found it necessary directly to confront the sophistic challenge to traditional piety in their plays.[22]

As a consequence of this decline in religious fervor, reverence lost much of its force, and a gap opened up between the public realm and the private. Many evidently welcomed the change. The Athenian general Nicias exhibited a piety that bordered on superstition. Yet, at a critical moment near the end of the disastrous Sicilian campaign in the late fifth century, he is said to have rallied his troops by reminding them that of all the various communities theirs was "the fatherland most free," and he specified what this freedom entailed by adding that Athens provided "to all an unregulated power (*anepíktatos exousía*) over the conduct of life."[23] That absence of regulation extended to the realm of opinion as well. A half-century after the Athenian invasion of Sicily, when Demosthenes delivered his first great public speech, he made a point of the fact that his compatriots had laws, customs, and a political regime that set them at odds with the Spartans and the Thebans, and he singled out for special notice the fact that, at Athens, one was free to heap praise on the laws and institutions of another city such as Sparta or Thebes.[24]

Concerning the unregulated character of Athenian life, others were less sanguine than Nicias. The Persian nobleman Otanes is said by Herodotus to have attacked monarchy as a form of tyranny because under it the ruler "is allowed without check to do whatever he wishes." With Athens in mind, Aristotle would later employ much the same phrase and write that the citizens of democracies are allowed to do whatever they please.[25] "The license to do whatever one wants" is ultimately undesirable, he elsewhere explains, because "it is unable to guard against the paltriness that is in all human beings."[26] Isocrates similarly complained that the fully developed Athenian regime educated its citizens in such a manner that they were inclined to confuse lack of discipline (*akolasía*) with democracy, lawlessness with freedom, and the power of doing everything they wished with happiness and success (*eudaimonía*).[27]

Plato anticipated this description of the Athenian regime. Struck by his native city's openness to "all sorts of human beings," he dubbed democracy with a double-edged irony "the fairest of regimes" and compared it with "a many-colored cloak decorated in every hue" because it was "decorated with every disposition." Such a polity, he tacitly acknowledged, admirably suited a man of Socrates' temper. It conferred on him "freedom of speech." It left him comparatively free "to organize his life privately in whatever way pleased him." And best of all, it was "a useful place in which to search out a regime" since, "thanks to its license" and the undiscriminating taste of the typical citizen, it exhibited the human soul in all its varieties and, in this sense, contained "all kinds of regimes." In Athens, there were tyrannical men, democratic men, oligarchic men, timocratic and even aristocratic or royal men: each type of human being was different in character, and each type was governed by an economy of desires peculiar to a particular political regime.[28] Moreover, where the Spartans were so cautious, so self-restrained and reticent that the term *laconic* came to be synonymous with *taciturn*, the Athenians were like drunkards: so convinced of their own wisdom and capacity to rule that they were notoriously willing to talk and so reveal themselves.[29] If Athens was of all the ancient cities the one most pleasing to Plato's Socrates, it is because her democratic regime best enabled him to undertake what he considered the true philosopher's principal task—the study of the soul: its virtues, its various dispositions, and what Plato might have been tempted to call its political economy.[30] In this way, it provided what was by ancient Greek standards a comparatively hospitable and dependable haven for those rare human beings who "alone without constraint, in accord with the dictates of their own nature (*autophuôs*), by divine dispensation (*theía moîra*) are truly and not at all by fabrication (*oúti plastôs*) good."[31]

Here, caution is needed: for what might appear, on Plato's part, to be a straightforward endorsement should not be taken as such. The polity most receptive to philosophy and best suited to providing for its needs was not deemed by this token well-ordered.[32] In a more straightforward fashion, Plato would in his final years pass judgment on Athens's democracy, arguing that a decline in reverence and fear had given rise to an excess of freedom and to a shamelessness that had undermined the friendship that was the foundation of the city's moral unity and its strength.[33] The Athenian's tastes as a philosopher and his concerns as a citizen were by no means simply one and the same.[34]

Plato was not the first to judge Athens deficient in reverence, shame, and *philía*. In the last years of the Peloponnesian War, Pericles' like-named son appears similarly to have lost faith in the democracy. His father had been prepared to compare his own city favorably with Sparta. He had celebrated her openness to the world, the absence of a civic regimen, and the citizens' penchant for overlooking one another's foibles, and he had asserted that his countrymen displayed on the battlefield an inborn valor in no way inferior to the courage which the Lacedaemonians learned through military drill and incessant toil (*pónos*). The great statesman had even argued that the city's comparatively tolerant demeanor in no way prevented a salutary dread (*déos*) from governing his compatriots' conduct in the public realm.[35] But where the older Pericles had been inclined to exalt the city of Athena, his son seems to have despaired of the Athenians' lack of *homónoia*. "Instead of working together for what is of advantage to themselves," he reportedly complained, "they are more abusive of each other and more envious among themselves than they are towards other human beings. In both public and private gatherings, they are the most quarrelsome of men; they most often bring each other to trial; and they would rather take advantage of each other than profit by cooperative aid. They treat public affairs (*tà koiná*) as matters foreign to themselves, and yet fight battles over these concerns and take the greatest pleasure in possessing the faculties for such strife."[36]

There is every reason to take this description of the ethos of late fifth-century Athens at face value. In the elder Pericles' day, Thucydides tells us, the city was extraordinarily well governed, for that statesman was a man of "rank, intelligence, and evident integrity" who proved capable of "restraining the people in the manner of a free man (*eleuthérōs*)." Because his motives were known to be worthy, Pericles had no need to say anything solely in order to please the *dêmos*. When in boldness the citizens bordered on *húbris*, he could admonish them; when in despair they lost heart, he could restore their spirits: "He was not led by them but they by him." In peacetime, he conducted the city's affairs in a measured fashion (*metríōs*), guarding its safety. With regard to the great war against the Spartans and their allies, he displayed remarkable foresight (*pronoía*). In his heyday, the Athenian polity was "a democracy in name" and "the rule of the first man in fact." But Pericles died not long after the war had begun. In that regard, he betrayed a lack of *pronoía*, for he made no provision for his own replacement. Among those who sought to fill his place, there was no one of comparable stature, intelligence, and integrity. They were, in fact, "more or less equal to one another"; and in the contest for preeminence, they conducted the city "in accord with popular pleasure and turned affairs over to the *dêmos*." These men were driven by "private ambition and a concern for personal profit (*katà tás ıdías phılotımías kaì ídıa kérdē*)"; and in pursuing "private vendettas arising from their struggle for the leadership of the people (*katà tás ıdías dıabolàs perì tês toû démō prostasías*)," they brought harm to the city and its allies, impairing the Athenians' capacity to resist the Peloponnesian foe, inspiring *stásıs*, and ultimately bringing the city to its knees.[37]

In their private affairs, the Athenians were as quarrelsome and combative as they were in public. Among other things, they were notoriously ready to drag one another into court.[38] And, as Theophrastus intimates, this is precisely what one would expect, for there is a connection between slander and backbiting on the one hand and freedom of speech, democracy, and liberty on the other.[39] It would be easy to suppose that the city of Athena had somehow become an open society, with an ethos similar in character to that of James Madison's increasingly litigious liberal republic, and it is not at all surprising that, in the wake of the French Revolution, Athens was romanticized and came to represent in the eyes of many the modern, liberal democratic ideal.[40] In our own day, especially among students of the classics, this vision retains considerable force.[41] Athens has even been represented as the primitive, premodern prototype of a working-class democracy.[42]

I . v i i . 3

And yet nothing could be further from the truth. The ancient democracies were, as Tocqueville remarked, "aristocracies of masters," and Athens was no exception. One could easily query the figures which Tocqueville gives for the number of slaves and of freemen in Attica: that he greatly exaggerates the former and underestimates the latter there can be no doubt. But objections of this sort are beside the point. For on the main issue Tocqueville was surely right. The "universal suffrage" which Athens extended to all adult, male citizens did not decisively set her apart from the less democratic regimes. The difference was simply a matter of degree. In the end, Athens's acceptance of slavery and its prevalence there made of that ancient city "an aristocratic republic"—albeit one "in which all the nobles had an equal right to the government."[43] Despite the growth of the market economy and the concentration of population in the town of Athens and in the port community that grew up at the Peiraeus, the ordinary Athenian remained a peasant smallholder caught up in village life and intent on achieving a measure of self-sufficiency;[44] and partly as a consequence of the campaigns against Persia, the incessant wars elsewhere, and the plentiful supply and low price of slaves, he seems to have been at least as well situated to become a slaveowner as his counterpart the dirt farmer of the American South.[45] Whether slavery dominated the productive sector of the economy or not is and will remain an open question.[46] But, in the end, the answer is of no great importance, for there is no reason to suppose that the mode of production is the only or even the most important force shaping the ethos of a society. What matters in this case is that, like their counterparts among the free white population in the American South, ordinary Athenians could and did take their own measure by comparing themselves favorably with the multitude of slaves in their midst.[47]

Democracy stood, in antiquity, for a limited extension of the circle of loyalty, not for a principled abandonment of the aristocratic sense of inborn superiority. The Athenians not only owned barbarian slaves in considerable numbers and excluded them from all participation in self-determination; they did so without any indication that they doubted the justice of their subjection. Furthermore, by the second half of the fifth century, they had transformed into a great empire of their own a league originally founded to defend the Greeks against Persia's appetite for dominion.[48] The citizens of Athens ruled—and even boasted that they ruled—over an extraordinary number of their fellow Hellenes.[49] As they were more than willing to acknowledge, this, too, involved a form of mastery and servitude.[50] No Athenian would have denied the accuracy of James Madison's claim that "the money with which Pericles decorated Athens, was raised by Aristides on the confederates of Athens for common defence, and on pretext of danger at Delos which was the common depository, removed to Athens, where it was soon regarded as the tribute of inferiors instead of the common property of associates, and applied by Pericles accordingly." Few seem to have worried that their dominion was unjust. The very fact that their allies tolerated this appropriation of the league monies was proof positive that these confederates were, indeed, inferiors and deserving of subjection. In short, the exercise of imperial dominion had much the same effect on Athenian morals and manners as slavery itself. "Dependent Colonies are to the superior State," Madison noted, "not in the relation of Children and parent according to the common language, but in that of slave and Master; and have the same effect with slavery on the character of the Superior." Like slaveholders, the citizens of an imperial community like Athens "cherish pride, luxury, and vanity. They make the labor of one part tributary to the enjoyment of another."[51]

There were, to be sure, other, more egalitarian influences on the ethos of Athens. Some Athenians did owe their livelihood to the despised professions of trade and industry. But, for the most part, these bourgeois pursuits were left in the hands of metics—and like the Jews of medieval Europe, these immigrants were kept on the periphery of the community: they were denied participation in politics, were refused the privilege of owning landed property, and were subjected to a resident alien's tax as a reminder of their low status.[52] Circumstances and the atmosphere created by democracy rendered the city of Athena somewhat more cosmopolitan than the other cities of Greece. At Athens, in the classical period, as at Sparta, even the rich were plainly dressed.[53] On the streets, we are told, one could hardly distinguish a citizen from a metic or slave, and the Athenians tolerated in both a freedom of speech purportedly unknown even to citizens in other communities.[54] But Athens's openness to the outsider should not be exaggerated: it was the radical democracy of the elder Pericles that tightened the requirements for citizenship, reacting to the permanent presence of immigrants in large numbers by insisting on the exclusion of their offspring from the political community and by reasserting with redoubled fervor the traditional emphasis on purity of blood.[55]

Centuries later, Dionysius of Halicarnassus looked back on the general Greek propensity for exclusiveness and expressly lumped Athens together with Sparta and Thebes. Like their less-democratic rivals, the Athenians were guilty of "harboring a claim to nobility of birth (*tò eugenés*)," and this claim was made manifest by their "sharing citizenship with none but the very few."[56] Dionysius would, in fact, have been justified in singling out Athens as an extreme case: for in contending that they were autochthonous—"always possessed of the same land" and even "born from the earth"—the Athenians cast aspersions on interlopers like the Spartans and the Boeotians,[57] and they asserted that they were of an origin considerably more ancient and aristocratic than these peoples,[58] that they were all brothers under the skin,[59] and that, in contrast with most other communities, they had an indefeasible, just, and rightful claim to their *pólis* and its attendant *chóra*.[60]

In the enforcement of morals, Athens was, at least when compared with other Greek *póleis*, quite notably lax. But the spirit that animated her regime was identical to that found elsewhere. Manliness and courage, public-spiritedness and piety—these were the standards by which the citizens as such were ultimately judged. James Madison summed up the difference between Sparta and Athens much as Plutarch had done: by juxtaposing not the goals but the approach taken by those who had framed laws for the two cities. "Lycurgus," he remarked, was "more true to his object," and he therefore placed himself "under the necessity of mixing a portion of violence with the authority of superstition; and of securing his final success, by a voluntary renunciation, first of his country, and then of his life." In contrast, "Solon . . . seems to have indulged a more temporising policy," for he "confessed that he had not given to his countrymen the government best suited to their happiness, but most tolerable to their prejudices."[61]

To Athenian temporizing, there were limits—and for obvious reasons: at no time in the classical period did the ethos of the citizen-warrior cease to be predominant. Thus, even at Athens, a man would forfeit his political rights as a citizen for throwing away his shield in battle or for compromising his manhood by allowing another to use him as a woman for pay.[62] Moreover, in that city, although the marketplace was left relatively unfettered by law, the force of custom and the ethos of civic friendship tended to prevent the interplay of supply and demand from dictating the price of services and goods.[63] Citizen morality also imposed other limits on behavior which may to us seem utterly strange. There is, for example, no reason to suppose that, in Athens, estates were ever inalienable, and there is no clear-cut evidence that there was any legal limit to the acreage that any individual could own.[64] But there was no real estate market and, in the democratic period, no public registry of property and contracts,[65] for land seems only rarely to have changed hands.[66]

Like other cities, Athens possessed sumptuary laws to prevent conspicuous consumption from inspiring jealousy.[67] There, under the democracy, custom came to dictate simplicity in dress and demeanor, and this development was perfectly consonant with the public policy of the democracy: for, in the aftermath of the Persian Wars, when the Athenians commissioned the Milesian architect Hippodamus to develop a plan for their new port city the Peiraeus, they were quite self-consciously choosing to build private homes equal in size and virtually identical in plan.[68] Moreover, in this period, as one would expect, the pressures on the wealthy to contribute to the public welfare through liturgies were not to be resisted.[69]

Like other cities, Athens gave women short shrift, relegating them almost entirely to the domestic sphere and, where economically feasible, confining them indoors.[70] In recording a universally acknowledged matter of fact, one client of Demosthenes told a jury, "For the sake of pleasure, we have courtesans; for the body's daily care, we have concubines; and for bearing legitimate children and faithfully guarding what lies within our homes, we have wives."[71] There was even a law at Athens disallowing wills made by those mentally incapacitated by insanity, old age, drugs, illness, or the influence of a woman.[72]

Similarly, despite her much-touted love of novelty[73] and her notorious openness to foreign cults, customs, and ways,[74] Athens was by our standards quite conservative. Prior to the scientific revolution, what was fresh and new was but rarely thought improved: in Attic Greek, the word *néos*, when applied to an event, actually connotes that which is unexpected, strange, untoward, and evil.[75] As one would then expect, Athens was intolerant of religious infractions: this was the *pólis* that sentenced the popular general Alcibiades to death for parodying the Eleusinian Mysteries in a private home;[76] this was the community that condemned the commanders victorious at Arginusae for failing to bury the citizen dead;[77] and this was the city that executed Socrates for not believing in the city's gods and for corrupting the youth by teaching them the same doctrine.[78]

It does not matter one whit that these particular prosecutions were politically motivated, as they all were.[79] Nor does it matter that the contest for public offices and honors generally accounted for charges being brought against those, such as Demosthenes' ally Timarchus, who had continued to exercise their rights as citizens after purportedly allowing themselves to be used as women by other men.[80] What counts above all else is that the rivals of Alcibiades, the opponents of the Arginusae generals, the enemies of Socrates, and the prosecutor of Timarchus had the religious and moral weapons ready to hand. No one—not even Socrates—ever dared to suggest that a man's religious beliefs and behavior were of no concern to the body politic, and no one argued that the city should concede full sexual freedom to all consenting adults. Not even in an emanation from its penumbra can one discern in the constitution of Athens a fundamental right to privacy. In that city, there were no effective institutional constraints on the exercise of popular will against those whose private demeanor had inspired public distrust; and to the best of our knowledge, none were ever even contemplated. Nor can one argue that these trials were isolated incidents. Though we are very poorly informed concerning day-to-day affairs in late fifth-century Athens, we do know that Diagoras of Melos was prosecuted for impiety, and there is evidence (some of it confused, but most of it quite plausible) that other philosophers and freethinkers suffered a similar fate.[81] Prosecutions for impiety were by no means unknown in the fourth century.[82]

As citizens, the Athenians exercised collective sovereignty, but they were not endowed with guarantees of civil liberty. Indeed, the body politic possessed in ostracism an instrument specifically designed to provide for the decade-long banishment of men guilty of no crime but the arousal of popular envy, fear, and distaste.[83] And when ostracism fell into abeyance, the popular courts remained fully capable of rigorously enforcing the citizen morality dictated by public opinion.[84] The orator Hyperides summed up the situation nicely in a speech prepared for one of his clients. "Do not form your judgment of me on the basis of the slanders made by the prosecutor," Hyperides' client urged the jury. "Do so, instead, on the basis of my entire life, examining the manner in which I have lived it. For no one in our city—neither the scoundrel nor the decent man—escapes the notice of the multitude, and the passage of time is the most precise witness for each man's way of conducting his affairs." [85]

It should not be surprising that Athenian defendants and plaintiffs displayed an almost obsessive penchant for introducing into their forensic orations matter extraneous to the issue in dispute but pertinent to the defense of their conduct in general. It made perfect sense for them to recount in detail the services that they had performed on the community's behalf.[86] Under Athenian law, any citizen could lay charges, and political disputes often played themselves out as contests in court.[87] Moreover, by the late fifth century, malicious prosecution was quite common;[88] and rich men, because they were envied and because many were suspected of harboring a sympathy for oligarchical rule, were easy marks.[89] Given the fact that orators were vulnerable to prosecution for accepting bribes and for making unlawful proposals and that the generals and the lesser magistrates were subject to an audit and judicial reckoning (*eúthuna*) at the end of their term of office, prudence dictated that the wealthy think hard before entering the political arena.[90] In anticipation of the day when a sycophant could not be bought off,[91] the prosperous were well advised to perform liturgies and other services designed to curry popular favor.[92] For, given the great size of the juries, to go on trial before a court was, in effect, to be judged as a citizen by the city itself.[93]

Benjamin Constant's analysis of the Athenian regime deserves heed. Athens did fail in practice to complete "the subjection of individual existence to the collective body"; she provided her citizens with much "greater individual liberty than Rome and Sparta"; and this phenomenon was intimately linked with the important role played by "commerce" and trade in her development. But by the same token, other aspects of Athenian life—the size of the polity, the laws and customs she inherited, the central importance accorded piety, the prevalence of slavery, the subjection of women, and the possession of an empire—served to make her illiberal not just in principle, but quite often in practice as well. As Constant put it: "We discover there vestiges of the liberty proper to the ancients. The people make the laws, examine the conduct of the magistrates, summon Pericles to render his accounts, condemn to death all the generals who had commanded at the battle of Arginusae. At the same time, ostracism, an arbitrary law much vaunted by all the legislators of the age, ostracism, which seems to us and should seem a revolting iniquity, proves that the individual was still very much subject to the supremacy of the social body at Athens—which he is not, in our time, in any free state of Europe." [94] Athens was not a liberal democracy occasionally subject to fits of aberrant behavior; she was a military, moral, and religious community reduced by circumstances and by conscious decisions to an advanced state of disarray and decay.

I . v i i . 4

Of course, one might wish to argue, as scholars caught up in the populist currents of our egalitarian age are wont to do, that the criticism leveled at Athens by Thucydides, the students of Socrates, Aristotle, and the other great thinkers of antiquity should be discounted as the antidemocratic posturings of embittered aristocrats deprived of what they take to be their birthright.[95] Moreover, from the funeral oration of the elder Pericles, one could easily enough construct a defense of Athens's democracy against that critique. This defense would, however, give cold comfort to those tempted to envisage Athens as a liberal regime. If Thucydides' report is to be trusted, Pericles did project a vision of an Athenian people tolerant of unorthodox and hedonistic behavior in private life. But in the same breath he asserted that they were still governed by dread (*déos*) and by shame (*aischúnē*) in their conduct of public affairs.[96] He acknowledged their cultivation of the arts but denied that it resulted in extravagance, and he praised them for their love of intellectual speculation, but only because this never reduced them to cowardly softness.[97]

Pericles' Athens was, by his own later admission, a tyrant *pólis*—the unwanted mistress of a great empire.[98] "We inspire wonder now," he observed, "and we shall in the future. We have need neither for the panegyrics of a Homer nor for the praises of anyone to whose conjecture of events the truth will do harm. For we have forced every sea and every land to give access to our daring; and we have in all places established everlasting memorials of evils [inflicted on enemies] and of good [done to friends]."[99] This Athens was a community of soldiers, not a bourgeois society of men "absorbed in the pursuits of gain, and devoted to the improvements of agriculture and commerce." Pericles' Athenians did not disguise their disdain for men of this stripe. "We do not think that a man who takes no part in politics is 'a man who minds his own business (*aprágmōn*),'" the statesman observed. "Alone we judge him utterly worthless."[100]

This contemptuous aside was not just a passing remark. On a later occasion, Pericles discussed the *aprágmōn* once more and made his reasoning clear. "Men of this sort," he argued, "would quickly destroy a city—here, if they persuaded others; elsewhere, if they set up an independent town for themselves. For 'the man who minds his own business' is saved only where posted with the man of action (*metà toû drastēríou*); and to seek safety in servitude, while it might suffice in a subject community, would not be of advantage in an imperial city."[101] Empire defined the Athens of Pericles. Empire constituted its greatness. Empire enabled it to become what Homer had once been: "the education of Hellas."[102]

In so warlike a commonwealth, the feminine virtues naturally counted for little: to be sure, Pericles did mention the wives and mothers of Athens in his funeral oration, but he did so only to say that the woman with the "best reputation" was the one "least talked about among men for praise or for blame."[103] The private pleasures of the household were judged far inferior to those of public life. "The love of honor is the only thing that never grows old," Pericles reminded his listeners, "and the greatest delight, when one is worn out with age, is not, as some say, turning a profit, but enjoying the respect of one's fellows."[104]

The emphasis on honor and shame runs through the entire address. Yet on the closely related subject of piety, Pericles is strangely silent. Despite the solemnity of the occasion, he apparently made no mention of the gods and heroes of the land; and though the circumstances were propitious, he neglected the opportunity for reasserting the ancestral and religious foundations of the community's solidarity in the war then under way. When Pericles did allude to the public sacrifices and to the festival games, he treated these religious events as entertainments adding to the dignity and pleasure of citizen life, not as ceremonies constituting the city's divine service.[105] There is much to link Pericles' celebrated address with the orations delivered in Athens on similar occasions.[106] But in its disdain for tradition and in its celebration of all that is recent in Athenian life, the great statesman's speech stands in stark contrast to the conventional rhetoric with which the Athenians were familiar.

One must, in fact, wonder whether James Madison had the funeral oration in mind when he wrote of the ancient democracies that "theoretic politicians, who have patronized this species of government, have erroneously supposed that by reducing mankind to a perfect equality in their political rights, they would, at the same time, be perfectly equalized and assimilated in their possessions, their opinions, and their passions." There is certainly no reason to suppose that Pericles thought it possible or would have deemed it desirable to eliminate the problem of faction by giving free rein to opinion and by encouraging the multiplication of special interests in the fashion later recommended by Madison himself. Only in modern times, after the publication of Machiavelli's unorthodox, institutional analysis of the Roman republic and the appearance of James Harrington's *Oceana*, John Locke's *A Letter Concerning Toleration*, and the second of his *Two Treatises of Government*, could a republican statesman write, "*Divide et impera*, the reprobated axiom of tyranny, is under certain qualifications, the only policy, by which a republic can be administered on just principles."[107] The Athenian orators were obsessed with the need for *homónoia*.[108] Even Democritus of Abdera, the figure most often cited as the ancient analogue to the modern liberal, believed that civic unity was indispensable. "It is *homónoia* that enables cities to do great deeds and to prosecute wars," he asserted. "Without it, they cannot."[109] If Pericles neglected the gods and heroes of the land, it was perhaps because Athens's great leader sensed that religious veneration and the respect for all that is ancestral no longer sufficed as guarantees of political like-mindedness and civic courage. Indeed, the funeral oration could be taken as evidence that he believed that he had discovered an adequate substitute in the *érōs* for glory.[110]

Toward the end of the speech, Pericles raised this issue directly. At the time that he delivered the address, he stood outside, near the cemetery at the Ceramicus, within easy view of the Parthenon and a number of the other temples which had been under construction on the acropolis and elsewhere prior to the outbreak of the war. The reader of Thucydides' brief summary of Pericles' most famous speech should perhaps conjure up the image of Athens's greatest orator pointing for effect to that collection of buildings as he exhorted his fellow countrymen:

> Fix your gaze daily on the power that actually belongs to the city—and become her *erastaí*! And when you have realized her greatness, keep in mind that those who acquired this were men of daring, men who knew what was demanded, men who were ashamed to be found wanting in action. . . . They gave their lives in common; and each on his own received in return both a praise that never grows old and the most remarkable of tombs—not that in which they lie buried, but rather that in which their reputation (*dóxa*) is laid up forever, always to be remembered on every occasion which calls for speech or for deed. For men graced with fame have the entire earth for a tomb: not only does the inscription on the columns in their own land mark them out; but, in foreign climes, an unwritten remembrance lives on in men's hearts though not graven on stone. Let these men be your model; and supposing happiness to be freedom and freedom to be stoutness of heart, take no notice of the dangers of war.[111]

In truth, Athens owed more to the Lacedaemonian example than Pericles was ever willing to admit. His Athenians are no less and in fact even more wholeheartedly dedicated to the pursuit of fame than the Spartans of Tyrtaeus. That much is evident from the remarks Pericles chose to deliver on the final occasion when he addressed his fellow citizens.

The extraordinary outburst that marks the beginning of the funeral oration's conclusion might conceivably be dismissed as a set of observations made in passing on an occasion that called for overblown rhetoric. But, according to Thucydides, Pericles returned to the same theme in his last speech to the Athenians—and this time with redoubled vigor. In the course of making his case, he not only joined the Spartan poet in emphasizing that the "shining glory" of the man who died for the community would by his fellow citizens be "never forgotten." He did not limit himself to the suggestion that the man's "name" would be "remembered" by those left behind in the city. Pericles went further, much further. Tyrtaeus's horizon had been entirely civic. His argument had been that within the city which the dead hoplite had defended his "tomb is pointed to with pride, and so are his children, and his children's children, and afterward all the race that is his." Unlike Tyrtaeus, Pericles was willing to contemplate the city's demise; he contended that even the annihilation of Athens would leave intact and unimpaired the golden memory of what her citizens had done:

> Remember that this city has the greatest name among all mankind because she has never yielded to adversity, but has spent more lives in war and has endured severer hardships than any other city. She has held the greatest power known to men up to our time, and the memory of her power will be laid up forever for those who come after. Even if we now have to yield (since all things that grow also decay), the memory shall remain that, of all the Greeks, we held sway over the greatest number of Hellenes; that we stood against our foes, both when they were united and when each was alone, in the greatest wars; and that we inhabited a city wealthier and greater than all. . . . The splendor (*lamprótēs*) of the present is the glory of the future laid up as a memory for all time. Take possession of both, zealously choosing honor for the future and avoiding disgrace in the present.[112]

One would be hard pressed to imagine an address more warlike in tone. It is no wonder that Alexander Hamilton denounced the republics of antiquity as "an infinity of little jealous, clashing, tumultuous commonwealths, the wretched nurseries of unceasing discord."[113] No modern liberal, acting in a manner consistent with liberal principles, could ever choose to defend a democratic regime in Periclean terms. And yet, as David Hume points out, the great statesman's panegyric of the city was, at least in this respect, typically Athenian.[114]

I. vii. 5

The illiberal character of the vision which Pericles projected cannot be gain-said, but one must wonder whether Athens ever actually achieved that at which her greatest statesman evidently aimed. It is characteristic of human affairs that deeds nearly always fall short of the aspirations advertised in speech. If the women of that city were little noticed in public, the position of prominence they occupied within the comparatively invisible world of the household should generally have given them an emotional leverage enabling them to counter in some measure the Athenian fascination with public affairs, and it may have conferred on them a certain indirect, covert influence over the political behavior of their fathers, brothers, husbands, and sons.[115] And yet, the natural allure of the domestic sphere seems to have counted for little when in competition with the erotic politics preached by Pericles—for if the ancient writers had been able to compare the polities of antiquity with those of our own time, there is one point on which they would have been agreed: the development of Athens's empire, the simultaneous and parallel elaboration of her democratic institutions, and the concomitant decay of the traditional ethos of reverence and shame really did unleash a mad and uncontrollable passion for dominion, for power, and for glory, one not just wholly foreign to the bourgeois temper of modern liberal democracy but, in fact, excessive even by the standards of ancient Greece. To begin to explore this phenomenon, one need only turn to the view expounded by the Corinthians.

In 432, on the eve of the Peloponnesian War, a Corinthian delegation appeared at Sparta to argue that an immediate war with Athens was essential if the Spartan alliance was to survive. The bulk of their presentation dealt with particulars and focused on the most recent Athenian provocations. But at the end, the Corinthians attempted to make clear to their allies just what they were up against, and in the process they provided an analysis of the Athenian character that, if borne out by Athens's behavior, would come close to justifying the most extreme of Pericles' pronouncements. The Athenians they depicted as "innovators, keen in forming plans, and quick to accomplish in deed what they have contrived in thought." In contrast, they claimed,

> You Spartans are intent on saving what you now possess; you are always indecisive, and you leave even what is needed undone. The daring of the Athenians exceeds their strength, they take risks against all reason, and in the midst of terrors they remain of good hope—while you accomplish less than is in your power, mistrust your judgment in matters most firm,

and think not how to release yourselves from the terrors you face. In addition, they are unhesitant where you are inclined to delay, and they are always out and about in the larger world while you stay at home. For they think to acquire something by being away while you think that by proceeding abroad you will harm what lies ready to hand. In victory over the enemy, they sally farthest forth; in defeat, they give the least ground. For their city's sake, they use their bodies as if they were not their own; their intelligence they dedicate to political action (*es tò prássein ti*) on her behalf. And if they fail to accomplish what they have resolved to do, they suppose themselves deprived of that which is their own— while what they have accomplished and have now acquired they judge to be little in comparison with what they will do in the time to come. If they trip up in an endeavor, they are soon full of hope with regard to yet another goal. For they alone possess something at the moment they long for it: so swiftly do they contrive to attempt what has been resolved. And on all these things they exert themselves in toil and danger through all their days of their lives, enjoying least of all what they already possess because they are ever intent on further acquisition. They look on a holiday as nothing but an opportunity to do what needs doing, and they regard peace and quiet free from political business (*hēsuchían aprágmona*) as a greater misfortune than a laborious want of leisure (*ascholían epíponon*).

The Corinthians conclude their diatribe by suggesting that "if someone were to sum the Athenians up by saying that they were born neither to allow themselves nor other human beings any peace and quiet (*hēsuchía*), that someone would speak the truth." [116]

There is no reason to doubt the testimony which Thucydides attributes to the Corinthians. The Athenians did everything that they could to live up to their reputation. In the last third of the fifth century, they fought a great war against the Spartans and their allies. In the first few years of that war, they lost approximately one-third of their population to the plague;[117] and after a decade of struggle, both parties to the conflict were driven by exhaustion to negotiate a peace that left all of the fundamental questions unresolved.[118] No one seriously expected the peace to last; and so, when Sparta encountered difficulties in the Peloponnesus, the Athenians provided considerable aid and comfort to Lacedaemon's ancient Argive enemy and to her rebellious allies.[119] When that venture failed, the Athenians proved incapable of remaining at rest, and despite the danger that failure might open the way for a renewed Spartan offensive, they accepted an appeal from a beleaguered barbarian community in Sicily and launched an expedition to seize Syracuse and conquer the distant island.

Alcibiades was the proponent of this venture, as he had been the proponent of renewing the struggle with Lacedaemon, and Nicias was his opponent, as he had been on that earlier occasion. We do not know what was said in the initial debate, but after the decision to send an expedition had been made, Nicias sought to have it reversed. He conceded at the outset that his "speech (*lógos*)" would be at odds with the Athenian character (*pròs mèn toùs trópous toùs humetérous*) and that it was highly unlikely that he would be able to persuade his countrymen "to preserve what they already possessed and not to risk what was ready to hand for prospects which lie hidden in future time." But he was resolved to make the attempt. And so he spelled out the dangers involved in undertaking such a venture while leaving so powerful an enemy behind, and he drew attention to the obstacles that lay in the way of conquering Sicily and to the virtual impossibility of holding on to an island so large and so far from home even if it were to fall into Athenian hands. He emphasized as well that it would be prudent, in the wake of the plague and the costly war that Athens had fought with Sparta, for the city to nurture its depleted manpower and build up its treasury with tribute from the empire it already possessed, and he sought to rally the older men in Athens's assembly in opposition to young men "in the grips of an unhealthy lust for what lies afar (*dusérōtas . . . tôn apóntōn*)."

In alluding to the ambitions of the young, Nicias referred disparagingly to the extravagance and the striving for personal brilliance (*idía ellamprúnesthai*) that characterized his rival Alcibiades,[120] and so it was quite predictable that the latter rise to his own defense. In doing so, he acknowledged that it was natural that he incur envy in making himself shine (*lamprúnomai*), but he suggested that the victories won by his teams in the chariot race at the Olympic games benefited the city by conveying an impression of strength. In their own lifetimes, he conceded, those who exhibit "brilliance (*lamprótēs*)" may by their example inflict a species of pain—especially on their equals and the others with whom they live. But when they are gone, jealousy gives way, men claim to be their relations, even when there is no truth in it, and the fatherland remembers them not as "strangers guilty of misdeeds but as compatriots who have done noble deeds (*hōs perì sphetérōn kaì kalà praxántōn*)." He had demonstrated his abilities in marshaling the Argives and Sparta's erstwhile allies against Lacedaemon, and with the help of the barbarians of the Sicilian hinterlands, he would prove his mettle once more in a struggle against cities composed of a promiscuous mix of peoples incapable of thinking and acting together and therefore wholly lacking in public spirit.

Alcibiades urged his compatriots to remember that Athens had acquired its empire as other communities elsewhere had done so: by coming to the aid of those who sought help, as he was now asking them to do. "It is not," he insisted, "possible to calculate, in the manner of a paymaster, just how large an empire we wish to rule, but it is necessary, as things stand, to conspire at new conquests and to retain what we have, for if we do not rule others we shall risk being ruled by them, and you Athenians cannot look on the quiet life (*tò hēsuchon*) as others do—unless you are going to change your practices and make them like theirs." By displaying their contempt for peace and quiet (*hēsuchía*), he averred, the Athenians would lay low the presumption of the Peloponnesians; and with what they gained in Sicily, they could hope to secure rule over all of Hellas. Nicias's policy of "minding one's own business (*apragmosúnē*)" and his attempts to divide the young from the old, Alcibiades denounced as foreign to Athenian custom. He suggested that, if the city were to "remain at rest (*hēsucházē*)," it would, like everything else, wear itself out, and its skill in all things would inevitably grow old and gray—while by struggle (*agōnizoménēn*) the *pólis* would add steadily to its experience, and it would become even more fully habituated to defending itself not in words but in deeds. "In general," he concluded, "I think that a city not minding its own business (*pólin mè aprágmona*) would quite swiftly bring itself to ruin by changing to a policy of minding its own business (*apragmosúnēs metabolē*), and I judge that those human beings live most safely who conduct their affairs in a fashion as little as possible divergent from their present character and customs (*toîs paroûsin éthesi kaì nómois*), even though these may be defective." [121]

It says much about the Athenians that the interchange between their two generals served only to increase their ardor for the expedition. It says even more that, when Nicias returned to the fray and sought to dissuade his compatriots by greatly magnifying the needs of the enterprise, his strategy backfired. According to Thucydides' report, "An *érōs* for the expedition fell upon all alike: the older men were persuaded that they would either subdue the places against which they were sailing or would come to no harm with so great a force; the young men in their prime were seized by a longing for the sights and spectacles of far-away places and were confident that they would return safe and sound. The great multitude and the ordinary soldier looked forward to earning money right away and to acquiring the power by which they might secure a permanent source of pay thereafter." [122] When in due course they put to sea, Thucydides tells us, everyone went down to the Peiraeus to see them off. It was the most splendid expedition ever mounted by any Greek city; and after reciting the customary prayers, singing the traditional hymn, and pouring their libations from cups of silver and gold, they set out by trireme in column and then raced to Aegina, joyfully making their way to a destination and contest from which only a handful of the men in their expedition and in the force sent to relieve it would ever return.[123]

One could, of course, query whether the debate reported by Thucydides ever took place in anything like the form in which he presents it. The speeches are his in style, and they are, in any case, far too compressed to have been intelligible to ordinary listeners. Moreover, the remarks attributed to Nicias and Alcibiades echo the orations of Pericles and the speech of the Corinthians at Sparta, and it can hardly be fortuitous that political *érōs* and the quest for *lamprótēs*, as opposed to *apragmosúnē* and the preference for *hēsuchía*, are as much at stake in the historian's account of the origins of the Sicilian expedition as they were in those earlier orations.[124] At the very least, Thucydides was selective in reporting what was said, as all historians are and must be, and he clearly chose to explore in his narrative and highlight in reporting the pertinent political debates the unfortunate consequences of Pericles' decision to instill in his compatriots a lust for civic glory. To the extent that the historian, intent above all else on accuracy, has given way to the artist, we find ourselves grappling not with Athens but with Thucydides' own reading of events and of his native city's peculiar bent.[125]

Fortunately, we possess another source of information in the plays of the poet Aristophanes. In *The Knights*, for example, he parodies Pericles' exhortation that the citizens become Athens's *erastaí*, and thereby he confirms the accuracy of Thucydides report in this vital regard.[126] More important, he chose to devote his play *The Birds* to a comic depiction of the same raging ambition and incapacity to leave well enough alone that so fascinated his older contemporary.[127] Moreover, it would be difficult to explain the Sicilian expedition itself without regard to the meddlesomeness that the comic poet, Thucydides, and their contemporaries customarily called *polupragmosúnē*,[128] and that great enterprise was not the first in which the Athenians had courted and wed disaster by allowing themselves to be diverted from the struggle with Sparta by the opportunity to seek their fortune on far-distant shores. In 460 or 459, when Athens was already involved in the First Peloponnesian War, Egypt revolted from Persian rule, and the Athenians sent a fleet of two hundred triremes to support the uprising and then another fifty ships to relieve that fleet—only to lose everything that they had wagered: a vast armada and something approaching fifty thousand men, not a few of them Athenian citizens.[129] Plutarch's contention that Pericles had found it necessary to dissuade his compatriots from undertaking other ventures in Egypt and Sicily is perfectly plausible. In the 420s, if not before, some Athenians favored an attempt to conquer Carthage.[130] Although she was remarkably cosmopolitan and relatively tolerant in her domestic relations most of the time, in the end, Athens was in her martial demeanor and in her insatiate lust for glory and for the profits of war exceedingly grim. When Plato's Socrates contends that, long before his young friend Alcibiades appeared on the scene, his countrymen had cast moderation (*sōphrosúnē*) to the winds under the leadership of Themistocles, Cimon, and Pericles, he states an opinion that Thucydides would have endorsed. The only Athenian in the latter's history to preach *sōphrosúnē* does so in the course of advocating genocide.[131]

Over time, the city's character may have softened somewhat. Athens's experience in the Peloponnesian War and her ultimate defeat were sobering. In the course of the war and in its immediate aftermath, she enacted a series of institutional reforms that appear to have been designed to discourage sycophancy, to restrain demagoguery, and to encourage prudence, moderation, and the rule of law.[132] In the first few decades that followed, she conducted her affairs with greater shrewdness and caution than hitherto had been her wont.[133] There is even evidence suggesting on the part of the Athenians an increasing absorption in the trials and tribulations of life within the confines of the domestic sphere.[134] But these changes arguably touched the surface, not the substance, of civic life; and there is much to be said for those critics of Athens's radical democracy, both ancient and modern, who charge that the city's legal and judicial system fostered a pattern of malicious prosecution, which made Athens unsafe for men of exceptional wealth, talent, or intelligence, and that her assembly provided a middle ground more conducive to passionate outburst than to rational deliberation, rendering Athenian politics so tumultuous, turbulent, and contentious that it was virtually impossible for a statesman to pursue a coherent foreign policy.[135] Certainly, at no time in this period did any Athenian concern, such as guaranteeing justice to the individual, securing the rule of law, or encouraging prudence and consistency in the conduct of diplomacy and war, rank higher than sustaining the sovereignty of the popular will; and except at rare moments of crisis, when a Thrasybulus or a Demosthenes might temporarily attain a preeminence comparable to that once occupied by the elder Pericles, the public arena at Athens was vigorously, bitterly contested ground.[136] Moreover, even in the fourth century, when her manpower had greatly diminished and she was constantly short of the requisite financial resources, the city was nearly always at war; and when Demosthenes rallied the Athenians against the threat from Macedon, they responded to his call and risked everything again and again over a period of years in the hope that they might retain full, untrammeled political freedom. Indeed, only when the democracy was itself destroyed did Athens succumb. At no time in human history has a people displayed so complete a commitment to the principle that man is by nature a political animal blessed with a capacity for *lógos* enabling him to discern and make clear to others what is advantageous, just, and good.

In a comedy no longer extant, the late fourth-century Athenian poet Menander summed up the outlook of the ancient citizen-soldier in a handful of words. "For me," one of his characters remarks, "the city is a place of refuge, a source of lawful order (*nómos*), and a master (*despótēs*)—judge of everything: of that which is just and of all that is unjust as well." To this observation, the man added a striking, if perhaps predictable conclusion, observing that "it is for the sake of (*pròs*) this one master that I must live." [137] Even at the very end, democratic Athens was in her fundamental principles as much a republic of virtue as twentieth-century Great Britain—with her monarchy and her House of Lords, with her nationalized industries and her welfare state—is a liberal, capitalist, bourgeois democracy. Every Greek *pólis* demanded from its citizens nothing less than everything—and as a consequence, philosophy could nowhere in Hellas find a truly comfortable home.

I.vii.6

The cause of philosophy's homelessness is relatively easy to ascertain. Largely because his pursuits were incompatible with *aidós*, and because they threatened the dominion of *nómos* and promised to undercut the *homónoia* which sustained the community in its particularity, the philosopher was destined to remain forever a stranger (*xénos*) in the ancient city's midst.[138] There was, to be sure, an intimate connection between the emergence of classical republicanism and the birth of philosophy, and this needs to be underlined. It is, for example, by no means fortuitous that the term *kósmos* and its cognates were employed with regard to man's capacity for establishing and maintaining political order in particular communities well before *kósmos* came to be used by philosophers to impute order to the universe as a whole.[139] The conceptual scheme applied by the pre-Socratics was in large part borrowed from the political sphere. Thus, while Hesiod confined justice (*díkē*) to mankind, Solon extended the notion to the sea, and Thales' immediate successor Anaximander of Miletus made giving "*díkē*" and making "reparation to one another for injustice (*tísis allélois adikías*) according to the ordinance of time (*katà tèn toû chrónou táxin*)" the principle governing the universe as a whole.[140] Soon thereafter, the Pythagorean medical writer Alcmaeon of Croton appropriated the term *isonomía*—which was coined in the sixth century to describe

a political regime marked by equality of participation and the rule of law—
and suggested that health resulted when there was an equilibrium (*isonomía*)
between wet and dry, hot and cold, bitter and sweet, and so forth, while
disease was the consequence when any one of them secured sole rule (*monarchía*).[141] In much the same fashion, colonization and the practice of founding
cities organized on an orthogonal grid seem to have prepared the way for
the sciences of astronomy and cartography:[142] Anaximander is said to have
been the *oikistḗs* of Apollonia on the Black Sea,[143] and he appears to have conceived of the universe on the model of a city laid out in a symmetrical space
geometrically defined—with the earth occupying a position of privilege and
authority in the middle ground.[144] Moreover, when he constructed a map of
the earth, he seems to have represented it as a short, flat cylinder comparable
to a column drum: at the center of the flat circle atop that cylinder lay Hellas
and, at the center of Hellas, Delphi—the common hearth of Greece.[145] It was,
therefore, entirely appropriate that Philolaus of Tarentum should later name
the middle position in the universe Hestia after the goddess synonymous
with the public hearth.[146]

Philosophy's debt to politics is more profound than even these examples
might seem to suggest, for the shift from cosmogony to cosmology was arguably inseparable from the decline of sacral kingship and the opening up of
the middle ground which constituted the *pólis* as a *res publica*.[147] It was the
trust in *lógos* presupposed and fostered by the practice of making political
decisions only after extended, public debate that made possible Greek speculative reason in the first place.[148] But if the assumption that man is somehow
godlike and therefore capable of employing *lógos* as a tool for understanding
underlay in similar fashion the ambition that inspired classical republicanism
and that which gave rise to Greek philosophy and science, there remained,
nonetheless, an almost unbridgeable gap between the demands of citizenship and those of philosophy.[149] Heraclitus had no difficulty in recognizing
the problem, and he alluded to it with his customary brevity and grace when
he summed up the credo of the philosopher by contending, "Those who are
to speak with understanding (*xùn nóōi*) must draw strength (*ischurízesthai*)
from what is common to all (*tōi xunōi pántōn*) as a city draws strength from
its law—only much more so (*polù ischurotérōs*): for all human *nómoi* are nourished by the one divine law, and it exercises sway (*krateî*) as far afield as it
wishes, and it suffices and more than suffices for all."[150] To a community
united by concord regarding loved things held in common, to a *pólis* driven
by a passion for the particular, to a people expected to fight for their own
city's *nómos* as fiercely as for its walls, so cosmopolitan an outlook had to

remain forever alien.[151] In carrying to its ultimate conclusion the logic underlying the primacy which the Greeks conceded politics, philosophy promised
to destroy the very conditions of political life.[152]

Initially, at least, the tension between the demands of philosophy and
those of citizenship took the form of what Plato's Socrates would later describe as "an ancient quarrel between philosophy and poetry."[153] By all accounts, the philosophers initiated the dispute. Aristotle intimates that Anaximander of Miletus and the first *phusiólogoi*—"those exercising *lógos* regarding
nature"—espoused a species of monotheism;[154] and in the surviving fragments, Xenophanes of Colophon dismisses the Olympian gods outright.
"One god there is," he contends, "greatest among gods and humankind
(*anthrópoisi*), in no way like mortals in body or in the thought of his mind
(*nóēma*)."

> In his entirety (*oûlos*), he sees; in his entirety, he thinks; in his entirety,
> he hears.
> Always in the same place, he remains, moving not at all; it is not fitting
> (*epitrépei*) that he should shift about now here and, then, elsewhere.
> But, holding aloof from toil, he sets all things a-quiver (*pánta kradaínei*)
> with the thought of his mind (*nóou phrení*).

Xenophanes knew perfectly well that "mortal men believe that gods are begotten, and that they have the dress, voice, and body of mortals." But for the
opinions of mankind he had little, if any, respect. "If oxen, horses, or lions
had hands with which to sketch and fashion works of art as men (*ándres*) do,"
he remarked, "then horses would draw the forms of gods like horses, oxen
like oxen, and they would each make their gods' bodies similar in frame to
the bodies that they themselves possess." Indeed, he observed, "the Ethiopi-
ans claim that their gods are snub-nosed and black; the Thracians, that theirs
are blue-eyed and red-headed." The critical element in Xenophanes' analysis
is the supposition that god does only what is "fitting." That is why he can
object that "Homer and Hesiod have attributed to the gods everything which
is deemed shameful and blameworthy among humankind: theft, adultery,
and deceiving one another."[155] Put simply, the god of the philosophers conforms to reason—if he is not, in fact, reason itself. While their fellow citizens
took it for granted that the fate of the community depended upon propitiating their ancestral gods, the early rationalists evidently shared the conviction, eventually given full articulation by Leucippus of Abdera, that "no
thing comes into being at random but all takes place in accord with reason
(*ek lógou*) and by necessity."[156] In short, they were devotees of what Leibniz
would later dub the Principle of Sufficient Reason.

In time, the poets rallied in defense of the city's cults and the horizon defined by its gods. Pindar accused the *phusiólogoi* of "plucking wisdom's fruit unripe," and Aristophanes charged that Socrates taught disbelief in the city's gods, that he undercut the foundations of justice, and that he thereby corrupted the city's youth and even prepared the way for his own demise. One poet reviled philosophy as a "bitch yelping and baying at her master"; another charged her with "being great in the empty speech of fools (*aphrónōn keneagoríaisi*)." One spoke of her disciples as a "mob of overly clever men holding sway" while another dismissed these "subtle ponderers" on the grounds that they were, if truth be told, "very poor indeed (*ára penóntai*)." There were, Plato remarks, "ten thousand indicators" of this "ancient antagonism."[157]

I.vii.7

Of course, nowhere in the poetry of archaic and classical Hellas do we find a god directly confronting a man, demanding that he gird up his loins, and asking him:

Who is this that darkeneth counsel by words without knowledge? . . .

Where wast thou when I laid the foundations of the earth? Declare, if thou hast understanding.

Who hath laid the measures thereof, if thou knowest? or who hath stretched the line upon it?

Whereupon are the foundations thereof fastened? or who laid the corner stone thereof;

When the morning stars sang together, and all the sons of God shouted for joy? . . .

Hast thou commanded the morning since thy days; and caused the dayspring to know his place; . . .

Hast thou entered into the springs of the sea? or hast thou walked in search of the depth?

Have the gates of death been opened unto thee? or hast thou seen the doors of the shadow of death?

Hast thou perceived the breadth of the earth? Declare if thou knowest it all. . . .

Canst thou bind the sweet influences of Pleiades, or loose the band of Orion?

Canst though bring forth Mazzaroth in his season? or canst thou guide Arcturus with his sons?

Knowest thou the ordinances of heaven? canst thou set the dominion thereof in the earth? . . .

Doth the hawk fly by thy wisdom, and stretch her wings toward the south?

Doth the eagle mount up at thy command, and make her nest on high.

Nowhere in the ancient corpus does one come upon an individual or a chorus posing the question "Where shall wisdom be found and where is the place of understanding?" and answering it in the following fashion:

Man knoweth not the price thereof; neither is it found in the land of the living.

The depth saith, It is not in me: and the sea saith, It is not with me.

It cannot be gotten for gold, neither shall silver be weighed for the price thereof.

It cannot be valued with the gold of Ophir, with the precious onyx, or the sapphire.

The gold and the crystal cannot equal it: and the exchange of it shall not be for jewels of fine gold.

No mention shall be made of coral, or of pearl for the price of wisdom is above rubies.

The topaz of Ethiopia shall not equal it, neither shall it be valued with pure gold.

Whence then cometh wisdom? and where is the place of understanding?

Seeing it is hid from the eyes of all living, and kept close from the fowls of the air.

Destruction and death say, We have heard the fame thereof with our ears.

God understandeth the way thereof, and he knoweth the place thereof.

For he looketh to the ends of the earth, and seeth under the whole heaven;

To make the weight for the winds; and he weigheth the waters by measure.

When he made a decree for the rain, and a way for the lightning of the thunder:

Then did he see it, and declare it; he prepared it, yea, and searched it out.

And unto man he said, Behold, the fear of the Lord, that is wisdom; and to depart from evil is understanding.

To find all of this, one must turn to the Book of Job.[158] But discussions of similar import can easily be discovered in the Greek tragedians.

Sophocles is a case in point. In a justly famous passage of *Antigone*, the chorus celebrates the intellectual and technical accomplishments of man, then intimates that those very accomplishments breed the intellectual arrogance that brings about his fall:

Much there is that is wondrous and terrible (*pollà tà deiná*)
But nothing more so than humankind.
This thing makes its way across the grizzled sea in the wintry storm,
Driving through the engulfing swell.
The eldest of the gods, the imperishable, untiring Earth
He wears out
As the plows go to and fro year upon year
Turning the soil with the horse's breed.

Over the tribe of light-witted birds he springs his trap
And drives nations of wild beasts and the salty offspring of the deep
With his net's meshy coils:
Hard-thinking man (*periphradès ánēr*).
With contrivances he rules the beast that roams the mountain wilds.
The shaggy-maned horse
And the unwearied mountain bull
He binds fast
With a yoke about the nape of the neck.

Speech and Thought,
As fast as the wind,
And the dispositions that order the town (*astunómoi orgaî*)
He has taught himself.
Refuge he has contrived from the inhospitable frosts of clear nights
And from the bolts of winter's storms.
Resourceful (*pantopóros*) he is: in approaching no future is he at a loss
    (*áporos*).
Escape from Hades—that alone—he cannot procure.
From disease without remedy he has devised an escape.

A cleverness he possesses in devising arts (*sophón ti tò mēchanóen téchnas*)
That surpasses all hope
And brings him sometimes to evil, sometimes to good.

If he honors the laws of the land (*nómous geraírōn chthonòs*)
And the justice sworn to the gods,
His city stands high.
But cityless (*ápolıs*) is the man
Who consorts with what is not noble (*tò mḕ kalòn*) for daring's sake.
Let him not be my hearth-mate (*emoì paréstıos*)
Nor think thoughts equal to mine
He who does these things.[159]

But it is not in this play that the poet dramatically explores the question in full. For that, one must turn to his *Oedipus Tyrannos*.[160] The protagonist of Sophocles' greatest masterpiece is neither a cosmologist nor a sophist. But he is a man who has managed to live almost entirely by his wits, and he evidences an implicit trust in the capacity of *lógos* to master events. When investigating the death of Laius, he persistently employs not just the technical language of forensic rhetoric and the Athenian courts but the precise terminology of pre-Socratic medicine and science.[161] Moreover, when confronted with the unwelcome wisdom of the prophet Teiresias, he and Jocasta resort to the familiar sophistic critique of prophecy, and eventually the logic of this argument drives Oedipus to renounce all dependence on the gods by describing himself as "the son of chance."[162] Finally, when he learns that his presumed cleverness is really folly, the chorus describes him as "equal to zero," and he completely reverses course: first, he deprives himself of the sense most closely linked with human pretensions to knowledge; then, he calls himself a "see-nothing, learn-nothing" man; and imperious to the very end, he insists that the will of the gods be done.[163] It would not be too much to call the play a critique of human reason.

Thus, if Sophocles never describes wisdom as "fear of the Lord," he nonetheless comes remarkably close. In *Antigone*, Haemon warns his father Creon that "whoever thinks that he alone understands (*phroneîn*) and has tongue and soul, come the unfolding, is seen all emptiness"; and as Creon is led away at the end, the chorus chants,

Understanding (*tò phroneîn*) is the first prerequisite for happiness
   (*eudaimonía*).
One must avoid all impiety towards the gods.
In inflicting great blows upon the proud,
Great speeches (*megáloi dè lógoi*) teach understanding to old age.[164]

In reasserting the ancestral faith, and in laying bare the pretensions of philosophy and of all those inclined to put their trust in the power of *lógos*, the poet sought to preserve that piety which formed the city's horizon and sustained its solidarity. In doing so, he set an example that his younger rival Euripides would follow in his last and greatest play.

Euripides' *Bacchae* is nothing if not an exploration of the relationship between piety and wisdom. The Greek term *sophía*—skill, cleverness, wisdom—and its cognates run through the play like a silver thread.[165] Even before Pentheus and Dionysus appear on the stage, the prophet Teiresias has delineated what is at stake. "In the eyes of the gods our sophistries are as nothing at all (*oudèn sophizómestha toîsi daímosin*)," he asserts. "The ancestral traditions (*patríous paradochás*), which have been ours time out of mind—no argument (*lógos*) can cast these down: not even if invented by the cleverness (*tò sóphon*) of the most exalted minds."[166] In similar fashion, when confronted with Pentheus's refusal to believe and with the sophistic rhetoric the young king deploys, the chorus chants:

> For mouths unbridled
> And lawless folly
> The end is misfortune.
> But the life of peace and quiet (*hesuchía*)
> And the good sense (*tò phroneîn*) that remains unshaken
> These preserve the households of men.
> For the gods of heaven
> Who dwell in the far-distant air
> Watch over the affairs of humankind.
> Cleverness (*tò sophón*) is not wisdom (*sophía*).
> To think thoughts not mortal is to render life brief.
> This being so, who would pursue great things
> And not put up with what is present to hand?
> To my mind, these are the ways
> Of madmen and of mortals cursed with ill counsel.

A few lines later, after invoking and praising the god of wine, they conclude on much the same note:

> It is wise to hold both heart and mind
> Aloof from overwise, over-curious men (*perissôn phōtôn*).
> The multitude—whatever the simpler sort
> Customarily think and do
> This would I approve and make my own.[167]

Eventually, even Pentheus learns where true wisdom lies, but only when it is already too late.[168] "What is wisdom?" the Bacchantes ask, as they prepare to tear him limb from limb; and in due course, the answer presents itself:

Slowly it proceeds
But trustworthy nonetheless
The might divine.
It calls to account (*apeuthúnei*) those among mortals
Who, with mad conviction, honor senselessness (*agnōmosúna*)
And fail to extol that which pertains to divinities.
The gods lie hidden in manifold ways
The lingering foot of time
And hunt the unholy (*ásepton*) down.
For never must a man think
And habitually do
That which is stronger (*kreîsson*) than law (*nómoi*).
For it is a light expense
To think this to have strength:
Whatever is divine.
That which remains lawful (*nómimon*) over a long span
Is lawful by nature (*phúsei*) for all time.[169]

When the young man's grisly fate has been revealed, Euripides leaves his reader the words of a witness to ponder: "Moderation (*tò sōphroneîn*) and reverence for that which pertains to the gods—this is best (*kálliston*). And I think it the wisest practice in use by mortal men."[170]

Euripides' argument would no doubt have been more persuasive had that student of the philosopher Anaxagoras not sounded a false note: in defending the gods, his play's chorus resorts to the very distinction that serves as the foundation for philosophy's claim to primacy—the distinction between those things which exist by nature (*phúsis*) and those which exist only in law, custom, and convention (*nómos*). The fact that, in the end, the argument of Aristophanes' *Clouds* rests on the same distinction suggests that the two Athenian poets were persuaded that they had no other recourse.[171] In any event, by arguing their case on ground chosen by the enemy, Aristophanes and Euripides made it relatively easy for their most acute readers to anticipate poetry's ultimate submission to philosophical hegemony, and they rendered it possible as well to foresee the manner in which poetry might be made to serve as an instrument of rhetoric in educating the *kaloì kagathoí* on behalf of a philosophy that had become politic and prudent, aware of its own vulnerability, conscious of the danger it posed to the *pólis*, and convinced of the necessity that it deploy the weapons of enchantment in defense of philosophy and the city alike.[172]

I . v i i . 8

The Athenian poets' failure of nerve also helps explain why the philosophers—who had initiated this dispute—had the last word as well. As is well known, Plato did not hesitate to confront the question head-on. In fact, in *The Republic*, Socrates does much more than defend his calling; he devotes a considerable part of his discussion to turning the tables on philosophy's adversaries. In particular, he suggests that Homer and his fellows, in depicting the gods and heroes as they do, miseducate the Greeks and render them as citizens worse. He even advocates the censorship of poetry on the grounds that such restrictions are essential for the prevention of *stásis* and the promotion of *homónoia*. To be admitted to a well-ordered city, he contends, poetry should be required to do more than exhibit its undeniable charms; it should be required to demonstrate its usefulness and worth and to make its apology before the philosopher's tribunal.[173]

Largely, no doubt, because of the general exhaustion and decline of the *pólis*, but partly, perhaps, as a result of Plato's efforts and those of the other Socratics, by the late fourth century, the general atmosphere in Athens and elsewhere seems to have changed somewhat, and it became possible—and perhaps even advisable—for the philosopher to pursue an alternative rhetorical strategy.[174] If, in *The Politics*, Aristotle virtually ignores religion's vital contribution to constituting the life of the *pólis* and if, in the *Poetics*, he gives hardly a hint of the central role the gods played in Greek tragedy, it is not a consequence of negligence, blindness, or folly on his part.[175] In similar fashion, without even a cursory attempt at explanation, he omits piety when he lists the moral virtues in his *Nicomachean Ethics*, *Eudemean Ethics*, and *Rhetoric*.[176] The peripatetic appears to have thought the gods more necessary and better suited to prepolitical, village life than to the good life made possible by the Greek *pólis*.[177] Moreover, as a philosopher mindful of the fate of Socrates and devoted above all else to fostering and protecting what he considered the best way of life,[178] Aristotle seems to have been less concerned with providing the well-to-do young gentlemen who attended his lectures with an historically accurate account of Greek politics and poetry than with discouraging and therefore downplaying the one feature of ancient civic life most likely to fuel the city's intolerance of free inquiry. In his work, as in that of many another great writer, what passes as description is often prescription as well.

Aristotle's ominous silence regarding religion testifies to the fanatical particularity evidenced in its heyday by the ancient Greek *pólis* no less and perhaps even more eloquently than Plato's celebrated renewal of the "ancient quarrel between philosophy and poetry." [179] The silence of the former in this regard and the outspokenness of the latter complement nicely the critique they both advanced against polities dedicated to war and the decision they both made to assign music and a reformed poetry a prominent role in the model regimes they devised.[180] As both philosophers recognized, it would not be possible to reduce the tension between the life of the mind and the needs of the *pólis* and to render the latter less prone to self-destruction without somehow softening the city's warlike character and providing ordinary, unphilosophical men with an antidote to the spiritedness that made it that way.[181]

In antiquity, that softening in some measure eventually took place, but only at the price of the city's freedom and autonomy. In the new age of despotism, inaugurated by the Hellenistic monarchs and eventually dominated by imperial Rome, the assumptions underlying the notion that man is a political animal remained, despite freedom's demise, very much alive—especially within the various philosophical schools. From these contending sects, as we shall soon see, the assumption that man is a being endowed with the faculty of *lógos* and thereby rendered capable of distinguishing the advantageous, the just, and the good was passed on as a legacy to the great religion that directed European life and thought for more than a millennium after antiquity had come to an end.

Fides Quaerens Intellectum

In the fifth century Christianity had conquered Paganism, and Paganism had infected Chris-
tianity. The Church was now victorious and corrupt. The rites of the Pantheon had passed into
her worship, the subtilties of the Academy into her creed. In an evil day, though with great
pomp and solemnity,—we quote the language of Bacon,—was the ill-starred alliance stricken
between the old philosophy and the new faith. Questions widely different from those which had
employed the ingenuity of Pyrrho and Carneades, but just as subtle, just as interminable, and
just as unprofitable, exercised the minds of the lively and voluble Greeks. When learning began
to revive in the West, similar trifles occupied the sharp and vigorous intellects of the Schoolmen.
There was another sowing of the wind, and another reaping of the whirlwind.—Lord Macaulay

More than two millennia separate the republics of ancient Hellas from those
of modern times. In the interim, two events took place of decisive importance for the history of self-government. To begin with, the followers of a
man whom Niccolò Machiavelli would have termed "an unarmed prophet"
brought to completion the work of political subversion initiated by the pre-
Socratics and carried forward by the Hellenistic monarchs and by Rome.
Then, more than a thousand years thereafter, a number of philosophers and
men of like mind staged a great rebellion against the rule of that unarmed
prophet and his disciples—a rebellion aimed at the establishment of what
Machiavelli called "new modes and orders" and destined to culminate in the
emergence of secular polities throughout the Christian West. Each of these
two events can best be described as a profound revolution, for each resulted
in the complete dissolution of the old regime and in the institution of an
entirely "new order of the ages." In each case, this new order was constituted by the creation of a new ruling element (*políteuma*) formed by a hitherto
unknown *paideía*—or, to restate the same point in Augustine's terms, it was
constituted by the transformation of "a multitudinous assemblage of rational
beings" into a "people . . . united by concord regarding loved things" never
before "held in common."

The first of these two revolutions excites little controversy because it was
an entirely public event and is relatively easy to discern and describe. If
the classical republicanism that survived in a dispirited and attenuated form
under Hellenistic and Roman domination finally succumbed entirely, it was
because a universal religion destroyed the little that remained of the ancient
city's particularist foundations. Friedrich Nietzsche was on to something
when he dubbed Christianity "Platonism for the people (*Volk*)," for it accom-

plished for the great body of ordinary folk what ancient philosophy had only threatened to do for a tiny and relatively inconsequential elite: it devalued the quest for office, for power, and for glory, and it rendered citizenship and civic loyalty at best a secondary concern.[1] Where Pericles' Athenians had been expected to "judge worthless" any "man who takes no part in politics" and could be described as "one who minds his own business (*aprágmōn*)," Paul's Thessalonians were enjoined, for the sake of respectability, "to find honor in being quiet (*philotimeîsthai hēsucházein*)" and "to mind" their own "private affairs (*prássein tà ídia*)."[2] Tertullian tells us that his fellow Christians remain "cold in the face of all ardor for glory and honor (*dignitas*)" and that they have "no need for political gatherings (*necessitas coetus*)" whatsoever. "There is nothing," he concludes, "more alien to us than the commonwealth (*nobis . . . nec ulla magis res aliena quam publica*)."[3] In making this last point, he no doubt goes too far—but not by much. To Christians inclined to take politics seriously, Augustine poses an unanswerable question: "In so far as concerns this life of mortal men, which is conducted and brought to conclusion within a few days, what does it matter under whose rule lives a man who is destined to die—as long as those who rule do not force him to commit impious and iniquitous deeds?"[4]

Not surprisingly, when the Bible replaced Homer, the lives of the martyrs and saints supplanted Xenophon's *Cyropaedeia* and Plutarch's biographies of the noble statesmen and warriors of ancient Greece and Rome.[5] Under the new dispensation, spiritual and temporal authority were both thought to descend from God; and so, properly speaking, men everywhere were subjects, not citizens. In fact, just as the Church was committed to its tutor the pope, so the kingdom was entrusted to its lawful ruler, and the city to its magistrates—all of whom ruled their charges by the grace of God.[6] In time, to be sure, representative assemblies were established in the various kingdoms of the Christian West, and civic republics reappeared in Italy and elsewhere. But it is striking that self-government was initially justified not with an eye to man's nature as a political animal and to the glorious role assigned the political community in completing and perfecting what nature had already offered men—but in terms of the far more prosaic principle governing the Roman law of private corporations as it had been applied in legal cases concerning the management of waterways: "What touches all in similar fashion shall be by all approved."[7]

The subsequent recovery of Aristotle's works, their translation into Latin by William of Moerbeke, and their gradual absorption occasioned second thoughts on the part of some humanists and even a jurist or two.[8] But if truth be told, the heightened civic consciousness which emerged in the republics of Renaissance Italy under the influence of Aristotle, Cicero, and the other ancient writers was never more than halfhearted, if that.[9] Within Christendom (and, even more so, the House of Islam), politics could never regain the primacy it had been accorded within the pagan polities of ancient Greece and Rome. For, as Machiavelli did not fail to recognize, no one who embraced a *paideía* grounded on the distinction between the city of God and the city of man could honestly and with full conviction repeat the dictum which Francesco Guicciardini had lifted from Gino di Neri Capponi and Machiavelli had subsequently made his own: "I love my native city more than my soul."[10]

And yet, if the *pólis* disappeared, much of its legacy did not. To conquer Rome, Christianity had to absorb classical culture and learning; and to do that, it had to confront and come to terms with a politic philosophy that had managed to defeat, accommodate, and, in some measure, even impose its hegemony on the poetry which served as a foundation for that culture and learning.[11] Tertullian might fulminate against the Christian propensity for employing "that wretched Aristotle, who introduced for the heretics dialectic, which is so expert at building up and tearing down, so crafty in its statements, so forced in its conjectures, so harsh in its arguments, so productive of strife (*operaria contentionum*)—an annoyance even to itself." He might ask, "What has Athens to do with Jerusalem?" He might wonder, "What has the Academy to do with the Church (*Ecclesia*)?" He might demand to know, "What have heretics to do with Christians?" And in the end, he might proudly assert: "Our education takes place at the Stoa of Solomon, who stipulated that the Lord must be approached in simplicity of heart. Off with those who have put forward a Stoic, Platonic, and dialectical Christianity. After Jesus Christ, we have no need for curiosity; nor do we need inquiry after the Gospel. When we believe, we desire to believe nothing more. For we believe this before all else: that there is nothing else that we ought to believe." Tertullian might repeat himself endlessly in the most eloquent Latin prose. He might cite Paul's injunction to the Colossians to beware lest "someone rob" them of the true faith "through philosophy and an empty deception in tune with (*katà*) human tradition, in tune with the elements of the cosmos, and not in tune with Christ."[12] But his efforts were of no avail.

Christianity was not, like Judaism and Islam, a religion of holy law; it was first and foremost a religion of faith. Moreover, the Gospel of John had identified the Godhead with speech, argument, and reason (*lógos*), and it had described Christ himself as the *lógos* made flesh.[13] Even Paul speaks of what is demanded by Christianity as "reasonable servitude (*logíkē latreía*)."[14] Of course, the author of the epistles to Timothy and Titus also denounced as "blind and demented" those who, "knowing nothing, betray a pathological

interest in inquiries (*zētéseis*) and the logical disputes (*logomachías*) which give
rise to envy, strife, blasphemy, base suspicions, and the violent contentions
of human beings corrupt in mind and deprived of the truth"; and in the first
epistle to the Corinthians, he juxtaposed "the Greeks" who "seek (*zētoûsi*)
wisdom" with the Christians who "preach Christ crucified." But, as even the
most vociferous opponents of philosophy were aware, in the Gospel of Matthew, Christ is said to have promised his followers: "Seek (*zēteîte*), and ye
shall find." [15] Just two centuries after Tertullian had passed from the scene,
when his fellow North African Augustine contended that "faith is nothing
if it is not thought through," he spoke for what had already become the
Christian mainstream. [16]

   Tertullian unwittingly provides testimony foreshadowing his own defeat,
for it is not without significance that, in the passage cited, he calls the Church
by the name given the public assembly in the ancient Greek *pólis*: whether he
liked it or not, the civic *ekklēsía* of classical Hellas lived on within the Christian congregation. The man's eloquence is itself a sign of the reappearance of
politics in a new guise. For this, the evidence is dramatic. In the late fourth
century A.D., when Gregory of Nyssa visited Constantinople, he found the
townspeople, to his great exasperation, debating the theological questions
pertinent to salvation with the same verve that their ancestors had reserved
for disputes touching on matters of political prudence. "If you were to ask
a shopkeeper for your change," he later remembered, "the man would phi-
losophize to you concerning what is begotten and what is not. If you were to
inquire concerning the price of bread, the baker would reply, 'The Father is
greater and the Son, inferior.' And if you were to ask whether your bath is
ready, the attendant would specify that the Son takes his being from no being
(*ex ouk óntōn tòn Huiòn eînai*)." [17] In the early fourteenth century, when Jacques
Fournier, the future Pope Benedict XII, became bishop of Pamiers in Ariège
in the Comté de Foix and conducted a severe inquisition in his diocese, he
found the peasants resident in the mountain village of Montaillou and the
illiterate shepherds who wandered back and forth across the Pyrenees in
search of work arguing about questions of faith with no less interest and intensity than had been evidenced by the shopkeepers, bakers, and bath atten-
dants of Gregory's Constantinople. [18] Nearly a millennium had passed, and
nothing had changed. Throughout the Middle Ages, Christianity remained
what it had been virtually from the start: a great debating society.

   The triumph of *lógos* within Christendom came at a price. As Edward Gibbon had occasion to remark, "The study of philosophy . . . was as often the
parent of heresy as of devotion." [19] Hilarius of Poitiers put his finger on
the problem soon after the trouble began. "It is a thing dangerous to us in the

highest degree," he warned the emperor Constantius, "and also lamentable that there now exist as many creeds as inclinations, as many doctrines as usages, and as many occasions for blasphemy as there are vices among us." Even, he sadly remarked, "though the creed may be inscribed as we wish, it is interpreted in a manner we do not like." And the results were clear for all to see: "We wander in uncertainty—caught up in a wind of doctrines—and either we teach and are confused, or we are taught and go astray. . . . Every month and every year, we decide on creeds concerning the Deity, we repent from what we have decreed, we defend those who repent, and we anathematize those defended. We either damn the dogmas of others in our own or our own in those of others—and in devouring one another, we are consumed and ruined in turn."[20]

The emperor Julian was not far wrong when he contended that "no wild beasts are as savage to mankind as are the majority of Christians in their ruinous hatred of one another." Indeed, in the last two centuries, he has been proven largely correct in his conviction that the establishment of religious freedom would set at odds those whom he contemptuously dubbed "the Galilaeans" and decisively weaken, if not cripple, Christianity itself.[21] As was already evident in the time of Constantine, the theological disputes of the Christian epoch were, if anything, more bitter than the political quarrels of the classical age. That this should be the case may seem strange to men born in an enlightened and comparatively irreligious age, but it made perfect sense to those who lived in earlier times. In the opinion of the men and women caught up in these religious controversies, much more was at stake in their disputes than in the ancient political quarrels—and they had a case. In a world in which salvation is universally held to depend on an acceptance of the true faith, the avoidance of heresy and the correct interpretation of doctrine are of greater concern than mere life and death. As a consequence, the petty squabbles of the philosophical sects, which had been in ancient times purely academic, assumed a practical importance and a dignity now hard to fathom; and from the moment that the first Christian emperor consolidated his rule, the public authority was drawn into doctrinal disputes.[22]

The Gnostic, Arian, Donatist, Nestorian, and Monophysite controversies were simply the beginning. By late antiquity, as Lord Macaulay would in due course observe, "Christianity had conquered Paganism, and Paganism had infected Christianity."[23] As in the classical past, *lógos* turned out to be a double-edged sword—so that, if speech and reason brought Christians together, argument and disputation conspired to drive them apart. To make matters worse, the marriage of Athens and Jerusalem, which produced Rome, was an uneasy alliance from the start. The fulminations launched against Artemon and his followers by a nameless contemporary of Tertullian exposed quite early on what would remain thereafter a constant temptation:

> Fearlessly, they have altered the Holy Scriptures and rejected the standard of ancestral faith. Christ they have ignored, inquiring not what the Holy Writ says but endeavoring with great industry that a syllogistic schema be found in confirmation of their godlessness (*atheótēs*). . . . Abandoning the Holy Scriptures of God, they pursue geometry; and under the pretext that they are of the earth, they prattle regarding the earth and ignore the One who comes on high. Euclid they geometrize laboriously. Aristotle and Theophrastus strike them with wonder. To Galen, in like manner, they practically make obeisance. Availing themselves of the techniques of the infidel to bolster their heretical opinions, they peddle the simple faith of the Holy Writ for the knavish trickery of the atheists (*hoi átheoi*).[24]

Even Augustine was prepared to admit that an individual who embarks "rashly (*temere*) and without disciplinary order upon the study" of the philosophical underpinnings of Christian theology "will become fussy (*curiosus*) rather than studious, credulous rather than learned, unbelieving rather than circumspect."[25] In retrospect, one can easily see that Tertullian's objections were not entirely without substance: in embracing philosophy, the Christian church had welcomed into its confines a Trojan horse.

For the horse, the situation would appear to have been considerably less awkward. Prior to modern times, no philosopher of any great stature ever seriously suggested that the common people might be receptive to philosophical enlightenment.[26] In fact, when Plato's Socrates denied that "the multitude (*tò plêthos*)" can ever become "devoted to wisdom (*philósophon*)" and insisted that "the many" are by their very nature hostile to the philosophical enterprise, he stated assumptions that would go effectively unchallenged for two thousand years.[27] These assumptions had profound implications for the comportment of philosophers within the political community.[28] For one must think it both possible and desirable that "the multitude (*vulgus*) be gradually enlightened (*eruditur*)," as did Thomas Hobbes, if one is to conclude that, "in order that philosophy might prosper, it ought to be free and subject to coercion neither by fear nor by shame."[29] In antiquity, therefore, and for a long time thereafter, politically astute philosophers were prepared to tolerate popular prejudice, to negotiate a compromise papering over the "ancient quarrel between philosophy and poetry," and in some cases even to propagate what Plato had called "noble" or "medicinal lies" and what Quintus Mucius Scaevola and Marcus Terentius Varro later dubbed "civil theology."

Mindful of the fate of Socrates and persuaded that no polity can long survive and prosper if unsupported by a civil religion, they took it for granted that it was both prudent and right that they accommodate themselves in one fashion or another to the needs and superstitions of their unphilosophical neighbors and that they do something with the help of the poets under their influence to reshape those superstitions in such a fashion as to render them less irrational, less conducive to vindictiveness and the persecution of philosophers, and more useful as a support for the political community.[30]

This fact goes a long way toward explaining why, at least initially, some of the philosophers should find Christianity attractive. When compared with the alternative civil theologies available, that religion appeared to have three not inconsiderable virtues. Its doctrine of Providence and the promise of reward and the threat of punishment in the afterlife rendered Christian theology similar in character to the politically salutary myths propagated by Plato in his *Phaedo, Republic, Timaeus,* and *Laws* and made it seem plausible to suppose that it would be particularly effective as an incentive to public-spiritedness. Its otherworldly orientation could arguably serve to moderate the political passions that had so disrupted civic life in the classical period. And, last but not least, Christianity was evidently receptive and, in some measure, even friendly to philosophical influence.[31] In fact, in practice, except when heretical doctrines threatened popular revolt, there was to be considerable intellectual freedom within the Christian church. So, at least, it must have seemed to Synesius of Cyrene.

In late antiquity, when he was offered the diocese of Ptolemais, this proud descendant of Sparta's Heraclid kings demurred on a variety of grounds. It was not just the fact that he had no intention of leaving his wife, that he entertained a great passion for hunting and other sports, and that he was happily engaged in his studies as a philosopher. These were serious concerns, but there was an additional problem as well; and so, as a reminder to his benefactor Theophilus, bishop of Alexandria, he added to his response a disclaimer which, he evidently hoped, would suffice to disqualify him for the post. By way of introduction, he made two points: that "philosophy is ranged against many of the dogmas that are the common talk," and that "it is difficult, if not utterly impossible to shake doctrines that have come into the soul through a knowledge founded in demonstration." Then he announced his own inability to believe three parts of Christian doctrine: that the soul is of later origin than the body, that the universe and its parts will be someday destroyed, and that the Resurrection actually took place. To be sure, he added, as a consolation, that he had no desire to undermine the prejudices of the common folk and that, like Plato, he recognized the necessity for medicinal lies. "Philosophic intelligence," he explained, "though an observer of truth, acquiesces in the use of falsehood. Just consider this analogy: light is to the truth as the eye is to the intellect. Just as it would be harmful for the eye to feast on unlimited light and just as darkness is more helpful to diseased eyes (*toîs ophthalmiôsi*), so, I assert, falsehood (*tò pseûdos*) is of advantage to the *dêmos* and the truth would be harmful to those not strong enough to peer steadfastly on the clear revelation of that which truly is (*hē tôn óntōn enargeía*)." In fact, he was prepared to sketch out a compromise between faith and reason that might be satisfactory to both. "I would be able to serve," he suggested,

> if the regulations of the priesthood, as they pertain to us, were to allow me this: to love wisdom at home, to embrace fables abroad (*tà mèn oíkoi philosophôn, tà d'héxō philomuthôn*)—neither teaching nor unteaching, but suffering men to remain in their previous notions. However, if anyone says that I must also undergo a change of mind and that the opinions of the *dêmos* and its priest must be the same, I would not escape being revealed to all. For what do the *dêmos* and philosophy have to do with one another? The truth must be left secret and unspoken (*apórrēton*), for the multitude (*plêthos*) are in need of another state of mind (*héxis*).[32]

It was on the basis of the compromise suggested by Synesius that Theophilus provided for the ordination of this talented infidel and for his consecration as bishop of the Libyan community of Ptolemais.[33]

Synesius's experience can hardly have been the norm, but his seems not to have been an entirely isolated case. The Neoplatonist Gregory of Nyssa was no less reluctant to enter the priesthood and be consecrated a bishop, and there is reason to wonder whether he was ever a sincere Christian.[34] In any event, there can be no doubt that the schools and universities which eventually grew up in the Christian West provided a relatively safe haven for heterodox speculation—at least for scholars willing to acquiesce in medicinal lies and pay lip service to approved doctrine.[35] Moreover, the division of authority between the Church and the great variety of temporal powers virtually guaranteed that dissidents as surefooted as Marsilius of Padua, John of Jandun, and William of Ockham would always have a place in which to seek refuge.[36] Thus, while philosophy managed with considerable difficulty and only moderate success to maintain an independent, if precarious and hermitlike existence on the margins of life within the House of Islam,[37] within Christendom, especially in the West, it flourished—almost as never before.

Or so it might seem. For, at the deepest level, the conflict between the pretensions of reason and the claims of revelation remained—and had to

remain—unresolved. Moreover, each of the three scriptural religions imposed on its adherents an intellectual regimen that made them much more
resistant to philosophy than their pagan predecessors,[38] and Christianity's
deep-seated concern with the individual's internal disposition and its desire
to promote sincere belief arguably rendered its embrace more dangerous to
philosophy than the open antagonism of Judaism and Islam. Synesius found
a comfortable place within the Church. But it is not without significance that
his beloved teacher, the celebrated Platonist Hypatia of Alexandria, was dis-
membered by a Christian mob—itself inspired, if not actually led, by the
firebrand Cyril, nephew to Synesius's patron Theophilus and the man's successor as bishop of Alexandria.[39] Jerome and Sidonius Apollinaris compare
philosophy with a beautiful girl of foreign extraction conquered and captured
in war. Just as Deuteronomy specified that a Jew could marry such a young
woman after she had shaved her head, pared her nails, doffed her prisoner's
garb, and mourned the loss of her parents, so the Church could form an
alliance with secular wisdom only after the latter's defeat, abject submission, and renunciation of idolatry, error, and illicit desire. Among genuine
Christians, philosophy's defenders were as intent upon her subjection as her
enemies were eager for her elimination.[40]

When viewed in light of the servile role which Christianity accorded philosophy, the trial of Galileo can hardly be dismissed as an aberration. Like his
infamous compatriot Machiavelli, the Florentine scientist thought of himself
as another Columbus. He knew something of "the envious nature of men."
He, too, was aware that it is "no less dangerous to discover new modes and
orders than to explore seas and lands unknown." As a consequence, his publications were largely political in purpose—drafted, to be sure, by the natural
philosopher himself, but edited by his allies at Rome and elsewhere chiefly
with an eye to the impact they were likely to have on the prospects afforded
the new science within those parts of Europe still subject to the great ecclesi-
astical polity. In his eagerness to free philosophy from slavery, the renowned
astronomer was prepared to assert that Scripture must be interpreted in light
of the dictates of reason and the new science. If he was condemned in the
end and placed under house arrest, it was, as the most perceptive of his contemporaries recognized, merely symptomatic of the ultimate incompatibility
of reason and faith. Everyone was cognizant of the risks which Galileo had
run—not least the man himself.[41]

Of course, in defending the Church's right to regulate science, her loyal
sons could note theology's status as queen of the sciences and point to
Anselm's thoroughly orthodox definition of that discipline as "*fides quaerens
intellectum*"—as faith in search of understanding.[42] The more militant among

them could even echo the thirteenth of St. Ignatius of Loyola's "Rules for Thinking in Conformity with the Church": "that I will believe the white which I see to be black if the hierarchical Church so determines."[43] In the thirteenth century, Bonaventure had reaffirmed the traditional understanding by making two observations. On the one hand, he specified that, while "those who love Holy Scripture embrace philosophy as well," they do so solely "in order that through it they might add strength to their faith." On the other, he condemned "philosophy" and compared it with *"the tree of the knowledge of good and evil"* on the grounds that in it "is mixed the false with the true."

> For if you emulate philosophy, you say: how could Aristotle be deceived? And you do not then love Holy Scripture; by necessity you fall away from the faith. If you speak of an eternal world, you know nothing of Christ. If you speak of there being a single intelligence in all things and say that there is no happiness after this life, no resurrection of the dead, if you eat from this *tree of the knowledge of good and evil*, you fall away from the faith. Those who study philosophy should watch out for themselves; all that is contrary to the doctrine of Christ one must flee as something fatal to the soul.[44]

In the strictures he issued, Bonaventure was in no way atypical. Thomas Aquinas was prepared to concede greater autonomy to philosophy within its proper sphere than any other mainstream medieval theologian.[45] But even he thought it appropriate to insist that "whatever is discovered in the other sciences must be condemned as entirely false if it is repugnant to the truth" of sacred doctrine.[46]

As Bonaventure's blunt warning would lead us to suspect, it was by no means clear to the most serious of philosophy's students that true understanding is compatible with faith and with a humble submission to the authority of a church or book. In fact, if we are to judge by the example of Socrates, it is the philosopher's proud awareness of his own ignorance, his irrepressible capacity for wonder, and his willingness to entertain what is radically unorthodox that sets him apart.[47] When the Reformation and the Counter-Reformation it inspired rendered the situation of freethinkers within the Christian West increasingly precarious, Europeans of philosophical temper began to reconsider the alliance of convenience forged with Julian's Galilaeans so many years before, and a considerable number answered Machiavelli's clarion call for the establishment of "new modes and orders" and flocked to the banner of revolt that he had unfurled. Of these, the ablest then began pondering just how someone—perhaps graced "with more *virtù*, more eloquence and judgment" than the Florentine—might "be able to satisfy" the great man's "intention"; and in time they devised a strategy for resolving the "ancient quarrel between philosophy and poetry" once and for all by recasting the former and equipping it with a new species of populist rhetoric so powerful as to virtually eliminate the multitude's need for poetry in the traditional sense.[48] Robert Molesworth, future leader and patron of England's radical Whigs, summed up their aim in the aftermath of the Glorious Revolution when he praised those countries which commit "the Government of their Youth to *Philosophers* instead of *Priests*," when he intimated that "the Character of *Priest*" must "give place to that of true *Patriot*," and when he suggested that, if the clergy "were once set upon the same foot the Philosophers of old were, . . . we should soon see them shift hands, and the Spirit of those *Philosophers* revive again in them."[49]

Philosophy's rebellion against clerical tutelage was destined to be of profound importance for the history of republicanism—for, as we shall see in the course of the next few chapters, the attack which Machiavelli and his successors launched against the Church was far more radical than the assault which the Latin Averroist Marsilius of Padua had made on the political pretensions of the Roman clergy.[50] Where the latter had looked for guidance to Aristotle and to the Islamic and Jewish philosophers of the more recent past, the former charted an entirely new course, aiming their attack at Christianity itself and elsewhere as well—above all, at the classical philosophy which lived on within the Church and thereby at the fundamental principle underlying not only that philosophy but the political practices of the ancient republics: the trust in man's double-edged capacity to reason and make speech concerning the advantageous, the just, and the good. In rejecting that principle as an unjustified presumption, Machiavelli and those who came after prepared the way for the emergence of a species of republican government hitherto unknown to man.[51]

Notes

ABBREVIATIONS AND BRIEF TITLES

In the notes, I have adopted the standard abbreviations for classical texts and in-scriptions and for books of the Bible provided in *The Oxford Classical Dictionary*[2], ed. N. G. L. Hammond and H. H. Scullard (Oxford 1970), and in *The Chicago Manual of Style*[13] (Chicago 1982) 388–89, as well as those for journals listed in *L'Année Philologique*. Where possible, the ancient texts and medieval and modern works of similar stature are cited by the divisions and subdivisions employed by the author or introduced by subsequent editors (that is, by book, part, chapter, section number, paragraph, act, scene, line, Stephanus page, or by page and line number). In some cases, where further specification is needed to help the reader to locate a particular passage, I have included in parentheses as the last element in a particular citation the page or pages of the pertinent volume of the edition used. For fragments surviving from works of the classical period now lost, I have followed the practice now standard among classicists of citing the author's name, the fragment or line numbers, and, in parentheses following those numbers, the surname of the editor of the collection. Superscripted numerals indicate the edi-tion of a book cited or the pertinent series of the journal. In referring the reader to earlier or later parts of my argument, I have cited volume, chapter, and section (for example, I.vii.3), indicating whether the pertinent passage appears above or below. For medieval and modern works and for journals, inscriptions, and texts not listed in the volumes cited above, the following abbreviations and short titles have been employed.

ABF
 The Autobiography of Benjamin Franklin, ed. Leonard W. Labaree et al. (New Haven 1964).
AJL
 The Adams-Jefferson Letters: The Complete Correspondence between Thomas Jefferson and Abigail and John Adams, ed. Lester J. Cappon (Chapel Hill 1959).
Alfarabi, *Aphorisms*
 Al-Fārābī, *Fuṣūl Al-Madanī: Aphorisms of the Statesman*, ed. and trans. D. M. Dunlop (Cambridge 1961).
———, *Opinions*
 Alfarabi, *The Principles of the Opinions of the People of the Virtuous City*. In *Al-Farabi on the Perfect State: Abū Naṣr al-Fārābī's Mabādi' Ārā' Ahl Al-Madīna Al-Fāḍila*, ed. and trans. Richard Walzer (Oxford 1985).
———, *Plato & Aristotle*
 Alfarabi's Philosophy of Plato and Aristotle[2], ed. and trans. Muhsin Mahdi (Ithaca 1969).
Annals of Congress
 Annals of Congress: The Debates and Proceedings in the Congress of the United States, ed. Joseph Gales (Washington, D.C., 1834–56).

APSR
  The American Political Science Review.
AQ
  American Quarterly.
Aquinas, *Summa theologiae*
  Thomas Aquinas, *Summa theologiae*, ed. Thomas Gilby, O.P., et al. (London 1964–76).
Aubrey, *Brief Lives* (ed. Clark)
  'Brief Lives,' chiefly of Contemporaries, set down by John Aubrey, between the Years 1669 & 1696, ed. Andrew Clark (Oxford 1898).
  ———, *Brief Lives* (ed. Dick)
  Aubrey's Brief Lives, ed. Oliver Lawson Dick (Harmondsworth 1982).
Averroes on Plato's Republic
  Averroes on Plato's Republic, ed. and trans. Ralph Lerner (Ithaca 1974).
Bacon, *Of the Advancement of Learning*
  In Francis Bacon, *The Advancement of Learning and New Atlantis* (London 1974).
Blackstone, *Commentaries*
  William Blackstone, *Commentaries on the Laws of England* (Oxford 1765–69).
Boccalini, *Ragguagli*
  Traiano Boccalini, *Ragguagli di Parnaso e scritti minori*, ed. Luigi Firpo (Bari 1948).
Burnet, *HMOT*
  Gilbert Burnet, *The History of My Own Time*, ed. Osmund Airy (Oxford 1897–1900).
CAF
  The Complete Anti-Federalist, ed. Herbert J. Storing (Chicago 1981).
Calvin, *Inst.*
  John Calvin, *Institutio christianae religionis* (1559). In *Joannis Calvini opera selecta* [3], ed. Peter Barth and William Niesel (Munich 1963–74) III–V.
Cato's Letters
  John Trenchard and Thomas Gordon, *Cato's Letters, or Essays on Liberty, Civil and Religious, and Other Important Subjects* [6] (London 1755).
CHJ
  Cambridge Historical Journal.
CJL
  The Correspondence of John Locke, ed. Esmond S. de Beer (Oxford 1976–   ).
CMPP
  A Compilation of the Messages and Papers of the Presidents, 1789–1897, ed. James D. Richardson (Washington, D.C., 1896).
Condorcet, *Esquisse*
  Marquis de Condorcet, *Esquisse d'un tableau historique du progrès de l'esprit humain*, ed. O. H. Prior and Yvon Belaval (Paris 1970).
DAH
  Documents of American History [7], ed. Henry Steele Commager (New York 1963).
Descartes, *Discours de la méthode*
  René Descartes, *Discours de la méthode*. In *WrRD* 125–79.
  ———, *Les passions de l'âme*
  René Descartes, *Les Passions de l'âme*. In *WrRD* 695–802.

DHFFC
 Documentary History of the First Federal Congress of the United States of America: March 4, 1789–March 3, 1791, ed. Linda Grant De Pauw (Baltimore, 1972–   ).
DHRC
 The Documentary History of the Ratification of the Constitution, ed. Merrill Jensen et al. (Madison, Wis., 1976–   ).
DSSC
 The Debates in the Several State Conventions[2], ed. Jonathan Elliot (Philadelphia 1876).
EcHR
 Economic History Review.
EHD
 English Historical Documents, ed. David C. Douglas et al. (Oxford 1953–   ).
EMM
 Les essais de Michel de Montaigne, ed. Pierre Villey and V.-L. Saulnier (Paris 1978).
Encyclopédie
 Encyclopédie, ou dictionnaire raisonné des sciences, des arts, et des métiers, ed. Denis Diderot and Jean Le Rond d'Alembert (Paris 1751–80).
Ep.
 Epistulae.
The Federalist
 Alexander Hamilton, James Madison, and John Jay, *The Federalist*, ed. Jacob E. Cooke (Middletown, Conn., 1961).
Ferguson, *EHCS*
 Adam Ferguson, *An Essay on the History of Civil Society*, ed. Duncan Forbes (Edinburgh 1966).
FSC
 The Federal and State Constitutions, Colonial Charters, and Other Organic Laws of the States, Territories, and Colonies Now or Heretofore Forming the United States of America, ed. Francis Newton Thorpe (Washington, D.C., 1909).
GHI 1
 Russell Meiggs and David Lewis, *A Selection of Greek Historical Inscriptions* (Oxford 1988).
GHI 2
 Marcus N. Tod, *A Selection of Greek Historical Inscriptions* II (Oxford 1948).
GHQ
 Georgia Historical Quarterly.
Grotius, *De iure belli ac pacis*
 Hugo Grotius, *De iure belli ac pacis libri tres* (Amsterdam 1646). In citing the Prolegomena, I have used the paragraph numbers added by subsequent editors.
———, *De iure praedae*
 Hugo Grotius, *De Jure Praedae Commentarius*, ed. James Brown Scott (Oxford 1950).
HJo
 Historical Journal.
HLQ
 Huntington Library Quarterly.

Hobbes, *Behemoth*
> Thomas Hobbes, *Behemoth, or The Long Parliament*[2], ed. Ferdinand Tönnies (New York 1969).

——— , *De cive*
> Thomas Hobbes, *De Cive: The Latin Version*, ed. Howard Warrender (Oxford 1983). Because I have been unable to improve on the translation *Philosophicall Rudiments Concerning Government and Society* published by an anonymous, contemporary admirer of Hobbes, I have used it throughout when quoting *De cive*. For a critical edition of the translation, see Hobbes, *De Cive: The English Version*, ed. Howard Warrender (Oxford 1983).

——— , *Dialogue*
> Thomas Hobbes, *A Dialogue between a Philosopher and a Student of the Common Laws of England*, ed. Joseph Cropsey (Chicago 1971).

——— , *Elements of Law*
> Thomas Hobbes, *The Elements of Law Natural and Politic*[2], ed. Ferdinand Tönnies (London 1969).

——— , *EW*
> *The English Works of Thomas Hobbes of Malmesbury*, ed. Sir William Molesworth (London 1839–45).

——— , *Leviathan*
> Thomas Hobbes, *Leviathan*, ed. C. B. Macpherson (Harmondsworth 1968).

——— , *LW*
> *Thomas Hobbes Malmesburiensis opera philosophica quae Latine scripsit omnia in unum corpus*, ed. William Molesworth (London 1839–45).

Hooker, *Laws*
> Richard Hooker, *Of the Laws of Ecclesiastical Polity*, ed. Georges Edelen, W. Speed Hill, and P. G. Stanwood (Cambridge, Mass., 1977–81).

HPT
> *History of Political Thought.*

Hume, *EMPL*
> David Hume, *Essays Moral, Political, and Literary*, ed. Eugene F. Miller (Indianapolis, 1985).

——— , *EPM*
> *An Enquiry Concerning the Principles of Morals.* In David Hume, *Enquiries Concerning the Human Understanding and Concerning the Principles of Morals*[2], ed. L. A. Selby-Bigge (Oxford 1902) 169–343.

——— , *THN*
> David Hume, *A Treatise of Human Nature*, ed. L. A. Selby-Bigge (Oxford 1888).

Hutcheson, *IMP*
> Francis Hutcheson, *A Short Introduction to Moral Philosophy in Three Books, Containing the Elements of Ethicks and the Law of Nature* (Glascow 1747).

——— , *SMP*
> Francis Hutcheson, *A System of Moral Philosophy in Three Books* (London 1755).

Hyper.
> Hyperides.

ICr
> *Inscriptiones Creticae opera et consilio Friderici Halbherr collectae*, ed. Margarita Guarducci (Rome 1935–50).

JAH
Journal of American History.
JBS
Journal of British Studies.
JCC
Journals of the Continental Congress, 1774–1789, ed. Worthington Chauncey Ford et al. (Washington, D.C., 1904–37).
JChS
Journal of Church and State.
JEcH
Journal of Economic History.
Jefferson, *NSV*
Thomas Jefferson, *Notes on the State of Virginia*, ed. William Peden (New York 1972).
——— , *MCPP*
The Memoirs, Correspondence, and Private Papers of Thomas Jefferson, ed. Thomas Jefferson Randolph (London 1829).
JER
Journal of the Early Republic.
JHO
James Harrington's Oceana, ed. S. B. Liljegren (Heidelberg 1924).
JMH
Journal of Modern History.
JP
Journal of Politics.
JSH
Journal of Southern History.
King, *Locke*
Peter King, *The Life of John Locke, with Extracts from his Correspondence, Journals, and Common-Place Books*[2] (London 1830).
La Rochefoucauld, *Maximes morales*
François, duc de La Rochefoucauld, *Réflexions ou sentences et maximes morales: Édition de 1678.* In *Oeuvres complètes*, ed. L. Martin-Chauffier and Jean Marchand (Paris 1964) 385–471.
——— , *Maximes supprimées*
François, duc de La Rochefoucauld, *Maximes supprimées*. In *Oeuvres complètes*, ed. L. Martin-Chauffier and Jean Marchand (Paris 1964) 483–98.
LBR
Letters of Benjamin Rush, ed. L. H. Butterfield (Philadelphia 1951).
LDH
The Letters of David Hume, ed. J. Y. T. Greig (Oxford 1932).
LJL
John R. Harrison and Peter Laslett, *The Library of John Locke*[2] (Oxford 1971).
Locke, *CU*
John Locke, *Of the Conduct of the Understanding.* In *WoJL* III 203–89.
——— , *ECHU*
John Locke, *An Essay Concerning Human Understanding*, ed. Peter H. Nidditch (Oxford 1979).

———, *EWrJL*
  The Educational Writings of John Locke, ed. James L. Axtell (Cambridge 1968).
———, *LCT*
  John Locke, *A Letter Concerning Toleration*, ed. Mario Montuori (The Hague 1963).
——— MSS
  Locke MSS, Lovelace Collection, Bodleian Library.
———, *QLN*
  John Locke, *Questions Concerning the Law of Nature*, ed. and trans. Robert Horwitz, Jenny Strauss Clay, and Diskin Clay (Ithaca 1990).
———, *RC*
  John Locke, *The Reasonableness of Christianity as Delivered in the Scriptures*, ed. George W. Ewing (Chicago 1965).
———, *Scritti inediti*
  Scritti editi e inediti sulla toleranza, ed. Carlo Augusto Viano (Turin 1961).
———, *STCE*
  John Locke, *Some Thoughts Concerning Education*, ed. John W. and Jean S. Yolton (Oxford 1989).
———, *TTG*
  John Locke, *Two Treatises of Government: A Critical Edition with an Introduction and Apparatus Criticus*[2], ed. Peter Laslett (Cambridge 1970)—as corrected by Nathan Tarcov, *Locke's Education for Liberty* (Chicago 1984) 229–30 n. 324, 253–54 n. 187.
———, *Two Tracts on Government*
  John Locke, *Two Tracts on Government*, ed. Philip Abrams (Cambridge 1967).
LWEP
  Letters Written by Eminent Persons in the Seventeenth and Eighteenth Centuries: To Which are Added, Hearne's Journeys to Reading, and to Whaddon Hall, the Seat of Browne Willis, Esq., and Lives of Eminent Men by John Aubrey, Esq., ed. Phillip Bliss and Rev. John Walker (London 1813).
Macaulay, *Essays*
  Thomas Babington Macaulay, *Critical, Historical, and Miscellaneous Essays* (New York 1860).
Machiavelli, *Discorsi*
  Niccolò Machiavelli, *Discorsi sopra la prima deca di Tito Livio*. In *WoNM* 73–254.
———, *Istorie fiorentine*
  Niccolò Machiavelli, *Istorie fiorentine*. In *WoNM* 629–844.
———, *Il principe*
  Niccolò Machiavelli, *Il principe*. In *WoNM* 255–98.
Maimonides, *Guide of the Perplexed*
  Maimonides, *The Guide of the Perplexed*, trans. Shlomo Pines (Chicago 1963).
Mandeville, *Fable of the Bees*
  Bernard Mandeville, *The Fable of the Bees*, ed. F. B. Kaye (London 1924).
Marsilius of Padua, *Defensor pacis*
  The Defensor Pacis of Marsilius of Padua, ed. C. W. Previté-Orton (Cambridge 1928).
MJQA
  Memoirs of John Quincy Adams, Comprising Portions of his Diary from 1795 to 1848, ed. Charles Francis Adams (Philadelphia 1874–76).

Montesquieu, *EL*
  Charles de Secondat, baron de La Bréde et de Montesquieu, *De l'esprit des lois.*
  In *WoM* II 225–995.
MPP
  Medieval Political Philosophy: A Sourcebook, ed. Ralph Lerner and Muhsin Mahdi
  (New York 1963).
N&Q
  Notes and Queries.
NEQ
  New England Quarterly.
PAH
  The Papers of Alexander Hamilton, ed. Harold C. Syrett (New York 1961–79).
PAmH
  Perspectives in American History.
PAR
  Pamphlets of the American Revolution, 1750–1776, ed. Bernard Bailyn (Cambridge,
  Mass., 1965–).
Pascal, *Pensées*
  Blaise Pascal, *Pensées.* In *Oeuvres complètes de Pascal,* ed. Jacques Chevalier
  (Paris 1954).
PBF
  The Papers of Benjamin Franklin, ed. Leonard W. Labaree et al. (New Haven
  1959–).
PGM
  The Papers of George Mason, ed. Robert A. Rutland (Chapel Hill 1970).
PGW
  The Papers of George Washington, ed. W. W. Abbot (Charlottesville 1983).
PJA
  Papers of John Adams, ed. Robert J. Taylor (Cambridge, Mass., 1977–).
PJJ
  The Correspondence and Public Papers of John Jay, ed. Henry P. Johnston (New
  York 1890–93).
PJM
  The Papers of James Madison, ed. William T. Hutchinson, William M. E. Rachal,
  et al. (Chicago 1962–77; Charlottesville 1977–).
PJoM
  The Papers of John Marshall, ed. Herbert A. Johnson et al. (Chapel Hill 1974–).
PMHB
  Pennsylvania Magazine of History and Biography.
PMHS
  Proceedings of the Massachusetts Historical Society.
PrStQ
  Presidential Studies Quarterly.
PSQ
  Political Science Quarterly.
PSR
  The Political Science Reviewer.
PSt
  Political Studies.

PTh
  Political Theory.
PTJ
  The Papers of Thomas Jefferson, ed. Julian P. Boyd (Princeton 1950–   ).
RFC
  The Records of the Federal Convention of 1787, ed. Max Farrand (New Haven 1911–
  37).
RP
  Review of Politics.
RPM
  The Renaissance Philosophy of Man, ed. Ernst Cassirer, Paul Oskar Kristeller, and
  John Hermann Randall, Jr. (Chicago 1948).
SAQ
  South Atlantic Quarterly.
SDUSC
  Sources and Documents of United States Constitutions, ed. William F. Swindler
  (Dobbs Ferry, N.Y., 1973–79).
Shakespeare
  All references are taken from William Shakespeare, *The Complete Works*, ed.
  Stanley Wells and Gary Taylor (Oxford 1986).
Smith, *TMS*
  Adam Smith, *The Theory of Moral Sentiments.* In *The Glasgow Edition of the Works
  and Correspondence of Adam Smith* (Oxford 1976).
——, *WN*
  Adam Smith, *An Inquiry into The Nature and Causes of the Wealth of Nations.* In
  The Glasgow Edition of the Works and Correspondence of Adam Smith (Oxford 1976).
Somers Tracts
  *Somers Tracts: A Collection of Scarce and Valuable Tracts, on the Most Interesting and
  Entertaining Subjects: But Chiefly such as Relate to the History and Constitution of
  These Kingdoms*[2], ed. Walter Scott (London 1809–15).
Spinoza, *Opera*
  Benedict de Spinoza, *Spinoza opera*, ed. Carl Gebhardt (Heidelberg 1925). In
  citing particular works, I have employed the divisions introduced in *Benedicti
  de Spinoza opera quae supersunt omnia*, ed. Carolus Hermannus Bruder (Leipzig
  1843–46), and generally used by editors since.
Sprat, *Royal-Society*
  Thomas Sprat, *The History of the Royal-Society of London, For the Improving of
  Natural Knowledge* (London 1667).
SRFC
  Supplement to Max Farrand's The Records of the Federal Convention of 1787, ed.
  James H. Hutson (New Haven 1987).
TAR
  Tracts of the American Revolution, 1763–1776, ed. Merrill Jensen (Indianapo-
  lis 1967).
Tocqueville, *DA*
  Alexis de Tocqueville, *De la démocratie en Amérique.* In *Oeuvres, papiers et corre-
  spondances*, ed. J.-P. Mayer (Paris 1951–   ) I, pts. 1–2.

Vico, *New Science*
  Giambattista Vico, *The New Science of Giambattista Vico*[2], trans. Thomas Goddard Bergin and Max Harold Fisch (Ithaca 1968).
VMHB
  Virginia Magazine of History and Biography.
WMQ
  William and Mary Quarterly.[3]
WoAL
  The Collected Works of Abraham Lincoln, ed. Roy P. Basler (New Brunswick, N.J., 1953–55).
WoDS
  The Collected Works of Dugald Stewart, ed. Sir William Hamilton (Edinburgh 1854).
WoFB
  The Works of Francis Bacon, ed. James Spedding, Robert Leslie Ellis, and Douglas Denon Heath (London 1857–74).
WoFN
  Friedrich Nietzsche, *Werke*, ed. Karl Schlechta (Munich 1966).
WoGS
  The Works of George Savile, Marquis of Halifax, ed. Mark N. Brown (Oxford 1989).
WoJA
  The Works of John Adams, ed. Charles Francis Adams (Boston 1850–56).
WoJH
  James Harrington, *Works: The Oceana and Other Works of James Harrington*, ed. John Toland (London 1771).
WoJJR
  Jean Jacques Rousseau, *Oeuvres complètes*, ed. Bernard Gagnebin and Marcel Raymond (Paris 1959–69).
WoJL
  The Works of John Locke (London 1823).
WoJP
  The Theological and Miscellaneous Works of Joseph Priestley, ed. John Towill Rutt (London 1817–32).
WoJSM
  Collected Works of John Stuart Mill, ed. John M. Robson et al. (Toronto 1963–   ).
WoJW
  The Works of James Wilson, ed. Robert Green McCloskey (Cambridge, Mass., 1967).
WoLB
  The Works of Lord Bolingbroke, with a Life Prepared Expressly for this Edition, Containing Information Relative to his Personal and Public Character (London 1844).
WoM
  Charles de Secondat, baron de La Bréde et de Montesquieu, *Oeuvres complètes de Montesquieu*, ed. Roger Caillois (Paris 1949–51).
WoNM
  Niccolò Machiavelli, *Tutte le opere*, ed. Mario Martelli (Florence 1971).
WoRB
  The Works of the Honourable Robert Boyle, ed. Thomas Birch (London 1772).

WoRD
René Descartes, *Oeuvres de Descartes*, ed. Charles Adam and Paul Tannery (Paris 1964–74).
WoRF
Sir Robert Filmer, *Patriarcha and Other Writings*, ed. Johann P. Sommerville (Cambridge 1991).
WoTJ
The Works of Thomas Jefferson, ed. Paul Leicester Ford (New York 1904–5).
WPQ
Western Political Quarterly.
WrEB
The Writings and Speeches of the Right Honourable Edmund Burke (Boston 1901).
WrGW
The Writings of George Washington, ed. John C. Fitzpatrick (Washington, D.C., 1931–44).
WrJD
The Political Writings of John Dickinson, 1764–1774, ed. Paul Leicester Ford (New York 1970).
WrJM
The Writings of James Madison, ed. Gaillard Hunt (New York 1900–1910).
WrRD
René Descartes, *Oeuvres et lettres*, ed. André Bridoux (Paris 1953).
WrSA
The Writings of Samuel Adams, ed. Harry Alonzo Cushing (New York 1904–8).
WrTA
Aquinas: Selected Political Writings, ed. A. P. D'Entrèves and trans. J. G. Dawson (Oxford 1948).
WrTJ (ed. Ford)
The Writings of Thomas Jefferson, ed. Paul Leicester Ford (New York 1892–99).
WrTJ (ed. Lipscomb and Bergh)
The Writings of Thomas Jefferson, ed. Andrew A. Lipscomb and Albert Ellery Bergh (Washington, D.C., 1903).
WrTJ (ed. Peterson)
Thomas Jefferson, *Writings*, ed. Merrill D. Peterson (New York 1984).
WrTJ (ed. Washington)
The Writings of Thomas Jefferson, ed. H. A. Washington (New York 1853–55).
WrTP
The Complete Writings of Thomas Paine, ed. Philip S. Foner (New York 1945).

Introduction

1. Winston S. Churchill, *Blood, Sweat, and Tears* (New York 1941) 55–66: The Munich Agreement, 5 October 1938.
2. For an examination of this question, see Francis Fukuyama, *The End of History and the Last Man* (New York 1992).
3. On this subject, much more could be said: see Frederick W. Marks III, *Wind Over Sand: The Diplomacy of Franklin Roosevelt* (Athens, Ga., 1988). On subsequent

blunders, see Amos Perlmutter, *FDR and Stalin: A Not So Grand Alliance, 1943–1945* (Columbia, Mo., 1993).

4. See Tocqueville, *DA* 2.2.11 (139), 13, 3.19 (254), with 2.3.13, 17–19, 21.

5. Note *JHO* 174–75; see Robert Molesworth, *An Account of Denmark, As It was in the Year 1692* (London 1694) Pref.; and consider Jean Louis de Lolme, *The Constitution of England*[3] (London 1781) 4–5.

6. The foundations for such comparisons have been laid by Claude Nicolet, *The World of the Citizen in Republican Rome*, trans. P. S. Falla (Berkeley 1980), and by Peter Riesenberg, *Citizenship in the Western Tradition: Plato to Rousseau* (Chapel Hill 1992) 87–186.

7. *WoM* II 1103: *Mes pensées* 399. See Montesquieu, *EL* 6.30.14.

8. Pl. *Tht.* 155c–d.

9. T. S. Eliot, *The Complete Poems and Plays, 1909–1950* (New York 1962) 145: "The Four Quartets, Little Gidding."

10. A number of works pertinent to the regime-analysis presented in this volume have appeared or come to my attention since the original edition of my book went to press.

Germane to my discussion (I.i.3–4, vii.4–7) of the role played within Greek life and thought by the questionable presumption that human beings are distinguished from the other animals by their capacity for reasoned speech (*lógos*) concerning the advantageous, the just, and the good are W. Robert Connor, *Thucydides* (Princeton 1984), and Daphne Elizabeth O'Regan, *Rhetoric, Comedy, and the Violence of Language in Aristophanes' Clouds* (Oxford 1992). Note, in this connection, Paul Cartledge, *The Greeks: A Portrait of Self and Others* (Oxford 1993). To the literature on women in classical Greece (I.i.2, notes 21–24, 27, 29), one can now add Lesley Dean-Jones, *Women's Bodies in Classical Greek Science* (Oxford 1993). To I.i.2, note 37, I would add Doyne Dawson, *Cities of the Gods: Communist Utopias in Greek Thought* (Oxford 1992). Pertinent to my account (I.ii.2–iii.5) of the ancient Greek economy and my passing remarks (I.vii.1–3, 5) concerning developments at Athens is Edward E. Cohen, *Athenian Economy and Society: A Banking Perspective* (Princeton 1992). Whether one finds Cohen's overall argument fully persuasive or not, one will want to take note of his discussion (41–60) of the distinction between "landed" and "maritime" yield and his account (61–110) of the underground economy and of the role played within this world of "invisible wealth (*aphanès ousía*)" by women, slaves, freedmen, and other resident aliens. In this connection, see also Xenophon, *Oeconomicus: A Social and Historical Commentary*, ed. and trans. Sarah B. Pomeroy (Oxford 1994), and Alison Burford, *Land and Labor in the Greek World* (Baltimore 1993). In connection with I.ii–iv, see Aineias the Tactician, *How to Survive Under Siege*, trans. David Whitehead (Oxford 1990). I would now add Carol Dougherty, *The Poetics of Colonization: From City to Text in Archaic Greece* (Oxford 1993), to the literature cited in I.iv.2, note 21, and Christopher A. Faraone, *Talismans and Trojan Horses: Guardian Statues in Ancient Greek Myth and Ritual* (Oxford 1992), to that cited in I.iv.3, notes 56–60. Pertinent to my discussion of character formation and piety in ancient Greece (I.iv.1–4, v.2–3) are Louise Bruit Zaidman and Pauline Schmitt Pantel, *Religion in the Ancient Greek City*, trans. Paul Cartledge (Cambridge 1992); N. R. E. Fisher, *Hybris: A Study in the Values of Honour and Shame in Ancient Greece* (Warminster 1992); and Douglas L. Cairns, *Aidōs: The Psychology and Ethics of Honour and Shame in Ancient*

Greek Literature (Oxford 1993). Note also Kevin Robb, *Literacy and Paideia in Ancient Greece* (Oxford 1994). To I.iv.3, note 50, I would now add *Philodemus on Piety: Critical Text with Commentary*, ed. and trans. Dirk Obbink (Oxford 1994). With regard to I.iv.5 and I.v.2–3, see M. L. West, *Ancient Greek Music* (Oxford 1992).

Students of Athenian affairs (I.vii) will want to consult Mark Golden, *Children and Childhood in Classical Athens* (Baltimore 1990); Jon D. Mikalson, *Honor Thy Gods: Popular Religion in Greek Tragedy* (Chapel Hill 1991); Jacqueline de Romilly, *The Great Sophists in Periclean Athens*, trans. Janet Lloyd (Oxford 1992); Jeremy Trevett, *Apollodoros the Son of Pasion* (Oxford 1992); Raphael Sealey, *Demosthenes and His Time: A Study in Defeat* (Oxford 1993); Nicole Loraux, *The Children of Athena: Athenian Ideas about Citizenship and the Division between the Sexes*, trans. Caroline Levine (Princeton 1993); Barry S. Strauss, *Fathers and Sons in Athens: Ideology and Society in the Era of the Peloponnesian War* (London 1993); Christian Meier, *The Political Art of Greek Tragedy*, trans. Andrew Webber (Cambridge 1993); and S. C. Todd, *The Shape of Athenian Law* (Oxford 1994).

Four new studies of Aristotle's political thought deserve attention: Arlene W. Saxonhouse, *Fear of Diversity: The Birth of Political Science in Ancient Greek Thought* (Chicago 1992); Judith A. Swanson, *The Public and the Private in Aristotle's Political Philosophy* (Ithaca 1992); William James Booth, *Households: On the Moral Architecture of the Economy* (Ithaca 1993) 15–93; and Bernard Yack, *The Problems of a Political Animal: Community, Justice, and Conflict in Aristotelian Political Thought* (Berkeley 1993). In this connection, see Aristide Tessitore, "Aristotle's Ambiguous Account of the Best Life," *Polity* 25 (1992): 197–215. Note also Zdravko Planinc, *Plato's Political Philosophy: Prudence in the Republic and the Laws* (Columbia, Mo., 1991).

In my brief discussion (I Epilogue) of the revival of public liberty in medieval and Renaissance Europe, I could have said more concerning the influence of Cicero and Seneca: see Quentin Skinner, "Ambrogio Lorenzetti: The Artist as Political Philosopher," *Proceedings of the British Academy* 72 (1986): 1–56. To I Epilogue, note 28, I would now add the following: Abū Bakr Muḥammad ibn Zakariyyā al Rāzī, "The Book of the Philosophic Life," trans. Charles E. Butterworth, *Interpretation* 20 (1993): 227–36, and Charles E. Butterworth, "The Origins of al-Rāzī's Political Philosophy," *Interpretation* 20 (1993): 237–57. In connection with I Epilogue, note 32, one may wish to consult *Ibn Taymiyya against the Greek Logicians*, ed. and trans. Wael B. Hallaq (Oxford 1993).

Prologue

1. Iris Murdoch, *The Nice and the Good* (London 1968) 165.

2. Alfred Zimmern, *The Greek Commonwealth*[5] (Oxford 1931) 215.

3. *WrTJ* (ed. Washington) VII 31–32: Letter to Isaac H. Tiffany on 26 August 1816.

4. Consider Tocqueville, *DA* 1.2.9 (316) in light of Robert P. Kraynak, "Tocqueville's Constitutionalism," *APSR* 81 (1987): 1175–95.

5. The connection between classical Sparta and the regime imagined by Rousseau is particularly evident in the famous chapter in *The Social Contract* dealing with the legislator: *WoJJR* III 381–84: *Du contrat social* 2.7.

6. For a brief exposition that brings out the reductionist character of this new

political science, see Albert O. Hirschman, *The Passions and the Interests: Political Arguments for Capitalism before Its Triumph* (Princeton 1977) 9–113.

7. Machiavelli, *Il principe* 15.

8. *WoGS* III 422.6–12: *Miscellaneous Maxims*. In the various tracts published while he was alive, Halifax cites by name as an authority only Machiavelli (whom he mentions but once). See *WoGS* I 241.29: *The Character of a Trimmer*. Elsewhere, in his *Nachlass*, the Florentine also appears—as do Montaigne, Bacon, and Tacitus: consider *WoGS* II 34.37, 185.20–22, III 166.6–9, 169.14, 236.10–12, 368.22–27 (with n. 1), 466.11: *Prerogative, Kings and Queens, Miscellanys, Miscellaneous Maxims,* and *Moral Thoughts and Reflections,* in light of II.i.3–5, below. For a brief biographical sketch, see Hugh R. Trevor-Roper, "The Marquis of Halifax," *Historical Essays* (New York 1957) 254–69. Hilda C. Foxcroft's full-length biography should be read in conjunction with the introductory essays that Mark N. Brown provides in his recent edition of Halifax's works: cf. Foxcroft, *The Life and Letters of Sir George Savile, Bart.* (London 1898) with *WoGS* I xix–xliii, 3–149, II 3–25, 115–34, 241–57, 335–62, 421–49, III 3–22. See also J. E. Parsons, Jr., "Halifax: The Complete Trimmer Revisited," *Essays in Political Philosophy* (Washington, D.C., 1982) 1–42.

9. August. *De civ. D.* 19.24. For a recent study that illuminates the difference between ancient and modern political science, see Harvey C. Mansfield, Jr., *Taming the Prince: The Ambivalence of Modern Executive Power* (New York 1989).

10. See *Essays on the Scientific Study of Politics*, ed. Herbert J. Storing (New York 1962). The much touted fact-value distinction rests upon a failure to recognize that, in political analysis, what counts as a fact depends upon prior evaluation: see Martin Diamond, "The Dependence of Fact Upon 'Value,' " *Interpretation* 2, no. 3 (Spring 1972): 226–35. Cf. Richard J. Bernstein, *The Restructuring of Social and Political Theory* (Philadelphia 1978).

11. This is the central insight of Allan Bloom's provocative study: *The Closing of the American Mind: How Higher Education Has Failed Democracy and Impoverished the Souls of Today's Students* (New York 1987) 25–67, 141–312, 336–82. Note also Bloom, "Western Civ," *Giants and Dwarfs: Essays, 1960–1990* (New York 1990) 13–31.

12. John K. Davies, *Wealth and the Power of Wealth in Classical Athens* (New York 1981) vii.

13. Nowhere is the inadequacy of this species of analysis more evident than in the repeated, wildly inconsistent, and largely incoherent attempts of Marx and Engels to make sense of contemporary developments in England, France, and Germany: see Richard F. Hamilton, *The Bourgeois Epoch: Marx and Engels on Britain, France, and Germany* (Chapel Hill 1991). The only element of continuity in these various analyses is their authors' fiercely partisan, polemical intent.

14. See, for example, G. E. M. de Ste. Croix, *The Class Struggle in the Ancient Greek World: From the Archaic Age to the Arab Conquests* (Ithaca 1981) 19–69, 81–98 (esp. 60).

15. See, for example, Eugene D. Genovese, "Materialism and Idealism in the History of Negro Slavery in the Americas" and "On Antonio Gramsci," *In Red and Black: Marxian Explorations in Southern and Afro-American History* (New York 1971) 23–52, 391–422 (esp. 32, 40, 406–9). The extraordinary power of the analytical scheme that Genovese deploys in *Roll Jordan Roll: The World the Slaves Made* (New

York 1974) owes far more to its explicitly Gramscian and, in fact, largely Aristotelian reading of the relationship between opinion and rule than to anything ever written by Marx himself.

16. *WoJSM* X 117–63 (at 133–34): "Coleridge." See *WoJSM* VIII 922–23: *A System of Logic*[8] VI.x.5.

17. In this connection, see Seth Benardete, *Herodotean Inquiries* (The Hague 1969). For one part of the story, see Stanley Rosen, "Philosophy and Revolution," *The Quarrel between Philosophy and Poetry* (New York 1988) 27–55.

18. See Leo Strauss, *The City and Man* (Chicago 1964) 139–241.

19. It is hard to see how anyone who has read the ancient political analysts with the sympathetic attention and care they deserve could conclude that they "lacked a 'conceptual framework' for the understanding . . . of long-range social change": cf. Moses I. Finley, "The Ancient Historian and his Sources," *Ancient History: Evidence and Models* (London 1985) 7–26 (at 18, 26). For an elegant inquiry into long-range social and political change self-consciously pursued in accord with Aristotelian principles, see Claude Nicolet, *The World of the Citizen in Republican Rome*, trans. P. S. Falla (Berkeley 1980).

20. See Strauss, *The City and Man* 236–41. Before considering I.vii.8, below, cf. Karl Mannheim, *Ideology and Utopia: An Introduction to the Sociology of Knowledge* (New York 1936), with Leo Strauss, "Introduction," *Persecution and the Art of Writing* (Glencoe, Ill., 1952) 7–21. As Nicolet, *The World of the Citizen in Republican Rome* 15, to his credit, readily acknowledges, his own study is similarly deficient in its treatment of religion.

21. Cf. Ste. Croix, *The Class Struggle in the Ancient Greek World* 409–52. It is not surprising that, in assimilating Aristotle to Marx, Ste. Croix should ignore Aristotle's respectful treatment of opinion and his insistence on subordinating economic to political analysis: cf. his defective account of the two thinkers (69–80) and that of Scott Meikle, "Aristotle and the Political Economy of the Polis," *JHS* 99 (1979): 57–73, with Harvey C. Mansfield, Jr., "Marx on Aristotle: Freedom, Money, and Politics," *RMeta* 34 (1980): 351–67, and see William James Booth, "The New Household Economy," *APSR* 85 (1991): 59–75. Soon after the Enlightenment took hold and popularized philosophy replaced religion as the principal source of the regnant opinion which everywhere serves as the element of civil society, the critique of ideology as a rationalization of class interest replaced the quite similar, Enlightenment critique of priestcraft: see Mark Goldie, "Ideology," in *Political Innovation and Conceptual Change*, ed. Terence Ball, James Farr, and Russell L. Hanson (Cambridge 1989) 266–91.

22. Cf. Hobbes, *Elements of Law* I.xiii.3, with Descartes, *Discours de la méthode* 1–6, and *La recherche de la vérité par la lumière naturelle*: *WrRD* 879–901.

23. Cf. Arist. *Top.* 100a18–101b4 (esp. 100b21–23) with *Eth. Nic.* 1098b9–12, 27–31, 1145b2–7, 1153b25–28; *Eth. Eud.* 1216b26–1217a18, 1235b13–18; *Pol.* 1280a9–25, 1281a42–b38; *Rh.* 1355a14–18, 1361a25–27, 1398b20–1399a6, 1400a5–14; *Metaph.* 993a30–b19. Note, in this connection, Aristotle's attitude regarding that which has been sanctioned by time: *Pol.* 1264a1–10, *Metaph.* 1074b1–15. The stated principle of Aristotle is entirely in keeping with the practice of Socrates in the Platonic dialogues. In this connection, one should consider the significance of Socrates' "taking refuge in rational speech (*lógous*)": cf. Pl. *Phd.* 96a–100b with *Resp.* 5.473a, and see *Leg.* 12.950b–c; note *Pol.* 262a–263b; and see Leo Strauss, *The Political Philosophy of Hobbes: Its Basis and Its Genesis* (Chicago 1952) 142–45; Ronna Burger,

The Phaedo: A Platonic Labyrinth (New Haven 1984) 135–60; and Seth Benardete, *Socrates' Second Sailing: On Plato's Republic* (Chicago 1989).

24. Consider Arist. *Eth. Eud.* 1216b26–1217a18, 1235b13–18, *Eth. Nic.* 1145b2–7 in conjunction with the famous claim of Eudemus recorded by Simplicius, *De Caelo* 488.18–24 (Heiberg), and see Harold Cherniss, "The Philosophical Economy of the Theory of Ideas," *AJPh* 57 (1936): 445–56; G. E. L. Owen, "*Tithenai ta phainomena*," in *Aristote et les problèmes de méthode,* ed. Suzanne Mansion (Louvain 1961) 83–103; and Martha Craven Nussbaum, "Saving Aristotle's Appearances," *The Fragility of Goodness: Luck and Ethics in Greek Tragedy and Philosophy* (Cambridge 1986) 240–63. Cf. Jonathan Barnes, "Aristotle and the Methods of Ethics," *RIPh* 34 (1980): 490–511.

25. This is particularly clear when a community comes to its testing time. What is at stake in war is the entire way of life of a people—and the sentiment which binds the classes together is almost always more telling than the economic interests which set them at odds. This is why the ordinary citizens of a nation or political community—except where there is extreme suffering of the sort inflicted on the cities of Greece by the Peloponnesian War (Thuc. 3.82–83)—have generally preferred the misrule of men of their own kind to a benevolent despotism exercised by foreigners. Cf. G. E. M. de Ste. Croix, "The Character of the Athenian Empire," *Historia* 3 (1954): 1–41, with its decisive refutation by Donald W. Bradeen, "The Popularity of the Athenian Empire," *Historia* 9 (1960): 257–69. The literature on this aspect of ancient history is vast and still growing; within it, a special place is reserved for the articles of Ronald P. Legon: see "Phliasian Politics and Policy in the Early Fourth Century B.C.," *Historia* 16 (1967): 324–37; "Megara and Mytilene," *Phoenix* 22 (1968): 200–225; and "Samos in the Delian League," *Historia* 21 (1972): 145–58. The view of politics which Legon elaborates in these articles is borne out by recent experience in the Third World: cf. Montesquieu, *EL* 2.11.2, with V. S. Naipaul, "A New King for the Congo: Mobutu and the Nihilism of Africa," *The Return of Eva Peron* (New York 1980) 171–204.

26. For these as definitions for the term *politeía,* see Schol. Pl. *Leg.* 1.625b and Isoc. 7.14.

27. This explains the prominence of *paideía* as a theme in both *The Republic* and *The Laws*: cf. Pl. *Resp.* 2.376c–4.445a, 6.487b–497a, 7.518b–541b, 8.548a–b, 554a–b, 559b–c, 10.600a–608b with *Leg.* 1.641b–2.674c, 3.693d–701b, 4.722b–9.880e, 11.920a–12.962e.

28. Cf. Arist. *Pol.* 1263b36–37 with 1276a8–b15.

29. Cf. Polyb. 6.19–58 with Xen. *Cyr.* 1.2.15. See *Vect.* 1.1; Pl. *Resp.* 8.544d–e, *Leg.* 4.711b–712a; Isoc. 2.31, 3.37, 7.14; Cic. *Rep.* 1.31.47, 5.3.5–5.7 (with *Leg.* 1.4.14–6.19, 3.1.2). See also Leo Strauss, *Natural Right and History* (Chicago 1974) 135–38.

30. In this connection, see Pl. *Ep.* 7.336d–337d.

31. Consider Pl. *Leg.* 3.691d–692a, 693a–b in light of 3.691c–d, 692b, 9.874e–875d, and see 4.712c–715d, 8.831c–832d. Note Aristotle's discussion and critique of "the techniques (*sophísmata*) of legislation": cf. *Pol.* 1297a14–41 with 1307b40–1308a2.

32. Consider Arist. *Eth. Nic.* 1109a28–35 in light of *Pol.* 1253a30–37, 1267b1–9, 1318b39–1319a1, 1323a36–38, *Rh.* 1382b4–5, *Eth. Eud.* 1216a23–27, and see Pl. *Leg.* 11.918a–920a (esp. 918d–e) with *Resp.* 9.583b–586d.

33. See Arist. *Pol.* 1280a7–1284b34, 1296a22–32, 1318a17–26, 1318b1–5, and con-

sider Pl. *Leg.* 3.689e–690d, 4.712e–715b, 8.832b–c in light of *Resp.* 5.473c–474a.

34. La Rochefoucauld, *Maximes morales* 218. Note Halifax, *WoGS* III 370.21–371.3: *Miscellaneous Maxims*.

35. For an earlier statement of the same point, see Montaigne, "De l'utile et de l'honneste," *EMM* 3.1 (790).

36. Consider the implications of La Rochefoucauld, *Maximes morales* 2–4, 39, 115, 119, 123, 150, 200, 234, 305, and *Maximes supprimées* 598.

37. *WoGS* III 370.21–371.8: *Miscellaneous Maxims*. Note *WoGS* I 302.26–35, III 328.6–9: *A Rough Draught of a New Modell at Sea* and *Miscellaneous Maxims*.

38. Otto Hintze, "Calvinism and Raison d'Etat in Early Seventeenth-Century Brandenburg," *The Historical Essays of Otto Hintze*, ed. Felix Gilbert (New York 1975) 88–154 (at 94).

39. Cf. Pl. *Resp.* 1.338d–339b with 1.331d–335e, and then consider 1.348b–352d. In this light, one should ponder *Leg.* 4.714b–715b.

40. Lewis Namier, "Human Nature in Politics," *Personalities and Powers* (New York 1955) 1–7 (esp. 4–5).

41. After reading Pl. *Resp.* 8.543c–9.592b and *Leg.* 3.689e–701b, 4.712b–715d, note 1.631d–632c, 3.696c–698a, 4.707a–d, 711b–d, and consider 6.752b–768e in light of 5.734e–735a, 6.751a–b, and 7.822d–824a (esp. 823a); then, cf. Arist. *Pol.* 1273a39–b1 and 1278b6–15 with 1295a40–b2; consider 1328b2–23 (esp. 13–14, 22–23—where I am inclined to adopt the reading of Lambinus) in light of 1328a35–b1; and see *Rh.* 1365b21–1366a22. And finally, note *Pol.* 1264a24–1266b38, 1276b1–13, 1277a12–b32, 1283a3–42, 1288a6–b4, 1289a10–25, 1292b11–21, 1294a9–14, 1297a14–b34, 1311a8–20, 1317a40–b17, 1323a14–1342b34; and see Cic. *Leg.* 3.12.28–14.32.

42. *The Federalist* 1 (3). See below, III Prologue and i.1.

43. After reading Arist. *Pol.* 1273a39–b1, 1278b6–15, 1289a10–25, 1292b11–21, 1295a40–b2, 1328a35–b23, and the rest of the material collected in note 41, above, cf. Pl. *Leg.* 3.683e with 686b, 4.709a–710d, 5.747c–e, 6.757d–758a, 780b; Cic. *Rep.* 2.33.57. In this connection, consider Pl. *Leg.* 10.886c–910d. Cf. *Resp.* 3.414c–4.427c, 5.449a–466d, 7.540b–541d with *Leg.* 5.739a–e. Cf. *Leg.* 4.713e–714a with *Resp.* 5.473c–474a and 9.591d–592b; then, cf. *Resp.* 7.515c–516b with *Phd.* 99d–100a, *Leg.* 10.897d–e, and Xen. *Mem.* 4.3.14, 7.7, and consider the material collected in I Epilogue, note 47, below. Note Pl. *Meno* 86e and *Resp.* 8.546a–547a.

44. As the notes to the first seven chapters should make clear, I have learned much from G. E. M. de Ste. Croix, Sir Moses Finley, and their students and admirers.

45. See Elizabeth Fox-Genovese and Eugene D. Genovese, "The Political Crisis of Social History: Class Struggle as Subject and Object," *Fruits of Merchant Capital: Slavery and Bourgeois Property in the Rise and Expansion of Capitalism* (Oxford 1983) 179–212, and Gertrude Himmelfarb, " 'History with the Politics Left Out,' " *The New History and the Old* (Cambridge, Mass., 1987) 13–32.

46. One can get some notion of what, I believe, needs to be done by perusing Nicolet's *The World of the Citizen in Republican Rome.* Note also, in this connection, the degree to which the argument of Ronald Syme in *The Roman Revolution* (Oxford 1939) is simply a logical construct out of the preliminary chapter he devotes to describing the predominant element within the Roman *políteuma* and the *paideía* that formed it and set it in motion.

47. August. *De civ. D.* 19.24.

Chapter 1

1. Finley Peter Dunne, *Observations by Mr. Dooley* (New York 1902) 271.

2. It should not, then, be surprising that the little reliable information which we do possess concerning the ancient Greek household and economy comes to us mainly from the law courts of Athens, where citizens were forced to divulge and to discuss in broad daylight matters that, under any other circumstances, they would have preferred to keep in the dark. Were it not for the corpus of fourth-century Athenian forensic orations, students of ancient Greek domestic life would be almost entirely at a loss. If we lacked this evidence, we would find it virtually impossible to interpret the little that can be gleaned from the archaeological remains, from the Greek inscriptions, from comedy, and from the rest of Greek literature.

3. Benjamin Constant, "De la liberté des anciens comparée à celle des modernes," *Cours de politique constitutionelle*, ed. M. Édouard Laboulaye (Paris 1861) II 547–48. For a thorough exploration of Constant's thinking in this and in other regards, see Stephen Holmes, *Benjamin Constant and the Making of Modern Liberalism* (New Haven 1984).

4. Xen. *An.* 5.4.30–34. See Hdt. 1.10.3, Thuc. 1.6.5, and Pl. *Resp.* 5.452c.

5. The phrase originates with Karl Polanyi: see "Societies and Economic Systems," "Aristotle Discovers the Economy," "Ports of Trade in Early Societies," and "On the Comparative Treatment of Economic Institutions in Antiquity with Illustrations from Athens, Mycenae, and Alalakh," *Primitive, Archaic and Modern Economies*, ed. George Dalton (Boston 1971) 3–37, 78–203, 238–60, 306–34; and *The Livelihood of Man* (New York 1977) 145–276. For bibliography and discussion, see Sally C. Humphreys, "History, Economics and Anthropology: The Work of Karl Polanyi," *Anthropology and the Greeks* (London 1978) 31–75. Polanyi's approach has influenced ancient historians chiefly through the work of Moses I. Finley: see, especially, "Aristotle and Economic Analysis," in *Studies in Ancient Society*, ed. M. I. Finley (London 1974) 26–52; *The World of Odysseus*[3] (New York 1978); "Land, Debt and the Man of Property in Classical Athens," "Technical Innovation and Economic Progress in the Ancient World," "Mycenaean Palace Archives and Economic History," "Homer and Mycenae: Property and Tenure," and "Marriage, Sale and Gift in the Homeric World," *Economy and Society in Ancient Greece*, ed. Brent D. Shaw and Richard P. Saller (London 1981) 62–76, 176–95, 199–245; and *The Ancient Economy*[2] (London 1985) 17–61, 150–83, 188–91, 196–207. Pierre Vidal-Naquet surveys Finley's earlier work in "Économie et société dans la Grèce ancienne: L'oeuvre de Moses I. Finley," *Archives européennes de sociologie* 6 (1965): 111–48. See also Michel M. Austin and Pierre Vidal-Naquet, *Economic and Social History of Ancient Greece* (Berkeley 1977). For further discussion, see below, note 7 and I.i.3, note 52.

6. Because they fail to recognize that the roots of this phenomenon are political, Polanyi and Finley (above, note 5) are inclined to underestimate the role played by economic analysis in the political thinking of Aristotle and of the Greeks in general: see Alan E. Samuel, *From Athens to Alexandria: Hellenism and Social Goals in Ptolemaic Egypt* (Louvain 1983) esp. 1–61.

7. Polanyi's formula (above, note 5) obscures the difference between warrior republics like those of classical Greece and subpolitical artisan communities of the sort so brilliantly described by Mack Walker in *German Home Towns* (Ithaca

1971). G. E. M. de Ste. Croix is able to avoid this difficulty by placing emphasis on the Greek employment of slave labor: *The Class Struggle in the Ancient Greek World: From the Archaic Age to the Arab Conquests* (Ithaca 1981). Moses I. Finley achieves much the same end by asserting the fundamental importance of the Greek peasantry's acquisition of political rights: see *Ancient Slavery and Modern Ideology* (London 1980) 67–149 and *The Ancient Economy*[2]. I would not wish to deny the importance of what they point out, but I doubt very much whether an interpretation of the *pólis* guided by Karl Marx or even by Max Weber can adequately answer the question posed by Mr. Dooley. To interpret instrumentally the fact that the Greeks placed such a high premium on the privilege of citizenship is to dismiss the Hellenic understanding of what made life worth living. See below, I.i.3–4.

8. And, even then, the kinship is distant. Early in the second century A.D., the Younger Pliny was dispatched to Bithynia-Pontus as the emperor Trajan's personal emissary. The letters which he wrote back to the emperor indicate that the various Greek cities of the province and their leading citizens had a propensity for bitter rivalry and for extravagant expenditure in a futile quest to outdo each other in constructing grand public edifices. Cf. *Ep.* 10.17a.3–4, 17b, 18, 23–24, 37–44, 70–71, 75–76, 81–82, 90–91, 98–99, 108, 113, 116–17 with A. N. Sherwin-White, *The Letters of Pliny* (Oxford 1966) 525–46, 580–728. Note, in particular, Trajan's disinclination (*Ep.* 10.34) to allow the formation of a *collegium* of firefighters at Nicomedia on the grounds that the cities of the province are already "disturbed by factions of this very kind." As he puts it, "Where men are drawn together for a common purpose, their organizations—whatever name we give them and for whatever purpose they exist—turn into political clubs (*hetaeriae*) in a short time." See also *Ep.* 10.92–93, 96.7. One gets much the same impression of affairs in the communities of the province from the civic orations of Pliny's contemporary Dio Chrysostom: *Or.* 38–51.

9. Consider Locke, *TTG* II.vii.87–viii.122, xix.211–243, in light of Harvey C. Mansfield, Jr., "The Religious Issue and the Origin of Modern Constitutionalism," *America's Constitutional Soul* (Baltimore 1991) 101–14.

10. This term was introduced by Machiavelli, who used *lo stato* to allude to "command over men," and it reached its full development in the political science of Thomas Hobbes, who would have accepted Max Weber's definition of the state as that entity which "(successfully) claims the *monopoly of the legitimate use of physical force* within a given territory": cf. J. H. Hexter, "The Predatory Vision: Niccolò Machiavelli. *Il Principe* and *lo stato*," *The Vision of Politics on the Eve of the Reformation: More, Machiavelli, and Seyssel* (New York 1973) 150–78, and Harvey C. Mansfield, Jr., "On the Impersonality of the Modern State: A Comment on Machiavelli's Use of *Stato*," *APSR* 77 (1983): 849–57, with Max Weber, "Politics as a Vocation," *From Max Weber: Essays in Sociology* (New York 1946) 78, and see Quentin Skinner, "The State," in *Political Innovation and Conceptual Change*, ed. Terence Ball, James Farr, and Russell L. Hanson (Cambridge 1989) 90–131. The state is an abstract entity constituted by power; and to the extent that it has a tangible existence, it is indistinguishable from the arms by which that power is exerted—the police forces, the standing army, and the bureaucracy that makes up the permanent government in every modern polity. The state is never synonymous with the body politic, and it is never itself a true community. This is evident enough from the manner in which it is consistently coupled with and

distinguished from the individual, the church, and society. In this connection, one would do well to ponder Nietzsche's observation (*WoFN* II 313: *Also Sprach Zarathustra* 1, "Vom neuen Götzen") that "State is the name of the coldest of all the cold monsters. Coldly as well does it lie; and this lie creeps out of its mouth: 'I, the State, am the People.'" As Nietzsche goes on to suggest, it is "a Faith and a Love," not the State, that constitute a People.

11. *The Federalist* 10 (61).

12. The references are collected by Charles Forster Smith, "What Constitutes a State," *CJ* 2 (1906–7): 299–302.

13. Alc. F112.10 and F426 (Lobel-Page).

14. See, for example, the inscriptions collected in *GHI* 1–2. In contrast, the Near Eastern texts customarily refer to those whom we are inclined to call the Babylonians as "the people of the territory of the city of Babylon." See Fritz Schachermeyr, "La formation de la cité grecque," *Diogène* 4 (1953): 22–39 (esp. 30–33).

15. See Yvon Garlan, *War in the Ancient World* (London 1975) 86–103. See also Xen. *Vect.* 2.3–4.

16. Austin and Vidal-Naquet, *Economic and Social History of Ancient Greece* 95–99. It took a special decree of the assembly to extend this right to a noncitizen: Jan Pecírka, *The Formula for the Grant of Enktesis in Attic Inscriptions* (Prague 1966).

17. See Stephen Holmes, "Aristippus in and out of Athens," *APSR* 73 (1979): 113–28, and his exchange with James H. Nichols, Jr. (129–38).

18. Arist. *Pol.* 1280a25–1281a4. See [Dem.] 25.16–17.

19. For the import of this distinction, see Ferdinand Tönnies, *Community and Society* (London 1955). The failure to grasp the importance of Tönnies's distinction for understanding the Greek *pólis* can lead one to attribute a confusion to Aristotle where none exists: R. G. Mulgan, *Aristotle's Political Theory* (Oxford 1977) 13–37.

20. As Aristotle on one occasion (*Eth. Nic.* 1162a16–29) acknowledged, the household is more natural than the *pólis* because it is prior to and more necessary than the political community. If he elsewhere (*Pol.* 1253a18–29) denies this, it is because the household lacks self-sufficiency (*autárkeia*) and can therefore survive and do its proper work in promoting virtue only as part of a much larger unit. The confusion caused by Aristotle's two statements is purely semantic in origin: from the perspective of efficient causation, the household holds priority; from that of final causation, the *pólis* is first. The household is a prerequisite for life; the *pólis*, for the good life. The inevitable tension between this private community and the public community is the background for the dramatic action of Aeschylus's *Eumenides*, Sophocles' *Antigone*, and Aristophanes' *Clouds*. It is no accident that Aristophanes' *Ecclesiazusae* makes no mention of procreation: a city without households would be a city that paid little or no attention to the rearing of children. For a defense of the household, see Aristotle's critique (*Pol.* 1261a4–1264b25) of Plato's abolition of the household in *The Republic*. Note also *Eth. Eud.* 1242a21–26. Consider Jean-Pierre Vernant, "Marriage," *Myth and Society in Ancient Greece*, trans. Janet Lloyd (New York 1988) 55–77, in light of Emile Benveniste, *Indo-European Language and Society* (Coral Gables, Fla., 1973) 193–97, and see Sally C. Humphreys, "*Oikos* and *Polis*," "Public and Private Interests in Classical Athens," and "The Family in Classical Athens: Search for a Perspective," *The Family, Women and Death: Comparative Studies* (London 1983) 1–32, 58–78.

21. The overall pattern is evident from Sarah B. Pomeroy's general survey: *Goddesses, Whores, Wives, and Slaves* (New York 1975) 16–148. See W. K. Lacey, *The Family in Classical Greece* (London 1968) 158–63, 167–70, 197–208, 212–16, 225–30; Jan N. Bremmer, "The Old Women of Ancient Greece," in *Sexual Asymmetry: Studies in Ancient Society*, ed. Josine Blok and Peter Mason (Amsterdam 1987) 191–215; and Claude Bérard, "The Order of Women," in *A City of Images: Iconography and Society in Ancient Greece*, trans. Deborah Lyons (Princeton 1989) 89–109.

22. The stark picture sketched by David M. Schaps, *Economic Rights of Women in Ancient Greece* (Edinburgh 1979), and Eva Cantarella, *Pandora's Daughters: The Role and Status of Women in Greek and Roman Antiquity*, trans. Maureen B. Fant (Baltimore 1987) 24–98, needs to be redrawn with an eye to Lin Foxhall, "Household, Gender and Property in Classical Athens," *CQ* n.s. 39 (1989): 22–44, and Raphael Sealey, *Women and Law in Classical Greece* (Chapel Hill 1990).

23. See David M. Schaps, "The Women Least Mentioned: Etiquette and Women's Names," *CQ* n.s. 27 (1977): 323–30; Alan H. Sommerstein, "The Naming of Women in Greek and Roman Comedy," *QS* 11 (1980): 393–418; and Jan Bremmer, "Plutarch and the Naming of Greek Women," *AJPh* 102 (1981): 425–26.

24. Consider Nep. *Praef.* 6–7 in light of Xen. *Hell.* 3.4.19, *Ages.* 1.28; Plut. *Ages.* 9.8, *Mor.* 209c; Polyaen. 2.1.5; and Ath. 12.550e. For the attempt to segregate women in one such community, see I.vii.3, note 70, below. In this connection, see Jean-Pierre Vernant, "Hestia-Hermes: The Religious Expression of Space and Movement in Ancient Greece," *Myth and Thought among the Greeks* (London 1983) 127–75. Needless to say, the homes of the wealthy were less squalid, dark, and damp than those of their poorer compatriots. But it is important to keep in mind that, even within the grander houses, the women were still confined to the women's quarters (*gunaikōnîtis*): always the least attractive part of the home. See R. E. Wycherley, *How the Greeks Built Cities*[2] (New York 1976) 175–97; Susan Walker, "Women and Housing in Classical Greece: The Archaeological Evidence," in *Images of Women in Antiquity*, ed. Averil Cameron and Amélie Kuhrt (Detroit 1983) 81–91; and Michael Jameson, "Private Space and the Greek City," in *The Greek City: From Homer to Alexander*, ed. Oswyn Murray and Simon Price (Oxford 1990) 171–95.

25. Consider Montesquieu, *EL* 1.7.9, in light of Soph. F583 (Radt) and Eur. *Med.* 230–51, and see Bernard Knox, "The *Medea* of Euripides," *Word and Action: Essays on the Ancient Theater* (Baltimore 1979) 295–322.

26. Plut. *Comp. Lyc. et Num.* 4.1.

27. In Crete (Ephorus *FGrH* 70 F149), an entire age-class of young men customarily took brides upon induction into manhood, but elsewhere it was unusual for a man to wed before his thirtieth year: this spaced out the generations so that a man would be likely to come into his inheritance at about the time that he married (Arist. *Pol.* 1335a32–34), and it left him relatively free from household responsibilities during the years when he was at the height of his physical powers and most useful to the city for the purposes of war. Women ordinarily reached menarche at about the age of fourteen: see Darrel W. Amundsen and Carol Jean Diers, "The Age of Menarche in Classical Greece and Rome," *Human Biology* 41 (1969): 125–32. No Greek writer commends marriage at so tender an age, but the eagerness of Greek men to insure a legitimate succession by marrying a virgin made this the norm everywhere except at Sparta: cf. Xen. *Lac. Pol.* 1.3–4 and Plut. *Lyc.* 15.3 with Hes. *Op.* 695–701; Solon F27 (West); Xen. *Oec.* 7.5;

Pl. *Resp.* 5.459b–460e, *Leg.* 4.721b–e, 6.772d, 785b (with 8.833c–d); and Arist. *Pol.* 1335a7–35 (with *Hist. An.* 544b14–27, 582a16–33, *Gen. An.* 766b29–37). There is evidence suggesting that the same pattern may have prevailed at Rome, but its interpretation is open to question: cf. Keith Hopkins, "The Age of Roman Girls at Marriage," *Population Studies* 18 (1965): 309–27, with Brent D. Shaw, "The Age of Roman Girls at Marriage: Some Reconsiderations," *JRS* 77 (1987): 30–46. The practice of marrying barely pubescent girls explains why an heiress became capable of acting as a vehicle for the transfer of her father's property at Athens (Arist. *Ath. Pol.* 56.7) and on Thasos (Jean Pouilloux, *Recherches sur l'histoire et les cultes de Thasos I: De la fondation de la cité à 196 avant J.-C.* [Paris 1954] 371: No. 141 [Inscr. Inv. 1032] line 22) when she was fourteen and at Gortyn when she was twelve (*ICr* IV 72 col. XII 6–19: *The Law Code of Gortyn*, ed. Ronald F. Willetts [Berlin 1967] 50). It may also explain why the exposure of female infants was common: as Mark Golden ("Demography and the Exposure of Girls at Athens," *Phoenix* 35 [1981]: 316–31) remarks, the propensity for men in their prime to marry adolescent girls would otherwise have resulted in there being a large population of unmarried women. Cf. Donald Engels, "The Problem of Female Infanticide in the Greco-Roman World," *CPh* 75 (1980): 112–20, with William V. Harris, "The Theoretical Possibility of Extensive Infanticide in the Graeco-Roman World," *CQ* n.s. 32 (1982): 114–16; then, see Engels, "The Use of Historical Demography in Ancient History," *CQ* n.s. 34 (1984): 386–93, and Cynthia Patterson, " 'Not Worth the Rearing': The Causes of Infant Exposure in Ancient Greece," *TAPhA* 115 (1985): 103–23. Though there seemed nothing odd about the marriage of a girl to a man twenty years her elder, sexual relations between the very young and the very old was a standard subject for mirth: cf. Ar. *Eccl.* 877–1111 with Ath. 13.559f–560a.

28. Cf. Lys. 1.6 with Hippoc. *De Virginibus* 1 (Littré VIII 464–71): because women were so rarely given the opportunity to speak for themselves, the latter passage may be the best evidence that we have for their outlook. It can be dismissed as the remarks of a man, but the absence of cant in the surrounding discussion suggests that we are dealing with behavior actually observed.

29. For further discussion of these issues, see Marylin B. Arthur, "Women and the Family in Ancient Greece," *The Yale Review* 71 (1982): 532–47, and Nicole Loraux, *Les enfants d'Athéna: Idées athéniennes sur la citoyenneté et la division des sexes* (Paris 1981) 75–117, 157–253. Cf., however, ibid., 119–53 with Cynthia Patterson, "Hai Attikai: The Other Athenians," *Helios* 13, no. 2 (1986): 49–67 (esp. 49–57).

30. For discussion of the subtle and understated manner in which the peripatetic explores the tension between the demands of justice and the appeal of the good life, see Mary P. Nichols, "The Good Life, Slavery, and Acquisition: Aristotle's Introduction to Politics," *Interpretation* 11 (1983): 171–83, and Wayne Ambler, "Aristotle on Nature and Politics: The Case of Slavery," *PTh* 15 (1987): 390–410. Note, in this connection, Harvey C. Mansfield, Jr., "Marx on Aristotle: Freedom, Money, and Politics," *RMeta* 34 (1980): 351–67, and William James Booth, "The New Household Economy," *APSR* 85 (1991): 59–75.

31. If the slaves had been given visibility, they might well have become politically articulate also. According to Seneca (*Clem.* 1.24.1), the Roman Senate once debated whether it would be prudent to require the slaves of the city to wear a special uniform. The senators ultimately decided against such a policy because they feared making the slaves aware of their own numbers. If this were the case, the opponents of the measure argued, the slaves would be prone to revolt.

Seneca's testimony on this matter may be suspect, but his point is well taken. The same eagerness to deny slaves every semblance of public existence lies behind the insistent recommendation of the ancient political commentators that the citizens of a community select their slaves from a variety of different nations lest the servile population be united by a common culture, religion, and tongue: Pl. *Leg.* 6.777c–d, Arist. *Pol.* 1330a25–28, [Arist.] *Oec.* 1344b18, Varro *Rust.* 1.17.5, Ath. 6.264f–265a. As the ancients recognized, rebellion is a political act—and successful political action presupposes the prior existence of that shared understanding of the nature of justice which constitutes the common way of life of a people. It can hardly be fortuitous that servile revolts have almost always had cultural, religious, or nationalist roots. Cf. Joseph Vogt, "The Structure of Ancient Slave Wars," *Ancient Slavery and the Ideal of Man* (Oxford 1974) 39–92, with Eugene D. Genovese, *From Rebellion to Revolution* (Baton Rouge 1979) 1–81. See below, I.i.4.

32. Eur. F1019 (Nauck[2]). The scholiast who cites this passage (Schol. Pind. *Pyth.* 4.71) goes on to remark that slaves are called *lusíponoi* because they do away with (*dialúousi*) toil (*pónous*) by their service (*therapeía*). Consider Heraclid. Lemb. *Pol.* 20 (Dilts) and Nicholas of Damascus *FGrH* 90 F58 in light of Olivier Picard, "Périandre et l'interdiction d'acquérir des esclaves," in *Aux origines de l'Hellénisme: La Crète et la Grèce: Hommage à Henry van Effenterre* (Paris 1984) 187–91.

33. Men. F560 (Koerte[3]). Note also Heraclid. Pont. F55 (Wehrli[2]).

34. Ath. 15.695f–696a. By Greek standards, the servile class of Crete was relatively free. Apart from being denied access to the assembly, its members suffered a number of deprivations particularly worthy of Greek notice: as Aristotle (*Pol.* 1264a20–22) observes, they were barred from the gymnasium and prohibited from the possession of arms. Compare the measures taken in some polities against the poor: *Pol.* 1297a29–35.

35. Tocqueville, *DA* 2.1.3 (22). See Moses I. Finley, "Was Greek Civilisation Based on Slave Labour?" *Economy and Society in Ancient Greece* 97–115; Ste. Croix, *The Class Struggle in the Ancient Greek World* 505–9; and Yvon Garlan, *Slavery in Ancient Greece: Revised and Expanded Edition*, trans. Janet Lloyd (Ithaca 1988) 55–69; and consider I.vii.3, note 46, below.

36. Cf. Arist. *Pol.* 1253b23–38 with Hom. *Il.* 18.373–81. The statue of Daedalus had one thing in common with the slave: its tendency to run away. See Eur. F372 (Nauck[2]); Pl. *Meno* 97d, *Euthphr.* 11b–c; Arist. *De An.* 406b18.

37. To the passages cited in note 36, above, one should add Crates F14–15 (Edmonds). It says something about the degree to which the quest for mastery over nature has supplanted the desire to participate in public life that the introduction of a myriad of labor-saving devices in the eighteenth century and after was accompanied by an increase, not a reduction, in the number of hours devoted to labor by the ordinary citizen. See E. P. Thompson, "Time, Work-Discipline, and Industrial Capitalism," *P&P* 38 (December 1967): 56–97. For the relation of work to time in premodern society, see Jacques Le Goff, *Time, Work, and Culture in the Middle Ages* (Chicago 1980) 29–52, and Edmund S. Morgan, "The Labor Problem at Jamestown, 1607–1618," *AHR* 76 (1971): 595–611. Cf. Ar. *Eccl.* 651–61, *Plut.* 510–26.

38. Heraclitus *Vorsokr.*[6] 22 B53. To the elder Cyrus, Xenophon attributes sentiments indistinguishable from those of Hybrias: *Cyr.* 7.5.78–79, 8.1.43–44.

39. There is one intriguing piece of evidence bearing on the proportion of houseborn slaves within the servile population of the classical period. The sur-

viving fragments (*IG* I³ 421, 426) of the Athenian inscriptions recording the sale of the property confiscated in 414 B.C. from those involved in the Herms and the Mysteries Scandals list forty-five slaves and specify the origins of thirty-five. Of these, only three were *oikogeneîs*: see *GHI* 1.79. In later times, if the Roman evidence is indicative, the houseborn came to make up a much larger proportion of the servile population: Ste. Croix, *The Class Struggle in the Ancient Greek World* 229–39. Unfortunately, though the manumission inscriptions from Hellenistic Delphi confirm the widespread suspicion that the *oikogeneîs* (some of them no doubt children of their masters) were the slaves most likely to be granted the privilege of freedom, they tell us little regarding the structure of the slave population as a whole. See Keith Hopkins (with P. J. Roscoe), "Between Slavery and Freedom: On Freeing Slaves at Delphi," *Conquerors and Slaves* (Cambridge 1978) 133–71 (esp. 140–41). The apparent dramatic increase over time in the proportion of manumitted slaves drawn from the ranks of the *oikogeneîs* may be an illusion. The difference could be accounted for by a change in reporting procedures: over the same period, there was a precipitous decline in the number of slaves whose origin is left unspecified in the inscriptions. For evidence concerning the enslavement of foundlings, see William V. Harris, "Towards a Study of the Roman Slave Trade," in *The Seaborne Commerce of Rome*, ed. John H. D'Arms and E. C. Kopff, *MAAR* 36 (1980): 117–40 (esp. 123). Their existence is presupposed by the conceits of New Comedy, but otherwise they are rarely even mentioned.

40. See Garlan, *Slavery in Ancient Greece* 45–55. Note also Moses I. Finley, "The Slave Trade in Antiquity: The Black Sea and the Danubian Regions," *Economy and Society in Ancient Greece* 167–75 (with Finley, *The Ancient Economy*² 187–88); Yvon Garlan, "Signification historique de la piraterie Grecque," *DHA* 4 (1978): 1–16; and D. C. Braund and G. R. Tsetskhladze, "The Export of Slaves from Colchis," *CQ* n.s. 39 (1989): 114–25.

41. Cf. Eur. F49 (Nauck²) with Sall. *Iug.* 85.41. Much the same charge could be leveled against a beggar (*ptōchós*). Consider the manner in which Homer uses the *gastér* of the *ptōchós* as a symbol for man's enslavement to the needs of the body: *Od.* 6.133, 7.211–21, 15.341–45, 17.226–28, 286–89, 468–76, 556–59, 18.1–3, 52–54, 360–64, 376–80.

42. Ar. *Plut.* 188–93. Consider the slave's failure to mention meat in light of Pl. *Resp.* 2.372a–373d, 404b–c.

43. Pl. *Resp.* 3.386a–387b. See also *Grg.* 483a–b.

44. *GHI* 2.204.24–51, Lycurg. 1.81, Diod. 11.29.2–4. Note Hdt. 7.132.2. See also Diod. 11.3.3, Polyb. 9.39.4–5.

45. Note Theopomp. *FGrH* 115 F153, and see Christian Habicht, "Falsche Urkunden zur Geschichte Athens im Zeitalter der Perserkriege," *Hermes* 89 (1961): 1–35.

46. Eur. F596 (Nauck²). See Sen. *Ep.* 77.15: *vita si moriendi virtus abest servitus est*.

47. For the relationship between courage, freedom, and the good life, see Thuc. 2.36.1, 43.4 (cf. 63.1), 4.126.2, 5.9.1, 9. Cf. what Tacitus (*Germ.* 20.2) has to say of the German tribes.

48. This is the theme of Hannah Arendt's *The Human Condition* (Chicago 1958). Though uncritical and misleading in certain crucial respects (see I.iv.1, note 4, below), Arendt's account of ancient Greek politics deserves much more attention from students of Greek antiquity than it has thus far received. As should be self-evident to those who take the trouble to read the article on which this chapter

is based, Patricia Springborg's recent discussion of my argument rests on a fundamental misinterpretation of my position: cf. Springborg, "The Primacy of the Political: Rahe and the Myth of the *Polis*," *PSt* 38 (1990): 83–104, with Paul A. Rahe, "The Primacy of Politics in Classical Greece," *AHR* 89 (1984): 265–93.

49. Xen. *Hiero* 4.3. See also Pl. *Resp.* 9.578d–579a. "*Quot servi,*" so goes the Roman proverb, "*Tot hostes.*" See Festus 314L, Sen. *Ep.* 47.5, Macrob. *Sat.* 1.11.13.

50. See, in particular, Philip Brook Manville, *The Origins of Citizenship in Ancient Athens* (Princeton 1990). In this connection, note also Kurt Raaflaub, *Die Entdeckung der Freiheit: Zur historischen Semantik und Gesellschaftsgeschichte eines politischen Grundbegriffes der Griechen* (Munich 1985). The best general discussion of the period is Oswyn Murray, *Early Greece* (Atlantic Highlands, N.J., 1980). Much can still be learned from Antony Andrewes, *The Greek Tyrants* (London 1956), and from W. G. Forrest, *The Emergence of Greek Democracy* (London 1966).

51. Nicostratus F29 (Edmonds). Cf. Dem. 21.123–25, where the struggle against exploitation gains dignity from being linked with the struggle for something nobler: political freedom. The evidence suggests that citizenship, honor, and material self-interest were so closely intertwined as to be inseparable: see Nick Fisher, "The Law of *Hubris* in Athens," and Oswyn Murray, "The Solonian Law of *Hubris*," in *Nomos: Essays in Athenian Law, Politics and Society*, ed. Paul Cartledge, Paul Millett and Stephen Todd (Cambridge 1990) 123–45.

52. Cf. Moses I. Finley, "The Freedom of the Citizen in the Greek World," *Economy and Society in Ancient Greece* 77–94, and *Politics in the Ancient World* (Cambridge 1983) esp. 39–49, 97–121, 134. I cite these two works because they represent the mature work of the ablest and most respected of the sociologically oriented historians of antiquity. As such, they exhibit admirably the virtues, the limits, and the ultimate inadequacy of the sociological approach. The disciples of Weber and Marx, in keeping with the propensity of social science and modern political practice since Hobbes, systematically depreciate the love of one's own and the desire for honor as human motives. As a consequence, they neglect or understate the central importance of civil religion, national culture, and public opinion in general and base their work on a distinction between materialism and idealism that cannot in the end be sustained: see Finley, "The Ancient City from Fustel de Coulanges to Max Weber and Beyond," *Economy and Society in Ancient Greece* 3–23, and *Ancient Slavery and Modern Ideology* 11–66. Among other things, materialism provides no foundation for making sense of the Greek hostility to marketplace concerns which Finley has himself done so much to unearth: see "Land, Debt, and the Man of Property at Athens," *Economy and Society in Ancient Greece* 62–76, and *Studies in Land and Credit in Ancient Athens, 500–200 B.C.* (New Brunswick, N.J., 1952). To understand why the Greeks had contempt for men of mercenary disposition and an aversion to the uninhibited quest for lucre, one must pay attention to what Aristotle means when he speaks of man as a political animal. By the same token, to understand the roots of that political apathy typical of modern republics, one must pay attention to the manner in which the modern preference for limited, representative government is grounded in a radically new understanding of the purposes for which constitutional government is established. Here again, the sociological approach is enlightening, but only to a degree: see Finley, *Democracy Ancient and Modern*[2] (London 1985), and consider Madison, *The Federalist* 10, in light of the argument advanced in II.i–vii (esp. iv–vii), below. In pointing out the inadequacy of Weber's account of the *pólis* as a political forma-

tion, Finley unwittingly exposes the weakness of any analysis grounded in the Hobbesian assumptions of modern social science: "Max Weber and the Greek City-State," *Ancient History: Evidence and Models* (London 1985) 88–103. Christian Meier's work on the Greek understanding of freedom is a useful corrective to the one-dimensional focus on "material benefits" and "material relations" in much of the recent scholarship: see "Die Politische Identität der Griechen," in *Identität*, ed. Odo Marquand and Karlheinz Stierle (Munich 1979) 371–406, and the essays collected in *The Greek Discovery of Politics*, trans. David McLintock (Cambridge, Mass., 1990).

53. In general, Aristotle is inclined to suppose that the end (*télos*) rather than the origin of an entity is determinative. As he (cf. *Ph.* 261a13–15 with 260b18–19) puts it, "What is posterior in the order of becoming is prior in the order of nature."

54. Arist. *Pol.* 1252b27–1253a39. See 1278b15–30, 1280a25–1281a10, 1283b42–1284a3; *Eth. Nic.* 1097a15–1098b8, 1169b16–18. Note Pl. *Leg.* 4.707d, 6.770c–e; Eur. F48 (Nauck²). See Peter Simpson, "Making the Citizens Good: Aristotle's City and Its Contemporary Relevance," *PF* 22 (1990): 149–66 (at 149–59). Consider, however, I.ii.1, below (esp. note 3). Cf. Richard Mulgan, "Aristotle and the Value of Political Participation," *PTh* 18 (1990): 195–215, with Catherine Zuckert, "Aristotle on the Limits and Satisfactions of Political Life," *Interpretation* 11 (1983): 185–206, and see P. A. Vander Waerdt, "Kingship and Philosophy in Aristotle's Best Regime," *Phronesis* 30 (1985): 249–73. From Aristotle's discussion of human nature, it follows that the one element most necessary to the *pólis* is "judgment (*krísis*) regarding the advantageous and the just": consider *Pol.* 1328b2–23 (esp. 13–14, 22–23—where I am inclined to adopt the reading of Lambinus) in light of 1328a35–b1, and see 1308a33–35. Cf. *Hist. An.* 487b33–488a13, where Aristotle uses the phrase *politikòn zôon* in a less precise sense to group human beings with bees, wasps, ants, and cranes, with *Part. An.* 673a8, where he specifies that man is distinguished by his capacity for laughter. With regard to the ultimate superiority accorded the philosophical life, note the similarity of phrasing at *Eth. Nic.* 1177b26–27 and *Pol.* 1253a2–5, and see *Eth. Nic.* 1177a12–1178a8 (with 1142a23–30 and *Metaph.* 982b1–983a20) and *Pol.* 1323a14–1325b32 (with 1333b29–35). Cf. John M. Cooper, *Reason and Human Good in Aristotle* (Cambridge, Mass., 1975), and Carnes Lord, "Politics and Philosophy in Aristotle's *Politics*," *Hermes* 106 (1978): 336–57; Richard Kraut, *Aristotle on the Human Good* (Princeton 1989); and the essays cited in I.vii.8, note 174, below. Cf. Marcel Détienne, *Dionysos Slain*, trans. Mireille and Leonard Muellner (Baltimore 1979) 53–67. Note Cicero *Off.* 1.16.50–17.58. For a discussion of the vital distinction between political or prudential speech and self-expression, see Harvey C. Mansfield, Jr., *The Spirit of Liberalism* (Cambridge, Mass., 1978) viii–ix, 16–27, 52–71. In this context, it is perhaps worth noting that Hobbesian man is modeled on Aristotle's inarticulate, hunted animal: cf. Hobbes, *Leviathan* I.13, with Leo Strauss, *Natural Right and History* (Chicago 1974) 172–74, and *What Is Political Philosophy?* (New York 1959) 176 n. 2, and see Locke, *TTG* II.ii.8, 10–11, iii.16, vii.79–80, 93, xix.228. This may explain why, in the liberal democracies of the twentieth century, freedom of expression has silently replaced freedom of speech. Where the latter is understood solely as an instrument and where it comes to be taken for granted, the concern for its preservation can easily be supplanted by a longing for the former.

55. He had even employed similar language: Isoc. 2.6–7.

56. Consider Alc. F130.16–25 (Lobel-Page) in light of Arist. *Pol.* 1253a1–18 with an eye to Hom. *Od.* 9.105–553; then, consider Euripides' treatment of the difference between human beings and the Cyclops in terms of the capacity of the former to engage in *lógos*, to be shaped by civic *paideía*, and to pursue the common good through *práxis*: cf. *Cyc.* 113–20 with 275–76, 286–355, and 476–82 after noting David Konstan, "An Anthropology of Euripides' *Kyklōps*," in *Nothing to Do with Dionysos? Athenian Drama in Its Social Context*, ed. John J. Winkler and Froma I. Zeitlin (Princeton 1990) 207–27. In translating Alcaeus's term *lukaimíais*, and in filling the lacuna in the papyrus, I have followed the lead of C. M. Bowra, *Greek Lyric Poetry*[2] (Oxford 1961) 145–47. For an alternative interpretation of the last two lines, see Denys Page, *Sappho and Alcaeus* (Oxford 1959) 198–209 (esp. 205–6). In this connection, one might wish to consider Walter Burkert, *Homo Necans: The Anthropology of Ancient Greek Sacrificial Ritual and Myth*, trans. Peter Bing (Berkeley 1983) 84–93.

57. Cf. Eur. *Phoen.* 385–442 with F313 (Nauck[2]), and see Theophr. *Leg.* F6a–b (Szegedy-Maszak). Cf. Madison, *The Federalist* 43 (297), with Hobbes, *Leviathan* I.13. See also Isoc. 14.49–50 where an exiled Plataean articulates what it means to have one's *pólis* destroyed. "The loss of our common life," he remarks, "causes each of us to have private hopes only. I think that you are not ignorant of the other sorts of *shame* which poverty and exile engender." It is perhaps worth noting that the Greek word *parrhēsía* makes its first appearance in the works of Euripides (*Hipp.* 422; *Ion* 672, 675; *Phoen.* 385–442; and F313 [Nauck[2]]) and Democritus (*Vorsokr.*[6] 68 B226). For a thorough survey of the Athenian evidence, see Kurt Raaflaub, "Des Freien Bürgers Recht der Freien Rede," in *Studien zur Antiken Sozialgeschichte: Festschrift Friedrich Vittinghoff*, ed. Werner Eck, Hartmut Galsterer, and Hartmut Wolff (Cologne 1980) 7–57. For a remarkably similar account of the import of exile, see Shakespeare, *Richard II* I.iii.133–85 (which should be read with II.i.149–51). Well into the Hellenistic period, when the individual cities of Greece had faded into relative insignificance, the classical view came under attack. Consider the defense of exile made by the Cynic philosopher Teles: F3 (Hense) ap. Stob. *Flor.* 3.40.8.

58. Phocylides F4 (Diehl).

59. I see no reason to doubt the authenticity of the inscription recording Darius's letter to the satrap Gadatas: *GHI* 1.12.4.

60. Cf. Aesch. *Pers.* 50, 74–75, 234, 241–42, 402–4, 584–97; Hdt. 7.101–4, 135–36; and Eur. *Hel.* 276, *Iph. Aul.* 1400–1401 with Isoc. 4.131–32, 150–52, 181–82, 5.107, 120–24, *Ep.* 3.5, 9.19; Pl. *Resp.* 4.435e–436a; Arist. *Pol.* 1285a15–29, 1313a34–b10, 1327b23–36. See also Hippoc. *Airs, Waters, and Places* 12, 16. Note Cic. *Rep.* 1.33.50.

61. For the pertinent evidence and a useful discussion, see Gabriel Herman, "The 'Friends' of the Early Hellenistic Rulers: Servants or Officials?" *Talanta* 12–13 (1980–81): 103–49. It deserves notice that, among those who served the various Hellenistic dynasts, Greeks predominated: see Christian Habicht, "Die herrschende Gesellschaft in den hellenistischen Monarchien," *Vierteljahrschrift für Sozial- und Wirtschaftsgeschichte* 45 (1958): 1–16.

62. Cf. Roland Kent, *Old Persian* (New Haven 1950) nos. DB I.19, II.19–20, 29–30, 49–50, 82, III.13, 31, 56, 84–85, V.8, with *GHI* 1.12.4. See Geo Widengren, *Der Feudalism im alten Iran* (Cologne 1969) 12–21, 32–34, 38. For the Persian empire as an *oikonomía éthnous*, see Arist. *Pol.* 1285b29–33.

63. Cf. Pl. *Ep.* 7.351a and Dem. 57.45 with Theog. 173–78, 181–82 (West). See Xen. *Hell.* 2.3.47–49 and Isoc. 14.50, and note Homer's treatment of the plight of the beggar: above, I.i.2, note 41.

64. Alc. F364 (Lobel-Page).

65. Cic. *Off.* 1.42.150. See also Isoc. 14.48. The passage from Cicero's *De Officiis* should be read in light of *Off.* 2.17.60, 3.2.7, and *Att.* 16.11.4: Cicero claims to have followed Panaetius closely, not simply translating the latter's book on moral obligation, but introducing only a few alterations. See Peter A. Brunt, "Aspects of the Social Thought of Dio Chrysostom and the Stoics," *PCPhS* 199 (1973): 9–34 (esp. 26–34).

66. When Socrates' old comrade Eutherus (Xen. *Mem.* 2.8.1–6) equates working as another's *epítropos* with slavery, he does so on the basis of an appeal to public opinion. For further discussion, see Claude Mossé, "Les salariés à Athènes au IVième siècle," *DHA* 2 (1976): 97–101. Throughout antiquity, personal service was equated with servitude: cf. Lucian, *De merc. cond.* esp. 7–9, 23–25, with Ulpian's allusion (*Digest* 43.16.1.16–19) to those who occupy "the place of slaves (*eos, quos loco servorum habemus*)" and must, therefore, be counted as members of the household (*familia*). One consequence was that full citizens could rarely, if ever, be found to manage a rich man's farm: cf. Rhona Beare, "Were Bailiffs Ever Free Born?" *CQ* n.s. 28 (1978): 398–401, with Gert Audring, "Über den Gutsverwalter (*epitropos*) in der Attischen Landwirtschaft des 5. und des 4. Jh. v. u. Z.," *Klio* 55 (1973): 109–16, and see Walter Scheidel, "Free-born and Manumitted Bailiffs in the Graeco-Roman World," *CQ* n.s. 40 (1990): 591–93. Artisans were thought slavish for similar reasons: see below, I.iii.3, note 74 and context. Cf. Lucian *Ap.* 11–12 with Tac. *Germ.* 25.3: where a monarchy had supplanted a popular regime and a single household (*res privata*) had absorbed the political realm (*res publica*), painful adjustments had to be made by those who coveted power and fame.

67. Cf. Montesquieu, *EL* 2.11.4 with 4.22.2; see 2.11.2–3, 5, 12.1–2; and then, consider 2.11.5–6 with an eye to the relationship between 12.3–13.20 and 1.5.6, 19, 7.1, 3.19.9, 26–27, 4.20.1–2, 4–8, 10, 12–14, 21, 23, 21.5, 6 (607, 609–10), 7, 12–16, 20, 22.2–3, 10–14, 17–19, 21–22, 23.8, 17 (695).

68. Montesquieu, *EL* 3.14.13, 19.27 (575–76); Tocqueville, *DA* 2.2.14, 4.1.

69. See *FSC* IV 2455, 2472 (New Hampshire, 1784, 1792); V 2637 (New York, 1777); V 3083 (Pennsylvania, 1776); VI 3740–41, 3753, 3763 (Vermont, 1777, 1786, 1793); and *SDUSC* II 198: Delaware's Declaration of Rights and Fundamental Rules, 1776.

70. After Pennsylvania ratified the federal constitution, the dissenting delegates drew up a list of objections that included the lack of an "exemption" from military service for "those persons who are conscientiously scrupulous of bearing arms." See *DHRC* II 617–39 (at 638): Dissent of the Minority of the Pennsylvania Ratifying Convention, 18 December 1787. A number of the delegates attending subsequent state conventions expressed similar misgivings. See *DSSC* I 335, II 549–56 (esp. 553), III 657–63 (esp. 659), IV 244: Ratification by Rhode Island, 29 May 1790; Maryland Ratifying Convention, 26–28 April 1788; Virginia Ratifying Convention, 27 June 1788; North Carolina Ratifying Convention, 1 August 1788. And, when the First Federal Congress paused to frame a bill of rights that would mollify the Anti-Federalists' misgivings, James Madison proposed giving conscientious objection constitutional sanction, and the majority of his colleagues in the House voted in favor. In the end, however, the majority seem to

have been prepared to concede some force to the arguments presented by those in the House who contended that, since conscientious objection was neither a natural nor a divine right, it was a matter best left to legislative grace—for, when the Senate rejected the pertinent clause and refused to budge, Madison and his colleagues gave way. Cf. *Annals of Congress* I 424–50 (esp. 434), 749–51, 767: 8 June and 17 and 21 August 1789, and *DHFFC* III 158–66: House of Representatives Journal, 21–22 and 24 August 1789, with *DHFFC* I 135–38 (esp. 136), 153–54, 167–68: Senate Legislative Journal, 25 August and 4 and 9 September 1789. Then, see *DHFFC* III 199, 216–18, 226, 228–29, 233: House of Representatives Journal, 10, 19, 21, and 23–25 September 1789; *Annals of Congress* I 913–14: 24 September 1789; and *DHFFC* I 181–82, 185–86, 189–90, 192: Senate Legislative Journal, 21 and 24–25 September 1789. Soon thereafter, the pertinent provision was dropped from Pennsylvania's constitution. See *FSC* V 3099–3101 (Pennsylvania, 1790).

71. See below, II.vi.6–7, Epilogue, III.iv.4–9.

72. The gap separating Ferguson's outlook from that of his friends is reflected in Hume's finding "almost every thing" in the former's *Essay on the History of Civil Society* so "exceptionable" that he was willing to "concur in any Method to prevent or retard the Publication." Regarding Ferguson's reflections, Hume wrote in a letter to a mutual friend, "I do not think them fit to be given to the Public, neither on account of the Style nor the Reasoning; the Form nor the Matter." See *LDH* II 12: Letter to Reverend Hugh Blair on 11 February 1766. The work's success surprised Hume and caused him to reconsider, but not to alter this judgment (*LDH* II 133: Letter to Reverend Hugh Blair on 1 April 1767). Apparently, Ferguson was too sympathetic to the rude and unpolished nations of ancient and not so ancient times to please a man of Hume's tastes. The latter reports with evident satisfaction the view of one reader that the style of the Highlander's essay (and, one must suspect, its substance as well) savored "of the country"—and not just "somewhat," but, in fact, "a great deal." Hardly anyone but a Scotsman, this worthy had remarked, "could write such a style." See *LDH* II 132: Letter to William Robertson on 19 March 1767. Cf. Ronald Hamowy, "Progress and Commerce in Anglo-American Thought: The Social Philosophy of Adam Ferguson," *Interpretation* 14 (1986): 61–87, with Richard B. Sher, "Adam Ferguson, Adam Smith, and the Problem of National Defense," *JMH* 61 (1989): 240–68, and consider, in context, the two passages cited as this chapter's epigraph: Ferguson, *EHCS* 1.5 (29), 5.3 (218).

73. Ferguson, *EHCS* 4.2 (186), 5.3 (221–22), 6.4.

74. Constant, "De la liberté des anciens comparée à celle des modernes" II 558.

75. Vico, *New Science* § 1008—where Vico cites Tac. *Ann.* 1.4, *Hist.* 1.1.

76. Hobbes, *Leviathan* I.13 (188).

77. *WoFN* I 1133: *Morgenröte* 3.179.

78. In this connection, one might consider James Bryce's celebrated discussion of the question "why great men are not chosen Presidents": *The American Commonwealth*[2] (London 1891) I 73–80.

79. Eur. *Supp.* 438–41 (to be read in the context of 399–462). For the formula ordinarily employed by the herald in Athens's assembly, cf. Eur. *Or.* 885 with Ar. *Ach.* 45, *Eccl.* 130; Dem. 18.170; Aeschin. 3.4. It is characteristic of Finley's Hobbesian reduction of ancient politics to the pursuit of "material benefits" that he manages to cite Theseus's reply to the herald and discuss at length the import of his speech while ignoring altogether what the Athenian leader has to say

about eminence and the desire to be *lamprós*: *Politics in the Ancient World* 136–39. The same one-dimensional focus is evident in precisely the same fashion in the most recent neo-Marxist discussion of the Greek understanding of *eleuthería*: Ellen Meiksins Wood, *Peasant-Citizen and Slave: The Foundations of Athenian Democracy* (London 1988) 126–37 (at 135).

80. See Theog. 495; Solon F10.2 (West); Hdt. 1.206.3, 3.80.2, 83.1, 4.97.5, 6.129.2, 130.1, 7.8.ô2, 8.74.2; Dem. 18.139.

81. Cf. Hdt. 3.142.3, 4.161.3, 7.164.1 with Archil. F91.30 and Theog. 678 (West), and see *IG* XII:5 872.27, 31, 38. Thus, what is placed *es méson* becomes community property to be held in common or parceled out (Hdt. 7.152; Eur. *Cyc.* 547; Plut. *Mor.* 483c–e; Lucian *Cronosolon* 19), and one might describe Aristophanes' *Congresswomen* as a comic exploration of the boundary between what is by nature private and what can, in fact, be placed *es méson*: note, especially, Ar. *Eccl.* 602–3. Compare the use of *tò koinón* and its cognates: note Aesch. *Supp.* 366, and cf. Hdt. 1.67.5, 5.85.1, 109.3, 6.14.3, 8.135.2, 9.117 with 3.82.3–4, 84.2; with 3.156.2, 5.109.3; and with 6.50.2, 9.87.2. Note what happens when men employ a *koinòs lógos*: 1.166.1, 2.30.3. See also 8.58.1, and note that *tò koinón* can be used to refer to the public treasury: 6.58.1, 7.144.1, 9.87.2. See Eur. *Ion* 1284.

82. Pl. *Pol.* 284e.

83. Cf. Hdt. 1.170.3 with Plut. *Sol.* 14.6, and see Ar. *Av.* 992–1009 (esp. 1004–9), Pl. *Ti.* 34a–c, and *Leg.* 10.886c–910d (esp. 893b–894a, 898a–b). Consider Alc. F129 (Lobel-Page) in light of Louis Robert, "Recherches épigraphiques. v: Inscriptions de Lesbos," *REA* 62 (1960): 285–315 (at 300–311), and see Victor Ehrenberg, *RE* XV:1 (1931) 1103–4. See also I.vii.6, below. Thus, to deny that Delphi is the world's navel (*omphalós*), lying at the center (*mésos*) of both land and sea, is to question the oracle's authority: Epimenides *Vorsokr.*⁶ 3 B11. In similar fashion, from quite early on, wisdom was linked with moderation, i.e., with keeping to the middle and avoiding the extremes. Note, for example, the role played by terms like *métron* and *metaíchmion* in the political thinking of Theognis (614, 694, 876 [West]) and Solon (F4c.3, 13.52, 16.2, 27.17, 37.9 [West]).

84. Sall. *Iug.* 11.3, Verg. *Aen.* 11.234–40, Plut. *Cic.* 2.2–3. Cicero (*Orat.* 15.50, *De or.* 2.77.313–14) recommends that a practitioner of rhetoric conceal those of his arguments that are least likely to be persuasive to the general public in the least exposed part of his work—the central section.

85. Pl. *Leg.* 12.968e–969a.

86. Consider Hdt. 3.83.3 in light of Hom. *Il.* 23.574, and see Hdt. 4.118.2, 8.22.2, 73.3 with 7.8.ô2.

87. Democr. *Vorsokr.*⁶ 68 B157.

88. To see what is implicit in the insistent Greek use of this term and its cognates, cf. Hdt. 1.30 with Thuc. 2.64. For the root meaning of *lamprós*, see Hdt. 4.64.3, 75.3 (with 2.96.3); Thuc. 7.44.2. See also Hdt. 1.30.4, 174.1, 3.72.2, 6.15.1, 9.75 where it is used with regard to the glory attached to particular deeds. For *lamprótēs* as renown, see 2.101.1. With the exception noted above, Thucydides uses this family of terms with an eye to everlasting fame: cf. 1.138.6, 3.59.2, 6.54.2, 7.55, 87.5; with 2.64.5, 4.62.2, 6.16.5, 31.6, 7.69.2, 75.6; with 6.16.3; and with 1.49.7, 2.7.1, 7.71.5, 8.67.3, 75.2. Note also Arist. *Ath. Pol.* 27.3.

89. See the seminal discussion of Marcel Détienne, "En Grèce archaïque: Géométrie, politique et société," *Annales (ESC)* 20 (1965): 425–41, and *Les maîtres de vérité dans la Grèce archaïque* (Paris 1990) 81–103. Note, in this connection. Claude

Mossé, "Ithaque ou la naissance de la cité," *AION(archeol)* 2 (1980): 7–19 (esp. 14–19).

90. Cf. Hom. *Il.* 7.381–84, 414–20, and *Od.* 2.6–259 (esp. 28–39, 146–54) with *Il.* 19.74–77, and see Hom. *Il.* 23.566–85 (esp. 574). Note, in this connection, Xen. *Cyr.* 7.5.46. For the circle of warriors, see 2.2.3.

91. Agamemnon makes reparation to Achilles by placing the compensation agreed upon back *es méson* for redistribution to the proper claimant: note Hom. *Il.* 1.124–26, 9.328–36; then, cf. 19.171–77, 240–65, 276–81, with Aesop 229 (Chambry), Theog. 677–79 (West), Xen. *Oec.* 7.26, and Herod. 2.84–91; and see Soph. *Phil.* 604–9.

92. Cf. Hom. *Il.* 23.506–13, 700–705, *Od.* 24.71–92 (esp. 86) with Theog. 993–96 (West); Xen. *An.* 3.1.21; Dem. 4.4–5; and Plut. *Mor.* 824e–f.

93. Note Hom. *Il.* 15.425–28, 23.257–73 (esp. 258, 273), 507, 685, 710, 814, *Od.* 8.260, 24.80–86; Hes. *Scut.* 310–13. Cf. Hom. *Il.* 23.704–5 with 798–800, 884–86, and note Hom. *Il.* 23.531, 24.1, *Od.* 8.200, 256–59.

94. Pl. *Resp.* 10.606e.

95. Note L. B. Carter, *The Quiet Athenian* (Oxford 1986) 1–25, and Blair Campbell, "The Epic Hero as Politico," *HPT* 11 (1990): 189–211, and see Jean-Pierre Vernant, "A 'Beautiful Death' and the Disfigured Corpse in Homeric Epic," "India, Mesopotamia, Greece: Three Ideologies of Death," and *"Panta Kala*: From Homer to Simonides," *Mortals and Immortals: Collected Essays*, ed. Froma I. Zeitlin (Princeton 1991) 50–91. It can hardly be fortuitous that Pericles had reportedly (Thuc. 2.41.1) employed the phrase appropriated by Plato. If Periclean Athens is to need no Homer (2.41.4), it is because she herself is to be the education of Hellas. That Thucydides is in agreement with Plato regarding Homer is suggested by his remark (1.3.3) that the first Hellenes were those who followed Achilles.

96. Cf. Hdt. 2.53 with Hes. *Theog.* 108–15, and see Hdt. 1.131. See also Xenophanes *Vorsokr.*⁶ 21 B14–16 and Arist. *Pol.* 1252b24–27.

97. See Cicero *Tusc.* 5.25.70–72—who argues that the human desire for immortality and that for virtue arise from meditation on the nature of the gods. With this in mind, consider what Augustine, drawing on Varro's *Antiquitates rerum divinarum*, has to say about the political import of the kinship between men and the gods of Rome: cf. *De civ. D.* 3.4 with 7.18. Note, in this connection, Pl. *Resp.* 6.501b. Cf. WoM II 210–11: Dossier des *Considérations*.

98. Pind. *Nem.* 6.1–7.

99. Hes. *Theog.* 950–55. See also 289–94, 313–18, 326–32, 526–34. For a thorough survey of the evidence concerning the various ways in which the poets, artists, and philosophers treat Hesiod's hero, see G. Karl Galinsky, *The Herakles Theme* (Oxford 1972) 1–125. See also Walter Burkert, *Structure and History in Greek Mythology and Ritual* (Berkeley 1979) 78–98, and the unpublished dissertation of Susan Woodford, "Exemplum Virtutis: A Study of Heracles in Athens in the Second Half of the Fifth Century B.C." (Columbia University 1966). For the ephebes, consider Ath. 11.494f in light of Pierre Vidal-Naquet, "The Black Hunter and the Origin of the Athenian *Ephebia*," and "Recipes for Greek Adolescence," *The Black Hunter: Forms of Thought and Forms of Society in the Greek World*, trans. Andrew Szegedy-Maszak (Baltimore 1986) 106–56; Vidal-Naquet, "The Black Hunter Revisited," *PCPhS* 212 (1986): 126–44; and John J. Winkler, "The Ephebes' Song: *Tragōidia* and *Polis*," in *Nothing to Do with Dionysos?* 20–62.

100. Cf. Hom. *Il.* 6.208 and 9.443 with *Od.* 11.488–91: in the story which he

tells Alcinous, Odysseus represents Achilles as having repudiated after death the heroic ethic by which he was guided in life. Achilles reportedly said that he would prefer the indignity of being a thete on earth—even a thete forced to serve a man so poor that he lacked an estate—to the privilege of being king over the dead.

101. Heraclitus *Vorsokr.*⁶ 22 B29. Note the juxtaposition of Heracles and the Dioscuri (heroes who achieved apotheosis) with Achilles and Ajax (heroes who did not) in Aristotle's Hymn to Virtue: F675 (Rose).

102. See Arist. *Eth. Nic.* 1095b19–31 (cf. Pl. *Resp.* 9.581c, 586a–b), Sall. *Cat.* 1.1. One might also want to reflect on the connection between the titles and the themes of Gustave Flaubert's *Madame Bovary* and his *Bouvard et Pécuchet*. According to Tocqueville, *DA* 2.4.6 (325), one consequence of the emergence of commercial society may be "to reduce each nation in the end to no more than a herd of timid and industrious animals, of which the government is the shepherd."

103. Cf. Aesch. *Pers.* 73–76, 241–42, 584–97 with Thuc. 1.70, 2.34–46, 60–64. See Pl. *Leg.* 3.694e–695a. In this connection, one should consider Hdt. 5.78.

104. Xen. *Hiero* 7.3.

105. Pl. *Leg.* 4.721b–c, where the emphasis is on procreation, but the implications of the claim are more extensive.

106. Pl. *Symp.* 207a–209a. See Tyrtaeus F12.31–32 (West), and Theog. 245–46 (West). Cf. Cic. *Rep.* 5.7.9, *Tusc.* 1.45.109–46.111, and Sall. *Cat.* 1.1–3.2.

107. See above, I Prologue.

108. Pl. *Symp.* 209a–e.

109. Cf. Pl. *Symp.* 210a–212a with *Resp.* 10.599b–608b; note Lycurg. 102–4; and see I.vii.6–8, below. Theognis was the first to depict the ship of state: it can hardly be fortuitous that he indicates that the poet himself rightly belongs at the helm. Cf. 667–82 with 543–47 (West). The term *aînós*—used by the poets to describe the stories, fables, and legends they recount—denotes legislation as well. Consider *WoFN* II 313: *Also Sprach Zarathustra* 1, "Vom neuen Götzen."

110. Cf. Arist. *Pol.* 1280b38–1281a3 with *Eth. Nic.* 1126b11–14.

111. The Spartan Tyrtaeus (cf. F12 [West] with Werner Jaeger, "Tyrtaeus on True Arete," *Five Essays* [Montreal 1966] 102–42) appears to have been the first to have conceived of the *pólis* in this fashion. The Athenians—and Pericles in particular—soon took up his idea: see Stesimbrotus of Thasos *FGrH* 107 F9, and cf. Thuc. 2.34–46 (esp. 41–44), 60–64 (esp. 64.3–6) and Ar. *Av.* 393–99 with Felix Jacoby, "Patrios Nomos," *Abhandlungen zur Griechischen Geschichtschreibung*, ed. Herbert Bloch (Leiden 1956) 260–315; Arnold W. Gomme, Antony Andrewes, and Kenneth J. Dover, *An Historical Commentary on Thucydides* (Oxford 1945–80) II 94–101; C. W. Clairmont, *Patrios Nomos: Public Burial in Athens during the Fifth and Fourth Centuries B.C.* (London 1983); and Nicole Loraux, *The Invention of Athens: The Funeral Oration in the Classical City*, trans. Alan Sheridan (Cambridge, Mass., 1986). See Cic. *Nat. D.* 3.19.49–50. In the fourth century, Plato's Athenian Stranger could even hint that the city existed for this precise purpose. "In approaching the end (*télos*) for the political regime (*politeía*) as a whole," he remarks, "the lawgiver should see in what manner it is fitting that there be funerals for each of those who have died—and he should observe what honors he ought to allocate to them": consider *Leg.* 1.632c in light of 7.801e, 12.947a–e, and Hdt. 1.30. In keeping with this understanding, Isocrates (8.120) attributes immortality (*athanasía*) to the *pólis*, and Cicero (*Rep.* 3.23.34) argues that a *civitas* should be ordered

with an eye to its lasting forever. See also Pl. _Leg._ 4.714a. Cf. Polyb. 6.53–55: at Rome, in a manner even more straightforward than in Greece, the family shared with the city the function of being the guarantor of commemoration. The Athenians, in fact, specified that funeral orations be delivered only at public funerals and, then, only by the man whom the city appointed for that purpose: Cic. _Leg._ 2.26.65.

112. Although Aristotle (cf. _Eth. Nic._ 1177b31–34 with Pl. _Tht._ 175d–177a) is here defending the attempt to live the philosophical life, his point applies with considerable force as well to the quest for eternal fame. Cf. the texts to which he is responding: Pind. _Isthm._ 5.13–16; Soph. F590 (Radt); Antiphanes F289 (Edmonds). Note Aristotle's treatment of this theme in the Hymn to Virtue that he wrote in memory of his friend Hermeias of Atarneus: F675 (Rose). For the impulse behind marriage and procreation, see Pl. _Leg._ 4.721b–c.

113. Arist. _Pol._ 1254a7: life is for action (_práxis_), not for production (_poíēsis_).

114. Consider Pind. F215 (Bowra) and Theog. 1104a–1106 (West) in light of Arist. _Eth. Nic._ 1123b35–1124a2.

115. Consider Isoc. 4.83–84 in light of Eur. _Tro._ 385–402, 1242–45; and, for further evidence, see Harald Fuchs, "Der Friede als Gefahr: Der Zweiten Einsiedler Hirtengedichte," _HSCPh_ 63 (1958): 363–85 (esp. 366–68 with nn. 44–65).

116. Cf. Pl. _Leg._ 2.660e–664c (esp. 662d–663b) with 12.950b–d. It is for the sake of virtue or human excellence (_aretḗ_) that _lógos_ has come into existence (Plut. _Mor._ 961f–963a [esp. 962a]); and, in the end, the love of honor may point beyond virtue, as commonly understood, altogether: see Arist. _Eth. Nic._ 1095b14–1096a2, and note 1120a23–31. In the absence of a common _lógos_ concerning _aretḗ_, ambition inevitably ends in tyranny: cf. Eur. _Phoen._ 499–506. In this connection, see Steven B. Smith, "Goodness, Nobility & Virtue in Aristotle's Political Science," _Polity_ 19 (1986): 5–26.

117. Hdt. 8.79–80. In the prepolitical world of Hesiod (_Op._ 11–29 [West]), competition is to be praised for the private advantages it confers; in the political world of Sophocles (_OT_ 879–80), it is to be valued solely for the contribution it can make to the good of the city as a whole.

118. Soph. F201b (Radt)—where I have adopted the emendation suggested by Reisig.

119. In recent years, scholars have become increasingly sensitive to the fact that the tragedy, comedy, and satyr drama of ancient Greece and Rome were as thoroughly embedded in the political community as was the ancient economy: consider Simon Goldhill, _Reading Greek Tragedy_ (Cambridge 1986), and the essays collected in _Nothing to Do with Dionysos?_ along with Peter Burian, "_Logos_ and _Pathos_: The Politics of the _Suppliant Women_," in _Directions in Euripidean Criticism_, ed. Peter Burian (Durham, N.C., 1985) 129–55, and Richard Seaford, "The Structural Problems of Marriage in Euripides," in _Euripides, Women, and Sexuality_, ed. Anton Powell (New York 1990) 151–76, in light of Bruno Gentili, _Poetry and Its Public in Ancient Greece: From Homer to the Fifth Century_, trans. A. Thomas Cole (Baltimore 1988); Walter Burkert, "Greek Tragedy and Sacrificial Ritual," _GRBS_ 7 (1966): 87–121; and Richard Seaford, "Dionysiac Drama and the Dionysiac Mysteries," _CQ_ n.s. 31 (1981): 252–75; and note David Konstan, _Roman Comedy_ (Ithaca 1983). Then, consider Jean-Pierre Vernant and Pierre Vidal-Naquet, _Myth and Tragedy in Ancient Greece_, trans. Janet Lloyd (New York 1988), in conjunction with Vernant, _Myth and Society in Ancient Greece_.

120. Ar. *Ran.* 1008–10. See 1030–36. The two quarrel not over the duty of the poet, but rather over what constitutes improving the citizens: 885–1465. Consider Pl. *Prt.* 326a, *Hp. Mi.* 363b, and Lycurg. 98–109 in light of Pl. *Resp.* 10.605c–d, Arist. *Rh.* 1408a23–24, *Pol.* 1339b42–1340b19, and ponder Jeffrey Henderson, "The *Dēmos* and the Comic Competition," and James Redfield, "Drama and Community: Aristophanes and Some of his Rivals," in *Nothing to Do with Dionysos?* 271–335.

121. Cf. Ath. 8.347e with 14.627c–d. See also *Vit. Aesch.* 120 (Westermann) and Plut. *Mor.* 604f.

122. Eur. *Supp.* 438–41. As a consequence of their preference for peace and quiet, these Athenians incurred contempt: see below, I.vii.4 (with particular attention to note 100) and I.vii.5, note 128.

123. Arist. *Pol.* 1280b10–12. See also Heraclitus *Vorsokr.*[6] 22 B102, Antiphon *Vorsokr.*[6] 87 B44.

124. Thomas Pownall, *A Memorial Addressed to the Sovereigns of America* (London 1783) 67–68. For a biographical sketch, see Caroline Robbins, "An Active and Intelligent Antiquary, Governor Thomas Pownall," *Absolute Liberty: A Selection from the Articles and Papers of Caroline Robbins*, ed. Barbara Taft (Hamden, Conn., 1982) 247–63.

125. In their eagerness to impute a liberal outlook to ancient democracy, Karl Popper, *The Open Society and Its Enemies I: The Spell of Plato*[5] (London 1966), and Eric A. Havelock, *The Liberal Temper of Greek Politics* (New York 1957), neglect to consider the missing dimension. Cf. Leo Strauss's detailed critique of the latter: *Liberalism Ancient and Modern* (New York 1968) 24–68, and note the degree to which orthodoxy conforms to the view advanced by Popper and Havelock: W. K. C. Guthrie, *The Sophists* (Cambridge 1971) 135–47. R. G. Mulgan, "Lycophron and Greek Theories of Social Contract," *JHI* 40 (1979): 121–28, comes remarkably close to isolating the source of their misunderstanding.

126. Xen. *Mem.* 2.1.1–34. Cf. Arist. *Pol.* 1324a5–1325b32 with Diog. Laert. 2.6–7, 8.63. See also Arist. *Eth. Nic.* 1179a13–16; Pl. *Hipp. Maj.* 283a; Plut. *Per.* 16.7–9: Aristippus was not unique. For "the new science of politics," cf. Tocqueville, *DA* 1 Introduction (5), with Hamilton, *The Federalist* 9 (51–52). Note that for Madison "the first object of Government" is "the protection" of the "different and unequal faculties of acquiring property": *The Federalist* 10 (58). Xenophon's account of Socrates' conversation with Aristippus does not rule out the possibility that a politic philosopher might discover a middle path of freedom and virtue, lying between slavery and rule and leading to true *eudaimonía*: note Leo Strauss, *Xenophon's Socrates* (Ithaca 1972) 32–39, and consider I.vii.6 (esp. note 138) and I.vii.7, below, in light of I.iv.3, note 82, and I Epilogue.

127. Montesquieu, *EL* 3.14.12–13, 19.27.

128. Cf. Montesquieu, *EL* 3.14.12–13, with 3.19.26–27, while keeping in mind his references to England's commercial character and his discussion of the impact of trade and luxury on politics, mores, and manners (1.5.6, 19, 7.1, 4.20.1–2, 4–8, 10, 12–14, 21, 23, 21.5, 7, 20); then, consider Tocqueville, *DA* 2.2.11 (139), 13, 3.19 (254), and see 2.3.13, 17–19, 21.

129. Tocqueville, *DA* 2.2.1–17.

130. Ferguson, *EHCS* 1.8 (49, 56–57).

Chapter 2

1. See Pascal, *Pensées* 295.

2. Cf. Pl. *Euthphr.* 7b–d, *Phdr.* 263a–b, and *Alc.* I 111b–112e with Arist. *Pol.* 1252b27–1253a29, and see Pl. *Pol.* 283b6–287b2 (esp. 284c1–7); cf. Hobbes, *Elements of Law* I.xiii.3 with II.x.8, and see *De cive* II.v.5; and then consider Madison, *The Federalist* 10 (57–60), in light of Hamilton, *The Federalist* 31 (194–95), and see III.i.3–8, below.

3. First, see Arist. *Hist. An.* 487b33–488a13 and *Pol.* 1252b27–1253a29; then, consider *Eth. Eud.* 1242b23–1243a1 in light of *Pol.* 1280b29–1281a8, *Eth. Nic.* 1159b25–1160a29, 1167a22–b16, 1170b33–1171a20, *Eth. Eud.* 1242a1–11, and Alfarabi, *Aphorisms* §§ 57, 94. Homer (*Il.* 7.271, 22.58, *Od.* 4.475, 8.233) uses *phílos*, almost as a possessive adjective, to denote a person or thing familiar and loved. In classical Greek parlance, a man's *phíloi* are those near and dear—first and foremost, his kin (Arist. *Poet.* 1453b19–1454a15), and then, by extension, also his friends: see Bernard M. W. Knox, *The Heroic Temper: Studies in Sophoclean Tragedy* (Berkeley 1964) 80–82. Note the link between *philía* and the spiritedness which gives rise to anger (*thumós*): *Pol.* 1327b38–1328a16. For a detailed exposition of the problem treated in the text, see Bernard Yack, "Community and Conflict in Aristotle's Political Philosophy," *RP* 47 (1985): 92–112, and "Natural Right and Aristotle's Understanding of Justice," *PTh* 18 (1990): 216–37. Consider as well the political import of Aristotle's exploration of the limits of nature's provision for man: see William J. Booth, "Politics and the Household: A Commentary on Aristotle's *Politics* Book One," *HPT* 2 (1981): 203–26, and Wayne H. Ambler, "Aristotle's Understanding of the Naturalness of the City," *RP* 47 (1985): 163–85. See also the material collected below, in I.iv.2, note 8, and see below, II.iv.

4. Hdt. 3.82.3–4. Herodotus's disclaimer notwithstanding (80.1), the so-called Persian debate (80–83) tells us considerably more about the arguments current in fifth-century Greece than about the state of public opinion in the Persia which came to be ruled by Darius the Great. For an earlier allusion to the distinction between rule by one man, rule by the few, and rule by the many, see Pind. *Pyth.* 2.86–88.

5. [Arist.] *Mag. Mor.* 1211a11–15. In this connection, see below, I.vi.2, note 45.

6. *The Federalist* 8 (47). See Smith, *WN* V.i.f.38–61 (esp. 58–59).

7. For the import of this fact, see Max Weber, *Economy and Society* (Berkeley 1978) II 1349–54, 1359–63; Sally C. Humphreys, "Economy and Society in Classical Athens," and "Homo Politicus and Homo Economicus," *Anthropology and the Greeks* (London 1978) 136–74; and Yvon Garlan, *Guerre et économie en Grèce ancienne* (Paris 1989).

8. The adjustment to the demands of commerce and industry was painful: see E. P. Thompson, "Time, Work-Discipline, and Industrial Capitalism," *P&P* 38 (December 1967): 56–97. For the relation of work to time in premodern society, see Jacques Le Goff, *Time, Work, and Culture in the Middle Ages* (Chicago 1980) 29–52, and Edmund S. Morgan, "The Labor Problem at Jamestown, 1607–1618," *AHR* 76 (1971): 595–611.

9. See Thuc. 2.14–17, Strabo 4.1.5. See also Moses I. Finley, *The Ancient Economy*[2] (London 1985) 95–149. For an extended discussion of the rural foundations of the ancient Greek *pólis*, see Robin Osborne, *Classical Landscape with Figures: The Ancient Greek City and Its Countryside* (Dobbs Ferry, N.Y., 1987).

10. See Xen. *Hiero* 4.3, Pl. *Resp.* 9.578d–e. For the central importance of slavery within the ancient Greek *pólis*, see above, I.i.2 (esp. note 35).

11. For the connection between agriculture and war, see Xen. *Oec.* 4.4, 5.4–5, 13–15, 6.4–10; [Arist.] *Oec.* 1343a26–b7; Cato *Agr.* Praef. 1–4; Cic. *Rep.* 2.4.7; Pliny *NH* 18.26; Veget. *De re milit.* 1.3.

12. Xen. *Oec.* 4.3, *Lac. Pol.* 7; Isoc. 11.18; Arist. *Pol.* 1277b1–7, 1278a25–26, 1321a28–29; *SEG* IX 1.43–50. Aeschines (1.27) takes it for granted that exclusion was the norm. See Pl. *Leg.* 8.846d–847a, 11.919d–920c (with 8.848e, 850b–c); Arist. *Pol.* 1319a4–39, 1328b37–1329a2. For Rome (as understood by a Greek), see Dion. Hal. *Ant. Rom.* 2.28 (with 9.25.2).

13. Hdt. 2.164–168 is the *locus classicus*. See Heraclid. Pont. *Pol.* 43 (Müller *FHG* II 224). See also Soph. *Aj.* 1121; Xen. *Oec.* 4.2–3; Pl. *Resp.* 9.590c, *Tht.* 176c, *Ep.* 7.334b; Arist. *Eth. Eud.* 1215a26–33, *Eth. Nic.* 1107b19, 1123a19, *Pol.* 1258b34, 1278a21, 1289b33, 1290b40, 1317b14, 1321a5, 1337b8–15, *Rh.* 1367a32–33; Plut. *Per.* 2.1–2. The fact that there had to be a law at Athens against heaping insults on those practicing a profession in the *agorá* indicates just how difficult it was to overcome this prejudice (Dem. 57.30–32). See Victor Ehrenberg, *The People of Aristophanes* [3] (New York 1962) 113–46; Kenneth J. Dover, *Greek Popular Morality in the Time of Plato and Aristotle* (Oxford 1974) 39–41, 172–74. In this connection, see André Aymard, "L'idée de travail dans la Grèce archaïque," *Journal de psychologie* 41 (1948): 29–45; Aymard, "Hiérarchie du travail et autarcie individuelle," *Études d'histoire ancienne* (Paris 1967) 316–33; and Jean-Pierre Vernant, "Work and Nature in Ancient Greece," *Myth and Thought among the Greeks* (London 1983) 248–70; and cf. I.i.2–4, above (esp. note 66 and context), with I.iii.3, below (esp. note 74 and context). Note also Cic. *Off.* 1.42.150–51.

14. Samuel Ricard, *Traité général du commerce* (Amsterdam 1781) 463; Montesquieu, *EL* 4.20.1–2; William Robertson, *The Progress of Society in Europe*, ed. Felix Gilbert (Chicago 1972) 67; Condorcet, *Esquisse* 148–49 (which should be read along with 122–23, 132–33, 227–30). Ricard's technical treatise was originally published in 1704 and then reedited again and again as the century progressed; the essay of William Robertson appeared in 1769. For further discussion, see Thomas L. Pangle, *Montesquieu's Philosophy of Liberalism* (Chicago 1973) 200–248, and Albert O. Hirschman, *The Passions and the Interests: Political Arguments for Capitalism before Its Triumph* (Princeton 1977) 9–113.

15. [François Veron de Forbonnais], "Commerce," in *Encyclopédie* III 690–99; Joseph Priestley, *Lectures on History and General Policy* . . . (Dublin 1788) 327–28; *WrTP* I 400: *The Rights of Man* 2.5 (February 1792); Benjamin Constant, *De l'esprit de conquête et de l'usurpation* I.2, *Oeuvres*, ed. Alfred Roulin (Paris 1957) 959–61. Cf. Hamilton, *The Federalist* 6 (31–36). The best brief discussion of the place of commerce in the liberal analysis of the causes of war is to be found in Thomas L. Pangle, "The Moral Basis of National Security: Four Historical Perspectives," in *Historical Dimensions of National Security Problems*, ed. Klaus Knorr (Lawrence, Kans., 1976) 307–72 (esp. 340–43). See also Michael Howard, *War and the Liberal Conscience* (New Brunswick, N.J., 1978).

16. Consider *GHI* 1.42; Hdt. 2.166–67; Thuc. 1.5–6, 6.62; Xen. *Mem.* 3.6.7, *Oec.* 4.1–4, 6.4–10; Arist. *Pol.* 1256a40–1257b39; and Plut. *Cim.* 9.3–6, 13.5–7 in light of Aymard, "Le partage des profits de la guerre dans les traités d'alliance antiques," *Études d'histoire ancienne* 499–512; Pierre Ducrey, *Le traitement des prisonniers de guerre dans la Grèce antique des origines à la conquête Romaine* (Paris 1968)

229–70; W. Kendrick Pritchett, *The Greek State at War* (Berkeley 1971–   ) I 53–100, II 126–32, V 68–504; Yvon Garlan, "Le partage entre alliés des dépenses et des profits de guerre," and Pierre Ducrey, "L'armée, facteur de profits," in *Armée et fiscalité dans le monde antique* (Paris 1977) 149–64, 421–32; and Humphreys, "Homo Politicus and Homo Economicus" 159–74. In this connection, see Yvon Garlan, "Signification historique de la piraterie grecque," *DHA* 4 (1978): 1–16. For a specific example of what Garlan has in mind, see Pierre Brulé, *La piraterie crétoise hellénistique* (Paris 1978).

17. Sprat, *Royal-Society* 3.34 (408).

18. Consider Mandeville, *Fable of the Bees* I 78–80, II 128–34, 147. See also I 41–57, 323–69.

19. Hume, *EMPL* 273: "Of Refinement in the Arts."

20. Smith, *WN* V.ii.f.6.

21. Montesquieu, *EL* 4.20.7–8. Gabriel Bonnot de Mably takes the foreign policy of Montesquieu's England as the model for the new science of diplomacy: *Principes des négotiations, pour servir d'introduction au droit public de l'Europe, fondé sur les traités, Collection complète des oeuvres de l'abbé de Mably* (Paris 1794–95) V 1–234.

22. For a brief survey of views held at the time, see Drew R. McCoy, *The Elusive Republic: Political Economy in Jeffersonian America* (Chapel Hill 1980) 86–90, and Felix Gilbert, *To the Farewell Address: Ideas of Early American Foreign Policy* (Princeton 1961) 44–75.

23. Cf. the comments of Thucydides' Alcibiades (6.18.3) regarding Athens with the famous remarks of Adam Smith (*WN* IV.vii.c.63) regarding Great Britain.

24. J. A. O. Larsen, "Freedom and its Obstacles in Ancient Greece," *CPh* 57 (1962): 230–34. To the material Larsen collected, one can add Pl. *Lys.* 207d–210d.

25. With England's happy experience in mind, Alexander Hamilton sounds this theme, arguing that America's natural insularity is conducive to the establishment and maintenance of a modern liberal republic: *The Federalist* 8.

26. Aristox. F8 (Müller *FHG* II 273).

27. Hdt. 8.3.1. This passage so caught the imagination that it inspired imitation: [Herod. Att.] *Perì politeías* 11–12 (Drerup). Compare the remark concerning Rome's civil wars attributed to Marcus Favonius: Plut. *Brut.* 12.3. The verb *homophronéō* and its cognates first appear in Homer (*Il.* 22.263; *Od.* 6.181–83, 9.456, 15.198) and in Hesiod (*Theog.* 60). See also *Theog.* 81; Pind. *Ol.* 7.6; Hdt. 7.229, 8.75, 9.2; Ar. *Av.* 632; Democr. *Vorsokr.*⁶ 68 B186; Xen. *Hell.* 7.5.7; Arist. *Ath. Pol.* 14.3; Dion. Hal. *Ant. Rom.* 9.45.

28. *The Federalist* 10 (58, 64).

29. Democr. *Vorsokr.*⁶ 68 B250; Lys. 18.17; Xen. *Mem.* 4.4.16; Pl. *Resp.* 1.351a–352a, *Alc.* I 126b–127d; Anaximenes *Rh.* 1424b15–18 (Fuhrmann); Arist. *Eth. Eud.* 1241a15–34, *Eth. Nic.* 1155a22–26, 1167a22–b16, *Pol.* 1330a9–23. See also Thuc. 8.75.2, 93.3; Andoc. 1.140; Lys. 2.63; Aeneas Tacticus 14.1; Hyper. F27 (Jensen); Arist. *Pol.* 1306a9; Paus. 5.14.9. *Homónoia* and its cognates are thought by some to have come into use at about the time of the Peloponnesian War—perhaps as a consequence of sustained reflection on the factional strife that broke out at the time (Thuc. 3.82–83). There is, in fact, another possibility: that these terms had long prior use in the ordinary speech of Athenians. Note the appearance of one such term in the Themistocles Decree (*GHI* 1.23.44)—which appears to be au-

thentic: see N. G. L. Hammond, "The Narrative of Herodotus VII and the Decree of Themistocles at Troezen," *JHS* 102 (1982): 75–93. Homer, Hesiod, Theognis, Pindar, and Herodotus employ *homophronéō* and its cognates instead. See above, note 27.

30. Arist. *Pol.* 1331a30–b3. See also Xen. *Cyr.* 1.2.3–5. See Roland Martin, *Recherches sur l'agora grecque* (Paris 1951) 279–446.

31. Cic. *Rep.* 1.32.49.

32. Xen. *Oec.* 6.4–8; Pl. *Leg.* 4.704d–705b, 5.741e–744a, 8.847d–e, 12.952d–953e; Arist. *Pol.* 1326b39–1327a40. See Alison Burford, *Craftsmen in Greek and Roman Society* (London 1972) 28–36.

33. Pl. *Leg.* 5.745b–e; Arist. *Pol.* 1330a9–25.

34. One example should suffice: regional divisions had plagued Athens in the sixth century, and Cleisthenes' tribal reform appears to have been aimed at reducing the political influence of geography by throwing residents of distant villages into the same religious, social, and political units: Hdt. 1.59–64, 6.66–70; Arist. *Ath. Pol.* 13–21. For the results, see John S. Traill, *The Political Organization of Attica* (Princeton 1975) 1–24, 35–58, 64–81, and Peter J. Rhodes, "Ephebai, Bouleutae and the Population of Athens," *ZPE* 38 (1980): 191–201.

35. Arist. *Pol.* 1330a20–23. Cf. Dem. 59.27, which records the decision of a publican to vote against a war because it would reduce trade and prevent him from recouping what he had bid for the right to collect the harbor tax.

36. Xen. *Oec.* 6.4.8, [Arist.] *Oec.* 1343a26–b7.

37. Harp. s.v. *aphanès ousía* is somewhat misleading: though real estate was virtually impossible to hide and was therefore almost always considered visible wealth, other categories of property would be described as visible if the owner gave public acknowledgment of ownership and as invisible if he practiced concealment. See A. R. W. Harrison, *The Law of Athens* (Oxford 1968–71) I 230–32; Louis Gernet, "Things Visible and Things Invisible," *The Anthropology of Ancient Greece*, trans. John Hamilton, S.J., and Blaise Nagy (Baltimore 1981) 343–51; and Vincent Gabrielsen, "*Phanerà* and *Aphanès Ousía* in Classical Athens," *C&M* 37 (1986): 99–114.

38. Cf. Montesquieu, *EL* 4.21.20, 22.13–14 with 4.20.4–5, 8, 10–11, 20, 23 (601) and 22.13. See Smith, *WN* II.v.14, III.iv.24, V.ii.f.6, k.80, iii.55.

39. See G. E. M. de Ste. Croix, "Greek and Roman Accounting," in *Studies in the History of Accounting*, ed. A. C. Littleton and B. S. Yamey (Homewood, Ill., 1956) 14–74. See also Richard H. Macve, "Some Glosses on 'Greek and Roman Accounting,'" in *Crux: Essays Presented to G. E. M. de Ste. Croix on His 75th Birthday*, ed. Paul Cartledge and F. D. Harvey (Exeter 1985) 233–64 (esp. 233–39, 262–64). What can be inferred from this is a matter of dispute: see below, I.iii.3, note 67.

40. In ordinary speech, invisible wealth was generally associated with fraud (Lys. 32.4, 19–29, F24.2 [Gernet/Bizos]; Isaeus 6.29–33, 8.35–37, 11.43; Isoc. 17.2–12; Dem. 27.56–57, 38.7–8, 48.9, 12–35, 56.1; Hyper. 5.4–12 [Jensen]) and with the evasion of civic responsibilities (Lys. 20.23, 33; Ar. *Eccl.* 601–2; Isaeus 7.35–40, 11.47; Dem. 5.8, 28.2–9, 45.66, 50.7–9, *Ep.* 3.41; Dein. 1.70). Note the contrast between the "visible friend" and "invisible wealth" at Men. *Dys.* 811–12. In this context, consider Lys. 3.24; Pl. *Resp.* 1.343d; Isoc. 7.31–35; Dem. 27.8, 28.3–4, 42.22–23; and Aeschin. 1.101. See also Andoc. 1.118; Lys. 12.83, F1.2 (Gernet/Bizos); and Isaeus F8.1.2 (Roussel).

41. *WN* V.ii.f.6.

42. For this reason, artisans (and merchants) were thought slavish: see below, I.iii.3, note 74 and context.

43. Systematic ravaging was the rule in Greek warfare and not the exception: Victor Davis Hanson, *Warfare and Agriculture in Classical Greece* (Pisa 1983), has collected and analyzed the relevant evidence. See also Yvon Garlan, *Recherches de poliorcétique grecque* (Athens 1974) 1–86.

44. Aphytis (Arist. *Pol.* 1319a14–19) is the best attested example. For the relevant evidence, see Georg Busolt, *Griechische Staatskunde*[3] (Munich 1963) I 352–58.

45. Cf. Lys. 34 with Eur. *Supp.* 238–45, *El.* 367–90, *Or.* 917–22. See R. Goossens, "République des paysans," in *Mélanges F. de Visscher* (Brussels 1950) III 551–77, and G. Mathieu, "La réorganisation du corps civique athénien à la fin du Ve siècle," *REG* 40 (1927): 65–116 (esp. 104–11).

46. Men. F408 (Edmonds).

47. Arist. *Pol.* 1258b27–33; [Arist.] *Oec.* 1343a25–b7.

48. See Ar. *Plut.* 510–16; Xen. *Mem.* 3.7.6.

49. A handful of craftsmen could provision a substantial community. In the fifth century, when the finer Athenian ware was prized not only at Athens but throughout the Mediterranean world and beyond, there were never more than one hundred vase painters with, say, three hundred assistants active in Athens at any given moment in time—and, of course, many of these were metics and slaves. See R. M. Cook, "Die Bedeutung der bemalten Keramik für den griechischen Handel," *JDAI* 74 (1959): 114–23 (esp. 118–19).

50. Amphis F17.2–3 (Edmonds).

51. Madison, *The Federalist* 10 (59). For the primacy of agriculture, note Arist. *Pol.* 1256a19–39, and see G. E. M. de Ste. Croix, *The Class Struggle in the Ancient Greek World: From the Archaic Age to the Arab Conquests* (Ithaca 1981) 120–33. In this connection, one can learn much from Fernand Braudel, *The Mediterranean and the Mediterranean World in the Age of Philip II*, trans. Siân Reynolds (New York 1972–73) I 25–102, 148–67.

52. Pl. *Resp.* 4.422e–423a. See also 8.551d.

53. Lys. 18.17.

54. Athens (cf. Solon F5, 34, 36–37 [West] with Arist. *A.P.* 2, 5–6, 11–12 and Plut. *Sol.* 13–16, 19.2–4) is the best-attested example from the period, but it was by no means an isolated case. There is evidence suggestive of similar agitation at Megara (Plut. *Mor.* 295c–d), Croton (Iambl. *Vit. Pyth.* 262), and Cumae (Dion. Hai. *Ant. Rom.* 7.8.1–2)—and these are likely to have been but the tip of the iceberg: consider the implications of Hdt. 4.162–64 (esp. 163.1). The issue was of sufficient concern that, after allotments had been fixed, the citizens of one Locrian community actually made it a capital crime under all circumstances short of a military emergency to propose or even vote in favor of a subsequent redistribution: see *GHI* 1.13 with David Asheri, "Distribuzione di terre e legislazione agraria nella Locride occidentale," *JJP* 15 (1965): 313–28, and Biagio Virgilio, "A proposito della lege locrese ozolia sulla distribuzione di terre (*IG* IX[2] I III, 609)," in *Philías Chárın: Miscellanea di studi classici in onore di Eugenio Manni* (Rome 1980) VI 2177–86. Similar prohibitions are attested later elsewhere: *SIG*[3] 141; *ICr* III iv 8. Where it was impossible or deemed imprudent to seize additional land in the immediate neighborhood of a community, the chief alternative to redistribution seems to have been forced expulsion and the launching of a colony (cf. Hdt.

4.150–51, 153 with Pl. *Leg.* 5.740b–e). Compare the Samnite practice: Dion. Hal. *Ant. Rom.* 1.16.1–4.

55. In that period, Athens was the exception: consider Arist. *Ath. Pol.* 40.3 (which should be read with Andoc. 1.88, Dem. 24.149, and Arist. *Ath. Pol.* 56.2) in light of what one can surmise from *Fouilles de Delphes* III.i.294; Diod. 15.58; Ael. 14.24; [Dem.] 17.15; *ICr* III.iv.8.21–24; Plut. *Dion* 37.5–7, 48.4–9. Note also Pl. *Resp.* 8.565e–566a, *Leg.* 3.684d–e, 5.736c–e; Isoc. 12.259; Anaximenes *Rh.* 1424a31–34 (Fuhrmann); Arist. *Pol.* 1305a3–7, 1309a14–20; Polyb. 4.9. Though perhaps muted, this impulse is by no means unattested in the fifth century: Thuc. 3.81.4, 5.4, 8.21. See Alexander Fuks, "Patterns and Types of Social-Economic Revolution in Greece from the Fourth to the Second Century B.C.," *Social Conflict in Ancient Greece* (Jerusalem 1984) 9–39.

56. The military strategy adopted by Pericles (Thuc. 2.13–23) at the beginning of the Peloponnesian War and followed thereafter by the Athenians generated tensions of this very sort. The Athenians withstood repeated Spartan invasions by abandoning the countryside for the safety of the city and of Long Walls that served as the umbilical cord linking it to its seaport the Peiraeus. Athens's control of the sea freed her from danger of siege, but the farmers paid a heavy price in devastation of their land (Ar. *Ach.* 183, *Pax* 628). To the desperately poor, war brought paid employment as oarsmen in the fleet (Thuc. 6.31.3); to the prosperous, it meant lost harvests and heavy civic exactions on their capital (Ar. *Eq.* 912, Lys. 21.6). As a consequence, the Athenians were divided along class lines over issues of foreign policy late in the fifth century ([Xen.] *Ath. Pol.* 2.14) and through much of the fourth century as well (*Hell. Oxy.* 6.2–3 [Bartoletti], Ar. *Eccl.* 197–98, Diod. 18.10.1). In this connection, see Josiah Ober, *Fortress Attica: Defense of the Athenian Land Frontier, 404–322 B.C.* (Leiden 1985).

57. Only within oligarchies (Pl. *Resp.* 8.556a–b) was it normal for a man to be allowed to do with his property whatever he wished.

58. For colonies founded in the archaic period, this seems to have been nothing out of the ordinary (Arist. *Pol.* 1266b18–23, 1319a10–11), and there are examples from the fifth, fourth, and third centuries as well: SIG^3 47, 141, 490; *Inschriften von Milet* I 3, no. 333e. The fragmentary sixth-century inscription recording the regulations imposed on the Athenian cleruchs sent to Salamis (*IG* I^3 1) should be read in conjunction with the similar fourth-century inscription dealing with those resident on Lemnos (III 73 b/c). As the latter indicates, the legislation for Lemnos was based on that for Salamis—so there is no reason to doubt that the cleruchs on Salamis, like their later counterparts on Lemnos, were denied the right to lease their lots, give them away, exchange them, or put them up as security for loans. The primacy of military concerns is explicit in the first of these two inscriptions. Cf. Pl. *Resp.* 8.552a–555c. The origins of this practice remain mysterious. As Moses I. Finley, "The Alienability of Land in Ancient Greece," *The Use and Abuse of History*[2] (Harmondsworth 1985) 153–60, has pointed out, the scattering of information available provides no support for the view that land was inalienable in Greece from the beginning and some evidence to the contrary. The early lawgivers from Corinth—Pheidon (Arist. *Pol.* 1265b10–16) and Philolaus (1274b1–5)—are thought to have been concerned that the number of households and citizens within a community be stable, and the early Corinthian colony Leucas (1266b20–23) is known to have been among the cities that stipulated that landed property be inalienable. It is just possible that these two figures originated

the notion. For the view that these arrangements are regime-specific, see David Asheri, "Laws of Inheritance, Distribution of Land, and Political Constitutions in Ancient Greece," *Historia* 12 (1963): 1–21. We are just beginning to sort out the techniques by which the boundaries of allotments were established. For the mute testimony of the archaeological remains, see Thomas D. Boyd and Michael H. Jameson, "Urban and Rural Land Division in Ancient Greece," *Hesperia* 50 (1981): 327–42.

59. Arist. *Pol.* 1266b14–18, 1319a6–9. There was apparently an absolute restriction at Thurii (1307a29–30), but not in Crete (Polyb. 6.46.1). The original allotments at Thurii were reportedly equal in size: Diod. 12.11.2. For land left undivided on the borders, see Diod. 12.11.1, 16.82.5; *SEG* IX 3; *SIG*³ 141. Land situated near the town was quite naturally more valuable than that lying nearer the borders: Xen. *Vect.* 4.50.

60. Arist. *Pol.* 1274b1–5: Philolaus at Thebes.

61. Public opinion discouraged the sale of land: Aeschin. 1.30–31, 96; Isaeus 7.31.

62. At Athens, a father could deny a son equal participation in dividing the inherited property only by repudiating him. See the evidence collected by Harrison, *The Law of Athens* I 75, 94, 130–32. Adopted sons shared equally only with the natural sons born after the act of adoption. At Massilia, there was a limit placed on the size of dowries: Strabo 4.1.5. At Gortyn (*ICr* IV 72 cols. IV.23–V.9, 29–54), the discretion of the parents was strictly limited. The father might specify who was to get what as long as his houses and cattle were divided equally among the sons and all of the offspring received shares of the rest—two parts each for the sons and one for the daughters. The property of the mother was divided in precisely the same fashion. To the same end, strict limits were placed on the size of the dowry (cf. Strabo 10.4.20) and on other gifts to the children: these were not, in any case, to exceed the anticipated inheritance. One hundred staters was set as the limit on gifts transferred from sons to mothers and from fathers to wives (cols. X.14–20, XII.1–5). Adopted sons received only a daughter's share and could easily be repudiated (cols. X.33–XI.23). Where an adopted son died without leaving behind legitimate children, his portion was divided among the heirs of the adopter. For a thorough discussion of the evidence, see *The Law Code of Gortyn*, ed. Ronald F. Willetts (Berlin 1967) 20–27, 29–31.

63. Aeschin. 1.30 should probably be read in light of Lys. F11 (Gernet/Bizos). See also Hdt. 2.177; Plut. *Sol.* 17, 31; Poll. *Onom.* 8.42.

64. Though attributed to Oxylus the legendary founder of Elis (Arist. *Pol.* 1319a12–14), this law must have been enacted after the invention of coinage. It may have been but one of a number of statutes designed for the protection of the smallholder: Polybius (4.73.6–10) paints an idyllic picture of country life in Elis. For the existence of similar laws elsewhere, see Diod. 1.79.5. In this context, one should consider Plato's description (*Resp.* 8.552a–555c) of the disease fatal to oligarchies.

65. The city was Gortyn: *ICr* IV 72 col. VI.2–7.

66. Diod. 1.79.3–5.

67. For the ordering principle and the chief source of confusion and disorder, cf. Pl. *Leg.* 11.923a–b and 12.942c with 11.925d–926d.

68. At Athens—the one city where pregnant widows are known to have been included—the eponymous archon (Lys. 26.12; Dem. 35.48, 43.75; Arist. *Ath. Pol.*

56.6–7; Aeschin. 1.158; Isaeus 7.30; Schol. Dem. 24.20; Poll. *Onom.* 8.89) performed this function, apparently with the aid of a board of *orphanistaí* (Soph. *Aj.* 512; *Suda* s.v. *orphanistôn*) or *orphanophúlakes* (Xen. *Vect.* 2.7 with Philippe Gauthier, *Un commentaire historique des Poroi de Xénophon* [Geneva 1976] 68–71). Similar boards are attested at Naupactus (*IG* IX 1² 624g, 628b, 643), at Ephesus (*SIG*² 510.29), at Delphi (*Fouilles de Delphes* III² 168), at Selymbria (*BCH* 36.549), at Gortyn (*ICr* IV 72 col. XII.7, 10–11: Willetts, *The Law Code of Gortyn* 27, 32, 50, 79), and on the Black Sea both at Gorgippia (B. Latyschew, *Inscr. ant. orae septentr. Ponti Ponti Euxini graecae et latinae* IV 434 F b–c.4) and at Istria (*Histria* I [Bucharest 1954] 557 No. 32: D. M. Pippidi, *I Greci nel basso Danubio* [Milan 1971] 85–86). Where the orphan's guardian was not eager to manage his ward's property, the archon would lease out the inheritance at auction so that the child would have a steady income. In such cases, it was the practice to evaluate, measure off, and set aside a parcel of the lessor's land as security (*apotimémata*) for the orphan's property and for the rent to be paid. Boundary stones (*hóroi*) recording this practice survive for Amorgos and for Naxos as well as for Athens: see Moses I. Finley, *Studies in Land and Credit in Ancient Athens, 500–200 B.C.* (New Brunswick, N.J., 1952) 38–44, 151–56, 189–90. The absence of evidence for this practice elsewhere is due to the failure of other cities to employ inscribed *hóroi* to mark encumbered land. Note the incomplete discussion of Iasos by Heraclides Ponticus: *Pol.* 40 (Müller *FHG* II 224). See also the provisions suggested by Plato: *Leg.* 11.924b–928d. It is revealing that, in Greece, the situation of the mother had no bearing on the status of her child: where the father was dead, the child was considered an *orphanós*.

69. For the elaborate legal safeguards established at Athens, see Harrison, *The Law of Athens* I 97–121. Cf. Plato's description of the problem (*Resp.* 8.554c), the solution he limns (*Leg.* 11.928c–d), and the provisions reportedly recommended by the lawgiver Charondas of Catana (Diod. 12.15). On fatherless children in general, see Hendrik Bolkestein, *Wohltätigkeit und Armenpflege im Vorchristlichen Altertum* (Utrecht 1939) 275–82, and A. Dorjahn, *RE* XVIII A (1942) 1197–1200.

70. Here again, the extreme case was Gortyn: see *ICr* IV 72 cols. VI.7–46, VIII.40–53, IX.3–24, XII.6–19.

71. Arist. *Pol.* 1274b1–5.

72. One should interpret Isaeus 2.13, 3.68, 4.16, 6.9, 7.24, 30, 9.2, 33, 10.4, 9, 11, 11.45; Dem. 20.102, 43.75, 44.14, 21–22, 26, 33, 64; Isoc. 19.49; Hyper. 5.17 (Jensen); Plut. *Them.* 32.1–2, *Mor.* 843a in light of Arist. *Pol.* 1266b14–17. For the meaning of *ápais*, see Hdt. 5.48. Where the deceased had a daughter, the adopted son was required to marry her: Isaeus 2.13, 3.42, 68, 10.13. For the requirement that an adoptive son intent on rejoining his natural father's household leave a son of his own behind to guarantee the continuation of his adoptive father's *oîkos*, see Isaeus 6.44, 10.11; Dem. 43.77–78 (with 13–14), 44.19–25. Plutarch (*Sol.* 21.3–4) misconstrues Solon's purpose. See David Asheri, "L'*oîkos érēmos* nel diritto successario attico," *Archivio Giuridico* 159 (1960): 7–24. There is no good reason to suppose that full testamentary freedom was ever extended to citizens with sons: see G. E. M. de Ste. Croix, *CR* 20 (1970): 389–90, and Robin Lane Fox, "Aspects of Inheritance in the Greek World," in *Crux* 208–32 (at 224–26).

73. The Attic orators take this motive as a given: see Isaeus 1.10–11, 2.10, 46, 6.51, 65, 7.29–32, 9.7, 36. A man claiming an inheritance would quite naturally seek to strengthen his case by showing that he had performed the requisite rites

(Isaeus 2.36, 4.7, 26, 8.21–24; Dem. 43.63–74, 44.2, 11, 32, 43, 66), and those opposing such a claimant would try to prove the opposite (Isaeus 4.19, 9.4). In anticipation, a claimant might even seek to prevent a potential rival from having access to the body (6.40–41, 8.21–27, 38–39). The same concerns are evident among the Aeginetans (Isoc. 19.31) and were probably shared by all the Greeks. In general, see Wesley E. Thompson, "Athenian Attitudes towards Wills," *Prudentia* 13 (1981): 13–23. For the religious duties attendant upon succession, see Donna C. Kurtz and John Boardman, *Greek Burial Customs* (Ithaca 1971); Margaret Alexiou, *The Ritual Lament in Greek Tradition* (Cambridge 1974) 4–14; and Robert Garland, *The Greek Way of Death* (Ithaca 1985) 21–37, 104–20. In Rome, these responsibilities were deemed a burden—so much so, in fact, that it was customary to speak of a windfall as a *sine sacris hereditas*: cf. Plaut. *Capt.* 775, *Trin.* 484 with Festus s.v. *sine sacris hereditas*, and see Alan Watson, *The Law of Succession in the Later Roman Republic* (Oxford 1971) 4–7. Something of the sort was presumably true in Greece as well. With regard to the family and religion, consider the classic account of Numa Denis Fustel de Coulanges, *The Ancient City* (Baltimore 1980) 7–108, in light of the recent reassessment by Arnaldo Momigliano and Sally C. Humphreys: see "Fustel de Coulanges, *The Ancient City*," in Humphreys, *The Family, Women and Death: Comparative Studies* (London 1983) 131–43. See also Humphreys, "Family Tombs and Tomb-cult in Classical Athens: Tradition or Traditionalism?" ibid., 79–130.

74. Dem. 46.20; Isaeus 8.31–32, 10.12–13, F25 (Thalheim); Hyper. F192 (Jensen); Men. *Aspis* 264–73. The *epíklēros'* son was sometimes formally initiated into her father's household or even that of a deceased brother by a posthumous adoption: Dem. 43.12–14; Isaeus 3.73, 7.31, 11.49. For the adoption of a daughter to function as an *epíklēros* after her adoptive father's death, see Isaeus 7.9, 11.8, 41.

75. Plut. *Sol.* 20.2–5 and *Mor.* 769a should be read in light of R. Dareste, "Une prétendue loi de Solone," *REG* 8 (1895): 1–6. For the *epidikasía* by which her relative could claim the *epíklēros*, see Isaeus 3.64, 10.12, 19; Dem. 46.22–23, 57.41; Ter. *Adel.* 650–59. A rich *epíklēros* might be a prize worth vying for (Andoc. 1.121; Isaeus 6.46; Dem. 30 hyp., 57.41; Arist. *Pol.* 1303b18–1304a13), but the victor in such a contest was not always left in an enviable position. The *epíklēros* had legal rights against abuse that gave her considerable leverage: one should read Men. F402–3, 585 (Edmonds) and Arist. *Eth. Nic.* 1161a1–3 in light of Isaeus 1.39, 3.46–47, 62; Dem. 37.45–46, 43.75; Arist. *Ath. Pol.* 56.6; Poll. *Onom.* 8.38; Harp. s.v. *kakôseōs*. There was reportedly similar legislation elsewhere: see Diod. 12.18.3–4 with Federica Cordano, "Leggi e legislatori Calcidesi," in *Sesta miscellanea greca e romana* (Rome 1978) 89–98. For a thorough discussion of these matters, see David M. Schaps, *Economic Rights of Women in Ancient Greece* (Edinburgh 1979) 25–47. See also G. E. M. de Ste. Croix, "Some Observations on the Property Rights of Athenian Women," *CR* 20 (1970): 273–78, and Raphael Sealey, *Women and Law in Classical Greece* (Chapel Hill 1990) 12–49. The prospect that a young *epíklēros* who lacked a son might be dragged from the arms of a loving husband by a greedy kinsman gave the comic playwrights an appealing theme to elaborate on. There is reason to suspect that an *epíklēros* who lacked a son and was tied to her husband by a deep, reciprocated love might work an informal deal in which her kinsman received monetary compensation or even the *klêros* itself (and retained his own wife) while she remained with her beloved: see Lane Fox, "Aspects of Inheritance in the Greek World" 225–30.

76. In the sixth century, only those disabled in war were eligible for public

support: Plut. *Sol.* 31.3–4. By the fourth century, this may no longer have been the case. I find it striking that none of the later sources (Lys. 24.1–26, Aeschin. 1.103–4 [with schol.], Arist. *Ath. Pol.* 49.4, Philochorus *FGrH* 328 F197) makes mention of any such restriction. In particular, one would expect the speaker in Lysias's oration to have said something about the sacrifices he had made for the city.

77. Diog. Laert. 1.55. Cf. Arist. *Ath. Pol.* 24.3, which attests to this being the custom just after the Persian Wars, with the epigraphical allusion (*SEG* X 6.121–25) to honors confered on orphans in about 460 B.C. The first absolutely dependable evidence is Thuc. 2.46. See Cratinus F171 (Edmonds), Lys. F6.1–2 (Gernet/Bizos), Pl. *Menex.* 248e–249c, Isoc. 8.82, Arist. *Pol.* 1268a8–11, Schol. Dem. 24.20, Aeschin. 3.154, Ael. Aristid. *Panath.* 368 (Lenz/Behr), Lesbonax *Protreptikos* 1.19. For the spirit of the law, see Lys. 2.75–76. For the *dokimasía* of orphans, see [Xen.] *Ath. Pol.* 3.4 and *Anecd. Bekk.* I 235.11. For metics, cf. Arist. *Ath. Pol.* 58.3. For a recent discussion of this practice, see Reinhard Stupperich, *Staatsbegräbnis und Privatgrabmal im Klassischen Athen* (Münster 1977) 239–44.

78. Arist. *Pol.* 1268a8–11. For the meaning of this passage, see W. L. Newman, *The Politics of Aristotle* (Oxford 1877–1902) II 300–301. For an alternative interpretation, cf. Willem den Boer, *Private Morality in Greece and Rome: Some Historical Aspects* (Leiden 1979) 43–55. By the end of the classical period, public maintenance of those left fatherless by war had become a standard technique for the encouragement of *homónoia* within democracies: Anaximenes *Rh.* 1424a35–39 (Fuhrmann). For Hippodamus's date and activities as a town planner, see below, I.ii.5 (esp. note 103).

79. Cf. the evidence for Athenian custom (Pl. *Menex.* 248e–249c, Isoc. 8.82, Aeschin. 3.154) with that for Rhodes (Diod. 20.84.3) and for Thasos (Jean Pouilloux, *Recherches sur l'histoire et les cultes de Thasos* I: *De la fondation de la cité à 196 avant J.-C.* [Paris 1954] 371–79 [no. 141: Inscr. Inv. 1032]). Public maintenance was deemed an honor: Arist. *Rh.* 1361a33–37.

80. Cratinus F171 (Edmonds). Note, in this connection, Aesch. *Sept.* 10–20. On Thasos (above, note 79) and at Athens as well (Schol. Dem. 24.20), these responsibilities devolved on the polemarchs or polemarch. As the title given these officials suggests, the care of such orphans was a matter related to war. See Sarah B. Pomeroy, "Charities for Greek Women," *Mnemosyne* 35 (1982): 115–35.

81. Diod. 20.84.3.

82. For the most recent survey of this period, see Peter Krentz, *The Thirty at Athens* (Ithaca 1982).

83. Cf. Lys. F6.1–2 (Gernet/Bizos) with *SEG* XXVIII 46: Ronald S. Stroud, "Greek Inscriptions: Theozotides and the Athenian Orphans," *Hesperia* 40 (1971): 280–301. As wages increased (cf. *IG* I² 373–74 with II² 1672), the pension for invalids kept pace (cf. Lys. 24.13, 26 with Arist. *Ath. Pol.* 49.4; Philochorus *FGrH* 328 F197). The same was presumably the case for the grants to children left fatherless by war.

84. For what follows, see Alexander Fuks, "Toîs aporouménois koinōneîn: The Sharing of Property by the Rich with the Poor in Greek Theory and Practice," *Social Conflict in Ancient Greece* 172–89. A number of scholars have recently attempted to situate the phenomenon of benefaction within the history of ancient institutions as a whole: see, especially, Paul Veyne, *Le pain et le cirque: Sociologie historique d'un pluralisme politique* (Paris 1976) 9–373 (esp. 185–373), and Philippe

Gauthier, *Les cités grecques et leurs bienfaiteurs (IVe–Ier siècle avant J.-C.): Contribution à l'histoire des institutions* (Paris 1985) esp. 7–15, 24–38, 66–128.

85. Democr. *Vorsokr.*^{6} 68 B245, B255.

86. Archytas *Vorsokr.*^{6} 47 B3.

87. Arist. *Pol.* 1320b7–11, 1329b39–1330a2.

88. Cf. Isoc. 7.31–36 with Lys. 16.14.

89. Cf. Theopomp. *FGrH* 115 F89, 135; Nep. *Cim.* 4.1–3; and Plut. *Cim.* 10, *Per.* 9.2 with Andoc. 1.147. I am not inclined to take the failure of Aristotle (*Ath. Pol.* 27.3–4) and Theophrastus (Cic. *Off.* 2.18.64) to mention that Cimon provided maintenance for all comers and not just for those from his own deme as proof that Theopompus, Nepos, and Plutarch exaggerate his hospitality; in any case, the first of the two peripatetic writers does emphasize that Cimon allowed anyone who wished to do so to join in harvesting the crops on his estates.

90. Ael. *VH* 14.24. For Olbia, see *SIG*^{3} 495.176–88; for Erythrae, see *Inschr. Erythrai-Klazomenai* 28; for Priene, see *Inschr. Priene* 108; for Samos, see *SEG* I 366; for Rhodes, see Strabo 14.2.5.

91. Theophr. *Char.* 23.5.

92. Anonymus Iamblichi *Vorsokr.*^{6} 89 B7.1–2, 8. In this connection, consider Thomas W. Gallant, *Risk and Survival in Ancient Greece: Reconstructing the Rural Domestic Economy* (Stanford 1991) esp. 113–96.

93. Pl. *Resp.* 9.578d–579a. Note also Xen. *Hiero* 4.3. For the existence of a class of country squires, cf. Xenophon's description (*Hell.* 5.2.7) of Mantineia with what Wesley E. Thompson, "The Regional Distribution of the Athenian Pentakosiomedimnoi," *Klio* 52 (1970): 437–51, has to say about Attica. Thompson's argument depends upon an assumption that is plausible but by no means certain: that the law setting aside certain offices for the wealthiest class of Athenians was still enforced in the second half of the fifth century—as it evidently was not in the decades that followed (cf. Arist. *Ath. Pol.* 7.4, 47.1 with Vincent Gabrielsen, *Remuneration of State Officials in Fourth Century B.C. Athens* [Odense 1981] 109–45). In this context, one should consider Strabo 14.2.5. In keeping with his tendency to give almost exclusive importance to "material relations," Moses I. Finley, *Politics in the Ancient World* (Cambridge 1983) 39–49, places great emphasis on local patronage. For a useful, if similarly reductionist treatment, see Paul Millett, "Patronage and Its Avoidance in Classical Athens," in *Patronage in Ancient Society*, ed. Andrew Wallace-Hadrill (London 1989) 15–47.

94. Plut. *Sol.* 18.6–7. Cf. Arist. *Ath. Pol.* 9.1, Dem. 21.45, Hyper. 3.11 (Jensen), Plut. *Mor.* 154d–e with Xen. *Lac. Pol.* 10.6.

95. For the notion and its relation to the privileges accorded resident aliens, see Aesch. *Supp.* 605–14. For particular examples, cf. Diod. 14.6.3 with Plut. *Lys.* 27.3, and see *GHI* 2.149.

96. The city was Cyme: Arist. F611.39 (Rose).

97. For the stake a man has in cultivating his neighbors, see Hes. *Op.* 342–51 (West), Cato *Agric.* 4, Columella *Rust.* 1.3.5–7, Pliny *NH* 18.44. Note Xen. *Hiero* 4.3–4. For further discussion of cooperative self-help, see Andrew Lintott, *Violence, Civil Strife and Revolution in the Classical City* (Baltimore 1982) 13–33.

98. Pl. *Leg.* 5.736c–e.

99. Cf. Arist. *Pol.* 1320a32–b12 with *Ath. Pol.* 16.2–6. See also Isoc. 7.32–35, 55; Ael. *VH* 9.25. For a discussion of Aristotle's proposal, see Claude Mossé, "Aris-

tote et le théorikon: Sur le rapport entre *Trophé* et *Misthos*," in *Philías Chárin* V 1603–12.

100. Arist. *Pol.* 1266a38–64. Note the policy attributed to the Samnites: Nicholas of Damascus *FGrH* 90 F103c.

101. Cf. Gorgias *Vorsokr.*⁶ 82 B5b, 8a with Philostr. *VS* 1.9; cf. Lys. 33.6–9 with Diod. 14.109.3; and see Isoc. 4.3, 15–17, 173–74, 181–88, 5.9, 12–16, 30–31, 95–97, 119–23, 126, 130, *Ep.* 2.11, 3.5, 9.8–10. See also Alexander Fuks, "Isokrates and the Social-Economic Situation in Greece," *Social Conflict in Ancient Greece* 52–79.

102. Consider Plut. *Tim.* 22–39; Nepos *Tim.* 1.1, 2.1–3.6, 5.2–4; and Diod. 16.66.1–68.11, 69.2–6, 70.1–6, 71.3, 72.2–73.3, 77.4–83.3, 90.1 in light of Pl. *Ep.* 7.335e–337d, and see H. D. Westlake, *Timoleon and his Relations with Tyrants* (Manchester 1952), and Richard J. A. Talbert, *Timoleon and the Revival of Greek Sicily, 344–317 B.C.* (Cambridge 1974). There is no evidence to prove that Timoleon was ever under Plato's influence, but it is hard to believe that, when the Corinthian arrived in Sicily, he was completely unaware of the efforts made by the philosopher to encourage recolonization just a decade before. One could "state with certainty that Timoleon's programme for the revival of Sicily owes nothing to Plato" only if one could demonstrate the truth of two propositions: that the Seventh Letter is a forgery, and that it in no way reflects what Plato was up to in the 350s. No one has ever provided evidence for the first proposition that would pass muster with anyone not already inclined to be hypercritical, and the second hypothesis rests on the supposition that the author of the letter knew little of Plato's relations with the Syracusan tyrant—which is demonstrably untrue. Cf. Talbert, 116–22.

103. Note Arist. *Pol.* 1267b21–1268a12, 1330b21–31; cf. Armin von Gerkan, *Griechische Städteanlagen* (Berlin 1924) 42–61, and Ferdinando Castagnoli, *Orthogonal Town Planning in Antiquity*, trans. V. Caliandro (Cambridge, Mass., 1971) 65–73, with Wolfram Hoepfner and Ernst-Ludwig Schwandner, *Haus und Stadt im klassischen Griechenland* (Munich 1986); see Pl. *Leg.* 5.739c–745b, 9.855a–856e, 877d, 11.923a–924a, 929b–e, with Alexander Fuks, "Plato and the Social Question: The Problem of Poverty and Riches in the Republic," "The Conditions of 'Riches' (*ploûtos*) and of 'Poverty' (*penía*) in Plato's Republic," and "Plato and the Social Question: The Problem of Poverty and Riches in the Laws," *Social Conflict in Ancient Greece* 80–171; and then note Arist. *Pol.* 1265a38–b12, 1335b22–23.

104. See Lin Foxhall and Hamish A. Forbes, "*Sitometreía*: The Role of Grain as a Staple Food in Classical Antiquity," *Chiron* 12 (1982): 41–90.

105. Such a statute is attested at Selybria ([Arist.] *Oec.* 1348b33–1349a3) and as part of Solon's legislation at Athens (Plut. *Sol.* 24.1–2). At a time of famine, there may well have been a similar law at Clazomenae ([Arist.] *Oec.* 1348b17–22), and it is likely that there was legislation of this sort on the books at Teos from the first half of the fifth century on: note the decree calling curses down on those guilty of preventing the import of corn or of arranging for it to be reexported: *GHI* 1.30.A (which should be compared with *SIG*³ 344). For further evidence, see Peter Garnsey, *Famine and Food Supply in the Graeco-Roman World: Responses to Risk and Crisis* (Cambridge 1988) 81–82.

106. This seems to have been the rule not just at Sparta (below, I.v.4) but in the various cities on the island of Crete (Ephorus *FGrH* 70 F149 ap. Strabo 10.4.16–22; Arist. *Pol.* 1271a26–36), and there is epigraphical evidence in Argive script suggesting the existence of such an institution in late seventh-century Tiryns:

see N. Verdelis, Michael Jameson, and J. Papachristodoulou, "Archaic Inscriptions from Tiryns," *Archaiologikē Ephēmeris* (1975): 150–205 (in modern Greek). It is conceivable that some such regimen had once been enforced in every Dorian community. Note the behavior of the colonists from Rhodes and Cnidus who settled in the Lipari islands: below, note 118.

107. There was nothing at all peculiar about the regulations proposed by Plato (*Leg.* 6.775a–b, 12.958d–960b): he was merely following a tradition established by the lawgivers of the archaic period and reasserted in later times. Legislation of this sort existed at Sparta (Plut. *Lyc.* 27), at Athens (see I.vii.3, note 67, below), at Syracuse (Diod. 11.38; Phylarchus *FGrH* 81 F45), at Massilia (Strabo 4.1.5), at Chaeronea (Plut. *Sol.* 21.7), at Delphi (Franciszek Sokolowski, *Lois sacrées des cités grecques* [Paris 1969] no. 77), at Iasos (Heraclid. Pont. *Pol.* 40 [Müller *FHG* II 224]), at Thasos (Sokolowski, *Lois sacrées: supplément* no. 64), at Nisyros (*IG*² XII 3, 87=*SIG*³ 1220), at Mytilene on Lesbos (Cic. *Leg.* 2.26.66), at Iulis on Ceos (Sokolowski, *Lois sacrées* no. 97; Ath. 13.610), at Gambreion near Pergamum (Franciszek Sokolowski, *Lois sacrées de l'Asie Mineure* [Paris 1955] no. 16), and no doubt elsewhere as well. The Roman parallel is well known (Kübler *RE* IV A [1932] 901–8), and there is suggestive evidence for Tegea (*IG*² V 2, 4), for Cleonae (*IG*² IV 1607), for Pautalia (Franciszek Sokolowski, "Loi sacrée de Pautalia," *BCH* 94 [1970]: 113–16), for Gortyn on Crete (*ICr* IV 22, 46, 76), and for the Chalcidian foundations in Sicily and Italy (cf. Stob. *Flor.* 4.2.24 [Hense] with Arist. *Pol.* 1274a23–24). In interpreting this evidence, most scholars stress the quest for political integration: see Santo Mazzarino, *Fra oriente e occidente: Ricerche di storia greca arcaica* (Florence 1947) 191–252 (esp. 192–94, 214–23, 236–42); Alexiou, *The Ritual Lament in Greek Tradition* 14–23; and Humphreys, "Family Tombs and Tomb-cult in Classical Athens" 85–87; and consider Carmine Ampolo, "Il lusso funerario e la città arcaica," *AION(archeol)* 6 (1984): 71–102, in conjunction with Umberto Cozzoli, "La *truphè* nella interpretazione delle crisi politiche," in *Tra Grecia e Roma: Temi antichi e metodologie moderne* (Rome 1980) 133–45, and Ampolo, "Il lusso nelle società arcaiche," *Opus* 3 (1984): 469–76. Apart from the fact that aristocrats remained prominent after the early lawgivers had done their work, there is not a shred of evidence to support the contention that the first Greek law codes were simply a clever ploy on the part of an embattled ruling class intent on bolstering its own solidarity and eager to dampen popular enthusiasm for more substantive reform: cf. Walter Eder, "The Political Significance of the Codification of Law in Archaic Societies: An Unconventional Hypothesis," in *Social Struggles in Archaic Rome: New Perspectives on the Conflict of the Orders*, ed. Kurt A. Raaflaub (Berkeley 1986) 262–300. Though, in some respects, the funerary regulations may have simply codified existing religious practice, I see no reason to doubt that the restrictions on participation, pomp, and display had a sumptuary function: cf. F. B. Jevons, "Greek Law and Folklore," *CR* 9 (1895): 247–50; and Mark Toher, "The Tenth Table and the Conflict of the Orders," in *Social Struggles in Archaic Rome* 301–26. That funerals can turn into political demonstrations was no less evident in antiquity than it is today: Polyb. 6.53–55. And, at least with regard to clothing, Greek religious and secular restrictions were in spirit one: see Harrianne Mills, "Greek Clothing Regulations: Sacred and Profane?" *ZPE* 55 (1984): 255–65.

108. Xenophon (*Oec.* 2.5–8) and Isaeus (6.60) briefly sum up the situation. See also Dem. 10.35–45, Arist. *Pol.* 1291a33–34, 1309a14–32, 1320a31–b11, 1321a31–b3. The institution seems to have been universal: J. Oehler, *RE* XII (1925) 1871–79,

found evidence for *leitourgíai* in some eighty-nine different communities in the classical period and after.

109. See Harrison, *The Law of Athens* II 236–38, and Vincent Gabrielsen, "The *Antidosis* Procedure in Classical Athens," *C&M* 38 (1987): 7–38. Note, however, Matthew R. Christ, "Liturgy Avoidance and *Antidosis* in Classical Athens," *TAPhA* 120 (1990): 147–69.

110. For the spirit of the laws, see Xen. *Oec.* 2.5–8; Lys. 19.61–63, 21.13–14; Dem. 10.45, 14.24–28; Isaeus 6.60–61, 7.39–40; Pl. *Leg.* 5.740a, 9.877d, 11.923a–b; Arist. *Pol.* 1262b37–1263b29, 1320a31–b11. Consider, in this connection, Lys. 19.9–10; Isoc. 15.158; Isaeus 5.41–45, F22 (Thalheim); Dem. 21.152–59, 38.25–26; Aeschin. 1.95–105.

111. Anaximenes *Rh.* 1424a20–26 (Fuhrmann). The ethos described is evident in Lys. 19.29, 42–43, 57–59, 21.1–5. Cf. [Xen.] *Ath. Pol.* 1.13. For further discussion, with particular attention given to the epigraphical evidence, see David Whitehead, "Competitive Outlay and Community Profit: *Philotimía* in Democratic Athens," *C&M* 34 (1983): 55–74.

112. The best-known case is Athens (Arist. *Ath. Pol.* 27.3–5, 41.3), but there were others as well: G. E. M. de Ste. Croix, "Political Pay Outside Athens," *CQ* n.s. 25 (1975): 48–52, has collected the evidence. Public provision was a standard feature of extreme democracies. The three obols a day paid Athenian jurors and, in due course, assemblymen was designed to encourage political participation on the part of the great multitude of those with meager resources (*hoi penétes, hoi áporoi*); the evidence leaves little doubt that this political stratagem was a great success: see Minor M. Markle III, "Jury Pay and Assembly Pay at Athens," in *Crux* 265–97.

113. [Xen.] *Ath. Pol.* 2.9–10.

114. From very early times, it was customary to wrap the bones of a sacrificial animal in its fat and to burn this as an offering to the divinity being honored; the edible parts of the animal were, then, roasted on a spit and consumed by those in attendance: Homer (*Il.* 2.421–31) provides the earliest and most elegant description of the ritual procedure, and Hesiod (*Theog.* 535–57), in trying to explain why the gods were shortchanged, vouches for its universal employment. Thus, when the Greeks spoke of sacrifice, they also had a barbecue in mind: cf. Hdt. 8.99.1 with Thuc. 2.38, and consider Athenaeus's description (4.138f–139a) of the festival of the *kopís* at Sparta along with Harmodius of Lepreon's discussion (*FGrH* 319 F1) of sacrificial customs at Phigaleia. The animals slaughtered at a festival could be numerous: for example, the Athenians sacrificed five hundred goats each year to Artemis Agrotera in commemoration of their victory at Marathon (Plut. *Mor.* 862a–c). We should not be surprised that Aristophanes associates the Panathenaia with indigestion (*Nub.* 386–87) and the Diasia with cooking (408–9); the poet (*Eq.* 652–63) does not hesitate to represent two demagogues as trying to outdo each other in increasing the number of animals slain. Rather than burn their victims entire in a holocaust as did the Jews, Theophrastus (ap. Porphyry *Abst.* 2.26) argued, the Greeks would give up sacrifice altogether. Some scholars believe that the ritual originated as a hunter's rite of expiation for the shedding of blood: see Karl Meuli, "Griechische Opferbräuche," *Gesammelte Schriften* (Basel 1975) II 907–1021 (esp. 948–1021), and Walter Burkert, *Homo Necans: The Anthropology of Ancient Greek Sacrificial Ritual and Myth*, trans. Peter Bing (Berkeley 1983) esp. 1–82. Others, noting that the Greeks sacrificed none but domestic animals, em-

phasize the role that sacrifice and communal meals centered on the consumption of cooked meat played in forming, defining, and sustaining the *pólis* as a community of human beings neither bestial nor divine: after reading the essays collected in *The Cuisine of Sacrifice among the Greeks*, ed. Marcel Détienne and Jean-Pierre Vernant (Chicago 1989), consider Jean-Pierre Vernant, "A General Theory of Sacrifice and the Slaying of the Victims in the Greek *Thusia*," *Mortals and Immortals: Collected Essays*, ed. Froma I. Zeitlin (Princeton 1991) 290–302.

115. Hdt. 3.57.2, 7.144.1; Arist. *Ath. Pol.* 22.7; Polyaen. 1.30.6; Philochorus *FGrH* 328 F119; Plut. *Per.* 37.4. See Xen. *Vect.* 4.33. See also Kurt Latte "Kollektivbesitz und Staatschatz in Griechenland," *Kleine Schriften* (Munich 1968) 294–312.

116. See P. A. Brunt, "Athenian Settlements Abroad in the Fifth Century B.C.," in *Ancient Society and Institutions: Studies Presented to Victor Ehrenberg*, ed. Ernst Badian (Oxford 1966) 71–92. See also Philippe Gauthier, "Les clérouques de Lesbos et la colonisation Athénienne au Ve siècle," *REG* 79 (1966): 64–88, and "A propos des clérouquies Athéniennes du Ve siècle," in *Problèmes de la terre en Grèce ancienne*, ed. Moses I. Finley (Paris 1973) 163–78; and note J. R. Green and R. K. Sinclair, "Athenians in Eretria," *Historia* 19 (1970): 515–27, and Eberhard Erxleben, "Die Kleruchien auf Euboea und Lesbos und die Methoden der Attischen Herrschaft im 5. Jh.," *Klio* 57 (1975): 83–100. For a general discussion of the advantages which empire brought Athens, see Moses I. Finley, "The Athenian Empire: A Balance Sheet," *Economy and Society in Ancient Greece*, ed. Brent D. Shaw and Richard P. Saller (London 1981) 41–61.

117. Arist. *Ath. Pol.* 24 should be read in light of Jack Martin Balcer, "Imperial Magistrates in the Athenian Empire," *Historia* 25 (1976): 257–87, and Mogens Herman Hansen, "Seven Hundred *Archai* in Classical Athens," *GRBS* 21 (1980): 151–73. See Gabrielsen, *Remuneration of State Officials in Fourth Century B.C. Athens*: even after the loss of her empire, Athens appears to have paid her officials when circumstances allowed. See Arist. *Pol.* 1317b35–38.

118. One should read Diod. 5.9.4–5 along with Livy 5.28.1–5 in light of Theodore Reinach, "Le collectivisme des Grecs de Lipari," *REG* 3 (1890): 86–96; R. J. Buck, "Communalism on the Lipari Islands," *CPh* 54 (1959): 34–39; and Thomas J. Figueira, "The Lipari Islanders and their System of Communal Property," *ClAnt* 3 (1984): 179–206.

119. Consider Dem. 10.45 in light of Pl. *Leg.* 5.740a. Note the anecdotes collected by [Arist.] *Oec.* 1348b17–1349a2, 9–10, 25–36, 1350a6–15, and consider the evidence indicating that a general subscription (*epídosis*) was conducted in Athens during the food crisis of 328/327: see *SIG*^{3} 304 with Adolphe Kuenzi, *Epidosis* (Bern 1923). Subscriptions of one sort or another may have been relatively common: Léopold Migeotte, "Souscriptions Athéniennes de la période classique," *Historia* 32 (1983): 129–48.

120. Aen. Tact. 14.1.

121. Cic. *Rep.* 2.4.7–9. See also Arist. *Pol.* 1327a10–15, 32–40. Consider Pl. *Leg.* 12.949e–953e in light of I.iv.5 (esp. at notes 108–109), vii.2, 6–8, below.

122. For a thorough discussion of the connection, see Georg Simmel, *The Philosophy of Money*, trans. Tom Bottomore and David Frisby (London 1978) 283–347, 429–45. In exploring the link, one should ponder Montesquieu's discussion of "communication": *EL* 3.19.5–6, 8–9, 12, 14, 27, 4.20.1–2, 4–14, 23, 21.5–7, 16, 20, 22.8.

123. See J. G. A. Pocock, "The Political Economy of Burke's Analysis of the

French Revolution," *Virtue, Commerce, and History: Essays on Political Thought and History, Chiefly in the Eighteenth Century* (Cambridge 1985) 193–212.

124. Heraclitus *Vorsokr.*⁶ 22 B90

125. Arist. *Pol.* 1259a6–36; Diog. Laert. 1.26.

126. Cf. Ar. *Nub.* 218–34, 333, 358–63, 1283–84 with Pl. *Ap.* 18b, 23d.

127. *SIG*³ 364.42, 46.

128. Consider Locke, *TTG* II.v.37, 46, 50 (esp. 46), xvi.184, and *WoJL* V 22: *Some Considerations of the Consequences of the Lowering of Interest, and Raising the Value of Money*, in light of Arist. *Eth. Nic.* 1133a29–32, *Pol.* 1257b10–14, and see Montesquieu, *EL* 4.21.20–22, 22.1–22.

129. Daniel Defoe, *Defoe's Review: Reproduced from the Original Edition, with an Introduction and Bibliographical Notes*, ed. Arthur Wellesley Secord (New York 1938) III 503: Facsimile Book 8, no. 126, 22 October 1706.

130. Pl. *Leg.* 4.704d–705b. See also Arist. *Pol.* 1327a32–40.

131. Hdt. 1.153.1–2.

132. In this connection, see *ABF* 181.

133. Montesquieu, *EL* 1.5.6, 3.19.27 (582), 4.20.2.

134. Cf. Anonymus Iamblichi *Vorsokr.*⁶ 89 B4 with Arist. *Pol.* 1257b1–1258a14.

135. Cf. *The Federalist* 43 (297) with Hobbes, *Leviathan* I.13 (188).

136. Cf. Arist. *Eth. Nic.* 1132b21–1133b28 with *Pol.* 1256b26–1258b8. After reading Marcel Mauss, *The Gift*, trans. Ian Cunnison (New York 1967), and Louis Gernet, "The Mythical Idea of Value in Greece," *The Anthropology of Ancient Greece* 73–111, consider Édouard Will, "Fonctions de la monnaie dans les cités grecques de l'époque classique," in *Numismatiques antique: Problèmes et méthodes*, ed. J.-M. Dentzer, Ph. Gauthier, and T. Hackens (Louvain 1975) 233–46, and see Will, "De l'aspect éthique des origines grecques de la monnaie," *RH* 212 (1954): 209–31, and "Réflexions et hypothèses sur les origines du monnayage," *RN* 17 (1955): 5–23. Cf. Karl Polanyi, "Aristotle Discovers the Economy," *Primitive, Archaic and Modern Economies*, ed. George Dalton (Boston 1971) 78–115, with Moses I. Finley, "Aristotle and Economic Analysis," in *Studies in Ancient Society*, ed. M. I. Finley (London 1974) 26–52, and see Thomas J. Lewis, "Acquisition and Anxiety: Aristotle's Case against the Market," *Canadian Journal of Economics* 11 (1978): 69–90; then cf. Scott Meikle, "Aristotle and the Political Economy of the Polis," *JHS* 99 (1979): 57–73, with Paul Millett, "Sale, Credit and Exchange in Athenian Law and Society," in *Nomos: Essays in Athenian Law, Politics and Society*, ed. Paul Cartledge, Paul Millett, and Stephen Todd (Cambridge 1990) 167–94, and see Alan E. Samuel, *From Athens to Alexandria: Hellenism and Social Goals in Ptolemaic Egypt* (Louvain 1983) 1–38.

137. Cf. Montesquieu, *EL* 3.19.27 (575, 582) and 4.20.2, with Cic. *Amic.* 16.59–60, and consider Soph. *Aj.* 678–83, 1328–67, Arist. *Rh.* 1389a3–1390a14.

138. Hdt. 1.155.4. Consider Caes. *BGall.* 6.24 in light of Strabo 4.1.5.

139. Consider Ferguson, *EHCS* 5.1–6.6, and Smith, *WN* V.i.f.48–61, in light of Richard B. Sher, "Adam Ferguson, Adam Smith, and the Problem of National Defense," *JMH* 61 (1989): 240–68.

140. *Pol.* 1280b10–1281a10. For a discussion of the measures that can be taken to head off such a degeneration, see Marvin Zetterbaum, *Tocqueville and the Problem of Democracy* (Stanford 1967). See also Martin Diamond, "Ethics and Politics: The American Way," in *The Moral Foundations of the American Republic*³, ed. Robert H. Horwitz (Charlottesville 1986) 75–108.

141. See Grotius, *De iure praedae* II 1: *qua gente non alia est honesti quaestus avidior.*
142. Cf. Mandeville, *Fable of the Bees* I 6–7, 25–26, with Locke, *TTG* II.v.42.
143. Tocqueville, *DA* 1.2.5 (231–33).
144. I cite "Shopkeepers at War" from Orwell's 1941 publication *The Lion and the Unicorn.* See the *Collected Essays, Journalism and Letters of George Orwell,* ed. Sonia Orwell and Ian Angus (New York 1968) II 82.

Chapter 3

1. Note Demaratus's remark to Xerxes: Hdt. 7.102.
2. For an extreme case, see Arist. *Ath. Pol.* 16.6.
3. For the degree to which the situation and the outlook of the ancient Greek peasant were comparable to those of peasants in other times and places, consider Hes. *Op.* 11–26, 32–34, 298–367, 394–413, 432–34, 453–57, 465–78, and 493–95, in light of the material collected by Paul Millett, "Hesiod and his World," *PCPhS* 210 (1984): 84–115, and see Edward C. Banfield, *The Moral Basis of a Backward Society* (Chicago 1958). Cf. Sydel F. Silverman, "Agricultural Organization, Social Structure, and Values in Italy: Amoral Familism Reconsidered," *American Anthropologist* 70 (1968): 1–20. Of course, in interpreting the late archaic and classical periods in light of Hesiod's *Works and Days,* one must keep in mind the profound transformation effected by the emergence of the *pólis.* The husbandmen of these later times were more than just peasants; they were citizen-soldiers.
4. Consider Peter Garnsey, *Famine and Food Supply in the Graeco-Roman World: Responses to Risk and Crisis* (Cambridge 1988) 3–86, in light of Robert Sallares, *The Ecology of the Ancient Greek World* (Ithaca 1991), and see Thomas W. Gallant, *Risk and Survival in Ancient Greece: Reconstructing the Rural Domestic Economy* (Stanford 1991). Note also Michael Jameson, "Famine in the Greek World," in *Trade and Famine in Classical Antiquity,* ed. Peter Garnsey and C. R. Whittaker, *PCPhS* Suppl. 8 (1983): 6–16, and Lin Foxhall, "Greece Ancient and Modern: Subsistence and Survival," *HT* 36 (July 1986): 35–43.
5. See Benedetto Bravo, "Le commerce des céréales chez les Grecs de l'époque archaïque," in *Trade and Famine in Classical Antiquity* 17–29, and John Boardman, "The Olive in the Mediterranean: Its Culture and Use," in *The Early History of Agriculture,* ed. J. Hutchinson (Oxford 1977) 187–96. To judge by what archaeology can tell us about land use and the demographic history of the southern Argolid, prosperity in all historical periods has depended on the agricultural specialization made possible by commerce: see Tjeerd H. van Andel and Curtis Runnels, *Beyond the Acropolis: A Rural Greek Past* (Stanford 1987).
6. Chester Starr, *The Economic and Social Growth of Early Greece, 800–500 B.C.* (New York 1977) 64–70, cites the relevant evidence. Copper, tin, and iron were in particularly short supply.
7. Consider Pl. *Phd.* 109a–b in light of the evidence suggesting that few, if any, *póleis* were genuinely self-sufficient: see Lucia Nixon and Simon Price, "The Size and Resources of Greek Cities," in *The Greek City: From Homer to Alexander,* ed. Oswyn Murray and Simon Price (Oxford 1990) 137–70.
8. Cic. *Rep.* 2.4.9.
9. See A. H. M. Jones, *The Later Roman Empire, 284–602: A Social, Economic, and Administrative Survey* (Norman, Okla., 1964) II 841–42, and Richard Duncan-

Jones, *The Economy of the Roman Empire: Quantitative Studies*[2] (Cambridge 1982) 366–69. Since the techniques of transport remained pretty much the same throughout antiquity, the evidence would apply to earlier times as well. For a somewhat more skeptical view of the reliability of the edict as a guide to real costs, see Keith Hopkins, "Models, Ships, and Staples," in *Trade and Famine in Classical Antiquity* 84–105 (esp. 102–5).

10. [Xen.] *Ath. Pol.* 2.6.

11. Gregory of Nazianzus *Or.* 43.34–35, esp. 34.4–7 (Migne, *PG* 36.541–44).

12. The Spartan example is well known: Xen. *Lac. Pol.* 7.5–6; [Pl.] *Eryxias* 400b; Plut. *Lyc.* 9, *Lys.* 16–17, *Mor.* 226c–d; Justin 3.2.11–12; Poll. *Onom.* 7.105, 9.79.

13. According to Aristotle (*Pol.* 1321b12–18), even a small *pólis* would find it necessary to appoint market regulators (*agoranómoi*); in a sizable, relatively commercial community, there might be a bewildering variety of such officials: cf. Arist. *Ath. Pol.* 51 with the Athenian regulations passed in 375/374 (Ronald S. Stroud, "An Athenian Law on Silver Coinage," *Hesperia* 43 [1974]: 157–88). The spirit of the oversight exercised is evident from Pl. *Leg.* 6.763e–764c, 11.917a–921d. The magistrates aimed not just at the execution of counterfeiters (cf. Dem. 20.167, 24.212 with the law in Hellenistic Dyme: *SIG*[3] 530) and the prevention of fraud (Arist. *Ath. Pol.* 51.1–2, Dem. 20.9, Hyper. 5.14 [Jensen], Theophr. *Leg.* F20–21 [Szegedy-Maszak]). They were concerned with just pricing as well (Arist. *Ath. Pol.* 51.2–4). Athens outlawed the hoarding of grain (Lys. 22.5–7) and even specified the markup which the grain dealers (*sitopólai*) could make (22.8, 13–16, 20, 22). For alternative readings of the pertinent oration, see Robin Seager, "Lysias against the Corndealers," *Historia* 15 (1966): 172–84, and Thomas Figueira, "*Sitopolai* and *Sitophylakes* in Lysias' 'Against the Corndealers,' " *Phoenix* 40 (1986): 149–71. Selybria prohibited the export of grain and fixed the price as well: [Arist.] *Oec.* 1348b33–1349a2. Cf. Pl. *Leg.* 11.917e, 920b–c: the *agoranómoi* of Magnesia were empowered to fix prices at a just level and to enforce them. Whether the stamps sometimes placed on ceramic ware used for the transport of wine have something to do with this sort of regulation of the market remains an open question: Virginia R. Grace, *Amphoras and the Ancient Wine Trade*[2] (Princeton 1979).

14. This was the policy not just at Sparta (Xen. *Lac. Pol.* 7.1–4; Plut. *Ages.* 26, *Mor.* 214a; Polyaen. 2.1.7), but apparently (Xen. *Oec.* 4.3) elsewhere as well.

15. In early times, prior to the emergence of extreme democracy (Arist. *Pol.* 1277a37–b7), craftsmen and others similarly offering their services to the public (*dēmiourgoí*) were excluded from office in quite a number of communities. Even in the fourth century, a deliberate policy of inclusion was deserving of note (Aeschin. 1.27). Thebes in particular seems to have had a law stipulating that anyone who made his living in the *agorá* was barred from office for ten years thereafter: Arist. *Pol.* 1278b25–26, 1321a26–29. Note the provisions later adopted in Ptolemaic Cyrene (*SEG* IX 1.43–50) and those which Aristotle thought appropriate for a well-ordered community (*Pol.* 1328b37–1329a2). The artisan or trader was to be treated as a stranger in his own land (1278a34–38).

16. Sparta restricted both travel by citizens and visits from foreigners (Ar. *Birds* 1012–13 [with scholia]; Thuc. 1.144.2, 2.39.1; Xen. *Lac. Pol.* 14.4; Isoc. 11.17–18; Pl. *Prt.* 342a–e; Arist. F543 [Rose]; Plut. *Lyc.* 27). Apollonia, which was reportedly governed by a closed and narrow oligarchy drawn from the colony's first settlers (Arist. *Pol.* 1290b8–14), is also known to have practiced *xenēlasía* (Ael. *VH* 13.16). See also Hdt. 3.148.2. Cf. the policy proposed by Plato (*Leg.* 12.949e–953e). The

geographical isolation of Crete served much the same function as *xenēlasía* elsewhere: Arist. *Pol.* 1272b16–23. At Rome, the expulsion of aliens served an entirely different purpose: Livy 39.3.4–6.

17. Plut. *Mor.* 297f–298a.

18. Arist. *Pol.* 1327a11–40. This idea was not radically new: Naucratis (Hdt. 2.178–79) had served Egypt as a port of trade in the Saite period, and Plato (*Leg.* 12.952e–953a) had made a proposal similar to Aristotle's some years before. For Naucratis, see Michel M. Austin, *Greece and Egypt in the Archaic Age* (Cambridge 1970). For other examples, see the essays collected in *Trade and Market in the Early Empires*, ed. Karl Polanyi, Conrad Arensberg, and Harry Pearson (Glencoe, Ill., 1957), esp. Robert B. Revere, " 'No Man's Coast': Ports of Trade in the Eastern Mediterranean" 38–63; Anne C. Chapman, "Port of Trade Enclaves in Aztec and Maya Civilizations" 114–53; Rosemary Arnold, "A Port of Trade: Whydah on the Guinea Coast" 154–76, and "Separation of Trade and Market: Great Market of Whydah" 177–87. See also Karl Polanyi, "Ports of Trade in Early Societies," *Primitive, Archaic and Modern Economies*, ed. George Dalton (Boston 1971) 238–60. The pattern persists: witness Hong Kong.

19. For the general pattern, see the definition given for *métoikos* by the Hellenistic lexicographer Aristophanes of Byzantium: F38 (Nauck). Gortyn (*ICr* IV 78) forced metics to live in Latosion. Athens and the cities nearby imposed a tax called the *metoíkion* on their resident aliens. For a detailed study of the location of the metics on the margin of Athens's political community, see the material cited in I.vii.3, note 52. For the metics of the other Hellenic cities, cf. Michel Clerc, "De la condition des étrangers domiciliés dans les différentes cités grecques," *Revue des universités du Midi* 4 (1898): 1–32, 153–79, 249–74, with David Whitehead, "Immigrant Communities in the Classical Polis: Some Principles for a Synoptic Treatment," *AC* 53 (1984): 47–59.

20. For a discussion of the degree to which the metics and other foreigners dominated overseas commerce, see Eberhard Erxleben, "Die Rolle der Bevölkerungsklassen im Aussenhandel Athens im 4. Jahrhundert v. u. Z.," in *Hellenische Poleis*, ed. Elisabeth Charlotte Welskopf (Berlin 1974) I 460–520, who tends to overstate the case.

21. Pl. *Leg.* 8.850a–c.

22. For a survey of the pertinent evidence and of the literature dealing with this vexed problem, see H. W. Pleket, "Technology and Society in the Graeco-Roman World," *Acta Historiae Neerlandica* 2 (1967): 1–25, and "Technology in the Greco-Roman World: A General Report," *Talanta* 5 (1973): 6–47. See also Moses I. Finley, "Technological Innovation and Economic Progress in the Ancient World," *Economy and Society in Ancient Greece*, ed. Brent D. Shaw and Richard P. Saller (London 1981) 176–95, and Alan E. Samuel, *From Athens to Alexandria: Hellenism and Social Goals in Ptolemaic Egypt* (Louvain 1983) esp. 39–61; and note J. G. Landels, *Engineering in the Ancient World* (Berkeley 1981), and Kenneth D. White, *Greek and Roman Technology* (Ithaca 1984). Cf. Andrea Carandini's preface to Jerzy Kolendo, *L'agricoltura nell'Italia romana: Tecniche agrarie e progresso economico dalla tarda repubblica al principato*, trans. C. Zawadzka (Rome 1980) ix–lv, with Finley, "Problems of Slave Society: Reflections on the Debate," *Opus* 1 (1982): 201–11. In this connection, see Jean-Pierre Vernant, "Some Remarks on the Forms and Limitations of Technological Thought among the Greeks," *Myth and Thought among the Greeks* (London 1983) 279–301.

23. Consider Arist. *Pol.* 1268a6–11, 1268b22–1269a27, in light of *Eth. Nic.* 1094a26–b11.

24. Hdt. 1.174. Note 7.22, 35, 8.97.

25. Cf. Xen. *Mem.* 4.7.2–8 with Pl. *Ap.* 18a–19d, and see Ar. *Clouds* 94–99, 133–251.

26. Plut. *Mor.* 219a.

27. For the character of Athens's fleet and its import, note Thuc. 1.121.3, 142.5–9, 7.63.3–4 with [Xen.] *Ath. Pol.* 1.19–2.8, 11–12; Arist. *Ath. Pol.* 24.3; and Plut. *Per.* 11.4. For Athens's dependence on imported grain, see I.iii.3, note 53, below.

28. Thuc. 1.70–71, 3.37.4–5, 38.4–6; Ar. *Clouds* 547–48, *Eq.* 111–20.

29. Pl. *Grg.* 512b–d.

30. Thuc. 3.37.3.

31. Dem. 24.139–41. For a somewhat different description of this statute, see Polyb. 12.16. See also Stob. *Flor.* 4.2.19 (Hense). Diodorus (12.17.1–5) attributes a similar Thurian law to the lawgiver Charondas.

32. For Dionysius, see Diod. 14.41.2–43.4. For the work done on behalf of the Ptolemies, see A. G. Drachmann, *Ktesibios, Philon and Heron* (Copenhagen 1948). The evidence suggests that the Greek subjects of the Ptolemies in Egypt were no less set in their ways than the Egyptians among whom they lived: see Samuel, *From Athens to Alexandria* 39–123.

33. Suet. *Vesp.* 18. See P. A. Brunt, "Free Labour and Public Works at Rome," *JRS* 70 (1980): 81–100 (esp. 81–83). Cf. Lionel Casson, "Unemployment, the Building Trade, and Suetonius, *Vesp.* 18," *BASP* 15 (1978): 43–51.

34. Cf. Petron. *Sat.* 51 with Pliny *NH* 36.195. For a variant, see Dio Cass. 57.21.7.

35. *De rebus bellicis* Praef. 3 (Ireland). For further discussion of this remarkable document, see E. A. Thompson, *A Roman Reformer and Inventor* (Oxford 1952).

36. See Ath. 12.518c–522a, and cf. Arist. F583 (Rose) with Phylarchus *FGrH* 81 F45. See also Jul. Africanus *Cest.* 293, Ael. *NA* 16.23.

37. S. H. A. *Pertinax* 8.7.

38. Hdt. 9.116–22.

39. As Plato (*Ep.* 8.355a) hints, the law was an educator before it was anything else.

40. Consider Arist. *Pol.* 1256b26–1258b8 with an eye to David Whitehead, "Aristotle the Metic," *PCPhS* 201 (1975): 94–99, and see Pl. *Leg.* 11.918a–919c. After reviewing the literature cited in I.ii.7, note 136, above, one may wish to ponder Wayne Ambler, "Aristotle on Acquisition," *Canadian Journal of Political Science* 17 (1984): 487–502.

41. Epicurus *Sententiae Vaticanae* F67 (Bailey).

42. It was perfectly respectable for an aristocrat to take to the seas in search of the metals he needed (Hom. *Od.* 1.180–89), but it was not honorable to earn one's livelihood as a trader (8.158–201).

43. See Paul Millett, "Sale, Credit and Exchange in Athenian Law and Society," in *Nomos: Essays in Athenian Law, Politics and Society*, ed. Paul Cartledge, Paul Millett, and Stephen Todd (Cambridge 1990) 167–94, and *Lending and Borrowing in Ancient Athens* (Cambridge 1991).

44. See Moses I. Finley, "Land, Debt, and the Man of Property in Classical Athens," *Economy and Society in Ancient Greece* 62–76. For a vigorous and helpful,

if not fully persuasive critique of Finley's argument, see Wesley E. Thompson, "The Athenian Entrepreneur," *AC* 51 (1982): 53–85. Note Finley's response: *The Ancient Economy*[2] (London 1985) 196–98.

45. This was the case not just at Athens (Dem. 36.6), but elsewhere as well: see Jan Pečírka, *The Formula for the Grant of Enktesis in Attic Inscriptions* (Prague 1966) esp. 137–49. Note, in particular, the fiscal strategies to which desperation drove the Byzantines: [Arist.] *Oec.* 1346b26–1347a3. A city that would—in exchange for one-third of the proceeds—allow foreign lenders to seize landed property when foreclosing on debts would sell its citizenship as well.

46. See [Arist.] *Oec.* 1349a3–8. In an emergency, this could pose severe difficulties: after civil strife prevented the citizens of Abydos from planting their crops, the metics refused to advance them loans until the *pólis* passed a decree empowering them to recover the debt by seizing the next harvest.

47. See Robin Osborne, "Social and Economic Implications of the Leasing of Land and Property in Classical and Hellenistic Greece," *Chiron* 18 (1988): 279–323.

48. For an exception to the rule, cf. Xen. *Oec.* 20.21–29: Xenophon's Ischomachus and his father were remarkable for their devotion to the acquisition of wealth. So, for that matter, was Xenophon himself: to be a mercenary soldier may sometimes have been profitable (*An.* 5.3.4–13); it can hardly ever have been a respectable profession for a citizen to pursue (3.1.4–7; Isoc. 4.167–68, 5.120–23, 8.44–48). Marx is not unjust when he speaks of Xenophon's "characteristic, bourgeois instinct." See Karl Marx, *Das Kapital: Kritik der politischen Ökonomie* (Frankfurt 1969–71) I 327–28. More typical is Xenophon's Socrates, who could be represented (*Symp.* 8.25) as having drawn a comparison between the boy (*erómenos*) a man loves and the property he owns: in each case, he desires to make better that which is most truly his. Such an outlook is hardly consistent with the intention to sell. For leased property, of course, one would feel no such attachment. Eventually, it might well pass into the hands of another. See also *Mem.* 1.1.8, Dem. 53.15.

49. [Arist.] *Oec.* 1344b32–34.

50. Cf. Xen. *Vect.* 4.7 with *Cyr.* 8.2.20–22, and consider the *pecunia otiosa* found in abundance by Pliny in Nicomedia (*Ep.* 10.54–55). Note Xen. *Cyr.* 3.3.3, and cf. Antiphon *Vorsokr.*[6] 87 B53–54 with Anonymus Iamblichi *Vorsokr.*[6] 89 B3–4, B7.1–2, 8: where the ancient writers have occasion to discuss the behavior of those governed by an excessive zeal for wealth, they mention hard work, self-denial, and hoarding—but not the intelligent investment of capital. See V. N. Andreyev, "The Structure of Private Wealth in Fifth and Fourth Century Athens," *VDI* 3 (1981): 21–48 (in Russian).

51. [Dem.] 34.51.

52. See G. M. Calhoun, "Risk in Sea Loans in Ancient Athens," *Journal of Economic and Business History* 2 (1930): 561–84; G. E. M. de Ste. Croix, "Ancient Greek and Roman Maritime Loans," in *Debits, Credits, Finance and Profits*, ed. Harold Edey and B. S. Yamey (London 1974) 41–59; and Paul Millett, "Maritime Loans and the Structure of Credit in Fourth-Century Athens," in *Trade in the Ancient Economy*, ed. Peter Garnsey, Keith Hopkins, and C. R. Whittaker (Berkeley 1983) 36–52. Virtually all of our evidence comes from the fourth century and after; but by 421 B.C., when bottomry loans are first clearly mentioned, they appear to have been nothing unusual: see F. D. Harvey, "The Maritime Loan in Eupólis' 'Marikas' (P. Oxy. 2741)," *ZPE* 23 (1976): 231–33. Furthermore, there is some reason

to suspect that the institution existed as early as 500 B.C.: see P. Calligas, "An Inscribed Lead Plaque from Korkyra," *ABSA* 66 (1971): 79–94. Given the general lack of evidence for economic practices in the archaic period, it would be a mistake to argue from the absence of early evidence that the institution was of late origin. Like many other practices, it may have come quite early to Corinth or to some other maritime center from Phoenicia or from elsewhere in the Near East.

53. For the grain trade, cf. Louis Gernet, "L'approvisionnement d'Athènes en blé au Ve et au IVe siècle," *Mélanges d'histoire ancienne* (Paris 1909) 270–391, with Sallares, *The Ecology of the Ancient Greek World* 50–107; see Philippe Gauthier, "De Lysias à Aristote (Ath. pol. 51, 4): La commerce du grain à Athènes et les fonctions des sitophylaques," *RD* 59 (1981): 5–28; and consider Peter Garnsey, "Grain for Athens," in *Crux: Essays Presented to G. E. M. de Ste. Croix on His 75th Birthday*, ed. Paul Cartledge and F. D. Harvey (Exeter 1985) 62–75, and *Famine and Food Supply in the Graeco-Roman World* 89–164. As Aristotle (*Rh.* 1360a12–13) makes clear, maintenance of the city's food supply was a matter of life and death: it was, therefore, a political, not just an economic, concern. See Arist. *Ath. Pol.* 43.4. In passing legislation dealing with this problem, Athens was by no means peculiar. Consider the curses which the citizens of early fifth-century Teos called down on anyone who obstructed the import of grain or arranged for its transhipment: *GHI* 1.30.A.

54. Cf. [Dem.] 34.38–40 (to be read in the context of the oration as a whole) with Andoc. 2.11–12, 17–21.

55. Theophr. *Char.* 23.2, 6.

56. [Arist.] *Pr.* 950a–b. For the general hostility to the charging of interest, see Dem. 37.52–54, 45.69; Arist. *Pol.* 1258a38–b8; Theophr. *Char.* 6.9 (with 5–6); Cic. *Off.* 1.42.150. Note that Plato (*Leg.* 5.742c) forbids all loans at interest in Magnesia. See also *Resp.* 8.555e–556b.

57. Note Antiphon 2.2.12: like the payment of exactions upon capital (*eisphoraí*) and the performance of liturgies as trierarch or *chorēgós*, the lending of money to friends (*eranízein*) was a sign of public-spiritedness and something to boast about. See Lys. 19.56; Isaeus 5.35–47; Dem. 45.69; Theophr. *Char.* 23.6 (with 1.5, 15.7, 17.9, 22.9). Note Andoc. 3.147, and consider Antiphon *Vorsokr.*^{6} 87 B54. See Johannes Vondeling, *Eranos* (Groningen 1961).

58. Cf. Thuc. 2.43.1 with Arist. *Pol.* 1332b35–41. For further discussion, see Louis Gernet, "Ancient Feasts" and "Law and Prelaw in Ancient Greece," *The Anthropology of Ancient Greece*, trans. John Hamilton, S.J., and Blaise Nagy (Baltimore 1981) 13–47, 143–215 (esp. 26–29, 149–59).

59. The overall pattern is evident from Moses I. Finley's classic work *Studies in Land and Credit in Ancient Athens, 500–200 B.C.* (New Brunswick, N.J., 1952). See, now, Paul Millett, "The Attic Horoi Reconsidered in Light of Recent Discoveries," *Opus* 1 (1982): 219–49. *IG* II^2 2762 (Finley, *Horos* no. 3) and *AD* 17 (1961–62): 35 no. 4 (Millett, *Horos* no. 12a) represent the only certain cases of borrowing for the purpose of purchasing or improving real property. Some might wish to add Finley and Millett *Horoi* nos. 18a and 114a.

60. This is suggested by Theophr. *Char.* 6.9 and confirmed by the fact that Athenians found it expedient to set aside time once a month for the hearing of *díkai aphormaí* (Arist. *Ath. Pol.* 52.2): lawsuits dealing with the disputes that arose regarding loans contracted for the purpose of doing business in the *agorá*. Hyper. 5.6, 9–11 (Jensen) is an example of this type of loan.

61. I know of four (Xen. *Mem.* 2.7.11–12; Lys. F38.1–4 [Gernet/Bizos]; Dem. 37, 40.52), just possibly five (Lyc. *Leocr.* 23 [to be read in light of 58]) loans of this sort in which citizens were involved—and, of these, the first and the last were secured in exceptional circumstances.

62. For the overall point, cf. Arist. *Ath. Pol.* 2.2, 6.1, 9.1; Plut. *Sol.* 15.2 with Diod. 1.79.3–5. Note also Ar. *Plut.* 147–48. In the fifth century, the subjection of citizens to debt-bondage is attested in Gortyn (*ICr* IV 41 cols. V–VI, 72 cols. I.56– II.2); in the Hellenistic period, the institution is found at Delphi (*SIG*³ 692a.48), in Arcadia (*Die Staatsverträge des Altertums*, ed. Hermann Bengtson et al. [Munich 1960–] No. 567.94), and in the cities of the Achaean League (Polyb. 38.11.10). Something of the sort may have existed in late fourth-century Athens (Men. *Her.* 18–40 [with *hyp.* 3–4], *Sic.* 133–40). Of course, Athenians had always been subject to seizure for failing to repay debts incurred when ransomed from captivity abroad ([Dem.] 53.11), and there is no reason to suppose that noncitizen debtors were ever protected against debt-bondage or even sale abroad by the laws of Athens (Ter. *Haut.* 600–607, 788–99) or those of any other community (Lys. 12.98, Isoc. 14.48). For further discussion, see Moses I. Finley, "Debt-Bondage and the Problem of Slavery," *Economy and Society in Ancient Greece* 150–66; David Asheri, "Leggi greche sul problema dei debiti," *SCO* 18 (1969): 5–122; G. E. M. de Ste. Croix, *The Class Struggle in the Ancient Greek World: From the Archaic Age to the Arab Conquests* (Ithaca 1981) 136–37, 162–70; and Andrew Lintott, *Violence, Civil Strife and Revolution in the Classical City* (Baltimore 1982) 27–28.

63. In this connection, see Paul Millett, "Patronage and Its Avoidance in Classical Athens," in *Patronage in Ancient Society*, ed. Andrew Wallace-Hadrill (London 1989) 15–47.

64. Cf. Cratinus F12 (Edmonds) in context (Schol. Lucian *Iupp. Trag.* 48) with Publilius Syrus F11 (Duff), and note Pherecrates F58 (Edmonds). See also Louis Gernet, "Mortgage Horoi," *The Anthropology of Ancient Greece* 303–11, and Ugo Fantasia, "ΑΣΤΙΚΤΟΝ ΧΩΡΙΟΝ," *ASNP* 6 (1976): 1165–75. For the meaning of *stígma*, see C. P. Jones, "*Stigma*: Tattooing and Branding in Graeco-Roman Antiquity," *JRS* 77 (1987): 139–55.

65. See L. M. Gluskina, "Some Aspects of Money and Credit Relations in Fourth Century Attica," *VDI* 113 (1970): 17–43 (in Russian). For the role played by the banks, see also Wesley E. Thompson, "A View of Athenian Banking," *MH* 36 (1979): 224–41, and Edward E. Cohen, "Commercial Lending by Athenian Banks: Cliometric Fallacies and Forensic Methodology," *CPh* 85 (1990): 177–90. Note Theophr. *Char.* 6.9: the professional usurer was evidently well known in the *agorá*.

66. Cf. Publilius Syrus F61 (Duff) with Xen. *Cyr.* 5.5.24–34 and Isoc. 15.39–40, 161–66.

67. See Gunnar Mickwitz, "Economic Rationalism in Graeco-Roman Agriculture," *EHR* 52 (1937): 577–89, and "Zum Problem der Betriebsführung in der antiken Wirtschaft," *Vierteljahrschrift für Sozial- und Wirtschaftsgeschichte* 32 (1939): 1–25. See also Moses I. Finley, *The Ancient Economy*² 104–22, 141–49, and "Documents," *Ancient History: Evidence and Models.* (London 1985) 27–46. Whether the absence of double-entry bookkeeping (above, I.ii.3, note 39) would greatly have impeded rational economic calculations regarding the relative profitability of the investment alternatives actually available to the ancient Greeks and Romans remains very much open to doubt: consider Duncan-Jones, *The Economy of the Roman*

Empire[2] 33–59, in conjunction with H. W. Pleket's review (*Gnomon* 49 [1977]: 55–
... "... mella's Vineyard and the Rationality of the
...77–204; note Finley's dismissive response (*The
...en, consider Richard H. Macve, "Some Glosses
g,'" in *Crux* 239–61.
Xen. *Cyr.* 8.2.5 and *Vect.* 4.6.

Note also 41–43.
vith Xen. *Hiero* 4.8, and see Democr. *Vorsokr.*[6]

e evidence: see the material collected by Ste.
Greek World 274–75 (with full annotation).
. 18.257–65, and see above, I.i.2–4 (esp.
er Nikolaus Himmelmann, *Archäologisches
\kademie der Wissenschaften und der Literatur
Sozialwissenschaftlichen Klasse* (Wiesbaden
-e Vernant, "Some Psychological Aspects
Thought among the Greeks 271–78. Note Pl.
st. *Pol.* 1328b24–1329a26.
Ploutos (Amsterdam 1925). Cf. Maurice
e in Ancient Greece," *G&R* 31 (1984): 140–
< contempt for idleness while mistaking its
ires the difference between toil on the city's
quired to meet the household's needs; he
ned; and he neglects the political logic illu-
ectability to the farmer generally denied
the craftsman (above, I.ii.2–3). Cf. Balme's treatment of the Choice of Heracles
(151–52) with I.i.5, above.

76. To the evidence collected and discussed by G. E. M. de Ste. Croix, *The Origins of the Peloponnesian War* (Ithaca 1972) 371–76, and K. J. Dover, *Greek Popular Morality in the Time of Plato and Aristotle* (Oxford 1974) 34–45, 109–12, one should add *Hell. Oxy.* 6.2–3 (Bartoletti), and Diod. 11.86.2–87.6

77. Arist. *Pol.* 1255b31–40. It was necessary to select the *epítropos* with great care, to encourage him, and to keep a watchful eye on his conduct of affairs: Xen. *Oec.* 9.11–13; [Arist.] *Oec.* 1344b35–1345a11. Note the example set by Pericles and by his steward Evangelos: Plut. *Per.* 16.3–7. See Gert Audring, "Über den Gutsverwalter (*epitropos*) in der Attischen Landwirtschaft des 5. und des 4. Jh. v. u. Z.," *Klio* 55 (1973): 109–16.

78. Xen. *Vect.* 4.14–16. See also Andoc. 1.38; Xen. *Mem.* 3.11.4; Hyper. 2.2 (Jensen); Dem. 27.20, 28.12, 53.20–21; Theophr. *Char.* 30.15–17; Plaut. *Curc.* 382–83, *Asin.* 441–43; Ter. *Ad.* 481–82. Diodorus's description of the plight of those working the mines of Egypt (3.12–14) and Spain (5.38.1) may well indicate something about the situation of the slaves laboring in a similar capacity in Greece. Cf. Strabo's discussion (12.3.40) of the quicksilver mines of Asia Minor.

79. Note Lys. 7.10, and cf. *IG* II[2] 10.1553–78 with L. M. Gluskina, "The Renting of Land in Fourth Century Attica," *VDI* 104 (1968): 42–58 (in Russian), who argues that the metic *geōrgoí* who rallied in such numbers to Thrasybulus at Phyle were freedmen working the land of their former masters. The ordinary peas-

ant had no extra land to rent out, and only citizens were allowed to lease the estates of orphans and the property owned by the city and its various gods. As a consequence, those metics interested in farming had no recourse other than the landed gentry. The high proportion of farmers among the metics who supported Thrasybulus's rebellion—one-quarter of the total number—is no doubt due to the location of Phyle on the border with Boeotia about as far away from the Peiraeus and from the town of Athens as one can get and still be in Attica. See also Ter. *Ad.* 949, which is almost certainly a translation of a line from Menander alluding to the practice of leasing out land in this fashion. This was common also at Rome: Ste. Croix, *The Class Struggle in the Ancient Greek World* 241–42.

80. See L. M. Gluskina, "Studien zu den Sozial-Ökonomischen Verhältnissen in Attika im 4. Ja. v. u. Z.," *Eirene* 12 (1974): 111–38 (esp. 121–23)—which summarizes a series of studies published some years before in Russian. For the original discussion of this particular issue, see "Die Freigelassenen in der athenischen Ökonomie des 4. Jahrhunderts," in *Ostcherki vseobschtschei istorii, Utschonnye zapiski LGPI im. A. I. Gerzena* CCCVII (Leningrad 1969) 278–95. It can hardly be fortuitous that the phrase *chōrìs oikoûntes* was used for freedmen (Dem. 4.36; [Dem.] 34.5–6, 10, 47.72; *Anekd. Gr.* I.316.11–13 [Bekker]) as well as for slaves (Andoc. 1.38, Aeschin. 1.97, Theophr. *Char.* 30.15, Men. *Epit.* 378–80 [Sandbach]). Manumission might alter the legal status of these men; it had little impact on the manner in which they actually conducted their affairs.

81. Cf. Yvon Garlan, "Les sociétés sans esclaves dans la pensée politique grecque," *Klio* 63 (1981): 131–40, with Joseph Vogt, "Slavery in Greek Utopias," *Ancient Slavery and the Ideal of Man* (Oxford 1974) 26–38.

82. *De Lapidibus* 58–59.

83. Cf. *Anth. Pal.* 9.418 with Vitr. *De Arch.* 10.5.2, and consider what one can infer from Suet. *Calig.* 39.1. See Marc Bloch, "Avènement et conquêtes du moulin à eau," *Annales d'histoire économique et sociale* 7 (1935): 538–63. Ausonius (*Mosella* 362–64) provides the earliest evidence that the water mill was used for anything other than the grinding of grain.

84. Cf. Vitr. *De Arch.* 5.10.1 with 10.1–16.

85. Cf. Xen. *Cyr.* 8.2.5 with Pl. *Resp.* 2.369e–370c. For a discussion of the import of this fact, see Marx, *Das Kapital* I 326–28. Finley ("Technological Innovation and Economic Progress in the Ancient World" 187) is not quite right in claiming that "no one has yet discovered a sentence in any Greek or Roman writer" bringing into "calculation the increase in quantity." Note also Aug. *De civ. D.* 7.4.

86. Scarcity of labor could no doubt sometimes be a prod: Pliny *NH* 18.300.

87. Consider Lynn White, Jr., *Medieval Technology and Social Change* (Oxford 1962); "Cultural Climates and Technological Advance in the Middle Ages," *Medieval Religion and Technology: Collected Essays* (Berkeley 1978) 217–53; and "Technological Development in the Transition from Antiquity to the Middle Ages," in *Tecnologia, economia et società nel mondo romano* (Como 1981) 235–51, in light of Gen. 1:1–2:25, 3:17–19; Deut. 5:12–15; Matt. 13:55; Mark 6:3; John 1:3, 5:5–17; Acts 18:3. Note also Exod. 31:1–5, 35:30–35; 2 Chron. 2:12–14; Isa. 54:16; 1 Thess. 4:11–12; 2 Thess. 3:8–11.

88. See Gen. 1:26–28, 3:17–19, 9:1, 6; Matt. 5:3–12, 6:19–34, 10:8–10, 16:25–26; Mark 4:19, 8:36–37, 10:17–27; Luke 6:17–25, 8:14, 9:2–3, 23–25, 10:3–8, 12:15–34, 14:8–11, 16:13, 17:33, 18:10–14, 18–27; John 12:25; 1 Tim. 6:1–18.

89. Cf. the evidence presented in this chapter with M. M. Postan, "Why Was Science Backward in the Middle Ages?" *Essays on Medieval Agriculture and General Problems of the Medieval Economy* (Cambridge 1973) 81–86.

90. See below, II.iii.3.

91. One should read Tocqueville, *DA* 2.1.10 in light of his description of the ancient democracies as "aristocracies of masters" at 2.1.3 (22).

92. Arist. *Pol.* 1259a6–36. Note Aristotle's dismissal (1258b33–39) of the detailed study of mining and the timber industry as a vulgar (*phortikón*) pursuit.

93. Plut. *Marc.* 14–17, 19; Livy 24.34, 25.31.9–10. See also Polyb. 8.3–7; Cic. *Fin.* 5.50; Val. Max. 8.7 ext. 7. The tomb was still intact (though weathered) in Cicero's time: *Tusc.* 5.64–66.

94. *De rebus bellicis* Praef. 6–7 (Ireland).

95. Note the first of this chapter's two epigraphs: Tocqueville, *DA* 2.2.18 (158). Then, see John H. D'Arms, *Commerce and Social Standing in Ancient Rome* (Cambridge, Mass., 1981); and consider the evidence suggesting that, in the archaic period, Greek aristocrats may have engaged in overseas trade through the agency of their dependents: Benedetto Bravo, "Une lettre sur plomb de Berezan: Colonization et modes de contact dans le Pont," *DHA* 1 (1974): 110–87, and "Remarques sur les assises sociales, les formes d'organisation et la terminologie du commerce maritime grec à l'époque archaïque," *DHA* 3 (1977): 1–59.

96. Xen. *Symp.* 4.35. In this connection, see also Plut. *Mor.* 236b–c.

97. The testimony of Xenophon (*Vect.* 4.3–7) is borne out by the *pōlētai* records: Margaret Crosby, "The Leases of the Laureion Mines," *Hesperia* 19 (1950): 189–312, and "More Fragments of Mining Leases from the Athenian Agora," *Hesperia* 26 (1957): 1–23. See also R. Hopper, "The Attic Silver Mines of the Fourth Century B.C.," *ABSA* 48 (1953): 200–254, and "The Laurion Mines: A Reconsideration," *ABSA* 63 (1968): 293–326.

98. Consider Arist. *Poet.* 1448a1–18; then, cf. Ar. *Plut.* 128–197 with 510–516, and note 254. See Pl. *Resp.* 4.421d.

99. *WoJJR* I 38: *Les confessions* 1 (near the end).

100. For the second of this chapter's two epigraphs, see Karl Marx, *Grundrisse der Kritik der Politischen Ökonomie* (Berlin 1953) 387.

101. Much of what Cato has to say in *De Agri Cultura* is ultimately derivative from treatises written centuries before by Greek students of the subject such as Charetides of Paros and Apollodorus of Lemnos (Arist. *Pol.* 1258b39–1259a5). Varro (*Rust.* 1.1.7–9) speaks of fifty Greek writers worth consulting and provides a list of names nearly that long.

102. For the colossal sums required if a man was to live without working, see Lionel Casson, "The Athenian Upper Class and New Comedy," *TAPhA* 106 (1976): 29–59. For the return on investments, see as well Wesley E. Thompson, "The Athenian Investor," *RSC* 26 (1978): 403–23.

103. Xen. *Lac. Pol.* 7.1. As Aristotle (*Pol.* 1257b30–1258a14) hints, it was often difficult to distinguish that form of money-making which was a legitimate part of household management from money-making per se.

104. Ferguson, *EHCS* 1.6 (31–32).

105. Hamilton, *The Federalist* 8 (47).

Chapter 4

1. *WoFN* II 735: *Jenseits von Gut und Böse* 9.262.
2. Smith, *WN* I.ii.1.
3. Madison, *The Federalist* 10 (61), 18 (111). See 38 (241).
4. In this fashion, Hannah Arendt exhibits an understandable desire to side-step the fanatical obscurantism to which her mentor Martin Heidegger lent his name: one should consider the omissions that characterize *The Human Condition* (Chicago 1958) in light of Lewis P. and Sandra K. Hinchman, "In Heidegger's Shadow: Hannah Arendt's Phenomenological Humanism," *RP* 46 (1984): 183–211. Whether the species of politics that she favored and her disciples still promote is, in the end, separable from the martial obsession and the radical particularity exhibited by the ancient Greek *pólis* and sought by Heidegger I very much doubt: consider I.iv.2–7, below, in light of I.i.1–5 and I.ii.1, above, and see George McKenna, "Bannisterless Politics: Hannah Arendt and Her Children," *HPT* 5 (1984): 333–60.
5. Consider Numa Denis Fustel de Coulanges, *The Ancient City* (Baltimore 1980) 109–215; Louis Gernet, "Political Symbolism: The Public Hearth," *The Anthropology of Ancient Greece*, trans. John Hamilton, S.J., and Blaise Nagy (Baltimore 1981) 322–39; and Irad Malkin, *Religion and Colonization in Ancient Greece* (Leiden 1987) 114–34, in light of the essays collected in *The Cuisine of Sacrifice among the Greeks*, ed. Marcel Détienne and Jean-Pierre Vernant (Chicago 1989). Note Jean-Louis Durand and Alain Schnapp, "Sacrificial Slaughter and Initiatory Hunt," in *A City of Images: Iconography and Society in Ancient Greece*, trans. Deborah Lyons (Princeton 1989) 53–70, and see Vernant, "A General Theory of Sacrifice and the Slaying of the Victims in the Greek *Thusia*," *Mortals and Immortals: Collected Essays*, ed. Froma I. Zeitlin (Princeton 1991) 290–302. In this connection, one may also wish to consult Stephen G. Miller, *The Prytaneion: Its Function and Architectural Form* (Berkeley 1978), and Vernant, "Hestia-Hermes: The Religious Expression of Space and Movement in Ancient Greece," *Myth and Thought among the Greeks* (London 1983) 127–75. See also Arist. *Pol.* 1328b11–13, 1329a26–34, 1330a9–16, 1331a24–26, 1331b16–17, 1335b14–16: although he follows Plato's *Republic* in reducing the sacred to the useful, Aristotle does acknowledge the city's need for gods.
6. For the gods and heroes of the land, see Thuc. 2.74.2, 4.87.2; Xen. *Cyr.* 2.1.1; Polyb. 4.20.8–9; Ap. Rhod. *Argon.* 2.1271–75 (with the scholia); Porph. *Abst.* 4.22; cf. Benjamin D. Meritt, "Inscriptions of Colophon," *AJPh* 56 (1934): 358–97 (esp. 361–63), with Louis Robert, "Études d'épigraphie grecque: xlvi. décret de Kolophon," *RPh* (1936): 158–68 (esp. 158–59); and note *ICr* III iii A. See also Aesch. *Supp.* 704–9, 893–94, 922, 1018–21, *Sept.* 14; Soph. *Trach.* 183, *OC* 53–63; Ar. *Eq.* 577; Thuc. 2.71.4, 4.98; Xen. *Hell.* 6.4.7–8, *Ages.* 11.1–2, *Oec.* 5.19–20; Pl. *Phdr.* 230b–c, *Leg.* 8.848d; Lycurg. 1.1–2; Cic. *Nat. D.* 3.18.45, 19.49–50; Paus. 6.20.2–6; Plut. *Arist.* 11.3; and Pap. Michigan inv. 3690: R. Merkelbach, "Die Heroen als Geber des Guten und Bösen," *ZPE* 1 (1967): 97–99. The evidence demonstrating the political import of hero cults particular to individual cities deserves special attention: consider, for example, Hdt. 1.66–68, 5.67, 89 (with Pind. *Isthm.* 8.23–29, Paus. 2.29.6–8, Schol. Pind. *Nem.* 5.94e); Paus. 4.32.3, 7.1.8, 8.9.3–4; Plut. *Thes.* 36.1, *Cim.* 8.3–6, *Arat.* 53, *Mor.* 302c; Polyaen. 6.53 (with Marsyas *FGrH* 135 F7),

in conjunction with Friedrich Pfister, *Der Reliquienkult im Altertum* (Giessen 1909–12) I 188–211. In general, see Lewis Richard Farnell, *Greek Hero Cults and Ideas of Immortality* (Oxford 1921), and Arthur Darby Nock, "The Cult of Heroes," *Essays on Religion in the Ancient World*, ed. Zeph Stewart (Cambridge, Mass., 1972) I 575–602. The archaeological evidence suggests that some of these cults may have originated in the Mycenaean period; others seem to be of later derivation. Homer takes for granted the existence of hero cults but lays no great stress on them: Theodora Hadzisteliou Price, "Hero-Cult and Homer," *Historia* 22 (1973): 129–44, and "Hero Cult in the Age of Homer and Earlier," in *Arktouros: Studies Presented to B. M. W. Knox on the Occasion of His 65th Birthday*, ed. Glenn W. Bowersock, Walter Burkert, and Michael J. Putnam (Berlin 1979) 219–28. The archaeological record indicates that the eighth century was distinguished by new dedications at Mycenaean tombs and by a stress on princely burials, and these changes may well be linked with the proliferation of the hero cults. This possibility has given rise to considerable speculation. Like Farnell (*Greek Hero Cults and Ideas of Immortality* 340–42), J. N. Coldstream, "Hero-Cults in the Age of Homer," *JHS* 96 (1976): 8–17, and *Geometric Greece* (London 1977) 341–57, stresses the inspiration occasioned by the diffusion of Homer's epics; Anthony M. Snodgrass, "Les origines du culte des héros dans la Grèce antique," in *La mort, les morts dans les sociétés anciennes*, ed. Gherardo Gnoli and Jean-Pierre Vernant (Cambridge 1982) 107–19, suggests that the new cults reflect attempts to establish rightful claim by free peasants recently settled on the land. I am struck by the fact that these changes appear to coincide with the emergence of the *pólis*: see Claude Bérard, "Récupérer la mort du prince: Héroïsation et formation de la cité," in *La mort, les morts dans les sociétés anciennes* 89–105; and François de Polignac, *La naissance de la cité grecque: Cultes, espace et société VIIIe–VIIe siècles avant J-C.* (Paris 1984). Note James Whitley, "Early States and Hero Cults: A Re-appraisal," *JHS* 108 (1988): 173–82. More generally, see Christiane Sourvinou-Inwood, "What is *Polis* Religion?" in *The Greek City: From Homer to Alexander*, ed. Oswyn Murray and Simon Price (Oxford 1990) 295–322.

7. The city requires justice if it is to function well (1.351a–e), and justice can only be established if the city becomes a household (3.416d–4.424a, 5.449a–464b). The notion that the citizens were "brothers born of a single mother" was a commonplace of Greek rhetoric: Pl. *Menex.* 239a. See also 244a and Dem. 25.87. Cf. Herodotus's description (4.104) of the Agathyrsi who "hold their women in common, so that they may be brothers of each other and, all being members of one household, not exhibit jealousy and hatred in their dealings with each other." Note Aristotle's critique (*Pol.* 1261b24–1262b35) of this notion, and see *Eth. Eud.* 1242a35–1242b2. See John Neville Figgis, *Churches in the Modern State*[2] (London 1914) 71–73.

8. Pl. *Resp.* 1.351a–d, 3.386a, 4.424a, *Menex.* 244a, *Alc.* I 126b–127d, *Leg.* 1.628a–c, 640b–d, 3.693c, 698a–701d, 5.729d, 743c, 6.757a, 8.837a–e; Arist. *Eth. Eud.* 1234b22–24, *Eth. Nic.* 1155a22–26, 1167a22–b16, *Pol.* 1262b7–10, 1280b38–40, 1295b21–27. See also *Eth. Eud.* 1241a1–34; *Eth. Nic.* 1159b25–1161b10. Because the citizens are numerous (*Eth. Nic.* 1170b33–1171a20) and because they are linked to each other by a common interest in mere self-preservation, their friendship is generally a friendship grounded in utility—but, because the city exists also for the promotion of virtuous living, the friendship of the citizens inevitably has an ethical dimension as well: cf. *Pol.* 1252b27–1253a29, 1280a25–1281a4, 1325a7–10

with *Eth. Eud.* 1242a1–11, 1242b22–1243a38. If the city were actually to become a circle of friends in the full sense of the word, it would cease to be a city. As Aristotle (*Eth. Nic.* 1155a26–27) remarks, there is no need for justice among friends: they are more than merely just in their relations with each other. For the foundations of true friendship, see Pl. *Ep.* 7.333d–334b. Note Emile Benveniste, *Indo-European Language and Society* (Coral Gables, Fla., 1973) 273–88, and see Joseph Cropsey, "Justice and Friendship in the Nicomachaean Ethics," *Political Philosophy and the Issues of Politics* (Chicago 1977) 252–73. See also John M. Cooper, "Aristotle on the Forms of Friendship," *RMeta* 30 (1977): 619–48. An occasional insight can be rescued from Horst Hutter, *Politics as Friendship: The Origins of Classical Notions of Politics in the Theory and Practice of Friendship* (Waterloo, Ontario 1978).

9. *De civ. D.* 19.24.

10. *Rep.* 1.25.39.

11. One should read Ennius *Annales* F467 (Warmington), Cic. *Rep.* 5.1.1–2, and Scipio F13–14 (ORF²) with [Arist.] *VV* 1250b16–24. For the appeal to the ancestral as a standard of conduct, see Hdt. 2.79.1, 3.31.3, 80 (esp. 5), 82.5, 6.60; *SEG* XIII 3; Ar. *Ach.* 1000, *Eccl.* 778; Thuc. 2.2.4, 16.2, 34.1, 3.58.5, 61.2, 65.2, 66.1, 4.86.4, 98.8, 118 (esp. 8), 5.18.2–3, 77 (esp. 5), 79, 7.21.3, 69.2, 8.76.6; Thrasymachus *Vorsokr.*⁶ 85 B1; Andoc. 1.83; Arist. *Ath. Pol.* 16.10, 29.3, 34.3 (with Diod. 14.3 and Xen. *Hell.* 2.3.2), 35.2 (with Schol. Aeschin. 1.39), 39.2; Xen. *Hell.* 3.4.2, 5.2.14, 6.5.6–7, 7.1.3–4; Pl. *Resp.* 7.538d, *Pol.* 295a, 296c–d, 298d–e, 299c–d, 300e–301a, *Hp. Maj.* 284b, *Leg.* 2.656e, 3.680a, 7.793a–c, *Ep.* 7.336c–d; Dem. 11.22, 18.90, 203, 19.64, 23.205, 24.139; Polyb. 4.20.8–9; Diod. 11.76.6; Stob. *Flor.* 4.2.19 (Hense). With rare exceptions (Aesch. *Supp.* 704–9, Eur. *Bacch.* 201), this usage of *pátrios* and its cognates is not found in Homer, Hesiod, Aeschylus, Sophocles, and Euripides. Note, however, the Spartan poem cited by Dio Chrysostom (59.2): *Carmina Popularia* F10.6 (PMG). For the religious roots of this fierce attachment to tradition, see Aesch. *Supp.* 704–9; Lys. 30.17–20; Andoc. 1.110–16; Xen. *Mem.* 1.3.1, *An.* 7.8.5; Isoc. 7.29–30; Pl. *Resp.* 4.427b–c, *Pol.* 290e, *Leg.* 12.959b, *Epin.* 985d; Dem. 21.51–54, 43.66; [Dem.] 59.75–85, 116; Lycurg. 1.97; Pl. *Leg.* 5.738b–c; Agatharchides of Cnidus *FGrH* 86 F5; Stob. *Flor.* 4.2.19 (Hense). In this connection, see also Hdt. 1.172.2, 4.180.2; Ar. *Ran.* 368; Thuc. 2.71.4, 3.59.2, 7.69.2; Xen. *Cyr.* 8.7.1, *Vect.* 6.1; Dem. 19.86. The preference for the ancestral is entirely in keeping with the Greek emphasis on filial piety: consider K. J. Dover, *Greek Popular Morality in the Time of Plato and Aristotle* (Oxford 1974) 273–75, in light of Aesch. *Supp.* 704–9. The virtue of the forefathers is consistently taken as a standard to be imitated: Aeschin. 3.178–87, 192–202; Dem. 3.30–36, 9.36–46, 18.317.

12. Consider Simon. F15 (West) and Eur. *Cyc.* 275–76 in light of Pind. F187 (Bowra), Soph. *OC* 919, and Thuc. 2.41.

13. See Pl. *Leg.* 5.738d–e.

14. Arist. *Pol.* 1303a25–b3. Such colonies were not uncommon: see A. J. Graham, *Colony and Mother City in Ancient Greece²* (Chicago 1983) 15–22. The ethnic quarrels to which colonies of mixed origin were vulnerable oftentimes turned on the identity (and ethnic origin) of the colony's founder (*oikistḗs*): see, for example, Diod. 12.35.1–3. In general, see Malkin, *Religion and Colonization in Ancient Greece* 254–60.

15. Pl. *Prt.* 322c.

16. See Thuc. 2.15.3 and Plut. *Pel.* 18.1–2 with Benveniste, *Indo-European Language and Society* 298–99, and consider Raoul Lonis, "*Astu* et *polis*: Remarques sur

le vocabulaire de la ville et de l'état dans les inscriptions attiques du Ve au milieu du IIe s. av. J-C.," *Ktema* 8 (1983): 95–109 (esp. 100–102).

17. Note Thuc. 2.15–16.

18. Thuc. 6.3.1 should be read in light of Pind. *Pyth.* 4.1–8, 257–62; Hdt. 4.150–65; *GHI* 1.5.7–11, 24–25; Thuc. 3.92.5; Kreophylus of Ephesus *FGrH* 417 F1; Antiochus *FGrH* 555 F10, 13; Hippys *FGrH* 553 F1; Diod. 8.17, 21.3, 23, 12.10.3–7; Strabo 6.2.4; Paus. 2.4.4 (with 5.18.8), 5.7.3, 7.2.1; Plut. *Mor.* 96b (with Hdt. 1.168, Plut. *Mor.* 812a, Ael. *VH* 12.9). Cf. Hdt. 4.144.2 with Strabo 7.6.2 and Tac. *Ann.* 12.63. Note also Hdt. 1.165.1 (with 167.4), 6.34.1–36.1 For further evidence and a full discussion of this phenomenon, see H. W. Parke and D. E. W. Wormell, *A History of the Delphic Oracle* (Oxford 1956) I 49–81 (with the collection of putative oracles in their second volume), and Malkin, *Religion and Colonization in Ancient Greece* 17–91.

19. Hdt. 5.39–48 (esp. 42.2).

20. Thuc. 5.16 should be read in light of Paus. 4.26–27 and Callim. *Aet.* 2.F43.56–67 (Pfeiffer). Note Aristophanes' parody of the rituals employed by the Athenians: *Birds* 809–991. For a brief allusion to these, see *GHI* 1.49.3–6. Note also *Etym. Magn.* s.v. *prutaneía* with Hdt. 1.146.2. See Malkin, *Religion and Colonization in Ancient Greece* 92–186.

21. Pind. *Pyth.* 5.87–95, *Ol.* 7.27–53, 77–81; Hdt. 1.168, 6.34.1–38.1; Callim. *Aet.* 2.F43.40–42, 46–56, 68–84 (Pfeiffer); Diod. 11.49.1–2, 66.4; Paus. 3.1.8; Plut. *Demetr.* 53; Schol. Pind. *Ol.* 1.149–93. See also Cic. *Nat. D.* 3.19.49–50. In this connection, one should perhaps consider Paus. 1.34.2. For the origins and import of this practice, see Malkin, *Religion and Colonization in Ancient Greece* 189–266. Its prevalence explains Thucydides' ability to list the οἰκισταί of the various Greek colonies in Sicily: 6.3–6. See also Strabo 14.1.3. Note Diod. 11.78.5. The savior of a city might sometimes be treated as its founder and given heroic honors: Thuc. 5.11 (with 4.102); Xen. *Hell.* 7.3.12; Diod. 20.102.2–3 (with Plut. *Demetr.* 25); Plut. *Tim.* 39 (with Diod. 16.90.1), *Arat.* 53 (with Polyb. 8.12). In this connection, one should perhaps consider Thucydides' enigmatic remarks (6.3.3) concerning Catania. Note also Thuc. 1.24–30 (esp. 25). A number of Greek cities claimed Apollo as their founder: for a list of examples, see the dissertation of Spyrídōn Paulou Lampros, *De conditorum coloniarum graecarum indole, praemiisque et honoribus* (Leipzig 1873) 8–20. In this connection, note Thuc. 6.3.1. For the duties of the οἰκιστές, cf. Hom. *Od.* 6.7–11 with Plut. *Mor.* 407f–408a, and see Graham, *Colony and Mother City in Ancient Greece*[2] 29–39, and Malkin, *Religion and Colonization in Ancient Greece* 17–186.

22. See, for example, Hdt. 1.163–70 (with Strabo 14.1.30 and Hdt. 6.8), 8.56–63 (esp. 61–62).

23. Heraclitus *Vorsokr.*[6] 22 B44.

24. Plut. *Mor.* 154e. Note Heraclitus's expression of profound respect for Bias: *Vorsokr.*[6] 22 B39.

25. Note Hdt. 1.170, and see Albert Debrunner, "Dēmokratía," *Festschrift für Edouard Tièche zum 70. Geburtstage* (Bern 1947) 11–24, and J. A. O. Larsen, "Cleisthenes and the Development of the Theory of Democracy at Athens," in *Essays in Political Theory Presented to George H. Sabine*, ed. Milton R. Konvitz and Arthur E. Murphy (Ithaca 1948) 1–16; cf. Victor Ehrenberg, "Origins of Democracy," *Historia* 1 (1950): 515–48 (esp. 515–24), with *POxy* 20 (1952): no. 2256 F3, and see Ehrenberg, *Sophokles und Perikles* (Munich 1956) 4 n. 2. See also Christian Meier,

"Die Entstehung des Begriffs Demokratie," *Die Entstehung des Begriffs Demokratie: Vier Prolegomena zu einer historischen Theorie* (Frankfurt am Main 1970) 7–69, and Raphael Sealey, "The Origins of *Demokratia*," *CSCA* 6 (1973): 253–95.

26. Pind. F152 (Bowra).

27. Even in the fourth century, diplomats might appeal to legendary connections: Xen. *Hell.* 6.3.6.

28. Paus. 5.5.12 should perhaps be read in light of *Die Staatsverträge des Altertums*, ed. Hermann Bengtson et al. (Munich 1960–) nos. 134, 147–48, 189, 193, 230, 297, and *GHI* 1.40.2–8, 46.41–43, 49.11–13, 69.55–58. Note also 1.40.2–8. See J. P. Barron, "Religious Propaganda of the Delian League," *JHS* 84 (1964): 35–48; Russell Meiggs, *The Athenian Empire* (Oxford 1975) 291–305. In this connection, see also Hdt. 1.141–51, 170, 6.7 and *Die Staatsverträge des Altertums* nos. 265, 308.

29. Thuc. 3.10.1.

30. Hdt. 8.144.

31. This can be inferred from the tone and emphasis of Thuc. 7.57.

32. For the continuity in cults, calendar, dialect, script, magistracies, and tribal divisions, see Friedrich Bilabel, *Die Ionische Kolonisation* (Leipzig 1920), and Krister Hanell, *Megarische Studien* (Lund 1934). In this connection, see also Angelo Brelich, "La religione greca in Sicilia," *Kokalos* 10–11 (1965): 35–54.

33. See Graham, *Colony and Mother City in Ancient Greece*² 4–8, 71–217. The subject has attracted considerable attention: see Édouard Will, "Sur l'évolution des rapports entre colonies et métropoles en Grèce à partir du VIᵉ siècle," *La Nouvelle Clio* 6 (1954): 413–60; Santo Mazzarino, "Metropoli e colonie," and Georges Vallet, "Métropoles et colonies: Leurs rapports jusque vers la fin du VIᵉ siècle," in *Metropoli e colonie di Magna Grecia*, ed. Pietro Romanelli (Naples 1964) 51–85, 209–29; Sally C. Humphreys, "Colonie e madre patria nella Grecia antica," *RSI* 78 (1966): 912–21; Robert Werner, "Probleme der Rechtbeziehungen zwischen Metropolis und Apoikie," *Chiron* 1 (1971): 19–73; and Roland Martin, "Relations entre métropoles et colonies: Aspects institutionnels," in *Philías Chárin: Miscellanea di studi classici in onore di Eugenio Manni* (Rome 1980) IV 1435–45.

34. Thuc. 1.25–88, 118–25 needs to be read in light of 1.13.4, 25.3–4, 38.3. In this light, one should also consider Hdt. 5.97.2, 7.46.2, 8.22.1, 9.106.3 (with 1.147.2). Note also Thuc. 5.89, 104, 106 with Xen. *Hell.* 2.2.3.

35. Pl. *Resp.* 5.469b–471c (with Xen. *Mem.* 2.2.2). Note Hdt. 7.131–32.

36. See Hdt. 3.38.

37. Cf. Pl. *Resp.* 1.332a–d with Thuc. 2.41.4–5. This ethic was in origin a reflection of the aristocratic individualism so visible in Homer's *Iliad*. To be able to repay one's debts to friends and enemies alike rendered one a god among men: Theog. 337–40 (West). Cf. Hom. *Od.* 6.180–85; Archil. 23.14–15, 126 (West); Theog. 869–72, 1032–33, 1107–8 (West); Pittakos *Vorsokr.*⁶ 10.3.e.8; Solon F13.5 (West); Pind. *Pyth.* 2.83–85, *Isth.* 4.52; Aesch. *Cho.* 120–23; Gorg. *Vorsokr.*⁶ 82 B11a.18, 25; Eur. *Med.* 807–9; Ar. *Av.* 416–26; Dissoi Logoi *Vorsokr.*⁶ 90.2.7; Lys. 6.7, 9.20; Xen. *Mem.* 2.3.14, 6.35, 4.5.10, *An.* 1.9.11, *Cyr.* 1.4.25, 8.7.7, 28, *Hiero* 1.34, 2.1–2, 6.12, 11.15; Pl. *Meno* 71e, *Cleitophon* 410a; Isoc. 1.26; and Arist. *Rh.* 1363a19–21, 33–34, 1399b36–37, with Xen. *Mem.* 4.8.11, Pl. *Cri.* 49b–c, and Matt. 5:43. Sophocles explores the logic of this understanding of human (and, by implication, civic) excellence in his *Ajax* and elsewhere: see Bernard Knox, "The *Ajax* of Sophocles," *Word and Action: Essays on the Ancient Theater* (Baltimore 1979) 125–60, and Mary

Whitlock Blundell, *Helping Friends and Harming Enemies: A Study in Sophocles and Greek Ethics* (Cambridge 1989).

38. Aesch. *Eum.* 976–87.

39. *The Federalist* 9 (52–53).

40. Pl. *Leg.* 1.626a. Characteristically, in assessing this phenomenon, Moses I. Finley, "War and Empire," *Ancient History: Evidence and Models* (London 1985) 67–87, stresses the profits that accrued from the successful conduct of war almost to the exclusion of other concerns.

41. His opinion can be inferred from Pl. *Resp.* 4.422e–423b.

42. See Montesquieu, *EL* 1.4.4–8.

43. Anaximenes *Rh.* 1424b15–21 (Fuhrmann).

44. Xen. *Cyr.* 8.1.2.

45. Pl. *Resp.* 2.368c–377b.

46. Arist. *Pol.* 1263b36–37.

47. Pl. *Resp.* 2.376e–3.392c. See also 3.392c–416c. Note, especially, 383c.

48. Critias *Vorsokr.*[6] 88 B25=*TrGF* 43 F19 (Snell). Note Protagoras *Vorsokr.*[6] 80 B4; cf. *PHerc.* 1428 F16 and 19 with Cic. *Nat. D.* 1.42.117–19; and see Albert Henrichs, "Two Doxographical Notes: Democritus and Prodicus on Religion," *HSCPh* 79 (1975): 93–123 (esp. 107–23), and "The Atheism of Prodicus," *Cronache Ercolanesi* 6 (1976): 15–21. For bibliography and a recent discussion, see Dana Sutton, "Critias and Atheism," *CQ* n.s. 31 (1981): 33–38. The fragment quoted is sometimes (wrongly, I think) attributed to Euripides: cf. Albrecht Dihle, "Das Satyrspiel 'Sisyphos,'" *Hermes* 105 (1977): 28–42.

49. Consider Arist. *Metaph.* 1074a38–b14 in light of *Pol.* 1252b15–30, and see Thomas K. Lindsay, "The 'God-Like Man' versus the 'Best Laws': Politics and Religion in Aristotle's *Politics*," *RP* 53 (1991): 488–509.

50. Isoc. 11.24–25; Polyb. 6.56.11–12, 10.2.10–12, 16.12.9; Diod. 34/35.2.47; Strabo 1.2.8. Compare Cic. *Rep.* 1.36.56, Plut. *Mor.* 763b–f, 879f–880a, Dio Chrys. *Or.* 12.39–41, 44, Euseb. *Praep. Evang.* 3.17.1–2, 4.1.2–4, and Aët. *Plac.* 1.6–9 with Tert. *Ad Nat.* 2.1.8–11, 2.1, 14 (Borleffs) and with what Augustine has to say about the Pontifex Maximus Scaevola (*De civ. D.* 4.27), about Varro (3.4, 9, 12, 18, 4.1, 9, 22, 27, 31–32, 6.2–10, 7.1, 3, 5–6, 9, 17, 22–28, 30, 33–35, 8.1, 5, 19.1–4), and about the distinction between mythical, civil, and natural theology which they espoused, and see Jean Pépin, "La 'théologie tripartite' de Varron," *REAug* 2 (1956): 265–94, and Ernest L. Fortin, "Augustine and Roman Civil Religion: Some Critical Reflections," *REAug* 26 (1980): 238–56. The discrepancy between what Cicero has to say regarding religion in his political works (*Rep.* 2.9.16–10.20, 14.26–27, *Leg.* 2.6.14–27.69) and what he says, in his own name, elsewhere (*Div.* 1.1.1–6.11, 2.3.8–72.150) is explicable in terms of his general purpose in composing those political works: consider *Leg.* 1.13.37–39, 2.14.35 in light of *Nat. D.* 1.1.2–4.7, 5.11–12, 22.61–23.63, 27.77, 30.84–31.87, 42.117–44.123, 2.1.2, 67.168, 3.1.1–4.9, 17.43, 19.50, 40.94–95, F1 (Müller), *Div.* 1.5.8–9; note *Nat. D.* 1.26.71, 2.3.8–9; and see August. *De civ. D.* 4.30, 5.9. In this connection, note the arguments which Cicero leaves unanswered: *Nat. D.* 1.16.42–43, 2.23.60–28.72, 3.4.10–6.17, 9.23–11.28, 15.39–39.93. Consider 1.21.57–22.60 in light of Pl. *Ti.* 28c. For further discussion, see W. Kendrick Pritchett, *The Greek State at War* (Berkeley 1971–   ) III 327–31, and Alan Wardman, *Religion and Statecraft among the Romans* (London 1982) 1–62 (esp. 52–62). It is by no means fortuitous that, in his *Laws*, Plato treats

theology in a digression from his discussion of penal law as it pertains to theft: consider 9.865d–866a, 870d–874c, 880a–881e, 10.884a–910b, 11.913d–914a, 916e–917d, 922c–923c, 931d–e, 12.943e, 958e–959d in light of Thomas L. Pangle, "The Political Psychology of Religion in Plato's Laws," *APSR* 70 (1976): 1059–77.

51. *Theog.* 1135–50 (West)—which I would emend in light of the suggestion of van Herwenden. See also 1179–82. Note the exhortation with which Zaleucus is said to have prefaced his code of laws: Stob. *Flor.* 4.2.19 (Hense).

52. Xen. *Mem.* 4.3.16, Pl. *Leg.* 6.762e. See also Isoc. 1.12–13.

53. Dem. 25.16. I see no reason to eject this oration from the Demosthenic corpus. The style is clearly that of the great orator, and we err if we suppose that the tone of every speech composed by a given man must be the same.

54. Dem. *Ep.* 1.1.

55. See the material collected by Jon D. Mikalson, *Athenian Popular Religion* (Chapel Hill 1983) 13–17. Note Cic. *Leg.* 2.3.7–4.8.

56. Cf. Verg. *Aen.* 1.68, 8.11 with Xen. *Cyn.* 1.15, and see Eur. *Heracl.* 347–52. In keeping with this conviction, the Spartans (Hdt. 5.75.2) carried the Tyndaridae into battle. Note the willingness of the Aeginetans (5.79–81) to lend the Aeacidae to their Theban allies. Every city had its own divine guardian: Ar. *Birds* 826–27. The importance accorded the city's divine patrons is particularly evident in Aeschylus: see *Sept.* 69, 91–95, 104–86, 211–29, 234–36, 251–87, 301–20, 582, 702–4, *Supp.* 704–9, 724–25, 732–33, 893–94, 1018–21. For an overview, see Ursula Brackertz, *Zum Problem der Schutzgottheiten griechischer Städte* (Berlin 1976).

57. Aesch. *Sept.* 217–22, 251–58, 304–20, 702–4; Soph. F452 (Radt); Eur. *Tro.* 23–27; Hdt. 8.41. It is with this in mind that one should read Hdt. 5.82–89, Thuc. 2.74.2, and Plut. *Sol.* 9. The Romans carried this notion one step further with their ritual of *evocatio*: Livy 5.15.1–12, 21.3–22.8, 30.1–3; Verg. *Aen.* 2.351–54 (with Servius ad loc.); Pliny *NH* 28.4.18; Macrob. *Sat.* 3.9.7. See, in this connection, Arn. *Adv. Gent.* 3.38. Note the similar Hittite practice: L. Wohleb, "Die altrömische und die hethitische Evocatio," *ARW* 25 (1927): 206–9; Vsevolod Basanoff, *Evocatio: Étude d'un rituel militaire romain* (Paris 1947). The various legends associated with the Trojan Palladion have similar roots: Cic. *Scaur.* 48; Dion. Hal. *Ant. Rom.* 1.69, 2.66; Ov. *Fasti* 6.433–54; Verg. *Aen.* 2.166–79 (with Servius ad 2.166, 3.407, 5.704); App. *Mithr.* 53; Strabo 6.1.14; Paus. 1.28.8–9, 2.23.5; Plut. *Camill.* 20; Conon *Narr.* 34 (*FGrH* 26 F1); Sil. *Pun.* 13.36–81. For further discussion, see M. van Doren, "Peregrina Sacra: Offizielle Kultübertragungen im alten Rome," *Historia* 3 (1955): 488–97, and L. Ziehen *RE* XVIII:3 (1983) 171–89 (esp. 186).

58. This practice was common in Greece and known in Phoenicia as well: Hdt. 1.26 (with Polyaen. 6.50), 5.83–84; Schol. Pind. *Ol.* 7.95; Pl. *Meno* 96d–97d; Diod. 17.41.7–8 (with Curtius 4.3.22, Plut. *Alex.* 24.3–4); Paus. 3.15.7, 8.41.6. See also Cratinus F74, Ar. F194, and Plato Com. F188 (Edmonds), as well as Menodotus *FGrH* 541 F1. For another view of this practice, see Karl Meuli, "Die gefesselten Götter," *Gesammelte Schriften* (Basel 1975) II 1035–81.

59. In stealing the bones of heroes and securing their patronage, the Spartans were particularly adept: see Hdt. 1.66–68; Paus. 7.1.8; Plut. *Mor.* 302c with C. M. Bowra, "Stesichorus in the Peloponnese," *CQ* 28 (1934): 115–19; D. M. Leahy, "The Bones of Tisamenus," *Historia* 4 (1955): 26–38; and George Huxley, "Bones for Orestes," *GRBS* 20 (1979): 145–48. Note also Paus. 3.14.1 with W. R. Connor, "Pausanias 3.14.1: A Sidelight on Spartan History, C. 440 B.C.," *TAPhA* 109 (1979): 21–27, and see Plut. *Arat.* 53. In this pursuit, the Spartans were by no means

alone: Plut. *Thes.* 36.1, *Cim.* 8.3–6; Paus. 8.9.3. In this connection, one should also read Hdt. 5.89.2 and Paus. 2.29.8.

60. See Mikalson, *Athenian Popular Religion* 18–26. Note also Theog. 1169–70 (West).

61. Pind. *Nem.* 11.1–10. Note Aesch. *Pers.* 347 and Xen. *Hell.* 7.4.34.

62. See Hom. *Il.* 1.8–101, 408–74, 16.384–92; Hes. F30.16–23 (Merkelbach/ West); Aesch. *Sept.* 597–614; Soph. *OT* 1–147; Antiphon 3.1.1–2, 3.11–12; Pl. *Leg.* 10.910b; Philostr. *VA* 8.5.

63. Hes. *Op.* 240–47 (West).

64. Pind. *Pyth.* 3.24–37.

65. Cf. Aesch. *Sept.* 602–4; Eur. *El.* 1349–56, F852 (Nauck²); Antiphon 5.81–83; Andoc. 1.137–39; Xen. *Cyr.* 8.1.25; [Lys.] 6.19; Hor. *Carm.* 3.2.26–32 with Jon. 1:1–16. For further evidence and discussion, see the dissertation of Dietrich Wachsmuth, *Pómpımos ho daímōn: Untersuchungen zu den antiken Sakralhandlungen bei Seereisen* (Berlin 1967). This deepseated reluctance is the unstated premise underlying the suspicions which some Athenians reportedly directed at the Corinthians on the eve of the Sicilian expedition in 416 at the time of the defacing of the Herms: Cratippus *FGrH* 64 F3, Philochorus *FGrH* 328 F133. They simply took it for granted that the sacrilege had been committed by enemies of Athens eager to prevent the sailing of the expedition.

66. See Pl. *Leg.* 10.910b. See also Antiphon 2.1.10–11, 3.9–11, 3.1.1–2, 3.11–12, 4.3.7; Andoc. 1.137–39; Xen. *An.* 4.8.25; Dem. 23.43. This concern explains the eagerness of the Athenians in 416 to identify and prosecute those guilty of defacing the Herms and of making a mockery of the Eleusinian Mysteries: Thuc. 6.27–29, 60–61. In general, see Robert Parker, *Miasma: Pollution and Purification in Early Greek Religion* (Oxford 1983). In this connection, see also Louis Gernet, "Sur la désignation du meurtrier," *Droit et société dans la Grèce ancienne* (Paris 1955) 29–50.

67. [Arist.] *VV* 1251a30–33. See also 1250b16–24. Note Stob. *Flor.* 4.2.19 (Hense).

68. Xen. *Hell.* 1.7.22, Lycurg. 1.113, 127.

69. Lycurg. 1.1, 129. Note Dinarchus 1.98, 3.14. In this connection, one should consider the references to piety and impiety at Dem. 8.8, 18.240, 323, 19.156; Lycurg. 1.34, 141.

70. Consider Aesch. *Pers.* 402–5 in light of 805–12, and see Hdt. 8.109.3.

71. Where we would expect to find reference to "the public and the private," the Greeks could speak of "the sacred and the private": Hdt. 6.9.3, 13.2.

72. Lycurg. 1.79. See Arist. *Ath. Pol.* 22.2, 31.1, 55.5; Dem. 24.150. Consider Pl. *Leg.* 12.948b–949c in light of I.vii.6–8, below. For the vital importance of oaths in Greek life, see the evidence presented by Mikalson, *Athenian Popular Religion* 31–38. See also Jean Rudhardt, *Notions fondamentales de la pensée religieuse et actes constitutifs du culte dans la Grèce classique: Étude préliminaire pour aider à la compréhension de la piété athénienne au IVme siècle* (Geneva 1958) 202–12.

73. Xen. *Mem.* 4.4.16.

74. *ICr* III iv 7. For a discussion of the circumstances under which the oath was imposed, see Ronald F. Willetts, *Aristocratic Society in Ancient Crete* (London 1955) 126–29. Note the use of oaths at a critical moment in Athenian history: Lys. 6.39, 45, 13.88, 25.23; Andoc. 1.90–91; Isoc. 18.19–21; Xen. *Hell.* 2.4.42; Aeschin. 2.176; Arist. *Ath. Pol.* 39.4. Note also Xen. *Hell.* 2.4.43, Justin 5.10.10–11.

75. *ICr* III iv 8. For evidence indicating that a similar oath was administered at Teos and Abdera in the tumultuous period subsequent to the Persian Wars, see *SEG* XXXI 984–85 with Peter Herrman, "Teos und Abdera im 5. Jahrhundert v. Chr.: Ein neues Fragment der Teiorum Dirae," *Chiron* 11 (1981): 1–30, and David M. Lewis, "On the New Text of Teos," *ZPE* 47 (1982): 71–72.

76. Cic. *Rep.* 4.3.3–4.4.

77. One should read *ICr* I viii 13, ix 9, xvi 5, xviii 9, xix 1, II v 24 in light of Ephorus *FGrH* 70 F149 (ap. Strabo 10.4.16–22). For briefer paraphrases of Ephorus's description, see Arist. F611.15 (Rose) and Heraclid. Pont. *Pol.* 3 (Müller *FHG* II 211–12). For the context in which these inscriptions should be understood, see Willetts, *Aristocratic Society in Ancient Crete* 110–26, 182–85.

78. *ICr* I ix 9.

79. The oath survives intact in an inscription posted by the deme Acharnae in the fourth century: *GHI* 2.204.6–20. For a brief summary, see Lycurg. 1.76–78. Note Dem. 19.303. For a less than entirely accurate text, see Poll. *Onom.* 8.105–6 and Stob. *Flor.* 4.1.48 (Hense). Note the reference to this oath at Plut. *Alc.* 15.7–8. Peter Siewert has drawn attention to a number of allusions to the oath in the literature of the fifth century and has argued forcefully for its origins early in the archaic period: see "The Ephebic Oath in Fifth-Century Athens," *JHS* 97 (1977): 102–11. For the *ephēbeía* as it existed in late fourth-century Athens, see Arist. *Ath. Pol.* 42. For the import of the young man's period of apprenticeship, see Pierre Vidal-Naquet, "The Black Hunter and the Origin of the Athenian *Ephebia*," and "Recipes for Greek Adolescence," *The Black Hunter: Forms of Thought and Forms of Society in the Greek World*, trans. Andrew Szegedy-Maszak (Baltimore 1986) 106–56, and "The Black Hunter Revisited," *PCPhS* 212 (1986): 126–44, as well as John J. Winkler, "The Ephebes' Song: *Tragōidia* and *Polis*," in *Nothing to Do with Dionysos? Athenian Drama in Its Social Context*, ed. John J. Winkler and Froma I. Zeitlin (Princeton 1990) 20–62. For a depiction of the ephebes taking the oath, see John Davidson Beazley, *Attic Red-Figure Vase Painters*[2] (Oxford 1963) II 1069: Thomson Painter no. 1.

80. Pl. *Resp.* 4.430b, *Phd.* 68d, *Leg.* 1.646e–649d. In paraphrasing a closely related discussion (2.666a–d, 671a–674c), Aulus Gellius (*NA* 15.2.5) translates *aidōs* and *aischúnē* with *pudor reverens*. Note Cic. *Rep.* 5.4.6.

81. Pl. *Leg.* 3.698b–699d. Consider in this light Aristotle's claim (*Pol.* 1331a35–41) that the oversight of the magistrates is very effective in engendering in men "true reverence (*tēn alēthinēn aidō*) and the fear that belongs to the free (*tòn tôn eleuthérôn phóbon*)." Note, in this connection, Pl. *Ep.* 7.336d–337d.

82. For the difference between the rational courage of the philosopher and the political courage of the citizen, cf. Pl. *Resp.* 6.485d–486b and 503b–506c (esp. 503e–504a, 506b) with 4.430a–c while noting *Leg.* 7.803a–804b, 11.922c–923b (with Ar. *Nub.* 223), and Alfarabi, *Aphorisms* §§ 71–75; cf. Pl. *Leg.* 12.963e with 2.658e–660a (esp. 659a–b); and, then, ponder *Ap.* 38a in conjunction with *Menex.* 246d–247c while considering *Resp.* 3.407a and Xen. *Ap.* 1.1, 4–9 in light of Pl. *Phd.* 67b–69e and *Leg.* 8.828c–d. See Arist. *Eth. Eud.* 1230a16–33. For the notion that some lives are not worth living (*abíōtos*), see also Pl. *Resp.* 3.407a–b, *Pol.* 299e (in context), and *Leg.* 11.926b with Alfarabi, *Plato and Aristotle* 2.7.30. In reading the ancient political philosophers, one must always keep in mind the distinction they maintain between virtue proper or philosophic virtue (which is rooted in nature) and demotic or political virtue (which is rooted in law or convention): con-

sider Pl. *Phd.* 68c–69c, 82a–84b, *Resp.* 4.430c, 6.500d, 7.518d–e, 10.619c–620c, *Leg.* 4.709e–710b (with 3.696d–e and 12.963e), 12.967d–968a, Arist. *Eth. Nic.* 1115a4–1117b21 (esp. 1116a17–b3), *Eth. Eud.* 1228b39–1230a36, *Rh.* 1366a23–1366b22 (with 1360b39–1361a10, 1365b1–20) in light of August. *Acad.* 3.17.37.

83. Timoth. F13 (PMG). Cf. Pl. *Tht.* 155c–d, *Leg.* 12.966d–967d, and Arist. *Metaph.* 982b12–983a22 with Xen. *Cyr.* 8.1.40–44 (esp. 42–43), and see Pl. *Ap.* 20c–24a, 29a–b, 33b–c, 41b.

84. For the relationship between fear, piety, reverence, shame, law-abiding-ness, justice, and political courage, see Aesch. *Eum.* 517–25, 681–706; Soph. *Aj.* 1071–84; Hdt. 7.104; Pl. *Leg.* 1.646e–650b, 3.699c, 12.943e; Isoc. 6.59, 11.24–25; Arist. *Eth. Eud.* 1229a13–14, 29–33, 1230a17–34, *Eth. Nic.* 1116a17–b3, *Pol.* 1314b38–1315a3, 1331a40–b1, *Rh.* 1366b11–12; Polyb. 6.56.11–12, 10.2.10–12, 16.12.9; Diod. 34/35.2.47; Plut. *Cleom.* 9, *Mor.* 1104b; Stob. *Flor.* 4.2.19 (Hense). The importance of piety is evident from the context of Pl. *Resp.* 4.430d. For its subordination to the *pólis*, see Pl. *Euthphr.* 14b2–7. Note the conjunction of fear, shame, and piety in Xenophon's discussion of sanity (*Mem.* 1.1.14), and consider Plato's analysis (*Euthphr.* 12a–c) of the relationship between fear, shame, and reverence. On the subject of divine wrath, see the material collected by Dover, *Greek Popular Morality* 246–68. On the importance of religion in war, see Pritchett, *The Greek State at War* III esp. 1–10, 327–31, and Raoul Lonis, *Guerre et religion en Grèce à l'époque classique: Recherches sur les rites, les dieux, l'idéologie de la victoire* (Paris 1979).

85. Ardant du Picq, *Battle Studies: Ancient and Modern Battle*, trans. John N. Greely and Robert C. Cotton (Harrisburg, Pa., 1946) 95–97, 110–11, 116, 140, 154, 226.

86. S. L. A. Marshall, *Men against Fire* (New York 1947) 149, 153, 161. See also du Picq, *Battle Studies* 154.

87. Marshall *Men against Fire* 162, 167.

88. For a comparison, see du Picq, *Battle Studies* 84–117.

89. See the discussion in John Keegan, *The Face of Battle* (New York 1976) 15–78, 285–336.

90. The statistical evidence collected by Marshall, *Men against Fire* 50–63, may well be inadequate as support for his assertion that rarely more than 25 per-cent of the troops ever fired their guns, and his claim may also be exaggerated somewhat. But his more general thesis concerning the prevalence of terror, the ordinary soldier's propensity to freeze, and the motives capable of causing him to risk his life is confirmed by what can be learned concerning behavior in combat in other places and times. Cf. Fredric Smoler, "The Secret of the Soldiers Who Didn't Shoot," *American Heritage* 40:2 (March, 1989): 36–45, with Bruce Catton, *America Goes to War* (Middletown, Conn., 1958) 48–67, and with Guy Sajer, *The Forgotten Soldier*, trans. Lily Emmet (New York 1971).

91. Marshall, *Men against Fire* 42. See also 148–56.

92. Consider Arist. *Pol.* 1326a5–b25 in light of Peter Laslett, "The Face to Face Society," in *Philosophy, Politics, and Society*, ed. Peter Laslett (Oxford 1956) 157–84. See Pl. *Resp.* 4.423a, 5.460a, *Leg.* 5.738d–e, 742d. Note also Thuc. 8.66.3, Isoc. 6.81, 15.171–72.

93. See Arist. *Eth. Nic.* 1170b31–32, *Pol.* 1276a22–30. Plato (*Leg.* 5.737d–738c) considered 5,040 a suitable figure for the number of citizens. See also *Resp.* 4.423a, 5.460a.

94. See the material collected by Alfred Zimmern, *The Greek Commonwealth*[5]

(Oxford 1931) 59–68. Even in the age of Hesiod, the *agorá* had its attractions (*Op.* 27–32), and men tended to gather about the smithy for conversation in winter (493–501). They were presumably even more gregarious in high summer—when the poet himself (582–96) thought relaxation appropriate.

95. Hesiod (*Op.* 303–20) praises labor, but only as a necessity (42–49, 90–105) imposed on men by the gods in recompense for Prometheus's theft of fire. Commendation was normally reserved for leisure: see Moses I. Finley, *The Ancient Economy*[2] (London 1985) 40–55, and Hannah Arendt, *The Human Condition* (Chicago 1958) 81–85.

96. Note I.v.6, below, and consider the punishment of *atimía* imposed on such men at Athens: Aeschin. 3.175–76. See also Dem. 24.103 (with 119). Cf. the regulations recommended by Plato: *Leg.* 12.943e–945b.

97. For the problem of provisions, see Pritchett, *The Greek State at War* I 30–52.

98. Note the remarks of Phormio to his men: Thuc. 2.89.10.

99. See Marcel Détienne, "La phalange: Problèmes et controverses," in *Problèmes de la guerre en Grèce ancienne*, ed. Jean-Pierre Vernant (Paris 1968) 119–42, and Victor Davis Hanson, *The Western Way of War: Infantry Battle in Classical Greece* (New York 1989). For the origins of this species of warfare early in the seventh century and for its import, see H. L. Lorimer, "The Hoplite Phalanx with Special Reference to the Poems of Archilochus and Tyrtaeus," *ABSA* 42 (1947): 76–138, and Anthony Snodgrass, "The Hoplite Reform and History," *JHS* 85 (1965): 110–22; cf. Paul Cartledge, "Hoplites and Heroes: Sparta's Contribution to the Technique of Ancient Warfare," *JHS* 97 (1977): 11–27, with John Salmon, "Political Hoplites?" *JHS* 97 (1977): 84–101, and see A. J. Holladay, "Hoplites and Heresies," *JHS* 102 (1982): 94–103 (esp. 97–103). The best collection of materials on Greek military practices by far is Pritchett's multivolume work *The Greek State at War*. See especially IV 1–93. J. K. Anderson, *Military Theory and Practice in the Age of Xenophon* (Berkeley 1970) is invaluable. Note also *Hoplites: The Classical Greek Battle Experience*, ed. Victor Davis Hanson (New York 1991). For a discussion of the relationship between artillery, cavalry, and infantry, see Paul A. Rahe, "The Military Situation in Western Asia on the Eve of Cunaxa," *AJPh* 101 (1980): 79–96. Note also W. R. Connor, "Early Greek Land Warfare as Symbolic Expression," *P&P* 119 (May 1988): 3–29; François Lissarrague, "The World of the Warrior," in *A City of Images* 39–51; and Jean-Pierre Vernant, "Artemis and Preliminary Sacrifice in Combat," *Mortals and Immortals* 244–57.

100. Dion. Hal. *Ant. Rom.* 7.9.3–5.

101. Montesquieu, *EL* 1.4.8 (272).

102. Hdt. 6.11.2.

103. Hdt. 6.7–18. Note, in this connection, 6.111–12, 7.104, 9.31.

104. Consider Xen. *Oec.* 4.4–25 in light of 5.4–5, 13, 20.2–15.

105. It is not fortuitous that, of the seven champions who assault Thebes in Aeschylus's play, only the reluctant Amphiaraus—who denounces his fellows for impiety—is described as *sōphrōn*. Nor is it an accident that Aeschylus fails to attribute anything like *lússa* to any one of the citizens picked to defend the city's seven gates. From the perspective of the *pólis*, the ferocity and the martial frenzy exhibited by Amphiaraus's six colleagues is a species of *húbris*. See Aesch. *Sept.* 42–54, 375–416, 422–51, 458–80, 486–580, 526–62, 568–625, 631–75. *Sōphrosúnē* is the quality required: 182–202.

106. For a helpful, if inadequate, overview, see Warren D. Anderson, *Ethos*

and Education in Greek Music: The Evidence of Poetry and Philosophy (Cambridge, Mass., 1968). See also Giovanni Comotti, *Music in Greek and Roman Culture*, tr. Rosaria V. Munson (Baltimore 1989), and Winkler, "The Ephebes' Song" 20–62. For an English translation of much of the pertinent evidence, see *Greek Musical Writings*, ed. Andrew Barker (Cambridge, 1984–89). See also Aristides Quintilianus, *On Music in Three Books*, trans. Thomas J. Mathiesen (New Haven 1983), and note the new critical edition and translation of the sixth book of Sextus Empiricus's *Adversus mathematikous*. See *Pros Mousikous: Against the Musicians (Adversus musicos)*, ed. and trans. Denise Davidson Greaves (Lincoln, Neb., 1986).

107. Consider Pl. *Resp.* 2.373e–415e in light of the shift in thought from 2.376e to 3.403c–412a, and read 4.424a–425a, 441e, 5.456a, 7.521d–522c, 539d, 8.546d–547a, 548b–549b, 9.591c–e, in conjunction with *Pol.* 305e–311c.

108. Pl. *Leg.* 1.642a, 2.653a–674c, 3.691a, 700a–701c, 4.722d–723b, 6.764c–766b, 7.795d–806c, 810e–817e, 8.828b–829e, 831b–832a, 834d–836c, 9.863b–c, 12.949a. Note, in this connection, Pl. *Ti.* 47c–e, 88b–c, and see William Shakespeare, *The Merchant of Venice* V.i.53–109.

109. Consider Arist. *Pol.* 1337a7–1342b34 and the passages cited in note 108, above, in light of 1323a14–1337a6 and Pl. *Leg.* 1.625c–632e, 2.660e–664a, 666e–667a, 3.688a–d; then, see Ernst Koller, *Musse und musische Paideia: Die Musikaporetik in der aristotelischen Politik* (Basel 1956); Carnes Lord, *Education and Culture in the Political Thought of Aristotle* (Ithaca 1982); and Stephen G. Salkever, "Tragedy and the Education of the *Dēmos*: Aristotle's Response to Plato," in *Greek Tragedy and Political Theory*, ed. J. Peter Euben (Berkeley 1986) 274–303. Note [Arist.] *Pr.* 919b26–920a8, 920b29–921a6, 922b10–27.

110. Aristox. *Harm.* 2.31–32 (Da Rios), F70, 75, 82, 85, 120a–d, 122–123 (Wehrli); Theophr. F87–93 (Wimmer); Chamaileon F3–6, 42 (Wehrli); Ptol. *Harm.* 1.12, 14, 16, 2.1, 6–7, 3.3–8 (Düring); Cic. *Tusc.* 1.2.4, 4.1.2–2.4, *Leg.* 2.15.38–39; Strabo 1.2.3, 8; Quint. *Inst.* 1.10.9–33; Plut. *Pel.* 19.1–2, *Mor.* 1131b–1147a (with 440d–452d); Aristid. Quint. 1.1–3, 12, 19, 2.1–19, 3.7–8, 16–17, 20–27 (Winnington-Ingram). For Varro, see Comotti, *Music in Greek and Roman Culture* 52.

111. Pind. *Pyth.* 5.63–69.

112. Consider Ar. *Nub.* 961–1104 (esp. 966–72, 984), 1321–1510 (esp. 1327–30, 1354–78) in light of *Ran.* 885–1465 (esp. 1008–10 and 1030–36) and *Thesm.* 146–73, and see Ath. 14.628f with Pl. *Phd.* 60c–d.

113. Pl. *Prt.* 324d–326e.

114. Damon *Vorsokr.*⁶ 37 A3–6, B6–7, 10.

115. Note *PHib.* 1.13 and Cic. *Leg.* 3.14.32; consider Phld. *De mus.* 1.1–3, 5–6, 9–10, 12–13, 15–23, 25–32, 3.3–6, 9–11, 14–17, 22–27, 32–37, 39, 41–42, 44–45, 48–56, 59–60, 73–77, 4.1b–38; Pap. 424, 1576 F1 (Kemke); and Sext. Emp. *Math.* 6.6–27 (Greaves) in light of Epicurus F5, 20 (Usener) and Cic. *Fin.* 1.21.71–72; and see Anderson, *Ethos and Education in Greek Music* 147–76.

116. In this connection, see Allan Bloom, *The Closing of the American Mind: How Higher Education Has Failed Democracy and Impoverished the Souls of Today's Students* (New York 1987) 68–137. See also John Adams Wettergreen, "Elements of Ancient and Modern Harmony," in *Natural Right and Political Right: Essays in Honor of Harry V. Jaffa*, ed. Thomas B. Silver and Peter W. Schramm (Durham, N.C., 1984) 45–61.

117. Polyb. 17.3–21.12. See Plut. *Pel.* 19.1–2 and *Mor.* 1131b–1147a. For an extended commentary on what "the judicious Polybius" has to say in the passage

cited, see Montesquieu, *EL* 1.4.8. Note, in this connection, Benjamin Rush, "Of the Mode of Education Proper in a Republic," *Essays, Literary, Moral & Philosophical* (Philadelphia 1798) 6–20 (at 13–14). Cf. Smith, *WN* V.i.f.39–41.

118. Democr. *Vorsokr.*[6] 68 B179.

119. See Kenneth J. Dover's seminal discussion of Aeschin. 1: *Greek Homosexuality* (Cambridge, Mass., 1978) 19–109. The last two chapters are less dependable, as Dover now acknowledges himself: *JHS* 104 (1984): 239–40. Note, by way of comparison, E. E. Evans Pritchard, "Sexual Inversion among the Azande," *American Anthropologist* 72 (1970): 1428–34; B. R. Burg, *Sodomy and the Pirate Tradition: English Sea Rovers in the Seventeenth-Century Caribbean* (New York 1984); and the non-Greek examples cited by Félix Buffière, *Éros adolescent: La pédérastie dans la Grèce antique* (Paris 1980) 29–45. Over the years, anthropologists have tended to sidestep this phenomenon, but, quite recently, ritualized homosexuality has begun to receive close attention: consider the remarks of Kenneth E. Read, "The *Nama* Cult Recalled," in *Ritualized Homosexuality in Melanesia*, ed. Gilbert H. Herdt (Berkeley 1984) 211–47, and see the publications cited in notes 121–22, below. That the practice of pederasty in ancient Greece, like the practice of heterosexual courtship in other places and times, should give rise to considerable social tension and ambivalence stands to reason, but David Cohen, "Law, Society and Homosexuality in Classical Athens," *P&P* 117 (November 1987): 3–21, exaggerates the importance of this phenomenon. His argument rests largely—though not entirely—upon the unstated and undefended assumption that Xenophon, Plato, and Aristotle speak for a great many of their contemporaries on this subject. He fails to recognize that the critique of pederasty adumbrated by Socrates' disciples and their greatest successor is part and parcel of the more general critique which these philosophers direct against the primacy of politics and war. For a later restatement of the philosophers' theme, see Plut. *Mor.* 990d–991a.

120. Consider H. I. Marrou, *A History of Education in Antiquity*, trans. George Lamb (London 1956) 26–35, and Harald Patzer, *Die griechische Knabenliebe* (Wiesbaden 1982), in light of Arnold Van Gennep, *The Rites of Passage*, trans. Monika B. Vizedom and Gabrielle L. Caffee (Chicago 1961). Though his adherence to Karl Otfried Müller's Dorian theory led him somewhat astray, Erich Bethe's "Dorische Knabenliebe," *RhM* n.s. 62 (1907): 438–75, is still of considerable value. The same can be said for Hutter, *Politics as Friendship* 57–90.

121. See, for example, Carl Strehlow, *Die Aranda- u. Loritja-Stämme in Zentral-Australien* (Frankfurt am Main 1907–20) IV:1 98; Gunnar Landtman, *The Kiwai Papuans of British New Guinea* (London 1927) 236–37; John Layard, *Stone Men of Malekula* (London 1942) 486–92; Jan van Baal, *Dema: Description and Analysis of Marind-Anim Culture (South New Guinea)* (The Hague 1966) 143–62, 351, 479–80, 669–75, 817–18, 950–52; Maurice Godelier, "Le sexe comme fondement ultime de l'ordre social et cosmique chez les Baruya de Nouvelle-Guinée," in *Sexualité et pouvoir*, ed. Armando Verdiglione (Paris 1976) 268–306 (esp. 276, 281–83); Raymond C. Kelly, "Witchcraft and Sexual Relations: An Exploration in the Social and Semantic Implications of a Structure of Belief," in *Man and Woman in the New Guinea Highlands*, ed. Paula Brown and Georgeda Buchbinder (Washington, D.C., 1976) 36–53 (esp. 40–41, 45–47, 50, 53 n. 7); Edward L. Schieffelin, *The Sorrow of the Lonely and the Burning of the Dancers* (New York 1976) 121–28, 170, 222; Raymond C. Kelly, *Etoro Social Structure: A Study in Structural Contradiction* (Ann Arbor 1977) 16; Jan van Baal, *Jan Verschueren's Description of Yéi-Nan Culture: Ex-*

tracted from the Posthumous Papers (The Hague 1982) 59–65; and Gilbert H. Herdt, "Fetish and Fantasy in Sambia Initiation," and Edward L. Schieffelin, "The *Bau a* Ceremonial Hunting Lodge: An Alternative to Initiation," in *Rituals of Manhood: Male Initiation in Papua New Guinea*, ed. Gilbert H. Herdt (Berkeley 1982) 44–98, 155–200. To date, the most detailed anthropological discussions of pederasty as a tribal institution are to be found in Gisela Bleibtreu-Ehrenberg, *Mannbarkeitsriten* (Frankfurt 1980); in Gilbert H. Herdt, *Guardians of the Flutes: Idioms of Masculinity* (New York 1981) esp. 203–94, 318–20; and in the remarkable collection of essays recently edited by Herdt: *Ritualized Homosexuality in Melanesia*. See, in particular, Herdt, "Ritualized Homosexual Behavior in the Male Cults of Melanesia, 1862–1983: An Introduction" 1–81; Michael R. Allen, "Homosexuality, Male Power, and Political Organization in Vanuatu: A Comparative Analysis" 82–127; Jan van Baal, "The Dialectics of Sex in Marind-anim Culture" 128–66; Herdt, "Semen Transactions in Sambia Culture" 167–210; Erich Schwimmer, "Male Couples in New Guinea" 248–91; Laurent Serpenti, "The Ritual Meaning of Homosexuality and Pedophilia among the Kimam-Papuans of South Irian Jaya" 292–317; Arve Søorum, "Growth and Decay: Bedamini Notions of Sexuality" 318–36; and Shirley Lindenbaum, "Variations on a Sociosexual Theme in Melanesia" 337–61.

122. See Francis Edgar Williams, *Papuans of the Transfly* (Oxford 1936) 158–59, 181–206, 308–9.

123. Ephorus *FGrH* 70 F149 (ap. Strabo 10.4.16–22). For briefer paraphrases of this passage, see Arist. F611.15 (Rose) and Heraclid. Pont. *Pol.* 3 (Müller *FHG* II 211–12). See also Pl. *Leg.* 2.666e. For additional evidence, much of it from inscriptions, see Ronald F. Willetts, *Ancient Crete: A Social History* (London 1965) 110–26. See also Henri Jeanmaire, *Couroi et courètes* (Lille 1939) 421–55. For Crete as the locus for the first Greek *politeía*, see Arist. F611.14 (Rose) and Heraclid. Pont. *Pol.* 3.1–2 (Müller *FHG* II 211). Perhaps with some reason, the Cretans claimed to be the source of nearly everything that was Greek: Diod. 5.77.3–8.

124. For the age of entry into the *agélē*, see Hesychius s.v. *apágelos*. See also Schol. Eur. *Alc.* 989 and Hesychius s.v. *skótioi*.

125. The same institution existed in Arcadia: Polyb. 4.20.12.

126. Ephorus *FGrH* 70 F149 ap. Strabo 10.4.16–22.

127. Equipment of this sort was quite commonly reserved for those who had passed the tests separating the men from the boys: according to Aristotle (*Pol.* 1324b15–18), a Macedonian warrior could not wear a belt until he had killed an enemy soldier in battle and there was a festival of the Scythians in which a drinking cup was passed about from which a man who had not killed someone in battle was not allowed to drink. In the same spirit, a Macedonian was also denied the privilege of eating while in a reclining position until he had speared a wild boar: Hegesandros *FHG* IV 419 (Müller) ap. Ath. 1.18a.

128. For Zeus as patron of ephebes, see the material collected by Ronald F. Willetts, *Cretan Cults and Festivals* (London 1962) 199–220. For his role as protector of the men's houses, see Hesychius s.v. *Zeus Hetaireîos*. The tale of Ganymede's abduction by Zeus was apparently of particular importance in Crete: according to Plato (*Leg.* 1.636d), the story was in this respect generally acknowledged to have been of Cretan invention. See *Anth. Pal.* 5.100. The historian Echemenes (*FGrH* 459 F1), who attributed the abduction to Minos instead of Zeus, was apparently out of step with his fellow Cretans. For pederasty in Crete, see also Arist. *Pol.* 1272a23–26, F611.15; Nep. *Praefatio* 4; Sext. Emp. *Pyr.* 3.199.

129. Ephorus *FGrH* 70 F149 ap. Strabo 10.4.16–22.

130. Sosicrates (Müller *FHG* IV 501) ap. Ath. 13.561e–f. Note Ael. *VH* 3.9.

131. Timaeus of Tauromenium (*FGrH* 566 F144) and Aristotle (F611.15 [Rose]) claim that the institution of pederasty originated in Crete and spread from there, and there is reason to suspect that they may be right. Pederasty was a custom particular to Greece: cf. Hdt. 1.135, Xen. *Cyr.* 2.2.28, Cic. *Tusc.* 5.20, Nep. *Alc.* 2.2 with the less credible material collected by Jan Bremmer, "An Enigmatic Indo-European Rite: Paederasty," *Arethusa* 13 (1980): 279–98. Plato (*Resp.* 5.452c) reports that the closely related (*Leg.* 1.636b–d; Ar. *Peace* 762–64, *Birds* 139–42; Cic. *Tusc.* 4.70–71; Mart. 4.55.6–7; Plut. *Mor.* 274d; cf. Pl. *Charm.* 155c–d and *Symp.* 217b–c with Aeschin. 1.12–13 and the attendant scholia) and, likewise, peculiarly Greek practice (Hdt. 1.10.3) of exercising naked in a public gymnasium first spread—not many generations before his own time—from Crete to Sparta and then on to the remainder of the Greek world. Thucydides (1.6.54) acknowledges that the latter custom distinguishes the Greeks from the barbarians; and, though he makes no mention of Crete, he does assert that the custom originated in Sparta and then passed from there to the rest of Hellas. See also Dion. Hal. *Ant. Rom.* 7.72.2–4, and note Pl. *Tht.* 169a–b. The conflict between the testimony of Plato and that of Thucydides is of little import—for the Spartans themselves (Hdt. 1.65 with Ephorus *FGrH* 70 F149 [ap. Strabo 10.4.17–19]) believed that their regime was modeled on the *politeía* which had emerged beforehand in Crete: see note 123, above. The notion that these two cities were the originators of much that was Greek was so widespread that Plato (*Prt.* 342a–343c) found it a ripe subject for parody. Orsippus of Megara (Paus. 1.44.1–2, Isidorus *Etym.* 17.2) may have been responsible for introducing athletic nudity to the Olympic games. See James A. Arieti, "Nudity in Greek Athletics," *CW* 68 (1975): 431–36. For further evidence indicating that the institution of pederasty came into being shortly after the emergence of ancient Greek republicanism, see below, note 160. It is perhaps worth mentioning that Timaeus's and Aristotle's accounts were not the only discussions of pederasty's origins: the other sources—perhaps including Euripides (Ael. *NA* 6.16)—resorted to legend (Pl. *Leg.* 8.836c, Ath. 13.602f). For Laius's abduction of Chrysippus, see Hellanicus *FGrH* 4 F157; Schol. Eur. *Phoen.* 60; Plut. *Pelop.* 19.1; Apollod. *Bibl.* 3.5.5.10. The story may have been told by Aeschylus: see Hugh Lloyd Jones, *The Justice of Zeus*[2] (Berkeley 1983) 119–23. The archaeological evidence for the archaic period provides strong support for the view that the classical Greek attitude to nakedness had its origins in that age: see Myles McDonnell, "The Introduction of Athletic Nudity: Thucydides, Plato, and the Vases," *JHS* 111 (1991): 182–93.

132. This can be inferred from Ael. *VH* 3.9.

133. See Gundel Koch-Harnack, *Knabenliebe und Tiergeschenke: Ihre Bedeutung im päderastischen Erziehungssystem Athens* (Berlin 1983), and Alain Schnapp, "Eros the Hunter," in *A City of Images* 71–87.

134. See the graffiti from Thera (*IG* XII:3 536, 549, 601, 1410, 1493) with Fritz Graf, "Apollon Delphinios," *MH* 36 (1979): 2–22. See also Walter Burkert, "Apellai und Apollon," *RhM* 118 (1975): 1–21.

135. Plut. *Mor.* 761b. See also Sext. Emp. *Pyr.* 3.199 (with *Anth. Pal.* 12.247).

136. Xen. *Symp.* 8.32–34; Plut. *Pel.* 18.2, *Mor.* 761b; Cic. *Rep.* 4.4.4. See Xen. *Lac. Pol.* 3.12, Pl. *Symp.* 182a–d, Joseph. *Ap.* 2.273. For the contest in male beauty

at Elis and for its military and religious significance, see Theophr. F111 (Wimmer); Ath. 13.565, 609. See also Paus. 6.24.8.

137. Onasander 24.

138. Plut. *Mor.* 761a–b. See Hesychius s.v. *Xalkıdízeın*; Ath. 13.601e–f.

139. Xen. *Symp.* 8.25–35, *Hell.* 4.3.39; Pl. *Symp.* 178e–179a, *Phdr.* 239a–b; Plut. *Pel.* 18, *Mor.* 760b–761e; Ath. 13.602a–603d, 604f–605a; Ael. *NA* 4.1; *Anth. Pal.* 13.22.3–8. See Xen. *An.* 7.4.8. Note also Theog. 1238a–b, 1377–80 (West).

140. Aesch. F134–39 (Radt); Ath. 13.600a, 602e; Plut. *Mor.* 760d–e. Aeschylus's version of the famous tale attracted general, but not universal, acclaim: cf. Pl. *Symp.* 179d–180b, Apollod. *Bibl.* 3.13.8, Arr. *Peripl. M. Eux.* 23.4, Sext. Emp. *Pyr.* 3.199, and Stella G. Miller, "Eros and the Arms of Achilles," *AJA* 90 (1986): 159–70, with Xen. *Symp.* 8.30–31, and see Aeschin. 1.132–33. For Sophocles' orientation, see the testimony of his acquaintance Ion of Chios (Müller *FHG* II 46 F1) and the story told by Hieronymus of Rhodes (Ath. 13.604d–f).

141. See Pl. *Alc.* I 121e–122b. For Sparta, see Cic. *Rep.* 4.3.3. In this connection, one might wish to consider Nietzsche's comments: *WoFN* I 604–5: *Human, All Too Human* I.v.259.

142. *Eth. Nic.* 1157a1–14, 1164a2–11.

143. Plut. *Mor.* 770b–c. Note what is assumed at Xen. *An.* 2.6.28.

144. F112 (Bowra). See also F108 (Bowra).

145. Ap. Ath. 13.601c. At Sparta (Plut. *Lyc.* 17.1) and apparently on Crete (Ael. *NA* 4.1), the *erastaí* were generally young men. For Athenian expectations, see Lys. 3.4.

146. Ath. 13.561d.

147. For the pertinent evidence, see Matthew Dickie, "Phaeacian Athletes," *Papers of the Liverpool Latin Seminar* 4 (1983): 237–76.

148. Arist. *Pol.* 1264a20–23.

149. They are consistently mentioned together: Aeschin. 1.138–39; Plut. *Sol.* 1.6, *Mor.* 152d, 751b.

150. Consider Schol. Pl. *Phdr.* 231e in light of I.iv.4, note 96 and its context, above: even if the scholiast is mistaken regarding the facts, his report is itself evidence that pederasty was popularly envisaged as an encouragement to civic virtue.

151. Pl. *Leg.* 1.636b (with *Tht.* 162b). See Ar. *Peace* 762–64, *Birds* 139–42; Plut. *Mor.* 274d. Note Martial's reference (4.55.6–7) to the "Ledaean wrestling grounds of libidinous Lacedaemon," and consider Montesquieu, *EL* 1.7.9, in light of 8.11 and 2.12.6.

152. Livy 1.57–60, 3.44–54.

153. Nepos (*Praefatio* 6–7) compares Greek mores with those of republican Rome. Lysias 1.6–14 elegantly illustrates the obstacles which seclusion posed for seduction at Athens. For a partial survey of the Athenian evidence, see J. P. Gould, "Law, Custom, and Myth: Aspects of the Social Position of Women in Classical Athens," *JHS* 100 (1980): 38–59. See also Sarah B. Pomeroy, *Goddesses, Whores, Wives, and Slaves* (New York 1975) 32–119. Sparta is a special case which I have reserved for discussion in I.v–vi. It is perhaps worth noting that in late antiquity seclusion became once again the norm: Peter Brown, *The Cult of the Saints* (Chicago 1981) 43–44.

154. It is not clear whether Antileon hailed from Heracleia in Lucania (Parth.

Amat. Narr. 7) or from the better-known Metapontum (Plut. *Mor.* 760c). For Mela-nippus and Chariton, see Plut. *Mor.* 760b–c, Ath. 13.602a–c, Ael. *VH* 2.4.

155. Hdt. 6.23; Thuc. 1.20.2, 6.53.3–59.4; Arist. *Ath. Pol.* 18–19.

156. See Arist. *Ath. Pol.* 58.1 with *IG* I² 77 (as revised by Wesley E. Thompson, "The Prytaneion Decree," *AJPh* 92 [1971]: 226–37), Isaeus 5.47, Din. 1.101. For the early evidence, see Anthony J. Podlecki, "The Political Significance of the Athenian 'Tyrannicide'-Cult," *Historia* 15 (1966): 129–41. See now M. W. Taylor, *The Tyrant Slayers: The Heroic Image in Fifth Century B.C. Athenian Art and Politics* (New York 1981). For the standard Athenian view, see Andoc. 1.96–98; Pl. *Symp.* 182b–d; Aeschin. 1.132, 140; Dem. 19.280, 20.159; Isaeus 5.47; Arist. *Rh.* 1401b. A tyrant could pay a high price for abuses of power in the sexual realm: Arist. *Pol.* 1311a28–b23.

157. Zimmern, *The Greek Commonwealth*⁵ 59–68, makes this comparison. See also Ernest Barker, *Greek Political Theory* (London 1918) 16. Tyranny requires a direct assault on the skein of personal relations that makes of the city a club: Arist. *Pol.* 1313a37–b5, Ath. 13.602d. Political participation fosters friendship; the tyrant cannot really have friends and cannot let others have them either: Xen. *Hiero* 1.32–38.

158. Eryxias, *The History of Colophon* (Müller *FHG* IV 106) ap. Ath. 13.561f–562a.

159. Zeno of Citium *SVF* I 61 F263 (ap. Ath. 13.561c).

160. For the view that Greek nudity and Greek pederasty both originated in historical times not long after the emergence of the *pólis*, Homer's depiction of Hellenic life provides vital support: though the tale of Ganymede's abduction (*Il.* 5.265, 20.231–35) and the story of the friendship linking Achilles with Patroclus (see above, note 140) offered him ample opportunity, the great poet nowhere made allusion to pederasty; and when he described athletic games in the *Iliad* (23.227–897), he had the contestants compete with girded loins (685, 710). Homer's silence regarding pederasty was noted in antiquity (Xen. *Symp.* 8.30–31, Aeschin. 1.141–42) and can hardly have been fortuitous. Archilochus exercised scant restraint in discussing and even celebrating his own heterosexual escapades (note especially F196a [West]), but he failed to mention pederasty or to evidence any interest in having relations with boys. Yet, by the time of Alcaeus (Cic. *Tusc.* 4.71, Hor. *Od.* 1.32.9–11), Solon (F23, 25–26 [West] with Plut. *Sol.* 1.6), Ibycus (F6–8, 28 [PMG]), Anacreon (F1, 12, 14–15 [PMG] with Maximus of Tyre 37.5) and Theognis (1017–22, 1063–68, 1231–1389 [West]), pederasty had become a major poetic theme. See also the Homeric *Hymn to Aphrodite* 203–12. I am inclined to suppose that Greek mores—and the rules of poetic decorum—had undergone a sea change in the interim. For a discussion of related issues, see above in context, notes 123 and 131.

161. For the decline of pederasty, see Joseph. *Ap.* 2.273–75.

162. Pl. *Phd.* 109a–b.

163. *The Federalist* 10 (59).

164. Cf. Ath. 14.627b–c with Plut. *Coriol.* 1.6.

165. Joseph. *Ap.* 2.225–26. Note Pl. *Resp.* 8.544c.

Chapter 5

1. Cf. *WoJJR* III 545–46: "[Histoire de Lacédémone]" with Montesquieu *EL* 1.3.4. For the second of this chapter's two epigraphs, see *WoJJR* III 510. For a recent discussion, see Arthur M. Melzer, *The Natural Goodness of Man: On the System of Rousseau's Thought* (Chicago 1990).

2. Arist. *Pol.* 1294b13–41.

3. Cf. 3.693d–e with 4.712d–e.

4. Cf. *Pol.* 1294b13–41 with 1293b7–1294a29. For the context, see 1289a26–1294b41 and 1299b20–30. See also 1270b17–25. Cf. Isoc. 7.61 with Dem. 20.107–8. See Stob. *Flor.* 4.1.138 (Hense).

5. See Elizabeth Rawson, *The Spartan Tradition in European Thought* (Oxford 1969) 139–241.

6. Victor Ehrenberg's 1934 radio address "A Totalitarian State" is particularly interesting: *Aspects of the Ancient World* (Oxford 1946) 94–104. See also H. I. Marrou, *A History of Education in Antiquity* (London 1956) 22–25, and even more recently, Richard Jenkyns, *The Victorians and Ancient Greece* (Oxford 1980) 225. For the decline of Laconophile sentiment, see Rawson, *The Spartan Tradition in European Thought* 241–367. For many, Athens was to be the liberal ideal: Nicole Loraux and Pierre Vidal-Naquet, "La formation de l'Athènes bourgeoise: Essai d'historiographie 1750–1870," in *Classical Influences on Western Thought A.D. 1650–1870*, ed. R. R. Bolgar (Cambridge 1979) 169–222.

7. Cf. Antony Andrewes, "The Government of Classical Sparta," in *Ancient Society and Institutions: Studies Presented to Victor Ehrenberg*, ed. Ernst Badian (Oxford 1966) 1, with Moses I. Finley, "Sparta and Spartan Society," *Economy and Society in Ancient Greece*, ed. Brent D. Shaw and Richard P. Saller (London 1981) 33. The latter essay was first published in 1968.

8. Thuc. 5.68.2.

9. Antony Andrewes, *Eirene* 12 (1974): 139.

10. F. Ollier, *Le mirage spartiate* (Paris 1933–43); E. N. Tigerstedt, *The Legend of Sparta in Classical Antiquity* (Stockholm 1965–78); and Rawson, *The Spartan Tradition in European Thought* 12–115.

11. Hume, *EMPL* 259: "Of Commerce."

12. See, for example, Pl. *Leg.* 1.630d–631b, 3.688a–d; Arist. *Pol.* 1269b29–1271b19. As Ephraim David, "Aristotle and Sparta," *AncSoc* 13–14 (1982–83): 67–103, points out, the two philosophers were generally in agreement. Despite appearances, there is reason to suspect that Xenophon may have shared their misgivings regarding Lacedaemon: see Leo Strauss, "The Spirit of Sparta and the Taste of Xenophon," *Social Research* 6 (1939): 502–36; W. E. Higgins, *Xenophon the Athenian: The Problem of the Individual and the Society of the Polis* (Albany, N.Y., 1977) 65–82, 115–22; and Gerald Proietti, *Xenophon's Sparta: An Introduction* (New York 1987).

13. Ferguson, *EHCS* 3.6.159.

14. For a thorough survey of the issues and of the literature published on this subject prior to the 1970s, see Pavel Oliva, *Sparta and Her Social Problems* (Amsterdam 1971); for a more recent survey, see Jean Ducat, "Sparte archaïque et classique: Structures économiques, sociales, politiques (1965–1982)," *REG* 96 (1983): 194–225. In general, see Humfrey Michell, *Sparta* (Cambridge 1964); Andrewes, "The Government of Classical Sparta" 1–20; Arnold Toynbee, *Some Problems of*

Greek History (Oxford 1969) 152–417; David M. Lewis, *Sparta and Persia* (Leiden 1977); W. G. G. Forrest, *A History of Sparta, 950–192 B.C.* [2] (London 1980); Finley, "Sparta and Spartan Society" 24–40; Stephen Hodkinson, "Social Order and Conflict of Values in Classical Sparta," *Chiron* 13 (1983): 239–81; J. F. Lazenby, *The Spartan Army* (Warminster 1985); Douglas M. MacDowell, *Spartan Law* (Edinburgh 1986); and Paul Cartledge, *Agesilaos and the Crisis of Sparta* (Baltimore 1987).

15. Pl. *Leg.* 2.666e, Isoc. 6.81, Plut. *Lyc.* 24.1. See Arist. *Pol.* 1324b5–9. In this connection, see also Pl. *Leg.* 1.625c–626c, 628e, 633a–d, 3.688a–d.

16. Thuc. 2.39.1; Xen. *Lac. Pol.* 14.4; Isoc. 11.18; Arist. F500 (Rose); Plut. *Lyc.* 27.6–9, *Agis* 10.3–8, *Mor.* 238d–e. See also Ar. *Av.* 1012–16, Thuc. 1.144.2, Plut. *Lys.* 19.7–21.1, Joseph. *Ap.* 2.259. Pl. *Leg.* 12.949e–953e is a commentary on and critique of this Spartan practice. Note the ironical discussion at Pl. *Prt.* 342a–d. See David Whitehead, "The Lakonian Key," *CQ* n.s. 40 (1990): 267–68.

17. Thomas Babington Macaulay, *The History of England* (Philadelphia 1861) I 273.

18. See Xen. *Lac. Pol.* 10.8, and note Arist. *Pol.* 1337a26–32. See also Joseph. *Ap.* 2.225.

19. Xen. *Lac. Pol.* 7.5–6; [Pl.] *Eryxias* 400b; Plut. *Lyc.* 9.1–3, *Lys.* 17, *Mor.* 226d; Justin 3.2.11–12; Porph. *Abst.* 4.3; Poll. *Onom.* 7.105, 9.79. Note the measures adopted in Plato's Cretan city: *Leg.* 5.741e–744a.

20. Xen. *Lac. Pol.* 7.1–2; Isoc. 11.18; Plut. *Lyc.* 24.2, *Ages.* 26.6–9, *Mor.* 214b, 239d; Polyaen. 2.1.7; Ael. *VH* 6.6. See also Plut. *Lyc.* 9.4–9, *Mor.* 226d. Though the evidence comes from the fourth century or thereafter, the prohibition was presumably adopted long before. Herodotus (2.167) specifies that the Spartans of his time were more contemptuous of the banausic trades than any other people. Given the absence of metics, the necessary arts and crafts were presumably practiced by landless *períoikoi* and by some of the helots (Plut. *Comp. Lyc. et Num.* 2.7) as well: see R. T. Ridley, "The Economic Activities of the Perioikoi," *Mnemosyne* 27 (1974): 281–92, which needs amendment in light of the rejoinder by Guy Berthiaume, "Citoyens spécialistes à Sparte," *Mnemosyne* 29 (1976): 360–64. For another view, see Paul Cartledge, "Did Spartan Citizens Ever Practice a Manual Tekhne?" *LCM* 1 (1976): 115–19. Note the measures which the Athenian Stranger devised for Magnesia: Pl. *Leg.* 5.743c–744a, 8.847d–e, 849c–d.

21. Plut. *Lyc.* 25.1.

22. Plut. *Comp. Lyc. et Num.* 2.6.

23. Thuc. 6.11.6.

24. Xen. *Hell.* 7.1.8.

25. Plut. *Lyc.* 16.1–3. Note the discussion by Pierre Roussel, "L'exposition des enfants à Sparte," *REA* 45 (1943): 5–17.

26. Polyb. 6.45.3, Justin 3.3.3, Porph. *Abst.* 4.3. See also Xen. *Lac. Pol.* 10.7, Pl. *Leg.* 3.684d–685a (with 683c–d). As Pavel Oliva, "On the Problem of the Helots," *Historica* 3 (1961): 5–34, and "Die Helotenfrage in der Geschichte Spartas," in *Die Rolle der Volksmassen in der Geschichte der vorkapitalistischen Gesellschaftsformationen*, ed. Joachim Herrmann and Irmgard Sellnow (Berlin 1975) 109–16, has repeatedly remarked, the peculiar form of property relations predominant at Sparta was intimately bound up with the peculiar status of the helots. In both cases, the political community asserted—at least in principle—its control over the means of securing a livelihood. There is no conflict between Plut. *Lyc.* 16.1–3 (with 8.1–9) and *Agis* 5.2: the elders of a man's tribe seem normally to have registered his

eldest son for the father's allotment at birth. Only if he completed the *agōgḗ* could he make good on his claim (*Mor.* 238e). Provision was presumably made for the man's younger sons from the allotments of those who had failed to produce suitable candidates for the succession, for Plutarch (*Mor.* 238e) makes it clear that anyone of citizen birth who successfully completed the *agōgḗ* had the right to an allotment. Note, in this connection, Teles F3 (Hense) ap. Stob. *Flor.* 3.40.8 (Hense). Cf. the regulations devised by Plato for the imaginary city of Magnesia on Crete (*Leg.* 11.923a–d). See also the stimulating discussion of Henri Jeanmaire, *Couroi et courètes* (Lille 1939) 481–90, who treats the public allotment as a species of fief conferred on the warriors of the community. On the helots in general, see Detlef Lotze, *Metaxù Eleuthérōn kaì Doúlōn* (Berlin 1959) 38–47, and Jean Ducat, "Aspects de l'hilotisme," *AncSoc* 9 (1978): 5–46.

I see no reason to follow those scholars who are inclined to dismiss the evidence cited above as nothing more than a reflection of legends invented by late fourth- and third-century propagandists. As Plutarch indicates, the origins of Sparta's peculiar property regime were contested—but all of those who commented on the dispute took for granted that regime's existence in the sixth and fifth centuries, and no ancient writer is known to have challenged this assumption. Herodotus and Thucydides do fail to comment on Lacedaemon's system of land tenure, to be sure, but they are silent concerning a great many well-attested features of Spartan life, and Plato (*Leg.* 3.684d–685a) is a witness to the persistence of an egalitarian distribution of property at Sparta. Unfortunately, Aristotle's *Lakedaimoniōn Politeía*, which (Arist. F611.12 [Rose]) appears to have discussed the history of Spartan property relations, is no longer extant. That work was, however, available to Plutarch, and given the biographer's customary practice, there is every reason to suppose that he would have told us if Aristotle's account had been in conflict with the story he recounts. The discussion in Aristotle's *Politics* (1270a16–39, 1271a29–37, 1272a12–21, 1307a34–36) is often cited by the skeptics, but it clearly refers to conditions in the philosopher's own time, and these reflect the consequences of the passage, shortly after the Peloponnesian War, of the law of Epitadeus (Plut. *Agis* 5)—which, in effect if not in intent, transformed the public allotments into private property: note David, "Aristotle and Sparta" 70–92 (esp. 80–92), and see I.vi.2, below. In general, cf. George Grote, *History of Greece*[2] (New York 1900–1901) II 393–416, and, most recently, Stephen Hodkinson, "Land Tenure and Inheritance in Classical Sparta," *CQ* n.s. 36 (1986): 378–406, with MacDowell, *Spartan Law* 89–110, and consider Thomas J. Figueira, "Population Patterns in Late Archaic and Classical Sparta," *TAPhA* 116 (1986): 165–213 (at 184–87). See I.v.4, note 141, below.

27. For the existence of and the rationale behind the regulations determining the rent to be paid, see Plut. *Mor.* 239e. For the precise amount paid to each Spartan master and for its distribution within the household, see Plut. *Lyc.* 8.7. The portion reserved for the wife corresponds closely with the monthly contribution made by her husband to the common mess: cf. Plut. *Lyc.* 12.3, who has converted the Laconian into Attic measures, with Dicaearchus F72 (Wehrli) ap. Ath. 4.141c. See also Porph. *Abst.* 4.4. This portion was roughly what a soldier or slave could expect in rations: see Hom. *Od.* 19.27, Hdt. 7.187.2, Thuc. 4.16.1, Polyb. 6.39.3, Diog. Laert. 8.18, Ath. 3.98e, 6.272b. The annual rent from the allotment seems to have been adequate for about seven persons. See Detlef Lotze, "Zu Einigen Aspekten des Spartanischen Agrarsystems," *JWG* 2 (1971): 63–76. For an am-

bitious and ingenious attempt to make sense of the available ancient statistics, see Thomas J. Figueira, "Mess Contributions and Subsistence at Sparta," *TAPhA* 114 (1984): 87–109. Earlier studies include Ulrich Kahrstedt, "Die Spartanische Agrarwirtschaft," *Hermes* 54 (1919): 279–94, and Auguste Jardé, *Les céréales dans l'antiquité grecque* (Paris 1925) 107–22. Cf. *Pol.* 1264a24–36 for Aristotle's criticism of the similar arrangement in Plato's *Republic*.

28. Arist. *Pol.* 1264a9–11, Plut. *Mor.* 239d–e. For the emphasis on courage, see Thuc. 2.39.1, Pl. *Leg.* 2.667a.

29. Plut. *Mor.* 217a.

30. Joseph. *Ap.* 2.228–31.

31. Arist. *Pol.* 1269a34–b12, *Rh.* 1367a28–33; Plut. *Lyc.* 24.2. See also Isoc. 11.20. All of the Spartans were *kaloì kagathoí*: Thuc. 4.40.2.

32. Xen. *Hell.* 3.3.5, *Lac. Pol.* 10.7, 13.1, *An.* 4.6.16; Arist. *Pol.* 1306b30; Dem. 20.107. See Hdt. 7.234.2, 9.62.3; Thuc. 4.40.2, who use the word playfully as an adjective in contexts where Sparta is being discussed. See also Xen. *Hell.* 3.3.11, Pl. *Leg.* 3.696a–b, Isoc. 7.61.

33. Madison's remarks, *The Federalist* 10 (59), can profitably be compared with Pl. *Leg.* 5.744d–745b and Arist. *Pol.* 1295b1–1296a21.

34. Note the distinction between the two types of landed property indicated by Arist. F611.12 (Rose) and Heraclid. Pont. *Pol.* 2.7 (Müller *FHG* II 211): it was illegal to sell one's civic allotment and shameful to sell one's privately owned farm. Note Plut. *Mor.* 238e–f.

35. As Aristotle (*Eth. Nic.* 1180a24–26) remarked, Sparta was exceptional in this. See *Pol.* 1337a31–32.

36. Xen. *Lac. Pol.* 2–4, Pl. *Leg.* 2.666e–667a, Plut. *Lyc.* 16.4–25. See Pl. *Leg.* 3.696a–b.

37. Xen. *Lac. Pol.* 5; Isoc. 11.18; Arist. *Pol.* 1263b36–1264a1, F611.13 (Rose); Plut. *Lyc.* 10, 12, *Mor.* 226d–227a, 236f; Porph. *Abst.* 4.4. See Pl. *Leg.* 8.842b. See also Alcman F98 (PMG) and Plut. *Mor.* 218d who call it the *andreîon*. Note also Justin 3.3.4.

38. Plutarch (*Mor.* 227f–228a) and Justin (3.3.8) seem to be describing the situation prior to the general liberalization of property law which took place in the fourth century. For this development, see Plut. *Agis* 5 and Arist. *Pol.* 1270a15–26. Note the emphasis which Justin places on the manner in which the absence of dowries limits the leverage of the wife and enables the husband to impose a discipline on her. In this connection, consider I.vii.5, note 115, below.

39. There is reason to suspect that, in this regard, Spartan arrangements regarding the inheritance of private property may have been similar to those at Gortyn—where, even when there were surviving sons, a daughter was entitled to inherit half a son's portion of the property left by their parents: see Hodkinson, "Land Tenure and Inheritance in Classical Sparta" 394–95, 398–404.

40. Plut. *Lys.* 30.6–7, *Mor.* 230a; Ael. *VH* 3.10, 6.4, 10.15. Note Pollux's reference (*Onom.* 3.48) to *díkē kakogamíou*. One should read Plut. *Ages.* 2.6 and *Mor.* 1d in light of Ath. 13.566a–b. See also 13.555c; Stob. *Flor.* 4.22.16 (Hense).

41. See, for example, Plut. *Lyc.* 13.5–7 (with Xen. *Ages.* 8.7), 27.1–5, *Mor.* 189e, 227c. See Arist. F611.13 (Rose) and Heraclid. Pont. *Pol.* 2.8 (Müller *FHG* II 211). There was evidently some sort of dress code as well, and it applied to both women (Arist. F611.13 [Rose]) and men (*Pol.* 1294b25–29; Plut. *Mor.* 237b, 239c; Justin 3.3.5). See also Plut. *Lyc.* 10.3.

42. See the material collected by G. E. M. de Ste. Croix, *The Origins of the Peloponnesian War* (Ithaca 1972) 137–38 (with 354–55).

43. Xen. *Lac. Pol.* 6.3–4, Arist. *Pol.* 1263a33–39. For their military use, see Xen. *Hell.* 6.4.10–11.

44. Thuc. 1.6.4, Xen. *Lac. Pol.* 7.3–4, Arist. *Pol.* 1294b19–29.

45. See Xen. *Hell.* 3.3.4–7; Pl. *Leg.* 6.776c–d, 777b–d; Arist. *Pol.* 1264a32–36, 1269a34–1269b12, 1272b16–22 (with 1330a25–28). To assess the impact on Spartan policy of the fear to which the helot danger gave rise, one should read Hdt. 7.235 (with Xen. *Hell.* 4.8.8, Diod. 14.84.5); Thuc. 4.3–5, 8–23, 26–41, 53–57, 5.35, 39.2–3, 44.3, 56.2–3, 115.2, 6.105.2, 7.18.3, 26.2, 86.3; Diod. 13.64.5–7 in light of Critias *Vorsokr.*[6] 88 B37; Thuc. 4.80 (with 1.132.4, 4.6, 41.3, 55.1, 5.14.3, 23.3, 35.6–7); Xen. *Lac. Pol.* 12.4; Plut. *Lyc.* 28, *Sol.* 22.1–3. The fact that the Spartans found the means to contain the helot threat should not be taken as evidence that it was not serious: cf. Richard J. A. Talbert, "The Role of the Helots in the Class Struggle at Sparta," *Historia* 38 (1989): 22–40.

46. For the emancipation of helots and their use as soldiers in war, see Ronald F. Willetts, "The *Neodamodeis*," *CPh* 49 (1954): 27–32; Yvon Garlan, "Les esclaves grecques en temps de guerre," in *Actes de colloque d'histoire sociale, 1970* (Paris 1972) 29–62 (esp. 40–48); K. W. Welwei, *Unfreie im antiken Kriegsdienst* (Wiesbaden 1974–77) I: *Athen und Sparta* 108–74; Teresa Alfieri Tonini, "Il problema dei *neodamodeis* nell'ambito della società spartana," *RIL* 109 (1975): 305–16; and Umberto Cozzoli, "Sparta e l'affrancamento degli iloti nel V e nel IV secolo," in *Sesta miscellanea greca e romana* (Rome 1978) 213–32. In this connection, one should perhaps also consider Detlef Lotze, "Mothakes," *Historia* 11 (1962): 427–35.

47. Plut. *Lyc.* 28.10.

48. At the time of the great earthquake of the 460s, the old helots of Laconia did rise up (note Thuc. 1.128.1, 132.4; then compare Diod. 11.63–64 and Plut. *Cim.* 16.4–7, 17.3 with Paus. 3.11.8; see also *Lyc.* 28.12); and after the Theban defeat of Sparta at Leuctra, many joined the invaders of Laconia: see Ephraim David, "Revolutionary Agitation in Sparta after Leuctra," *Athenaeum* 68 (1980): 299–308. Note also Thuc. 7.26.2. In general, see Ducat, "Aspects de l'hilotisme" 5–46 (esp. 24–38), and Paul Cartledge, "Rebels and Sambos in Classical Greece: A Comparative View," in *Crux: Essays Presented to G. E. M. de Ste. Croix on His 75th Birthday*, ed. Paul Cartledge and F. D. Harvey (Exeter 1985) 16–46 (esp. 40–46). For a somewhat different estimate of the situation in Laconia, see Arlette Roobaert, "Le danger hilote?" *Ktema* 2 (1977): 141–55, and James T. Chambers, "On Messenian and Laconian Helots in the Fifth Century B.C.," *The Historian* 40 (1977–78): 271–85.

49. Arist. *Pol.* 1269b36–39.

50. See Xen. *Hell.* 3.3.4–7; Pl. *Leg.* 6.776c–d, 777b–d; Arist. *Pol.* 1269a34–1269b12, 1272b17–22 (with 1330a25–28); Ath. 6.264f–265a. According to Strabo (8.4.10), the Spartans defeated the Messenians in war on four different occasions: at the time of the original conquest in the late eighth century, again some two generations later at the time of the revolt which Tyrtaeus helped crush, and then twice thereafter. Strabo no doubt had in mind the well-known uprising which took place in the wake of the great earthquake of the mid-460s, continued for a decade thereafter, and ended not with a Spartan victory but with a negotiated withdrawal of the rebels: Thuc. 1.101.1–103.3; Diod. 11.63–64, 84.8; Plut. *Cim.* 16.4–17.3; Paus. 1.29.8–9, 4.24.5–7; [Xen.] *Ath. Pol.* 3.11; Ar. *Lys.* 1138–44 with

the scholia; note also Lewis, *Sparta and Persia* 46 with n. 135. The timing of the
fourth war is less certain, but there is reason to accept Plato's claim (*Leg.* 3.692d,
698d–e) that the helots were also in revolt on the eve of Marathon: see W. P.
Wallace, "Kleomenes, Marathon, the Helots, and Arkadia," *JHS* 74 (1954): 32–35,
who makes a strong case for the view that the events described at Paus. 4.23.5–10
took place at this time and not in the seventh century. In this connection, see also
E. S. G. Robinson, "Rhegion, Zankle-Messana and the Samians," *JHS* 66 (1946):
13–20, and *GHI* 1.22. Herodotus's silence concerning the revolt (6.120) is a token
of the effectiveness of Spartan attempts to maintain strict secrecy (Thuc. 5.68.2)
concerning internal matters.

51. For the importance of Argive hostility, see Arist. *Pol.* 1269a39–1269b5.
The recent discovery of a new fragment of Tyrtaeus (*POxy.* 3316=F23a [West])
confirms the contention of Pausanias (2.24.7, 3.2.2–3, 7.3–6, 4.5.1–3, 10.1, 6–7,
11.1–8, 14.1, 8, 15.7, 17.2, 7, 8.27.1) that Argos was already hostile to Sparta in
the very early years of the archaic period. Note also Xen. *Hell.* 3.5.11, Strabo
8.4.10. Cf. Thomas Kelly, "The Traditional Enmity between Sparta and Argos:
The Birth and Development of a Myth," *AHR* 75 (1970): 971–1003. The hatred did
not wane with the passage of time. For the battle of champions in about 546 B.C.,
see Hdt. 1.82 and Paus. 2.38.5. The battle of Sepeia occurred either shortly before 519 (see Paus. 3.4.1 with Hdt. 6.108.2, Thuc. 2.68.5, and Arnold W. Gomme,
Antony Andrewes, and Kenneth J. Dover, *An Historical Commentary on Thucydides*
[Oxford 1945–80] II 358) or—more likely—about 494 (Hdt. 6.76–83, 7.148). For
subsequent relations, see Hdt. 7.148–53, 8.72–73, 9.12, 35.2; Thuc. 2.27.2, 4.56.2,
57.3, 5.14.4, 41, 69–83, 6.7.1–2, 95.1, 105, 7.26, 57.9, 8.25, 27.6, 86.8–9; Xen. *Hell.*
1.3.13, 2.2.7, 3.5.1, 11, 4.2.17–23, 3.15–17, 4.1–14, 19, 5.1–2, 7.2–7, 8.15, 5.1.34–36,
6.5.16–50, 7.1.29–33, 45, 2.1–10, 4.27–30, 5.5; Diod. 12.75.5–7, 77.2–3, 78.1–80.3,
14.82, 86, 92, 97.5, 15.23.4, 40.3–4, 62–65, 68, 70.3, 75.3, 84–85, 16.34.3, 39.

52. This can be inferred from Hdt. 9.10.1, 28.2, 29.1 (which match the claim
made at 61.2 nicely). As the population of *hómoioi* declined (I.v.4, note 141,
below), the situation became worse. Consider Xen. *Hell.* 3.3.4–5. Even after Messenia had become independent, the helots remained numerous. Plutarch (*Cleom.*
18.3) claims that Aetolians invading the region in the third century were able
to run off with fifty thousand slaves; the observation made by one Spartan that
these invaders had helped the city by lightening its burden indicates that virtually all of those taken were helots. The extent of that burden in earlier times
helps explain the intensity of the Spartan eagerness to conserve manpower:
Hdt. 7.205.32; Thuc. 4.15, 19.1, 5.15; Diod. 13.52.3; Andem *FGrH* 324 F44;
Plut. *Ages.* 30. Figueira, "Mess Contributions and Subsistence at Sparta" 87–
109, doubts whether the cultivable land available to the helots and their Spartiate masters could support the population implicit in the ratio seven-to-one. He
would reduce the proportion to something like 4.38-to-one, and to make sense of
Herodotus's testimony, he suggests that the Spartans must have taken virtually
every adult male helot with them to Plataea. His argument is grounded on too
many questionable estimates—concerning the age-structure of the population,
the amount of land available to the Spartiates, the carrying capacity of that land,
and so forth—to be accorded great weight.

53. For the hostility of the *períoikoi* to Sparta, see Xen. *Hell.* 3.3.6, and note the
manner in which they comported themselves when the opportunity for rebellion presented itself: Thuc. 1.101.2; Xen. *Hell.* 6.5.25, 32, 7.2.2, *Ages.* 2.24; Plut.

Ages. 32.12. See also Paul Cartledge, *Sparta and Lakonia* (London 1979) 178–93, and Ephraim David, "Revolutionary Agitation in Sparta after Leuctra" 299–308. On the *períoikoi* in general, note also Franz Hampl, "Die Lakedaemonischen Perioeken," *Hermes* 72 (1937): 1–49.

54. Sparta formed her alliance system within the Peloponnesus gradually in the course of the second half of the sixth century. The Lacedaemonians first defeated Tegea, persuaded her to deny refuge to fugitive helots, and made of her an ally: see Hdt. 1.65.1, 66–69 with Plut. *Mor.* 292b as interpreted by Felix Jacoby, "*Chrēstoùs Poieîn* (Aristotle fr. 592R)," *Abhandlungen zur Griechischen Geschichteschreibung,* ed. Herbert Bloch (Leiden 1956) 342–43. See also D. M. Leahy, "The Spartan Defeat at Orchomenus," *Phoenix* 12 (1958): 139–65. Then, step by step, they extended their area of control, using a crusade against tyranny as a pretext: see Hdt. 1.68.6; Thuc. 1.18.1; Plut. *Mor.* 859b–d; *FGrH* 105 F1; and Paus. 7.1.8 with D. M. Leahy, "Chilon and Aeschines: A Further Consideration of Rylands Greek Papyrus fr. 18," *BRL* 38 (1955–56): 406–35, and "The Bones of Tisamenus," *Historia* 4 (1955): 26–38. In general, see G. L. Huxley, *Early Sparta* (London 1962) 67–76. Perhaps as a result of Sparta's abortive attempt to extend her control beyond the Peloponnesus (Hdt. 5.55–95), her most important Peloponnesian allies (apart from Corinth) showed signs of serious disaffection in the 490s and 480s. For Tegea, see Hdt. 6.74–75, 9.37.4. Mantineia withdrew from Thermopylae before the battle (7.202, 222), and both Mantineia and Elis arrived late for the struggle at Plataea (9.77)—a failure which cost the former, but not the latter (*GHI* 1.27; Paus. 5.23.1–4), credit for participating in the struggle against the Mede. Elis escaped public censure but presumably only because one of the two thank-offerings was set up and inscribed at Olympia, which she controlled. The battle at Plataea was not unexpected, and the late arrival of the Eleians and Mantineians can hardly have been accidental. See Antony Andrewes, "Sparta and Arcadia in the Early Fifth Century," *Phoenix* 6 (1952): 1–5. Though the extent and precise character remain in doubt, trouble erupted once again in the 460s: see the admittedly speculative arguments of W. G. G. Forrest, "Themistocles and Argos," *CQ* n.s. 10 (1960): 221–41, and "Pausanias and Themistokles Again," *Lakonikai Spoudai* 2 (1975): 115–20, and note the criticism made by J. L. O'Neil, "The Exile of Themistokles and Democracy in the Peloponnese," *CQ* n.s. 31 (1981): 335–46. The alliance fell apart once more in the aftermath of the Peace of Nicias (Thuc. 5.13–83; Diod. 12.75.1–76.3, 77.2–3, 78.1–80.3, 81.2–5; Plut. *Alc.* 14–15). Corinth broke away for a time in the early fourth century (Xen. *Hell.* 2.4.30, 3.2.25, 5.1–2, 5, 17, 23, 4.2.9–23, 3.15, 4.1–19, 5.1–19, 8.10–11, 5.1.29–36; Diod. 14.17.7, 82, 86, 92.1–2, 97.5, 110.2–3; Plut. *Ages.* 16.6–19.4, 21.1–23.5); and, of course, the alliance collapsed altogether after Sparta's defeat at Leuctra: Xen. *Hell.* 6.5, 7.1–5; Diod. 15.59, 62–72, 77–78, 82–89; Plut. *Ages.* 30–35. At that time, Messenia regained her independence: Diod. 15.66, Plut. *Ages.* 34.1–2.

55. Xen. *Hell.* 4.2.11–12.

56. Cf. Xen. *Hell.* 7.1.10 and Arist. *Pol.* 1270a29–34 with *WoM* II 173: *Considérations sur les causes de la grandeur des Romains et de leur décadence* 18.

57. Thucydides (cf. 8.40.2 with 24.4) hints at this. So does Isocrates (12.177–81). See Lys. 33.7. For the salutary effect of such fear, see Pl. *Leg.* 3.699c, Arist. *Pol.* 1308a24–30. What the helot threat did for the citizens of Sparta, the Etruscans, Samnites, Gauls, and Carthaginians accomplished for the Roman aristocracy: cf. Sall. *Iug.* 41.3 with Jochen Martin, "Dynasteia," in *Historische Semantik und Begriffs-*

geschichte, ed. Reinhart Koselleck (Stuttgart 1978) 228–41. See Preston H. Epps, "Fear in Spartan Character," *CPh* 28 (1933): 12–29.

58. Thuc. 1.23.6, 68–71, 88, 118.2, 5.107, 109.

59. See, for example, Hdt. 9.46–48 and Thuc. 5.63–65. When successful in routing the foe, the Spartans were more concerned with minimizing their own losses than with making their victory complete. Thus, where the Athenians were inclined to charge forward, press home their advantage, and slaughter or capture as many as possible of those who had taken to heel, the Spartans tended to hold back and to remain in formation under the protection afforded by their phalanx: cf. Thuc. 1.70.2–5 with 5.73.4, and see Paus. 4.8.11; Plut. *Lyc.* 22.9–10, *Mor.* 228f. For similar reasons, the Lacedaemonians were prohibited from dispersing to strip the bodies of the enemy dead: Plut. *Mor.* 228f–229a and Ael. *VH* 6.6.

60. Cf. the charge made at Thuc. 5.105.3–4 with the pattern of behavior evidenced at 3.52–68.

61. Even among their allies, the Spartans were notorious (Hdt. 9.54.1) for thinking one thing and saying another. They were even supposed (Paus. 4.17.2) to have invented the stratagem of securing victory by bribing key figures on the enemy side. Note also Plut. *Ages.* 32.14, *Marc.* 22, *Mor.* 238f: it was considered more glorious to win by trickery than in a pitched battle.

62. Plut. *Cleom.* 9.1–2. In this connection, note Ernst Bernert, *RE* XX:1 (1941) 309–18.

63. Paus. 3.5.8. The evidence for Spartan piety is ubiquitous: see Hdt. 1.65–70, 5.42–46, 62–75, 90–93, 6.52–86, 105–7, 120 (cf. Pl. *Leg.* 3.698c–e, Paus. 4.15.2, Strabo 8.4.9), 7.133–37, 204–6, 220–21, 239, 8.141, 9.7–11, 19, 33–38, 61–62, 64–65, 73, 78–81, 85; Thuc. 1.103, 112, 118, 126–34, 2.74, 3.14–15, 92, 4.5, 118, 5.16–18, 23, 30, 49–50, 54, 75–76, 82, 116, 6.95, 7.18, 8.6; Xen. *Hell.* 3.1.17–19, 23–24, 2.21–31, 3.1–5, 4.3–4, 6, 11, 15, 18, 23, 5.5, 23–25, 4.2.20, 3.14, 21, 5.1–2, 11, 6.10, 7.2–5, 7, 5.1.29, 33, 3.14, 19, 27, 4.37, 41, 47, 49, 6.4.2–3 (cf. 7–8), 15–16, 5.12, 17–18, 7.1.31, 34, *Lac. Pol.* 8.5, 13.2–5, 8–9, 15.2–5, 9, *Ages.* 1.2, 10–13, 27, 31, 2.13–15, 17, 3.2–5, 8.7, 11.1–2, 8, 16. See also Plut. *Pel.* 21.3.

64. Pl. *Leg.* 1.634d–e. See Dem. 20.106. For the divine origins of Spartan law, see Tyrtaeus F4 (West); Hdt. 1.65.2–3; Xen. *Lac. Pol.* 8.5; Pl. *Leg.* 1.624a, 632d, 2.662c–d, 3.691d–692a, 696b; Polyb. 10.2.9–13; Cic. *Div.* 1.43.96; Strabo 10.4.19; Plut. *Lyc.* 5.4, 6.1–6; Justin 3.3.10; August. *De civ. D.* 2.16. See also Pl. *Leg.* 6.762e. Note also Justin 3.3.11–12.

65. Soph. *Aj.* 1073–84.

66. Consider Robert Parker, "Spartan Religion," in *Classical Sparta: Techniques behind Her Success*, ed. Anton Powell (Norman, Okla., 1988) 142–72 with an eye to Xen. *Symp.* 8.35. For an intriguing attempt partially to explain why the Spartans were so exceptionally pious, see Paul Cartledge, "Seismicity and Spartan Society," *LCM* 1 (1976): 25–28. Note Hodkinson, "Social Order and Conflict of Values in Classical Sparta" 273–76.

67. Though originally published in 1912, Martin Nilsson's essay "Die Grundlagen des spartanischen Lebens," *Opuscula Selecta* (Lund 1952) II 826–69 (esp. 826–49), remains valuable—particularly for its discussion of the similar institutions to be found in the tribes of Africa and the South Seas. See also Jeanmaire, *Couroi et courètes* 147–227, 463–588, with Louis Gernet, "Structures sociales et rites d'adolescence dans la Grèce antique," *Les Grecs sans miracle*, ed. Riccardo di Donato (Paris 1983) 201–11. Recent work paying particular attention to the

relevant anthropological literature includes Angelo Brelich, *Paides e parthenoi* I (Rome 1969) 113–207; Pierre Vidal-Naquet, "The Black Hunter and the Origin of the Athenian *Ephebia*" and "Recipes for Greek Adolescence," *The Black Hunter: Forms of Thought and Forms of Society in the Greek World*, trans. Andrew Szegedy-Maszak (Baltimore 1986) 106–56; and Jean-Pierre Vernant, "Between Shame and Glory: The Identity of the Young Spartan Warrior," *Mortals and Immortals: Collected Essays*, ed. Froma I. Zeitlin (Princeton 1991) 220–43.

68. Pl. *Leg.* 2.666e–667a, Plut. *Lyc.* 16.7–9. See also Xen. *Lac. Pol.* 2.1–11.

69. See Plut. *Lyc.* 24.1. See WoJJR III 381–82: *Du contrat social* 2.7.

70. Plut. *Lyc.* 21, 24.5. Note Thuc. 5.69.2. For the dances, see Henri Jeanmaire, "La cryptie lacédémonienne," *REG* 26 (1913): 143 n. 2. Note Paus. 3.11.9.

71. Consider Xen. *Lac. Pol.* 2.3–9, *An.* 4.6.14–15; Arist. F611.13 (Rose); Plut. *Lyc.* 16.10–14, 17.4–18.2, *Mor.* 237e–f, 239d in light of Pl. *Leg.* 1.633b–c.

72. See Thuc. 5.69.2–70, Polyb. 4.20.6, Val. Max. 2.6.2, Plut. *Mor.* 238b, Ath. 14.630e–631c (with 627b–d, 628e–f). See also Pl. *Leg.* 1.633b–c, 2.654a–662c. One should probably interpret what we are told (Paus. 3.14.8–10, Cic. *Tusc.* 5.27.77, Lucian *Anach.* 38, Plut. *Mor.* 290d) of the mock battles among the Spartan youth in light of the parallel discussion in Ephorus (*FGrH* 70 F149 [ap. Strabo 10.4.18, 20]) and Aristotle (F611.15 [Rose]) of the practice on Crete. It is clearly not fortuitous that, at Sparta, flute playing was an hereditary office: cf. Hdt. 6.60 with Thuc. 5.70. See, in this connection, Everett L. Wheeler, "*Hoplomachia* and Greek Dances in Arms," *GRBS* 23 (1982): 223–33, and "The *Hoplomachoi* and Vegetius' Spartan Drillmasters," *Chiron* 13 (1983): 1–20. Note Lillian B. Lawler, *The Dance in Ancient Greece* (Middletown, Conn., 1964).

73. Ath. 14.632f–633a.

74. Pind. F189 (Bowra).

75. Terpander F6 (Bergk) should be read with Hellanicus *FGrH* 4 F85; Plut. *Mor.* 1134b–c, 1146b–c; Ath. 14.635f. See also Arist. F545 (Rose).

76. Alcm. F41 (PMG).

77. Pratinas F2 (PMG).

78. For the details, see Felix Bölte, "Zu Lakonischen Festen," *RhM* 78 (1929): 124–43. Note also H. T. Wade Gery, "A Note on the Origin of the Spartan Gymnopaidiai," *CQ* 43 (1949): 79–81. In this connection, one should also consult Jeanmaire, *Couroi et courètes* 513–40; Angelo Brelich, *Guerre, agoni et culti nella Grecia arcaica* (Bonn 1961) esp. 22–39, 74–84; and Jean-Pierre Vernant, "Une divinité des marges: Artémis Orthia," in *Recherches sur les cultes grecs et l'occident* II (Naples 1984) 13–28.

79. See Plut. *Mor.* 1146b–c with 779a. In judging what may seem an extravagant claim, one should consider the parallel testimony of Polybius concerning Arcadia: 4.17.3–21.12.

80. Pind. *Pyth.* 5.63–81.

81. Arist. *Pol.* 1339b2–4. See also Pl. *Leg.* 2.659d–661d, 666e.

82. In this connection, one should ponder the role assigned to the Spartan Dracontius by the Ten Thousand: Xen. *An.* 4.8.25–28.

83. Consider the testimony of Plato: *Resp.* 2.375b–403c, 10.606e–608b, *Leg.* 2.654c–671a, 3.700a–701b, 4.719b–e, 7.801a–804b, 810b–813a, 817a–d, 8.829c–e, 10.890a, 11.935e–936b, 12.941b.

84. Johann Peter Eckermann, *Gespräche mit Goethe* (Jena 1905) II 298–99: Conversation held 1 April 1827.

85. For a restatement of the ancient position, see Alfarabi, *Aphorisms* §§ 50–52, with William F. Boggess, "Alfarabi and the Rhetoric: The Cave Revisited," *Phronesis* 15 (1970): 86–90. Note Lycurg. 98–109.

86. Plut. *Lyc.* 21.2. See also *Mor.* 238a–b; Ath. 14.632f–633a.

87. Pl. *Leg.* 3.680c–e. Of course, if forced to choose between Homer and Hesiod, the Spartans would embrace the former as their poet and relegate the latter to their helots: Plut. *Mor.* 223a.

88. Plato (*Leg.* 1.629a–630d, 2.666e–667a, 9.858e) treats Tyrtaeus as the poet supreme in Lacedaemon. See Dio Chrys. *Orat.* 2.29.

89. Cf. Ath. 14.630f with Thuc. 5.69.2, and see Plut. *Mor.* 238b.

90. Philochorus *FGrH* 328 F216.

91. Tyrtaeus F2 (West).

92. Deut. 8:7–8. The rigor of Spartan life caused some Jews to suppose that Spartan law derived from Abraham: 1 Macc. 12; Joseph. *AJ* 12.225–27, 13.164–70. See Michael Ginsburg, "Sparta and Judaea," *CPh* 29 (1934): 117–22.

93. Tyrtaeus F4 (West).

94. Tyrtaeus F5–7 (West).

95. Consider Myron of Priene *FGrH* 106 F2 in light of Theognis 53–58 (West); Ar. *Nub.* 69–72, *Lys.* 1150–56, *Eccl.* 720–24; and Poll. *Onom.* 7.68, and see Plut. *Lyc.* 28.8–10, *Demetr.* 1, *Mor.* 239a–b. In this connection, one should read Pl. *Leg.* 7.816d–e. Note also Theopomp. *FGrH* 115 F13. See Jean Ducat, "Le mépris des hilotes," *Annales (ESC)* 29 (1974): 1451–64, and Ephraim David, "Laughter in Spartan Society," in *Classical Sparta* 1–25. Those who find the ancient books on the interpretation of dreams no more outlandish than those by Sigmund Freud may still find something of use in Georges Devereux's discussion of the relations between the helots and their masters: "La psychanalyse et l'histoire: Une application à l'histoire de Sparte," *Annales (ESC)* 20 (1965): 18–44.

96. For an overview, read Xen. *Lac. Pol.* 2–3, *An.* 4.6.14–15, 4.8.25 (with 4.7.16); Isoc. 12.211–17; Paus. 3.16.7–11; Plut. *Lyc.* 16–18, 21, 28, *Mor.* 237a–238d, 239d; Lucian *Anach.* 38; Ael. *VH* 7 (with Stat. *Theb.* 4.233, Philostr. *VA* 6.20, Tert. *Ad Martyras* 4, Libanius *Or.* 1.23, and Themistius *Or.* 21.250a); and Hesychius *Boúa*, *Bouagór*, in conjunction with R. C. Bosanquet, "Excavations at Sparta, 1906: 5. The Sanctuary of Artemis Orthia," *ABSA* 12 (1905–6) 303–17 (esp. 312–17); K. M. T. Chrimes, *Ancient Sparta: A Re-examination of the Evidence* (Manchester 1949) 84–136; and Françoise Frontisi-Ducroux, "La *bomolochia*: Autour de l'embuscade à l'autel," in *Recherches sur les cultes grecs et l'occident* II 29–49. For evidence pertinent to the dances and the masks worn, consider Hdt. 6.129–30; Ar. *Nub.* 553–56, *Eq.* 697, *Lys.* 82, 1242–76, 1296–1308, *Plut.* 279 (all with the attendant scholia); Schol. Eur. *Hec.* 934; Xen. *Hell.* 4.5.11, *Ages.* 2.17 (with *An.* 6.1.11); Sosibius *FGrH* 595 F7 (ap. Ath. 14.621d–f); Verg. *G.* 2.487–88; Lucian *Salt.* 10–12; Libanius *Or.* 64.17; Ath. 14.629f–631d, 15.678c; Poll. *Onom.* 4.99–107 (with Ar. *Nub.* 540–48 and the attendant scholia, Theophr. *Char.* 6.3, Paus. 6.22.1), 150–51 (with Ar. *Plut.* 1050–94); Hesychius s.v. *Brudalícha, Brullichistaí, deikēlistaí* (with Plut. *Ages.* 21.8, *Mor.* 212f, and Schol. Ap. Rhod. *Argon.* 1.746), *thermastrís, kalabís, kórdax, kordakízeia, kordakismoí, koruthalístriai* (with Ath. 4.139a–b), *kulínthion, kúnthion, kúrithra, kurittoí, turbasía*, and Phot. *Bibl.* s.v. *kallabís, móthōn* (with Ath. 14.618c), in light of R. M. Dawkins, "Excavations at Spartan, 1906: 6. Remains of the Archaic Greek Period," and Bosanquet, "7. The Cult of Orthia as Illustrated by the Finds," *ABSA* 12 (1905–6) 318–30 (esp. 324–26), 331–43 (esp. 338–43); Guy

Dickins, "The Terracotta Masks," in *The Sanctuary of Artemis Orthia at Sparta*, ed. R. M. Dawkins (London 1929) 163–86 (with plates xlvii–lxii); and Arthur Pickard-Cambridge, *Dithyramb, Tragedy and Comedy*[2], rev. T. B. L. Webster (Oxford 1962) 132–87 (esp. 132–37, 162–69). After digesting this material, peruse Pl. *Rep.* 3.412e–414a and *Leg.* 1.633a–2.674c (esp. 671b–d), 7.812b–817d (esp. 815c–d, 816d–e), and ponder the seminal discussion of Vernant, "Between Shame and Glory: The Identity of the Young Spartan Warrior" 220–43. Note, in this connection, Vernant and Frontisi-Ducroux, "Features of the Mask in Ancient Greece," in Vernant and Pierre Vidal-Naquet, *Myth and Tragedy in Ancient Greece*, trans. Janet Lloyd (New York 1988) 189–206 (esp. 195–201). For comparative data from other Greek cities, see Frontisi-Ducroux, "L'homme, le cerf, et le berger: Chemins grecs de la civilité," *TR* 4 (1983): 53–76, and Denise Fourgous, "Gloire et infamie des seigneurs de l'Eubée," *Metis* 2 (1987): 5–30; and consider H. J. Rose, "Greek Rites of Stealing," *HThR* 34 (1941): 1–5, with Hdt. 3.48.

97. Consider Plut. *Cleom.* 2.4 in light of Tyrtaeus F10 (West). Cf. Plut. *Mor.* 235f with 959a–b.

98. Tyrtaeus F11 (West).

99. Cf. Tyrtaeus F12 (West) with Hom. *Il.* 11.784 (cf. 6.208–9) and *Od.* 1.1–3. See, in particular, Werner Jaeger, "Tyrtaeus on True Arete," *Five Essays* (Montreal 1966) 103–42. See also H. James Shey, "Tyrtaeus and the Art of Propaganda," *Arethusa* 9 (1976): 5–28; Charles Fuqua, "Tyrtaeus and the Cult of Heroes," *GRBS* 22 (1981): 215–26, and Theodore A. Tarkow, "Tyrtaeus 9D: The Role of Poetry in the New Sparta," *AC* 52 (1983): 48–69.

100. Tyrtaeus F12.1–9 (West).

101. Tyrtaeus F12.10–22 (West).

102. See P. A. L. Greenhalgh, "Patriotism in the Homeric World," *Historia* 21 (1972): 528–37, and compare Hom. *Il.* 22.38–76 (esp. 71–76) with Tyrtaeus F10.23–27 (West).

103. Arist. F611.13 (Rose).

104. See, for example, Paus. 3.12.9, 14.1, and note R. Ball, "Herodotos' List of the Spartans Who Died at Thermopylai," *MusAfr* 5 (1976): 1–8, and W. R. Connor, "Pausanias 3.14.1: A Sidelight on Spartan History, C. 440 B.C." *TAPhA* 109 (1979): 21–27. Only those who died in battle had their names inscribed on their tombstones: consider *IG* V 1 701–3, 706–7 in light of Plut. *Lyc.* 27.3, *Mor.* 238d, and see Franz Willemsen, "Zu den Lakedämoniergräbern im Kerameikos," *MDAI(A)* 92 (1977): 117–57. Those who distinguished themselves in so dying might receive the prize of valor (*aristeîa*) and even become the subject of song: see W. Kenrick Pritchett, *The Greek State at War* (Berkeley 1971–   ) II 285; note Plut. *Lyc.* 21.2 and Ael. *VH* 6.6; and consider Bölte, "Zu Lakonischen Festen" 124–32 (esp. 130 n. 6), and Wade Gery, "A Note on the Origin of the Spartan Gymnopaidiai" 79–81 (esp. 80 n. 4), in conjunction with Hdt. 1.82. The bodies of those who fought well would be crowned with olive wreaths; those granted the prize of valor (*hoi dè teléōs aristeúsantes*) would be buried in a purple cloak. For a somewhat different approach, see Nicole Loraux, "La 'belle mort' spartiate," *Ktema* 2 (1977): 105–20.

105. Tyrtaeus F12.23–34 (West). Note Xen. *Hell.* 5.4.33.

106. There were formal mechanisms for selecting those who had distinguished themselves: consider Hdt. 8.124 and Thuc. 2.25.2 in light of Lewis, *Sparta and Persia* 42 n. 102, and see Plut. *Ages.* 34.8–11 (with Ael. *VH* 6.3 and Polyaen. 2.9), 35.1–2.

107. Tyrtaeus F12.35–44 (West).

108. These practices were also designed to discomfit and terrify the foe: cf. Hdt. 7.208–9 with 1.82, and see Xen. *Lac. Pol.* 11.3, 13.8; Plut. *Mor.* 238f; Ael. *VH* 6.6. According to Tacitus (*Germ.* 38), the Suevi wore their hair long for similar reasons and their chiefs prepared for battle in a similar fashion.

109. For the consumption of wine and its purpose, see Xen. *Hell.* 6.4.8 (with Plut. *Dion* 30.5). Throughout history, soldiers have tended to fortify themselves with drink or drugs just before confronting the foe: see John Keegan, *The Face of Battle* (New York 1976) 113–14, 181–82, 241, 326. For the use of the flute, see Thuc. 5.70 and Plut. *Mor.* 238b with I.v.2, note 72, above. For the purpose of the paean, see Aesch. *Sept.* 270; Thuc. 5.70; Diod. 5.34.5; Plut. *Lyc.* 21.4, 22.5–7, *Mor.* 238b. See also Pritchett, *The Greek State at War* I 105–8.

110. Plut. *Lyc.* 21.7, *Mor.* 238b. In this connection, see also Dio Chrys. *Or.* 2.31M, 92R; Val. Max. 2.6.2.

111. Martin Nilsson's reconstruction ("Die Grundlagen des spartanischen Lebens" 826–49) of the stages of the *agōgē* needs adjustment in light of the arguments and evidence presented by Aubrey Diller, "A New Source on the Spartan *Ephebeia*," *AJPh* 62 (1941): 499–501; Chrimes, *Ancient Sparta* 84–117; C. M. Tazelaar, "PAIDES KAI EPHEBOI: Some Notes on the Spartan Stages of Youth," *Mnemosyne* 20 (1967): 127–53; Hodkinson, "Social Order and Conflict of Values in Classical Sparta" 249–50; and MacDowell, *Spartan Law* 159–67. Cf. Albert Billheimer, "Tà déka aph hébēs," *TAPhA* 77 (1946): 214–20, and H. I. Marrou, "Les Classes d'age de la jeunesse spartiate," *REA* 48 (1946): 216–330. For comparative material, see Heinrich Schurtz, *Altersklassen und Männerbünde: Eine Darstellung der Grundformen der Gesellschaft* (Berlin 1902), and Bernardo Bernardi, *Age Class Systems: Social Institutions and Polities Based on Age*, trans. David I. Kertzer (Cambridge 1985).

112. For the stages through which a young Spartan advanced, cf. Xen. *Lac. Pol.* 2–4 with *Hell.* 5.4.32; see Plut. *Lyc.* 16.1–2, 7, 12, 17.3–4, 22.1–6; and consider the evidence contained in the so-called Herodotus and Strabo glosses (which are conveniently reprinted by MacDowell, *Spartan Law* 161) in light of the literature cited in note 111, above. The existence of a formal *dokimasía* by the magistrates stands to reason and can be inferred from occasional allusions in the ancient texts. We are told of the scrutiny that took place shortly after a child's birth (Plut. *Lyc.* 16.1–2); there is evidence (Ael. *VH* 6.3, which should be read with Plut. *Ages.* 34.8–11) suggesting that, at one or more stages in the course of his education, each *paîs* could expect to be given a formal looking over. That he would again be subjected to scrutiny when he became a *paidískos* can be inferred from Xenophon's reference (*Hell.* 5.4.25) to someone who had just graduated *ek paídōn* as *eudokimótatos*, and Plutarch's reference (*Lyc.* 17.1) to *hoi eudokímoi néoi* suggests that those who entered adulthood and came to be called *hoi hēbôntes* or *hoi néoi* were once again put through a *dokimasía*: consider Xenophon's use of the word *eudokímos* at *Lac. Pol.* 13.9 with this possibility in mind, and see Willem den Boer, *Laconian Studies* (Amsterdam 1954) 284–88, in conjunction with notes 122 and 125, below.

113. See Plut. *Lyc.* 16.7–19.13.

114. Pl. *Leg.* 1.633b–c (with the scholia); Arist. F538, 611.10 (Rose); Heraclid. Pont. *Pol.* 2.4 (Müller *FHG* II 210); Plut. *Lyc.* 28.2–4, *Cleom.* 28.4. See Justin 3.3.6–7. Henri Jeanmaire, "La cryptie lacédémonienne" 121–50, elucidates the nature of this institution by drawing attention to African parallels. Consider Jeanmaire, *Couroi et courètes* 510, 550–69, and Chrimes, *Ancient Sparta* 374–76, in light

of Arnold Van Gennep, *The Rites of Passage*, trans. Monika B. Vizedom and Gabrielle L. Caffee (Chicago 1961). See below, note 121.

115. See Xen. *Lac. Pol.* 10.7 with Plut. *Mor.* 238e and with Arist. *Pol.* 1271a26–36. See also Teles F3 (Hense) ap. Stob. *Flor.* 3.40.8 (Hense).

116. Plut. *Lyc.* 12.3, Porph. *Abst.* 4.4. Cf. Schol. Pl. *Leg.* 1.633a, where the number of members mentioned is ten, and Plut. *Agis* 8.4, where the reinstituted *sussitía* of the late third century is to include hundreds of members.

117. Consider Hdt. 1.65.6; Plut. *Mor.* 226d–e; Polyaen. 2.1.15, 3.11, in light of Xen. *Cyr.* 2.1.28. The members were called tentmates (*súskēnoi*): Xen. *Lac. Pol.* 7.4, 9.4, 15.5. See also Pl. *Leg.* 1.625c–626b, 633a.

118. Plut. *Lyc.* 12.9–11.

119. Persaeus *FGrH* 584 F2.

120. Consider Critias *Vorsokr.*[6] 88 B32–37; Xen. *Lac. Pol.* 5.2–8; Pl. *Leg.* 1.637a (with 639d–e); Sosibius *FGrH* 595 F19; Plut. *Lyc.* 12, 25.4 (with *Cleom.* 9.1), *Mor.* 224d; and Ath. 141a–e in light of N. R. E. Fisher, "Drink, *Hybris* and the Promotion of Harmony in Sparta," in *Classical Sparta* 26–50, and see David, "Laughter in Spartan Society" 1–4. Cf. Hdt. 6.84.

121. For the existence of a system of garrisons headed by harmosts, see H. W. Parke, "The Evidence for Harmosts in Laconia," *Hermathena* 46 (1931): 31–38. The institution of the *agronómoi* devised by Plato (*Leg.* 6.762e–763c, 778d–779a) is apparently a close imitation of the Spartan arrangement: see *PLondon* No. 187—which is discussed by Paul Girard, "Sur la cryptie des Lacédémoniens," *REG* 11 (1898): 31–38, and "*Krypteia*," in *Dictionnaire des antiquités grecques et romaines d'après les textes et les monuments*, ed. Charles Victor Daremberg and Edm. Saglio (Graz 1962–63) III:1 871–73, who confuses the system of garrisons with the *krupteía*. While in his twenties, a Spartan could expect to spend two years on patrol. Without some such arrangement, it is inconceivable that the Spartans could have maintained their dominion—particularly that in Messenia (above, note 114). Although the Athenian ephebes performed some functions comparable to those performed by the Spartans doing garrison service (Aeschin. 2.167, Arist. *Ath. Pol.* 42.2–5), they had more in common with the Spartans undergoing the *krupteía*: see Vidal-Naquet, "The Black Hunter and the Origin of the Athenian Ephebia," *The Black Hunter* 106–28; John J. Winkler, "The Ephebes' Song: *Tragōidia* and *Polis*," in *Nothing to Do with Dionysos? Athenian Drama in Its Social Context*, ed. John J. Winkler and Froma I. Zeitlin (Princeton 1990) 20–62; and Pierre Vidal-Naquet, "The Black Hunter Revisited," *PCPhS* 212 (1986): 126–44. Cf. Arist. *Pol.* 1331a19–23, 1331b14–17, which is an adaptation of Spartan practice to the needs of a walled city.

122. See Plut. *Lyc.* 15.7–8. See also Xen. *Lac. Pol.* 1.5, Plut. *Mor.* 228a–b, *Suda* s.v. Lukourgos. Within the ordinary Greek city, it was customary to refer to those under thirty as "the young men (*hoi néoi*)" (Xen. *Mem.* 1.2.35, Polyb. 4.20.7), and we know that, at Sparta, those under that age were subject to special restrictions: Plut. *Lyc.* 25.1. This has led scholars to presume that the *néoi* referred to at Plut. *Lyc.* 15.7–8 are Spartiates in their twenties: see, for example, MacDowell, *Spartan Law* 78–79. However, in classifying citizens among the *neótēs*, as in so many other things, Sparta was an exception: consider Hdt. 7.234.2, 9.10.1, 12.2 in light of H. T. Wade Gery, "The Spartan Rhetra in Plutarch, *Lycurgus* VI," *Essays in Greek History* (Oxford 1958) 82, and note Thucydides' use (2.8.1 and, in one manuscript, 4.80.3) of the same term; then see Cartledge, *Agesilaos and the Crisis*

of Sparta 21, and consider Xenophon's claim (*Ages.* 1.6) that Agesilaus was *éti néos* when he became king in about 400 in light of the fact (*Hell.* 5.4.13) that he was over sixty in 379 and in light of the evidence (*Ages.* 2.28, Plut. *Ages.* 36.3, 40.3) indicating that he was in his eighties and had been king for more than forty years when he died in or shortly after 360. This peculiar, technical use of the term *néos* and its cognates by the Spartans almost certainly underlies the report which Diodorus (13.76.2) drew on when he claimed that Kallikratidas was quite young (*néos*) when he became navarch in 407/406, and Plutarch (*Lyc.* 22.1–6) clearly uses these terms in this fashion. The *néoi* or, as they are sometimes (e.g., Xen. *Hell.* 3.3.8–9) called, the *neóteroi* appear to have been distinguished from the *presbúteroi* of classical Sparta in much the same fashion as the *iuniores* were distinguished from the *seniores* of ancient Rome. The fact that all the men under forty-five slept with their tentmates helps explain why so many Greeks looked on Sparta as an armed camp: above, I.v.2, note 15. If the comparative data gathered by ethnologists is any guide, Jeanmaire, *Couroi et courètes* 483, may be correct in arguing that the young men of a set of *sussítia* shared sleeping quarters. This would, in any case, stand to reason. Not all of the fifteen or so men who belonged to a particular mess will have been under forty-five, and the remainder will have spent their nights at home. It is conceivable, but improbable, that a man graduated from the *néoi* when he reached the age of fifty (rather than forty-five): cf. Figueira, "Mess Contributions and Subsistence at Sparta" 101–2 n. 47, and "Population Patterns in Late Archaic and Classical Sparta" 165–213 (at 167–69).

123. Dion. Hal. *Ant. Rom.* 2.23.3. For the *sussítia* as a religious institution, note Alcman's use of the word *thíasos* in connection with the *andreîon*: F98 (PMG).

124. Xen. *Lac. Pol.* 4.3–4. See Hdt. 1.67.5, 8.124.3; Thuc. 5.72.4; Xen. *Hell.* 3.3.9–11, 6.4.14 (where, with Stephanus, I read *hippeîs* rather than *híppoi*); Ephorus *FGrH* 70 F149 (ap. Strabo 10.4.18); Dion. Hal. *Ant. Rom.* 2.13.4; Plut. *Lyc.* 25.6, *Mor.* 231b; Stob. *Flor.* 4.1.138 (Hense); Hesych. s.v. *hippagrétas*. See also Jeanmaire, *Couroi et courètes* 542–50. Cf. Thuc. 4.55 and Xen. *Hell.* 4.4.10–12 with Ephorus *FGrH* 70 F149: the three hundred *hippeîs* were apparently not a cavalry unit in the strict sense, but rather an elite hoplite unit that accompanied the king—perhaps on horseback—to and from engagements. See P. A. L. Greenhalgh, *Early Greek Warfare* (Cambridge 1973) 94–95. Victory in the Olympic games apparently guaranteed election by the *hippagrétai*: consider Xen. *Hell.* 2.4.33 in light of Plut. *Lyc.* 22.8. During the march of Xenophon's Ten Thousand to the sea, the Spartan Cheirisophus appears to have organized a similar elite unit: Xen. *An.* 3.4.43. In this connection, one might want to consider the various groups of three hundred Spartan warriors mentioned in the sources: Hdt. 1.82.3, 7.202, 205.2 (which should be read with 220.3–4), 9.64.2; Xen. *Hell.* 6.5.31. Institutions of similar import are instanced elsewhere: see Marcel Detienne, "La phalange: Problèmes et controverses," in *Problèmes de la guerre en Grèce ancienne,* ed. Jean-Pierre Vernant (Paris 1968) 134–42; Pritchett, *The Greek State at War* II 221–25; and Geneviève Hoffmann, "Les choisis: Un ordre dans la cité grecque?" *Droit et cultures* 9–10 (1985): 15–26, and note Tac. *Germ.* 13.3–14.1.

125. Hdt. 1.67.5. There is no evidence specifying when a Spartiate ceased to be a *hébôn.* In ordinary speech, the term is used to refer to those who have become adults but have not yet reached old age: see Tazelaar, "PAIDES KAI EPHEBOI" 143–46, 150. Most scholars, nonetheless, assume that a man would leave the royal bodyguard when he reached his thirtieth birthday: see, most recently,

Tazelaar, "PAIDES KAI EPHEBOI" 150; Hodkinson, "Social Order and Conflict of Values in Classical Sparta" 242, 244–47; MacDowell, *Spartan Law* 66–68; and Cartledge, *Agesilaos and the Crisis of Sparta* 204–5. There are two reasons for doubting that this was the case. There is evidence that the Spartans employed the terms *néoi* and *neóteroi* to distinguish warriors under the age of forty-five from the *presbúteroi* (above, note 122), and in the *Hellenika* (3.3.8–11), Xenophon appears to use both terms, as synonyms for *hēbôntes*, to designate the *hippeîs* commanded by the *hippagrétai*. Furthermore, in the *Lakedaimoníōn Politeía* (4.3), he not only tells us that the *hippagrétai* were chosen from among the *hēbôntes*; he adds that they were selected from among the *akmázontes*. In ordinary Greek parlance, the last-mentioned term would normally be used to refer to a man over thirty years in age: Pl. *Resp.* 5.460e–461a. It is hard to believe that a people notorious for being inclined to honor their elders would think that a man had reached his *akmé* earlier than that, and it is even harder to believe that they would be willing to entrust the royal guard to the command of men so young.

126. Cf. Xen. *Lac. Pol.* 4.6–7 with 2.2. If my hypothesis as to the central importance of a man's forty-fifth birthday is correct, the exclusion of all but *presbúteroi* from political office would be yet another sign of the exaggerated respect that the Spartans showed to those of advanced age. Note that it was contrary to custom (*paranómōs*) for the Spartans to send *hēbôntes* abroad as governors (*archóntes*) of allied cities: Thuc. 4.132.3. In this connection, see Arist. *Pol.* 1332b12–1333a16.

127. One should read Plut. *Lyc.* 15.6–10 and *Mor.* 228a in conjunction with note 122, above. For the treatment of inveterate bachelors, see Clearchus of Soli F73 (Wehrli); Plut. *Lyc.* 15.1–3, *Lys.* 30.7, *Mor.* 227e–f; Stob. *Flor.* 67.16; Poll. *Onom.* 3.48, 8.40. Cf. Hdt. 2.80.1, Xen. *Lac. Pol.* 9.4–5.

128. Plut. *Comp. Lyc. et Num.* 4.1. For a general discussion of relations within Spartan marriages, see Martin Nilsson, "Die Grundlagen des spartanischen Lebens" 849–62. Josephus (*Ap.* 2.273) described the Spartan regime as unsociable and accused the Lacedaemonians of slighting matrimony.

129. For a useful discussion and collection of material, see Paul Cartledge, "The Politics of Spartan Pederasty," *PCPhS* 207 (1981): 17–36. See also Brelich, *Paides e parthenoi* I 113–26; and Claude Calame, *Les choeurs de jeunes filles en Grèce archaïque* (Rome 1977) I 350–57.

130. Plut. *Lyc.* 16.12–18.9, *Mor.* 237b–c; Ael. *VH* 3.10, 12. Xenophon's description (*Lac. Pol.* 2.12–14) of Spartan practice in this regard may well be ironic. His claim that the relations of the pair were strictly platonic is belied by the testimony of Plato himself (*Leg.* 1.636a–b, 8.836b–c) and by that of Martial (4.55.6–7). If Cicero (*Rep.* 4.4.4) is to be trusted, the law allowed the two to embrace and to share a bed, but not to remove their cloaks: that no doubt set the limit on what others were allowed to witness.

131. See Cic. *Rep.* 4.3.3, Plut. *Lyc.* 18.8–9, Ael. *VH* 3.10.

132. See Theoc. 12.13 and Callim. F68 (Pfeiffer) with the scholia. See also Plut. *Cleom.* 3.2; Ael. *VH* 3.10, 12; and Hesych. s.v. *empneî*. In this connection, one should note Xenophon's use of *empneîn* at *Symp.* 4.15. The notion that insemination is a means for transferring manliness and strength is commonplace in societies practicing ritual pederasty: see the works cited above, in I.iv.6, notes 121–22: esp. Raymond C. Kelly, *Etoro Social Structure: A Study in Structural Contradiction* (Ann Arbor 1977) 16; Gilbert H. Herdt, *Guardians of the Flutes: Idioms of Masculinity* (New York 1981) 203–94, 318–20; Jan van Baal, *Jan Verschueren's Description*

of Yéi-Nan Culture: Extracted from the Posthumous Papers (The Hague 1982) 60–63; Gilbert H. Herdt, "Fetish and Fantasy in Sambia Initiation," and Edward L. Schieffelin, "The *Bau a* Ceremonial Hunting Lodge: An Alternative to Initiation," in *Rituals of Manhood: Male Initiation in Papua New Guinea*, ed. Gilbert H. Herdt (Berkeley 1982) 55–84, 162–63, 177–79; and Gilbert H. Herdt, "Ritualized Homosexual Behavior in the Male Cults of Melanesia, 1862–1983: An Introduction"; Michael R. Allen, "Homosexuality, Male Power, and Political Organization in Vanuatu: A Comparative Analysis"; Jan van Baal, "The Dialectics of Sex in Marind-anim Culture"; Gilbert H. Herdt, "Semen Transactions in Sambia Culture"; Kenneth E. Read, "The *Nama* Cult Recalled"; Laurent Serpenti, "The Ritual Meaning of Homosexuality and Pedophilia among the Kimam-Papuans of South Irian Jaya"; Arve Sørum, "Growth and Decay: Bedamini Notions of Sexuality"; and Shirley Lindenbaum, "Variations on a Sociosexual Theme in Melanesia," in *Ritualized Homosexuality in Melanesia*, ed. Gilbert H. Herdt (Berkeley 1984) 17, 22, 28–29, 34–35, 40–41, 67, 120–23, 131–36, 163, 167–69, 172–78, 181–94, 197–208, 220–21, 226–29, 236–44, 304–17, 319, 322–26, 331–36, 339–52. It is perhaps worth adding that it is quite possible, but by no means certain, that the Spartans followed the Thessalian practice (Theoc. 12.14) of using the term *aítas* or "hearer" to designate the *erómenos*; they are known to have used the term in the archaic period for describing young girls: Alkman F34 (Page) with scholia.

133. Consider Plut. *Lyc.* 15.4–6 in conjunction with 16.11. The abduction could be more than a ritual: Hdt. 6.65.2.

134. See George Devereux, "Greek Pseudo-Homosexuality and the 'Greek Miracle,' " *SO* 42 (1968): 69–92. In this connection one should perhaps ponder the Argive law concerning married women adorned with beards: Plut. *Mor.* 245f.

135. Plutarch (*Comp. Lyc. et Num.* 3.1–4) suspected that indifference on the part of the husband was the norm.

136. It can hardly be an accident that Plato (*Leg.* 1.636a–b) links pederasty with the existence of the *sussitía* and equates Spartan practice in these matters with that on Crete (8.836b–c).

137. One should, I suspect, interpret Xen. *Hell.* 4.8.37–39 with this supposition in mind.

138. Consider Ath. 13.561e in light of Onasander 24.

139. Consider *WrTJ* (ed. Lipscomb and Bergh) XV 482: Letter of 31 October 1823 to A. Coray in light of the first of this chapter's two epigraphs: Montesquieu, *EL* 1.5.2. In eighteenth-century France, Jefferson's opinion was widely held: Rawson, *The Spartan Tradition in European Thought* 256–60.

140. Groups smaller than ten are often ineffective; those larger than twenty are subject to faction: note the findings of E. J. Hobsbawm, *Primitive Rebels* (New York 1965) 18–19, and *Bandits*[2] (New York 1981) 16, 20. Col. N. G. L. Hammond served behind the German lines in Macedonia during the Second World War. In a conversation held on the twenty-second of March 1981, he remarked to me that in 1943 the standard number of men assigned to a unit within the ELAS guerrilla army was fifteen. As the leaders of that body of soldiers understood, the critical factor is that the men be familiars in the full sense of the term: see S. L. A. Marshall, *Men against Fire* (New York 1947) 42, 123–56.

141. According to Aristotle (*Pol.* 1270a36–37), ten thousand was the largest figure given anywhere for the adult male citizen population. At some point in the archaic period, there may well have been as many as nine thousand households

(Plut. *Lyc.* 8.3, 16.1). In 480, there were approximately eight thousand Spartiate *ándres* available for combat (Hdt. 7.234.2); of these, five thousand were classified as *néoi* and could be spared for service at Plataea (9.10.1, 11.3, 12.2, 28.2, 29.1). Prior to the Persian Wars, Sparta appears to have suffered from overpopulation: cf. Cartledge, *Sparta and Lakonia* 308–10, with Figueira, "Population Patterns in Late Archaic and Classical Sparta" 170–75. At some point after the Persian invasion, the number of Spartiate warriors began a well-attested and, I suspect, initially precipitous decline: see Xen. *Lac. Pol.* 1.1; Arist. *Pol.* 1270a29–34, 1270b1–4; Plut. *Agis* 5.4. With regard to the decline itself, cf. Gomme, Andrewes, and Dover, *An Historical Commentary on Thucydides* IV 110–17, with Forrest, *A History of Sparta*[2] 131–37, and see, most recently, Lazenby, *The Spartan Army* 3–62 (esp. 5–20, 24 n. 31, 41–48, 53–54, 57–60), and Figueira, "Population Patterns in Late Archaic and Classical Sparta" 167–70, 175–210. For the causes of that decline, consider Ludwig Ziehen, "Das spartanische Bevölkerungsproblem," *Hermes* 68 (1933): 218–37, in light of the discussion by Toynbee, *Some Problems of Greek History* 346–52, and cf. Hodkinson, "Land Tenure and Inheritance in Classical Sparta" 386–406 (esp. 386–94), and Robin Lane Fox, "Aspects of Inheritance in the Greek World," in *Crux* 211–23, with Lazenby, *The Spartan Army* 58–60, and with Figueira, "Population Patterns in Late Archaic and Classical Sparta" 177–79, 181–87, 192–99, 201–4.

I am inclined to interpret the initial demographic drop in terms of the earthquake and helot revolt of 465. Some twenty thousand Lacedaemonians are said to have lost their lives as a consequence of the tremor (Diod. 11.63.1–3), and there is reason to suppose that Sparta was the quake's epicenter and that those most likely to be indoors in the daytime (women and young children) suffered the most: for we are told that the city's ephebes were all killed when a building collapsed and that the *neaniskoi* accidentally escaped the very same fate (Plut. *Cim.* 16.5), and we can draw our own conclusions from the report that only five houses were still standing after the event (Plut. *Cim.* 16.4, Polyaen. 1.41.3, Ael. *VH* 6.7). There is also evidence suggesting that Sparta may have suffered heavy casualties during the initial stages of the helot revolt that followed: Hdt. 9.64.2. There is even reason to suspect that, as a consequence of a dramatic decline in population, more land could be employed to support the breeding of horses: see Stephen Hodkinson, "Inheritance, Marriage and Demography: Perspectives upon the Success and Decline of Classical Sparta," in *Classical Sparta* 79–121 (at 95–105).

The continued decline of Sparta's citizen population after the Peloponnesian War can almost certainly be traced to Epitadeus's liberalization of property relations—which opened the way for the concentration of land in the hands of a few wealthy families and resulted in the impoverishment of a great many Spartans who were thereafter unable to pay the requisite *sussitía* dues: consider Arist. *Pol.* 1270a16–39, 1271a29–37, 1272a12–21, 1307a34–36 in light of Plut. *Agis* 5, and see below, I.vi.2.

142. According to Stobaeus (*Flor.* 3.7.29–30 [Hense]), Aristotle attributed this famous admonition to Gorgo, the daughter of Cleomenes and wife of Leonidas, who figures prominently in Herodotus's narrative (5.51, 7.205, 7.239); with one exception, it is elsewhere attributed to an unnamed Spartan mother sending her son off to battle. For the *locus classicus*, see Plut. *Mor.* 241f. I see no reason to doubt that Aristotle could have been Stobaeus's source, and I am therefore less inclined

than some scholars to suppose that, in his text, Aristotle is a corruption for Ariston. For the most recent discussion of this scholarly problem, and for a useful list of the passages in which this admonition figures, see Mason Hammond, "A Famous *Exemplum* of Spartan Toughness," *CJ* 75 (1979–80): 97–109.

143. Hdt. 7.101–4.

144. See Plut. *Mor.* 240c–242b.

145. One should read Hdt. 3.148, 5.51.2, 6.50.2, 72, 82.1, 8.5.1; Thuc. 1.76.4, 95, 109.2, 2.21.1 (note Plut. *Per.* 22.2 and Diod. 13.106.10), 128–30, 5.16.3, 8.45.3, 50.3; Ephorus *FGrH* 70 F193; and Plut. *Per.* 22.4, *Lys.* 16.1–17.1 in light of Thuc. 1.77.6; Eur. *And.* 451; Ar. *Pax* 623–24; Xen. *Lac. Pol.* 14; and Arist. *Pol.* 1270b6–12, 1271a1–5, F544 (Rose). Note Pausanias's expectations at Thuc. 1.131.2. An exception to the rule was deemed worthy of note: Thuc. 4.81.

146. See *WoJJR* III 381–82: *Du contrat social* 2.7. Rousseau made the same point in even stronger terms in his initial draft: III 313. Note also *WoJJR* III 957: *Considérations sur le gouvernement de Pologne* 2. From the constant constraint imposed on the individual Spartan, Rousseau argued, "there was born in him an ardent love of the fatherland which was always the strongest or rather the unique passion of the Spartiates, and which made of them beings above humanity."

147. Simon. F111 (PMG).

148. Dion. Hal. *Ant. Rom.* 20.13. For evidence confirming Dionysius's claim concerning the attitude of the Athenians, see Dem. 18.132, 22.51–52.

149. Pl. *Alc.* I 122c7. Cf. *Resp.* 8.548c.

150. Pl. *Resp.* 8.548a should be read in light of 544c, 545a. See also Isoc. 8.95–96, 11.20; Plut. *Mor.* 239e–f.

151. Pl. *Alc.* I 122e–123a. See *Hipp. Maj.* 283d. Individual Spartans were known to have large sums on deposit in Arcadia and at Delphi: Posidonius *FGrH* 87 F48c. See Plut. *Lys.* 18.2.

152. Pl. *Resp.* 8.548a–b. See also Xen. *Hell.* 6.5.27, Diod. 15.65.5, Paus. 9.14.6.

153. Arist. F611.13 (Rose).

154. Arist. *Pol.* 1269b12–1270a14, 1271a18, 1271b17. On the lack of self-control exhibited by Spartan women, see also Pl. *Leg.* 1.637c, 6.780d–781d, 7.804c–806c, and note Dion. Hal. *Ant. Rom.* 2.24.6; Plut. *Comp. Lyc. et Num.* 3.5–9. See James Redfield, "The Women of Sparta," *CJ* 73 (1977–78): 146–61; Paul Cartledge, "Spartan Wives: Liberation or Licence," *CQ* n.s. 31 (1981): 84–105; Alfred S. Bradford, "Gynaikokratoumenoi: Did Spartan Women Rule Spartan Men," *AncW* 14 (1986): 13–18; and Barton Kunstler, "Family Dynamics and Female Power in Ancient Sparta," *Helios* 13, no. 2 (1986): 31–48. Note Xen. *Hell.* 6.5.28.

155. See below, I.vi.2 (esp. note 58).

156. Arist. F544 (Rose), Diod. 7.12.5, Plut. *Mor.* 239f. For additional citations, see Joseph Fontenrose, *The Delphic Oracle: Its Responses and Operations with a Catalogue of Responses* (Berkeley 1978) 272: Q10.

157. Isoc. 6.59.

158. Hdt. 7.205.2 should be read in light of 220.3–4.

159. Lycurg. 1.129–30.

160. Xen. *Lac. Pol.* 9.4–6, 10.7.

161. Consider Plut. *Ages.* 30.2–4 in light of Hdt. 2.121, and see David, "Laughter in Spartan Society" 1–25 (esp. 13–17).

162. Cf. Hdt. 7.232 with 229–31, 9.71, and see Tyrtaeus F11.14 (West) with Plut. *Ages.* 30.2–4.

163. Hdt. 1.82.

164. Xen. *Hell.* 4.5.11–19 (esp. 14).

165. Thuc. 4.37–40.

166. Thuc. 5.34.2, Diod. 12.76.1. See Thuc. 4.19.1, 108.7, 5.15–24.

167. Plut. *Ages.* 30, *Mor.* 191c; Polyaen. 2.1.13.

168. Xen. *Hell.* 6.4.16. See Plut. *Ages.* 29. Xenophon reports much the same phenomenon in connection with the disaster at Lechaeum: *Hell.* 4.5.10.

169. For the Spartan dedication to *homónoia*, see Isoc. 12.177–79, Dem. 20.107–8, Polyb. 6.48.2–5. Note also 6.46.6–8. In this connection, see Arist. *Pol.* 1306a9–12.

Chapter 6

1. Lewis Namier, *The Structure of Politics at the Accession of George III*[2] (London 1957) x–xi. I cite the preface of the first edition, published in 1928.

2. This aspect of Namier's argument has attracted considerable criticism: see Harvey C. Mansfield, Jr., "Sir Lewis Namier Considered," *JBS* 2 (November 1962): 28–55; cf. Robert Walcott, " 'Sir Lewis Namier Considered' Considered," *JBS* 3, no. 2 (May 1964): 85–108, with Mansfield, "Sir Lewis Namier Again Considered," *JBS* 3, no. 2 (May 1964): 109–19; and note Quentin Skinner, "The Principles and Practice of Opposition: The Case of Bolingbroke versus Walpole," in *Historical Perspectives: Studies in English Thought and Society in Honour of J. H. Plumb*, ed. Neil McKendrick (London 1974) 93–128.

3. See below, II.iv–vii, III.i–vii.

4. For an attempt to do just that for Namier's period, see John Brewer, *Party Ideology and Popular Politics at the Accession of George III* (Cambridge 1976).

5. Ferguson, *EHCS* 3.6 (160–61).

6. *WoJJR* III 372: *Du contrat social* 2.3.

7. See Harvey C. Mansfield, Jr., *Statesmanship and Party Government: A Study of Burke and Bolingbroke* (Chicago 1965). Note also Brewer, *Party Ideology and Popular Politics at the Accession of George III* 55–95.

8. The word *stásis* refers not to a political party in the modern sense, but to a faction—or, to be precise, to the men who "stand together."

9. See Pl. *Resp.* 6.489b–500e (*hoi polloí*), Thuc. 3.82.1 (*hoi olígoi*), Arist. *Ath. Pol.* 34.3 (*hoi dēmotikoí* and *hoi gnórimoi*), Thuc. 7.8.2 (*ho óchlos*), and Pl. *Resp.* 8.569a4 (*hoi kaloì kagathoí*).

10. Plut. *Per.* 10.1–3, 14.1. See Lys. 12.64, Xen. *Hell.* 6.4.18. Such a political grouping, if aristocratic in character, might be referred to as an *hetairía*. See Thuc. 3.82, Lys. 12.55, Isoc. 4.79, Pl. *Resp.* 2.365d, Arist. *Pol.* 1272b34.

11. See, for example, Thuc. 5.46.4, Plut. *Lys.* 17.4, and Xen. *Hell.* 5.4.25.

12. See Peter A. Brunt, "Spartan Policy and Strategy in the Archidamian War," *Phoenix* 19 (1965): 255–80 (at 278–80). Note Plut. *Ages.* 5.3–4.

13. For the dark side of *philotimía*, see Hdt. 3.53.4; Eur. *Phoen.* 531–67, *IA* 337–42, 527; Ar. *Thesm.* 383–94, *Ran.* 280–82, 675–85; Thuc. 2.65.7, 3.82.8, 8.89.3; Lys. 14.21; Isoc. 3.18, 12.81–82; Pl. *Resp.* 8.548c–550b, 9.586c; Dem. 8.71; Arist. *Eth. Nic.* 1107b21–34, 1125b1–25. For an extreme view, see Men. F620 (Koerte[3]).

14. *Pol.* 1271a14.

15. *Ages.* 5.5. In this connection, see Xen. *Cyr.* 8.2.26–28 and Dem. 20.108.

16. Pind. F198 (Bowra). For the source, see Plut. *Mor.* 457b. I have followed Plutarch's editors Pohlenz and Sieveking in adopting the reading *hístasın*—which is found in manuscripts G, X³, and S²—rather than the more common *è stásın*.

17. This was, of course, the goal elsewhere as well: for a *philotımía* aimed at public service, see Lys. 16.18–21, 19.55–57, 21.22–25, 26.3; Isoc. 2.29–30, 6.35–36, 8.93, 18.61; Isaeus 7.35–40; Pl. *Smp.* 178d–e, *Ep.* 7.338d–e; Dem. 18.257, 19.223, 20.5–6, 21.159–67, 28.22, 42.24–25, 45.66–67, 50.64, 51.22; Aeschin. 1.129, 196, 2.105, 3.19–20; Lycurg. 1.15, 140; Arist. *Pol.* 1324a29–32. In this connection, see also Aeschin. 1.160.

18. Arist. *Pol.* 1270b17–25, 1294b13–41. See also Pl. *Leg.* 691d–e, Polyb. 6.3–10, Cic. *Rep.* 2.23. Note Xen. *Hell.* 7.1.32. For a general discussion, see Édouard Will, Claude Mossé, and Paul Goukowsky, *Le monde grec et l'orient* (Paris 1972–75) I 438–44.

19. For a useful survey of the evidence, see Paul Cloché, "Sur le rôle des rois de Sparte," *LEC* 17 (1949): 113–38, 343–81. See also Carol G. Thomas, "On the Role of the Spartan Kings," *Historia* 23 (1974): 257–70, and Pierre Carlier, *La royauté en Grèce avant Alexandre* (Strasburg 1984) 240–324.

20. Polyb. 6.45.5.

21. Plut. *Ages.* 1. Cf. Stob. *Flor.* 3.40.8 (Hense).

22. Xen. *Hell.* 5.3.20.

23. See Hdt. 6.57.5, Thuc. 1.20.3, Arist. *Pol.* 1270b35–1271a6, Plut. *Lyc.* 5, 26. Herodotus appears to claim that each king had two votes, but Thucydides denies that this was the case. While the king was a minor, a regent (*pródıkos*)—usually the nearest agnatic male relative—exercised his prerogatives: see Xen. *Hell.* 4.2.9, Paus. 3.4.9, Plut. *Lyc.* 3, Hesychius s.v. *prodıkeîn*. One should probably interpret Paus. 3.6.2–3 in this light. There is reason to suspect that Herodotus's discussion (6.56–58) of the kings' powers draws on a Spartan document listing their prerogatives: see Carlier, *La royauté en Grèce avant Alexandre* 250–52.

24. Xen. *Lac. Pol.* 15.2. See also Hdt. 6.56.

25. Hdt. 5.74–75, 6.48–50, 9.10.2; Xen. *Lac. Pol.* 15.2. In an emergency, of course, another man could stand in for a king: Herodotus (7.137.2, 8.42.2) mentions two such occasions during the Persian Wars and alludes to their exceptional character by drawing attention to the fact that the commanders were not members of either royal house.

26. One should interpret Hdt. 5.70–75 and perhaps 6.49–51, 61–74 in light of 6.56.

27. Arist. *Pol.* 1271a18–26, 39–40, 1285a3–10, 14–15, 1285b26–35. See also Justin 3.3.2.

28. Hdt. 8.114.2. Note also the connection with the Dioscuri: 5.75.2.

29. For the Arcadians, see Hdt. 8.73.1 (which should be read with 2.171.3 and Thuc. 1.2.3), Hellanicus *FGrH* 4 F161, Xen. *Hell.* 7.1.23, Dem. 19.261, Paus. 5.1.1, Cic. *Rep.* 3.15.25, Schol. D. Ael. Aristid. *Panath.* 103.16 (Dindorf). For the Athenians, see II.vii.3, note 57, below.

30. Isocrates' Archidamus (6.16–33) elegantly summarizes the legend. See also Apollod. *Bibl.* 2.8.2–4, and note especially Hdt. 5.43. For further allusions to the import of descent from Heracles and Zeus, see 1.7, 13–14, 91, 7.208, 8.137, 9.26–27, 33; Thuc. 5.16.2; Xen. *Lac. Pol.* 15.2. In this connection, see Walter Burkert, "Demaratos, Astrabakos und Herakles: Königsmythos und Politik zur Zeit der Perserkriege (Herodot 6, 67–60)," *MH* 22 (1965): 166–77.

31. Plut. *Agis* 19.9.

32. Xen. *Hell.* 3.3.1. For the import of these rites, see Hans Schaefer, "Das Eidolon des Leonidas," in *Charites: Studien zur Altertumswissenschaft*, ed. Konrad Schauenburg (Bonn 1957) 223–33, and Paul Cartledge, *Agesilaos and the Crisis of Sparta* (Baltimore 1987) 331–43.

33. See Tyrtaeus F7 (West), Hdt. 6.58–59, Heraclid. Pont. *Pol.* 2.5 (Müller *FHG* II 210), Paus. 4.14.4–5. According to Aristotle (F611.10 [Rose]), nothing was sold for three days and the market was strewn with chaff.

34. Xen. *Lac. Pol.* 15.9.

35. Hdt. 5.39.1–42.2, Xen. *Hell.* 3.3.2, Nep. *Ages.* 1.2–5, Paus. 3.6.2–3. The royal title descended, as directly as possible, down the male line. Where the legitimacy of an heir was in dispute, Delphi might be consulted, but the decision lay in principle with the *pólis* and with its magistrates: Hdt. 6.61–66, Xen. *Hell.* 3.3.1–4, Paus. 3.6.2–3, 8.8–10.

36. Hdt. 6.59, Thuc. 5.16.3.

37. Plut. *Lyc.* 6.2. For the meaning, see Tyrtaeus's paraphrase of the oracle: F4 (West). For the term *archagétēs*, see Pind. *Ol.* 7.79 (with 30); *GHI* 1.5.11, 26; Eur. *Or.* 555; Thuc. 6.3.1; Pl. *Lys.* 205d; Xen. *Hell.* 6.3.6, 7.3.12; Ephorus *FGrH* 70 F118; Arist. *Ath. Pol.* 21.5–6; Polyb. 34.1.3 (ap. Strabo 10.3.5); *ICr* III iii A; *IDelos* nos. 30, 35 (with F. Robert, "Le sanctuaire de l'archégète ANIOS à Delos," *RA* 41 [1953]: 8–40; and with Georges Daux, "Chronique des fouilles et découvertes archéologique en Grèce en 1961," *BCH* 86 [1962]: 629–978 [at 959–62], and "Chronique des fouilles et découvertes archéologique en Grèce en 1962," *BCH* 87 [1963]: 689–878 [at 862–69]); Strabo 14.1.46; Paus. 10.4.10; Plut. *Arist.* 11.3, *Demetr.* 53, *Mor.* 163b–c. See also Irad Malkin, *Religion and Colonization in Ancient Greece* (Leiden 1987) 241–50.

38. Hdt. 5.39–41, 6.61–70; Xen. *Hell.* 3.3.1–4.

39. Plut. *Agis* 11.2. I see no reason to accept the view, advanced by Cartledge, *Agesilaos and the Crisis of Sparta* 96, that the prohibition against a Heraclid's having children *ek gunaikòs allodapês* is a prohibition against marrying anyone not of Heraclid stock. There is no evidence suggesting that the descendants of Heracles were a separate caste; in ordinary circumstances, the pertinent adjective refers to those from foreign parts; and, in the passage cited, the prohibition under discussion here is linked with another barring settlement abroad on pain of death. Moreover, it is most unlikely that the Spartans were worried that a son born to a non-Heraclid woman would somehow not be a Heraclid. In general, the Greeks were inclined to suppose that mothers contributed little, if anything, to the biological make-up of their own progeny: see G. E. R. Lloyd, *Science, Folklore and Ideology: Studies in the Life Sciences in Ancient Greece* (Cambridge 1983) 66, 86–111. What the Spartans did, of course, fear was the corrupting influence of foreigners. And, believing, as they did, that their own right to Laconia and Messenia rested on a divinely sanctioned Heraclid claim, they were terrified at the prospect that a legitimate claimant to either throne might be born abroad to a foreign woman, reared among an alien people, and groomed as a champion against Lacedaemon. In this connection, consider Hdt. 6.74.1–75.1 in conjunction with W. P. Wallace, "Kleomenes, Marathon, the Helots, and Arkadia," *JHS* 74 (1954): 32–35.

40. The discussion of royal patronage that follows recapitulates in brief the argument of my unpublished dissertation: see Paul A. Rahe, "Lysander and the Spartan Settlement, 407–403 B.C." (Yale University 1977). As Cartledge, *Agesi-*

laos and the Crisis of Sparta 99–112, 139–59, 242–73, has recently shown, Agesilaus made ample use of the patronage power available to the king.

41. See Arist. *Pol.* 1285a3–7, Xen. *Lac. Pol.* 13.2–5, 8, 11. Note also Hdt. 9.61.2–3, Xen. *Hell.* 3.4.3–4, 23, 4.2.20.

42. See Hdt. 9.10.3, Xen. *Hell.* 5.4.15 (with 25), and Arist. *Pol.* 1285a7–9 (with Plut. *Ages.* 32.6–11), and note Thuc. 5.66.2–4, 8.3, 5.

43. Thuc. 5.60 (cf. 63), 71–72.

44. To get some feel for the role that a king or regent could play, one need only survey Herodotus (3.148, 5.49–54, 6.50–84, 9.106 [with 90–91, 104]), Thucydides (1.79–85, 94–96, 128–35, 2.12–13, 18, 71–75, 5.16–17, 19, 59–60, 63, 8.5, 8, 70–71), and Xenophon (*Hell.* 2.2.11–13, 4.28–39, 3.2.21–31 [with Paus. 3.8.3–6, Plut. *Mor.* 835f, Lys. 18.10–12], 4.2–29, 5.17–25, 4.1.1–2.8, 3.1–23, 4.19–5.18, 6.1–7.7, 5.1.32–34, 2.3–7, 32, 37, 3.8–25, 4.13–18, 20–41, 47–59, 6.3.18–20, 4.1–16, 5.3–5, 12–21, 7.5.9–14). This list of pertinent passages is by no means intended to be exhaustive.

45. For doubts as to the connection between *xenía* and *proxenía*, cf. Christian Marek, *Die Proxenie* (Frankfurt 1984) 387–88. For a useful attempt to make sense of these two institutions in light of the comparable institutions brought to light by comparative ethnography, see Gabriel Herman, *Ritualised Friendship and the Greek City* (Cambridge 1987). Networks of *xénoi* were, in all periods, the exclusive preserve of the rich and wellborn. From the outset, the tie of *xenía* was deemed sacred, and in the age when the *pólis* was ascendant, many a prominent Greek caught up in the bitter political rivalries of the day (above, I.ii.1) turned to his *xénoi* abroad for help against his enemies at home. This explains why the *dêmos* might regard with considerable suspicion those wealthy and ambitious citizens who maintained close connections with monarchs or foreign statesmen known to be hostile to the city. But it can hardly be sufficient to justify Herman's all-encompassing conclusion (160) that "the upper classes *did* display more solidarity with those of their kind outside their communities than they did with the lower classes inside them." For further evidence, see Herman, "Nikias, Epimenides, and the Question of Omissions in Thucydides," *CQ* n.s. 39 (1989): 83–93, and "Patterns of Name Diffusion within the Greek World and Beyond," *CQ* n.s. 40 (1990): 349–63.

46. In general, see Paul Monceaux, *Les proxénies grecques* (Paris 1886); Fritz Gschnitzer, *RE* Supp. XIII (1973) 629–730; and Marek, *Die Proxenie* 1–385. For the origins, see M. B. Wallace, "Early Greek *Proxenoi*," *Phoenix* 24 (1970): 189–208. For the political import of the position, see Russell Meiggs, "A Note on Athenian Imperialism," *CR* 63 (1949): 9–12, and Shalom Perlman, "A Note on the Political Implications of Proxenia in the Fourth Century B.C.," *CQ* n.s. 8 (1958): 185–91. See also André Gerolymatos, *Espionage and Treason: A Study of the Proxenia in Political and Military Intelligence Gathering in Classical Greece* (Amsterdam 1986).

47. The caution evidenced by the Spartans in this regard helps explain why Pausanias (7.10.1–3) could single out Lacedaemon as the only city never to have been ruined by treachery on the part of its own citizens.

48. It is not likely to have been fortuitous that, in 398, the Spartan *próxenos* at Elis was the *xénos* of Agis: Paus. 3.8.4.

49. Hdt. 6.57.2. The city represented apparently had to ratify the choice made by the two kings before it could properly take effect (*IG* I² 106), and, in practice, *proxenía*, like the relationship of *xenía* on which it was modeled, tended to be

hereditary both at Sparta (Pl. *Leg.* 1.642b–c) and abroad (Thuc. 6.89.2). I see no reason to accept the suggestion advanced by D. J. Mosley, "Spartan Kings and Proxeny," *Athenaeum*[2] 49 (1971): 433–35, that the royal prerogative in this sphere was merely meant to supplement the arrangements made on their own behalf by other communities.

50. Hdt. 6.57, Xen. *Lac. Pol.* 15.5, Cic. *Div.* 1.43.95, *Suda* s.v. *Púthioi.* In this connection, see also Plut. *Pel.* 21.3.

51. For the political manipulation of religion at Sparta, see Polyb. 10.2.9–13. Note also August. *De civ. D.* 2.16. See Thuc. 5.16.2.

52. Hdt. 5.62–75, 90–93, 6.50–84.

53. Hdt. 6.57.4–5. Herodotus's use of the verb *hiknéetai* in this passage suggests that, in choosing a husband for a Spartan *patroûchos*, the kings were expected to abide by certain principles of law or policy, but everything that we know about the position accorded the family within the Lacedaemonian polity militates against the view, advanced by Evanghelos Karabélias, "L'épiclérat à Sparte," in *Studi in onore di Arnaldo Biscardi* (Milan 1982) II 469–80, that they would ordinarily follow the Athenian practice and award her to her nearest surviving male relation. It is worth noticing that Herodotus's characterization of the power exercised by the kings in this sphere precludes the possibility that their decisions were subject to review by a higher authority. I am inclined to suppose that—at least in the period prior to the passage of Epitadeus's law—the kings were expected to award a *patroûchos* to the younger son of a Spartan who was not in a position to inherit his father's public allotment.

54. Macaulay, *Essays* IV 362: "Leigh Hunt."

55. Plut. *Ages.* 15.7.

56. For the houses of the Spartans, cf. Plut. *Lyc.* 13.5–7, *Mor.* 189e, 227c, 285c, 997c–d, and F62 (Sandbach) with Xen. *Ages.* 8.7, and see Pl. *Resp.* 8.548a–b.

57. Arist. *Pol.* 1270a26–29. I find Stephen Hodkinson's attempt, "Land Tenure and Inheritance in Classical Sparta," *CQ* n.s. 36 (1986): 378–406 (at 394–98), to reconcile this passage with Hdt. 6.57.4–5 as implausible as his earlier insistence (378–79, 384–85) that Plut. *Lyc.* 8.3–6 and 16.1 cannot be reconciled with *Agis* 5.2–3.

58. Plut. *Agis* 5. For the results, see Arist. *Pol.* 1270a18–21. In this connection, note Pl. *Leg.* 11.922a–929e (esp. 922d–923b). See also David Asheri, "Sulla legge di Epitadeo," *Athenaeum* 39 (1961): 45–68; Pavel Oliva, *Sparta and Her Social Problems* (Amsterdam 1971) 188–93; Jacqueline Christien, "La loi d'Epitadeus: Un aspect de l'histoire économique et sociale à Sparte," *RD*[4] 52 (1974): 197–221; Ephraim David, "The Conspiracy of Cinadon," *Athenaeum* 57 (1979): 239–59, and *Sparta between Empire and Revolution (404–243 b.c.): Internal Problems and their Impact on Contemporary Greek Consciousness* (New York 1981) 5–10, 43–77; and Gabriele Marasco, "La retra di Epitadeo e la situazione sociale di Sparta nel IV secolo," *AC* 49 (1980): 131–45.

59. Arist. *Pol.* 1271a26–36.

60. Arist. *Pol.* 1270a15–26, 1307a34–36. In this connection, note also 1269b–1270a14, 1271a18, 1271b17. Dowries were forbidden in earlier times: Plut. *Mor.* 227f–228a, Justin 3.3.8. It is worth noting that Justin explicitly links the prohibition of dowries with the husband's capacity to keep his wife under control. Stephen Hodkinson's suggestion (I.v.2, note 39, above) that the daughter of a Spartan had inheritance rights comparable to those of her counterpart at Gortyn

seems quite plausible (at least with regard to the private property of her parents), and, as he points out, such a supposition makes sense of the proportion of land that came to be concentrated in the hands of Sparta's women in Aristotle's day (after, I would insist, the public allotment had come to be treated, in effect, as private property). From the outset, the rules of inheritance will no doubt have affected the pattern of marriage alliances and encouraged restrictions on the number of offspring within the small circle of families which possessed an abundance of private property. After the public allotments were in effect privatized, this behavior seems to have become universal. See Hodkinson, "Inheritance, Marriage and Demography: Perspectives upon the Success and Decline of Classical Sparta," in *Classical Sparta: Techniques behind Her Success*, ed. Anton Powell (Norman, Okla., 1988) 79–121 (esp. 82–95, 109–14).

61. Aristotle no doubt had Sparta in mind when he suggested the oligarchies should deny a man the right to leave his land to whomever he pleases: *Pol.* 1309b20–25.

62. Xen. *Lac. Pol.* 15.3.

63. Cf. Hdt. 9.81 with Phylarchus *FGrH* 81 F56, and see Hdt. 6.56.

64. Pl. *Alc.* I 123a–b with Strabo 8.5.4.

65. Arist. *Pol.* 1272b38–1273a2.

66. Cic. *Rep.* 2.33.57–58, *Leg.* 3.7.15–16.

67. *WoJJR* III 454: *Du contrat social* 4.5.

68. See H. D. Westlake, "Reelection to the Ephorate?" *GRBS* 17 (1976): 343–52.

69. Cf. Xen. *Ages.* 1.36, Arist. *Pol.* 1272a6–7, Paus. 3.11.2, and Plut. *Ages.* 4.3 with Xen. *Hell.* 2.3.9–10.

70. Xen. *Hell.* 2.3.34, 4.29. Note Arist. F611.10 (Rose).

71. Plut. *Agis* 12.1. Cf. Arist. *Rh.* 1419a31 with *Pol.* 1271a6–8. Whether the retiring ephors were jailed while their conduct was under review, as seems to have been the case with the *basileîs* at Cyme, is unknown: Plut. *Mor.* 291f–292a. For the procedures followed in Athens, see Arist. *Ath. Pol.* 4.2, 48.3–5, 54.2, with P. J. Rhodes, *A Commentary on the Aristotelian Athenaion Politeia* (Oxford 1981) 114–15, 155, 313, 316–18, 547–48, 560–64, 597–99.

72. Xen. *Hell.* 3.3.8. The context leaves little doubt that we should identify Xenophon's "little assembly" with the *gerousía*. His point is that the ephors, instead of summoning the *gerousía* proper, unobtrusively consulted those of the *gérontes* who happened to be nearby. If they had actually called a meeting of the *gerousía*, they might have tipped off Cinadon's conspirators that something was afoot. See also Hdt. 5.40. Some scholars believe that the Spartans held a great assembly once a year and argue that "the little assembly" was the regular monthly meeting of the *ekklēsía* mentioned by schol. Thuc. 1.67.3: see W. G. G. Forrest, *CR* 83 (1969): 197 n. 1, and Walter Burkert, "Apellai und Apollon," *RhM* 118 (1975): 1–21 (esp. 8–10). On the basis of Ephorus *FGrH* 70 F149 (ap. Strabo 10.4.18) and Stob. *Flor.* 4.1.138 (Hense), a number of scholars conclude that the *hippeîs* constituted "the little assembly": see Henri Jeanmaire, *Couroi et courètes* (Lille 1939) 544–45; Marcel Détienne, "La phalange: Problèmes et controverses," in *Problèmes de la guerre en Grèce ancienne*, ed. Jean-Pierre Vernant (Paris 1968) 119–142 (at 135–40); and Geneviève Hoffmann, "Les choisis: Un ordre dans la cité grecque?" *Droit et cultures* 9–10 (1985): 15–26 (at 21).

73. Xen. *Hell.* 2.2.19, Plut. *Agis* 9.1.

74. Xen. *Hell.* 2.2.19, 5.2.11–24; Plut. *Agis* 5.3–4, 8.1–9.1. For the role played

by the *gerousía*, see Diod. 11.50; Plut. *Lyc.* 6. A. H. M. Jones provides a useful discussion of the issues in "The Lycurgan Rhetra," in *Ancient Society and Institutions: Studies Presented to Victor Ehrenberg*, ed. Ernst Badian (Oxford 1966) 165–75. To the secondary literature he cites, one should add W. G. Forrest, "Legislation in Sparta," *Phoenix* 21 (1967): 11–19.

75. For the regular monthly meeting, see schol. Thuc. 1.67.3 with Plut. *Lyc.* 6.1–4 and Hdt. 6.57.2. In this connection, one should consider Burkert, "Apellai und Apollon" 1–21.

76. See Plut. *Mor.* 214b, 801b–c.

77. Thuc. 1.87.1–2.

78. Xen. *Hell.* 2.4.38, 3.2.23, 4.6.3. See Antony Andrewes, "The Government of Classical Sparta," in *Ancient Society and Institutions* 1–21 (at 13–14), and Jones, "The Lycurgan Rhetra" 165–75. See also Hdt. 5.40.

79. Arist. *Pol.* 1322b12–16.

80. Thuc. 1.144.2, 6.88.9, 8.12.1–3; Xen. *Lac. Pol.* 14.4; Plut. *Lyc.* 27.6–9; *Agis* 10.3–8 should be read in light of Hdt. 3.148.2; Thuc. 1.131.1–2; Xen. *Hell.* 2.2.13, 19; Plut. *Lys.* 19.7–21.1.

81. Thuc. 5.36–38, 6.88.7–93.3, 8.5–6 should be read in light of Hdt. 3.46, 148.2, 6.106, 9.6–11; Thuc. 1.90.5; Xen. *Hell.* 2.2.11–13, 17–19, 4.28–29, 35–38, 3.1.1, 5.2.9, 11–24; Theopomp. *FGrH* 115 F85; Polyb. 4.34; Plut. *Them.* 19.1–3, *Cim.* 6.3, *Lys.* 14.5–8.

82. For the appointment of a harmost, see Xen. *Hell.* 4.8.32. For the supersession of a commander, see Xen. *Hell.* 2.4.28–29. For orders to commanders, see Thuc. 1.131.1–2; Xen. *Hell.* 3.1.1, 7, 2.12; Plut. *Lys.* 19. See also Thuc. 8.6.3, 12.1–3; Xen. *Hell.* 3.2.6–7, 5.4.24. Needless to say, a strong king could influence the choices made: Plut. *Mor.* 212d.

83. Xen. *Hell.* 3.2.23–25, 5.6, 4.2.9, 5.3.13, 4.47, 6.4.17, 5.10. For a full discussion, see Andrewes, "The Government of Classical Sparta" 10–12 and notes: sometimes the ephors were implementing a decision of the assembly; at other times, they were no doubt acting on their own authority. Similarly, sometimes the assembly picked the commander; at other times this detail seems to have been left to the ephors. See Hdt. 9.10; Thuc. 8.12; Xen. *Hell.* 2.4.29, 5.1.33, 4.14, *An.* 2.6.2.

84. Xen. *Lac. Pol.* 11.2, *Hell.* 6.4.17.

85. Plut. *Agis* 10.5–8, Ael. *VH* 14.7.

86. Agatharchides *FGrH* 86 F10, Ael. *VH* 14.7.

87. Xen. *Lac. Pol.* 4.3–4. See above, I.v.4 (with notes 122–24).

88. Plut. *Agis* 16.1.

89. Diod. 13.106.8–9, Plut. *Lys.* 16. The Spartans normally sold captured men and goods on the spot. The profits were public property. See W. Kenrick Pritchett, *The Greek State at War* (Berkeley 1971–   ) I 85–92.

90. Plut. *Agis* 16.1.

91. Arist. F538, 611.10 (Rose). See also Plut. *Lyc.* 28. For the murder of helots, see Thuc. 4.80, Myron of Priene *FGrH* 106 F2. Most scholars doubt Isocrates' assertion (12.181) that the ephors could execute *períoikoi* without trial. I am hesitant to reject his statement out of hand.

92. Arist. F539 (Rose). For the archaic practice, see Ath. 4.143a. See also Humfrey Michell, *Sparta* (Cambridge 1964) 126 n. 5.

93. *Cleom.* 9.3.

94. Arist. *Pol.* 1271a6–8. That they examined the magistrates of the preceding year and not their fellow magistrates follows from their examining the ephors of the preceding year.

95. Xen. *Lac. Pol.* 8.4.

96. Arist. *Pol.* 1275b8–10.

97. Xen. *Lac. Pol.* 8.4, Arist. *Pol.* 1270b28–31.

98. Xen. *Lac. Pol.* 10.2; Arist. *Pol.* 1270b39–40, 1273a19–20, 1275b10, 1294b33–34; Plut. *Lyc.* 26.2, *Mor.* 217a–b should all be read in light of Paus. 3.5.2, which shows the ephors joining the *gerousía* in a capital case involving a king. For a conduct of the *anákrisis* and prosecution by the ephors, see Thuc. 1.95.3–5, 131; Xen. *Hell.* 5.4.24, *Lac. Pol.* 8.4; and the new Theophrastus fragment: John J. Keaney, "Theophrastus on Greek Judicial Procedure," *TAPhA* 104 (1974): 179–94 (at 189–91). See also Robert J. Bonner and Gertrude Smith, "Administration of Justice in Sparta," *CPh* 37 (1942): 113–29. Note the appearance of a king in a judicial role: Plut. *Mor.* 213d.

99. Xen. *Lac. Pol.* 15.6, Nicholas of Damascus F114.16 (*FHG* Müller III 459), Plut. *Mor.* 217c. Cf. Arist. F611.10 (Rose).

100. Thuc. 1.131; Plut. *Lyc.* 12.5 (to be read in light of *Mor.* 226f–227a), *Lys.* 30.1, *Ages.* 2.6, 4.2–5.4, *Cleom.* 10, *Mor.* 1d, 482d. The king was required by law to answer the third summons. See also Thuc. 5.63, Ephorus *FGrH* 70 F193. Whether these last two references record the work of the ephors remains unclear. There must have been some limit to the fines they could impose: an extremely large fine was tantamount to banishment.

101. Xen. *Lac. Pol.* 13.5. See Hdt. 9.76.3, Xen. *Hell.* 2.4.36. When the expedition took the king far away from Lacedaemon for an extended period, the city could send a board of advisors (*súmbouloi*) instead: Xen. *Hell.* 3.4.2, 20, 4.1.5, 5.3.8. When the judgment of a king inspired distrust, the same procedure could be followed even when the struggle was nearer home: Thuc. 5.63.

102. Plut. *Mor.* 211c.

103. Nicholas of Damascus F114.16 (*FHG* Müller III 459).

104. Xen. *Lac. Pol.* 15.7.

105. Plut. *Agis* 11. See H. W. Parke, "The Deposing of Spartan Kings," *CQ* 39 (1945): 106–12.

106. Hdt. 6.82, Thuc. 1.131, Plut. *Agis* 18–19. Cf. Hdt. 5.40.1 with Paus. 3.5.2.

107. The references are collected at G. E. M. Ste. Croix, *The Origins of the Peloponnesian War* (Ithaca 1972) 350–53.

108. Herodotus (6.75, 85, 7.205) places Cleomenes' death and Leonidas's succession shortly before the battle of Marathon in 490. When Leonidas's reign came to an abrupt end at Thermopylae in 480 (7.224), Pleistarchus—his son by Cleomenes' daughter Gorgo (5.48, 7.205, 239)—became king. Pleistarchus was a minor at the time of the battle of Plataea in 479 (9.10) and remained so for a considerable time thereafter (Thuc. 1.132). His mother Gorgo was only eight or nine years old in 499 at the time of the Ionian Revolt (Hdt. 5.51) and cannot have given birth to a child before 493 at the earliest. See Darrel W. Amundsen and Carol Jean Diers, "The Age of Menarche in Classical Greece and Rome," *Human Biology* 41 (1969): 125–32. Indeed, since the Spartans did not normally marry off their daughters at menarche, but usually waited a few years until they were fully grown (Plut. *Lyc.* 15), it is probable that Gorgo did not marry Leonidas much, if at all, before 490. This suggests that Pleistarchus reached the age of thirty and took

on the full responsibilities of kingship (cf. Xen. *Mem.* 1.2.35 with Mary White, "Some Agiad Dates: Pausanias and his Sons," *JHS* 84 [1964]: 140–152 [at 140–41]) only shortly before his death—which took place sometime before the battle of Tanagra in 457 when Pleistoanax had already succeeded him (Thuc. 1.107.2; Arnold W. Gomme, Antony Andrewes, and Kenneth J. Dover, *An Historical Commentary on Thucydides* [Oxford 1945–80] I 270). This supposition is confirmed by Pausanias's report (3.5.1) that Pleistarchus died very soon after taking up the kingship. Cf. Diod. 13.75.1 with White, "Some Agiad Dates" 140 n. 3.

109. According to Theophrastus (Plut. *Ages.* 2.6, *Mor.* 1d), Archidamus was once fined for choosing too short a wife. See also Ath. 13.566a–b, and note Pollux's reference (*Onom.* 3.48) to *díkē kakogamíou*. I do not share the skepticism of Andrewes, "The Government of Classical Sparta" 19 n. 17; Ste. Croix, *The Origins of the Peloponnesian War* 352; and Cartledge, *Agesilaos and the Crisis of Sparta* 20, regarding this anecdote. The Spartans had every reason to concern themselves with the physical qualities of the offspring of their kings. Cf. Thuc. 2.18 with 5.63: Archidamus courted disaster in 431.

110. See Keaney, "Theophrastus on Greek Judicial Procedure" 181–82, and note the example reported by Plutarch: *Mor.* 775c–e. Cf. Xen. *Lac. Pol.* 4 with Moses I. Finley, "Sparta and Spartan Society," *Economy and Society in Ancient Greece*, ed. Brent D. Shaw and Richard P. Saller (London 1981) 32–33.

111. Arist. *Pol.* 1270b13–17.

112. Note Xen. *Ages.* 1.36.

113. Polyb. 23.11.4.

114. Xen. *Lac. Pol.* 8.4, Pl. *Leg.* 4.712d2–e5, and Arist. *Pol.* 1270b14.

115. See Paul A. Rahe, "The Selection of Ephors at Sparta," *Historia* 29 (1980): 385–401. I am not persuaded by P. J. Rhodes's defense, "The Selection of Ephors at Sparta," *Historia* 30 (1981): 498–502, of the orthodox view that the ephors were directly elected.

116. For the relationship, in general, between favors accepted and dependency, see Xen. *Cyr.* 5.5.25–34. For a Spartan king's practice of the art of gaining adherents in this fashion, see Plut. *Ages.* 20.6, *Mor.* 212d. In this connection, note Xen. *Hell.* 5.4.15–34, 6.4.14.

117. Arist. *Pol.* 1270b8–10.

118. On the manner in which a strong king could influence the ephors, see Plut. *Ages.* 4.3–6. He could deal with his opponents by the same means (Cic. *QFr.* 1.2.7; Plut. *Ages.* 5.2–4, 20.6, *Mor.* 212d, 482d). Note Xen. *Ages.* 11.11–12.

119. At least in the third century, some Spartans were willing to argue that the ephors were intended to be arbiters between the two kings and that, when the kings were in accord, the ephors lacked the legal power to act against them: Plut. *Agis* 12.2–3. Note Hdt. 6.56.

120. Dion. Hal. *Ant. Rom.* 4.73.4.

121. Hdt. 6.52.8, Arist. *Pol.* 1271a25–26. In this connection, note Plut. *Mor.* 215f. It may be worth mentioning that the tombs belonging to the two Heraclid houses lay in the vicinity of different villages (Paus. 3.12.8, 14.2–3, 6) and that we do not hear of any intermarriage. Only in a revolutionary situation would both kings be chosen from the same house: Plut. *Cleom.* 11.5.

122. The most obvious case in point is Phlius (Xen. *Hell.* 5.3.10–17, 20–25. Cf. Diod. 15.19.4). There are strong indications that this was true at Mantineia (Xen. *Hell.* 5.2.1–7, 6.5.4) and at Elis (Xen. *Hell.* 3.2.21–31, Paus. 3.8.3–6, Plut. *Mor.*

835f, Lys. 18.10–12) as well. In each case, one can observe links, on the one hand, between the proponents of democracy and the Agiad house and, on the other, between the supporters of oligarchy and the Eurypontid house. This probably means that the Agiad kings favored local autonomy, not democracy, and were therefore tolerant of the democratic regimes that their Eurypontid colleagues were eager to destroy. Note also the ties linking Agesilaus with leading figures at Tegea: Xen. *Hell.* 6.4.18; *Ages.* 2.23.

123. Note, for example, Xen. *Hell.* 5.4.25.

124. See Tyrtaeus F1–4 (West); Plut. *Lyc.* 6.4, 7.1–3, 8.3; Arist. *Pol.* 1313a26–28. See W. G. G. Forrest, "The Date of the Lykourgan Reforms in Sparta," *Phoenix* 17 (1963): 157–79, and *A History of Sparta, 950–192 B.C.* [2] (London 1980) 40–68.

125. See Hdt. 6.50–84.

126. Thuc. 1.79–88. Pleistoanax was then in exile (Thuc. 5.16 with Plut. *Per.* 22.3) and his son Pausanias was a minor (Thuc. 3.26). In light of what we know of the career of Pleistoanax both before (Plut. *Per.* 22.3) and after (Thuc. 5.16) his exile and of what we know of Pausanias's subsequent activities (Plut. *Lys.* 21.1–4, Xen. *Hell.* 2.4.29–43, Diod. 14.33.5–7, Paus. 3.5.1–3, Lys. 18.10–12), it seems unlikely that Cleomenes, Pausanias's regent and Pleistoanax's brother, was in favor of war or could have swung the adherents of his brother and nephew behind a policy that must have been repugnant to them. This cannot, however, be ruled out as a possibility. For another view, see W. Robert Connor, "Pausanias 3.14.1: A Sidelight on Spartan History, C. 440 B.C.," *TAPhA* 109 (1979): 21–27.

127. Plut. *Dion* 53.4.

128. Dem. 20.107.

129. Dion. Hal. *Ant. Rom.* 2.14.2.

130. Dem. 20.107, Arist. *Pol.* 1270b23–25, Plut. *Lyc.* 26.

131. Plut. *Mor.* 801b–c.

132. Plut. *Lyc.* 26.1–5, *Ages.* 4.3. Note Polyb. 6.45.5. For the selection of the *gérontes* from among the members of a sacerdotal aristocracy, see Rahe, "The Selection of Ephors at Sparta" 386–87 (with notes).

133. Plut. *Lyc.* 6. See *Agis* 8–9. See Forrest, "Legislation in Sparta" 11–19.

134. Paus. 3.5.3. Note also Plut. *Mor.* 217b. For this reason, the *gerousía* (presumably with the ephors as well) judged homicide cases: Arist. *Pol.* 1275b10. See, however, note 136, below.

135. Cic. *Div.* 1.43.95–96.

136. I am not inclined to follow Ephraim David, "The Trial of Spartan Kings," *RIDA* [3] 32 (1985): 131–40, in supposing that the assembly ordinarily exercised jurisdiction where the kings were involved—but the evidence he presents does suggest the possibility that it may normally have met to confirm (or, in rare cases, overturn) the verdict when a jury of ephors and *gérontes* found a king guilty of a capital crime.

137. Arist. *Pol.* 1271a10–18.

138. Isoc. 12.154.

139. See Justin 3.3.2. In this connection, note Isocrates' claim (12.154) that the *gerousía* exercised precisely the same power which the Council of the Areopagus had once exercised in Athens.

140. See *RFC* I 288–89, 309–10: 18 June 1787.

141. Arist. *Rh.* 1389a2–b12.

142. Arist. *Rh.* 1389b13–1390a22. Cf. Soph. *Aj.* 1328–67 with 678–83.

143. Note Thuc. 4.132.3.

144. Arist. *Pol.* 1329a2–17.

145. See Hdt. 2.80.1; Xen. *Mem.* 3.5.15; Plut. *Lyc.* 15.2–3, 20.15, *Mor.* 227f, 232f, 235c–f, 237d; Justin 3.3.9. Cf. Plato's depiction of Athens: *Resp.* 8.562e–563a.

146. Plut. *Mor.* 795e–796a.

147. Plut. *Mor.* 237c. See also *Lyc.* 17.1–2.

148. Diod. 11.50. On rare occasions, the division between young and old could even become a ground for civil strife in a city: Polyb. 4.53.3–55.6.

149. In this connection, consider this chapter's epigraph: Montesquieu, *EL* 1.5.7.

150. His example is Sparta: Arist. *Pol.* 1294b13–41. In this connection, one might wish to ponder Aristotle's discussion of the fashion in which the distribution of offices within a polity can be at odds or in tension with its *agōgē* and ethos: *Pol.* 1292b11–20.

151. Note Isoc. 7.61, 12.178–79.

152. Note Isoc. 7.61.

153. Cf. Tac. *Ann.* 4.33 with *Dial.* 40, and see *Ann.* 3.26–27 with *Hist.* 2.38.

154. *WoJSM* XI 302–3: "Grote's History of Greece [I]."

155. See Meyer Reinhold, "Philhellenism in America in the Early National Period," *Classica Americana: The Greek and Roman Heritage in the United States* (Detroit 1984) 214. John Dickinson spoke of the Spartans as having been "as brave and as free a people as ever existed." See *WrJD* 324: *Letters from A Farmer in Pennsylvania* (1768).

Chapter 7

1. Hdt. 2.166–67.

2. Hdt. 1.165.1.

3. See Thuc. 1.13 and Strabo 8.6.20–23. For the dragway, see Thuc. 3.15, 8.7. For the trade routes to Corinth, see Hdt. 7.147.2–3, Thuc. 3.86.4–5, Lycurg. 1.26. See also Cic. *Rep.* 2.4.7–9. The best general studies are Édouard Will, *Korinthiaka* (Paris 1955); J. B. Salmon, *Wealthy Corinth: A History of the City to 338 B.C.* (Oxford 1984); and Donald Engels, *Roman Corinth: An Alternative Model for the Classical City* (Chicago 1990). See also A. J. Graham, *Colony and Mother City in Ancient Greece*[2] (Chicago 1983) 118–53. For the dragway, see R. M. Cook, "Archaic Greek Trade: Three Conjectures," *JHS* 99 (1979): 152–55 (esp. 152–53).

4. Cf. Cic. *Rep.* 2.4.7 with Montesquieu, *EL* 4.20.7–8.

5. Thuc. 1.103.4 (with 105–6) and then 24–88, 118–25. Note Hdt. 5.93.1. Of the two Corinthian ports, Kenchreai lay on the Saronic Gulf which Athens dominated with ease (Thuc. 1.105, 115.1, 2.93, 3.51, 4.42–45, 66–74, 8.10–11, 14.2, 15, 20.1, 23), and Lechaeum lay on the Corinthian Gulf. During the Peloponnesian War, the Athenians used their base at Naupactus to blockade the Corinthian Gulf: see Thuc. 2.69.1 (with 80–92, 7.19.5, 31.4–5, 34). Naupactus was almost certainly used in a similar fashion in the earlier struggle as well: 1.103.1–3, 107.3. The Athenians initially involved themselves in Sicilian affairs with an eye to cutting off grain imports into the Peloponnesus: 3.86.4–5. One should probably read Polyaen. 5.13.1–2 in this connection.

6. Arist. *Pol.* 1291b22–24 should be read with Ath. 6.264e–266f (which includes

Theopompus *FGrH* 115 F122 and Nymphodorus *FGrH* 572 F4); Hdt. 1.165.1, 8.105; and Thuc. 8.40.2. See, in this connection, Carl Roebuck, "Chios in the Sixth Century B.C.," and Th. Ch. Sarikakis, "Commercial Relations between Chios and Other Greek States in Antiquity," in *Chios: A Conference at the Homereion in Chios, 1984*, ed. John Boardman and C. E. Vaphopoulou-Richardson (Oxford 1986) 81–88, 121–31.

7. Thuc. 8.24.4 should be read with 40.2.

8. See Hdt. 6.1–32 (esp. 15 where Herodotus attributes to them *tà érga lamprá*—"shining deeds"), 8.132, 9.106.

9. Compare Thuc. 1.96–99 (note Hdt. 8.3.2); Arist. *Ath. Pol.* 23.3–24.2; Diod. 11.44–47; Plut. *Arist.* 23.1–25.3, and *Cim.* 6.1–3 with Thuc. 1.19, 2.9, 3.10.5, 50, 6.43, 85.2.

10. Note Thuc. 4.51, and see Thuc. 8.5–12, 14–20, 22–24, 28, 30–34, 36–45, 55–57, 61–64, 79, 100–101; Xen. *Hell.* 1.1.32, 6.3–38, 2.1.1–17; Diod. 13.34.1–2, 38.7, 65.3–4 (with Xen. *Hell.* 3.2.11), 76.3–4, 99.6, 100.5, 104.3. Note also Diod. 14.84.3. For further evidence and a somewhat different reading of Chian behavior, cf. J. P. Barron, "Chios in the Athenian Empire," in *Chios* 89–103.

11. See Alfred French, *The Growth of the Athenian Economy* (London 1964), which traces this development. Cf. the review by Moses I. Finley, *The Economic Journal* 75 (1965): 849–51.

12. Xen. *Hell.* 2.3.24. There is reason to think that the postwar population was less than half of what it had once been: see Barry S. Strauss, *Athens after the Peloponnesian War: Class, Faction, and Policy, 403–386 B.C.* (Ithaca 1986) 70–86 (with 179–82). Things had come to such a pass before the war's end that, for the purposes of producing legitimate children on the city's behalf, the citizens were in effect allowed two wives: consider Arist. F93 (Rose), Callisthenes of Olynthos *FGrH* 124 F43 and Demetrius of Phaleron *FGrH* 228 F45 (ap. Plut. *Arist.* 27.1, Ath. 13.555d–556b, and Diog. Laert. 2.26) as well as Aul. Gell. 15.20.6 in light of Ar. *Lys.* 591–97. There is evidence suggesting that Pericles' restrictive citizenship law (see I.vii.3, note 55, below) was also annulled at this time to allow the legitimation of offspring born to citizens and metic or slave women: note Dem. 23.53, and cf. Dem. 57.30, Carystius of Pergamum F11 (*FHG* IV 358) ap. Ath. 13.577a–c with Eumelos *FGrH* 77 F2 ap. Schol. Aeschin. 1.39. As Aristotle (*Pol.* 1278a26–34) points out, such liberality is often a sign of a shortage in men.

13. The evidence presented by Josiah Ober for the purpose of showing that Athens defied Roberto Michels's "Iron Law of Oligarchy" belies what his book's title would lead one to expect: see *Mass and Elite in Democratic Athens: Rhetoric, Ideology, and the Power of the People* (Princeton 1989).

14. Cf. Peter Laslett, "The Face to Face Society," in *Philosophy, Politics, and Society*, ed. Peter Laslett (Oxford 1956) 157–84, with Thuc. 8.66.3 and Isoc. 15.171–72. Athens did not meet Aristotle's criterion (*Pol.* 1326a5–b25) that a *pólis* be easily surveyed. For the size and character of Attica, see Alfred Philippson, *Die Griechische Landschaften* I:3 (Frankfurt 1952) 753–939. Only Sparta controlled a larger territory, and her citizens resided together in the central plain of the Eurotas valley; except in time of invasion, the great majority of Athens's citizens were dispersed throughout Attica: see I.vii.3, note 44, below. A. H. M. Jones's discussion of Athens's citizen population, *Athenian Democracy* (Oxford 1957) 161–80, needs to be adjusted in light of Mogens Herman Hansen, "Demographic Reflections on the Number of Athenian Citizens, 451–309 B.C.," *AJAH* 7 (1982): 172–89;

Hansen, *Demography and Democracy: The Number of Athenian Citizens in the Fourth Century B.C.* (Herning, Denmark 1985); and Strauss, *Athens after the Peloponnesian War* 70–86. For the foreigners resident in Attica during the second half of the fifth century, see R. P. Duncan-Jones, "Metic Numbers in Periclean Athens," *Chiron* 10 (1980): 101–9.

15. In this connection, see Philip Brook Manville, *The Origins of Citizenship in Ancient Athens* (Princeton 1990).

16. Consider Arist. *Ath. Pol.* 43–69 (with an eye to 4.3, 7.3–8.1, 9, 22.2, 5, 26) and Aeschin. 3.13 in light of [Xen.] *Ath. Pol.* 1.3, and see Hdt. 3.80.6; Pl. *Resp.* 8.557a; Arist. *Pol.* 1294b7–13, 1317b17–1318a11 (esp. 1317b17–21), *Rh.* 1365b30–33. See as well the extremely terse, abstract, and difficult discussion in Arist. *Pol.* 1300a8–b12, and note the use of the lottery as an anticorruption device: *Ath. Pol.* 63–69. Consider the critical remarks in Xen. *Mem.* 1.2.9 and Isoc. 7.21–22 in light of Pl. *Leg.* 6.756e–758a, and see Arist. *Pol.* 1303a13–16 (with *Ath. Pol.* 30–31) and Anaximenes *Rh.* 1424a12–20, 1424a39–b3 (Fuhrmann).

17. Arist. *Ath. Pol.* 62.3. Note Dem. 24.150, and see P. J. Rhodes, *A Commentary on the Aristotelian Athenaion Politeia* (Oxford 1981) 696–697.

18. Consider Arist. *Ath. Pol.* 62.2 in light of 24, 27, 28.3, 29.5, 30.2, 33.1, 42.3. See Mogens Herman Hansen, "*Misthos* for Magistrates in Classical Athens," *SO* 54 (1979): 5–22, and Vincent Gabrielsen, *Remuneration of State Officials in Fourth Century B.C. Athens* (Odense 1981). Note Arist. *Pol.* 1300a1–3.

19. See Thuc. 2.37.2, 7.69.2; [Xen.] *Ath. Pol.* 1.10–12. Excessive freedom is the theme of Plato's description of democracy (*Resp.* 8.557b–558c, 562c–564a) and of his discussion of Athens's decline (*Leg.* 3.698b–701e). Note Theophr. *Char.* 28.5–6.

20. Indeed, Athens's circumstances may have had much to do with her development into a democracy in the first place, and they certainly reinforced her democratic tendencies thereafter. Town life brought a comparatively large proportion of the common people together and thereby fostered the class consciousness that gave rise to that peculiar brand of populism that took "the power of the people (*dēmokratía*)" as its slogan; similarly, town life afforded those who enjoyed it relative anonymity and thereby undermined the ethos of deference and shame that maintained the old aristocratic order. As a consequence, throughout Hellas, the larger civic communities tended to become democracies (Arist. *Pol.* 1286b20–22, 1320a17–18) while those articulated into villages and lacking urban centers were generally governed by the gentry. Cf. the advice given oligarchs in this regard by Anaximenes (*Rh.* 1424b7–10 [Fuhrmann]) with Arist. *Pol.* 1311a13–15. This principle is elegantly illustrated by the history of Mantineia: in the fifth century, after its synoecism (Strabo 8.3.2), it is a democracy (Thuc. 5.29.1); in the fourth century, its *dioikismós* into villages is associated with the establishment of an oligarchy (Xen. *Hell.* 5.2.3–7, 6.4.18); and, when the democracy is restored, the *pólis* undergoes a second synoecism (6.5.3–5). In this connection, see Stephen and Hilary Hodkinson, "Mantineia and the Mantinike: Settlement and Society in a Greek Polis," *ABSA* 76 (1981): 239–96. Note also L. B. Carter, *The Quiet Athenian* (Oxford 1986) 76–98.

21. Aesch. *Eum.* 696–703 (which should be read with 516–24).

22. Aristophanes did so explicitly by devoting an entire play—*The Clouds*—to the issue. Sophocles (*OT* 707–25, 848–58, 964–72) and Euripides (cf. *Bacch.* 215–62 with 267–327, and see 343–57, 451–514, 642–76, 777–809) did so indirectly by

attributing arguments central to the sophistic critique of traditional religion to their characters Oedipus, Jocasta, and Pentheus. For the intellectual causes of unbelief, see Pl. *Leg.* 10.886a–890b. See I.vii.6–8, below.

23. Thuc. 7.69.2. Note also 2.37.2. For the excessive piety of Nicias, see 7.50.3–4; Diod. 13.12.6; Plut. *Nic.* 3–5, 23–24, *Comp. Nic. et Crass.* 5.3.

24. Dem. 20.105–11. Note Dem. 22.51.

25. After noting Hdt. 3.80.3, consider Arist. *Pol.* 1310a28–36, 1317b10–14, in light of Ar. *Vesp.* 546–49. See, in context, Arist. *Pol.* 1280a5, 1281a6, 1291b34–35, *Rh.* 1366a2–22. Note also R. G. Mulgan, "Aristotle and the Democratic Conception of Freedom," in *Auckland Classical Essays Presented to E. M. Blaiklock,* ed. B. F. Harris (Auckland and Oxford 1970) 95–111.

26. Arist. *Pol.* 1318b39–40.

27. Isoc. 7.20.

28. Consider Pl. *Resp.* 8.557a–558a in light of 561a–d.

29. Consider Pl. *Leg.* 1.641e–642a and 4.721e in light of 3.700a–701b, cf. 1.645b–649c (esp. 649b) and 2.671a–d, and see 1.649d–650b. Note Arist. F611.13 (Rose), Plut. *Lyc.* 19.1–2.

30. Pl. *Cri.* 51c–53a should be read in light of Socrates' claim that, as a physician of the soul, he is a master of rhetoric and the only true statesman in Athens: cf. *Grg.* 462b–465e and 500b–527e with *Leg.* 1.643a–650b (esp. 649a–650b), 4.719e–720e, 9.857c–e, and see *Resp.* 8.544d–e.

31. Pl. *Leg.* 1.642c–d. In pondering the class of men whom Plato has in mind when he has the Spartan Megillus employ the phrase *theía moîra,* consider *Resp.* 6.487b–497b (esp. 491a–b, 492a–493a, 496a–497b), *Leg.* 9.874e–875d, and *Epin.* 984d–985e in light of *Ap.* 33c and *Phdr.* 244a–257b (esp. 244b), 265a–266b, 279a, and see *Meno* 99e–100c; then, note *Resp.* 6.499b–500d, 9.591e–592b, *Ep.* 7.326a–b, 337b–e; and consider *Prt.* 322a and *Criti.* 121a–b. Cf. *Ap.* 22b–c with *Ion* 534b–c, 535a, 536c–d, 542a, and see *Phdr.* 229e–230a; then, cf. *Phd.* 58e with *Ap.* 40a–c, and see *Phd.* 67d–e; and, finally, after noting *Resp.* 6.496c, ponder the connection between *Theag.* 127c–128b and 128d–130e, and consider the manner in which that between *Symp.* 177d and 199c–212c (esp. 199e–201c) enables one to resolve the apparent contradiction between *Ap.* 20c–23b and 38a along the lines suggested by *Leg.* 3.687a–688d.

32. Nowhere does Plato attribute *eunomía* to Athens: see *Cri.* 52e, 53b–c, *Hipp. Maj.* 283e–284b, *Resp.* 2.380b, 3.406b, 4.425a, 5.462e, 10.605b, 607c, *Tim.* 20a, 23c, 24d, *Pol.* 293e, *Soph.* 216b, *Leg.* 1.638b, 2.656c, 4.712a, 713e, 7.815b, 11.927b, 934e, 12.950a–d, 951b, 960d. In fact, from the time of Tyrtaeus (F1–4 [West]) on, *eunomía* was a codeword for Sparta—a city no more open to philosophy than Plato's heavenly city *Kallípolis* would have been to traditional poetry (*Resp.* 2.376c–398b, 10.606e–608b). Needless to say, Pl. *Hipp. Maj.* 283e–286a and *Prt.* 342a–343c exemplify the customary irony attributed to Socrates at *Symp.* 216e–219a and *Resp.* 1.337a.

33. Cf. Pl. *Leg.* 3.698b–701e with 1.646e–649c.

34. Recognition of this fact allows one to reconcile the various, apparently contradictory remarks concerning democracy found in the Socratic corpus, and it obviates the need to engage in the dubious enterprise of singling out certain Platonic dialogues as somehow more accurately Socratic than the other Platonic dialogues and the works of Xenophon: cf. Gregory Vlastos, "The Historical Socrates and Athenian Democracy," *PTh* 11 (1983): 495–516, with Ellen Meiksins Wood

and Neal Wood, "Socrates and Democracy: A Reply to Gregory Vlastos," *PTh* 14 (1986): 55–82, and see I.vii.6–8 and Epilogue, below.

35. Thuc. 2.37.2–3, 39.

36. Xen. *Mem.* 3.5.16–17.

37. Consider Thuc. 2.65.5–13 in light of Donald Kagan, *Pericles of Athens and the Birth of Democracy* (New York 1990), and see Isoc. 15.316–17 and Arist. *Ath. Pol.* 28. After pondering developments in the democracy at Syracusa (Thuc. 6.32.3–41.4, 72–73, 103; Xen. *Hell.* 1.1.27–31; Diod. 13.4.1–2, 11.3–6, 18.3–6, 19.4–33.3, 34.4–35.5, 39.4, 63.1–6, 75.2–9, 91.1–96.4), consider the remarkably similar pattern of events at Athens (Thuc. 4.65, 102–8 [with 5.26.5], 6.26.1–32.2, 53–61 [with 74, 88.7–93.3, 7.18.1–2, 8.6–109; Xen. *Hell.* 1.4.10–20, 5.10–17], 7.47–49 [with Plut. *Nic.* 22]; Xen. *Hell.* 1.6.19–7.35 [with Diod. 13.97.1–103.2], 2.1.20–32 [with Diod. 13.104.8–106.7]; and Andoc. 3.33–35 [with Philochorus *FGrH* 328 F149a]) in light of Machiavelli, *Discorsi* 1.28, 31, 53, with an eye to Nathan S. Rosenstein, *Imperatores Victi: Military Defeat and Aristocratic Competition in the Middle and Late Republic* (Berkeley 1990). On the phenomenon of demagoguery, see W. Robert Connor, *The New Politicians of Fifth-Century Athens* (Princeton 1971), and Ober, *Mass and Elite in Democratic Athens.*

38. Consider Thuc. 1.77 in light of Ar. *Pax* 505, *Av.* 41, 109, *Nub.* 206–9; [Xen.] *Ath. Pol.* 1.16; Isaeus 8.4. For one dimension of the problem, see Matthew R. Christ, "Liturgy Avoidance and *Antidosis* in Classical Athens," *TAPhA* 120 (1990): 147–69.

39. Theophr. *Char.* 28.5–6.

40. See Nicole Loraux and Pierre Vidal-Naquet, "La formation de l'Athènes bourgeoise: Essai d'historiographie 1750–1870," in *Classical Influences on Western Thought A.D. 1650–1870*, ed. R. R. Bolgar (Cambridge 1979) 169–222, and Frank Turner, *The Greek Heritage in Victorian Britain* (New Haven 1981) 187–263.

41. Cf. Georg Jellinek, *Allgemeine Staatslehre*[3] (Berlin 1914) 292–312; Blair Campbell, "Constitutionalism, Rights and Religion: The Athenian Example," *HPT* 7 (1986): 239–73, and "Paradigms Lost: Classical Athenian Politics in Modern Myth," *HPT* 10 (1989): 189–213; Raphael Sealey, *The Athenian Republic: Democracy or the Rule of Law?* (University Park, Pa., 1987); and Mogens Herman Hansen, *Was Athens a Democracy?: Popular Rule, Liberty and Equality in Ancient and Modern Political Thought* (Copenhagen 1989), with the more sensible and nuanced discussion in Richard Mulgan, "Liberty in Ancient Greece," in *Conceptions of Political Liberty in Political Philosophy*, ed. Zbigniew Pelczynski and John Gray (New York 1984) 7–26. Hansen's case, though forcefully argued, rests on special pleading throughout. It would collapse altogether were he to acknowledge the martial character of the Athenian democracy and to recognize as anomalous in modern democracies phenomena which are clearly illiberal vestiges of the premodern world: slavery, the exclusion of women from political life, the refusal to naturalize immigrant laborers and assimilate their offspring, and the absence of a written constitution expressly limiting the sphere of public control. Because he takes Dem. 22.51–52 at face value, Hansen fails to recognize that respect for the privacy of the household is no more an Athenian than a Spartan phenomenon: see I.v.5, above.

42. To do so, one must resolutely avert one's gaze from the prevalence of slavery, the subjection of women, and the lust for empire: see Ellen Meiksins Wood and Neal Wood, *Class Ideology and Ancient Political Theory: Socrates, Plato, and Aristotle in Social Context* (Oxford 1978) esp. 13–80, and Ellen Meiksins Wood,

Peasant-Citizen and Slave: The Foundations of Athenian Democracy (London 1988). The latter book is of particular interest because it provides an instructive example of just how far an able and highly intelligent scholar can be led astray by the inclination to emphasize material relations and class struggle to the point of effectively denying the capacity of opinion concerning honor and the good life to contribute decisively to shaping the ethos of a community. For her methodological predilections explain Wood's inability to see why a more or less self-sufficient peasant smallholder would be inclined to harbor contempt for artisans, merchants, and laborers dependent upon customers, and the same can be said for her failure to appreciate the central importance of war for the Greeks and consequently to recognize that those in Hellas who worked the land had reason to distrust those who depended for their livelihood on exportable skills or on the investment of movable wealth: cf. *Peasant-Citizen and Slave* 81–144 with I.ii.1–3, iii.3, above.

43. Tocqueville, *DA* 2.1.3 (22), 15 (67).

44. For the situation in the early years of the Peloponnesian War, see Thuc. 2.14–17. For the relatively small number of Athenians without land at the end of that struggle, see Lys. 34 with Dion. Hal. *Lys.* 32. For recent discussions of the importance of peasant smallholding and village life, see Robin Osborne, *Demos: The Discovery of Classical Attika* (Cambridge 1985), and David Whitehead, *The Demes of Attica, 508/7–ca. 250 B.C.: A Political and Social Study* (Princeton 1986).

45. The 1860 census reveals that in the Old South on the eve of the American Civil War there were considerably fewer than four hundred thousand slaveholders and just over one and a half million white households; nearly three-quarters of the free population had no direct, familial connection with slavery at all: Kenneth M. Stampp, *The Peculiar Institution: Slavery in the Ante-bellum South* (New York 1956) 29–30. In Attica, all but the poor seem to have been in a position to own slaves (Lys. 24.6), and enough availed themselves of the opportunity for it not to seem bizarre for an orator in court to speak as if every member of the jury was a slaveholder: Dem. 45.86.

46. Given the paucity of pertinent evidence (especially regarding the countryside) and the difficulties posed by its interpretation, we cannot be certain that slavery was the predominant form of labor in agriculture: cf. Michael H. Jameson, "Agriculture and Slavery in Classical Athens," *CJ* 73 (1978): 122–45, with Ellen Meiksins Wood, "Agricultural Slavery in Classical Athens," *AJAH* 8 (1983): 1–47; Wood, *Peasant-Citizen and Slave* 42–80, 173–80; and Robert Sallares, *The Ecology of the Ancient Greek World* (Ithaca 1991) 53–60; then see Thomas W. Gallant, *Risk and Survival in Ancient Greece: Reconstructing the Rural Domestic Economy* (Stanford 1991) 30–33.

47. The bulk of the pertinent evidence cited in I.i.2, above, is Athenian. In this connection, cf. Chester Starr, "An Overdose of Slavery," *JEcH* 18 (1958): 17–58, with Carl Degler, "Starr on Slavery," *JEcH* 19 (1959): 271–77, and see Gallant, *Risk and Survival in Ancient Greece* 30–33.

48. See Russell Meiggs, *The Athenian Empire* (Oxford 1975) 1–305.

49. See ibid., 152–74 (with 425–27).

50. Aristophanes seems to have exploited this theme in his *Babylonians* and was unsuccessfully prosecuted by Cleon for slandering the city in front of foreigners: consider Ar. *Ach.* 377–82, 502–6, 515–16, 641–45, 659–64 (with the scholia) in light of G. Norwood, "The Babylonians of Aristophanes," *CPh* 25 (1930): 1–10.

51. Cf. *PJM* XIV 164–65: "Notes for the *National Gazette* Essays," ca. 19 December 1791–3 March 1792, with Montesquieu, *EL* 3.15.1–19, and Jefferson, *NSV* 18 (162–63). Madison drew on these notes in an essay that the editors of the pertinent volume of *PJM* failed to recognize as his. See Colleen A. Sheehan, "Madison's Party Press Essays," *Interpretation* 17 (1990): 355–77 (esp. 356–57, 376–77): "Dependent Colonies," *National Gazette*, 12 December 1791.

52. See David Whitehead, *The Ideology of the Athenian Metic* (Cambridge 1977), with Whitehead, "The Ideology of the Athenian Metic: Some Pendants and a Reappraisal," *PCPhS* 212 (1986): 145–58.

53. Consider Thuc. 1.6.3–5, Ar. *Eq.* 1321–24, Herakleides Pontikos F55 (Wehrli), and Schol. Hom. *Il.* 13.685 in light of Diog. Laert. 6.90 and Schol. *Eq.* 580; then, see Arnold W. Gomme, Antony Andrewes, and Kenneth J. Dover, *An Historical Commentary on Thucydides* (Oxford 1945–80) I 101–6, and A. G. Geddes, "Rags and Riches: The Costume of Athenian Men in the Fifth Century," *CQ* n.s. 37 (1987): 307–31.

54. Cf. [Xen.] *Ath. Pol.* 1.10–12 and Dem. 9.3 with Theophr. *Leg.* F6a–b (Szegedy-Maszak), and see Pl. *Resp.* 8.562c–563b.

55. Consider Arist. *Ath. Pol.* 26.4 (in context); Plut. *Per.* 37; and Ael. *VH* 6.10, 13.24, F68 in light of Arist. *Pol.* 1326b20–21, and see Cynthia Patterson, *Pericles' Citizenship Law of 451–50 B.C.* (New York 1981) 1–139, and Rhodes, *A Commentary on the Aristotelian Athenaion Politeia* 331–35. For the law's enforcement, see also Philochorus *FGrH* 328 F119. The Periclean law was still in effect as late as 414: Ar. *Av.* 1649–52. It was reenacted in 403: Eumelos *FGrH* 77 F2 (ap. Schol. Aeschin. 1.39). For the large number of immigrants permanently resident in late fifth-century Athens, see Thuc. 7.63.3 with 1.121.3, 143.1.

56. Dion. Hal. *Ant. Rom.* 2.17.1.

57. Hdt. 7.161.3 (with 8.55); Eur. *Ion* 29–30, 589–92 (with 20–21, 265–70, 999–1000), F360 (Nauck²); Ar. *Vesp.* 1075–80; Thuc. 1.2.5–6, 2.36.1; Lys. 2.17; Pl. *Menex.* 237d, 239a, 245d–e, *Ti.* 23d–e, *Criti.* 109c–e; Isoc. 4.23–25, 12.124–25; Dem. 19.261, 60.4; Lycurg. 1.41 (with 21, 47–48, 85); Hyper. 6.7 (Jensen); Paus. 2.14.4; Cic. *Rep.* 3.15.25; Ael. Aristid. *Panath.* 30 (Lenz/Behr); Schol. D. Ael. Aristid. *Panath.* 103.14 and 16 (Dindorf); Harpocration s.v. *autochthónes*. In this connection, see Emil Ermatinger, *Die attische Autochthonensage bis auf Euripides* (Berlin 1897); Walter Burkert, "Kekropidensage und Arrhephoria: Vom Initiationsritus zum Panathenäenfest," *Hermes* 94 (1966): 1–25; Claude Bérard, *Anodoi: Essai sur l'imagerie des passages chthoniens* (Neuchâtel 1974) 31–38; Nicole Loraux, *Les enfants d'Athéna: Idées athéniennes sur la citoyenneté et la division des sexes* (Paris 1981) 7–26, 35–73; Arlene W. Saxonhouse, "Myths and the Origins of Cities: Reflections on the Autochthony Theme in Euripides' *Ion*," in *Greek Tragedy and Political Theory*, ed. J. Peter Euben (Berkeley 1986) 252–273; and, most recently, Vincent J. Rosivach, "Autochthony and the Athenians," *CQ* n.s. 37 (1987): 294–306.

58. Cf. Hdt. 7.161.3; Isoc. 4.23–25; Hyper. 6.7 (Jensen); Arist. *Rh.* 1360b31–38 with Ar. *Av.* 466–92, 687–704; Pl. *Ti.* 34b–c.

59. Pl. *Resp.* 3.414d–e, 470d.

60. Lys. 2.17, Cic. *Rep.* 3.15.25.

61. Cf. *The Federalist* 38 (241) with Montesquieu *EL* 1.3.4–6, 3.19.21, and see Plut. *Sol.* 15.1–2, 22.1–3.

62. Consider Aeschin. 1.21, 3.175–76, and Dem. 24.103 (with 119) in light

of the ethos made visible by Pierre Vidal-Naquet, "The Tradition of the Athenian Hoplite," "The Black Hunter and the Origin of the Athenian *Ephebia*," and "Recipes for Greek Adolescence," *The Black Hunter: Forms of Thought and Forms of Society in the Greek World*, trans. Andrew Szegedy-Maszak (Baltimore 1986) 85–156, and François Lissarrague, *L'autre guerrier: Archers, peltastes, cavaliers dans l'imagerie attique* (Paris 1990). For two recent and thought-provoking, if sometimes fanciful, discussions of the sexual protocols for citizen-men, see David M. Halperin, "The Democratic Body: Prostitution and Citizenship in Classical Athens," *One Hundred Years of Homosexuality and Other Essays on Greek Love* (New York 1990) 88–112, and John J. Winkler, "Laying Down the Law: The Oversight of Men's Sexual Behavior in Classical Athens," *The Constraints of Desire: The Anthropology of Sex and Gender in Ancient Greece* (New York 1990) 45–70—the latter with note 80, below. In this connection, note also Mark Golden, "Slavery and Homosexuality at Athens," *Phoenix* 38 (1984): 308–24.

63. See Paul Millett, "Sale, Credit and Exchange in Athenian Law and Society," in *Nomos: Essays in Athenian Law, Politics and Society*, ed. Paul Cartledge, Paul Millett, and Stephen Todd (Cambridge 1990) 167–94, and *Lending and Borrowing in Ancient Athens* (Cambridge 1991).

64. See Moses I. Finley, "The Alienability of Land in Ancient Greece," *The Use and Abuse of History*[2] (Harmondsworth 1985) 153–60, and Gustave Glotz, *La solidarité de la famille en Grèce* (Paris 1904) 329–30, who demonstrated long ago that Arist. *Pol.* 1266b17 does not attribute to Solon a statute restricting the ownership of land.

65. Consider Theophr. *Leg.* F21.1–3 (Szegedy-Maszak) in light of Pl. *Leg.* 5.745a–d, 8.850a, 9.855a–b, 11.914c, and Arist. *Pol.* 1321b34–40; and see William Scott Ferguson, "The Laws of Demetrius of Phalerum and Their Guardians," *Klio* 11 (1911): 265–76, and Sterling Dow and Albert H. Travis, "Demetrius of Phaleron and His Lawgiving," *Hesperia* 12 (1943): 144–65. Note also Hans-Joachim Gehrke, "Das Verhältnis von Politik und Philosophie im Wirken des Demetrios von Phaleron," *Chiron* 8 (1978): 149–92. Cf. Moses I. Finley, *Studies in Land and Credit in Ancient Athens, 500–200 B.C.* (New Brunswick, N.J., 1952) 177–81.

66. This fact was no doubt closely linked with the persistence of the peasant smallholder throughout the classical period: see V. N. Andreyev, "Some Aspects of Agrarian Conditions in Attica in the Fifth to the Third Centuries B.C.," *Eirene* 12 (1974): 5–46. See also Gert Audring, "Über Grundeigentum und Landwirtschaft in der Krise der athenischen Polis," in *Hellenische Poleis*, ed. Elisabeth Charlotte Welskopf (Berlin 1974) I 108–31, and "Zur wirtschaftlichen und sozialen Lage der attischen Bauern im ausgehenden 5. und im 4. Jahrhundert v. u. Z.," *Jahrbuch für Wirtschaftsgeschichte*, Sonderband: *Studien zur Athenischen Sozialstruktur und römischen Wirtschaftspolitik in Kleinasien* (Berlin 1977) 9–86. As a consequence of the unwillingness of Athenian peasants to part with their farms, the extremely wealthy—men like Nicias, Hipponicus, and Philemonides—are much less well known for their holdings in land than for investing their excess capital in armies of slaves whom they set to work in the city's silver mines: Xen. *Vect.* 4.14–16.

67. See Dem. 43.62; Cic. *Leg.* 2.23.59, 25.63–27.69; Plut. *Sol.* 12.8–9, 20.6, 21.5–6; Ath. 6.245a–c. Cf. Pl. *Minos* 315c–d. In the list of Athens's sumptuary laws, one should no doubt also include the restrictions that Solon is said to have placed on the honors and privileges conferred on those victorious in the great Panhellenic games: see Xenophanes *Vorsokr.*[6] 21 B2, and cf. Plut. *Sol.* 23.3 and

Diog. Laert. 1.55 with Diod. 9.2.5. Note, in this connection, Plut. *Sol.* 24.5; Ath. 4.137e.

68. Consider Geddes, "Rags and Riches" 307–31, in light of Wolfram Hoepfner and Ernst-Ludwig Schwandner, *Haus und Stadt im klassischen Griechenland* (Munich 1986) esp. 1–21, 247–75.

69. One should consider Isaeus 6.59–61 in light of Xen. *Oec.* 2.5–8; interpret Dem. 1.28, 10.35–45, 21.211, 22.51, 24.111, 42.17–23 with an eye to Thuc. 6.39.1 and Dem. 14.25–28; and see Theophr. *Char.* 26.6. Note Dem. 3.34–35 and Isoc. 15.151–52.

70. Consider Eur. *Tro.* 645–56; Xen. *Oec.* 3.11–16, 7.17–43; Pl. *Phdr.* 239c–d; Men. F546 (Edmonds); and Stob. *Flor.* 4.1.502 (Hense) in light of J. P. Gould, "Law, Custom and Myth: Aspects of the Social Position of Women in Classical Athens," *JHS* 100 (1980): 38–59; Roger Just, *Women in Athenian Law and Life* (New York 1989); and David Cohen, "Seclusion, Separation, and the Status of Women in Classical Athens," *G&R* 36 (1989): 3–15, and "The Social Context of Adultery at Athens," in *Nomos* 147–65.

71. Consider Dem. 59.122 in light of Pl. *Leg.* 7.805d–806c and Arist. *Pol.* 1277b20–25, and see Raphael Sealey, *Women and Law in Classical Greece* (Chapel Hill 1990) esp. 1–49, 151–60.

72. Lys. F230 (Sauppe); Dem. 46.14, 16; Arist. *Ath. Pol.* 35.2; Isaeus 4.16, 6.9, 21; Hyper. 5.17 (Jensen); Plut *Sol.* 21.4, *Mor.* 265e.

73. See Thuc. 1.70, 3.37–38 (with Ar. *Nub.* 331–34, 547–48). Note Acts 17:21. It is not fortuitous that Thucydides (2.35) represents Pericles as having opened the funeral oration with a critique of tradition.

74. For Athenian *philoxenía* and the ridicule it incurred, see [Xen.] *Ath. Pol.* 2.7–8, Strabo 10.3.18 (with Pl. *Resp.* 1.327a–328a, 354a). In this connection, one should reread Cic. *Rep.* 2.4.7–9 and Pl. *Leg.* 4.704d–705b.

75. *LSJ*⁹ II.2 s.v.

76. Thuc. 6.27–29, 53, 60–61, 8.53.2.

77. The testimony of Xenophon (*Hell.* 1.6.19–7.35) and Diodorus (13.97.1–103.2) is in some respects inconsistent, and the interpretation of the battle and trial is a subject of scholarly dispute: see, for example, Antony Andrewes, "The Arginousai Trial," *Phoenix* 28 (1974): 112–22, and Donald Kagan, *The Fall of the Athenian Empire* (Ithaca 1987) 325–75.

78. Xen. *Mem.* 1.1.1, *Ap.* 10–13, 17–20; Pl. *Ap.* 24b–c, 35e–38d, 42a, *Phd.* 116e–118a; Diog. Laert. 2.39–44.

79. This was true even in Socrates' case, for he was held responsible for the misdeeds of his students Alcibiades and Critias: consider Xen. *Mem.* 1.2.12, Aeschin. 1.173, and Hyper. F55 (Jensen) in light of the assumptions voiced by Plato Comicus: see F191 (Kock) with Plut. *Per.* 4.1–4. In this connection, note Richard A. Bauman, *Political Trials in Ancient Greece* (London 1990) 61–67, 69–76, 105–16.

80. Cf. Winkler, "Laying Down the Law" 45–70, who makes rather more of the gap between the ascetic ideal embodied in the law and what can be surmised regarding actual standards for Athenian behavior than I think justified. It stands to reason that public figures should be more vulnerable to prosecution than their less well known compatriots, and it is in keeping with the spirit of Athenian democracy that the citizens should in other cases be less than rigorous in their enforcement of the reigning political morality; but this does not indicate that the Athenians had somehow inscribed in the law an ideal at odds with their deepest

interests and feelings. The fact that Aristophanes (*Nub.* 1066–1104) can elicit a laugh by suggesting that all of those in his audience are guilty of the pertinent infraction can hardly be taken as evidence that a great many were.

81. For a characteristically thorough, but excessively skeptical survey of the evidence, see K. J. Dover, "The Freedom of the Intellectual in Greek Society," *Talanta* 7 (1975): 24–54. This essay, its title notwithstanding, refers to Athens alone. Dover is eager to exonerate ancient democracy of every hint of illiberality but finds himself forced to admit Diagoras's prosecution. Though hardly as solid as one might wish, the evidence for the persecution of freethinkers other than Socrates and Diagoras is, in fact, as good as virtually all of the evidence from the period pertinent to subjects other than politics, diplomacy, and the conduct of war. Note Bauman, *Political Trials in Ancient Greece* 37–49, 67–68.

82. Among those tried and convicted were Archias (Dem. 59.116–17), Ninos (Dem. 19.281 [with the scholia], 39.2, 40.9), Phryne (Hyper. F171–80 [Jensen]), and Theoris (Dem. 25.79–80, Philochorus *FGrH* 328 F60). For additional examples, see Bauman, *Political Trials in Ancient Greece* 105–27.

83. See Thuc. 8.73.3; Plut. *Arist.* 7.7–8, *Nic.* 11. See also Arist. *Ath. Pol.* 22, *Pol.* 1284a17–22, 1284b15–22, 1302b15–21, 1308b16–19; Demetrius of Phaleron F95 (Wehrli). For the procedures, see Arist. *Ath. Pol.* 43.5 and Theophr. *Leg.* F18a–b (Szegedy-Maszak) with Diod. 11.55.2, Plut. *Arist.* 7.5–6, Poll. *Onom.* 8.20, Schol. Ar. *Eq.* 855, Philochorus *FGrH* 328 F30. When ostracism was first introduced, the power of banishment may have been exercised by the Athenian *Boulē* rather than by the *dêmos* itself. See J. J. Keaney and A. E. Raubitschek, "A Late Byzantine Account of Ostracism," *AJPh* 93 (1972): 87–91: MS Vat. Gr. 1144, 222^{r-v}. For the surviving *ostraka*, see *GHI* 1.21. Similar institutions existed at Argos (Arist. *Pol.* 1302b18), at Miletus and Megara (Schol. Ar. *Eq.* 855), and, for a brief spell, at Syracuse (Diod. 11.86.5–87.6).

84. See Claude Mossé, "De l'ostracisme au procès politique: Le fonctionnement de la vie politique à Athènes," *AION(archeol)* 7 (1985): 9–18. Note also Svend Ranulf, *The Jealousy of the Gods and Criminal Law at Athens: A Contribution to the Sociology of Moral Indignation* (London 1933) esp. I 132–42, and Mossé, "Les proces politiques et la crise de la démocratie Athènienne," *DHA* 1 (1974): 207–36.

85. Hyper. 2.14–15 (Jensen). See Hyper. 3.22 (Jensen); Aeschin. 1.179, 2.145, 150. In consequence, witnesses were less often summoned to the city's courts to establish the facts than to testify to a man's character as a citizen and householder and to demonstrate by their presence the respectability of his associations: consider Sally C. Humphreys, "Social Relations on Stage: Witnesses in Classical Athens," *History and Anthropology* 1 (1985): 313–69, and "Kinship Patterns in Athenian Courts," *GRBS* 27 (1986): 57–91, in light of Humphreys, "The Evolution of Legal Process in Ancient Attica," in *Tria Corda: Scritti in onore di Arnaldo Momigliano*, ed. E. Gabba (Como 1983) 229–56, and see Stephen Todd, "The Purpose of Evidence in Athenian Courts," in *Nomos* 19–39.

86. See, for example, Antiphon 2.2.12; Lys. 3.46, 4.19, 5.3, 7.30–33, 41, 12.38, 18.20–21, 19.9, 56–64, 21.1–10, 26.3; Andoc. 1.132; Isoc. 18.63; Dem. 21.152–74, 28.19–20, 42.17–23, 50.2, 7–36; Isaeus 5.41–42, 6.59–61, 7.36; Lycurg. 1.139; Hyper. 2.16–18 (Jensen).

87. Consider Arist. *Ath. Pol.* 9.1 and Plut. *Sol.* 18.6–7 in light of Robin Osborne, "Law in Action in Classical Athens," *JHS* 105 (1985): 40–58, and see Bauman, *Political Trials in Ancient Greece* 12–127. For an amusing attempt to reconstruct a

particularly bizarre case, see Paul Cartledge, "Fowl Play: A Curious Lawsuit in Classical Athens (Antiphon XVI, frr. 57–9 Thalheim)," in *Nomos* 41–61.

88. After reading Arist. *Ath. Pol.* 25 alongside Craterus *FGH* 342 F12 (ap. Plut. *Arist.* 26), consider Xen. *Hell.* 2.3.12, Lys. 12.5, Arist. *Ath. Pol.* 35.3, and Diod. 14.4.2 in light of Lys. 25.25–30, and see Pl. *Rep.* 8.565a–c and Theophr. *Char.* 26.3–6. Then, note [Xen.] *Ath. Pol.* 1.14 and Ar. *Av.* 1420–35, and see Antiphon 3.2.1; Ar. *Ach.* 685–88, 911–22, *Vesp.* 894–994, F198 (Kock); Lys. 7.1, 18.18–19, 20.12; Isoc. 15.314, 21.8–15; Dem. 18.138, 55.33, 57.34, 58.61–63; Aeschin. 2.145; and Lycurg. 1.31 with an eye to what can be inferred concerning the pattern of malicious prosecution from the disclaimers voiced at Antiphon 1.1; Lys. 12.3, 19.55; Isaeus 1.1, 8.5, 9.35, 10.1; Isoc. 15.26; Dem. 27.2, 29.1, 41.2, 48.1, 55.2; Hyper. 2.19, 3.13 (Jensen); and elsewhere.

89. Consider Lys. 27.1–2, Xen. *Hell.* 2.3.12, Isoc. 21.8–15, Hyper. 3.33–36 (Jensen), and Nep. *Chabrias* 3 in light of Arist. *Pol.* 1279b17–1280a6, 1309b35–1310a37, 1311a15–22; and consider the resentments and fears to which the speaker is appealing in Isoc. 20.20; Dem. 18.102–8, 320, 19.295, 21.66–67, 112, 124, 133, 138, 142–46, 153–59, 198–204, 210–13, 23.208, 24.112, 36.45, 38.27, 40.50–51, 42.31, 45.67, 51.11, *Exordia* 2; Aeschin. 1.195; and Lycurg. 1.139–40 in conjunction with Lys. 3.9, 31.8–14, and Isaeus 5.35–45. Cf. Robin Osborne, "Vexatious Litigation in Classical Athens: Sykophancy and the Sykophant," in *Nomos* 83–102, with David Harvey, "The Sykophant and Sykophancy: Vexatious Redefinition?" in *Nomos* 103–21, and see Ober, *Mass and Elite in Democratic Athens* 192–247.

90. Just as oligarchies denied active citizenship to the poor, so also an extreme democracy might reward the well-to-do for political quiescence. If *apragmosúnē* was ever generally thought a virtue, it was the virtue not of the rulers but of the ruled: cf. Donald Lateiner, " 'The Man Who Does Not Meddle in Politics': A *Topos* in Lysias," *CW* 76 (1982–83) 1–12, with Carter, *The Quiet Athenian* 26–130 (esp. 99–130), and see Thuc. 8.68.

91. This was apparently common: consider Plut. *Nic.* 4 and Isoc. 21.8–15 in light of Ar. *Eq.* 259–65 (with the attendant scholia); Antiphon 5.80; Xen. *Mem.* 2.9.1–8 (with *Hell.* 1.7.2, Lys. 14.25, and Ar. *Ran.* 417); Lys. 25.25–26; Dem. 58.33, 61–65; Hyper. 2.1–2 (Jensen).

92. Consider Lys. 20.30–31, 25.12 (with 18.23, 21.15, Isoc. 18.66–67, and Isaeus 7.41), and Xen. *Oec.* 2.5–6 in light of [Xen.] *Ath. Pol.* 1.13–14.

93. Consider the manner in which Plato's Socrates (*Ap.* 29c–35d, 38c–39b) represents his trial as a confrontation with the *pólis* constituted by "the Athenians"; note Dem. 43.72; and ponder the willingness of jurors to make public display of their displeasure with a litigant just as they were wont to do in the assembly when they disapproved of the remarks of an orator: see Victor Bers, "Dikastic *Thorubos*," in *Crux: Essays Presented to G. E. M. de Ste. Croix on His 75th Birthday*, ed. Paul Cartledge and F. D. Harvey (Exeter 1985) 1–15. Cf. Mogens Herman Hansen, "*Demos, Ecclesia* and *Dicasterion* in Classical Athens," *The Athenian Ecclesia: A Collection of Articles, 1976–83* (Copenhagen 1983) 139–60, with Ober, *Mass and Elite in Democratic Athens* 324 n. 16, and see Ober, 141–48, 299–304.

94. Benjamin Constant, "De la liberté des anciens comparée à celle des modernes," *Cours de politique constitutionelle*, ed. M. Édouard Laboulaye (Paris 1861) II 542, 546–47. Cf. Arist. *Pol.* 1284a3–b33 and Montesquieu, *EL* 5.26.17, 6.29.7, with Andoc. 4.1–6.

95. The most recent effort along these lines has the great virtue that it lays bare

and, in fact, proudly exhibits the untenable assumption underlying all attempts to explain away the efforts of the greatest minds of the past as a mere rationalization of interest and prejudice: the conviction that all thought is inextricably partisan and polemical. In the process, it nicely illustrates the degree to which such a presumption undermines in its proponents even the pretense to scholarly impartiality and thereby encourages in them a tendency to neglect or cavalierly dismiss evidence contrary to their own inclinations, a propensity to distort the evidence they deign to present, and a proclivity to resort to special pleading of the most transparent sort. Cf. Wood and Wood, *Class Ideology and Ancient Political Theory* esp. 1–12, 81–265, with the review by Gregory Vlastos: *Phoenix* 34 (1980): 347–52 (esp. 348–52).

96. Thuc. 2.37.2–3.

97. Thuc. 2.40.1.

98. Thuc. 2.63.2. Note 3.37.2, Ar. *Eq.* 1111–14.

99. Thuc. 2.41.4. See I.iv.2, note 37, in context above.

100. Cf. Thuc. 2.40.2 with Hamilton, *The Federalist* 8 (47). For those who exhibited the tendency which Pericles denounced, see Carter, *The Quiet Athenian* 26–130. In this connection, see also R. K. Sinclair, *Democracy and Participation in Athens* (Cambridge 1988).

101. Thuc. 2.63.3.

102. Cf. Thuc. 2.41.1 with Pl. *Resp.* 10.606e, and see Thuc. 1.3.3.

103. Thuc. 2.45.2.

104. Thuc. 2.44.4.

105. Thuc. 2.38.1.

106. For a systematic comparison, see Nicole Loraux, *The Invention of Athens: The Funeral Oration in the Classical City*, trans. Alan Sheridan (Cambridge, Mass., 1986). Note also C. W. Clairmont, *Patrios Nomos: Public Burial in Athens during the Fifth and Fourth Centuries B.C.* (London 1983).

107. Cf. *The Federalist* 10 with *PJM* X 212–14: Letter to Thomas Jefferson on 24 October 1787, and see II.v.7, 10–11, vi.4–5, 7, Epilogue, III.i.3–6, below.

108. See, for example, Andoc. 1.106–9, 2.1; Lys. 2.13, 17–18, 24, 63–65, 18.17–18, 25.21–23, 30; Isoc. 6.67, 7.31, 69, 8.19, 12.178, 258, 18.44, 68; Aeschin. 3.208; Dem. 9.38, 19.298, 25.89–90; Hyper. 3.37 (Jensen); Deinarchus 1.99, 3.19.

109. Democr. *Vorsokr.*⁶ 68 B250. For Democritus as a liberal democrat, see Eric A. Havelock, *The Liberal Temper in Greek Politics* 12, 17–18, 32–33, 70, 115–56, 165–67, 171–85. For a closer look at this thinker, see Cynthia Farrar, *The Origins of Democratic Thinking: The Invention of Politics in Classical Athens* (Cambridge 1988) 192–264, and J. F. Procopé, "Democritus on Politics and the Care of the Soul," *CQ* n.s. 39 (1989): 307–31, and "Democritus on Politics and the Care of the Soul: Appendix," *CQ* n.s. 40 (1990): 21–45.

110. Consider Francis MacDonald Cornford, *Thucydides Mythistoricus* (Philadelphia 1971) 201–20, in light of Hdt. 5.32, and see Michael Palmer, "Love of Glory and the Common Good," *APSR* 76 (1982): 825–36.

111. Thuc. 2.43.1–4.

112. Cf. Thuc. 2.64.3–6 with the material presented in I.v.3, above.

113. *The Federalist* 9 (52–53).

114. For this chapter's epigraph, see Hume, *EPM* VII.

115. Consider Eur. *Tro.* 654–56, Xen. *Oec.* 3.11–16, Lycurg. 1.141–42, Dem. 59.107–15, and P. Didot I (Sandbach) in light of Hdt. 1.37.3 and Xen. *Cyr.* 6.4.9,

and see Georges Raepsaet, "Sentiments conjugaux à Athènes aux Vᵉ et IVᵉ siècles avant notre ère," *AC* 50 (1981): 677–84. Women were undoubtedly more influential than their legal status would seem to suggest. Where, by divorce, they could deprive their husbands of a substantial dowry, this was doubly true. Consider Pl. *Leg.* 6.774c–d in light of Lin Foxhall, "Household, Gender and Property in Classical Athens," *CQ* n.s. 39 (1989): 22–44 (esp. 32–43), and see I.v.2, note 38, above. There is much to be said for Winkler's contention that, in these matters, nothing is ever quite as simple as public prescription makes it seem: "Introduction," and "The Laughter of the Oppressed: Demeter and the Gardens of Adonis," *The Constraints of Desire* 1–13, 188–209.

116. Thuc. 1.70.

117. This can be inferred by comparing Athenian hoplite losses with the figures that we are given for the city's heavy infantry force at the beginning of the war: cf. Thuc. 3.87 with 2.13.6, and see Strauss, *Athens after the Peloponnesian War* 75–76 (with the notes: esp. 84 n. 33).

118. Consider Thuc. 2.1–5.24 with Donald Kagan's discussion of the remaining evidence and the secondary literature: *The Archidamian War* (Ithaca 1974).

119. Consider Thuc. 5.13–83 in conjunction with Donald Kagan's discussion of the remaining evidence and the secondary literature: *The Peace of Nicias and the Sicilian Expedition* (Ithaca 1981) 17–155.

120. Thuc. 6.9–14.

121. Thuc. 6.16–18.

122. Cf. Thuc. 6.19–26 with Eur. *IA* 808–9.

123. Thuc. 6.30–32.2 For subsequent events, see 6.32.3–53.2, 60–7.87 with Kagan, *The Peace of Nicias and the Sicilian Expedition* 157–372.

124. For an exploration of these themes, see Steven Forde, *The Ambition to Rule: Alcibiades and the Politics of Imperialism in Thucydides* (Ithaca 1989).

125. The passage in which Thucydides describes the procedure that he followed in composing the speeches that adorn his narrative is notoriously difficult to interpret: 1.22.1–3. It would, however, be fair to say that four themes predominate: his eagerness to summarize the arguments actually presented, the virtual impossibility in many cases of securing complete and accurate information after the fact, his special interest in reporting the speeches delivered by those who best succeeded in enunciating what was demanded by the situation in which they found themselves, and his willingness to embellish on what was said without departing from the overall argument. See Clifford Orwin, "Thucydides' Contest: Thucydidean 'Methodology' in Context," *RP* 51 (1989): 345–64.

126. Ar. *Eq.* 730–32. For further evidence indicating that the historian did not invent this particular oration out of whole cloth, see Carter, *The Quiet Athenian* 195–96.

127. An Athenian in search of a place that is *aprágmōn* will soon attempt the establishment of an empire: cf. Ar. *Av.* 27–45, 113–61 with 162–208, 252–59, 316–24, 366–640, 809–1765.

128. Cf. Ar. *Av.* 471 with 44, and see Eur. *Supp.* 576 and Thuc. 6.87. See also Ar. *Ach.* 833, *Plut.* 913; Lys. 1.15–16, 24.24; Isoc. 15.98, 230, 237; and consider Victor Ehrenberg, "Polypragmosune: A Study in Greek Politics," *JHS* 67 (1947): 46–67, and A. W. H. Adkins, "*Polupragmosune* and 'Minding One's Own Business': A Study in Greek Social and Political Values," *CPh* 71 (1976): 301–27.

129. After considering M. Amit, *Athens and the Sea: A Study in Athenian Sea-*

Power (Brussels 1965) 30–49, cf. Thuc. 1.104, 109–10, and Isoc. 8.86 with Diod. 11.71.3–6, 74–75, 77.1–5; Ctesias *FGrH* 688 F14; and Justin 3.6.6–7; and see J. M. Libourel, "The Athenian Disaster in Egypt," *AJPh* 92 (1971): 605–15, and Meiggs, *The Athenian Empire* 92–151, 473–76. In this connection, see Hdt. 3.12.4, 160.2 (with 7.82, 121.3), 7.7. Even those who believe these figures inflated concede that something like one Athenian citizen in five died in the Egyptian campaign: see A. J. Holladay, "The Hellenic Disaster in Egypt," *JHS* 109 (1989): 176–82.

130. Consider Plut. *Per.* 20.4 in light of Ar. *Eq.* 172–78, 1300–1315, *Peace* 250, and see H. D. Westlake, "Athenian Aims in Sicily, 427–424 B.C.," *Historia* 9 (1960): 385–402.

131. Pl. *Grg.* 518e–519d, Thuc. 3.37.3. Cf. 4.28.5, 6.29.2, 8.53.3.

132. See Martin Ostwald, *From Popular Sovereignty to the Sovereignty of Law: Law, Society, and Politics in Fifth-Century Athens* (Berkeley 1986), and the various studies devoted to aspects of this question by the preeminent contemporary student of Athenian political institutions: Mogens Herman Hansen, *The Sovereignty of the People's Court in Athens in the Fourth Century B.C. and the Public Action against Unconstitutional Proposals* (Odense 1974); *Eisangelia: The Sovereignty of the People's Court in Athens in the Fourth Century B.C. and the Impeachment of Generals and Politicians* (Odense 1975); and *The Athenian Assembly in the Age of Demosthenes* (Oxford 1987). Note also the articles collected in Hansen, *The Athenian Ecclesia*, as well as "Initiative and Decision: The Separation of Powers in Fourth-Century Athens," *GRBS* 22 (1981): 345–70; "The Number of *Rhetores* in the Athenian *Ecclesia*," *GRBS* 25 (1984): 123–55; and "The Political Powers of the People's Court in Fourth-Century Athens," in *The Greek City: From Homer to Alexander*, ed. Oswyn Murray and Simon Price (Oxford 1990) 215–43. For background, see Chester G. Starr, *The Birth of Athenian Democracy: The Assembly in the Fifth Century B.C.* (New York 1990).

133. See Strauss, *Athens after the Peloponnesian War* 89–178.

134. Consider, in this connection, Sally C. Humphreys, "*Oikos* and *Polis*," "Public and Private Interests in Classical Athens," and "The Family in Classical Athens: Search for a Perspective," *The Family, Women and Death: Comparative Studies* (London 1983) 1–32, 58–78.

135. See J. A. O. Larsen, "The Judgment of Antiquity on Democracy," *CPh* 49 (1954): 1–14, and II.iv.3–III.i.8, iii–v, below. Cf. G. E. M. de Ste. Croix, *The Origins of the Peloponnesian War* (Ithaca 1972), and *The Class Struggle in the Ancient Greek World: From the Archaic Age to the Arab Conquests* (Ithaca 1981) 70–71, 76, 141–42, 188–91, 278–326, 345–46, 603–7, and Moses I. Finley, *Democracy Ancient and Modern*[2] (London 1985), and *Politics in the Ancient World* (Cambridge 1983), who are as quick to excuse or deny the blunders and sins of the Athenians as they are to point out and condemn those of the Spartan foe.

136. See Ober, *Mass and Elite in Democratic Athens* esp. 95–103, 141–48, 295–309. The rough outlines of the satirical depiction in Aristophanes' *Knights* of the relationship between the demagogues and the dêmos of Athens is borne out by Ober's discussion (esp. 104–292). For an enlightening analysis of "the political character of adjudication" at Athens, see Dennis Peter Maio, "*Politeia* and Adjudication in Fourth-Century B.C. Athens," *American Journal of Jurisprudence* 28 (1983): 16–45 (esp. 21–44). Maio is quick to dismiss as an "empty myth" the supposition, fundamental to modern republican jurisprudence, that "adjudication . . . can" and should "be independent from the basic ordering of political society." As a consequence, he finds it all too easy to ignore the force of the Whig denial

(below, II.i–ii, iv–III.i) that a "direct democracy" can function as "liberal state" and effectively safeguard "personal freedom."

137. Men. F566 (Koerte³).

138. Cf. Hdt. 3.38 with 1.7–13; see I.i.5, ii.6, and iv.3, above; note Eur. *Med.* 294–301; then, consider Xen. *Ap.* 2–9 and *Mem.* 4.8.4–10 in light of *Cyr.* 3.1.13–40; and see Pl. *Grg.* 485d–486d, 521d–522c, *Ap.* 17c–18a, 31c–33a, *Resp.* 6.487b–497a, 9.591e–592b; Arist. *Metaph.* 995a1–6, *Pol.* 1324a14–1325b32; Cic. *Tusc.* 5.37.106–9; and Plut. *Mor.* 605a–d. The position adopted by Anaxagoras and the dramatic exploration of this question by his student Euripides deserve attention: cf. Eur. F910 and F1023 with F1113; note F184–88, F219, F395; and see F193–94, F196, F198–99, F200–202 (Nauck²)—all in conjunction with Carter, *The Quiet Athenian* 142–50, 163–73. Carter's overall attempt (131–86) to explicate Plato's discussion of the theoretical life as "a philosophic rationalization of the social and political phenomenon of *apragmosyne*" rests on his inability to appreciate the unavoidable tensions between the uninhibited quest for the truth and the demands of ancient citizenship. Only if one recognizes that there is more to the contemplative life than *apragmosúne* "bedecked with speculative trimmings" can one even begin to assess Plato's deliberate, literary exploitation of this phenomenon on philosophy's behalf. In this connection, see I.vii.6–8, Epilogue, and II Prologue, below.

139. In late antiquity, it was disputed whether Pythagoras, Parmenides, or some earlier figure was the first natural philosopher to appropriate the term *kósmos*: consider Diog. Laert. 8.48; note Anaximenes *Vorsokr.*⁶ 13 B2 (with Arist. *Ph.* 203b14–30 [esp. 25–28]); Heraclitus *Vorsokr.*⁶ 22 B30, 89; Empedocles *Vorsokr.*⁶ 31 B134; and see Xen. *Mem.* 1.1.11. It is quite conceivable that the term goes back to Thales, Anaximander, and Anaximenes: see Charles H. Kahn, *Anaximander and the Origins of Greek Cosmology* (New York 1960) 219–30. Compare Hom. *Il.* 1.16, 375, 2.655, 806, 3.1, 236, 10.472, 12.87, 14.379, *Od.* 18.152; Theog. 677, 947 (West); Solon F13.11 (West); Simon. F26.9 (PMG); Timoth. F12 (PMG); Hdt. 1.59.6, 65.4; Thuc. 4.76.2, 8.72.2. In the cities on the island of Crete, the magistrates responsible for the maintenance of order were themselves called *kósmoi* (Arist. *Pol.* 1272a4–12, 27–b15); and, as it happens, the earliest surviving written Greek law stipulates that a citizen of Dreros who has served as *kósmos* be ineligible for reelection until he has been out of office for at least ten years: see *GHI* 1.2.

140. Cf. Hes. *Op.* 274–80 with Solon F12 (West), and see Anaximander *Vorsokr.*⁶ 12 B1. See Gregory Vlastos, "Solonian Justice," *CPh* 41 (1946): 65–83, and "Equality and Justice in Early Greek Cosmologies," *CPh* 42 (1947): 156–78. Note Kahn, *Anaximander and the Origins of Greek Cosmology* 166–96.

141. Cf. Alcmaeon of Croton *Vorsokr.*⁶ 24 B4 with *Carmina Convivialia* F10–13 (PMG) and with Hdt. 3.80.2–82.5, 142.3, 5.37.2, and see Gregory Vlastos, "Isonomia," *AJPh* 74 (1953): 337–66 (esp. 347–66), with Hoepfner and Schwandner, *Haus und Stadt im klassischen Griechenland*. Those interested in the political uses of the term *isonomía* may also wish to consult Vlastos, "Isonomia Politikē," *Platonic Studies* (Princeton 1981) 164–203, and Martin Ostwald *Nomos and the Beginnings of the Athenian Democracy* (Oxford 1969) 96–136. The term subsequently played a considerable role in the arguments of Epicurus: Cic. *Nat. D.* 1.19.50, 39.109. In similar fashion, *isokratía* emerged in political parlance before being taken over by the scientists and philosophers: see Martin Ostwald, "Isokratia as a Political Concept (Herodotus, 5.92α.1)," in *Islamic Philosophy and the Classical Tradition: Essays*

Presented by His Friends and Pupils to Richard Walzer on His Seventieth Birthday, ed.
S. M. Stern, Albert Hourani, and Vivian Brown (Columbia, S.C., 1973) 277–91
(esp. 277–82).

142. See Georges Vallet, "Espace privé et espace public dans une cité coloniale
d'occident: Mégara Hyblaea," in *Problèmes de la terre en Grèce ancienne*, ed. Moses I.
Finley (Paris 1973) 83–94; cf. Roland Martin, *L'urbanisme dans la Grèce antique*[2]
(Paris 1974) 97–126, with 289–329; and consider David Asheri, "Osservazioni
sulle origini dell'urbanistica Ippodamea," *RSI* 87 (1975): 5–16, in light of what we
can now surmise concerning the innovations introduced in the fifth century by
the town planner Hippodamus of Miletus: see I.ii.5, above (at note 103).

143. Anaximander *Vorsokr.*[6] 12 A3.

144. Note Thales *Vorsokr.*[6] 11 A2; then, compare Anaximander *Vorsokr.*[6] 12
A1–2, 4, 6, 10, 11.3–5, 18–19, 21–22, 26 (esp. 2–3, 11.3, 26) with Hdt. 3.142.3; Pl.
Phd. 108e–109a, *Ti.* 62d–63a; and, finally, see Ar. *Av.* 992–1009. In this connec-
tion, see Kahn, *Anaximander and the Origins of Greek Cosmology* 53–63, 75–118, and
Jean-Pierre Vernant, "Geometry and Spherical Astronomy in the First Greek Cos-
mology," *Myth and Thought among the Greeks* (London 1983) 176–89; then, cf. Jan
Janda, *Eirene* 5 (1966): 202–5 (esp. 204–5), with Vernant, "Geometrical Structure
and Political Ideas in the Cosmology of Anaximander," *Myth and Thought among
the Greeks* 190–211; and see Vernant, "Space and Political Organization in Ancient
Greece," *Myth and Thought among the Greeks* 212–34.

145. Cf. Agathemerus 1.1–2 (GGM) with Hdt. 4.136, and see Kahn, *Anaximander and the Origins of Greek Cosmology* 81–84.

146. Consider Philolaus *Vorsokr.*[6] 44 B7 and 17 in light of Rudolph E. Siegel,
"On the Relation between Early Greek Scientific Thought and Mysticism: Is
Hestia, the Central Fire, an Abstract Astronomical Concept?" *Janus* 49 (1960):
1–20, and see the material collected in I.iv.2, note 5, above.

147. For a thorough and persuasive discussion of this question, see Jean-Pierre
Vernant, *The Origins of Greek Thought* (Ithaca 1982), along with Marcel Détienne,
Les maîtres de vérité dans la Grèce archaïque (Paris 1990). Note Pierre Vidal-Naquet,
"Greek Rationality and the City," *The Black Hunter* 249–62; and consider Marcel
Détienne and Jean-Pierre Vernant, *Cunning Intelligence in Greek Culture and Society*,
trans. Janet Lloyd (Chicago 1991), and Louis Gernet, "Aux origines de la pensée
grecque: En relisant P.-M. Schuhl," *Les Grecs sans miracle*, ed. Riccardo di Donato
(Paris 1983) 212–22, and "The Origins of Greek Philosophy," *The Anthropology of
Ancient Greece*, trans. John Hamilton, S.J., and Blaise Nagy (Baltimore 1981) 352–
64, as well as Vernant, "The Formation of Positivist Thought in Archaic Greece,"
Myth and Thought among the Greeks 343–74, and "Les origines de la philosophie,"
*Mythe et pensée chez les Grecs: Étude de psychologie historique—nouvelle édition revue
et augmentée* (Paris 1985) 403–10. For a recent study of one transitional figure, see
Hermann S. Schibli, *Pherekydes of Syros* (Oxford 1990).

148. Consider II.iv.3–8, below, in conjunction with Pl. *Tht.* 175d–177a and *Resp.*
6.501b; and cf. G. E. R. Lloyd, *Magic, Reason and Experience: Studies in the Origins and Development of Greek Science* (Cambridge 1979) 226–67 (esp. 246–64), with
Hugh Lloyd Jones, *The Justice of Zeus*[2] (Berkeley 1983) 179–84.

149. It is not fortuitous that Plato's Socrates compares himself by implication
with Heracles (*Ap.* 22a) and explicitly with Achilles (28b–d); in the *Apology* (17d–
18a, 20e–23b, 29c–38b), in the *Gorgias* (cf. 452d–e with 463d–467b, 481b–522e [esp.
484c–500d, 511c–513d, 521b–522a], 526b–c), and in *The Republic* (1.345e–347e,

2.357a–368c, 5.473c–9.592b [esp. 6.492a–497a, 498a–500d, 7.514a–521c, 9.571a–592b]), he presents the life of philosophy devoted to the pursuit of wisdom as an alternative to the life of active citizenship devoted to the pursuit of honor. Aristotle juxtaposes the same two options in a similar fashion: see I.i.3, note 54, above. Consider also Eur. F910 (Nauck²).

150. Heraclitus *Vorsokr.*⁶ 22 B114.

151. With this problem in mind, one should ponder the distinction which the ancient political philosophers drew between demotic or political virtue and its philosophic counterpart (above, I.iv.3, esp. note 82); one should consider the tension between the patriot's spirited, thumotic love of his own and the philosopher's uninhibited, erotic love of the good while reading Pl. *Symp.* 189a–193d and 198a–212c in light of 205d–206a, *Leg.* 5.731e–732a, and Arist. *Pol.* 1327b38–1328a17; and then, after perusing Hdt. 1.8–13 (esp. 8) and Pl. *Leg.* 7.797a–799b, one should ponder the tension between 11.863e–864b and 863c–d; one should compare *Ap.* 24b–25b and Xen. *Mem.* 1.1.1 with Arist. *Metaph.* 995a1–6, while keeping in mind Abū Bishr's discussion of this passage (quoted in Shlomo Pines, "A Tenth Century Philosophical Correspondence," *Proceedings of the American Academy of Jewish Research* 24 [1955]: 103–36 [at 119–20 n. 71]) and that of Averroës and Maimonides (quoted and discussed in Shlomo Pines, "The Limitations of Human Knowledge According to Al-Farabi, ibn Bajja, and Maimonides," in *Maimonides: A Collection of Critical Essays*, ed. Joseph A. Buijs [Notre Dame, Ind., 1988] 91–121 [at 111–15]); and one should see Pl. *Resp.* 9.591d–592b and *Leg.* 6.770c–e.

152. Cf. Numa Denis Fustel de Coulanges, *The Ancient City* (Baltimore 1980) 344–88 (esp. 344–52) with 3–6, and see Alfarabi, *Aphorisms* § 93.

153. Pl. *Resp.* 10.607b.

154. Arist. *Ph.* 203b3–15.

155. Xenophanes *Vorsokr.*⁶ 21 B11–12, 14–16, 23–26. See B10, 18, 32; Heraclitus *Vorsokr.*⁶ 22 B14–15, 32, 40, 42, 56–57, 106, 128; Empedocles *Vorsokr.*⁶ 31 B27–29, 132–34; and Diog. Laert. 8.21; and consider the passages cited in I.iv.3, notes 48–50, above.

156. Leucippus *Vorsokr.*⁶ 67 B2.

157. Cf. Pind. F197 (Bowra) with Ar. *Nub.*, and see Pl. *Resp.* 10.607b and *Leg.* 12.967c–d. In Cicero's day, ordinary men could take it for granted that the philosophers did not believe in the gods: Cic. *Inv. Rhet.* 1.29.46.

158. Job 28:12–28, 38:1–39:30. Note Prov. 9:10. These passages help explain why Spinoza could later depict the Jews as loathing philosophy: see *Tractatus theologico-politicus* XI.24: *Opera* III 158, with Leo Strauss, "Introduction," *Persecution and the Art of Writing* (Glencoe, Ill., 1952) 20–21.

159. Soph. *Ant.* 332–75.

160. In this connection, see Bernard Knox, *Oedipus at Thebes: Sophocles' Tragic Hero and his Time* (New York 1971); Seth Benardete, "Sophocles' *Oedipus Tyrannus*," in *Ancients and Moderns: Essays on the Tradition of Political Philosophy in Honor of Leo Strauss*, ed. Joseph Cropsey (New York 1964) 1–15; and Arlene W. Saxonhouse, "The Tyranny of Reason in the World of the Polis," *APSR* 82 (1988): 1261–75.

161. See Knox, *Oedipus at Thebes* 107–58.

162. Cf. Soph. *OT* 380–403, 707–25, 945–49, 964–88, 1076–85 (esp. 1080–81) with 883–910. For further discussion, see Knox, *Oedipus at Thebes* 159–84.

163. Soph. *OT* 1189, 1251–79, 1422–58, 1484–85, 1517–21. Note 441–42.

164. Cf. Soph. *Ant.* 707–9 with 1348–52.

165. Eur. *Bacch.* 30, 179, 200–204, 266, 395, 480, 641, 655–56, 824, 839, 877, 1150–53, 1190.

166. Eur. *Bacch.* 200–204.

167. Eur. *Bacch.* 386–401, 417–32.

168. Eur. *Bacch.* 824.

169. Eur. *Bacch.* 877–96.

170. Eur. *Bacch.* 1150–53.

171. Cf. Ar. *Nub.* 889–1104 with 1303–1475, and pay careful attention to the reversal of roles which takes place at 1425–32, where, albeit unwittingly, Strepsiades not only manages to defeat his son in argument but forces him to fall back on a lame appeal to authority—and does so by elaborating a new understanding of the *phúsis* of man and the foundation of *nómos* of the very sort that Xenophon and Plato (if not, in fact, a Socrates grown older and wiser) will in due course employ to secure victory for the just over the unjust argument. Note also the similarity between Aristophanes' description of himself (547) and the wording of the charge lodged against Socrates (Xen. *Mem.* 1.1.1, Pl. *Ap.* 24d); then see *Leg.* 7.797a–799b (with an eye to the phrasing at 797c).

172. With regard to the emergence of political philosophy, consider note 171, above, in conjunction with Paul Kraus, "Raziana I. La conduite du philosophe: Traité d'éthique d'Abū Muhammad b. Zakariyyā Al-Rāzī," *Orientalia* 4 (1935): 300–334 (esp. 322–34); Alfarabi, *Plato & Aristotle* 2.10.36–38; and Muhsin Mahdi, "Man and His Universe in Medieval Arabic Philosophy," in *L'homme et son univers au moyen âge*, ed. Christian Wenin (Louvain-la-neuve 1986) I 102–13 (at 112–13): Alfarabi, *Paraphrase of Aristotle's Topics* MS, Bratislava, no. 231, TE 40, fol. 203; then, see Strabo 1.2.8, and consider William F. Boggess, "Alfarabi and the Rhetoric: The Cave Revisited," *Phronesis* 15 (1970): 86–90, and Muhsin Mahdi, "Alfarabi on Philosophy and Religion," *PF* 4 (1972): 5–25. Poetry can easily become an instrument of philosophy because the stories it tells need not be irrational. In fact, as Aristotle (*Poet.* 1451a36–1452a10) emphasizes, at its best, poetry is akin to philosophy. The historian is called upon to relate what has actually happened— even if the actual course of events is simply "one damned thing after another." But the poet is in a different position. To be effective, he must shape his plot in a fashion that surprises spectators and readers, to be sure. But, in the end, that plot has to make perfect sense. In short, it must bring to light the hidden logic which underlies human events. For this reason, poetry can do more than serve as an instrument for enchanting and instructing the nonphilosophic multitude; its study can be a kind of preparation for philosophy—which, in similar fashion, tries to make sense of what is unexpected in the familiar: Strabo 1.2.3, 8; Plut. *Mor.* 14e–37b. Virgil's *Aeneid* is arguably the best ancient example of the philosophical poetry that later appeared. For a discussion of one early example of what I have in mind, see Carnes Lord, "Aristotle, Menander, and the *Adelphoe* of Terence," *TAPhA* 107 (1977): 183–202.

173. One should consider the role assigned poetry in Plato's *Laws* in light of Pl. *Resp.* 2.376e–3.415e, 4.424a–425e, 430a–b, 441e, 8.548b–549b, 9.591c–e, 10.595a–608b (esp. 607c).

174. For an analysis of this strategy, see the work of Aristide Tessitore: "Aristotle's Political Presentation of Socrates in the *Nicomachean Ethics*," *Interpretation* 16 (1988): 3–22; "A Political Reading of Aristotle's Treatment of Pleasure in the *Nicomachean Ethics*," *PTh* 17 (1989): 247–65; and "Making the City Safe for Phi-

losophy: *Nicomachean Ethics*, Book 10," *APSR* 84 (1990): 1251–62. Note Richard H. Cox, "Aristotle's Treatment of Socrates in the *Nicomachean Ethics*: A Proem," in *Politikos: Selected Papers of the North American Chapter of the Society for Greek Political Thought* (Pittsburgh 1989–) I 122–53.

175. In both cases, Aristotle substitutes the natural for the divine: see Wayne H. Ambler, "Aristotle's Understanding of the Naturalness of the City," *RP* 47 (1985): 163–85 (esp. 179–81), and Bernard M. W. Knox, *The Heroic Temper: Studies in Sophoclean Tragedy* (Berkeley 1964) 96–97. Cf. Anne P. Charney, "Spiritedness and Piety in Aristotle," in *Understanding the Political Spirit: Philosophical Investigations from Socrates to Nietzsche*, ed. Catherine H. Zuckert (New Haven 1988) 67–87, with Thomas L. Pangle, "The Political Psychology of Religion in Plato's Laws," *APSR* 70 (1976): 1059–77 (esp. 1062–65), and see I.iv.3, note 49, above.

176. Arist. *Eth. Nic.* 1105b28–1106a1, *Eth. Eud.* 1219b38–1221b10, *Rh.* 1366a23–b22. Note [Arist.] *VV* 1250b16–24.

177. See Arist. *Pol.* 1252b15–30.

178. One should keep Arist. *Eth. Nic.* 1172a19–1178b31 in mind when pondering the biographical tradition, which asserts that Aristotle was charged with impiety and withdrew from Athens to Chalcis in 323 B.C., remarking that he had no desire to give the Athenians the opportunity to sin against philosophy a second time. Consider *Vita Aristotelis Marciana* 41–42, *Vita Aristotelis Vulgata* 19–20, *Vita Aristotelis Latina* 43–44, Ael. *VH* 3.36, Origen *c. Cels.* 1.380, and Elias *In Cat. prooemium* (*CIAG* XVIII:1 123.15) in conjunction with Diog. Laert. 5.5–9, Sen. *Dial.* 8.8.1, Ath. 15.696a, Eust. *Od.* 7.120–21, *II Vita Aristotelis Syriaca* 3, 7, *II Vita Aristotelis Arabica* (Al-Mubashir) 20–23, *IV Vita Aristotelis Arabica* (Ibn Abi Usaibia) 7–11, 15–21. All of the pertinent evidence is readily accessible in Ingemar Düring, *Aristotle in the Ancient Biographical Tradition* (Göteborg 1957). The animus aimed at Aristotle and his school no doubt had something to do with his not inconsiderable services to Philip of Macedon and his successors: note Diog Laert. 5.38 (with Ath. 11.508f, 13.610e–f), and see Anton-Hermann Chroust, *Aristotle: New Light on His Life and on Some of His Lost Works* (Notre Dame, Ind., 1973) I 73–91, 117–76 (esp. 145–76).

179. The divergent rhetorical strategies adopted by the two Greek philosophers had an unforeseeable consequence more than a millennium thereafter. In general, the philosophers belonging to what came to be known in the West as the Averroist school followed Aristotle. Alfarabi, the founder of that school, had access to at least part of *The Politics* in some form: see Shlomo Pines, "Aristotle's *Politics* in Arabic Philosophy," *The Collected Works of Shlomo Pines* (Jerusalem 1979–) II 146–56. But precisely because, for the most part, Aristotle ignored religion while Plato adumbrated a strategy for coping with its presence and for incorporating it into a scheme presupposing the primacy of philosophy, Alfarabi and the other *falāsifa* found the latter's political doctrine better suited rhetorically to detailed elaboration as a public teaching in a setting dominated by a revealed religion which presents itself first and foremost as holy law. See Leo Strauss, *Philosophy and Law: Essays toward the Understanding of Maimonides and His Predecessors*, trans. Fred Baumann (Philadelphia 1987) 53–58, 79–110; "Some remarks on the Political Science of Maimonides and Farabi," *Interpretation* 18 (1990): 3–30 (esp. 4–7); and "On Abravanel's Philosophical Tendency and Political Teaching," in *Isaac Abravanel: Six Lectures*, ed. J. B. Trend and H. Loewe (Cambridge 1937) 95–129 (esp. 95–100); consider Leo Strauss, "Introduction" 7–21, and Miriam Gal-

ston, *Politics and Excellence: The Political Philosophy of Alfarabi* (Princeton 1990); and read through Alfarabi, *Plato & Aristotle*. To indicate that he is fully conscious of what he is doing, Alfarabi initially lays out an Aristotelian account of the status and character of political science in his *Enumeration of the Sciences* and then silently replaces it with a Platonic account. Consider *MPP* 24–26: *The Enumeration of the Sciences* 102–6 in light of Muhsin Mahdi, "Science, Philosophy, and Religion in Alfarabi's *Enumeration of the Sciences*," in *The Cultural Context of Medieval Learning*, ed. John Emery Murdoch and Edith Dudley Sylla (Dordrecht 1975) 113–47. In this connection, see also Muhsin Mahdi, "Remarks on Alfarabi's *Attainment of Happiness*," in *Essays on Islamic Philosophy and Science*, ed. George F. Hourani (Albany, N.Y., 1975) 47–66. For a popular presentation of this public teaching, see Alfarabi, *Opinions*. As a consequence of the political strategy adopted by the early *falāsifa*, Aristotle's *Politics* received comparatively little attention within the House of Islam; and, in Averroës' time, it was unavailable in the Muslim West in any form: *Averroes on Plato's Republic* 22.3–5. In this connection, note Avicenna's contention that Plato's *Laws* is a book about prophecy and the holy law: *MPP* 97: *On the Divisions of the Rational Sciences* 108. It may not be fortuitous that Alfarabi appears in Raphael's School of Athens as a musician. Direct divine inspiration is strikingly absent from the prophetology of the *falāsifa*—even in Alfarabi's most popular tract. In fact, religion is treated as nothing more than a poetic or imaginative approximation to philosophical truth useful for directing the multitude: see Alfarabi, *Opinions* 4.14.1–11 (esp. 7–9), 5.17.1–6 (esp. 2–4), which should be read with Richard Walzer's commentary (413–23, 471–81) and with Walzer, "Al-Fārābī's Theory of Prophecy and Divination," *Greek into Arabic: Essays on Islamic Philosophy* (Cambridge, Mass., 1962) 206–19. Note, in this connection, Muhsin Mahdi, "Averroës on Divine Law and Human Wisdom," in *Ancients and Moderns* 114–31. See also Shlomo Pines, "The Arabic Recension of *Parva Naturalia* and the Philosophical Doctrine Concerning Veridical Dreams According to *al-Risāla al-Manāmiyya* and Other Sources," *The Collected Works of Shlomo Pines* II 96–145. As Strauss emphasizes in the essays cited above, Maimonides' prophetology owes much to Alfarabi: see *Guide of the Perplexed* II 32–48. See also Leo Strauss, "Der Ort der Vorsehungslehre nach der Ansicht Maimunis," *Monatsschrift für Geschichte und Wissenschaft des Judentums* 81 (1937): 93–105 (esp. 101–2). In this connection, see Alexander Altmann, "Maimonides and Thomas Aquinas: Natural or Divine Prophecy?" *Association for Jewish Studies Review* 3 (1978): 1–19. In general, see I Epilogue (esp. note 30), below.

180. See the material cited in I.iv.5, note 109, above. Aristotle's evident preference for republican regimes would seem at odds with his apparent willingness to serve and advise Hellas's Macedonian conquerors (above, note 178) were there not evidence suggesting that he hoped that Macedon's hegemony might serve as an antidote to the self-destructive propensities inherent in classical republicanism: note IV *Vita Aristotelis Arabica* (Ibn Abi Usaibia) 15–21, and consider *Pol.* 1296a22–b1 (esp. the implications of Aristotle's use of the word *sunepeísthē* at 1296a38–39) in light of [Dem.] 17.15. In this connection, consider P. A. Vander Waerdt, "Kingship and Philosophy in Aristotle's Best Regime," *Phronesis* 30 (1985): 249–73, and W. R. Newell, "Superlative Virtue: The Problem of Monarchy in Aristotle's 'Politics,'" *WPQ* 40 (1987): 159–78, with an eye to the manner in which politics points beyond itself: see Delba Winthrop, "Aristotle on Participatory Democracy," *Polity* 11 (1978): 151–71; Winthrop, "Aristotle and Theories of

Justice," *APSR* 72 (1978): 1201–16; and P. A. Vander Waerdt, "The Political Inten-
tion of Aristotle's Moral Philosophy," *AncPhil* 5 (1985): 77–89. Note also Carnes
Lord, "Aristotle's Anthropology," in *Essays on the Foundations of Aristotelian Political
Science*, ed. Carnes Lord and David O'Connor (Berkeley 1991) 49–73.

181. It is in this connection that one should consider what they have to say
concerning the relationship between women and men: see Stephen G. Salkever,
"Women, Soldiers, Citizens: Plato & Aristotle on the Politics of Virility," *Polity*
19 (1987): 232–53, and *Finding the Mean: Theory and Practice in Aristotelian Political
Philosophy* (Princeton 1990) 165–204.

Epilogue

1. Cf. *WoFN* II 566: *Jenseits von Gut und Böse* Vorrede with Numa Denis Fustel
de Coulanges, *The Ancient City* (Baltimore 1980) 344–88, and see *WoM* II 1098:
Dossier de *L'esprit des lois* 380.

2. Cf. Thuc. 2.40.2 with 1 Thess. 4:11–12, and see Thuc. 2.63.3.

3. Tert. *Apol.* 38 (Migne, *PL* 1.526–31).

4. August. *De civ. D.* 5.17.

5. In this connection, see Pascal, *Pensées* 714.

6. See Walter Ullmann, "Juristic Obstacles to the Emergence of the Concept of
the State in the Middle Ages," *Annali di storia del diritto* 12–13 (1968–69): 43–64.

7. Cf. *Cod. Iust.* 5.59.5.2 with *Dig.* 39.3.8, and see Gaines Post, "Corporate
Community, Representation, and Consent," in *Studies in Medieval Legal Thought*
(Princeton 1964) 27–238. See also Yves M.-J. Congar, "Quod omnes tangit ab
omnibus tractari et approbari debet," *RD*[4] 36 (1958): 210–59; Peter N. Riesenberg,
"Civism and Roman Law in Fourteenth-Century Italian Society," *Explorations in
Economic History* 7 (1969): 237–54; and Riesenberg, "Citizenship at Law in Late
Medieval Italy," *Viator* 5 (1974): 333–46.

8. See Ronald Witt, "The Rebirth of the Concept of Republican Liberty in Italy,"
in *Renaissance Studies in Honor of Hans Baron*, ed. Anthony Molho and John A.
Tedeschi (Dekalb, Ill., 1971) 173–99; Joseph P. Canning, "A Fourteenth-Century
Contribution to the Theory of Citizenship: Political Man and the Problem of Created Citizenship in the Thought of Baldus de Ubaldis," in *Authority and Power:
Studies on Medieval Law and Government Presented to Walter Ullmann on His Seventieth Birthday*, ed. Brian Tierney and Peter Linehan (Cambridge 1980) 197–212;
and Canning, "The Corporation in the Political Thought of the Jurists of the
Thirteenth and Fourteenth Centuries," *HPT* 1 (1980): 9–32.

9. Figures such as Coluccio Salutati and Leonardi Bruni were attracted by the
example of classical antiquity, as Hans Baron, *The Crisis of the Early Italian Renaissance: Civic Humanism and Republican Liberty in an Age of Classicism and Tyranny*[2]
(Princeton 1966), suggests—but as a Christian, Salutati evidenced a marked ambivalence regarding the relative value to be placed on political life of a sort more
typical of his contemporaries and their successors than the single-mindedness
to be found in unbelievers such as Guicciardini or Machiavelli: see Ronald G.
Witt, *Hercules at the Crossroads: The Life, Works, and Thought of Coluccio Salutati* (Durham, N.C., 1983). Even among the humanists, the latter were the exception, not
the norm: Paul Oskar Kristeller, *Renaissance Thought: The Classic, Scholastic, and
Humanist Strains* (New York 1961) 70–91.

10. Consider Francesco Guicciardini, *Dialogo del reggimento di Firenze*, ed. Roberto Palmarocchi (Bari 1932) 162, in light of Gianfranco Folena, " 'Ricordi' politici e familiari di Gino di Neri Capponi," in *Miscellanea di studi offerta a Armando Balduino e Bianca Bianchi per le loro nozze* (Padua 1962) 29–39 (esp. 35), and see Renzo Sereno, "The *Ricordi* of Gino di Neri Capponi," *APSR* 52 (1958): 1118–22; then, cf. Machiavelli, *Istorie fiorentine* 3.7 and *WoNM* 1250–51: Letter to Francesco Vettori on 16 April 1527, with August. *Ep.* 91.1, and see Machiavelli, *Discorsi* 1 *Proemio*, 4, 2.2, 3.1, 27, 31, 43. Note, in this connection, Montesquieu, *EL* 1.4.4, and *WoJJR* III 460–69: *Du contrat social* 4.8.

11. See Paul Wendland, *Die hellenistisch-römische Kultur in ihren Beziehungen zum Judentum und Christentum*[4] (Tübingen 1972); Johannes Geffcken, *Das Christentum im Kampf und Ausgleich mit der griechisch-römischen Welt: Studien aus seiner Werdezeit*[3] (Leipzig 1920); Pierre Champagne de Labriolle, *History and Literature of Christianity from Tertullian to Boethius*, trans. Herbert Wilson (New York 1925); Werner Jaeger, *Early Christianity and Greek Paideia* (Cambridge, Mass., 1961); and Peter Brown, *The World of Late Antiquity, A.D. 150–750* (London 1971) 82–95. Cf. Charles Norris Cochrane, *Christianity and Classical Culture* (New York 1959). Note also Ernest L. Fortin, *Christianisme et culture philosophique au cinquième siècle: La querelle de l'âme humaine en Occident* (Paris 1959).

12. Cf. Tert. *De praescr. haeret.* 7 (Migne, *PL* 2.22–23) with Col. 2:8. For an explication of this and the other pertinent passages from Tertullian, see André Labhardt, "Tertullien et la philosophie ou la recherche d'une 'position pure,' " *MH* 7 (1950): 159–80.

13. John 1:1–34. Cf. Gen. 18:16–19:29 with 21:1–22:18 and Job 28:12–28, 38:1–42:17, and see I.vii.7, above.

14. Rom. 12:1.

15. Cf. 1 Tim. 6:4–5 and 1 Cor. 1:21–23 with 1 Tim. 1:4, 2 Tim. 2:23, and Titus 3:9; and see Matt. 7:7; then, consider Jean Daniélou, "Recherche et tradition chez les Pères du IIe et du IIIe siècles," *NRTh* 94 (1972): 449–61.

16. August. *De praedestinatione sanctorum* 5 (Migne, *PL* 44.963). See *Ep.* 120.1–5, *De doctrina Christiana* 2.40.60–61, and note 42, below.

17. Gregory of Nyssa, *De deitate filii et spiritus sancti* (Migne, *PG* 46.557).

18. See Emmanuel Le Roy Ladurie, *Montaillou: The Promised Land of Error*, trans. Barbara Bray (New York 1978).

19. Edward Gibbon, *The History of the Decline and Fall of the Roman Empire* (London 1776–88) l 514. For the early heresies, see I 449–586, II 179–310, 504–14, III 10–102, 505–55, IV 28–33, 532–620, V 88–133, and A. H. M. Jones, *The Later Roman Empire, 284–602: A Social, Economic, and Administrative Survey* (Norman, Okla., 1964) I 80–97, 112–19, 164–66, 208–16, 285–87, 360–62, 406–7, II 950–70.

20. Hilarius *Ad Constantium Augustum* 2.4–5 (Migne, *PL* 10.566–67). Note, in this connection, Amm. Marc. 21.16.18.

21. See Amm. Marc. 22.5.3–4, and consider II.vi.4–5 in light of III.i.5, iv.5–6, and vi.2–4, below.

22. See Gibbon, *The History of the Decline and Fall of the Roman Empire* II 179–263, and Jones, *The Later Roman Empire* I 80–97.

23. Consider this epilogue's epigraph (Macaulay, *Essays* III 443–44: "Lord Bacon"), in light of *WoFB* III 596: *Cogitata et visa de interpretatione naturae*.

24. Euseb. *Hist. Eccl.* 5.27.1–28.19 (esp. 28.13–15) should be read in light of Richard Walzer, *Galen on Jews and Christians* (Oxford 1949) esp. 75–86.

25. August. *De ordine* 2.5.17 (Migne, *PL* 32.1002). See 1.11.31 (Migne, *PL* 32.992–93).

26. Mere moralists, such as the Stoic Musonius Rufus (2–5 [Hense]), can hardly be said to fit the bill: see *WoFN* III 434.

27. Note Pl. *Resp.* 6.487a–501a (esp. 494a), 7.520a–b, 9.581c–592b, *Phd.* 64b, *Grg.* 485d–486d, 521d–522c, *Ep.* 7.324c–345a (esp. 328e, 331c–d, 332d–e, 338b–345a), *Ti.* 51e, *Phlb.* 52b; consider Xen. *Ap.* 2–9 and *Mem.* 4.8.4–10 in light of *Cyr.* 3.1.13–40; and see Arist. *Eth. Nic.* 1179b4–19; Cic. *Tusc.* 2.1.1–4; Strabo 1.2.8; Sen. *Ep.* 5.2; Alfarabi, *Plato & Aristotle* 1.2.34–36, 3.40, 4.50–62, 2.3.7, 5.14–6.25, 7.29, 10.38, 3.1.2, 12–13, 15–16; *Averroes on Plato's Republic* 23.6–9, 24.6–9, 25.13–32, 48.19–29, 61.20–72.33 (esp. 62.7–64.2), 74.14–29, 78.26–79.9, 103.25–104.10; *RPM* 350–77 (esp. 350–57, 363–65, 373–75): Pietro Pomponazzi, *De immortalitate animae* 14. One should interpret Maimonides, *Guide of the Perplexed* II 36 (371–72) in light of 40 (381–82) and I Introduction, 14, 31, 33–34, III 8, 27 (510), 51, 54. Note the prudent fashion in which Marsilius of Padua (*Defensor Pacis* 1.13.1–8) skirts the issue which is playfully raised by the dramatic confrontation depicted at Pl. *Resp.* 1.327a–328b.

28. In this light, one should consider Pl. *Phd.* 62b, 89c–90d, *Phlb.* 15d–17a, *Phdr.* 274b–278c, *Tht.* 155e–156a, 180c–d, *Ep.* 2.312d, 313c, 314a–c; Arist. *Eth. Nic.* 1124b26–30; Cic. *Tusc.* 5.4.10–11, *De Or.* 2.67.270; Strabo 1.2.8; Sen. *Ep.* 5.1–3, 14.14; Diog. Laert. 4.2; Clem. Al. *Strom.* 5.9.56–59; Origen *c. Cels.* 4.39; August. *De civ. D.* 8.4 (with *De vera religione* 1.1–2.2, 5.8), *De doctrina christiana* 4.9.23, *De ordine* 2.10.28–29 (Migne, *PL* 32.1008–9), *Ep.* 1.1, 118.17–33; Paul Kraus, "Raziana I. La conduite du philosophe: Traité d'éthique d'Abū Muhammad b. Zakariyyā Al-Rāzī," *Orientalia* 4 (1935): 300–334 (at 322–34)—translated into English by A. J. Arberry, "Rhazes on the Philosophic Life," *The Asiatic Review* (1949): 703–13; Alfarabi, *Plato & Aristotle* 1.4.60–61, 2.10.36–38; *MPP* 83–85: Alfarabi, *Plato's Laws* Introduction 1–3: Muhsin Mahdi, "Man and His Universe in Medieval Arabic Philosophy," in *L'homme et son univers au moyen âge*, ed. Christian Wenin (Louvain-la-neuve 1986) I 102–13 (at 112–13): Alfarabi, *Paraphrase of Aristotle's Topics* MS, Bratislava, no. 231, TE 40, fol. 203; *Averroes on Plato's Republic* 77.12–29; Maimonides, *Guide of the Perplexed* I Introduction, 17, 31–35, 59, 68–69, II 29 (346–48), III Introduction. Note Cic. *Acad.* F21 (Müller) with August. *Conf.* 5.10.19 and *Acad.* 2.13.29, 3.7.14, 17.37–20.43, and see Cic. *Nat. D.* 1.5.10–6.14, 7.17, 21.57, 22.60, 2.1.2–3. Cf. Pl. *Phd.* 69c–d and *Symp.* 209e–212c, 215a–222b with Ar. *Nub.* 140–44, 250–509 (esp. 250–60, 497–99); then, see *II Vita Aristotelis Arabica* (Al-Mubashir) 37 with Cic. *Fin.* 5.4.10–5.14, Aul. Gell. *NA* 20.5, Plut. *Alex.* 7, Gal. *De substantia facultatum naturalium fragmentum* IV.757–58 (Kühn), Themistius *Or.* 26.385 (Dindorf), and the other material collected in Ingemar Düring, *Aristotle in the Ancient Biographical Tradition* (Göteborg 1957) 426–43. To think these passages revealing, one need not suppose that the ancient political philosophers and their successors privately espoused "secret doctrines" that they never even intimated in their published works. Cf. Pl. *Phdr.* 275e–278c and *Ep.* 7.340b–341e with *Leg.* 12.968d–e, and see *Resp.* 7.518b–519b with Maimonides, *Guide of the Perplexed* I Introduction (17–20), 17, 33–34, III Introduction; then, see George Boas, "Ancient Testimony to Secret Doctrines," *PhR* 62 (1953): 79–92; note Thomas More's allusion to the philosophy of the schools and his contention that there is "another, more politic philosophy (*alia philosophia civilior*)," which seeks to achieve its goals within the public sphere by an "indirect" or even "devious ap-

proach (*obliquo ductu*)": *The Complete Works of Thomas More* IV: *Utopia*, ed. Edward Surtz, S.J., and J. H. Hexter (New Haven 1965) 86–102 (esp. 98–100); and consider Clem. Al. *Strom.* 1.1.7, 9–10 (with 6.7.61, 15.131), 11, 14–16, 18, 2.20, 12.53 (with 6.1.2, 7.18.110–11), 55, 4.2.4–5, 7.8.50, 9.53 in light of Ernest L. Fortin, "Clement of Alexandria and the Esoteric Tradition," *Studia Patristica* 9 (1966): 41–56. In this connection, see note 32 in context, below.

29. Cf. Hobbes, *LW* II: *De homine* XIV.13, with *LW* V 92: *Lux mathematica* Ep. Ded. In this connection, note *LW* I: *De corpore* I.7; consider *De cive* Ep. Ded. [6]–[7] and *Leviathan* II.18 (233), 30 (382–85), in light of II.31 (407–8); and see Hobbes, *Behemoth* 70–71. The first of the two passages quoted is said to have been much favored by Friedrich Engels: Ferdinand Tönnies, *Thomas Hobbes*[3] (Stuttgart 1925) 195.

30. One should consider the various ancient discussions of "civil theology" cited in I.iv.3, notes 48–50, above, in light of Pl. *Ti.* 28c and *Resp.* 3.414b–415d, and then see 1.331b–c, 2.376e–3.398b (esp. 382c–d, 389b–c), 5.459c–d, 6.489a–c, 7.535d–e, 8.564b–c, *Leg.* 2.663d–664d, 12.959a–c. Cf. Plut. *Nic.* 23.3–6 with Hobbes, *Leviathan* IV.46 (692); Locke, *RC* § 238; *WoM* I 1546–47: *Mes pensées* 2097; *WoJJR* III 46n: "Observations de Jean-Jacques Rousseau de Genève"; *WrEB* VII 31–32: Speech on a Bill for the Relief of Protestant Dissenters, 17 March 1773; and Condorcet, *Esquisse* 51–58, 81–82; note Grotius, *De iure belli ac pacis* III.i.6–17; then, see Pascal, *Pensées* 294. In this connection, note Varro's adherence to the Old Academy: August. *De civ. D.* 19.1–4. Consider Posidonius's opinion of Epicurus: Cic. *Nat. D.* 1.30.85, 44.123–24. Note also Origen *c. Cels.* 4.19. See I.vii.7, note 179, above; consider *Alfarabi's Book of Letters (Kitāb al-Hurūf)*, ed. Muhsin Mahdi (Beirut 1970) 131.4–134.15, 153.13–157.3 (translated by Lawrence V. Berman, "Maimonides, the Disciple of Alfārābī," *Israel Oriental Studies* 4 [1974]: 154–78 [at 171–78]), in light of Muhsin Mahdi, "Alfarabi on Philosophy and Religion," *PF* 4 (1972): 5–25; and see Alfarabi, *Plato & Aristotle* 1.3.38–4.63, 3.1.13, 2.15–16 (with 1.1.3–4, 2.33, 2.3.7, 3.1.12); *MPP* 36–37, 40–41: Alfarabi *The Political Regime* 49–50, 55–56; and *Averroes on Plato's Republic* 25.13–32, 29.9–33.5, 39.27–42.1, 60.26–61.1, 65.29–67.8, 77.12–29. It is in this light that one should consider Maimonides' account of the claim that man is made in "the image and likeness of God" and his bold reinterpretation of the Fall (*Guide of the Perplexed* I 1–2), his insistence on God's incorporeality and on his creation of the universe (I 35, II 13–31), his enigmatic defense of providence and his unorthodox reading of the story of Job (III 17–18, 22–23, 51), his depiction of the peculiar status of Moses as a prophet (II 33–36, 39, 45), his discussion of the aims of Holy Law (III 27), and his frank treatment of the doctrine of divine retribution for injustice simply and solely as a "belief . . . necessary for the sake of political welfare": cf. III 28 with I 26, 47, 50–54. The same concerns explain the character of Averroës' public rhetoric in defense of philosophy (*MPP* 164–85: *The Decisive Treatise; Averroes' Tahafut al-tahafut [The Incoherence of the Incoherence]*, trans. Simon Van den Bergh [London 1954]) and account for the difference between what the *falāsifa* say in their public works concerning the afterlife and the doctrine they teach elsewhere: cf. Alfarabi, *Opinions* 5.16.2–11 (esp. 8) with *MPP* 37–39: Alfarabi, *The Political Regime* 51–53, and consider the various reports regarding the claims he advanced in his commentary on Aristotle's *Nicomachean Ethics*: *MPP* 140: Ibn Tufayl, *Hayy the Son of Yaqzan* 13–14; Moritz Steinschneider, *Al-Farabi (Alpharabius) des arabischen Philosophen Leben und Schriften* (St. Petersburg 1869) 94, 102, 106; and Ibn Bajja MS Bodleian Library,

Pococke 206, fol. 126b: Shlomo Pines, "The Limitations of Human Knowledge According to Al-Farabi, ibn Bajja, and Maimonides," in *Maimonides: A Collection of Critical Essays*, ed. Joseph A. Buijs (Notre Dame, Ind., 1988) 91–121 (at 91–93). Then, cf. *Averroes' Tahafut al-tahafut* 585.3–6 with *Averroes on Plato's Republic* 31.7–25, 105.14–25, and consider the material collected in II Prologue, notes 12–15, below. In passages artfully scattered through his book, Marsilius of Padua acknowledges the necessity that there be a civil theology, asserts that no one but the temporal ruler is empowered to suppress heretical speech, and suggests that he rightly does so only when that speech contravenes "human law," which is restricted to promoting man's welfare in this world: consider *Defensor pacis* 1.4.3, 5.2, 10, 12–14 (esp. 14), 9.2, 2.4.6, 30.4 in light of 1.4.4, 5.11, 10.3, and see 1.5.4, 7, 2.2.4, 8.5, 9.11, 10.4, 9, 17.8. One can, I think, make sense of the above only in light of the last sentence of 1.1.7. With this in mind, see 1.6.8–9, and consider II Prologue, note 62, below.

31. Its potential as a civil religion was appreciated by philosophic infidels under Platonic influence at least as early as Galen: see Walzer, *Galen on Jews and Christians* esp. 15–16, 56–74, 87–98.

32. Synesius of Cyrene *Ep.* 105 (Hercher, *Epist. Gr.*). See also *Ep.* 96. For a similar statement stressing the need to keep secret the truths of philosophy, see *Ep.* 143. Compare the passages cited in notes 27–30, above. There is an obvious connection between the politic philosophy Synesius seems to have been taught in Alexandria and what, in Europe, later came to be called Averroism. Alfarabi, the actual founder of that school of thought, tells us that Muslim Arabs first learned philosophy from Monophysite Christian instructors whose predecessors had abandoned Alexandria for Antioch after the Arab conquest and then moved on later to Harran and ultimately Baghdad—where, in due course, he was a student himself. For the Arabic text and a summary in German, see Steinschneider, *Al-Farabi (Alpharabius) des arabischen Philosophen Leben und Schriften* 211–13 (with 85–89). See also Max Meyerhof, *Von Alexandrien nach Bagdad: Ein Beitrag zur Geschichte des philosophischen und medizinischen Unterrichts bei den Arabern* (Berlin 1930), and consider Miriam Galston, *Politics and Excellence: The Political Philosophy of Alfarabi* (Princeton 1990). In this light, one should note the close, if not exact, correspondence between the Christian doctrines which Synesius could not accept and the Muslim doctrines which Al-Ghazali accused Alfarabi and Avicenna of denying: *MPP* 171–74: Averroës, *The Decisive Treatise* 9–12; *Averroes' Tahafut al-tahafut* 587.1–6. In this connection, see Muhsin Mahdi, "Alfarabi against Philoponus," *JNES* 26 (1967): 233–60.

33. For his outlook and career, see Ulrich von Wilamowitz-Moellendorff, "Die Hymnen des Synesios and Proklos," *Sitzungsberichte der Königlich Preussischen Akademie der Wissenschaften* 14 (1907): 272–95, and Jay Bregman, *Synesius of Cyrene: Philosopher-Bishop* (Berkeley 1982). Cf. H. I. Marrou, "Synesius of Cyrene and Alexandrian Neoplatonism," in *The Conflict between Paganism and Christianity in the Fourth Century*, ed. Arnaldo Momigliano (Oxford 1964) 126–50.

34. See Harold Fredrik Cherniss, *The Platonism of Gregory of Nyssa* (New York 1930). Cf. Jean Daniélou, *Platonisme et théologie mystique: Essai sur la doctrine spirituelle de Saint Grégoire de Nysse* (Paris 1944).

35. I incline to the older view which sees in Latin Averroism a cloak for freethinking: see Pierre Félix Mandonnet, *Siger de Brabant et l'averroïsme latin au XIIIme siècle*[2] (Louvain 1908–11) I 142–95. Cf. Fernand van Steenberghen, *La philoso-*

phie au XIIIᵉ siècle (Louvain 1966); Maître Siger de Brabant (Louvain 1977); and *Thomas Aquinas and Radical Aristotelianism* (Washington, D.C., 1980) 75–110. Even Étienne Gilson, who doubts that this was universally true, acknowledges its likelihood in the case of John of Jandun and suspects that he was one among many: see "La doctrine de la double vérité," *Études de philosophie médiévale* (Strasbourg 1921) 51–75 (at 60–68). Cf. Stuart MacClintock, *Perversity and Error: Studies on the "Averroist" John of Jandun* (Bloomington, Ind., 1956) esp. 69–99. See, especially, Ernest L. Fortin, *Dissidence et philosophie au Moyen Age: Dante et ses antécédents* (Montreal 1981). Note Aryeh L. Motzkin, "Elia del Medigo, Averroes, and Averroism," *Italia* 6 (1987): 7–19.

36. See Richard Hofstadter and Walter P. Metzger, *The Development of Academic Freedom in the United States* (New York 1955) 3–77 (esp. 3–40).

37. As Richard Walzer points out, Alfarabi and his successors repeatedly depict the philosopher condemned to live in the ignorant city as a *gharīb* (i.e., *xénos*) in its midst: consider his commentary in Alfarabi, *Opinions* 468–71 in light of I.vii.6 (esp. note 138), above; and see Alfarabi, *Aphorisms* § 88; *MPP* 127–28, 132: Avempace, *The Governance of the Solitary* 10–11, 78; and *Averroes on Plato's Republic* 63.5–64.27; then, cf. Maimonides, *Guide of the Perplexed* II 36 (372) with I 34 (79), and see III 51 (618–21). The standard surveys of Islamic philosophy resolutely ignore the evidence indicating that the *falāsifa* found it necessary to practice dissimulation in composing their books, take at face value the claims prudently advanced by the *falāsifa* for the ultimate compatibility of philosophy and Islam, and overlook the brief indications they give that this is simply not the case. In similar fashion, because their authors tend to confuse originality with brilliance, these surveys understate the thoughtfulness of the *falāsifa*. Cf. Richard Walzer, "Islamic Philosophy," *Greek into Arabic: Essays on Islamic Philosophy* (Cambridge, Mass., 1962) 1–28, "The Achievement of the Falasifa and their Eventual Failure," *Correspondance d'Orient* 5 (1962): 347–59, and "Early Islamic Philosophy," in *The Cambridge History of Later Greek and Early Medieval Philosophy* (Cambridge 1970) 643–69, and E. I. J. Rosenthal, *Political Thought in Medieval Islam: An Introductory Outline* (Cambridge 1968) esp. 84–223, with Leo Strauss, "Introduction," *Persecution and the Art of Writing* (Glencoe, Ill., 1952) 7–21, and see Muhsin Mahdi, "Introduction, 1962 Edition" in Alfarabi, *Plato & Aristotle* 3–10, and Ralph Lerner, "Introduction," *Averroes on Plato's Republic* xiii–xxviii. Despite this critical deficiency, there is much to be learned from Walzer's essays (*Greek into Arabic*) and from the introduction and commentary in his edition of Alfarabi, *Opinions* 1–18, 331–502—especially with regard to the ancient precursors of the *falāsifa*.

38. Cf. Arist. *Metaph.* 995a1–6 with Maimonides, *Guide of the Perplexed* I 31, and see Pines, "The Limitations of Human Knowledge According to Al-Farabi, ibn Bajja, and Maimonides" 111–15.

39. See Praechter, "Hypatia," *RE* IX:1 (1914) 242–49 (esp. 247–49). Note also Gibbon, *The History of the Decline and Fall of the Roman Empire* IV 545–50.

40. Cf. Jerome *Ep.* 70.2 (Labourt) and Sid. Apoll. *Ep.* 9.9 (Migne, *PL* 58.622–26) with Deut. 21:10–13, and see André Labhardt, "Sur une page de saint Jérôme," in *Hommage et reconnaissance: Recueil de travaux publiés à l'occasion du soixantième anniversaire de Karl Barth* (Neuchâtel 1946) 56–62. See also Fortin, *Christianisme et culture philosophique au cinquième siècle* 64–74, and Roger Mehl, *La condition du philosophe chrétien* (Neuchâtel 1947).

41. See Pietro Redondi, *Galileo Heretic*, trans. Raymond Rosenthal (Princeton

1987). For Galileo's subordination of scriptural exegesis to the discoveries of science, see *Discoveries and Opinions of Galileo*, trans. Stillman Drake (Garden City, N.Y., 1957) 173–216: Letter to the Grand Duchess Christina, 1615. For the phrases quoted, see Machiavelli, *Discorsi* I Proemio.

42. As Anselm explains in the preface to his *Proslogion*, this Latin phrase was the original title of that work: *St. Anselm's Proslogion*, ed. and trans. M. J. Charlesworth (Oxford 1965) 105–6. In this connection, Augustine (*De libero arbitrio* 1.2.4, 2.2.6, *Ep.* 120.5) was fond of quoting Isa. 7:9. For a helpful introduction to Anselm's thought, see H. Liebeschütz, "Anselm of Canterbury: The Philosophical Interpretation of Faith," in *The Cambridge History of Later Greek and Early Medieval Philosophy* 611–39. Cf. Karl Barth, *Anselm: Fides Quaerens Intellectum: Anselm's Proof of the Existence of God in the Context of his Theological Scheme* (Richmond, Va., 1960) with M. J. Charlesworth, "Introduction," *St. Anselm's Proslogion* 3–47 (esp. 22–47).

43. *Obras completas de San Ignacio de Loyola*, ed. Ignacio Iparraguirre, S.J., and Candido de Dalmases, S.J. (Madrid 1982) 288–89: Ejercicios espirituales.

44. *Sancti Bonaventurae opera omnia* (Quaracchi 1882–1901) IX 63: Sermones de tempore, Dominica 3 Adventus, Sermo 2.

45. See Ernest L. Fortin, "Thomas Aquinas and the Reform of Christian Education," *Interpretation* 17 (1989): 3–17.

46. Aquinas, *Summa theologiae* Ia q.1 a.5–6.

47. Consider Pl. *Ap.* 20c–24a, 29a–b, 33b–c, 41b in light of *Symp.* 204a–c, and note *Tht.* 155c–d and Arist. *Metaph.* 982b12–983a22. See also Pl. *Leg.* 12.966d–967d.

48. One should consider Carlo Ginzburg, "High and Low: The Theme of Forbidden Knowledge in the Sixteenth and Seventeenth Centuries," *P&P* 73 (November 1976): 28–41, in light of Machiavelli, *Discorsi* I Proemio.

49. Robert Molesworth, *An Account of Denmark, As It was in the Year 1692* (London 1694) Pref.

50. Marsilius's purpose had been to adapt Aristotle's political teaching to meet the danger posed by clerical ambition within a polity based on a revealed religion which made salvation dependent on an adherence to the true faith: *Defensor pacis* 1.1–7. See Alan Gewirth, *Marsilius of Padua, the Defender of the Peace* (New York 1951) I: *Marsilius of Padua and Medieval Political Philosophy*.

51. Thus, where Quentin Skinner gives great prominence to Marsilius of Padua and argues for continuity between classical antiquity and modernity while tracing the roots of modern statecraft to the revival within Latin Christendom of the secular political philosophy of Aristotle, I give primacy to Machiavelli, Montaigne, Bacon, and Hobbes and argue for a decisive break while seeking the foundations of the modern state in a phenomenon wholly unprecedented: the attempt to refound political prudence and establish political science on a philosophical repudiation of moral and political reason. Cf. Skinner, *The Foundations of Modern Political Thought* (Cambridge 1978), with Harvey C. Mansfield, Jr., *Taming the Prince: The Ambivalence of Modern Executive Power* (New York 1989), and see II.i–vii, below. Skinner comes far closer to appreciating Machiavelli's radical break with the past when he abandons his contextualist method and focuses his attention on what the Florentine wrote himself: *Machiavelli* (New York 1981).

Index